URBAN RESEARCH

and

POLICY PLANNING

Volume I, URBAN AFFAIRS ANNUAL REVIEWS

INTERNATIONAL EDITORIAL ADVISORY BOARD

URBAN RESEARCH and POLICY PLANNING

Edited by

LEO F. SCHNORE

and HENRY FAGIN

Volume I URBAN AFFAIRS ANNUAL REVIEWS

For information address:

SAGE PUBLICATIONS, INC.
275 South Beverly Drive
Beverly Hills, California 90212

SAGE PUBLICATIONS LTD
St George's House / 44 Hatton Garden
London E C 1

Printed in the United States of America

International Standard Book Number 0-8039-0030-9

Library of Congress Catalog Card No. 67-18420

THIRD PRINTING

Contents

Part II POLICY PLANNING

Preface

THIS IS THE INITIAL VOLUME in a planned series of annual reviews. To start the series with a measure of historical perspective, however, the editors have been asked to arrange this time not for a one-year retrospective but rather for a survey of what has been occurring in the twenty-year period since World War II.

We have chosen to concentrate on two closely interwoven subjects: urban research and policy planning. The distinction is perhaps more one of orientation than of substance. Part I, which focuses on urban research as such, is organized largely around the academic disciplines. Part II, addressed to policy planning, cuts across disciplinary lines and looks at action-oriented research mainly from certain institutionally derived perspectives, i.e., from the standpoint of the planning process or of social programs or of transportation or housing or urban development.

Although it is the first in a series of annuals, this volume might be regarded as a companion to *The Study of Urbanization,* edited by Philip M. Hauser and Leo F. Schnore for the Social Science Research Council, and published by John Wiley and Sons in 1965. When he was approached by Sage Publications, the senior editor was reminded of two themes that recurred again and again during a four-day Chicago conference based on the Hauser-Schnore volume. The first of these themes was that the earlier book was very parochial in a geographic sense.

> *Participants in the conference, 33 in number, included the members of the Committee on Urbanization, the other contributors to the volume who were not members of the committee itself, a few American guests, and 13 scholars from outside the United States . . .*
>
> *There was widespread consensus among the participants on the need for systematic, comparative inquiry into the problems of urbanization. It generally was agreed that* The Study of Urbanization *itself represents a somewhat parochial and ethnocentric view of research on urbanization and the problems of cities, although it was recognized that the original charge to the committee was to survey the state of the field, particularly in the United States . . .*
>
> *The desirability exists, therefore, for a number of further conferences oriented toward more intensive exploration of particular problems; toward the applied aspects of scholarly research on the city; toward the more intensive examination of issues on a comparative basis as revealed in one or several countries, in contrast to a world view; and toward the expansion of intradisciplinary communication particularly in those fields characterized by a marked cultural bias, on one hand, or by lack of communication among regional specialists within it, on the other (Ginsburg, 1965b, pp. 49-50).*

The reference in this passage to work directed "toward the applied aspects of scholarly research on the city" is the basis that lies behind the first part of this volume. The present volume has not corrected for "American parochialism," but it does represent what we hope will be a large step in the direction of removing the limitation mentioned above — an absence of attention to policy issues.

The scope and limits of this book are easily identified. The first half attempts a survey of the social science disciplines engaged in urban research. It is made up of five pairs of chapters. The first pair of chapters in Part I comprises essays by Leo F. Schnore and Eric E. Lampard on "Social Science and the City: A Survey of Research Needs" and by Lyle W. Shannon and Magdaline Shannon on "The Assimilation of Migrants to Cities." The second pair deals with social psychology and social welfare and consists of a chapter by Anselm L. Strauss on "Strategies for Discovering Urban Theory" and a chapter by Eleanor P. Wolf and Charles N. Lebeaux on "Class and Race in the Changing City." The third pair turns to economics and regional science; Wilbur R. Thompson has contributed a chapter looking "Toward an Urban Economics," and John F. Kain has summarized recent research on "Urban Travel Behavior." The fourth pair takes up history and geography; Charles N. Glaab provides "Historical Perspective on Urban Development Schemes" and Harold M. Mayer surveys "Urban Geography and City and Metropolitan Planning." The last pair of chapters in the first half of the book consists of essays by a political scientist and a political sociologist; Norton E. Long's chapter takes up "Political Science and the City" and Robert R. Alford surveys some recent research in "The Comparative Study of Urban Politics." In almost every instance, the first chapter in a pair deals with general problems, while the second chapter takes up specifics.

The second half of the book, Part II, surveys the changes that have occurred in the general field of public policy planning in terms of concepts, technology, and organization. There are five pairs of chapters in Part II. In a manner similar to Part I, the chapters in each pair tend to move from the more general to the more particular. The first pair in Part II demonstrates substantial expansion in the horizon of planning and consists of a chapter by Henry Fagin on "The Evolving Philosophy of Urban Planning" and one by Lyle C. Fitch on "Social Planning in the Urban Cosmos." The second pair deals with technology in transition; it contains a chapter by Britton Harris on "The New Technology and Urban Planning" and another by Melvin M. Webber on "Transportation Planning for the Metropolis." The third pair turns to the design of the physical world and the human environment with a chapter by Henry Fagin and Carol H. Tarr on "Urban Design and Urban Development" and a chapter by Robert D. Katz on "Urban Housing and Site Design." The fourth pair takes up the sequence from policy formulation to action; Robert T. Daland discusses the relations between "Public Administration and Urban Policy" and then William L. C. Wheaton discusses "Moving from Plan to Reality." The final pair of chapters consists of essays written from the vantage points of the United Nations staff and the United States cabinet; Ernest Weissmann's chapter probes "The Role of the United Nations in Urban Research and Planning," and Robert C. Weaver's chapter states and projects "The Evolving Goals of the Department of Housing and Urban Development."

Reflecting on this second half of the book, the junior editor finds notable the recurrence of several themes from essay to essay. It is evident that the development of public planning in the past twenty years has taken two seemingly divergent directions. First, there has been a trend toward differentiation: toward a multiplicity of planning specialties. This reflects partly the professional specialization that grows from the need for great depth in narrow bands of concern and partly the proliferation of administrative institutions — of special districts and agencies to handle new problems or new complexities in old problems. In response, a number of distinct urban planning orientations have emerged in what used to be thought of as a field *par excellence* for the born generalist. Throughout the chapters the rise of expertise is traced in planning for such functional areas as transportation, housing, urban renewal, land use, economic development, and social welfare.

The second trend, also discussed recurrently in the essays, has been toward consolidation — toward the better integration of policies that interact. The current emphasis on overall systems development is an expression of this concern for focusing simultaneously on the various aspects of public policy — economic, social, and political. Here the emphasis is on viewing the physical, financial, programmatic, manpower, and interest-group components of decisions within unified and comprehensive frameworks.

Another interesting common thread in the essays is the quiet acceptance of modern technology as a means of coping with modern problems. One senses a determination to lay hold of the entire gamut from the softest of software to the hardest of hardware to deal with the intractable welter of cause and effect and accident, of social and economic and cultural and political forces that intertwine at their most intense levels where men lead urban lives. There is a shift back and forth throughout the chapters in Part II between moods of affluence and moods of crisis. There is an awareness of the great need for planning and of the great gap between, on the one hand, our present knowledge of what to plan and how to plan it, on the other hand, the awesome mushrooming of the world's population from year to year and from decade to decade.

The first volume appears, then, at a crucial time in the history of urban affairs. A long struggle to have urban affairs recognized as a major element of national and state concern appears to have been won. With the creation of the federal Department of Housing and Urban Development, a rapidly growing number of state agencies charged with primary responsibility for the well-being of our urban centers, and the continued expansion of local governmental efforts, there has come a large demand for personnel trained to grapple with urban problems. There is also increasing need for research to clarify what has been happening and to identify the options that might exist in the future. Paradoxically, the current war reinforces the need for substantially higher levels of competence in dealing with urban affairs precisely because the contingent shortages of resources demand the most effective possible use of what we do have to work with in our urban areas.

With a very few exceptions, noted at appropriate points in the text, the materials here assembled are original essays prepared specifically for this first annual review. The editors hope and believe that the volume will make a contribution to the urban literature in three respects: (1) by engendering heightened interest in urban affairs on the part of scholars working in the many disciplines to which we look for enriched understanding; (2) by clarifying responsibilities and needs in the development of urban public policy; and (3) by hastening the solution of urban problems through the substantive insights offered here.

We are indebted to our publisher, Sara Miller, for her encouragement and cooperation at every step of the way. We are also deeply obliged to Carol H. Tarr for her very efficient work as editorial associate; the relative completeness of the bibliography is mainly due to her diligence. We would also like to acknowledge the valuable assistance rendered by Janice Deneen, Joy Oren, and Ann Wallace. Finally, our greatest debt is to our 21 collaborators — the authors of the various individual chapters. It is literally true that without their unfailingly cheerful cooperation this book would not have been possible.

LEO F. SCHNORE

HENRY FAGIN

Madison, Wisconsin

January, 1967

Part I

URBAN RESEARCH

Some Research Priorities

THE FIRST PAIR OF CHAPTERS in Part I presents essays by Leo F. Schnore and Eric E. Lampard on "Social Science and the City: A Survey of Research Needs" and by Lyle W. Shannon and Magdaline Shannon on "The Assimilation of Migrants to Cities: Anthropological and Sociological Contributions."

In Chapter 1, Schnore and Lampard survey the various academic disciplines represented in Part I. According to the authors, the various disciplinary statements in this book are marked by a high degree of ethnocentrism, for American problems are emphasized in all but one case — that of geography. Chapter 1, then, represents a deliberate effort to right the balance in favor of research in other parts of the world. Both writers were associated with the Social Science Research Council Committee on Urbanization (1958-1964), and both were contributors to *The Study of Urbanization* (Hauser and Schnore, 1965).

Schnore and Lampard begin with a distinction between the dual concepts of *research priorities* and *research emphases.*

> *The notion of research priorities is an intriguing one that has great appeal to policy-makers and the purposeful organizations which nowadays sponsor urban research. Scholars, on the other hand, have conventionally surveyed existing knowledge and have asked themselves the question: "What do I need to find out in order to discover this or that which I would like to know?" They are concerned with a question or hypothesis, in short, and they hope to devise an appropriate set of operations that will furnish a reliable answer or test.*

Lampard and Schnore go on to make the following assertion: "Serious scientific research must continue to be concerned with fundamental questions of understanding the whole urban phenomenon and not just those aspects that currently appear to be problems to the social engineers. And here it is a matter of appropriate *emphases* rather than *priorities*."

Accordingly, the balance of Chapter 1 is given over to the consideration of possible emphases in a half-dozen fields: (1) demography, (2) sociology, (3) anthropology, (4) economics, (5) history, and (6) political science.

In Chapter 1 it is held that the two leading subjects for anthropological study are "(1) the effects of urbanization on family life, and (2) the acculturation of migrants to the city." Shannon and Shannon take up the latter problem in Chapter 2, reviewing the very substantial anthropological and sociological literature that has accumulated since World War II.

Chapter 2 is more than a bibliographic essay, however, for Shannon and Shannon interweave the results of past research on the subject within a framework of analysis that is their own. Their approach draws upon both anthropological and sociological sources and represents a new and highly original synthesis. What they advocate is, in essence, a merging of (1) *anthropological methods of field research* with (2) *a sociological perspective.* They have placed emphasis "on the organization of society as a determinant of how successful a migrant is in becoming assimilated, rather than on his individual characteristics." This is in keeping with their basic sociological premise with respect to the fate of the individual migrant: "Whether society is going to assimilate him or not assimilate him will depend more on how it is organized than on how he behaves as an individual."

Another new element in the authors' treatment of the subject is the adaptation of the well-known theory of differential association to the problem of migrant assimilation. This theory, originally developed by the late Edwin H. Sutherland (1883-1950), was an attempt to account for the acquisition of delinquent and criminal attitudes. It specified four facets of interpersonal association as crucial: the primacy of priority, frequency, duration or continuity, and intensity of contact (Sutherland, 1939; Sutherland, 1956). Shannon and Shannon use this theory as a point of departure for the development of eight new propositions about migrant assimilation. One example will illustrate their approach:

Assimilation is more likely to take place if interaction is intense. Migrants engaging in primary group interaction with members of the larger society are more likely to be assimilated than those who have had only contacts of a secondary group nature. To the extent that integrated education, as contrasted to segregated education, makes for assimilation into the larger society, we have an indication of the relationship of intensity of interaction to assimilation.

It is such ideas as these that provide the basis for a number of practical recommendations by Shannon and Shannon. For example, "We must put our welfare workers behind the bar, in the poolroom, on the street corner, in the rooming-house lobby, and any other place where the migrant and others in need of assistance may be found as they arrive and attempt to adjust in the urban-industrial milieu." All in all, the authors are concerned "to develop new solutions based on the best behavioral science research available." Chapter 2 represents a step in that direction. At the same time it illustrates the relationship between Parts I and II of this volume. The development and verification of propositions about cities might be designated primarily as *urban research,* with the applications of research in effective action programs being labelled *policy planning.* A hallmark of our epoch is the intertwining of these two emphases.

—*L.F.S.*

1

Social Science and the City

A Survey of Research Needs

LEO F. SCHNORE
and ERIC E. LAMPARD

☐ IT WILL QUICKLY BECOME EVIDENT to the reader of this volume that the first half, which focuses on urban research, is given over almost entirely to "disciplinary" considerations of the urban scene in the United States. Future editions of this yearbook will have to break out of these narrow contexts – substantive and geographic.

More will have to be done in the way of reporting on urban research topics in terms that transcend disciplinary boundaries. An indicator of the newness of an interdisciplinary interest in urban research is the very recent appearance of two books on methods of studying cities. Although both are edited by sociologists, the two editors have not confined themselves to urban sociological research as such (Gibbs, 1961; Hauser, 1965a).

We shall also have to abandon the comforts of an American parochialism and consider the city in all its manifestations around

AUTHORS' NOTE: *Earlier versions of parts of this chapter were delivered by the senior author as lectures at St. John's University (New York) on December 9, 1966 and at The Colorado College on January 12, 1967. Some of the ideas set out here appeared earlier in considerably different form in Lampard and Schnore, 1961. The senior author (an urban sociologist specializing in demography and human ecology) is mainly responsible for the sections dealing with sociology, anthropology, and politics. The junior author (an economic historian who focuses on the study of population redistribution) is chiefly responsible for the sections on economics and history. Both contributed to the discussion of demography and to the introductory materials on research priorities and emphases.*

the world. The basic materials for expanding our horizons are only now becoming available. For most American urban researchers, for example, Africa has until recently remained a dark continent indeed; they have had no means of knowing just what has been done in the way of social science investigations of African cities. Now, however, English-language bibliographies are providing at least the basis for a more informed approach to the subject (see, for example, Simms, 1965, and Department of Social Anthropology, University of Edinburgh, 1965).

In this chapter we shall attempt at least partially to offset the parochialism built into the rest of the book. We shall emphasize research needs drawn as much from other places as from the American experience. (For further materials in this vein, see Chapter 19 by Ernest Weissmann.)

It is presumptuous, of course, for anyone to specify what the next steps in urban research should be. Nevertheless, we think that listing some things that the social sciences *can* do may be useful in helping individual social scientists decide what they *will* do. (Another attack on the same broad problems may be found in a recent and excellent paper by Gutman and Rabinovitz, 1966.)

RESEARCH PRIORITIES

The notion of research priorities is an intriguing one that has great appeal to policy-makers and the purposeful organizations which nowadays sponsor urban research. Scholars, on the other hand, have conventionally surveyed existing knowledge and have asked themselves the question: "What do I need to find out in order to discover this or that which I would like to know?" They are concerned with a question or hypothesis, in short, and they hope to devise an appropriate set of operations that will furnish a reliable answer or test. But the more "bureaucratized" concern of the research entrepreneur – whether government official or foundation executive – implies that knowledge is not enough, that research should be pertinent to desirable action or goals, and that the urgency of the actions and objectives will determine the order or time sequence in which research should be undertaken.

In the case of urbanization, many research entrepreneurs have become exercised about the "problems" of cities, rather narrowly constructed. Their objective is the amelioration of certain city conditions, and they ask such questions as "What can be done with urban environments to prevent political disorder and the possible spread of subversive influence?" While solutions to such problems are understandable objectives of policy, the research horizons they set are extremely low. Answers to such questions are perhaps more appropriately sought by the applied researchers called planners than by academic social scientists operating in the name of basic research. Sufficient answers may be found by sending out teams of experts from the richer countries on such matters as housing, sanitation, and materials, under the direction of educated planners who try to see the local problem whole. Together with local officials and specialists in local color, such teams might explore local sentiments, appraise local resources, and estimate the strategic points at which ameliorative actions can begin.

In other words, alien problem-solvers are faced with a complex local situation; they must bring it into an intelligible focus and recognize that the specialized approaches suitable at home are inadequate, if not dangerous, when used alone. If housing and shelter are adjudged a critical point of entry, it is necessary to understand local traditions affecting property rights, mortgage facilities, and the cost of land in relation to surface structures; the possibilities of using local labor and materials; the availability of sanitary services, schools, and transportation access to and from proposed housing settlements; and so on. Many experts feel that such activities should be supplemented by urban community development teams which foster "self-help" and citizen participation as these terms are understood in some Western countries (Clinard, 1966). The outcome of such on-the-spot investigations should be an appraisal of local situations, programs for suitable actions and for legislation, and a budget for meeting the costs of the actions proposed. (It goes without saying that such investigations should be undertaken only at the request of the local government concerned, and should be carried on with local involvement. Wherever possible, the local government should hire indigenous personnel to participate in the studies and to supervise the implementation of any program that is developed.)

From an operational standpoint, "urban action programs" should receive high priority and they do. But they can be successful only if citizens can secure an urban livelihood and maintain their families with some hope for the future. This qualification, however, immediately brings us to the larger questions of urbanization and social change. Cities are apparently part of the evolving social "infra-structure" necessary for economic growth. That is, they involve whole complexes of transportation facilities, housing, schools, public utilities, etc.

Serious scientific research must continue to be concerned with fundamental questions of understanding the whole urban phenomenon and not just those aspects that currently appear to be problems to the social engineers. And here it is a matter of appropriate *emphases* rather than *priorities*. What does urbanization do to the growth, structure, and behavior of populations in town *and* country? What forms of economic activity are most advantageously located in cities? What patterns of urban growth are most conducive to total economic growth in the light of rising population pressures? It is only when such general questions have been answered that economic and social advances in particular places can be made secure. Questions about the extent to which scarce productive resources can be used for housing, education, health and welfare must be tested not only against the criterion of their relative contributions to growth but also against other criteria, e.g., controlling human fertility, which is a critical determinant of output per capita.

EMPHASES IN URBAN RESEARCH

Recently, Philip M. Hauser has set out a demographic conception of urbanization as population concentration (Hauser, 1965b). But urbanization is a complex societal process that has many concomitants which are not encompassed by a minimal definition of this type. Large and densely settled agglomerations exhibit internal structural features significantly different from those in smaller communities, but it is no less apparent that highly urbanized societies are vastly different, in economic, social, and political structures, from those in which city-dwellers are in a distinct minority. Such "structural" or "organizational" aspects of urbanization tend to be neglected in the demographic emphasis of much sociological research on the city.

However, two further considerations make us hesitant about using broader — and seemingly more "realistic" — conceptions of urbanization. (1) Little research has been directed at the non-demographic side of urbanization, and it is likely that we have an extremely biased sample on which to base inferences about urban structure. The whole sociological discussion of "urbanism as a way of life," for example, rests upon an empirical base that is narrow indeed, being largely drawn from a few scattered case studies and impressionistic accounts of city life, mainly in the United States. (2) On methodological grounds, we want to avoid building a large number of variables into our basic conception of urbanization, so that we might let them vary independently. (An enlightening review of alternative definitions of urbanization may be found in Reiss, 1964.)

It is our feeling that a definition that includes both demographic and organizational aspects virtually precludes any subsequent analysis of the interrelations between the two. Issues that are problematic are thus prematurely resolved by fiat. There would be no possibility of testing hypotheses regarding the interconnection between, say, population concentration and industrial-occupational structure, since a complex definition of urbanization might prejudge the matter by assuming a relationship that may or may not hold under all circumstances. As Kingsley Davis has argued, "Our preference is to define the city in demographic and spatial terms. In this way a consistent conception can be stated which is not only close to usage but also leaves open the question of the socioeconomic causes and consequences of urbanization" (Davis, 1961, p. xvi).

Now most urban research is "disciplinary" in the extreme, despite our frequent pious assertions about the value of interdisciplinary research. Actually, a *demographic* conception of urbanization is most "neutral," in the sense of being suited to the needs of many disciplines. We might begin, then, by considering possible demographic emphases in urban research.

DEMOGRAPHIC EMPHASES IN URBAN RESEARCH

One disputed question in demography is the current speed of urbanization. *Rates* of recent urban growth are not as easy to compare as *levels* of urbanization. On the basis of more or less informal observation, several writers have indicated that the developing areas are exhibiting extremely high rates of urban growth, and even "abnormal" or "cancerous" growth. A few writers have gone further and have suggested that cities in developing areas are growing at rates substantially above those achieved by the advanced nations when they were in a comparable stage of development. This is perhaps a problem that requires the acuity of a statistically sophisticated urban historian together with the usual mathematical skills of the demographer. (See Gibbs and Schnore, 1960, for citations of the relevant literature.)

Kingsley Davis has suggested that urbanization

> refers. . . to the proportion of the total population concentrated in urban settlements, or else to a rise in this proportion. A common mistake is to think of urbanization as simply the growth of cities. Since the total population is composed of both the urban and rural, however, the "proportion urban" is a function of both of them. Accordingly cities can grow without any urbanization, provided that the rural population grows at an equal or greater rate (Davis, 1965, pp. 41-42).

Davis thus defines urbanization as a *level,* the ratio of urban to total population at any time U_t/P_t, or as a rise in that ratio $\triangle$ (U/P). The latter expression is simply a measure of the percentage of total population removed to the urban sector within a given period. It measures *absolute* changes over time in the urbanization ratio or the "structural" shift from rural to urban residence as these categories are defined by the census authority. But for some purposes this quantification of structural shift might be less significant than a measure of the growth of urban population *relative* to the growth of total population in a given period. This seems to be what Davis has in mind when he writes of the growth of cities "without any urbanization." In his example, urban population grows but total population grows more rapidly in the same interval; hence the "proportion urban" falls and, in fact, the structural shift is urban to rural. Something like this apparently happened in the United States in the course of the decade 1810-1820, and it was probably not an uncommon occurrence in pre-industrial times when the "proportion urban" was almost always low, say, 10 per cent or under. At the other extreme, when the "proportion urban" is virtually 100 per cent, all incremental population growth will be located in cities; cities will grow "without any urbanization," in Davis' sense, but rural population growth in the same period will be zero.

Something approaching this "end of urbanization" could conceivably occur in the United States or some other highly urbanized country, like Great Britain or Australia, unless census definitions and categories were modified. The day of reckoning could easily be postponed, of course, by simply raising the dichotomous rural-urban "cut-off" point, say, from $U_t \geq 2{,}500$ to $U_t \geq 10{,}000$! Meanwhile, inter-urban migration is already of greater interest for certain purposes than rural-to-urban shifts, and in most economically advanced countries the focus of census concern is with the metropolitan areas.

The growth of urban population relative to total population is, nevertheless, of greater analytical and policy interest than either the Davis case of "negative" urbanization or the "end of urbanization" case. Thus, the measure $\frac{\Delta U}{\Delta P} \Big/ \left(\frac{U}{P}\right)$ represents a *relative* growth rate in contrast to the *absolute* rate represented above by $\Delta\left({}^{U}\!/_{P}\right)$. The former measure $\left(\frac{\Delta U}{\Delta P_{t+1}}\right) \Big/ \left(\frac{U_t}{P_t}\right)$ can be expressed as $\frac{\Delta U_{t+1}}{U_t} \Big/ \frac{\Delta P_{t+1}}{P_t}$ which relates, so to speak, the "marginal" rate of urbanization in any period to the "average" rate. This last expression and the measure from which it derives is but one among several alternatives which will give a rate of urban growth standardized by the rate of population growth. The point is that the "marginal" rate of urbanization, in this sense, may be significant in any short period as an indicator of important economic and social changes in an underdeveloped country or in some historical period of early industrialization when *all* incremental urbanization is from the typical low $\frac{U}{P}$ base of a largely agrarian society (Williamson, 1965). If attention were focused exclusively on the $\Delta\left({}^{U}\!/_{P}\right)$ measure, according to the Davis definition, the critical moment of industrial "take-off" or discontinuity with the past would probably be obscured.

In developed countries, of course, the research analyst works with a set of highly refined labor force data, by occupation and industry, and his empirical operations are not restricted to the manipulation of crude proxy variables which tend to identify urbanization of population with industrialization of the economy. The development economist or economic historian, on the other hand, is fortunate indeed to have a rough and ready population census at hand and, lacking other data, he must be prepared to exploit the rural-urban population dichotomy for all it is worth. But since industrial revolution or "take-off," to adopt the jargon of Walt W. Rostow, involves deep-seated social reorganization, as well as greater occupational and locational specialization, acceptance of the rural-to-urban shift as a reliable proxy for the "modernizing" agricultural-to-manufacturing and service shifts probably begs the question. The rural-urban population dichotomy may not be worth all that much.

Thus the transfer from a relatively undifferentiated, low-productivity, pre-industrial society or sector to the relatively specialized, high-productivity, industrial society or sector is by no means coterminous with the move from rural-to-urban residence, nor even co-extensive with our contemporary notion of the shift from agricultural to non-agricultural employments. In a time of "take-off," division of labor is still too rudimentary and economic structure insufficiently articulated to warrant the full imposition of concepts and measures appropriate to advanced industrial-urban society. But the demographic concept of urbanization treated above may distort the processes of early industrialization and social change far less than the more inclusive and (in the long run) more "realistic" structural concept. For most historical and comparative purposes, therefore, demographic definitions and measures of urbanization are preferred, for all their shortcomings.

In addition to the study of levels and rates of urbanization, there is much to be done in the comparative analysis of urban structure in a demographic sense. Recent work on "primary cities" analyzes what is perhaps the simplest aspect of structure – the distribution of cities by size – and seeks the determinants of variations therein (Berry, 1961; Berry, 1965). Other aspects of structure, as represented in the concept of a "system of cities," require more comprehensive flow data in order to describe interrelations between parts of the whole network, and this work is not as far advanced as it might be, given the extraordinary amount of multidisciplinary effort that has gone into it (Berry and Pred, 1965). Some of the urban transportation studies described by John F. Kain and Melvin M. Webber, however, are beginning to yield both the essential data and analytical models for such work. (See Chapters 6 and 14 in this volume.)

SOCIOLOGICAL AND ANTHROPOLOGICAL EMPHASES IN URBAN RESEARCH

The interests of certain sociologists and anthropologists tend to overlap in considering the broader social aspects of urbanization in a comparative framework. But urban anthropology is a new field and the "social" study of the city has been mainly pre-empted by the urban sociologist. Thus, it is a source of some embarrassment for us to admit that the comparative study of urbanization is not very far advanced. Gideon Sjoberg has argued that the dominant sociological approach has depended upon a seriously biased sample of Western cities and, as a consequence, has failed to come to grips with comparative questions (Sjoberg, 1959). His view seems to imply that there may be general "laws" that fit all cities in all places; perhaps it would be more accurate to say that the limits of extant generalizations have not been specified very carefully in the past.

It is true that there has not been a full-scale comparative study of urbanization by an American scholar since Adna F. Weber's doctoral dissertation was published at the turn of the century (Weber, 1899). The resulting deficiency in perspective can be seen in a quick examination of the standard texts in urban sociology which are largely unchanged since the pioneer volumes of the late 1920s. Most of them depend upon data from scattered studies of North American cities. The professional journals provide little more; most of the articles devoted to cities outside of the United States are superficial accounts of certain obvious departures from North American patterns. In short, far too much time has been devoted to the surface manifestations of American cities and to detailing the infinite behavioral nuances of "urbanism" writ large. The only American sociologists to study the determinants and consequences of urbanization and the conditions that give rise to differences between cities and societies have been those working within a narrow demographic framework. The result has been a body of descriptive material that is badly out of balance, lacking proper weight to important organizational elements and other phenomena that are not discoverable by means of demographic analysis alone.

One obvious subject for comparative study is that of the spatial structure of urban areas in various parts of the world. There are intriguing research questions concerning the shape of cities in the developing countries (see Hauser and Schnore, 1965, Chapter 10). For example, consider different patterns of land use in large Indian cities; they differ from each other in many respects as much as they do from North American cities. Another instance is provided by patterns of internal segregation. It has repeatedly been remarked by observant travellers that even large cities in underdeveloped countries tend to lack unity, and consist of whole clusters of contiguous quarters that remain relatively isolated from each other despite their proximity; they are frequently separated by walls and joined only by gates. This pattern of internal segregation, very often along lines of religion, language and color, should be of considerable interest to sociologists and others concerned with organizational matters. For one thing, such a pattern is a direct physical representation of the internal "segmentation" that Emile Durkheim viewed as the hallmark of the undifferentiated social structure (Durkheim, 1933). In addition, knowledge of the day-to-day functioning of these constituent parts of cities in the underdeveloped areas would seem to be essential. Just as modern metropolitanism seems to represent *a social and economic community composed of many politically defined cities,* the form of urbanism on view in backward areas (and even in some Western cities) may consist of *politically defined cities composed of many social and economic communities.*

Another question that has yet to be satisfactorily answered is the urban occupational destination of farm laborers and other rural migrants who abandon the countryside. This obviously has grave implications for the political attitudes of the new urban populations. Scattered evidence from the United States suggests that they enter the urban occupational structure near the bottom (Lipset, 1955; Freedman and Freedman, 1956). There are also fragmentary data suggesting that sheer length of residence in the community of destination is a critical variable with respect to a variety of behaviors on the part of individual migrants (Zimmer, 1956).

Closely related is the question of the extent to which so-called "social-class" differentials in fertility may be attributed to more fundamental rural-urban differentials. The possibility occurs that the widely observed tendency for the lower urban strata to reproduce at higher rates may be partially explained by the disproportionately large representation of recent rural migrants that they contain. Former residents of rural areas certainly bring their children with them, and they may also carry along fertility patterns more appropriate to an agricultural setting. Snapshot surveys at a single point in time may merely reflect basic rural-urban differentials (Goldberg, 1959).

Anthropological methods are especially suited to studying the effects of urbanization on community life and organization in town and country. Thus, the investigations of the British sociologist R. P. Dore in Japan combine the virtues of sociological, anthropological, and historical research in both urban and rural settings (Dore, 1958; Dore, 1960). Not all of the observed decline and disintegration of traditional systems, of course, can or need be attributed to urbanization. The loose associations of clans and extended families in some parts of Africa, for example, were already being undermined by migratory invasion, slave traffic, religious penetrations, and gunpowder, long before the onset of rapid urbanization. The same applies to the centrally organized chiefdoms and other indigenous political systems of sub-Saharan Africa (United Nations, 1957a; International African Institute, 1956). The rise of "nationalism" in such places as Léopoldville (Kinshasa) however, suggests that rapid migration to a metropolis may indeed have political implications.

The two leading subjects for anthropological study, perhaps, are (1) the effects of urbanization on family life, and (2) the acculturation of migrants to the city (or the "deculturation" of migrants from the country). We have a great deal of evidence concerning the "deviant" city life of male migrants when separated from their village-family life. What does all this movement do to personal relations and the established tradition of family authority? The Japanese family apparently rode out the early transition very well – much better than the family in the United States if urban sociologists are to be believed. World War II and its aftermath probably produced more serious dislocation in Japan than urbanization itself. Comparative family studies under standardized conditions would no doubt help to clarify some of these more obscure issues.

Does urbanization necessarily produce personal breakdown and a rise in mental illness? Fragmentary evidence suggests that it does *not* (Goldhamer and Marshall, 1953). This, of course, raises a crucial question which affects analyses of almost all urban phenomena: by what *methodological* means are case study and other microscopic materials related to the macroscopic societal processes of population concentration (Srole, *et al.*, 1962, pp. 253-281)? For what they are worth, however, a few limited case studies have discovered instances of "urbanization without breakdown" (Lewis, 1952; Desai, 1954). And in West African cities, certain voluntary associations appear to have played a crucial role in helping unattached migrants as well as families adapt to urban life and the market economy. They help the newcomer find jobs, housing, necessary goods and services, etc., and thereby cushion the impact of moving from an old social structure to a new one (Little, 1957; Little, 1965; Kuper, 1965).

ECONOMIC EMPHASES IN URBAN RESEARCH

A great deal more information is required on the present and past economic bases of cities, on linkages and clustering of activities, and on the potential advantages and disadvantages of clustered versus dispersed development. Studies must also be made of proposed expenditures on water, sewers, streets, transportation, housing, education, health, welfare, etc., compared with alternative possibilities, e.g., on the basis of different assumptions about the opportunity cost of capital, drains on balance of payments, and rates of obsolescence.

One revealing clue to the changing economic bases of cities and to the organizational dynamics of developing societies is to be found in the structure of the urban labor force (Pitts, 1962). It has been argued that Western nations have experienced a rather regular transition in the industrial composition and organization of their labor forces, characterized by a shift from largely "primary" activities (mainly agriculture) to a predominance of manufacturing ("secondary") activities and the eventual numerical preponderance of service ("tertiary") activities when high levels of development have been reached (Fisher, 1939; Clark, 1940). There is some evidence, however, that a number of developing countries at the present are skipping the second stage, at least in the sense that the fastest gains are being registered in the tertiary sector while manufacturing languishes. Assuming the validity of the measures employed, this fact not only calls into question the entire primary-secondary-tertiary sequence as an appropriate conceptual scheme for summarizing the development process, but suggests the very strong possibility that the expansion of tertiary activity in backward areas does not reflect the Western pattern of up-grading in levels of living (Bauer and Yamey, 1963). This trend may, in fact, mirror the wholesale transfer of rural poverty to the urban setting in face of population pressures. The greatest growth in the tertiary sector sometimes occurs in the most poorly paid and least productive activities, such as those of itinerant pot menders, street vendors, and household servants (Mehta, 1961). These changes are not so much the concomitants of massive structural developments, therefore, as they are the outcome of gradually worsening conditions in both town and country.

Students of the economics of urbanization would do well to examine the subject of population distribution in greater detail. Where great numbers of agriculturists are piled up on the land, rapid development is correspondingly difficult, depending on the type of farming; it is hard to get such people off the land. A redundant rural population, moreover, is ordinarily found in an organizational context that has built-in pressures to persist without radical structural change. Here are found the institutional arrangements regarding property and its inheritance that lead to further fragmentation of holdings and preclude rational land-use. Here also are discovered structural forms that encourage continued high fertility — forms that apparently arose as part of an ecological adaptation that once took a heavy toll in mortality. The demographic consequence of such organizational regimes are even heavier population pressures; its economic consequences are further barriers to modernization.

Now it may appear that the "solution" is obvious: expand employment opportunities in the non-agricultural sectors and large numbers of peasants will give up agriculture. But the difficulty is at once apparent when one considers the alternatives implied by substituting the word "urban" for "non-agricultural" in the formulation of the above solution. Hence, the possibilities of village industry are widely debated in the development literature. Some authorities contend that a system of manufactures dispersed in small plants or "garden cities" will avoid some of the disutilities and disruptions that attend rapid urbanization: crime, delinquency, desertion and divorce, and the high costs of misdirected migration (Aubrey, 1951). The heavy investment in large factories and urban housing would also be avoided. This is an intriguing hypothesis for which there is some support, but at the moment it is no more than a hypothesis. Village industry may certainly serve as a "holding operation" to moderate rural-to-urban flows and, if itself made the subject of "extension-type" educational effort, might provide a useful proving ground for entrepreneurial talent. Small-scale improvements in agriculture, agricultural processing, rural manufactures, and some types of public works – highways, drainage, irrigation, sanitary installations, schools, etc. – may be constructed in small stages without capital-intensive techniques. (A most informative case study is to be found in Moore, 1951.)

The possibility occurs, however, that full-fledged dependence upon a village system might result in total failure. For one thing, a system of dispersed industry foregoes most of the hypothetical economies of concentration that can only be realized with actual urbanization. Secondly, the specification of small-sized plants means rejection of economies of scale that only accrue to very large establishments. Third, such a scheme presupposes the existence of a complex communications and transport network of far greater efficiency than most developing areas may hope to achieve in the immediate future (Harris, 1959). Finally, a system of decentralized village industry may provide too many opportunities for peasants to slip back into traditional agriculturism on at least a part-time or seasonal basis. Along with this goes the continuance of high "non-economic" outlays for funerals, dowries, and other rites of passage. Indeed, what may well be required is a massive structural upheaval that uproots large numbers and transplants them in new habitats. Thus, some degree of urban concentration may actually be a functional prerequisite of agrarian reorganization and of real modernization. Exponents of "big push" development have founded their case upon a need for large *initial* increases in the rate of saving and investment and heavy outlays on manufacturing. Whether their argument applies, however, must depend on the circumstances. Some of the force of their case is lost when it is remembered that such facilities require very different gestation periods for their construction. If producers of goods are allowed to *export* some of their output, moreover, their technically fixed minimum investments need not be excessive relative to aggregate demand, and overhead charges per unit of output will be correspondingly reduced. Large inputs of private capital from abroad might be attracted into these industries and, if certain safeguards were forthcoming, development might continue along such lines at a modest pace, making for a more gradual absorption of migrants from the countryside.

The foregoing discussion, of course, is almost entirely speculative and is not to be taken as the result of accomplished research. Nonetheless, some of these ideas – given further clarification and elaboration – might serve as the bases for testable hypotheses regarding the place of urbanization in economic development. The real world presents us with such a rich variety of situations that it should not prove terribly difficult to find a series of varying cases that exhibit sufficient contrast to comprise a kind of "natural experiment." If it should turn out that the hunches enumerated here have any real validity, their implications for practical developmental programs would be fully as useful as the propositions that would become candidates for inclusion in a full-fledged abstract theory of economic development. Practically, the findings would be extremely helpful in industrial location programs and in planning for the assimilation of migrants to the cities. Theoretically, a demonstration of the interconnections between urbanization and modernization would fill a large gap in the contemporary understanding of economic development.

A common focus of much of the literature on economic development is found in such topics as savings, investment, and capital formation. Until recently, population factors have been given only a minor role, despite the strong demographic interest exhibited within classical economics. If the reader will trust the judgment of two amateur economists, this deficiency can be attributed to an extraneous factor or, more properly speaking, to a set of circumstances that have no necessary relevance to theory. We refer to the "actionist" bias of contemporary economics. Distrustful of palliatives and panaceas, the economist seems to have fastened upon capital formation as the bedrock fundamental of development. Assuming no large reserve of underemployed resources, something must be set aside out of current production and diverted to areas and sectors with little or no prospects of immediate return, in order for future output to surpass existing levels. These are undeniable "facts" of accounting logic but their implications are various. For one thing, the analyst need not focus exclusively on capital formation itself; rather, he may turn to a study of the *external conditions* under which capital accumulation proceeds most rapidly. Granted the necessity for reducing life to sets of national accounts and slices of diagrammatic pie, it is well for planners to remember that chunks of saving that go directly into manufactures have often been quite limited in the past compared with chunks that go into the "infra-structure." Some of the great surges in the economic growth of Western Europe and North America were apparently connected with railroad construction, street railway development, urban building, electrification, and so on. We need to know much more about the kinds of diversions of capital which offered greater or lesser returns at various times, their capacities for absorbing urban labor force increments, and their individual multiplier effects (Lampard, 1955).

The same narrow preoccupation with saving and investment has produced a kind of economic psychologist, immersed in the problem of "inducements" to save, and caught in sterile debate regarding human "propensities" to behave in this or that manner. Without a more sophisticated behavioral and experimental apparatus than most economists currently display, this sort of amateur psychologizing may prove to be one of the least promising byways down which economists have wandered in their search for "realism." In any event, the actionistic bias of contemporary economics, when it is considered alongside the microscopic drift of social science generally, has yielded a peculiar conceptual set; concern with the process of capital accumulation and its psychological ramifications has proceeded without much reference to the contextual situation. Add to this the manipulative interest of the orthodox Keynesian, and his tendency to avoid long-run questions, and one current dilemma of economics becomes understandable.

To find economists tending to ignore the implications of urbanization in their analyses is no great surprise. But the disturbing thought occurs that the current preoccupations with the practical aspects of capital accumulation may actually hinder the understanding of development as a "natural" phenomenon. The actionist orientation of economics is certainly not to be derided as a fault in itself. We hope to bridge the gaps between urban research and policy planning. What *is* to be criticized is the tendency to allow practical goals to obscure the objectives of scientific research, and to permit action-oriented assumptions to enter in the guise of theoretical postulates. As a consequence, we have only recently reached the point (through the efforts of Harvey Leibenstein, Ansley J. Coale, Simon Kuznets, Edgar M. Hoover, and a few others) where there is a growing appreciation of the significance of population growth and composition for economic development (Leibenstein, 1957; Coale and Hoover, 1960). It is in no small part the achievement of a mere handful of economists to have effected the "exile's return" of demographic factors to economics. While it is not always possible to accept his solutions, Leibenstein's work provides a convincing demonstration of the relevance of changes in both population size and composition to economic development. One misses, however, a corresponding treatment of changes in *population distribution,* and especially urbanization, in the development literature. Except for the work of Bert F. Hoselitz and a few others, one would have to say that the topic has been almost entirely neglected by economists (Hoselitz, 1953; Hoselitz, 1960; Perloff, *et al.,* 1960; Williamson, 1965).

It is apparent that economic policies are being promulgated in a vacuum of knowledge regarding urbanization in both Western and non-Western settings. It is of the first order of importance to learn the extent to which efficient large-scale production and distribution systems still require a concentrated labor force and market, or whether new means of power generation, transport and communications, reinforced by traditional elements, have lessened the need for the huge agglomerations that were created during the nineteenth-century industrialization of the West. On the labor force side, we need to know whether or not modern urban-industrialism can function effectively on the basis of seasonally migrant labor, to what extent trade union activities affect the rudimentary factor markets of developing countries, and the ways in which management organization and policies operate in the same context of economic transition (Moore, 1964).

What is the effect, moreover, of urbanization on the consumption habits of recent migrants? According to some writers, urbanization has the effect of increasing imitative consumption; goods and services bought with new income are often less desired for their functional use than for their prestige value. As a community assumes elements of the consumption patterns of more advanced societies, it probably becomes easier to adopt additional elements later on (Holton, 1960). Imitative consumption is thus *self-reinforcing* and, as T. R. Malthus noted, "a decided taste for the conveniences and comforts of life" stimulates a man's efforts over and beyond the amount necessary to insure his food supply; he seldom begrudges working overtime for it is "inconsiderable compared with the commodities it will purchase." Case study materials in themselves, however, do little more than document the insights of Malthus that were achieved more than a century and a half ago, when the English country folk were first becoming committed to the standards and styles of the town.

Another important area for investigation – in view of the critical importance of the population problem – is the possible impact of urbanization on fertility. We are aware that family separation and a surplus of adult males in cities apparently increases the incidence of prostitution, delinquency, and crime. But what does it do to the birth rate in town and country? By the time he published his *Principles of Political Economy* in 1820, Malthus thought that the movement of families to the towns and their pursuit of modest improvements in consumption might lower the tendency to reproduce. In a more technical way, economists like Harvey Leibenstein expect a similar outcome. If anything, we know a little more about the effects of non-agricultural employment on the fertility of women in the country than in the town, and what we know is disquieting. A study by A. J. Jaffe and Koya Azumi, based on limited data from Puerto Rico and Japan, concludes that from a fertility standpoint, "the most desirable industries to be introduced . . . would be those using large quantities of female labor away from home, in modern factories, stores, offices, etc. If enough women were so occupied the birth rate would be lowered considerably" (Jaffe and Azumi, 1960). So far as it goes, this evidence does not augur well for the possibility of reducing the social costs of urbanization by planned developments of dispersed cottage industry.

HISTORICAL EMPHASES IN URBAN RESEARCH

The interest of contemporary social scientists in the problems of "modernization" in developing countries has given a fillip to research in historical aspects of urbanization. Scholars turn to the record of the economically advanced countries of Western Europe and North America in the hope of gaining new insights into the complexities of the developmental process today. The experience of a country such as England, the first to carry through the industrial revolution and the first to transform itself into an industrial-urban society, would seem to have special relevance for all students of the city. The urbanizing experience of countries like the United States, Germany, Japan, or Russia, which achieved their industrial revolutions out of a fusion of indigenous and induced elements, and with greater or lesser awareness of their predecessors' examples, appears to be even more germane to the task of putting "modernization" in historical perspective (T. C. Smith, 1960). That this is no naive exercise in historicist thinking should be clear from our previous concern with comparative studies that might comprise a "natural experiment." In this regard, the "uniqueness" of discrete situations becomes a distinct methodological advantage; since the true comparativist is always as much concerned with differences as with similarities, he is ultimately in the best position to see the generic potential of cultures and societies realized in the specific performances and contexts of particular historical cases. No two cities are alike in all respects any more than any two persons; nevertheless, with proper intellectual safeguards, comparisons in time are possible and useful.

In light of the interest in, and promise of, historical studies of urbanization, it is somewhat disappointing to report that our knowledge of man's past experience with urban life is rather limited. This is notably true for the period of industrial urbanization since the eighteenth century. There is, to be sure, a growing literature of histories of individual cities and of case studies of particular aspects of urban life in different countries and periods (Dawson and Warner, 1963) but owing to the fragmentary character of this work such studies provide little cumulative or generalized knowledge about urbanization. The social scientist who turns, therefore, to the historical literature on urbanization and cities is likely to seek in vain.

For the most part, writings in urban history can be classified as local history. While the work of the local historian is often reported in monumental and (for the specialist) indispensable detail, it is nevertheless true that most local studies only assume wider significance when their subject is itself important by virtue of its size and political status, or because of the outstanding events and historical personalities associated with it. National capitals are obvious examples.

Even when the less parochial scholar writes a comparative history of two or more places having some experience in common, his frame of reference is usually limited in time or narrow in focus, he very rarely treats the societal movements that create cities or give a generic character to the urban life of a period. The dominant concern with urbanization and society in modern times, in fact, has come from outside the confines of local history and originates in a derivative kind of social history that is a by-product of research and writing in intellectual or economic history. The emphasis in such studies is usually placed upon urban *problems* and reform movements rather than upon the *processes* of social change and adaptation (Lampard, 1963; Briggs, 1963, pp. 11-54).

Relations between the burgeoning city populations of the nineteenth century and the larger society are conceived in terms of "the impact" of the dynamic urban-industrial order upon the relatively stable rural-agrarian order, resulting in the disintegration and eventual disappearance of the latter after a prolonged and bitter conflict between opposing "ways of life." In focusing so much upon the politicized problems of urbanization and neglecting the formative societal process, the "urban impact" historians adopted many of the same lines of inquiry, asked broadly similar questions of the same types of data, and came up with much the same conclusions as their more action-oriented forebears in the social sciences. As a consequence, historians of recent times have contributed very little to our general knowledge of the changing structure and organization of the world's first industrial-urban societies (Kuznets, 1966). Here research could very well be directed into the societal process of *differentiation* which appears to be intensified under industrialism in the form of three interrelated population movements:

(1) growth and redistribution of population in space, notably via rural-to-urban migration;

(2) growth and differentiation of the labor force, notably by the shift out of relatively undifferentiated agricultural occupations into more specialized and full-time non-agricultural occupations (mining, manufactures, and service categories);

(3) the achievement of higher socioeconomic status for larger numbers of people, notably by the more widespread distribution of property and/or education (the formation of the "middle classes").

To the extent that these interrelated social movements are contingent upon agrarian reorganization and political-legal emancipation of the individual, such research would begin to throw more light upon the institutional "prerequisites" for social change under early industrialism and its incremental manifestations.

If the climax of the first industrial revolution in England during the late eighteenth and early nineteenth centuries represents the crossing of a threshold into industrial-urban society, social historians in general and students of economic development in particular will have to concern themselves with what lay on the far side of that great benchmark in the history of society. It was in this pre-industrial era, presumably, that the fundamental changes occurred which constituted the "preconditions," albeit unspecified, on which Walt W. Rostow (1960) erected the rather brittle structure of his "stages of economic growth." Surprisingly enough, more is known in some respects about the role of cities in pre-industrial societies, European and non-European, than in the industrial era itself. We will give only two recent examples available in the English language: (1) Gustave von Grunebaum (1955) has focused on social institutions of Islamic cities, and (2) Carl H. Kraeling and Robert McC. Adams (1960) have brought together recent findings and suggested future lines of research into the role of urbanization in the cultural development of the ancient Near East. Of more immediate interest to social scientists concerned with the role of cities in the commercial development of Europe are the scholarly, though very uneven, chapters contributed to the *Cambridge Economic History*, Volume 3, (Postan, Rich, and Miller, 1963). They treat such topics as the rise of towns, organization of trade, markets and fairs, urban economic policies, guilds, the policies of state governments towards the towns, public credit in the towns, and changing conceptions of economy and society. Much of the more detailed and up-to-date historical research on urbanization in antiquity and the European medieval period is not available in English, but nonspecialists will find an excellent bibliographic orientation and a useful typology of pre-industrial cities in a recent essay by Robert S. Lopez.

Lopez suggests four different historical types of urban settlement – "with different attitudes toward technology and economy" – the stockade city, the agrarian city, the market city, and the industrial city. Of special importance for the development of European *bourgeois* society is the market city in which the merchant, for the first time, becomes the social leader. Although markets had existed in the agrarian city and even, intermittently, in the stockade city, the true market city appears "when market and public square became one thing, that is, when the superiority of the land owner was eliminated . . . Wealth rather than birth thus became the main basis of class distinction" (Lopez, 1963, p. 34).

It should be noted at this point, perhaps, that the celebrated thesis of Henri Pirenne (1925) regarding the revival of medieval trade and the origins of cities has been modified somewhat by more recent research which treats the medieval urban experience over wider areas of Europe; emphases are now placed upon regional divergences from the Pirenne pattern, greater continuity with antiquity, and upon the numbers of manorial officials and landholding nobility, as well as "new" mercantile men, who formed the urban patriciate (Ennen, 1956; Hibbert, 1953; Tikhomirov, 1959). The comparative historian, moreover, cannot fail to note that sizable mercantile cities flourished in parts of sub-Saharan Africa during the European medieval period, although the social transformations and political structures of the more autonomous market cities of Europe were not repeated elsewhere (Davidson, 1959; Freeman-Grenville, 1962). Hence Max Weber's notion that the *conjuratio*, or oath-bound fraternity of contracting individuals, provides a uniquely moral-contractual basis for the self-governing territorial corporations of medieval Europe, still stands. Nothing among the diverse Greek *poleis* nor among the teeming cities of the Orient quite resembled this remarkable, albeit untypical and short-lived, mode of European community.

The social and spatial structures of pre-industrial market cities in late medieval Europe appear to differ somewhat from other preindustrial centers which have market functions situated within them or attached to them. Likewise political structures and jurisdictions differ strikingly from region to region and in varying degree from the corresponding structures and jurisdictions of certain non-European cities and city-states. Thus it is difficult for the historian, especially an urban specialist, to agree with the rigorous statement of the sociologist Gideon Sjoberg (1960) that the structural correlates of *all* pre-industrial or "feudal" cities (as he uses the term) are more or less constant and alike, while their "specific cultural content" varies widely. To be sure, some of the evidence for diversity cited above might be dismissed as "merely cultural" or, alternatively, Sjoberg might categorize the capitalistic market cities of Europe as "modernizing" and "transitional" to his original dichotomy of types (Sjoberg, 1965).

But again, it is not easy to accept the postulate that technology — which for Sjoberg involves tools, sources of energy, and the "know-how" connected therewith — is the primary determinant of both structural similarities and change (Reynolds, 1961). According to Robert S. Lopez, it was chiefly for the reason of insufficient demand that the burgeoning commercial centers of Europe stopped short of industrial self-transformation: the pressures of demand did not "warrant a greater investment in labor saving devices for all stages of production" (Lopez, 1963, p. 35). It is precisely this insensitivity to structural divergences which reflect organizational or cultural variances that has led a specialist in the historical cities of Southeast Asia (Wheatley, 1963) to doubt the usefulness of Sjoberg's carefully constructed pre-industrial type as a tool in comparative historical research.

The question of the build-up to the threshold of the industrial-urban revolution leads conveniently to that other great watershed in historical studies of urbanization, namely *the* "urban revolution" of so-called neolithic times (Childe, 1950). Knowledge of men's first approaches toward urban life has recently been enlarged by the expansion of archeological research and the adaptation of certain natural science techniques to the examination of archeological evidence. The still very incomplete record of eleven Old World and seven New World areas from the late Pleistocene Era after 15,000 B.C. suggests a variety of "cultural build-ups" leading to what Robert J. Braidwood and Gorden R. Willey (1962) call incipient urbanization and the first thresholds of urban civilization. Each of the areas in question experienced a cumulative sequence from loose-knit food collecting systems through more or less effective food production to a point of definitive urbanization. There were, however, not only significant variations among them in climate, topography, vegetation, crops and animals, but also in reliance upon irrigation works, in the emergence of cult and ceremonial centers, in social stratification, and in size and density of settlements as well.

Not least variable were the time spans involved: "definitive" urbanization was achieved in Mesopotamian Iraq and "the fertile crescent" by the fourth millennium B.C.; in the Indus valley and Huangho basin from the third to the second millennia B.C.; in Mesoamerica very late in the first millennium B.C.; in the Central Andes, Northern Europe, and possibly in sub-Saharan Africa during the first millennium A.D. The technological achievement of agriculture and the social organization of the agrarian village underlie all documented cases of incipient urbanization, but they do not guarantee the entire sequence or even acceleration of changes in a definite direction. Some populations appear to have lived too abundantly from part-time cultivation, gathering, and fishing, for example, ever to submit fully to the regimen of village agriculture; in other areas, climatic extremes or uniformity of physical environment (jungle, forest, steppe, etc.) may have combined with social conditions to inhibit either the achievement of village agriculture or succession beyond it.

The abstract criteria for the urban revolution, which V. Gordon Childe (1950) deduced from archeological evidence, indicate that urbanization is a social as well as a cultural process. The relevance of social organization has been stated most succinctly by Robert McC. Adams (1960) in his treatment of the immediate origins of cities in Southwest Asia. "The rise of cities," he maintains, ". . . was pre-eminently a social process, an expression more of changes in man's interaction with his fellows than in his interaction with his environment." The novelty of the city consisted in "a whole series of new institutions and the vastly greater size and complexity of the social unit, rather than basic innovations in subsistence." (See also Adams, 1966.)

Recent work has, therefore, reduced the decisive significance attaching to hydraulic engineering in the older literature and, in light of experience in pre-Columbian America, has even questioned the indispensability of elaborate writing and script systems. Eric E. Lampard (1965) concludes that "definitive urbanization" was a "culmination of primordial tendencies in the additional and *alternative* form of social organization: the definitive city. By means of its capacity to generate, store, and utilize social saving, the definitive city artifact is capable of transplanting itself out of its native uterine environments" (Lampard, 1965, p. 523). This "classic" mode of urbanization endures and ramifies in different parts of the world in circumstances and under constraints which tend to moderate and, indeed, check both the growth of population and urban centers. The threshold of "industrial" urbanization is not, in fact, crossed until the moderating constraints are finally relaxed through the build-up of *organizational* as well as technological capacities for unprecedented population concentration. Then by means of its novel capacity to convert and control high per capita levels of inanimate heat energy, the industrial-urban city establishes itself outside of its uterine setting in Western Europe in ever-widening reaches of social and physical environment.

Thus, out of the changing relations of urban populations to their social and physical environments stem some of the major research problems of the new social history. The language which Oscar Handlin (1963) used in his consideration of "the modern city as a field of historical study" is applicable to far wider ranges of time and place. We need to know more about: (1) the differential organization of social space; (2) the creation of a social order within a population; and (3) the adjustment by the human personality to the continuing reorganization of the social environment. If historical studies of urbanization are to contribute more to our understanding of the "modernization" process, it may be by exploring these larger questions of a common and comparative nature within the renovated framework of human ecology suggested by Otis Dudley Duncan (1964).

POLITICAL EMPHASES IN URBAN RESEARCH

One of the striking things about the substantial increases in the urban parts of developing nations is their juxtaposition with (a) extremely youthful populations, (b) certain elements of modern technology, and (c) social, economic and political structures that are formally unchanged from past decades. These aspects of rapid urban growth assume particular significance in the context of the widespread poverty in which they usually appear. In brief compass, however, the problem is as much "political" as it is "economic" and "social."

The main facts of political life seem to be these. In the first place, a growing majority of the population in some underdeveloped areas has no real stake in the *status quo*; this would seem especially true in the cities. Much of the urban populace is young and not yet established; the age distribution, ethnic composition, and rapid natural increase alone would be enough to produce and intensify this explosive situation. The effect of urbanization – in the sense of simple population agglomeration – is to concentrate large numbers of unattached youth, and to transfer the poverty of the over-crowded village to the teeming city streets. Added to this, however, is the disquieting fact that very few benefit from the operation of the *ancien régime.* Much of the real wealth is siphoned off by a small indigenous elite and/or by compatible foreign interests (Schnore, 1960-61).

The element that supplies a fuse for this powder keg is the presence of certain pieces of strictly twentieth-century technology. Radios and movable loudspeakers can be utilized to reach great numbers, literate or otherwise; buses and trucks can assemble them quickly; the transistor radio and movies can thrust across a propaganda-laden message much as the newspaper did in Western countries, but with far more devastating impact. In this context, it takes only a clever and willful demagogue to whip into a frenzy the barely latent discontent of the new urban masses; some demagogues have learned these techniques of crowd management from successful Western exemplars (Rudé, 1965). Different leaders – not all of them semiliterate Marxists – offer alternative panaceas, vying for the fickle support of mobs in the street. Small wonder, then, that recent years have witnessed political turmoil in the cities of the underdeveloped world. Most of the basic ingredients for violent upheaval are at hand, and some of them serve multiple functions. The mass media, for example, may vividly portray a way of life previously beyond the power of the untutored imagination. The motion pictures – and American and European films, in particular – may have an "anti-Western" effect, by displaying a glamor-tinged image of life in this part of the world. Thus may be fostered "the revolution of rising expectations," to use a descriptive phrase so appropriate that it has quickly passed into the public domain. Add to this the "conspicuous consumption" of local elites and their Western partners and expectations are transformed into a rising surge of resentment. In the presence of the new technology, the poverty-ridden youthfulness of the urban populace takes on an entirely new aspect.

Lest our language have the appearance of concern for the *status quo,* we must admit to the feeling that very little in the way of true development and modernization will take place in the absence of radical changes in the social structure of many underdeveloped nations – in the cities no less than in the countryside. However, the likelihood that the new leaders, hard pressed by domestic difficulties, will be catapulted into rash adventures at home or abroad must lead even the most remote "scientific" observer to see these cities and their potential for explosion as menacing the peace of an uncertain era. Even if revolutions sometimes begin in the countryside, they will surely move on the cities. The goal – in policy as well as in research – is to gain some understanding of the forces that have been set loose in a world of stark contrasts between poor and rich, illiterate and educated, earthbound and airborne, starving and affluent, rustic and urban.

2

The Assimilation of Migrants to Cities

Anthropological and Sociological Contributions

LYLE W. SHANNON
and MAGDALINE SHANNON

☐ THE UNITED STATES IS IN AN ADVANCED stage of worldwide transition from an agricultural to an industrial society. In the early years of the twentieth century this transitional process was accompanied by the emigration of millions of young adults from other countries to the United States, some with rural and some with urban antecedents, and more recently by the internal migration of persons from farms and villages to urban areas. (For a comprehensive review of the literature see Kahl, 1959.)

MIGRATION AS A MAJOR SOURCE OF URBAN GROWTH

THE IMPRESSION OF DECLINING IMPORTANCE

During the peak period of emigration from other countries more than a million immigrants entered the United States each year, an estimated 40 million arriving in the United States between 1820 and 1950, and 38 million of these in the one hundred-year period between 1830 and 1930. Although almost a third of the newcomers left the United States over the years, about 29 million remained. As the years have gone by the relative numbers of the foreign-born in the United States have markedly declined. For example, in 1920 there was one foreign-born person in the United States for every eight inhabitants, in 1940 one for every eleven inhabitants, and in 1960 there was one for every 15 inhabitants. The diverse fortunes of some who remain have recently been narrated in *Beyond the Melting Pot: The Negroes, Puerto Ricans, Jews, Italians and Irish of New York City* (Glazer and Moynihan, 1964). One might conclude from immigration and migration data alone that the social impact on cities of (1) rural-reared immigrants from foreign lands, and (2) migrants from villages and rural farm or nonfarm areas in the United States has largely passed. But to the contrary and central to this chapter is the fact that internal migration, much of it of a problem-generating type, has remained a major source of the growth of cities in the United States.

THE NEW IMPACT OF MIGRATION TO URBAN AREAS

The Changing Source of Urban Growth

Our position is that a decline in the proportion of foreign-born in cities or in the number or proportion of persons involved in cityward migration does not necessarily mean that the impact of migration on urban areas is decreasing. Quite apart from either real or perceived benefits, or added life burdens for individual migrants, the nature of contact and interaction between either new arrivals and members of the urban society, or between different ethnic and racial groups within urban society, indicates that far-reaching public consequences of both earlier and latter-day population movements are continuing to be generated.

Just as the countries of origin of immigrants changed over the years, so has the source of migration to Northern cities shifted disproportionately to the South and Southwest and rural regions within these areas. Despite the fact that as many as three-quarters of the persons migrating to cities in the United States today have nonfarm origins and destinations, that portion which comes to Northern industrial cities from urban and rural regions in the South and Southwest has become an important element in the urban population.

As Southern white, Negro, and Mexican-American migrants and their offspring increase in numbers and proportion in the cities, the problem will become more acute. They will continue to increase since those at the lowest levels in the South and Southwest are only beginning to awaken. Added to this is the concentration of migrants in the inner core of our cities (Sharp and Schnore, 1962; Schnore and Sharp, 1963). And as migrants attempt to translate their desires for a higher level of living into reality through action, it will be better realized how incorrect is the notion that the transition from rural to urban has passed its period of maximum interest in the United States. Rather than being concerned about the optimum size of cities or the most desirable rate of change (Shannon, 1961a) we will be forced to turn our attention to the development of workable techniques for absorbing into the economy the migrant who will likely have increasingly less to offer in the complex urban-industrial milieu.

Laboratories for the Study of Social Change

Another error is to assume that if one wishes to study societies in transition or the processes of social change, the only remaining research sites are undeveloped countries where urbanization and industrialization are in their incipient stages. (For example, see Abu-Lughod, 1961, on Cairo and Pearse, 1961, on Rio de Janeiro.) Essentially the same process has also been described by Sheila Patterson in *Dark Strangers* (Patterson, 1964) in her account of the absorption of West Indian immigrants to London (also see Maddox, 1960). Such sites are, of course, more exotic or physically attractive than others, and funds may even be readily available for studies of industrialization in them. Under such circumstances it takes little imagination to understand the bored Midwestern sociologist who decides that it is essential for him to journey to far places for his research. Furthermore, cross-cultural checking of our hypotheses should be encouraged (Peterson and Scheff, 1965, p. 171).

Were one selecting a laboratory for the study of migration, and the process of acculturation and assimilation in individuals and groups that takes place as a consequence, there would be no better setting than Northern industrial cities, the way stations to which migrants first move, and the depressed areas from which they come. Although some research is now being conducted in the urban industrial communities in which these migrants find themselves, less work is being done in the way stations such as Memphis, or places of origin, such as South Texas and Mississippi.

CONCEPTUALIZING ACCULTURATION AND ASSIMILATION

Cultural Integration

Discussions of assimilation have usually revolved around the terms to be used in referring to some larger social process and the position that this or that concept takes on a continuum with cultural pluralism and assimilation at its opposite poles. Notable among these has been the Social Science Research Council Summer Seminar on Acculturation in 1953 (SSRC, 1954). Other excellent reviews of acculturation and assimilation have been completed by Spiro (Spiro, 1955) and Peterson and Scheff (Peterson and Scheff, 1965). As we see it, acculturation and assimilation are points on a continuum, extending from a point of maximum difference between people to one where either two groups are no longer distinguishable, or members of an immigrant group have become indistinguishable from members of the host society.

Acculturation refers to the acquisition or borrowing of certain cultural traits from one society by people in another – it may be a two-way process. Persons may have multiple behavior patterns – old and new. Richardson (Richardson, 1961, p. 20), however, has defined acculturation as the process of acquiring or adopting behavior patterns similar to those in the whole society. He sees it as a one-way process in which the minority acquires some of the characteristics of the majority – a process that involves the acceptance of beliefs, (Butterworth, 1962) going further than food habits, dress, or other cultural items. This definition of acculturation implies more than borrowing cultural traits and is consistent with our position that it is a point on the processual continuum leading to assimilation. Acculturation involves not only a change in behavior but even a change in the conception of oneself. There is also a time element involved in that acculturation may take place in a relatively short period of time while assimilation is considered to be a longer, and more gradual process.

Plural societies would be at one end of the continuum to which we refer and at the other would be societies in which the migrant has completely conformed to the host or dominant society. This leads us back to our original point – that emphasis should be on the process whereby the migrant acquires behavioral patterns of the larger society and learns how to play the major roles appropriate to his position in the society, that is, the roles assigned to him in the social order of which he is a part (Taft, 1953).

Economic Absorption

S. N. Eisenstadt has conceptualized the process of absorption as follows: "... the process of absorption from the point of view of the individual immigrant's behavior, entails the learning of new roles, the transformation of primary group values and the extension of participation beyond the primary group in the main spheres of the social system" (Eisenstadt, 1954, p. 15). This process may be observed on three different levels – acculturation, institutional integration, and personal adjustment (Eisenstadt, 1953). Acculturation can take place without integration into the major social institutions and without personal adjustment. Whether integration into the major social institutions is a requisite for personal adjustment is debatable, but the work of orientation of migrants indicates that integration into the economic institution would be paramount. Reasonable security of employment is probably essential for fuller cultural integration (Borrie, 1959, p. 101).

From a practical standpoint, then, we shall place considerable emphasis on the process of economic absorption. Economic absorption, to repeat, is one measurable facet of the total absorption process or cultural integration. While "cultural integration" refers to integration into the whole gamut of institutional life, "economic absorption" refers to the process of securing work and becoming part of the regularly employed labor force.

The Problem of Measurement

Lack of Sensitivity in Scales

Sociology probably has fewer instruments for measuring what it perceives to be the appropriate variables than any other discipline with pretensions of rigor, except perhaps cultural or social anthropology. Operational definitions of variables that have been translated into reliable ordinal measures, let alone cardinal measures, are scarce. Even the most cursory review of the measuring devices that have been used in assimilation research suggests that conclusions must be tentative.

One major shortcoming of existing measuring devices (appropriate scales for assimilation research) is that they measure variations among individuals in the host society fairly well, but are constructed in such a manner that migrants are so skewed toward one end of the scale that changes among them tend to remain relatively imperceptible. While differences are found within the host society as we move from those at the lowest to the highest level of living, and from those who have an active to those who have a passive world view, gradations of variation within migrant groups are not as nicely measured. Migrants usually tend to cluster at the lower end of the continuum. This brings us to the problem of sub-cultural bias.

Cultural Bias in Measuring Devices

It might be imagined that a relatively simple measure of the degree of economic absorption or cultural integration could be devised from responses to questions about occupation and income, food habits, dress, associations, or the individual's view of his physical and social environment. This does not turn out to be the case. Sociologists usually develop an instrument based on items selected from the larger culture, with the goal of discerning behavioral or attitudinal modification in the migrant as a consequence of contact with the larger culture. Since the items are representative of the larger culture, and the migrant is at least initially far from the level of living and focal concerns of the average person in the larger society, the changes that occur immediately or within a few years of his arrival in the urban industrial society are either not those anticipated by the researcher, or as we have just suggested, are almost imperceptible.

Only with time in the community, and that may mean a generation or two, is change of the type expected or of observable magnitude readily seen. Any perceptive person who has grown up in a community with the first generation of either the foreign-born or migrants from the South or Southwest knows how those in his own generation differ from the previous generation, and even more noticeably, from the often remarkably well assimilated third generation. It is this generational change that is more readily measurable than change within persons who have moved from the South or the Southwest and have been in the urban-industrial community only a short period of time.

A Bias Introduced by the Passage of Time and by Invention

Aside from the difficulties encountered in measuring accumulation, assimilation, or integrative behavior there are special pitfalls when attempting to measure economic absorption. Increasing complexity and specialization in the systems of production and distribution of goods has changed the relative proportion of people at different occupational levels in the society. Differences between the urban North and rural South and Southwest have been accentuated over a period of time. The transitional process from labor-intensive production with skilled or unskilled labor, to mass production and assembly lines, and finally to automation, has had, as its consequence for urban dwellers, a rather continuous upward movement in the occupational hierarchy. Traditionally this has left positions at the lowest level for new arrivals, but the lowest levels have also been moving up in terms of the years of formal education required for a regular place in the economic order. This also means that the proportion of workers that can be absorbed into the economy as completely unskilled laborers is decreasing.

Thus, on an integrational basis, sons who migrate (Scudder and Anderson, 1954) are at higher levels than their fathers, but even those who do not migrate are likely to be at higher levels than their fathers for the simple reason that fewer people work at the lowest occupational levels than in each previous generation (Duncan, 1966; Kahl, 1959, pp. 58-61). Migration from rural to urban, or village to city, changes the migrant's job classification so that occupational mobility seems to have taken place. Actually the migrant may be working at the lowest level in the urban industrial society but at a higher level on the scale of occupations for the total society only because the urban industrial society has relatively few positions comparable to those in the rural or small town society from which he came.

THE SAD STATE OF KNOWLEDGE ABOUT THE PROCESS OF ASSIMILATION

A Static versus a Dynamic Approach

Depending on one's viewpoint, we know either an amazing lot about the process of assimilation of migrants to cities or astoundingly little. Perhaps it would be more appropriate to say that our knowledge is greater or less, depending on whether we are interested in static or dynamic aspects of the problem.

Failure to Study Assimilation in Relation to Social Organization

To make the situation even more disappointing, sociologists have ignored or paid only lip service to the fact that some knowledge of the social organization of the host city and the community of origin is crucial to an understanding of the process of assimilation and the success or failure of migrants to be assimilated. (For a notable exception among the mobility-oriented studies see Lipset, 1955). Although even an anthropologist would agree that the city is the place to start (Mayer, 1962), studies of assimilation have neither adequately dealt with the social organization of the host communities nor the area from which migrants come as determinants of what takes place when they arrive in the host community. There is one exception in this respect; Rubin went to Chicasaw County, Mississippi, in 1956, and interviewed 114 heads of households concerning the migration patterns of their siblings and children (Rubin, 1960). He selected the locale because it had provided a considerable number of Negro migrants to Beloit, Wisconsin, the site of Omari's study (Omari, 1956).

A plethora of studies have focused their attention on the individual characteristics of the migrants at the time that they leave their place of origin, their characteristics at the time that they enter the city (Turner, 1949), their adjustment at some later point in time, (Killian, 1953), and in at least one case, their adjustment upon return to place of origin (Form and Rivera, 1958). To summarize the findings of studies dealing with the characteristics of migrants we need only say that the migrant comes to the city with little in the way of marketable skills (Benewitz, 1956; Shannon and Krass, 1964) but with kinship attachments that will enable him to survive (Blumberg and Bell, 1959; Abu-Lughod, 1961; Pearse, 1961;

Morrill, 1963) while he becomes acquainted with the simplest demands of urban life.

Whether the proportion of migrants without marketable skills is essentially the same as in the past or is increasing is irrelevant for the simple reason that the demand for unskilled workers has declined and the demand for workers with special skills has increased. Even though the bulk of those who move to the city may be better than average in their home community, the question is whether or not they will be readily absorbed into the industrial economy. The characteristics of migrants are of interest in relation to changes in the organization of production because of the consequences of these characteristics for the society and the migrants, but not in a purely ethnographic sense as far as the sociologist is concerned.

Emphasis has tended to be on the characteristics of the individual migrants or the status of the group in comparison with persons who have always lived in the community, rather than upon what was happening where the migrants came from, what was going on in the city when they arrived, what was taking place in the city at the time that the study was being conducted, and how each of these increases or decreases the likelihood of assimilation. For example, how are the chances for assimilation increased at the time that the migrant arrives if every foundry or other heavy industry is working three shifts as contrasted to being at half its usual employment level? Or, what happens if migrants settle in an industrial community shortly before automation in the foundries and other heavy industry? And to take an even simpler variable, how does the rural-reared or migrant proportion of a city's population influence the life chances of new arrivals? Already one-third of Cairo's permanent residents were born outside Cairo (Abu-Lughod, 1961). Is it possible to assimilate migrants with ease, all other things being equal, whether ten per cent or fifty per cent of the population consists of migrants? And which is most important, the characteristics of the migrant or those of the host community, considering communities with varied proportions of their population consisting of migrants?

Internal versus External Determinants of Assimilation

Our contention is that the crucial determinants of success or failure to assimilate rapidly lie to a very large extent outside individuals. That the determinants of success are (1) lodged in the minds of the migrants, or (2) are learned behavior patterns, has been erroneously concluded by many laymen and professionals. Perusal of the assimilation literature indicates that the individual characteristics of migrants explain relatively little of their assimilation, leaving most of the variation in the degree to which individuals and groups have been assimilated to be explained by unobserved characteristics, possibly internal but probably external to the migrant. Even a psychologist commences by stating that one must know something about the nature of the contact between groups when attempting to understand the acculturation process (Doob, 1957), and if the migrant has internalized attitudes that make him receptive to change he has them as a consequence of social experience (Gonzalez, 1965, p. 278).

Having directed our initial criticism at the work of sociologists and anthropologists, it should be said that both have tended to exploit the available data as much as possible. However much their desire to conduct research of one type or another in order to learn more about social processes, the sociologists have often as not been forced to accept the data that they could lay their hands on with little or no excuse, and what better data could they find than the United States census – the greatest survey of all time (for example, Freedman, 1950). This has resulted in what we have characterized as a static approach, the use of census data to describe the individual characteristics of migrants at various points in time. Anthropologists, by contrast, and also limited in their resources, have dealt with relatively few people and often in rather unsystematic fashion. The traditional anthropological sin is one of employing small, non-representative samples and data that cannot be replicated.

Basically, the sociological emphasis has been on gaining knowledge of the characteristics of migrants as contrasted to non-migrants and some of the variation that takes place in migrant streams from one region to another and from one time to another. By now we are well informed on how the newly arrived migrant differs from his urban-reared counterpart at the time of arrival as well as how he may still differ after a period of time in the community (Freedman and Freedman, 1956).

The Failure to Exploit a Sociological or Anthropological Approach

But what we know in terms of the characteristics of migrants at various points in time could equally well have been discovered by someone other than a sociologist. As we have contended, these are the static aspects of the problem, as distinguished from the more dynamic or processual aspects. Our concern is double; we believe that a sociological orientation is necessary if we are to understand the process of assimilation but at the same time we are apprehensive because sociologists have utilized non-sociological, individualistic orientations, in their research, a concern shown by Jones over ten years ago (Jones, 1956). What we need to know is under what conditions assimilation most readily takes place and under what conditions it is most difficult. How the Mississippi Delta Negro will be assimilated in the Northern industrial community we cannot presume to say; such a process may take generations. What we are probably concerned with is the chain of events through which he will become acculturated and then assimilated into the urban Negro community and eventually integrated into the larger society.

Migrants from the South and Southwest may have experienced socialization in an almost totally different environment from that of Northern industrial areas. They have acquired local images and expectations of persons playing various roles in the local and the larger society, just as members of dominant groups in the local and the larger society have internalized ideas about them (Simmons, 1961). Their early school years may be their first and most memorable experience in contact with the dominant group in the society from which they came (Senter and Hawley, 1946). What we need to know is how they can be resocialized in facilitating the process of assimilation. But even if assimilation is not the goal of all ethnic or racial groups or subcategories of them, there can be little argument about the migrant's eagerness to be absorbed into the economy and the need for more adequate knowledge about the absorption process.

Not only must we learn something about the factors that make for success or failure to assimilate, but likewise we must know what conditions preclude absorption into the economy and eventual assimilation or cultural integration.

PRELIMINARY SUMMARY OF THE RESEARCH ON ASSIMILATION

The most carefully organized of the attempts to summarize the research on the assimilation of migrants to urban areas is "Theory, Method, and Findings in the Study of Acculturation," a review by Claire L. Peterson and Thomas J. Scheff. They evaluate the existent theoretical and empirical studies utilizing systematic data. They have organized their findings in terms of background variables, and these may include handicapping characteristics, personal orientations, characteristics of the migrants, (both of the latter categories are likely to be of relatively less importance when the basic problems of American cities are viewed), and the social situation into which migrants have moved. They have also referred to the social situation from which the migrants come, the nature of the host, and the external relations of the migrants. The nature of the research that they are summarizing results in not much being said about the consequences of entering the occupational structure at the bottom of the ladder. Migrants are unlikely to settle in a community if the general economic situation is unfavorable, but the newly arrived migrant's experience may very well be determined by forces (strikes, recessions, etc.) over which he has no control once he is in the community that gave promise of opportunity.

Peterson and Scheff conclude their summary of the literature by pointing out that some studies seem to indicate no relationship between certain variables and assimilation and other studies fail to mention negative results. They contend that measures of variables may sometimes be so crude that real and existing relationships are hidden. If we take this position, then not only must we say that research has failed fully to describe the assimilation process, but that it has also done a less than adequate job on the more static aspects of assimilation (Peterson and Scheff, 1965).

ANOTHER LOOK AT THE RESEARCH ON ASSIMILATION

Stacking the Cards Against the Migrant

As we have stated, there are essentially three groups of migrants to Northern urban industrial areas with whom we should be concerned – Southern whites, Negroes, and Mexican-Americans. The

Mexican-American migrant has a two-fold problem of adjustment, adjustment involving minority group background and adjustment in terms of rural background. Being a member of this minority is also likely to involve early training in Spanish rather than in English. Southern Negroes have a racial handicap and in many cases a language handicap.

When attempting to assess the adjustment of rural-reared migrants in urban areas, the usual approach has been to show how the migrant is faring in comparison with his urban-reared counterpart. Ronald and Deborah Freedman (Freedman and Freedman, 1956) found that the farm-reared are overrepresented in low status positions whether the measure of status is education, occupation, family income, or self-perception of status. Farm-reared people held low status jobs and had low incomes. These findings remained even when age, sex, color, and region were held constant. Not only did the Freedman study show that the rural-reared were lower on the average in terms of external criteria of adjustment, but also that their self-concept was lower than that of their urban-reared counterparts, that they had a lower level of political participation and a lower sense of political efficacy than did the nonfarm-reared. The data indicated that the rural-reared migrant had neither been integrated nor economically absorbed. Were these differences only in reference to participation in organized groups there would not be quite so much concern, since numerous studies have shown that urban working-class families do not usually participate extensively in formally organized voluntary associations (Axelrod, 1956).

The nature of the migrant's participation may be such as to influence personal adjustment but not increase the likelihood of absorption into the economy. Sectarianism among lower level migrants may assist them in adjusting personally (Dynes, 1956) but does it go beyond that? Tilly and others (Tilly, 1965, pp. 1-3 and 36-37) have indicated that what the migrant transfers to the city may facilitate or impede assimilation. If the migrant has little in the way of skills or status, his chances are reduced (Griffin, 1962).

While this approach has yielded some provocative results, it tends to be misleading because the cards are stacked against the migrant (Shannon, 1961b). The measures of assimilation that have been employed are almost certain to show the host at a higher level, and this is to be expected considering the social system from which the migrants come as contrasted to the social system in which they are now interacting. Studies with such a design tend to foster the impression that the rural dweller is an unassimilable rustic who cannot make out in the city. In actuality some rural-reared migrants ultimately rise above the median of their urban-reared counterparts (Beers and Heflin, 1945).

The Mitigating Influence of Time in the City

Other studies have altered this impression by examining the adjustment of rural-reared urban migrants according to the length of time they have been in the city. Differences in adjustment that at first seemed to be so great between the rural-reared and urban-reared tended to wash out over a period of time. Omari's (Omari, 1956, pp. 47-53) study of 200 Negro migrants in Beloit, Wisconsin, demonstrated that length of residence in Beloit was more highly correlated with socioeconomic status and community satisfaction than any of a dozen or more other variables that were hypothesized to have some relationship to adjustment.

Rural-reared manual workers have been found to belong to fewer formal organizations than the urban-reared, but the former increase their membership with time in the city; rural-reared manual workers do not reach the level of officership positions in organizations that natives do, but the difference is not great (Zimmer, 1955, pp. 214-224). Voter registration follows the same pattern with the percentage of manual workers registered increasing with length of time in the community. One must conclude that the migrant's failure to appear integrated into the larger society is in part a reflection, of (1) the low rate of participation of people at their economic level regardless of origin, and (2) failure to take into consideration the length of time the migrant has been in the city.

Slow though integration into the formal and informal social organization of urban areas may be for the migrant, we should not conclude that he is helpless and in a sea of secondary contacts. This is only another myth, for indeed the city is not in all respects such a contrast to his former home. In discussing the rural-urban dichotomy, such a distinction is frequently and incorrectly made; in some respects primary group contact is more a characteristic of urban life than of rural-farm or rural-nonfarm life. Reiss' sample of Nashville, Tennessee, and adjacent rural-farm and rural-nonfarm respondents revealed that the average urban, employed male spent significantly greater time in primary contact than did his rural-nonfarm or rural-farm counterpart (Reiss, 1959). Axelrod (Axelrod, 1956) observed widespread mutual aid among urban friends and relatives.

There has been some concern about the development of personality types in rural settings that are inappropriate for city life. Inhibiting "personality" characteristics of migrants, if they exist, are likely to inappropriately be labelled "rural." If the migrant does possess attitudes that inhibit assimilation-facilitating responses it is just as likely that these are not rural attitudes, but attitudes acquired in the process of interacting in a situation where he has been defined as inferior. And he becomes even more "inferior" in the industrial setting, particularly if he has been a farm worker and the attitudes of the Anglo toward ethnic farm workers become known to him (McDonagh, 1955).

The long and the short of it is that the rural-reared migrant, whether he be native American or foreign-born, must go through a period of transition during which he learns about the new statuses and roles that are found in urban-industrial societies. During this period he is bound to have some difficulty, but the adaptability of people has resulted historically in only a relatively small proportion of the migrants being neither absorbed nor integrated into urban industrial society, if allowed to engage in the appropriate activities. The validation of acculturation is a precondition to assimilation (Broom and Kitsuse, 1955). Absorption into the economy is made difficult, if not impossible, if Negroes are barred from craft or other unions (Patten, 1963) or are forced to work below the highest level at which they are qualified in order to preserve tranquility among potential white co-workers (Hope, 1952).

The Complex Influence of Education

As far as the economic absorption of rural-reared youth is concerned, it would be unrealistic to expect them to compete as effectively, at least initially, as their urban-reared counterparts, for every study has shown that rural-reared migrants are at a disadvantage educationally. Education has been shown to be related to first job in place of origin, and to present job. This is not a simple relationship, however, and it is here that the social organization of the larger society is of crucial importance in determining just how much education is necessary for absorption at various levels and how much education is important in terms of integration into either the larger culture or integration into a sub-culture primarily composed of persons from one's own ethnic or racial group.

We have indicated elsewhere (Shannon and Krass, 1963a) that education and occupational level of first job and present job have been related for various samples of Anglo, Negro, and Mexican-American migrants as well as non-migrants. In the case of Mexican-Americans, education and occupation were correlated within a limited range at the lowest end of the occupational level scale, but this relationship was not present when the entire range of occupations was considered. In other words, the barrier or ceiling on occupations only took effect if Mexican-Americans had "too much" education. Education and occupation were significantly related for Anglos but not for Negroes. When persons with nine through twelve years of education were compared, Anglos had significantly higher level jobs than either Negroes or Mexican-Americans and the difference was greater than at any other educational level. Furthermore, in this educational group, differences between Anglos and Negroes or Mexican-Americans were greater for Anglos who had lived longest in the community. A high school education is not always an equalizer.

While the Negro and Mexican-American migrant is absorbed and integrated with time in the community, he doesn't seem to catch up with the Anglos, even if he is educated and attempting to run on a "fast track." In essence, the Negro and Mexican-American migrant with little education finds it easier to become like his urban Anglo counterpart than does the Negro and Mexican-American with a high school education.

The Migrant's Choice

The migrant's decision to compete in the larger society or to compete in the Negro or Mexican-American community may depend on the amount of education and experience that he has, and how he perceives this as facilitating absorption and integration into the larger community rather than into the ethnic community. The development of a sub-culture may be a more practical approach, as suggested in the Yankton Indian case (Hurt, 1962).

But in many cases there may be no real choice; barriers to interaction in the larger society may be so formidable that the choice is made for the migrant. If the migrant has been systematically segregated residentially, or even unsystematically segregated, his probability of assimilation is reduced through lack of contact with the host population in the school, the neighborhood, the church, and other institutions. Lieberson found most dimensions of assimilation in American cities to be correlated with residential segregation (Lieberson, 1961).

To presume that the migrant has a completely free choice, aside from that more or less dictated by the existing situation or the organization of the community in which he finds himself, is also an error. His total experience in the society of origin may have been such that he finds it easy to accept a limited area of competition and decision-making. This would seem to be the case for the Mexican-American who has lived under the patron-peon system in the Southwest (see Knowlton, 1962) and who now finds himself in a Northern industrial community with an employer or union representative taking the role of the patron.

External versus Internal Criteria of Success

If we do decide to use some external criterion of change such as occupational status, we are allowing our own values to intervene by assuming that movement upward on an occupational level scale is the most important evidence of assimilation. We are in effect judging the occupational dimension to be the most critical dimension for measurement. We are presuming that the migrant has the same set of values that we have, and that his activities are oriented in the same direction as those of occupationally oriented Anglos. If, in observing changes in behavior, food habits, dress, level of aspiration for oneself and one's children, we assume these changes to be indicators of cultural integration, we are presuming that these specific measures of integration are evidence of success on the part of the migrant. On the other hand, the migrant may be moving in the direction of the norms of the larger society along quite different vectors.

Instead of examining only indicators of assimilation which members of the host society value we might look at some measures suggested by the migrants themselves. During a three-year period from 1955 to 1958 in Alcorn County, Mississippi, of 161 families interviewed, 32 per cent left farming and 66 per cent of these stated that they did so in order to make money (Baird and Bailey, 1958, p. 5). The average annual income of those still farming in 1958 was $541 while that of those who had left farming was $679. A change in the direction expected and hoped for by those who had left farming had taken place.

When migrants are asked why they have come to a specific industrial community they sometimes respond in neither economic nor job-oriented terms. This should not be construed as evidence contrary to the general notion of economic push or pull for the simple reason that a response, "to be with my family" may mean "to work with my family." The respondent came to be with his kin after he had been assured that economic gain would take place. A response need not be in strictly monetary or work-oriented terms for economic factors to be crucial in the decision to join with kin. Kinfolk presented the opportunity for economic advancement but the move was rationalized as a desire to be with kin.

Systematic studies have not yet been made, but they would probably show chains of migration between Southwestern or Southern cities and their Northern industrial targets. The residents of communities losing their population to Northern industrial cities may take comfort in the rationalization that out-migration takes place on a basis of kin-ties, rather than "facing up" to their declining economic position or oppressive social organization. The ability to leave the community in itself may be defined as success by the migrant. As one middle-aged Negro lady in Mississippi replied to one of the authors in the summer of 1966, "Who would want to stay here if they could leave?"

Another measure of economic absorption may be constructed from work records of migrants contrasted with those of persons who have always lived in the urban-industrial community. In Almond's study, little difference was found in the work records of persons with farm and nonfarm backgrounds in two major manufacturing plants in a predominantly agricultural area; no matter whether the workers were reared on the farm or in town, had industrial or farm experience, they had essentially the same employment records (Almond, 1956, pp. 828-836).

It is also possible to utilize an internal criterion in measuring assimilation – the migrants' perception of how well they are doing in the community. If migration was for essentially economic reasons, then the migrants' judgments may well be based on how they perceive themselves to be succeeding in the world of work. If they moved in order to remove themselves from a community in which they were not satisfied with their position in the power structure, then their responses would be based on how they perceived themselves to be situated in the new community. Migrants' perception of the relationship between themselves and the police in the new community as contrasted to the old might in itself be the basis for some expression of satisfaction. It is, of course, problematical whether a changed relationship of this nature can be considered evidence of assimilation, but if migrants perceive their life as having changed as a consequence of the move, and they feel themselves more like members of the host society than they felt in the community from which they came, then they indeed have undergone a certain type of assimilation.

THE CRUCIAL DETERMINANTS OF ASSIMILATION

The Role of Communication

Assuming that measures of cultural integration and its subcategory, economic absorption, have been constructed, and that we are willing to accept them as measures of the larger process of assimilation, what are the factors that explain the difference in the rate at which migrants are assimilated?

Communication receives more emphasis than does any other factor in the literature on assimilation. The ability to communicate seems to be the most important precondition or requisite for successful assimilation; language permits the individual to engage in symbolic interaction with others and thereby allows him to acquire the values and goals that characterize the dominant group. Unless the individual knows the language he may adopt only the superficial cultural traits of the dominant culture with which he has contact, but he will not become familiar with the world view of those in the larger society. He may modify his dress or change his food habits, but he wil remain outside the most meaningful interaction system of the larger society. A study of the personal and social adjustment of migrants from rural Mississippi to Pittsburgh (Windham, 1961) reported that identification measures correlated with level of education and social participation as well as other variables.

Scheff (Scheff, 1965) in noting that Warner and Srole distinguished between the internal and external system of migrants in Yankee City (Warner and Srole, 1945) proposed language as a measure of change in the internal and external systems of migrants. The decision or willingness to shift from Spanish to English more quickly in public use than in private use was held to be indicative of slowness or failure of migrants in Racine, Wisconsin, to change their internal system, thus impeding absorption into the host society.

The Organization of Society

As we have previously stated, absorption into the economy is the basis for assimilation into the larger society. Probably the most important single factor in determining if a group will be assimilated is whether or not its members are able to secure employment in which they have contacts with the larger society, and by this is not meant merely physical contact, but contacts requiring communication.

When the only work available to migrants was unskilled labor there was often little chance for interaction with members of the host society while on the job, however much contact there might have been with other new arrivals. To the extent that more communication is possible and necessary than in earlier systems of production on the job and in job-related activities, the migrant who does find employment has a greater likelihood of interacting with members of the host society than previously.

It is for this reason that we have placed so much emphasis on the organization of society as a determinant of how successful a migrant is in becoming assimilated, rather than on his individual characteristics. Whether society is going to assimilate him or not assimilate him will depend more on how it is organized than on how he behaves as an individual.

Communication is perceived, not as a process succeeding or failing on the basis of the individual characteristics of the migrants or members of the host society, although there are individual variations, but as something that takes place or does not take place on the basis of how people are organized in relationship to or in contact with each other. Communication thus becomes the province of the sociologist rather than the psychologist. The variable of major importance therefore becomes the nature of the associations likely to take place within the organization of society. It is here that the organization of the community into voluntary associations and kinship groups open to the migrant may play a crucial part (the Ibo in Nigeria, Morrill, 1963). Welfare and other agencies, if they render propitious assistance, may also make the difference between successful integration into the network of exchange relationships or complete failure in the complex bureaucratic milieu (Shannon, 1963).

Communication, of course, does not involve direct person-to-person association alone, but also consists of indirect associations through the written word, the spoken word, and the visual image combined with the spoken word as in the case of television. The major problem, then, is to specify the general nature of the social experiences that make for the transmission of values and behavioral patterns followed by the types of social experiences that are most likely to facilitate this process in any given society, depending on its social organization.

Dimensions of Association as Determinants of Assimilation

An adequate theory of assimilation must specify the effect of varying amounts of social distance between interacting individuals or groups and its pertinence to the process of assimilation. It must also identify the role of the initiator of interaction, the immediate consequence of interaction, and how the interactional situation is perceived in terms of past experiences by those currently interacting with each other.

To the extent that the migrants' interaction set and responses to the larger society influence assimilation, a theory specifying the nature of interaction resulting in assimilation could begin by spelling out Edwin H. Sutherland's "dimensions of association" as they apply to migrants and members of the host community. Sutherland's "differential association theory," elaborated and modified considerably since its earliest formulation, specified four facets of association in reference to the process of acquiring delinquent and criminal attitudes and subsequent behavior: primacy, frequency, duration, and intensity of contact. Those values and behaviors will be assimilated which are first encountered, most frequently encountered, encountered for the longest period of time, and encountered in the most meaningful fashion. Our detailed specifications of these and related propositions follow:

1. Assimilation takes place if migration to the city has been early in a person's life time. In other words, assimilation takes place more readily among those who arrive in the host society at an early age.

2. Assimilation is more likely to take place if migrant interaction with members of the host society is frequent. If the relation of education to assimilation is considered, the first two propositions seem generally acceptable since years of education in the host society are related to assimilation.

3. Assimilation is more likely to take place if interaction is intense. Migrants engaging in primary group interaction with members of the larger society are more likely to be assimilated than those who have had only contacts of a secondary group nature. To the extent that integrated education, as contrasted to segregated education, makes for assimilation into the larger society, we have an indication of the relationship of intensity of interaction to assimilation.

4. Assimilation is more likely to take place if contact is carried out over a lengthy period of time. Time in the community has consistently been related to various measures of assimilation.

5. Assimilation is greatest when the social distance between the interactors is not so great that the lower-status person cannot conceive of himself in the position of the upper-status person. Similarity of migrants and hosts has been related to successful assimilation, particularly if the migrant perceives himself to be similar to the host.

6. Assimilation is more likely to take place if the role of the interaction initiator is favorably defined by the lower-status person. Assimilation-facilitating behavior on the part of migrants is more likely to take place if interaction initiators are co-workers rather than policemen.

7. Assimilation is more likely to take place if the consequences of past interaction have been defined as favorable by the migrant. Rewards rather than problems lead to further interaction and assimilation.

8. Assimilation is more likely to take place if the migrant anticipates favorable consequences from interaction.

The empirical literature inclines one to accept these propositions, but it would be incorrect to say that they have been tested explicitly by the research that has been conducted. Existent research does suggest, however, that tests designed for these hypotheses would be likely to result in positive findings.

As we have indicated, the research that has been conducted to date on the assimilation of migrants to urban areas tends to indicate whether or not migrants hold comparable occupational positions, whether or not migrants are learning the language, and how migrants compare with members of the host community in terms of level of living and level of aspiration. While such descriptive information is valuable, it does not present us with the facts that we need if we are to facilitate the process of assimilation.

SUMMARY AND CONCLUSIONS

Although the impression may have been created that the problems deriving from the movement of persons from rural to urban settings in the United States are pretty much a thing of the past, this could only be true in reference to the sheer volume of movement. The population movements that are taking place today and that will continue to take place are transpiring under quite different conditions than during the early stages of urbanization and industrialization; problems generated by these migration streams will become of increasing rather than decreasing importance. Furthermore, the organization of people for production and distribution has become increasingly complex so that there is relatively scant need for unskilled migrants and less opportunity for them to be absorbed into the economy at even the lowest levels than previously. And economic absorption, we have indicated, is necessary in order to facilitate the process of assimilation.

In essence, although millions of foreign-born immigrants are no longer appearing on the urban-industrial scene in America, the assimilation of new migrants to urban industrial areas, whether they be Mexican-American, Negro, or Southern white, will present formidable but certainly soluble problems if we recognize what is involved in the process of assimilation rather than merely considering the problem in terms of the individual characteristics of migrants.

We know a good deal about the characteristics of migrants at different stages in the process of migration but have not conducted sufficient research on what may be termed "experiential chains."

Experiential chains have been referred to as movement through role paths and event sequences by Ozzie G. Simmons and his colleagues in their ongoing research on the urbanization of migrants at the University of Colorado. They too have concluded that although we pay lip service to the dynamic or processual characteristics of acculturation, assimilation, and migration, the approaches and concepts thus far used in research have been static. They have emphasized the importance of studying not only the role paths but also studying the characteristics and behavior of the "gate-keepers" and other key agents who stand at crucial points in the role paths taken by migrants as they move from rural society to the urban industrial milieu (Simmons, 1961).

These "gate-keepers" are the persons whose decisions, for all practical purposes, determine the extent to which migrants will be allowed to participate in activities of the community which are crucial to economic absorption and cultural integration. These "gate-keepers" very often have no formal position in the status structure of the community but the nature of their positions – social agency personnel, bartenders, landlords, health and welfare workers and in some cases police and court officials – enable them to go beyond their official duties. They have the decision-making power that either facilitates integration into the community or completely thwarts it.

When the interrelationships of a multitude of variables in the larger society are examined, the correlations between level of aspiration, education, and other abilities on one hand, and measures of economic absorption, level of living and income on the other, tend to be relatively high. It is for this reason that we often presume that Mexican-Americans, Negroes, or Anglos who have made relatively less progress than others toward middle-class goals, are in the position that they are because they have neither the ability nor desire to be otherwise. But when the larger society is broken down into its component parts and into various sub-cultural groups, we find quite different relationships of these variables to each other, relationships which would, and probably do, disappoint and frustrate the minority group members, including migrants, who believe that things should work out for them just as they do for persons in the larger society.

There are essentially two reasons why these relationships do not prevail in all groups. A sub-cultural group may be organized differently from the way that the larger society is organized and its members may be working toward dissimilar goals. Should this be the case, we would say that the migrant must be made aware of the fact that he has the choice of working toward integration into either the larger society or into the social organization of the subcultural group of which he is a member. If the latter is the case, then he must be made aware of the costs and consequences of his decision.

On the other hand, should the migrant wish to be absorbed and integrated into the larger society, we must be concerned with the fact that "gate-keepers" may prevent certain categories of people from access to opportunities available to other categories of people. If this is the case, we should then determine if there is an acceptable rationale for the decision-making process or if the basis for deprivation is unrelated to capability.

Our first recommendation is that we conduct research more pertinent to the process of economic absorption and cultural integration, concerning ourselves less with the characteristics of migrants at any given period. This will necessitate studying migration utilizing other than census reports, although it cannot be denied that many important questions may be answered through sophisticated analysis of census data. Other types of data may be obtainable only if the researcher is able to follow the experiential chains of the migrants quite closely. It may well be that researchers ought to combine sociological and anthropological approaches in an effort to obtain more adequate data and eventually a more sophisticated description of the behavior that takes place as people move from their place of origin to the urban-industrial milieu. What we may need is very intensive participant observation of the group situations in which these crucial decisions are made.

Aside from the inadequacies of existing research, what we do know is not taken into consideration in planning programs for newcomers to the city. We know that most welfare agencies have relatively little contact with persons who are entering the economic order at the bottom of the ladder. We know that social workers and others concerned with the problems of the less fortunate in our society, have become less interested in people at the lowest levels and more interested in middle-class clients whom they find more responsive to their suggestions. Unfortunately, professional personnel in our social welfare institutions have become more oriented toward those who least need their assistance. Those whom they find it rewarding to assist are often already on the way up, and would make it by themselves in one manner or another.

Only recently has this problem been recognized and then we have trod carefully rather than injure the finer sensitivities of our dedicated social workers. The least fortunate in our society, among them newly arrived migrants to the city, perceive the organization of the city less accurately than do others; they have difficulty communicating with appropriate persons in the complex urban-industrial bureaucratic milieu. Yet the representatives of welfare and other organizations concerned with the problems of the less fortunate often reduce their availability by locating their offices in places inaccessible to likely clients. And when they do sally forth to the natural habitat of the less fortunate, they frequently deport themselves in such a fashion as to present either a fearsome or condescending image.

In spite of our knowledge of the relative ineffectiveness of existing welfare organizations, due not only to the manner in which they are organized but to the orientation of the personnel who staff them, we have been slow to modify or replace them. Only during the past few years, particularly with the advent of the so-called "War on Poverty," have we attempted to set up parallel structures based on a grass-roots approach. Although we have been concerned previously and have attempted to approach these problems through the indigenous inhabitants in the community, these approaches have been few compared to the traditional professional approaches. The cry for a back-of-the-yards approach has been small indeed compared to requests for a saturation approach by professionals. Perhaps most amazing of all is the fact that so little evidence exists for the effectiveness of our traditional professional approaches and that year after year funds for these programs are increased.

If we are to have any success whatsoever in reaching the migrant we must be where he is. Therefore, it is recommended that increased use be made of informal grass-roots non-professional approaches in communicating with those who have migrated to the city from other areas. We must put our welfare workers behind the bar, in the poolroom, on the street corner, in the rooming-house lobby, and any other place where the migrant and others in need of assistance may be found as they arrive and attempt to adjust to their new environment.

3

Strategies for Discovering Urban Theory

ANSELM L. STRAUSS

☐ THIS IS A PROGRAMMATIC CHAPTER whose aim is to stimulate types of research which will lead to the discovery of an integrated and maximally useful urban theory about American cities. There is no such theory today, any more than there was eight years ago when Gideon Sjoberg remarked that the dominant theoretical orientations in urban sociology could "hardly be termed full-fledged theories" and that "a consistent general theory of urbanism, though perhaps unattainable, should be the goal toward which we strive" (Sjoberg, 1959, p. 356).

This chapter will not offer a blueprint for launching specific researches nor develop a theory by which to approach urban data. My intent is rather to suggest a set of strategies – which together constitute a stance – for studying cities and their people so as to discover which problems are most relevant for developing a general but grounded urban theory. Many of the specific suggestions for organizing research arise from, or are implied in, my earlier work (Strauss, 1961). Readers who find themselves stimulated, but also just as probably frustrated, by the necessarily truncated treatment in this chapter, may wish to refer to the longer discussion. The present set of strategies is not, however, suggested there.

AUTHOR'S NOTE: *For their critical reading of a first draft of this chapter, and for stimulating discussions about city life, I am much indebted to Howard S. Becker, Fred Davis, Barney Glaser, Virginia Olesen, Leonard, Schatzman, and Louis Schaw.*

THE PARK AND WIRTH PROGRAMS

The two most influential programs for studying the American city from a sociological and social psychological – rather than essentially an ecological or demographic – perspective undoubtedly were Robert E. Park's "The City: Suggestions for the Investigation of Human Behavior in the Urban Environment" (Park, 1916) and Louis Wirth's "Urbanism as a Way of Life" (Wirth, 1938). Although Wirth succeeded in presenting a systematic view of city life, his paper seems to have had its impact on sociologists largely because it reaffirmed attitudes widespread among them about cities as places characterized by much anonymity, impersonality, segmentalism and rationality. But a postwar generation, accustomed to comparative studies, has turned a questioning eye on his American-bound, if not Chicago-bound, generalizations (Reiss, 1955, Janowitz, 1952; Sjoberg, 1959; Kolb, 1954; Gans, 1952).

The impact of Park's paper was much greater and its substance more interesting. Park offered a loosely strung series of comments about various facets of the city combined with lists of researchable questions about how cities functioned and how people lived and acted in them. Admirably transcending, for the most part, the reformism of his predecessors and contemporaries, Park stimulated urban research at the University of Chicago and elsewhere for over a decade, in accordance with ideas expressed in his early paper. The impetus he gave to urban sociology (ecology aside) came principally through his students' studies of urban types, occupations, and communities (Zorbaugh, 1929; Wirth, 1928; Hughes, 1940; Anderson, 1923; Cressey, 1932; Thrasher, 1927; Frazier, 1931; Shaw and McKay, 1929).

The hallmark of these studies was their descriptive power. Their weakness was their relatively unsophisticated methodology which today allows many readers to dismiss them as merely journalistic. A more serious weakness was their relatively sparse and unintegrated theory – a characteristic shared by Park's own program, at least until later when he refined his ideas about ecology in relation to social organization. Although Park's papers on cities are still read his program no longer seems to stimulate much research, although undoubtedly third and fourth generation impulses are still emanating from it. For instance, some of the work in "deviance" can easily be traced to Park through Everett C. Hughes, a student of Park's, as in the work of Howard S. Becker and Erving Goffman who did their graduate studies at the University of Chicago.

Its waning influence is not surprising: our cities and their problems seem changed, and anyhow perhaps a majority of significant sociological researches are relevant to understanding social relations in an urbanized nation. There may be considerable truth in both those assertions; but it is also true that many facets of urban life have not changed quite so much since Park's death, and that our contemporary studies do not add up to a concentrated focus on city life (Reiss, 1957). Neither do they add up to an integrated sociological theory about urban life, assuming such a theory might be achieved. Park's program at least had the virtue of concentrating on a wide range of related issues. His early paper on the city bears rereading not so much for its rewarding nuggets as for reminding us that the program is still unfulfilled, if not in detail at least in scope. I shall later touch by implication on the relevance of its unfinished business to a program appropriate to the contemporary urban scene.

IDEOLOGY AND ITS CONSEQUENCES

As a first step, I suggest that urban sociology (and/or social psychology) could profit greatly from a critical scutiny of itself and its past. The conceptions which inform sociologists' writings are essentially identical to, and not always more sophisticated than, those found in the popular media (Strauss, 1961, pp. 255-259). Indeed, virtually all the important urban sociologists during any decade, from Henderson or Zueblin at the turn of the century to Greer today, can, without stretching credulity, be viewed as articulate spokesmen, excellent rhetoricians, for less sophisticated versions of the same views about cities. What C. Wright Mills demonstrated for the rural biases of "social problems" literature (Mills, 1943), could just as easily be demonstrated for the relevant biases in contemporary sociological writing about poverty, urban race relations, delinquency, suburbia and other public issues. The "all-too-American" views of cities held by sociologists have had at least two major consequences for their urban sociology. I only mention these consequences here, since the remainder of this chapter deals with their implications.

In the first place, a remarkably small range of potentially relevant topics has been studied from sociological perspectives. A corollary is that sociologists have bunched their research around relatively few topics or areas. Thus, we have an abundance of research about major cities (where "social problems" have been so obvious) but comparatively little about life as lived in regional centers, in small cities, or in specialized cities like Reno, Flint or Birmingham. We have writing far out of proportion to its probable import for urban theory about poverty, vice, delinquency and urban crime, while the recent spate of interest in middle-class suburbs flows from the same ideological source: concern with a social problem. The occupations we know best through many researches either have not been much studied with direct focus on their urban aspects (medicine, nursing, for instance); or have been studied because they relate to reformistic concerns (prostitution, political bossism, teaching, real estate brokerage).

The case of the realtor is particularly instructive: he has been studied somewhat in relation to race relations and to city planning, but we know almost nothing about the network of social relationships within which he and his clients operate, say, in suburbs and suburban counties. Except from personal experience, no sociologist could begin to write a systematic account of relationships which exist among realtors, bank employees, contractors, local politicians, investment brokers (professional and amateur) and other relevant parties to realtors' transactions. In short, an unfortunate consequence of sociologists' commitments to ideological positions or of their concern with public issues has been to limit severely the areas which they have studied, and possibly has led them also to overconcentrate on certain other areas.

The character of theory about urban social relations has also been negatively affected for the same reasons. Anyone who has taught a course or read through available textbooks in urban sociology must know that "hodge-podge" is an accurate description of urban theory, at least those portions of it that deal with social relations in the city. When sociologists are relatively consistent in their views of city life, then their theories are deeply colored by one or more ideological positions. When they are eclectic, as in the textbooks, then their ideological positions shift from chapter to chapter and sometimes from paragraph to paragraph. The elements of urban theory tend merely to be refinements of common sense conceptions about urban social relations, however sophisticated the language and however "data-based" are the supporting facts (Strauss, 1961). I shall not attempt to demonstrate these assertions: I make them only as an introduction to the statement of a position.

STRATEGIES FOR URBAN RESEARCH

The cardinal strategies that I shall suggest and discuss – quite aside from specific areas of research also to be discussed later – are as follows.

First, study the unstudied. The reasoning behind this strategy is not merely that already too much is known about too small a range of topics, but that quite literally we do not know the most fertile topics for developing a powerful urban theory. I do not mean to suggest that nothing can be learned through further studies of the police, skid-row residents, or delinquents, or of any other repeatedly studied subject; but these may have less pay-off for understanding our cities and the social relations within them than many another area of research.

Second, study the unusual. The reasoning behind this strategy is that urban sociologists have assumed that they knew the important topics for developing theory, but this assumption is questionable, if only because they have been captives of their ideological postions and their concerns with reform. Whether questionable or not, however, the assumption can be checked only through deliberate study of topics which not only have been untouched but may seem so trivial as not to warrant study.

Third, study an area which is enmeshed in public debate only after taking steps to minimize ideological entrapment. The reasoning behind this strategy is: if the sociologist is interested in entering the public debate as such, he need not be concerned with research except for rhetorical purposes; but if he is interested in urban theory – and in contributing to the public issue through the application of theory – then he *must* guard against ideological commitments. Later I shall suggest a specific tactic for doing this.

Fourth, where possible study any topic comparatively. This strategy is not always feasible, but I advocate it. While single case studies are useful, a comparative procedure yields more urban theory, and more quickly. For instance, the study of a number of suburban banks will yield more theory than the study of one or two banks "in depth." If the banks are sampled according to theoretical considerations, then the theoretical yield is likely to be still greater (Glaser and Strauss, 1966). This "theoretical sampling" should be directed by theory, but it should pertain less to banks as organizations than it does to banks as they relate to urbanization and urbanites. In addition, the strategy of comparative analysis implies that the scattered literature on a great variety of urban groups, communities, institutions and processes be reconceptualized in accordance with a concerted attempt to develop a systematic and integrated theory of urban social relations.

This set of strategies does not lead automatically to a specific number of areas of research; but it does imply a redirection of sociologists' energies and perspectives, and to some extent a broadening of their methods. A further implication is that the redirection leads to new intersections with the urban studies of colleagues in other fields. It is remarkable how little interchange there is between urban sociologists and urban historians, or with economists whose work sometimes bears directly on social relations in metropolitan areas. The overlapping work of sociologists and political scientists, both of whom are interested in urban politics, is much better developed. The recent writing of Norton Long seems especially to have stimulated sociologists.

The remainder of this chapter will consist of a relatively few suggestions bearing on the kind of research implied by the four strategies. My remarks about research areas should not be regarded as more than suggestions. Each reader will doubtless find other areas that impress him as more interesting and possibly as more fruitful for theory development. What is of more importance than the specific research areas is the general perspective implied by the set of strategies.

UNSTUDIED AREAS

VARIETIES OF CITIES

Since the terrain that is still relatively unstudied or untouched is very great, perhaps its discussion might begin with a rather glaring omission in our urban studies. Sociological generalizations about urban social relations are based principally on studies of large American cities and a few smaller ones. Some inkling of what has been omitted, besides differentials in size, is suggested by a series of articles about American cities which appeared in the *Saturday Evening Post* during the late 1940s: over 100 cities, from all sections of the nation, were covered. Even a casual scrutiny of the articles suggests a range of potentially relevant dimensions which bear on urban social relations.

There are cities which are generally considered by their citizens and neighbors to be regional centers – representative of their geographic area. There also are cities located "in" a region, many of whose citizens are symbolically as well as actually linked closely with non-regional geography. There are specialized cities: for sin, for more regular transient recreation, for resort living, for old folks, for conventions, for manufacture of a small range of products, for turning out legislative business. There are towns which have had glorious histories but have dim futures; there are towns with little history but great futures; towns with minor histories and seemingly little future. There are cities which consider themselves rivals of certain nearby cities, and ones which rival distant cities. There are cities which are run by outsiders, and ones which are governed by insiders – by old elites or by new elites. There are cities which seem to be entirely surrounded by middle-class suburbs, and cities with an enormous variety of suburbs. According to Gans, "The primary task for urban (or community) sociology seems to me to be the analysis of the similarities and differences between contemporary settlement types" (Gans, 1952, p. 627). He confines himself to a thoughtful exploration of suburbs with the city's "inner" and "outer" areas.

Finally, all cities bear the marks of their geography, in style, as well as in predominant business – river cities, agricultural towns, mining towns, mountain cities, seaports. (Since agriculture or mining are very different in different regions, even such terms imply multiplicity.) Sociologists need not have gone overseas to challenge Wirth's generalizations about city life! Indeed, an immense amount of popular writing implicitly or explicitly has challenged the "impersonality" and heterogeneity views of "the city" (White, 1927; White, 1924; Nicholson, 1904; Welsh, 1946).

In recent years, probably due largely to the more scattered location of sociologists themselves, a number of researches have been done on populations within a greater variety of cities. The implications of this material for urbanism have yet to be worked out for simple empirical purposes, let alone for urban theory, but any good introductory textbook (e.g., Gouldner and Gouldner, 1963) lists a number of such studies (Herring, 1939; Hunter, 1952; Smith, 1954; Dalton, 1950; Lazarsfeld and Merton, 1954; Hollingshead, 1948; Useem, 1942; West, 1945; Cottrell, 1939).

URBAN ICONS

The dimensions I have touched on should readily suggest some foci around which research might be organized. Two others — implicit in the above — are especially worth emphasis, the more so as they fall somewhat outside the usual attention of sociologists. Cities might well be studied, contemporaneously and historically, in terms of their icons. These are important — at least for various groups within a given city — for helping to set the city's style, for bringing a sense of belonging to citizens, for representing the city to outsiders, even for giving direction to planning and to the evolution of its institutions. The symbolism of Washington for the nation, and the prominence of its icons (the Capitol, the White House, and so on) is an obvious instance. A less obvious example is the complex of meanings represented by Chicago's various prominent icons. Chicago's business spirit and cosmopolitanism formerly were represented by such visual icons as Marshall Field's, the railroad depots, State Street, the "Loop," and skyscrapers like the Wrigley Building and the Tribune Towers. Although these Chicago icons still function for some populations, no doubt, nowadays the bustling commercialism and cosmopolitanism are more likely to be represented by Michigan Avenue, Rush Street, the double-towered apartment building complete with marina at its base, the lake front, and O'Hare Airport — claimed to be the nation's busiest air terminal. Chicago is represented through these icons on countless posters and postcards, in the mass media, and in the speech of natives and visitors alike: "crossroads of the nation," "second city," and bustling "forward-looking" business mart.

Of course, different populations emphasize different icons, including some I have not mentioned. What is needed for the development of urban theory is a series of cumulative studies of different types of icons, for different cities, and for different populations within those cities. And since the meanings of these icons are never static, we need a focus on change also: for instance, it would be interesting to know what happened in Brooklyn just before and after the Dodgers left.

Symbolism of Time

Another perspective from which cities might usefully be studied is in terms of their symbolism of time. Actual time and symbolic time are not always closely associated; in any event, they are different items. Thought and speech about cities are replete with temporal imagery. Cities are represented as oriented toward the past, the present, or the future; as being old or young; as settled or conservative; or are referred to by other temporal terms. American cities frequently are characterized according to a future-oriented growth model ("expanding," "increasing," or "progressing") or an inverse growth model ("declining" or "decreasing"). They can also be described in terms of a metaphor of biological development, losing and gaining attributes rather than merely more or less of the the same thing. The very terms used to describe city development are borrowed from the language of human development. For decades, Chicago has been described as "adolescent," but Milwaukee, which is about the same age, tends to be described as middle-aged and settled.

A great many questions are raised by this temporal and metaphorical treatment of cities. When does a city stop being represented as being young and become adolescent, why, and by whom? How long can a city exist without being regarded as old, or even middle-aged and settled down? When a city changes, what must be done before a claim legitimately can be made, or safely supported, that a new stage in city development has been reached? What happens to temporal symbolism when a city is invaded by new waves of immigrants: is it conceived to be the same city, a different one, and in what degree, and by whom? There are a whole battery of research questions which bear on how different segments of a city may attempt to make public their temporal conceptions, make them predominate in the mass media, and stamp them into the city's physical structure. (Pittsburgh's recent "rejuvenation" is a nice instance, and one that has implications for the temporal aspect of urban theory.)

Leonard Schatzman has suggested to me that fruitful studies might be made of how different populations regard "what the city used to look like and what it looks like now." For instance, old-time natives in San Francisco sometimes complain bitterly about the high-rise apartments that are "spoiling" the old skyline; while newcomers usually do not know what the older city looked like, and so may (some do) find the skyline enchanting or exciting. Such temporal considerations unquestionably affect the public battles over a city's physical aspects.

Symbolism of Space

Another area of research is the symbolism of space: it is relatively unstudied by urban sociologists, despite the many ethnic, "natural area," stratification and even suburban studies. These studies have been confined principally to large cities – a point I shall not emphasize except to suggest that research on the same ethnic group (say of Jews or the Irish) in diverse cities (say, Norfolk, Milwaukee, Santa Fe, Stockton, Lincoln, and Meridian, Mississippi) might show some surprising things about the range of urban experience and the use and symbolism of space. A wonderfully suggestive study of space was published some years ago, although it has been little referred to since, by Christen Jonassen who described the ecology and successive movements of a Norwegian community in Brooklyn, with an appropriate focus on the Norwegians' rural symbolism of space (Jonassen, 1949). His study illustrates both the potential value of research on symbolic space per se and the value of choosing little-known urban and suburban groups for study. Most of our community studies pick up something of how people perceive and use urban space, but few studies are much focused on the more subtle meanings of space for the city's residents.

As I write these lines, Chicago Poles bitterly assail the police who protect Negro demonstrators on their march through Polish areas. Negroes' desire for housing there runs afoul of a fierce sense of possession of land – which is not simply a bunch of streets but village parishes. Ten years ago, another Chicago parish defended itself against invaders by constantly stationing armed guards at major entry points for some weeks.

Any city — any metropolitan region — might be viewed as a complex related set of symbolized areas. Any given population will be cognizant of only a small number of these areas: most will lie outside of effective perceptions; others will be conceived in such ways that they will hardly ever be visited and will even be avoided. When properly mapped, any given area will be symbolized differently by several, if not by numerous, populations. In consequence, our cumulative research tells us more about the symbolic meaning of space for simple residential areas than for complex areas used and symbolized by diverse groups. One urgent task of urban theory is to develop categories and related hypotheses about the differential symbolism of space, and the differential behavior associated with that symbolism. This aspect of theory has rather obvious implications for land use, recreation, urban aesthetics, and so on. The exploratory research suggested by Lynch is especially worth perusing in this regard (Lynch, 1960).

Worlds Which Transcend Space

One great gap in Park's original program — one which still exists in urban sociology — was failure to take cognizance of the many social worlds which are not closely linked with specific urban spaces. Ethnic groups are spatially locatable, so it makes sense to study them in terms of space. But many urban worlds are diffusely organized and difficult to pin down definitely in space, since their members are scattered through several or many urban (and rural) areas. Although the chief institutions of an urban world (fashion, jazz, drama, chess, art, bridge, stamp collecting, baseball, or lesbianism) are necessarily located somewhere, the important attributes pertain more to the shared interests and activities of "members" of those worlds. I venture to say that the standard sociological concepts are not especially suited to understanding either these worlds or the behavior of their members.

Probably, we shall even have to discover the most useful kinds of research questions to ask about these worlds (Shibutani, 1955). Perhaps these questions might include how the local, national, and international versions of a given world (like chess) interlock; and how the margins of certain worlds (homosexual and ballet) overlap. The existence of mass media (magazines for sports fishermen or hi-fi enthusiasts) and special institutions (the Museum of Modern Art or the New York Metropolitan Opera House) to specified worlds is more obvious than their meanings for their various consumers. The relationship of a world's professionals and amateurs is perhaps another good research question. These worlds are far more absorbing to, and so better covered by, popular writers than by sociologists; but one can hardly be content with popular description and explanation.

American Symbolism: Urban and Cultural

In a stimulating article Lois Dean recently analyzed the psychological gestalt of a community which she named "Minersville" (Dean, 1965). The people of this community share a feeling of belonging to a golden vanished century, and an almost complete alienation from a federal government which they believe is antagonistic and non-responsive to their values. Dean concludes that planning which operates on the principle of federal collaboration with local initiative is unlikely to work well, if at all, with such communities. Translated into the language of the preceding discussions of city-types and the sociology of time, space, and social worlds, we can see the more easily that Minersville and other towns and cities require study in terms of where they fit – temporally as well as regionally, symbolically as well as physically – into the American scene. Granted that people who are located differentially in a city's social structure inevitably differ in their views of the city, in their actions toward it, in their styles of living within it, and in what they wish to preserve or forget about its past; nevertheless, those cities can be studied globally in relation to the American scene.

Chicago is a good example. As I have documented in *Images of the American City*, Chicagoans from the very beginning thought of their city as destined to become a world center, not simply a regional city (Strauss, 1961). Fairly quickly it overtook other cities in population and resources, and was not surpassed by any other city until recently; now Los Angeles contests Chicago's right to be called "the second city." Since Chicago overtook St. Louis (after the Civil War) it has had New York as its key rival – but not vice versa. Chicagoans are still sensitive to judgments by New Yorkers that Chicago and the Midwest are only "the provinces." Chicago shares a regional suspicion of the East as epitomizing distinctions of class, as over against the more equalitarian and democratic spirit of a region established under conditions of frontier democracy. Chicago also shares in the ambiguous definition of "the midwest" – a region which shifted, in fact and in symbol, from being the nation's breadbasket to being one of our greatest industrial areas.

I do not claim that all Chicagoans are bathed in all of this symbolism, but only that they and their city (and metropolitan region) can profitably be studied in such terms. Regional and urban historians are more apt to bring such considerations into their research, but only for more strictly historical or chronological purposes. Urban sociologists either are unaware of such considerations or do not thoroughly explore what such considerations might imply. The final book in Lloyd Warner's Yankee City Series goes further in this direction that almost any other study of an American city by a sociologist or anthropologist, although the earlier volumes are not consistently informed by the later insights about symbolism (Warner, 1959). A steady focus on matters of symbolism, I suggest, would teach us a great deal about social relations in given urban settings. Comparative studies, as will be suggested below, would also build such a focus on a theory of urban relations in America.

STUDY OF THE UNUSUAL

Since there is no end to the suggestions that can be made for studies of the unstudied, I turn now to the related second strategy: studying the unusual. This strategy should lead ingenious researchers to groups and institutions whose study might more quickly develop aspects of urban theory than research on less "regular" areas. Again, convinced readers will wish to devise their own list of researches, after reading the few suggested below. Howard Becker has suggested to me that even the somewhat studied underworld still is largely *terra incognita.*

THE TRIVIAL

First of all, we should take seriously the game of studying phenomena which seem trivial. For instance, I have engaged in some fieldwork at shops where wigs are sold and quickly found categories suggested by the data that bear, for instance, on matters of urban privacy (how salespeople and customers, reciprocally and respectively, handle potentially embarrassing exposure; how breakdown of protective maneuvers fail and with what consequences), and public display (how customers learn to display themselves through wigs; for what audiences; and how the wigmaker or salesman teaches display). Fieldwork at second-hand furniture auctions suggests the fruitfulness of studying the more sociological aspects of little-noted economic behavior. Careful observation of spatial movements on a bus route suggests ways of maintaining distance, reserve, dignity, and privacy under crowded urban conditions. Twenty-four hour vigils, by students, at a downtown street corner suggest a number of hypotheses about the use and symbolism of space, as well as ideas about nighttime careers. Similar observation and interviewing in a variety of parks reveals a number of unsuspected personal careers and urban worlds.

THE ODD

A corollary tactic is to choose the "odd" or "different." For instance, rather than studying the usual occupations, or those that seem important to the city's functioning, why not study those that are little noted, even in popular magazines? They might turn out to be strikingly informative about city life. For instance, we might study bill collectors if only because they visit virtually all sectors of the metropolitan area, and probably experience some not-so-ordinary encounters. Everett Hughes' suggestion of some years ago that sociologists study the "low" occupations (garbage collection) or the "dirty-work" of the professions (abortionist physicians, ambulance-chasing lawyers) is also a guideline to discovery of the unusual urban worker. Barney Glaser has pointed out to me that most of the city's functionaries whose services keep its physical structure "going" have scarcely been studied, if at all, by urban researchers: for instance, garbage collectors, firemen, electricians, and workers in the sewerage and water systems. The subway guard, the bus driver, the garage mechanic, the nighttime office cleanup lady are among the more lowly, unusual workers; but higher occupations like professional fund-raisers or radio announcers might also prove to be informative subjects for research.

Minor Economic Activity

An associated tactic is to choose some category of economic activity, or some business, which is not likely to be studied for its importance to the city. (One of the most informative urban studies I ever read, a thesis at the University of Chicago, was about Chinese laundries and laundrymen.) Once this tactic is stated, the studies almost suggest themselves: auctions of all types (art, antique, industrial); second-hand sales of various goods (clothes, furniture, yachts); varieties of land purchase and sales (as suggested earlier); and so on. Some of these businesses and markets are much studied by economists, but their sociological aspects are yet to be explored, especially as they might pertain to urban social relations.

Study of the Streets

One more suggestion for studying the unusual: it would certainly be productive to study systematically the social relationships that exist on certain types of streets. What network of social relations exists on the Negro main streets which parallel the white main streets in many a Southern small city? What about the recognizable evolution of certain streets as they change from "far-out-bohemian" to what might be termed "shoppers' bohemian?" In fact, what about the change of any business street in any characteristic direction whether upward in the standard scale of business or downward? Again, I know from study of certain streets that unusual relationships, businesses, and functions can be discovered: for instance, in a Negro neighborhood a "basement store" was by day also a nursery for the children of recent migrants and at night a gathering place for teen-age jazz enthusiasts and a kind of social club for adults. Of course, such studies should not be confined to purely business streets. Even fairly conventional streets, if studied in terms of an evolving urban theory, probably would be highly profitable, especially in types of cities that are not yet much studied. Students in urban sociology courses, according to Virginia Olesen, continually raise the question: "How does urban life, e.g., San Francisco, differ from so-called suburban life, for those of similar status and education?" One efficient way to find out is to study a number of streets where similar people, of comparable status and education, live and shop.

MINIMIZING IDEOLOGICAL COMMITMENTS

Some pages ago, I remarked that urban sociologists had allowed their ideological commitments profoundly to affect their research. If a researcher wishes to study some aspect of urban relations that is quite involved in public debate, his best defense against his own (usually unwitting) commitments is to undertake an initial research into the various ideological commitments which others have made about the phenomenon – poverty, let us say, or social mobility – including those made in previous decades by sociologists, as well as laymen. A historical perspective on the rhetoric of public issues is necessary because rhetoric has historical roots; arguments have a way of getting repeated with slight variations of imagery, emphasis and language. Contenders in the current forum can thus be "placed" and their arguments treated as behavior, to be taken into account in studying "the topic" – one that the researcher will inevitably then define differently than when he began his inquiry.

Although space does not permit extended discussion of this strategy, perhaps a brief example will induce others to use it. Louis Wirth's "impersonality of urban relations," mentioned some pages ago, is a popular theme not only in the writings of many sociologists but in the speech and writing of others, laymen and specialists alike. Variants of the theme are easy to find in the nineteenth- and twentieth-century literature, whether by journalists or ministers or novelists or farmers. Some urban dwellers have had their styles and behaviors crucially affected by this view of cities; others have rejected it, or never even encountered it. The sociologist's task is to determine the variants of this impersonality theme (and there are many); to discover which kinds of groups, and under what specified conditions, see segments of urban life in those terms, and with what consequences to themselves, their institutions, and other groups. Explicit studies with such a focus are rare (Davis, 1959; Stone, 1954; Lopata, 1965).

This means that sociologists who have written and acted on the assumption of urban impersonality are also fair game for study – especially those who, like Wirth, have influenced city planners or, like C. Wright Mills, have affected popular thought. Other influential exponents of urban impersonality, like Lewis Mumford, should be studied by urban sociologists, rather than ignored or treated as remote founts of wisdom.

I cannot resist adding that the controversy over "popular culture," in which many social scientists have become embroiled, can be conceived as embodying views of the city as depersonalized, impersonal, and anomic. That assertion, whether true or not, suggests that urban imageries or themes intertwine in marvelously complex ways. Part of the task of urban sociology – both for its own development and minimizing researchers' ideological commitments – is to trace out the connections among those imageries. Just what difference has it made to Americans and their cities that some cities have been visualized as especially corrupting to rural migrants who failed to conquer it, but also especially conducive to rural migrants' making it up the social ladder? What kinds of institutions have been spawned by the intersection of themes like "opportunities in the city," "education for the urban masses," and "the city as a rational marketplace" (Strauss, 1961; Fisher, 1965)? What has been the impact on urban planning of versions of the city as "depersonalizing;" "aesthetically depressing;" "morally corrupting;" as antagonistic to physical health, but at the same time as conducive to the very highest civilization? Perhaps these questions seem a light-year away from the discussion of the protective strategy against ideology with which this section started, but just these kinds of questions are necessary, I believe, for transcending the arguments which usually backstage the research we do in "hot" public areas.

COMPARATIVE STUDIES

The fourth strategy that I suggest should guide many urban studies is the deliberate use of comparative method. Most studies of urban social relations have been case studies: one or two suburbs, one or two occupations, a neighborhood, a city institution, or a type of institution. Case studies are certainly useful for various purposes, but they are deficient for *discovering* a systematic, integrated theory about urban social relations. They are deficient because the researcher finds himself extrapolating to more general theory, buttressing his own data with occasional data or interpretations drawn from selected studies, but without developing the *grounds* of that more general theory. He may even attempt little or no wider interpretation of his data, thereby throwing the burden on those of his readers who are interested in wider theory. I believe this case approach to be a chief reason for the disparate character of theory of urban relations.

Where we are weak is not in how to *verify* theory, but in how to *discover* theory. Thus, I draw a distinction between discovery and verification. The line between the two activities is not sharp, and is not hard and fast. Certainly research can embody both activities. But during the last few decades sociologists have tended to develop the verification side much further than the discovery side. In the eyes of methodologists, case studies tend to be thought of as only preliminary, affording hypotheses to be tested by more rigorous methods. I am asserting just the opposite view: case studies give great depth of knowledge, and therefore are probably very good for verifying theoretical formulations. I do not think they take us very far, or very fast, in discovering and formulating integrated theory. They tend to give bits and pieces of relatively unrelated theory. Their accumulation affords inventive readers the opportunity to formulate some generalizations, which they may use in lectures or research, but these hardly add up to integrated or fully public theory. To continue the piling up of informative case studies would seem an unwarranted act of faith, if we are interested (to use Sjoberg's phrase) in a consistent, general theory.

Insofar as theory is the goal (not for its own sake, simply, but also for its pragmatic consequences), the alternative is a self-conscious use of comparative method. Space does not permit detailing how comparative studies are best carried out for purposes of developing theory, but some recent work illustrates the comparative method (Glaser and Strauss, 1965).

In accordance with initial hunches or hypotheses, the researcher can begin to "theoretically sample" various groups or institutions. For instance, even without sophisticated hypotheses, one might wish to study realtors in various kinds of urban or suburban areas, to see what similarities and differences in their behavior, relationships, and institutions would quickly become apparent. At a more sophisticated level, one might wish to sample urban or suburban locales where he suspected various urban images might predominate among the population: for instance, a rural imagery, an impersonality imagery, a class-conflict imagery, a status-climbing imagery, a city-as-fun imagery; or any combination of such imageries.

In this kind of study — because his aim is the discovery and *not* the verification of theory — the researcher need not know everything about realtors or everything about the locale; he only needs to know enough to feel quite certain about the phenomena directly at the center of his interests. This kind of comparative focus "rather quickly draws the observer's attention to many similarities and differences . . . these contribute to the generation of theoretical categories, to their full range of types or continua, their dimensions, the conditions under which they exist . . . and their major consequences. . . . The observed differences and similarities speedily generate generalized relations among the theoretical categories, which in turn become the hypotheses soon integrated into the . . . theory" (Glaser and Strauss, 1965, p. 290). All the research problems or areas suggested earlier are amenable to this type of theoretical sampling and comparative analysis.

In this kind of comparative research for discovering theory, data that are already published become highly relevant — not for buttressing a researcher's theoretical formulations, but as relevant as his own first-hand data for the discovery of theory. For this purpose, researchers are thoroughly warranted in drawing on published data. Thus anyone who might wish to study the symbolic use of space will find plenty of material in the sociological literature. Most of it would be inadequate for testing theory, but it is quite adequate for stimulating the development of theory. Some of the published data are not in the form of another researcher's conclusions, but will actually be his raw data, including quotations from his informants. A good example of such data is the hobo's conceptions and uses of urban space, as detailed descriptively in Anderson's early monograph on the hobo (Anderson, 1923). Use of all these data for general comparative purposes — a form of secondary analysis — is perfectly legitimate when one's aim is the development of theory (Glaser, 1963).

A NOTE ON METHOD

It should be readily apparent that many of the research areas suggested in this paper probably require extended field observation, and even some measure of participant observation. One should not, however, foreclose on any alternate method which appears appropriate for an area under study. But I call attention to field observation precisely because the monographs of the early "Chicago school" were based mainly on that method. Since their publication, field methods have greatly developed and should be used wherever deemed helpful or necessary.

There is perhaps more point to my urging that historical and humanistic documents be used as data. Although little used by American urban sociologists, these documents can be of considerable value for exploring the forms, functions and meanings of cities. In fact, if readers take seriously any of my suggested strategies or research areas, they will find themselves turning to such documents. Some of our needed urban research simply cannot be accomplished without such materials – abjuring them only leads to the impoverishment of our theory and even of our descriptive knowledge. As I have remarked elsewhere, comparative studies cannot do without documentary research if only because use of documents – found in the library and elsewhere – is sometimes speedier and more efficient than first-hand collection of observational, interview, or questionnaire data. A recent study in urban history that should be of considerable interest to urban sociologists, and which illustrates the kinds of documents available besides those found in libraries, is Warner's study of three Boston suburbs (Warner, 1962). While historians make excellent use of such documentary materials, they do not address themselves to the same range of problems as those noted above, although there is much overlapping of interest, of course, between them and urban sociologists. Indeed, use of such materials would almost certainly bring historians, sociologists, political scientists, economists, and humanists closer together in their separate explorations of "urban problems," as well as provide correctives for their separate types of blindness. That planners, architects, statesmen, and other practical men of affairs might also profit from such collaboration seems very probable.

4

Class and Race in the Changing City

Searching for New Approaches to Old Problems

ELEANOR P. WOLF
and CHARLES N. LEBEAUX

☐ BY NOW, EVERYONE IS AWARE OF those changes in the population of the central city which have combined with a number of other factors to create the current concern about American urban life. In the pages which follow we will examine two kinds of responses to the so-called "crisis of the city." First, we will consider the efforts to halt, reverse, or otherwise exercise some control over the population trends of the city so that it will not become overwhelmingly the abode of disadvantaged people. We might describe these as efforts to affect the spatial distribution of "haves" and "have-nots." Second, we will examine some of the present trends in our efforts to improve the situation of the poor, especially those efforts usually categorized under the heading of social welfare programs, but including education.

RETAINING AND RECAPTURING THE "HAVES"

RETAINING MIDDLE-CLASS HOUSEHOLDS

Almost ten years ago the late Morton Grodzins warned that "many central cities of the great metropolitan areas of the United States are fast becoming lower class, largely Negro slums" (Grodzins, 1959). During the ensuing years programs striving to halt this process have been many and varied, but all of them either have tried to keep white middle-class groups from leaving the city (or certain areas within it), and/or have tried to entice advantaged households not living in the city to locate within its political boundaries.

Much of the effort to retain white middle-class households has taken the form of attempts to "stabilize" racially changing neighborhoods. These efforts have been largely conducted by local residents' groups. This is a rather interesting example of American voluntary organizations aimed at exercising social control over population movements, an area of life which, in this country, has tended to be left to the operations of the market and the entrepreneurs working within it. These local citizens' groups (the Hyde Park-Kenwood organization in Chicago was a leading forerunner) have developed programs of considerable scope and variety. Their avowed purpose has generally been both to prevent "deterioration," i.e., maintain the middle-class character of these areas, and prevent "re-segregation," the succession to all or predominantly Negro occupancy. It was this double emphasis which reputedly led Mike Nichols to satirize the Hyde Park-Kenwood effort as "black and white, shoulder-to-shoulder, united against the lower classes." Some of these programs have been aimed at halting the exodus of white households from such neighborhoods, while others have concentrated on attracting a sufficient number of new white households to prevent transition to a largely Negro-occupied area. These two kinds of programs, of course, influence each other; that is, residents' decisions about leaving such an area are markedly affected by observation of what kind of people are moving in, and decisions about entering are influenced by knowledge of what those already residing in the area seem to be doing.

Some of the programs designed to halt or slow the exodus of white households, sometimes described as "flight," or, if apparently rapid, as "panic," are discussed in the following pages.

Attempts to Control Real Estate Solicitation

Neighborhood organizations are united in (and by) their resentment of the high-pressure tactics of many real estate brokers. Although the social researcher may declare himself unable to specify the impact of these activities upon racial transition, to the resident (especially if he is active in these neighborhood associations) the relationship between constant solicitation and the sprouting of *For Sale* signs is clearly that of cause and effect. Earlier efforts to cope with the presumed impact of these activities mainly took the form of pleas to brokers and the "pressure of public opinion." Recently there have been attempts to secure laws and city ordinances aimed at controlling real estate practices, and some groups have sought to use the state licensing authority to halt unethical high-pressure tactics or appeals to bigotry. While legislation which regulates such matters as the size and number of signs which can be posted on a piece of property can be reasonably well-enforced (if aided by vigilant citizens), what passes in the private conversation between the agent and those he serves is much more potent and, if couched in suitably discreet language, almost impossible to control. It seems likely that the mere appearance of large numbers of brokers has a discouraging and perhaps self-fulfilling effect. Their presence is a sign from those professionally expert that "the neighborhood is changing." It must be noted, however, that this activity cannot cause an exodus when the market conditions are unfavorable, as was the case, for example, is a northwest Detroit area between 1960 and 1962 (Wolf, 1965).

Maintaining and Enhancing Neighborhood Standards

Most of these local organizations have successfully functioned as pressure groups to secure adequate city services (such as garbage collection and tree-trimming) and facilities (such as libraries and playgrounds). They have also effectively represented their areas before zoning boards, usually in opposition to changes in land use. (Neighborhood council leaders are either unfamiliar with, or unconvinced by, Jane Jacobs' arguments against homogeneous land use.) These councils have also occasionally approached individual residents or the owners of shops at commercial boundaries of their areas, with appeals or pressure to conform to the prevailing standards of upkeep or propriety. Although these activities have often been conducted quite successfully, the physical standards of an area seem to play a minor role in the residential decisions of white households, at least in comparison with the importance of the social characteristics of the area's population. There are, of course, a number of largely Negro-occupied areas in many cities which present an excellent appearance. However, this was not sufficient to maintain the racial mixtures which such areas did possess at one time in the past.

The overwhelming importance of the social characteristics of residents, as compared with the importance of community facilities, may be seen by observing population movements and can be revealed by insightful interviewing as well. Yet programs of neighborhood stabilization often place greater stress on facilities than they do on people, perhaps because facilities are easier to obtain. Government-sponsored programs of neighborhood conservation are based in part on the belief that people who can choose would decide to remain in certain areas of the city if other people would do a better job of property upkeep. Thus, conservation programs have, at least in the past, consisted of rather unsuccessful attempts to propagandize people with inadequate incomes into fixing up their deteriorating homes, even if it required applying for loans. The so-called successful programs of "rehabilitation" have, up to now, consisted of converting run-down housing in very desirable locations into more expensive dwellings, thus changing the population living there by making it too expensive for those of more modest means.

Ventilation and Education

Many of these groups show a noteworthy capacity for imaginative and sustained educational activities aimed at correcting distorted stereotypes of Negroes, myths of the "inevitable" decline of property values, and irrational fears of rowdyism and crime. They have attributed great importance to correcting false information concerning area change and to dispelling false rumors. Block meetings of white residents faced with a move-in by a Negro family have offered opportunities for prejudiced whites to air their fears and become aware of other viewpoints, some now given considerable support by government and religious leaders.

Our own studies do not support the notion that these activities make a decisive contribution to racial stabilization. In fact, our data suggest that after an initial flurry of false rumors, white residents tend to form reasonably accurate appraisals of the number and characteristics of their Negro neighbors. However, the impact of these efforts appears wholly constructive and beneficial, developing an increasing number of enlightened and concerned citizen leaders.

Building Neighborhood Morale and Cohesion

Perhaps as a consequence of a growing pessimism regarding the possibility of long-term stabilization of many biracial areas, there has been some tendency of late to minimize preoccupation with numbers and percentages of Negro households and stress instead building "neighborhood spirit." This attempt at a revived localism often sits oddly upon the sophisticated urbanites who espouse it; "neighborliness," understandably, becomes a virtue if one's neighbor is a Negro. Neighborhood fairs and festivals have been organized, and other attempts to emulate the booster spirit attributed to suburban communities have been promoted.

The relationship, however, between neighborly interaction, residential mobility and stabilization of racial mixture is not at all clear. There is little evidence that neighborliness has a serious impact on household decisions to leave a changing neighborhood and some of the small number of areas which have demonstrated long-term stability of racial mixture are rental areas of rather high mobility. It may be noted also that *mobility* per se is not viewed as a problem in middle-class areas. It is only in those instances where the newcomers are of lower social or economic status that acute concern about residential stability develops.

Efforts to Influence the Nature of Incoming Population

In some cities the increased supply of housing available to middle-income Negro households has lessened the concentration of demand, thus decreasing the pressure on any single area. (This increased supply of dwellings is, of course, one outcome of the outward movement often bemoaned as "flight" or "exodus.") It may also be true that the growing proportion of older people among white residents of the city has meant a less mobile population, especially since in many instances they are already in peripheral areas and the next move must be to a suburb. Perhaps the activities of the citizens' groups *have* held some households longer than would have been the case without these efforts. Yet even in those instances where white households have departed at rates similar to (or even lower than) that which occurred when there were no Negro families in residence, the usual pattern is for most of the homes sold to be sold to Negroes. The white buyer still tends to be a minority in the "neutral" or established racially mixed city neighborhood. (This is not true of the redevelopment areas to be discussed later, nor is it true in certain areas where there is a considerable amount of rental property.)

Citizen leaders of the integrated neighborhood associations have become increasingly aware of the fact that even if all departures of resident households were for "normal" – i.e., non-racial – reasons, without a constant supply of new white buyers the area would eventually follow the traditional pattern of racial succession. We suspect that the customary practice of real estate brokers in promoting and showing property along racial lines (with mixed areas considered as part of the Negro housing market) is more influential in maintaining racial separation in housing than is the excessive solicitation described earlier. The assumption by brokers that prospective purchasers will want to conform to established patterns of racial occupancy tends to be accurate, one would suppose, on a probability basis, but it ignores the existence of important deviant preferences and crystallizes some considerable amount of unformed opinion.

In an effort to counteract these effects many of the citizens' councils have devoted an increasing amount of their energies to the search for white buyers. In some instances they have opened offices and assumed the role of real estate agencies in bringing buyers and sellers together. (As long as no fees or commissions are involved they are free of state regulation.) Many have advertised or otherwise promoted their neighborhoods quite widely, some even on a national basis, in hopes of capturing the attention of transferred business executives and the like. The search for a large enough supply of white buyers has been a difficult one in many cases, and a common finding has been that it is much easier to discover white households willing, even eager, to *rent* in racially mixed areas. This permits a trial, without a more permanent commitment, and does not require that the entrants make a prediction about the area's *future*, which they view with some misgivings.

Efforts to Increase the Residential Dispersion of Negroes

While searching for new white buyers, some integrated neighborhood associations have sought to discourage the entrance of "too many" Negroes, although they would not be likely to describe their efforts in such language. (A few years ago there was considerable interest in the use of benign quotas, an approach now largely viewed as either impractical or in violation of fair housing measures.) Some have made open efforts to prevent inundation. ("I'm doing my darndest to keep Negroes from moving into my neighborhood," the *Wall Street Journal* quotes a Negro leader in the racially-mixed Cleveland suburb of Ludlow.) A more indirect and slower approach is simply that of encouraging the movement of Negroes to lily-white suburbs and any similar remaining city neighborhoods. Some new allies of open-occupancy legislation have come from local councils convinced by the logic of their own experience while trying to stabilize their areas, that success requires the existence of a truly open housing market. To this end, in addition to endorsing legislation aimed at this goal, they have added their support to the established civil rights organizations pressing for better police protection for Negro families moving into new territory, and have given encouragement and assistance to suburban human-relations groups working on behalf of housing integration. Some suburban mayors have been pressed into public declarations asserting the right of "all races" to move into their communities.

The participation of these integrated homeowners' groups on behalf of fair housing legislation, their opposition (often unsuccessful) to such fair-housing repeal measures as California's Proposition 14, and their support of fair listing services to aid dispersion is a somewhat new emphasis as compared with the more localistic efforts of ten or fifteen years ago. The fair listing service attempts to bring Negro buyers who are willing to move into predominantly white areas together with owners who are willing to sell to them. It often happens that there are more of the latter than there are of the so-called pioneers. The reluctance of isolated Negro families to move into possibly hostile areas has prompted the suggestion that such efforts be organized into moving on a group basis, with a number of households undertaking the venture simultaneously.

It must also be noted that while the movement of Negroes into suburban areas is desirable on a number of counts, it is by no means clear that racial residential patterns will be different from what they are in comparable areas within the city limits. There is no magic in the suburban air which insures racial stabilization of the desired proportions, and suburbs where Negroes have lived for many years often show a tendency to racial concentration much like that found in comparable city neighborhoods.

There is a measure of ambivalence in the response of Negroes to programs which stress racial stabilization and mixture rather than the mere insistence upon open occupancy. This is understandable, especially when the emphasis shifts from encouraging the continued presence of whites to *discouraging* the presence of "too many" Negroes. "Is one race more welcome than another in northwest Detroit?" asked a Negro newspaper recently apropos the selective recruitment of white buyers being undertaken by the community councils striving for racial stabilization, as opposed to racial "resegregation" of their areas. All of the unresolved ambiguities regarding Negro identity, assimilation, amalgamation, and group-belonging are touched where efforts shift from the mere *right* to occupy any dwelling one can pay for, to the *value* or *need* of interracial mixture.

The consequences of white flight are by no means wholly negative. If an exodus of white owners is really hasty and large-scale it may have the effect of making good homes available to Negroes at somewhat lower prices than would otherwise be the case. (This effect is, of course, defined by fearful whites as the threat of declining property values.) And the residential concentration of Negroes has made possible political power which might not have been achieved with a more scattered residential pattern.

School Problems in Changing Neighborhoods

Schools are of crucial importance in the residential choices of parents whose resources are such that the term "choice" is appropriate. Negro parents, perhaps especially those of middle-class status, are acutely concerned about what is usually described as "standards" of the schools which their children attend. This concern is shown both in their residential choices and the focus on schools in various displays of social protest in recent years. White parents are similarly aware of the importance of their children's educational achievement. In their case, concern may more often be centered on the problem of admission to prestige colleges.

Efforts to retain white middle-class households in racially changing areas, as well as attempts to attract such families to buy in such neighborhoods, must reckon with this concern about schools. Attempts at promotion usually recite their advantages, often in terms of curriculum, facilities, staff qualification, and plant. Early formulations of the problems besetting schools in changing areas were described largely, if not entirely, by such phrases as "educational neglect" or "declining quality," with inadequate attention given to the precise variables involved. Sometimes changes which *accompanied* population change, e.g., a rapid increase in pupil enrollment which also increased class size, were assumed a priori to be the *cause* of whatever differences in achievement began to be visible, although one rarely hears of drops in achievement produced by suburban schools suffering similar upsurges in pupil enrollment. Not enough studies have been conducted of schools in areas undergoing population changes to state whether the alleged changes *within* the school (staff transfers, teacher hostility and resentment, discrimination in school supplies, increased class size) or changes in the scholastic aptitude of the entering pupil population are primarily responsible for the declining school standards often cited as the chief reason for the white middle-class exodus from changing neighborhoods. Our own observations and a study of such areas in Detroit suggest that changes in pupil composition are probably more important than the "school variables" in affecting changes in education performance.

Racial change in occupancy involves shifts in the social class proportions of an area more often than is ordinarily realized, at least by proponents of civil rights. Once again, we are confronted with what seems to us the single most important factor in the interrelated problems we are considering: The social class distribution of the American Negro. The supply of middle-class Negro households entering what have been middle-class all-white areas is smaller than ordinarily estimated. In many instances a substantial proportion of the entering Negro households will be "respectable working class"—often with both husband and wife employed. Especially if the area (as has often been the case) was formerly occupied to a large extent by Jewish households, the difference in average school performance may be noticeable. If these changes are accompanied by even small increases in the proportion of pupils who are rowdy, physically aggressive, or otherwise threatening to middle-class standards of language and other behavior, former residents may decide to leave. This experience has been a serious handicap in developing support for plans to achieve more racially balanced school assignment, a program which has run into great difficulties in northern cities whenever attempts to implement it on a large scale have been undertaken. (This is not to suggest that all, or even most, of these parental objections can be attributed to the realities of social class differences.)

If differences in pupil behavior and educational performance are not very great, the latter could perhaps be handled by vigorous programs of educational assistance, especially in the lower grades. But big city school systems, operating in a chronic state of financial crisis, and hard pressed to deal with the overwhelming needs of the children of poverty, have shown scant success in working even such small miracles. Some changes in behavior (in the direction of middle-class styles) are likely to occur as a consequence of interaction in the new social climate if the proportion of new pupils of somewhat lower social status is small. However, the wish of most aspiring parents, Negro and white, to immerse their children in an atmosphere where they are surrounded by models of higher achievement and "better" behavior is so strong that those who can manage to do this will most certainly try. Thus, the typical middle-class neighborhood undergoing racial change often retains users of parochial schools, or older people without children, after most families with young children using the public schools have long since departed for areas which they believe will be "better for the children."

Recapturing White Middle-Class Households

In some quarters there has been, and perhaps still is, much hope that the outward movement of white middle-class households with children could be stemmed or even reversed by the creation of attractive housing in the core area of the central city. For the most part, such housing has been built only with government assistance as part of urban renewal programs. Typically, such efforts have involved what is usually called slum clearance, followed by construction of dwellings and other facilities for a much higher-income population on the valuable lands thus made available. As critics have pointed out, to describe this as slum clearance is misleading, since thus far Congress has been unwilling adequately to subsidize homes for poor people above the public-housing level. Slum clearance has perforce consisted of razing substandard dwellings and offering those dislodged (usually poor Negroes) varying degrees of help in finding whatever happens to be vacant elsewhere, in the same housing market and with the same inadequate income which caused these persons to be living in substandard housing at the outset. Proponents of these programs, while often deploring the lack of housing for the poor, nevertheless believe that the prospect of central cities becoming ever more heavily poor-and-Negro is so grim that the program is justified. Some stress the city's grave financial needs, its declining tax base, and its loss of civic leadership. Others are most concerned with the need to protect important public investments in core city medical and educational facilities, now menaced by what is usually called "blight" – by which is meant, it appears, the concentration nearby of very poor people, some of whom display various kinds of undesired behavior. Others attribute much importance to the presumed gains in morale derived from these symbols of urban vitality.

Perhaps the most important contribution of core-city residential redevelopment has been the creation, in some cities where this has not existed before, of neighborhoods which maintain their racial mixture. Several factors – including high cost, selective promotion and marketing practices, and the availability of some rental housing – appear to be involved in this success. These urbane and civilized enclaves have demonstrated conclusively – if such demonstrations are still needed – that racial heterogeneity is easily handled when people have similar incomes and life-styles. In short, racial differences in behavior are imaginary, but social class differences are real. Of course, they have made it possible for many Negro families to occupy new housing, in a friendly social climate, and have offered a glimpse of what an integrated society might be like in the United States some day.

To what extent have these new core-city residential redevelopment areas stemmed the tide of outward movement? Gross population figures do not confirm enthusiastic claims, and the majority preference of white households with children still tends to be for a suburban location. Of course, it is reasonable to assume that some families moving from one metropolitan area to another come to live in a downtown redevelopment area instead of going to a suburb, and some households with children – apparently not very many – have moved back to the central city after a suburban sojourn. But their numbers are still too small to reverse the trend, despite the rejoicing of those whom Scott Greer describes as "ideologists of return." It is also difficult to say how much of this reverse movement would have taken place without the government assistance given to these redevelopment programs. There have always been some well-to-do families who preferred central city living and who sent their children to private schools, as well as a larger group of middle-aged couples who, when the last child left them, moved back from a suburban or peripheral neighborhood into a city apartment or town house (Foote, 1960).

An interesting feature of these efforts at residential redevelopment is the varying degree of emphasis upon mixed-class housing, and/or the sharing of some facilities – notably schools – with surrounding slum-dwellers. The attempts to attract upper-income households to the core-city raises at once the whole issue of heterogeneity: Will privileged groups elect to live near the very poor? How privileged? How poor? How many? And with what degree and kind of interaction? As in the case of those living in changing neighborhoods, it appears that preferences about physical space and facilities can be compromised more readily than concerns about the social characteristics of near-dwellers. For the most part, only those who can manage to substitute social for physical distance (the old Gold Coast and the Slum) will choose to place themselves in situations where they are surrounded by very poor people – the more so if they are Negroes.

Although there has been considerable discussion of the issue of mixed-class urban redevelopment, especially in the planning stages of such ventures, the absence of comprehensive provisions for the rehousing of displaced slum-dwellers on their former sites has made these discussions largely academic. One can imagine the controversies which would ensue if, for example, all core-city residential redevelopment ventures were required to have, let us say, half or more of their dwellings earmarked for families with an annual income under $5,000. Although liberals tend to lump them together, efforts to reduce race and class segregation often work against each other. The most stable, and (to participants) the most satisfactory, instances of racial mixture are those where social class is fairly uniform and comfortable.

In the absence of the much-needed housing programs for the poor the focus of controversy has tended to be the school system. If pupil assignment is based on place of residence, and if the school district covers a large enough area (as it tends to beyond the elementary school level), the children of upper-middle-class residents will be assigned to schools which have large percentages of children from very poor households. In many, if not in most cases, the poorer children will be Negroes. There seems little doubt that reluctance on the part of parents to consent to such arrangements has kept many families with school-age children (both white and Negro) from moving into such areas, unless they are able and willing to use private schools. Of course, if low-income populations continue to be removed from the urban core and replaced by the more prosperous this problem will gradually diminish from the perspective of the middle-class parent. The impoverished families, of course, will simply be living – with their problems – somewhere farther away, and using other schools.

In summary, what can be said of these attempts to control trends in the population composition of central cities? At the moment, neither programs of neighborhood stabilization nor residential redevelopment seem likely to halt the tendency for many of them to become more and more Negro-occupied. While this tendency is usually discussed as a disaster it is just possible that it may be the means whereby Negro alienation and powerlessness will be overcome. The gradual assumption of much of the management of American cities may make it possible for an increasing number of Negroes to exercise responsible power in our society. This may have disastrous consequences, however, if the present social class distribution of the Negro population remains unchanged, although it may develop that the control of cities will yield enough political power to achieve changes in the class structure. While we can see only dimly the future outlines of Negro group identity, the ominous consequences of continued poverty are already clearly visible. In the next half of this chapter some of the attempts to deal with this problem will be considered.

UPGRADING THE POOR: TRENDS AND ISSUES IN SOCIAL WELFARE AND EDUCATION

Efforts to deal with poverty and its consequences are inherently full of dilemmas, for a fundamental question to society is at stake: the relations between the social classes. Both the older, traditional social welfare programs and the newer departures in anti-poverty, strike against the barriers raised in the natural operation of an open-class stratification system; the newer programs today, especially in urban areas, try also to deal with the effects of a closed-class or caste-like system, the race relations problem.

GROWTH AND LIMITATIONS OF THE TRADITIONAL WELFARE PROGRAMS

Compared to all other industrialized, Western nations the United States lags markedly in the development of social welfare as measured by allocation of national resources. For example, in 1957 for roughly comparable "social security" programs the United States spent 5.5 per cent of national income while France spent 17.3 per cent, West Germany 17.3 per cent, Italy 13.2 per cent, Canada 8.8 per cent, and so on (Gordon, 1963, Table 4, p. 15). Yet the expansion of welfare provision under public auspices has been persistent and massive, as can be seen from the following figures on expenditures.

TABLE 1

TWO DECADES OF WELFARE EXPANSION*

	1944-45	1949-50	1964-65
Social Insurance	$1,419	$ 4,873	$28,098
Public Aid	1,031	2,496	6,259
Health and Medical	2,331	2,087	6,651
Other Welfare Services	160	458	2,703
Veterans Programs	892	6,381	5,979
Public Housing	10	15	309
Sub-Total	$5,843	$16,310	$49,999
Education	3,018	6,698	27,726
Total	$8,860	$23,008	$77,726

*Figures in millions of unadjusted dollars, rounded to nearest thousand.
SOURCE: Merriam, 1965, Table 1, p. 8.

The largest increase in the two decades since World War II has been in social insurance, most of it accounted for by the maturation and increasing scope of Old Age, Survivors, Disability and Health Insurance (OASDHI, or "Social Security"), which will jump again by about 6 billion dollars when the 1965 amendments including health protection become operative (Ball, 1965, p. 20). Outlays for education, also mounting rapidly, are shown here since public education, in origin a part of "social welfare," is again becoming heavily "welfarized," especially in the problem-laden cities, which is a notable trend in social service. As Merriam observes:

> Increasing concern with school dropouts, the quality of education in slum areas, and the interrelationships of social and economic circumstances with educational aspirations and achievements, however, again point up the relevance of education to social welfare (Merriam, 1965, p.4; see also Sheldon and Glazier, 1965).

These impressive increases in expenditures in the traditional program represent more than just an expansion of the economy and population, or price, inflation; larger shares of national resources have been allocated to social purposes:

TABLE 2

SOCIAL WELFARE EXPENDITURES

	As Percent of Gross National Product	Per Capita 1964-65 Prices
1944-45	4.2	$104.56
1949-50	8.7	198.05
1954-55	8.5	224.83
1959-60	10.6	302.94
1964-65	12.0	394.57

SOURCE: Merriam, 1965, Tables 2 and 3, pp. 7-8.

With all this expenditure, why should we now be faced with the need for a new revolution in social welfare? Have all these programs, along with the booming economy, failed to deal with the problem of poverty? Not completely. There is no question but that for most people real levels of living are much higher now than they were ten or twenty years ago. Using the $3,000 poverty level employed by the Council of Economic Advisers for families, and using fixed 1962 dollars, the proportion of families in poverty dropped from 32 per cent in 1947 to 19 per cent in 1963. At the rate of progress of the last few years only about ten per cent of families will remain under this poverty line in 1980 (Miller, 1964, p. 82). Thus, measured in the real goods of food, clothing, housing, medical care, and education, poverty in this country has been and is being substantially reduced.

Further, the traditional welfare programs, particularly social insurance, as well as playing a part in this reduction and preventing much poverty, could in the judgment of their administrators cure a good part of the remaining problem. Thus, United States Commissioner of Social Security Robert M. Ball estimated: "Perhaps a third to a half of the poverty that exists in the United States could be prevented by the improvement and broader application of the social insurance principle" (Ball, 1965, p. 20). Such improvements could include, in OASDHI, the already legislated health and hospital care of the aged, extension of medical care to other age groups, expansion of the scope of the disability programs, liberalization of the retirement test, extension of coverage, raising benefits and reducing interstate differences in unemployment insurance, establishing in all states the temporary disability insurance now operating in just four states, the humanizing of the administration of workman's compensation so that long delays and losses due to litigiousness are controlled, and the like.

But why does not the 34 billion dollars of social insurance and public assistance, already in effect, cure poverty? This sum is, after all, about three times the 12 billion dollar "poverty gap" (what it would take per year to raise the incomes of all those below the poverty line up to it). The reasons are generally of two kinds: many of the poor are not covered by insurance and assistance programs for the conditions which now make them poor; and benefits, even when forthcoming, are often too little to lift people out of poverty.

Lampman, for example, makes the following estimates of the numbers among the 35 million poorest who did and did not receive OASDHI and Unemployment Compensation in 1963.

TABLE 3

SOCIAL INSURANCE AMONG THE POOR (1963)

	On Social Insurance*	Not on Social Insurance*	Total*
Aged	6	2	8
Children	3	12	15
Not Aged, Not Children	3	9	12
Total Poor	12	23	35

***Figures in estimated millions.**
SOURCE: Lampman, 1966, p. 18.

Thus, only about one-third of the poor get social insurance payments (and this number is inflated by the six million aged who are not as poor on the average as the younger groups), either because there is no established provision for their particular ills or because they are not sufficiently "workforce attached" to qualify for benefits — farm labor, migratory workers, domestic help, unmarried and deserted mothers with children, and the like. It comes out that of the 27 billion dollars paid out in social insurance benefits in 1963, only 4 billion dollars went to the 35 million poor (Lampman, 1966, p. 4).

In contrast, all of the approximately 6 billion dollars per year now spent on public assistance goes to them — yet only 8 million receive such aid, a smaller percentage than gets social insurance payments. The reasons for this "lack of coverage" are, first, about half of the 35 million are *too rich* to qualify for relief under the still-prevalent rule of "less eligibility" descended from fifteenth century England, whereby no dependent person shall be maintained at public expense at a standard higher than that enjoyed by the poorest, "last eligible," independent person. The remaining 8 million ". . . are virtually as poor in terms of income less assistance and . . . poorer in terms of income including assistance . . ." than those getting aid (Lampman, 1966, p. 2), but are either self or administratively disqualified by the myriad deterrent features designed into the administration of poor relief (e.g., residence requirements, property lien laws, relatives' responsibility provisions, moral "suitability" regulations), or they live in states where there is no effective general relief program. In the 1965-66 hearings of the

Federal Advisory Council on Public Welfare the director of the Oklahoma Department of Public Welfare said:

> While the law authorizes we can make a $35 payment, we don't have the money in our funds. The maximum monthly payment that we make to any family is $20, and $10 to a single person . . . with further limitations of only two payments, except in the extreme case. So, you might say we have little or no general assistance program in Oklahoma (Department of Health, Education, and Welfare, Welfare Administration, 1966, p. 25).

Thus, altogether, only about half of the poor get any social insurance *or* public assistance payments. Those who do, frequently get amounts that are only enough to keep them alive in poverty. Relief is, as we have noted, by design almost always pegged at a destitution level – e.g., in recent years the average yearly grant for a member of a family receiving Aid to Dependent Children was less than $400. Social insurance benefits are usually larger but still are often not adequate for those without other income: in February 1966 the average monthly benefit in OASDHI for retired workers was $84.13, for a widow $73.83, for a child of deceased workers $61.39. These are averages and the poor, having earned less, get less. Such sums reflect the original and still dominant philosophy of social insurance in America: that it should provide a basis for income security, not the whole of it.

THE CHANGING CLIENTELE

Probably the most important social welfare development in cities in the post-World War II period has been the emergence of nonwhites, mainly Negroes, as the predominant and problem population. Their social conditions of life account on the one hand for much of the ineffectiveness of the traditional welfare measure described above, and on the other, for many of the issues and dilemmas which crop up in the new poverty programs.

The facts of Negro poverty need only be highlighted here. (Moynihan, 1965a; Drake, 1965; Fein, 1965; and Hauser, 1965c.) Under the usual classification of the 35 million poor by "poverty-linked" characteristics (age, race, education, marital status, etc.) Negroes, who are about 11 per cent in the general population, comprise 20 per cent of the Country's poor. But this drastically underestimates the Negro component because it does not allow for chronicity of poverty; Herman Miller calculates *that among families having substandard incomes for just two successive years, 40 per cent are Negro* (Miller, 1966, p. 4).

For children the situation is worse. It is estimated that in recent years 56 per cent of Negro children have been on AFDC (Aid to Families with Dependent Children) assistance at some time while growing up, compared to eight per cent of white children (Office of Planning and Research, U.S. Department of Labor, 1965, p. 12). In big families with five or more children, *94 per cent* of nonwhite children are being reared in poverty as measured by the U.S. Department of Agriculture "low cost" food plan, the usual standard in relief budgeting (Hauser, 1965, p. 862). In northern industrial cities – Chicago, Cleveland, Detroit – 80 to 90 per cent of the family-type relief caseloads (AFDC, general assistance) are Negro. Moynihan estimates that in 1963 there were only about 45,000 Negro males in the whole country who earned over $10,000 per year – enough, that is, to populate but a small part of the middle-class area of one city like Detroit (Moynihan, 1965, p. 756).

The implication for social welfare policy of the changed clientele is succinctly illustrated in two of the most hopeful programs from the 1930s – public housing and Aid to Dependent Children. Largely white, largely stable working- or genteel lower middle-class, the first public housing tenant populations were proud of their homes and were proudly served by public officials. In today's central cities, however, population movement has concentrated masses of problem-laden families in institutional warrens that even many of the poor avoid. Similarly, ADC was designed for white families of widows and children of the type who had been supported by the predecessor "Mothers Aid" programs – respectable, above scandal, thrifty and skilled in home management, needing only cash grants and a yearly eligibility reinvestigation. In big cities today this program has turned into the main support of the whole bottom layer of Negro society, a population marked by all the wretched characteristics of the very poor and discriminated-against.

Slowly, hesitantly, carrying the burden of much public disfavor, both public housing and ADC (exemplifying a wider movement among health, education and welfare agencies) now seek to redesign themselves to fit the changed social scene – in public housing, disposal of units, rent subsidy, attempts to reduce class segregation; in ADC, services, training and jobs, counseling, acceptance of the "subculture of poverty." Much of the new direction in the older programs, though it may be but the realization of old dreams of old welfare workers, reflects the social philosophy of the new anti-poverty movement, symbolized in the already battered slogan "participation of the poor."

NEW ANTI-POVERTY PROGRAMS – SOME ISSUES AND PROBLEMS

Compared to the tens of billions of welfare dollars that stream from the Federal and state governments, from Social Security and Welfare Administrations, via traditional programs, those spent by Economic Opportunity programs are but a trickle. But the attention of the nation is properly caught by the latter, for they represent the essence of the War on Poverty, the ferment of new ideas which aggravate old issues or bring new ones into view.

Participation of the Poor

It would be useful, if not altogether accurate, to categorize all the new anti-poverty efforts in terms of "participation," for they envision involvement of the poor not only in jobs, on advisory and policy boards to poverty programs, and as political activists, but in the much larger range of roles and activities suggested by Head Start and Higher Horizons; the slum-siting of Community Action Centers, the short-circuiting of established agencies and scorning of established social service professions, Upward Bound and educational parks, Medicare and the negative income tax. All of these attempt to push or pull the poor, especially the black city poor, into society's mainstream. (Even those few observers who see much to admire and preserve in the life-styles of the poor and thus reject the negative implication of "participation" that poverty's children need rescue from a satisfactionless oblivion, accept the need for most of the affluence- and status-sharing programs.)

Participation is, however, usually more narrowly conceptualized in terms of employment and of direction of anti-poverty efforts, exemplified in such roles as:

Social and political action – neighborhood organization for pressure on political bodies, action through political parties, rent strikes;

Policy and power positions – placement of poor persons on policy committees, administrative committees, in administrative and executive positions in program operations;

Knowledge sources, consulting and research – use of the poor on advisory committees, as consultants to programs, as key informants and respondents in social surveys, as researchers and interviewers in surveys;

Employment – creation of jobs for the poor to fill, finding jobs, training for jobs, use of nonprofessionals on an extensive scale.

The theory of the push for participation derives from the trends discussed above, that the new urban poor – in a way that was never true of the earlier European immigrant poor – are effectively excluded from the economic and status rewards of the society both by their distinctive minority status and by a changed economy with its ever-dwindling demand for manual labor. Participation can help overcome two evils – feelings of resentment and apathy as well as economic deprivation.

While it is recognized that a great deal of resourceful experimentation with new social devices will have to be done to put these worthwhile ideas into practice, some approaches to participation have been so ill-conceived or over-aggressively pushed as to have already suffered a backlash. For example, the "ombudsman" idea – that the government employ agents to protect individuals against itself – has precedent in this country in such forms as the Public Defender and is being further developed in anti-poverty legal aid programs. But in some quarters the goal of organizing the poor for political action has taken the form of a demand that the government finance a kind of guerrilla warfare against itself. Likewise, it seems a good idea to elect or appoint poor persons to community action center advisory and policy boards and to appropriate administrative positions, both to symbolize the country's recognition of their potentials and as a means of exploiting the special knowledge the poor have of their own problems. But to demand that poverty be the primary qualification for appointment to top anti-poverty executive positions and to controlling majorities and policy boards makes neither administrative nor democratic sense.

The trend toward participation of the poor in advisory and policy roles was hardly two years old in the spring of 1966 when government officials, both locally and in Washington, were having second thoughts about it. All sides have been prone to exaggerate the ideological components at issue – that the vested interests and bureaucrats are leagued against the poor on the one side, that the revolutionaries and intransigents are out to kill the anti-poverty program at all costs, on the other. The fact is that participation of the poor at *this level* conceals many complexities and ambiguities that need to be worked at and studied: roles have been unclear, wrong expectations have been created, unwise promises have been made. Sheer confusion plays a large part – "middle-class bureaucrats" in community action centers are often blamed for rebuffs of the poor which are actually administered by other poor employed in the center who do not understand how to communicate with and help people. With patience and will, such defects can be overcome.

There has been more experience and more success in achieving participation of the poor through employment. It is hardly novel. "Work relief" (not to mention "the workhouse") runs back for many centuries in welfare history (de Schweinitz, 1961) and continues down to the present as a more or less client-hated feature of general relief in the United States. Inadequate financial support and unimaginative administration of some Great Society work programs have let them in for similar opprobrium – in 1966 unemployed youth in Detroit were scornfully (and probably rightly) rejecting $1.25 per hour Neighborhood Youth Corps job offers as "cheap jobs" with low status, low pay, no future (Wolf and Lebeaux, 1965, Vol. II).

Such miscarriages in the execution of work programs, and others as bad in training and work-finding projects, have cast some shadows on the whole philosophy of "employment as participation"; and even the idea of work as an important social role was in the early and middle 1960s under attack from the disciples of the Triple Revolution whose theory of productive glut led them to emphasize novel measures of distributing income (e.g., the negative income tax) rather than gainful employment as the important social goal for this era.

Most attractive and promising in the participation-through-work movement were the ideas that Riessman and others began putting forth in the 1960s – millions of semi- and non-professional jobs in schools and social and health agencies, which would give good pay and dignified status to the job holders and would accomplish important work left undone by the shortage of professionals. Prototypes of these jobs were developed by Mobilization for Youth (MFY) in the early 1960s and by 1966 tens of thousands of community, teacher, and health aides were at work in the country. For a time excessive claims regarding the value of the work performed by the poor as non-professionals seemed to induce resistance from professionals, and this threatened further development of the idea. For example, many of the advantages claimed for the "indigenous worker" – poor persons used for client-contact work in poor neighborhoods – evaporate under close examination. MFY experience showed that the most successful workers were also the most middle-class; ability to help was not related to "distinctive lower-class insight"; alleged knowledgeability about the exploitiveness of lower-class culture led to refusal of service; special know-how in low-income survival techniques turned out to be either not very special or to be lacking in value base, e.g., how to buy cheaply in the "hot stuff" market, and so on (Barr, 1966).

Overzealous claims of this sort were, however, soon abated and the more important anti-poverty aspects of the non-professional job role came more clearly into focus: its use as a vehicle for training and education of the poor, for inducting them into careers via the work role, and its effectiveness for enhancing the personal dignity and self-respect of the "underdog." Nevertheless, even these feasible and very necessary objectives cannot be achieved, it now appears, without great care and large investment of thought and money in training and supervision. Otherwise "cheap jobs" result. There is a particularly painful rub here. To the poor person it looks as though poverty funds are being drained off to pay the professionals, the teachers of Head Start, the trainers of the counselors aides, and the "trainers of the trainers." To the professional it seems that there is an inadequate allocation of time and money for the supervision of the non-professional. Both are right; both witness the need for a much more massive investment in anti-poverty.

Anti-Establishment – The Case of Social Work

Bureaucracy and professionalism – the first term already a full-fledged epithet, the second fast becoming one – are the typical organizational means for task accomplishment in our society and, as such, are the natural targets for attack when expectations go unmet. Such complaints are not new; one suspects that there was already in the Neolithic village enough red tape and helplessness at the hands of organized specialists to foster revolt. But it is much worse in the organizational society.

Some of the resentment is directed against the very nature of bureaucracy (specialization of function, defined roles, hierarchy, formality, routines) as though it were possible in today's society to dispense with it. More reasonable are the complaints about "bureaupathology," interminable waiting lists, clerical coldness, a smother of regulation which mark particularly the operations of large government offices like the employment service and public assistance.

Resentment of bureaucracy is a constant for most organizations in the social welfare establishment. During the 1960s a new trend in criticism was leveled rather specifically at the voluntary social agencies and at the profession of social work (distinguishable but historically related phenomena usually lumped together in the view of the anti-poverty ideologists) on some or all of the following grounds:

> *Abandonment of the poor* – geographic shift of many private agencies to middle-class areas and suburbs, movement of social workers into non-poor-serving settings (e.g., psychiatric clinics), requirements which rebuff the poor (e.g., having to prove "motivation for treatment" by coming to the agency);
>
> *People-changing rather than society-changing in outlook* – adherence to psychodynamic as opposed to economic and socio-cultural theories of change, individual and one-by-one or family emphasis as contrasted to mass and institutional change approach, stressing problems and weaknesses rather than strengths and normality of the poor;
>
> *The middle-class–lower-class cultural gap* – lack of understanding of the lower-class culture, imposition of middle-class behavior standards, mutual distrust and fear, inappropriate diagnosis and treatment techniques;
>
> *"Welfare colonialism"* – encouragement of dependency, paternalism, support of the status quo, seeking adjustment to unjust conditions;
>
> *Remedial rather than preventive* – spending all resources on the already damaged (e.g., multi-problem families) rather than seeking out basic social causes.

These "new" criticisms have long been debated and, to a considerable extent, have been accepted within the profession. Social work has a strong tradition of commitment to social reform as a professional responsibility which makes social workers highly sensitive to such allegations. Yet in sociological perspective there was probably less substance to these criticisms than either the profession or its attackers realized. There are a number of reasons why social work developed along these lines, perhaps the major one being that it could not possibly be an exception to the dominant middle-class pressures in the whole society.

This is not to deny that ideological commitments and social movements are also "social forces," dynamic parts of the social system, e.g., the War on Poverty aims to alter some of the ways in which our society operates. To the extent that the social work professionals in the private agencies wish to participate in that War more than they already have, they will have consciously to turn away from the easy-to-serve and toward the hard-to-serve, to keep their agencies in the hard-core areas, to adjust theories and techniques to the culture of poverty and the alienation of lower-class Negroes, to get imaginative and enthusiastic about using non-professionals. A considerable move in this direction by the private agencies is already evident. Even larger has been the shift of social work professionals into public agency employment – relief, economic opportunity, and school programs – where poverty is the key, and hopes have been lifted by allocation of funds for these purposes.

But too much may be expected. Both within and without the profession there appears to be an exaggerated notion of the power of social workers and of the voluntary social work agencies to affect welfare practice and achieve social reform. The voluntary agencies dispense only a minuscule portion of the social welfare budget in this country, while the entire social work profession numbers just 45,000 persons of low pay, lower prestige, and but medium talents. Saddled with a name and with a self (and public) image which promise too much, social work makes an easy butt; but such recriminations, which can as easily fall on every side, are an ill-afforded luxury in a war which may well be far sterner than any had anticipated.

Problems in Education

Public schools in central cities have had a constantly increasing proportion of children from poor (and especially poor Negro) households. This is the single most crucial factor in accounting for our present crisis in urban education. Not that the educational problems of poor children are created by the city. Indeed, the collection of such pupils in urban schools has compelled the recognition of needs which were hidden from our sight in the rural South or, when such children were a minority in the urban North, concealed within the average achievement scores in the big city school systems of the past. It is true that decreased demand for unskilled labor makes inadequate education more handicapping now than it was 25 years ago, but then too it contributed to keeping such groups in inherited poverty.

That inequality in the conditions of families works against equality of opportunity for children is an ancient insight. Those who cherish the latter must constantly struggle to minimize the damaging effects both of a bad start in life and of continuing unfavorable conditions through childhood and adolescence. In the public school system, children marked by both the physical and psychological consequences of poverty are confronted by the demands, the standards, and the values of American society. No other institution involves an encounter between social classes on such a scale and under such conditions. The encounter is universal, with no filter of self-selection involved. The school receives the child as his family and his community send him, and must return him to that life, which often undermines educational aims, at the end of each school day.

Children in school are graded, sorted and labeled in accordance with their school performance, which has already been – and which continues to be – deeply affected by their lives outside the classroom. Because the use of absolutely uniform requirements and grading standards, without regard for resources for school achievement, would be demoralizing for all participants, this harsh procedure tends to be modified. School personnel in very poor areas tend (as do college professors) to adjust their criteria to what seems reasonable under the circumstances, so that they and their students can experience some feeling of success. This is the "lowering of standards" which has been so criticized, and understandably so, for, although it makes life more tolerable temporarily, the pupil is still disadvantaged in competition with others from more fortunate circumstances. Thus, it comes about that the child who got good grades in a slum elementary school is ill-prepared for a more inclusive high school, and high school graduates with "B" averages or better cannot meet admission requirements for a good college.

A few years ago, in the earlier stages of the new concern for the education of disadvantaged children, analyses of this problem tended to be made wholly in terms of educational inequality. Much attention was directed to the existence of inequalities within school systems, an additional injustice wherein a number of factors conspired to give least to those who needed most (e.g., Sexton, 1961). The usual pattern in a city school system was (and in some cases, still is) that pupils in the core areas were using old and unattractive buildings, obsolete equipment, were assigned staff whose numbers included a larger proportion of less-experienced teachers, as compared with more prosperous areas, and often were taught in somewhat larger classes.

In some cities, most of these blatant inequalities have been corrected, and in a few instances more educational services are now provided for disadvantaged children than for others within the same system. However, although research evidence is still unavailable, it appears probable that these educational inequalities are inadequate to explain the very marked under-achievement of children from very poor families. Their educational problems exist when they are not subject to the gross discrimination described above, and even when they are attending the same schools, sometimes in the same classrooms with children from privileged backgrounds. When one reflects that the skills and general behaviors wanted in school are constantly taught, practiced and reinforced within the middle-class environment, this is not surprising. Liberals are often reluctant to concede the destructive effects of the poverty they deplore, perhaps because it seems to denigrate the poor, more likely because to do so might be construed as an excuse for inaction on the part of those agencies whose task it must be to meet such needs.

How can the impact of social class differences upon school achievement be made to vanish or be greatly minimized? Can children learn equally well, even while living (and having lived) so unequally outside of school? One kind of response to this problem consists of attacks upon schools — their staff, materials, curriculum, and criteria of achievement — for "middle-class bias." Current proposals for the abolition of intelligence and aptitude tests are an example of this line of criticism. Of course, if such test scores or other kinds of performance are used as indicators of innate ability their users claim what science cannot validate. But beyond this kind of criticism there is confusion: Are schools at fault because they *do* try to help poor children to compete more successfully within this society (for surely this requires the skills and behavior described as middle-class)? Or are they being criticized because they are not successful *enough* in doing so? The latter is a question of appropriate techniques and methods of achieving the same results that can be achieved quite readily with other children. But to accept, for example, the language of lower-class Negro pupils, and not to attempt to change it because it is "equally valid" or "worthy" is surely to consign these pupils permanently to some kind of underclass in this country.

Another line of attack on this problem involves placing poor children in heterogeneous situations, where they can interact with others of higher social status. Some advocates of this approach stress the need for social class mixture, others for racial balance, and some stress both. Often the benefits to children from privileged strata are asserted, but this appears to be mainly an attempt to assuage opposition to this method of improving the educational situation of poor children. Some of these plans incorporate the view that all schools should be composed of certain proportions of pupils in such a way as to prevent Negro percentages from rising above a certain level.

There are numerous plans for securing more heterogeneity within a few nearby schools: for example pairing, and its variations. A proposal recently adopted in Hartford, Connecticut, will use one-way busing of Negro pupils away from the core area to some white suburban schools. At present there is much interest in the idea of educational parks, that is, the clustering of a number of schools in one location so that facilities may be shared, and a larger and more heterogeneous mixture of the pupil population of a city gathered in one place. This avoids some of the unfortunate connotations of busing and pairing, with their distasteful calculations of how many Negroes are "tolerable." Although there appears to be somewhat less emphasis within the civil rights movement on the problem of *de facto* segregation in public schools than there was a few years ago, there is considerable support from some quarters within the federal government and from some professional educators (mainly in universities) for what is termed "affirmative action" in this area. There is as yet no definitive constitutional decision on this question, but at present the prevailing interpretation seems to be that while racial concentrations arising from residential partterns may be altered by school boards if they *wish* to do so, they are not legally *required* to take such action.

Once again, the skewed class distribution of the Negro population both complicates the issue, and, in the eyes of those who strongly oppose class segregation, makes it all the more urgent that racial imbalance be corrected. To evaluate the research data on interracial contact alone is a formidable task far beyond the scope of this chapter (Williams *et al.*, 1964, Chapter 7). What is the impact of contact upon behavioral differences associated with differing social class levels? To what extent is contact the "cure" for inequality? Some of the recent work by Herbert Gans, Alan Wilson, William Sewell and others has begun to examine the complex dimensions of this question which, of course, will not be settled solely on a basis of the weight of research evidence. There is not very much support from middle- or working-class white parents for large-scale programs of school balancing which involve contact with any considerable numbers of lower-class children, especially if they are all or mainly Negro. Just how important this issue is to Negro parents is difficult to estimate, once the issue of educational inequality is removed, and assuming that uniform rules of pupil assignment which ignore race are operative. To some, especially among the middle-class, this sort of contact may have important symbolic value. At present, the participation of suburban (white) school systems would be required to implement the elimination of *de facto* school segregation because in so many large cities the majority of public school pupils is either already nonwhite, or seems soon to be so. Already, some school systems using pupil-assignment procedures to achieve certain kinds of mixes have been plagued by parental struggles over who gets what proportions of the scarce high-achievers. In addition, the goal of retaining and recapturing middle-class whites and the goal of upgrading children from poor families are often in conflict.

Experimental evidence on the effects of contact is scarce, and in field research it is difficult to isolate test variables. In fact, since most of these plans are sold to apprehensive middle-class parents by promising that they will incorporate many educational improvements in addition to pupil mixture, it becomes impossible to evaluate the impact of the latter factor alone. Stressing the provision of "quality education for all children," "integration and quality education," etc., has helped to soften parental opposition to pupil mixture plans, but it is doubtful whether, if implemented, this would improve the *competitive* position of children of the very poor. It seems more likely that a general improvement in education (like general wage and salary increases) tends to maintain the existing gap between average levels of performance.

There is growing support for programs of compensatory education, although the financial investment in these efforts has been small indeed in comparison with the dimensions of the task. To begin to equalize opportunity for the children of the very poor will require highly *unequal* education – in their favor – and even this may not be sufficient to offset general inequality of condition. A *massive program* (as yet untried) of compensatory education and child-welfare services together with provision of a wide range of anti-poverty measures, would probably make a substantial improvement in school achievement. For a minority of poor children some kind of boarding-school arrangement may well be necessary, for one suspects that as long as they remain where they are, they cannot learn in any conventional school. If the results (e.g., of Head Start, Higher Horizons, Great Cities, and other programs) have not been striking, the most likely explanation is that we are dealing with very weak variables. Too little or too late – or both. Perhaps, however, no school program can sufficiently offset the extent and degree of inequality of American society and we must move toward a generally more egalitarian reward system.

In this chapter we have repeatedly stressed what seems to us the crucial factor in the social problems of American cities today: the concurrence of poverty and race. The destructive impact of the concentration in urban core areas of millions of poor people, creating costs the less bearable in proportion to the outflux of the more affluent, is not simply added to, but is multiplied and rendered explosive by, the consciousness of rejection because of race. Efforts to redistribute in urban space the increasing proportion of this group do not appear to hold much promise. Similarly, programs of social insurance and social welfare, at least as presently conceived, range from those which are merely inadequate to those which do not touch at all the people whose needs are greatest. It is possible that even full employment, housing subsidies, increased health and education services, and programs of "economic opportunity" – our current weapons against poverty – will not be as successful as we now estimate in normalizing the social class distribution of Negroes in the United States. It is troubling to learn that, according to Richard Titmuss, despite all of the reforms associated with the welfare state in Britain, inequality there may be growing more rather than less pronounced, apparently as an outcome of persistent class differences in usage and practice, and of the ability of the "haves" to retain and enhance their status (Titmuss, 1962 and 1965).

American society, it would appear, can sustain a large degree of social inequality as long as sufficient numbers of have-nots can move into the higher ranks, and are not overwhelmingly concentrated in a group set apart by race. We hazard the hope that the Negro-dominated central city, itself the outcome of racial exclusion and poverty, may prove – given the required social and economic conditions – to be the instrument by which these evils will be overcome.

Economics and Regional Science

THE THIRD PAIR OF CHAPTERS consists of essays by Wilbur R. Thompson and John F. Kain; they are entitled "Toward an Urban Economics" and "Urban Travel Behavior" respectively.

In looking toward an urban economics, Thompson begins by asserting that we need a new location theory. Location theory is one of the main antecedents of urban economics, but it stands in need of revision in order to take account of locational developments since World War II. Thompson describes location theory as "a form of industry economics which seeks out the most efficient or least cost spatial arrangement for a given industry." As he notes, most of the theoretical constructs of location economics are "framed in terms of the single-product, single-plant firm which is (implicitly) owner controlled, while a very large and growing share of economic activity is conducted by multi-product, multi-plant corporations which are management controlled, following from the typical pattern of many scattered stockholders."

Thompson feels that this kind of theoretical up-dating would be of great service to another field related to urban economics — the field of "regional economics." Regional economics is much newer than location theory, and it has been undergoing rapid change since World War II as the result of a concerted effort on the part of a small but growing number of American economists, many of whom have operated under the aegis of "regional science" (Isard, 1956; Isard, 1960). Regional income analysis is another area of special interest that is contributing to a viable urban economics, especially as it analyzes the impact of the local "industry mix" on local income characteristics.

In the second half of Chapter 5, Thompson turns to another intellectual challenge: how to move from an urban-regional economics to an intra-urban economics. The latter field, he contends, is currently well out of the mainstream of modern economic thought, but it deserves close attention despite that fact. The structure of urban land use is especially in need of increased attention because of its bearing upon urban planning. One example will suffice: "In our urban renewal planning one misses incisive analysis of what might be expected to occupy the core area block of blighted structures scheduled for demolition."

Still other topics covered in Thompson's chapter are (1) the relationship between growth rates and the patterns of urban blight; (2) factors affecting the size of the slum; (3) the trade-off between political and economic democracy in cities; (4) rationalizing the spatial pattern of local government, including metropolitan government; and (5) urban price policies. In each case, Thompson elaborates on the themes developed in his path-breaking book, *A Preface to Urban Economics* (Thompson, 1965).

In Chapter 6, Kain provides a very useful survey of empirical findings on urban travel behavior. This is an area in which economists and others (especially transportation planners) have made giant strides since World War II.

As Kain observes, "the postwar period has been characterized by a truly phenomenal outpouring of data, empirical findings, and research on urban travel. Urban travel has proved to be an immensely difficult, complex, and interdependent set of phenomena and has stubbornly resisted efforts to comprehend it, but significant progress has been made in understanding at least its grosser dimensions." It might be added parenthetically that Kain himself has contributed enormously to this understanding by his own work, most notably in his efforts to clarify *The Urban Transportation Problem* (Meyer, Kain, and Wohl, 1965).

The structure of Chapter 6 is deceptively simple. Beginning with a review of data sources, especially origin-and-destination studies, Kain turns to two main types of analysis: (1) aggregate or descriptive models of travel behavior, and (2) micro or behavioral analyses of urban travel.

Under the first rubric—aggregate or descriptive models—Kain considers such topics as city-size variations in urban travel, time and trip-purpose profiles, and variations in mode of travel. Among the findings are these: (1) per capita trips to the central business district are much more numerous in smaller than in larger cities; (2) roughly 40 per cent of all urban trips either begin or end at a workplace; (3) the private automobile dominates noncommuter travel in all but the very largest city in the United States — New York City — and is increasing in importance over time. Some of these facts are well known, but their implications are less widely appreciated, and Kain renders a valuable service in giving some of the implications considered attention.

Under the second heading — micro or behavioral analyses — Kain takes up the determinants of automobile ownership, the sources of trip generation, the relationship between the journey to work and residential location, and the matter of transit use and choice of travel mode. The following findings are illustrative. Automobile ownership is associated with income, net residential density, distance from the central business district, and the size of the city or metropolitan area. Different volumes of travel are generated by different uses of land, and within land-use categories (e.g., residential) such variables as household size play an important role in trip generation. White households tend to balance transportation costs and the costs of site occupancy in a manner that has been summarized as the dilemma of "spacious living versus easy access." Comparisons of the travel behavior of Negroes and whites reveal important effects of residential segregation by race upon tripmaking. (Kain's own work suggests that residential segregation, combined with high travel costs from central ghettos, may even be a cause of Negro unemployment.) Metropolitan transportation studies nearly always conclude that automobile ownership is the most important factor in determining whether or not mass transit facilities will be used. These are but a few of the empirical findings cogently summarized in Chapter 6, which should serve as a very convenient overview of what we have learned about travel behavior in American cities since World War II. (For another perspective on urban transportation, see Chapter 14 by Melvin M. Webber.)

— *L.F.S.*

5

Toward an Urban Economics

WILBUR R. THOMPSON

☐ LOCATION THEORY, AS DEVELOPED by economists, is largely an extension of price theory; the study of the allocation of scarce resources among competing ends is extended to allocation in space. The conceptual framework is quite similar, building on a rational model of the profit-maximizing private firm producing a standardized product and selling in competitive markets. The relatively thin literature in this field seldom treated goods which created significant social costs in their production or consumption nor those which conferred important social benefits, or at least the literature ignored such "spillovers" and "externalities" as do exist. These analyses, therefore, can be regarded as "normative" locational economics – what *ought* to be where – only for fully private goods, or as "positive" locational economics – what *is* there – if social costs and/or benefits do exist and do escape the profit calculus of the private entrepreneur.

FROM LOCATION THEORY TO REGIONAL ECONOMICS

TOWARD A NEW LOCATION THEORY

Location theory is one of the main antecedents of the new field of "urban economics," perhaps even its theoretical taproot, and the analysis of these "little economics" should exploit the modest but significant legacy in this field. But urban economics is at least as much a creation of some of the most compelling issues of the day: slum versus suburb, local fiscal autonomy versus grants-in-aid, the depressed areas as the new "farm problem," and traffic jams. Destined to be a policy field, urban economics will emphasize the spillover of social costs and benefits, the provision of "pure public goods" and the public sector in general, making it into a more comprehensive and normative spatial economics. The location theory which underlies this new field must seek to capture the social costs and benefits of locational change, such as houses and schoolrooms standing vacant in small towns, and rural areas suffering net out-migration, while overcrowded schools on half-day sessions plague the cities "enjoying" great in-migration, costs which largely escape the private locational decision.

Location theory also deserves to be up-dated considerably to reflect the economic, technological and institutional facts of mid-twentieth century life. Most of the theoretical constructs of this field are framed in terms of the single-product, single-plant firm which is (implicitly) owner controlled, while a very large and growing share of economic activity is conducted by multi-product, multi-plant corporations which are management controlled, following from the typical pattern of many scattered stockholders. Again we need to expand the analysis beyond that of finding the least-cost location of an operation using one (or at most two) fixed sources of inputs and a fixed market for its output, given distances and the structure of freight rates on both the materials and product.

What we may come to see as our locational analyses become more comprehensive is that while the theoretical solution becomes much more complex, if not indeterminate, the practical approximation of a least-cost location for a multiple-input, multiple-output operation is at or very near a multiple-mode transportation center. The larger urban places, are, of course, our principal transportation nodes, or these nodes will soon become our larger cities. The larger urban area generates a volume of traffic that leads to lower unit costs, assuming expensive, indivisible facilities, such as tracks and terminals, which create heavy fixed costs and therefore significantly lower unit costs with larger outputs. These bigger places tend also to be served both by a number of carriers of a given mode and a number of different modes to the end that flexibility is greater, risk is lessened and rivalry ensures that much or most of the reduced cost of volume operations will be passed on to the shipper. (Below-cost rates are not uncommon between transportation centers, for example, the old issue of long-haul railroad rates below short-haul rates.)

A number of other forces are reacting to reinforce the advantage of the larger urban area in the competitive struggle for industry, forces which merit more intensive examination in the new location theory. A trend away from material-orientation and toward market-orientation has been noted by a number of observers but it has been created as an empirical phenomenon without extended analysis. Certainly we are all keenly aware of the decreasing share of employment in the extractive industries, especially the dramatic decline of the farm share, and we are at least vaguely aware that the early-stage, material-processing industries, such as smelting of ore and steel and textile mills, are losing share to the later stage, product-fabricating industries, such as automobile production and assemblage, and apparel industries (Perloff, *et al.*, 1960). But to what extent is this major shift in industrial structure due to:

a. a twist in the transportation rate structure against materials and in favor of finished goods?

b. growing mass affluence and the demand for more differentiated (stylized) products that are best manufactured in close contact with the mass markets of "megalopolis" (Gottmann, 1961)?

c. a more rapid rate of labor-saving technological change in the earlier stages of production displacing workers there more than proportionately, certainly the case in much of agriculture and probably also in forestry, fishing, smelting and processing "mills" in general?

d. shifting demands away from products with relatively heavy costs of materials (e.g., foods, wood and leather products) and toward highly finished and complex products with minor material costs (e.g., instruments, plastics), including both "autonomous" changes in taste preference and changes in consumption patterns induced by rising income (i.e., different income elasticities of demand)?

While the trend to market orientation may well have been, up to now, largely a result of the shift from intensive material processing to intensive product fabricating within manufacturing, the power of the mass market may, in coming decades, rest more on the coming dominance of the high services, or Jean Gottmann's "quaternary industries" (Gottmann, 1961, especially Chapter 11). Extractive industries gain from being dispersed to avoid the diminishing returns of very intensive cultivation or extraction, while manufacturing operations, and services even more, seem to experience a rather long stage of increasing returns with high densities. Manufacturing at large scale requires the assembling of large workforces, and the movement of persons (commuting) is, on the whole, more expensive than the transportation of materials or product. (Location literature did not pay much attention to the costs of transporting the worker; the very elegant web of August Lösch was spun without using this critical thread, nor does Edgar M. Hoover's illuminating work shine into this dark corner.) The service industries need, moreover, to weigh the costs of movement of both the producer (lawyer, doctor, teacher) and the consumer (client, patient, student), although these are sometimes substitutive (the "house call"). A dense cluster of people – a city – is almost by definition a physical manifestation of a planned arrangement for heavy personal interaction, especially characteristic of the service industries.

The new location theory may also come to explain better the growth of megalopolis and the economic flowering of the natural garden spots of our country when it incorporates the pervasive impact of the labor union. Industry after industry is finding wage rates to be spatially invariant as the union fixes a standard rate across the whole country. With this most important cost everywhere the same, the industry becomes increasingly footloose. (Remember, too, that the large corporation finances largely out of retained earnings and its own depreciation reserves and borrows in a national credit market to the end that the cost of capital – the interest rate – is also spatially invariant.) In effect, managers become increasingly free to locate where they would like to live. Plant location as a personal consumption decision of the head of the business is not a new phenomenon. Many, perhaps most, family firms were initiated in the home town and stayed there because that was where the owner preferred to live (Greenhut, 1956). The difference would seem to be that of the manager (not owner) group choosing the place to live, with income and education rather than birthplace and family circle dominating the choice.

All in all, the new location theory that is to underlie urban economics will need to come to grips with the amazing growth and vitality of metropolis and megalopolis. We need to understand much better, moreover, not merely the inter-urban spatial economics of the struggle between metropolis and town, but the intra-urban spatial economics of great city size as well.

Urban Economics as Regional Economics

While location theory has a literature thinly spread over more than a hundred years, "regional economics," another well-spring of urban economics, is much younger and busier. That part of urban economics which treats the performance of the urban area as a whole within the context of a national system of cities, focusing on inter-urban flows of goods and persons and inter-urban competition, is essentially "urban-regional economics." Most of the recent activity in urban-regional economics has stressed "macro-economics," tracing out the income and employment characteristics of industrial specialization. Essentially this is a form of "short-run" economics which takes as given the local industry-mix or export base and draws out its welfare implications, ordinarily expressed in terms of the level, distribution, and stability of income and employment.

Considerably less active in recent years is the study of the inter-regional variations in factor prices that, in the long run, cause industrial relocations. Perhaps the high and rising mobility of capital, leading to interest rates that are more nearly the same everywhere, and the spread of unionism which simulates the spatial price pattern of mobile labor by equalizing wage rates among regions, has contributed to the decline of interest in "regional micro-economics." Even that hardy perennial, the taxes-and-location study has faded noticeably with time, either because taxes have seldom (never?) been found to be a major locational factor, at least as between urban regions, in contrast to site selection within politically fragmented metropolitan areas, or because tax differentials are narrowing as the public service levels demanded by increasingly educated and affluent urbanites also narrow.

In any event, urban-regional income and employment analysis seems almost certain to continue as one of the principal foci of economists' interest through the formative years of this new field. Certainly, the economist, on leaving the national economy in which he feels most comfortable, finds it hard to establish rapport with any "region" below the national level, short of that spatial unit which serves as the primary unit of income generation – the local labor market, defined as the commuting range about a cluster of workplaces. Unquestionably, the economist's newly-found interest in this urban region, closely approximated by the Standard Metropolitan Statistical Area, has lagged behind the "discovery" by economic geographers and ecologist-sociologists of this powerful spatial unit for physical and social analysis. While geographers and sociologists have probably led the way in defining regions, excepting the work of August Lösch and a few other economists, and busied themselves most with the empirical materials, it is the economist who is most prepared to draw out the welfare implications of the structure that exists within these urban regions. It is only a slight exaggeration to observe that even now there is more interest and activity in defining regions than in doing anything with these regions once defined. But this failing must be laid more at the doorstep of the economist who professes expertise in industrial and income analyses, but who has ignored the local labor market as an analytical unit, to the point where much of the urban-regional growth and income analysis has been done by non-economists.

Economists' contribution to the work of delineating regions in space would not seem to carry the highest priority. The new breed of urban geographers are well trained in statistical techniques, mingle with economists in such organizations as the Regional Science Association and are, therefore, quite capable, and prone to press forward the work of defining economic regions. Apparently though, it is the economist alone who fully appreciates the urban region as the primary unit of economic welfare. This very basic unit of income and employment analysis becomes by easy extension a local housing market and transportation surface as well as a labor market, especially in light of the fact that the journey from home to work usually constitutes the peak demand on the transportation system and thereby fixes the required investment in capacity. Clearly, the skills of the economist are called for in the rationing of movement in the given system and in all allocation of new resources to urban movement in the long run.

Again, all residential subdivisions are not equally preferred by the householder but they are (imperfect) substitutes, and it is the economist whose business it is to rationalize this system of housing sub-markets so that *social* costs and benefits as well as private are considered in residential locational decision-making. To the extent that we can regard families on public assistance as rejects of the local labor market, financial responsibility for their well-being would seem to rest on the taxpayers (workers) of the whole urban area rather than the resident-taxpayers of the particular municipality in which they chance to reside, if equity is to be served. Not only is the region a primary unit of income generation and thereby a potential entity for income redistribution, but the urban area also becomes the logical range within which to rationalize various "pure public goods," such as air pollution and police protection. Local labor market, transportation surface, housing market, public economy – the economist cannot help but feel at home in the study of the urban region, as soon as he finds his way there.

Regional Income Analysis

The impact of the local industry-mix on local income characteristics will not be pursued in any appreciable depth here, both because the material is so rich and the author has had his say at great length elsewhere (Thompson, 1965 and 1966). Much of the standard lore of economics is transferable with little or no alteration. High-income regions are in large part the sites of high-wage industries, therefore, the urban-regional economist expects to find local affluence where the local industries make heavy use of high skills and higher education, such as in research centers or university towns, or where considerable monopoly power rests, such as in the automobile and the oil cities. In the latter case, it takes both the "administered prices" of oligopoly coupled to the monopoly power of the trade union to ensure that high prices will lead to high wages as well as high profits, for it is only the wages which are sure to remain in town.

The degree of income inequality also shows the influence of the local industry specialty. Manufacturing areas typically combine a relatively narrow range of skills, especially characteristic of the more routine assembly operations in the branch-plant cities, with the egalitarian influence of the trade union, to produce a relatively low degree of inequality. Again, the existence of jobs for women acts to reduce inequality in that working wives come more proportionately from the lower income groups. Because a high female labor force participation rate is associated more with commercial, financial and government centers, while manufacturing areas usually have a lower-than-average rate, the overall pattern of income inequality is quite complex, but no less a function of the local industry-mix for its intricacy.

The economist has such overpowering evidence that durable goods are more cyclically unstable than non-durables, which are in turn more unstable than services, that he falls quite naturally into the hypothesis that durable goods areas should have the heaviest cycle. It is, therefore, quite disconcerting to see empirical returns that do not verify this presumption. This early in the game, the economist might be excused his inclination to accept the hypothesis and reject the data. Still, the lesson to be learned is that the region is something more than simply a bundle of industries in space.

Then again, perhaps it is just that industry-income linkages are very subtle. There is some evidence, in fact, that the local industry-mix operates in part through the local growth rate as it wends its casual way toward local instability. Industries whose products are subject to demands which increase more than in proportion to increases in income – "income elastic demands" – experience secular increases in sales and production at a greater than average rate, leading to a relatively rapid growth of local employment and population, assuming average labor productivity changes. But the same income elasticity that engenders rapid growth may also cause sharp slumps along the rapidly rising trend line, as consumption of the product also *decreases* more than proportionately when per capita income slips temporarily on its inexorable way upward. Again, rapid local growth builds an enlarged construction sector, as plants, houses, stores, and schools are being added to accommodate both the natural increase in the population plus a high rate of net in-migration. Construction activity is, of course, one of the most unstable activities, both because of the durability of the product and its speculativeness.

The industry-mix does have a most pronounced effect on the local growth rate as brought out above, but the "mix-effect" is placed in perspective by relating it to the "share-effect." Clearly a region may grow either due to the presence of fast-growing industries or by gaining shares of the slower-growing ones. North Carolina has grown by attracting the textile industry from New England, and the Boston area has come back with fast-growing electronics, higher education, and research. A hypothesis comes easily to mind that the larger urban areas probably grow at a moderate rate by combining a fast-growing mix of new industries in the early, rapid growth stage of exploiting a new market, with a steadily falling share of their more established industries, going through the usual stage of decentralization. The smaller urban areas, less industrially sophisticated, tend more to grow by gaining shares of industries which are leaving the larger urban areas in search of lower wages, taxes, or land costs but only when these industries have matured to the point where they use only routine skills. The smaller urban areas continually complain that they never get their share of growth industries.

We might hypothesize a general tendency for industries to filter down through the national system of cities, a hypothesis which can now be tested with the "shift-share" county-level employment calculations recently released by the U.S. Department of Commerce. Probably even more socially significant would be to determine whether this filtering-down of industries across regions is accompanied by an up-grading of regions across industries. That is, is each successive industry passed down to a given urban region at a successively higher stage of technology than that at which the previous one was received, so that these smaller areas do progress technologically? Or does the industrially underdeveloped urban region run along a treadmill, trading low-skill, dying industries for increased shares of just as low-skill, mature industries? Location theory needs to be integrated with regional economics.

FROM NATIONAL LOCATIONAL EFFICIENCY TO REGIONAL WELFARE

Location theory is a form of industry economics which seeks out the most efficient or least cost spatial arrangement for a given industry. Some attention has been given to linkages between industries – Walter Isard's "industrial complex analysis" – but for the most part industries are handled in splendid isolation analogous to the partial equilibrium analysis of elementary price theory ("demand and supply"). There is virtually no literature treating the impact on regions of the many industry patterns in aggregate. Imagine a dot map of the United States for each industry and then imagine superimposing them one on top of another, like planner's overlays. If a circle representing the normal commuting radius is drawn around each of the more important clusters of workplaces, we would have a system of urban regions exhibiting a wide variety of industry-mixes. The regional economics described above is a provincial view of one such bundle of industries. A great unexplored national question is whether a better set of patterns might not be arranged.

Each industry might assume its optimal pattern, considering only the private costs and benefits that filter through the market or are directly assessed by government, and appear, therefore, to satisfy the criteria for allocative efficiency in space at the national level. But the aggregative effect of all the industry patterns may produce grave regional distortions. Some regions may have a preponderance of industries with sharp summer peaks and other industries with winter peaks; steel cities lack jobs for women while national and state capitals have an excess. Some places need moderate to high skill manufacturing jobs as stepping stones for Negroes (for example, Washington, D.C.) while others lack unskilled and part-time work. Could national industrial-regional planning mesh complementary patterns so that some would be better off with no one worse off (the very conservative Paretian Welfare criterion) or even many better off with only a few worse off (a very bold prescription, routine to decision-makers)?

The marketplace might come tolerably close to accomplishing such a re-allocation of resources in space if all the values could be squeezed into prices which must be borne or might be earned by private enterprises. If, that is, unemployed women in steel towns would work for less or the local governments of summer seasonal towns would reduce tax rates or public service charges for winter peak businesses, it is conceivable that a near-perfect dissemination of some set of highly sophisticated differential prices might produce better balanced urban-regional economies. But the sophistication and integrity needed by labor union leaders, local public administrators and the inevitable federal review board, charged with preventing destructive price cutting, staggers the imagination.

Perhaps the solution to the problem of distributing industry in space so as to create desirable regional economies will be resolved automatically by the trend toward very large metropolitan areas with highly diversified economies, producing near national average income and growth patterns. A nation of relatively few very large urban areas might not call for much federal intervention in matters of industrial location, except perhaps to assist in providing easy access within these very large, densely-populated clusters. Federal financial aids in highways and mass transit may then be seen as the cutting edge in national industrial-employment-manpower planning.

To the extent, however, that a national policy to limit the size of the largest cities is formulated and implemented, then the great-size solution to a balanced regional industry mix is sacrificed and the need to juggle the set of local industries returns. The decision to limit the size of cities would probably derive from the judgment that the (marginal) social costs of another plant or office, as reflected in traffic congestion, sprawl, pollution, *anomie*, or whatever, would exceed the (marginal) social benefits of that addition to local scale, as reflected in an increasing range of choice in goods or occupations or a spreading of the overhead costs of facilities with some idle capacity. Thus, it would be the social costs of intra-urban form and flow that would be substituted for the social costs of urban-regional industrial and labor market imbalance, as the policy criteria. Clearly, we would benefit from a "modelling" of the metropolis in which both intra-urban and urban-regional social costs and benefits were introduced as instrumental or policy variables.

FROM URBAN-REGIONAL TO INTRA-URBAN ECONOMICS

FROM INDUSTRY-MIX TO LAND USE

If we have lacked for analyses which trace through the effect of the industry-mix on the income characteristics of the urban area, we have even less work that extends this good beginning one step farther into the implications of that mix and income pattern on the land-use pattern of the urban area. Economists from the mainstream of thought will find intra-urban economics much less familiar ground than regional income analysis. While mainstream economists have in passing made a few contributions to our knowledge of intra-urban location, only the urban land economists based in the real estate programs of the business schools have tended this patch over the years. Furthermore, talented and productive middle-generation urban land economists seem much less numerous than the elders of this field (Fisher, Ratcliff, Weimer, *et al.*) and a younger generation is hard to recruit or even identify.

In our urban renewal planning one misses incisive analysis of what might be expected to occupy the core-area block of blighted structures scheduled for demolition. If, for example, the local indus-

SCHEMATIC DIAGRAM OF SOME IMPORTANT LINES OF LINKAGE RUNNING FROM INDUSTRY-MIX TO PERSONAL DEVELOPMENT

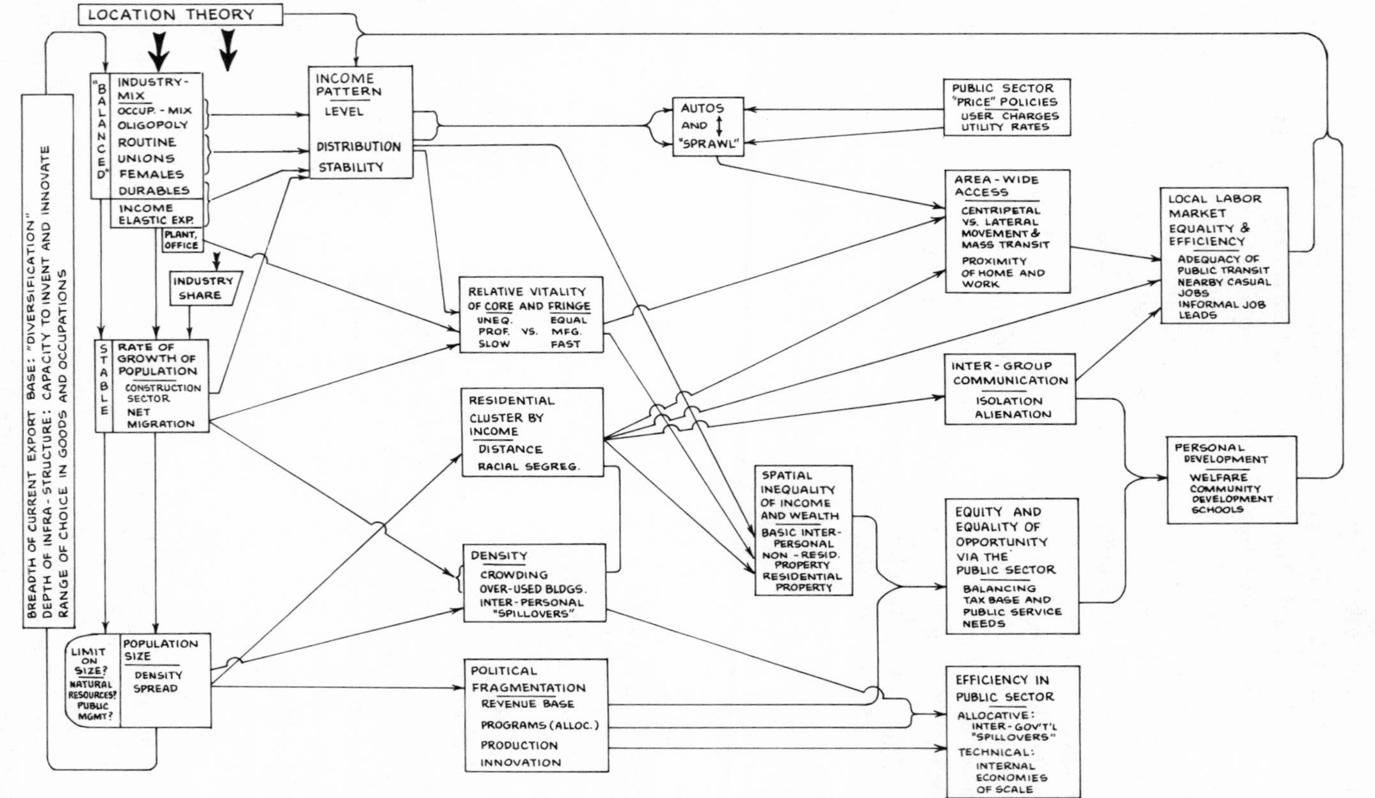
LOCATION THEORY
"BALANCED"
INDUSTRY-MIX
OCCUP. - MIX
OLIGOPOLY
ROUTINE
UNIONS
FEMALES
DURABLES
INCOME ELASTIC EXP.
PLANT, OFFICE
INDUSTRY SHARE
STABLE
RATE OF GROWTH OF POPULATION
CONSTRUCTION SECTOR
NET MIGRATION
LIMIT ON SIZE? NATURAL RESOURCES? PUBLIC MGMT?
POPULATION SIZE
DENSITY
SPREAD
BREADTH OF CURRENT EXPORT BASE: "DIVERSIFICATION"
DEPTH OF INFRA-STRUCTURE: CAPACITY TO INVENT AND INNOVATE
RANGE OF CHOICE IN GOODS AND OCCUPATIONS
INCOME PATTERN
LEVEL
DISTRIBUTION
STABILITY
AUTOS AND "SPRAWL"
PUBLIC SECTOR "PRICE" POLICIES
USER CHARGES
UTILITY RATES
RELATIVE VITALITY OF CORE AND FRINGE
UNEQ. PROF. SLOW VS. EQUAL MFG. FAST
RESIDENTIAL CLUSTER BY INCOME
DISTANCE
RACIAL SEGREG.
DENSITY
CROWDING
OVER-USED BLDGS.
INTER-PERSONAL "SPILLOVERS"
POLITICAL FRAGMENTATION
REVENUE BASE
PROGRAMS (ALLOC.)
PRODUCTION
INNOVATION
AREA-WIDE ACCESS
CENTRIPETAL VS. LATERAL MOVEMENT & MASS TRANSIT
PROXIMITY OF HOME AND WORK
INTER-GROUP COMMUNICATION
ISOLATION
ALIENATION
SPATIAL INEQUALITY OF INCOME AND WEALTH
BASIC INTER-PERSONAL
NON-RESID. PROPERTY
RESIDENTIAL PROPERTY
EQUITY AND EQUALITY OF OPPORTUNITY VIA THE PUBLIC SECTOR
BALANCING TAX BASE AND PUBLIC SERVICE NEEDS
EFFICIENCY IN PUBLIC SECTOR
ALLOCATIVE: INTER-GOV'T'L "SPILLOVERS"
TECHNICAL: INTERNAL ECONOMIES OF SCALE
LOCAL LABOR MARKET EQUALITY & EFFICIENCY
ADEQUACY OF PUBLIC TRANSIT
NEARBY CASUAL JOBS
INFORMAL JOB LEADS
PERSONAL DEVELOPMENT
WELFARE
COMMUNITY DEVELOPMENT
SCHOOLS

URBAN-REGIONAL ECONOMICS

INTRA-URBAN ECONOMICS

trial trend is toward more manufacturing industries, especially those inclined toward one-story ramblers with lots of parking, then the core-area land-conversion prospects are less bright. Not only will these new plants move to the suburbs directly and not provide a demand for the newly vacated core areas, but other core-area plants of similar character, not in the current demolition area, may soon be moving out to join them in the suburbs, further increasing the already redundant supply of core-area land. Probably of much greater quantitative importance, manufacturing acts indirectly to favor the fringe area by generating high and equal distribution of income. An upper-middle income class is ordinarily oriented toward suburban living. Suburban residences, moreover, minimize the manufacturing worker's journey to work, in both time and money, further weakening residential demands for the cleared core land.

Consider, however, the prospect of area industrial development more heavily weighted with professional employment. Office buildings are a much better prospect for the new core-area sites and, indirectly, are more likely to give rise to strong demand for core-area residential units because of their tendency to generate both very high- and very low-paying work. High-income persons are more likely to be attracted to the urbanity of the core area and low-income persons are more likely to be forced into the older housing and better public transportation of the core. Again, difficult or costly transportation tends to bring home and work together, especially for the very skilled person for whom time is the scarce factor and also for the low-income person for whom money is scarce.

Considerable contract research linking the local industry-mix and land-use patterns — basic real estate analysis — may lie hidden in confidential reports, but a scholarly literature, especially one built on careful quantitative work, is not clearly evident. Almost certainly a better feel for the influence of the industry-mix on the form of the city would alter the character of our very expensive urban renewal program to fit the local situation.

Growth Rates and Urban Blight Patterns

The local industry-mix has another indirect impact on the land-use pattern of the area, operating through its effect on the local growth rate. Local specialization in fast-growing industries boosts the demand for labor in the local market, raises wage rates, generates overtime hours, and generally attracts in-migrants. A high rate of net in-migration plus the natural increase in the local labor force would almost surely outrun the increase in the the stock of housing in the area. The housing shortage will be greatest in the low-income districts, assuming the usual case where the in-migrants are predominantly the poor, which in the larger eastern and midwestern metropolitan areas will ordinarily be located in the inner ring near downtown. Core-area housing will, under rapid growth, be kept in use a little longer and the low-income concentric ring will expand outward as usual, but without moving away from downtown.

If, on the other hand, the rate of local job formation is less than the rate of depreciation in the local housing stock such that houses in the next concentric ring out from the center filter down to prices within reach of the lowest income group in amounts equal to or in excess of the number of such houses needed, the very lowest income group will move *outward* in space from the innermost ring of housing as well as *upward* in quality out of the most dilapidated housing.

Certainly, one of the main reasons why the cores of our central cities have become so "blighted" is that the very high rates of postwar migration from rural areas and small towns to the big cities have kept the pressure on the metropolitan area housing stock, overcrowding and overloading it. Thus, the oldest part of the housing stock is aged prematurely and then this blighted housing is kept in service unusually long. Tight housing markets have also held the most blighted residential areas close to downtown even while they grew larger and expanded outward. A reduced rate of in-migration in the future, now that our rural areas have largely emptied out, offers the prospect that the rate of "filtering down" of the housing in successive rings out from the CBD will more than accommodate net new household formation in the lowest income class and cause the slum to move outward away from the core.

All this would seem to suggest the usefulness of a relatively simple econometric model of the local housing market which, among other virtues, would bring together:

a. The current rate of growth in output and employment in various local industries and their probable preference for central versus fringe area plant sites, together with estimated land-to-worker ratios;

b. The predicted income distribution generated by their wage and salary disbursements, together with the expected residential preferences of the employees by location, using income as a proxy for occupation and education characteristics or adding these extra dimensions;

c. The balancing of the local rates of net natural increase and net in-migration (net new household formation) with the rate of house filtering (and new) low-cost housing, to map the spatial migration of the slum.

The prospects for renewing the central business district would seem to be most favored by: (1) the expansion of professional services, (2) income inequality, and (3) a moderate rate of aggregate growth. Urban decentralization and the decline of the role of the core would seem to most likely follow from a rapid rate of job formation in moderately well-paying manufacturing work. But we need careful quantitative work here.

The author has outlined elsewhere a complementary study which would age the whole housing stock and predict the income of the families that would inhabit that housing at a given future date (Thompson, 1965, Chapter 3). The future spatial pattern of income of an urban area would seem to be quite easily ascertainable; few things are as knowable as the value of a given house ten years hence, where it will be, and, by extension, the income of the inhabitants. Further, if we can predict the future spatial pattern of income, we can predict which local governments of the politically fragmented metropolitan area will be most hard pressed. Consider the suburban area built-up en masse with $12,000 housing in the early postwar years which can do nothing but age into a slum, lacking the commercial and industrial base which keep our central cities' public sectors barely afloat.

On the Optimum Size of a Slum

The more one reflects on the web of urban problems, the more one is struck with the centrality of the typical pattern of residential clustering by income. Since the separation of slums from "nice neighborhoods" is a very old urban form (although far from universal in either time or space), it is the scale of the separation which is at issue. As the distance between homes and neighborhoods of different socioeconomic classes has increased from a few blocks to many miles, the erosion of inter-group access and interaction has had an adverse effect on employment opportunities, formal and informal education, public safety and, indeed, almost every facet of urban life. There is a very great impressionistic literature on the harmful effects of tough neighborhoods, backward slum schools, and the lack of jobs, especially jobs that develop new skills. But not nearly enough measurement, especially spatial measurement.

What is the optimum size of a slum? We need not be afraid to ask this question so bluntly if our purpose is to arrive at that slum size which is most likely to reduce if not eliminate environments which destroy aspiration and expression and generally degrade urban life. Perhaps slums can be too small to create the minimal clustering of "one's own kind" that produces a base of emotional security from which one can venture more safely and experiment more tentatively. Again, certain public services, rendered especially to the poor, may be performed more efficiently if the poor are clustered a little; for example, consider community development activity stressing political participation and leadership experience.

But surely slums are most often far too big. A slum that exhausts a grade-school district puts the child about two grades behind by the end of the sixth grade so that even if he transfers to a mixed junior high school he carries a handicap from which he probably will never fully recover. Now that our biggest city slums have grown to high-school district size, unemployability is almost ensured. A neighborhood, moreover, which breeds a conniving, mistrusting youth seeking only the quick payoff and self-preservation will hardly prepare him to be a disciplined laboratory technician in a cooperative scientific venture.

Besides, from whom will he hear of these new fields? Which neighbor can provide him with the informal job contacts and "pull" that usually provide the entering wedge into the better job markets? The slum youth finds, moreover, few nearby part-time jobs into which he may bump on a chance stroll and to which he could easily and cheaply commute. At least they are few in absolute number, for what neighbor can afford to have his grass cut, or even has grass? They are fewer still in relative measure, for he must compete with desperate adults for the few jobs that do exist nearby.

For all the familiarity of this oft- and better-told tale, we suffer for the lack of numbers here. We need to know how many acres and families of "R-5" we can pack together and what are the social costs and benefits of income clustering and income mixing at various fineness of grain. The economist is not, however, used to working with such small "regions" as the block or even the census tract, but the issues are there and the data, too, to attract the econometrician.

The Trade-off Between Political and Economic Democracy

Because the residential pattern by income is so intimately involved with equality of opportunity, the residential pattern gets highly entangled with the spatial structure of government. This is not surprising for we look to government to redress much of the inequality which free enterprise produces and family ties perpetuate. Let us pose the problem of equality of opportunity and the structure of government in the large metropolitan area as a difficult choice among four partly conflicting goals and four rough paths toward them. If we infer the preference function of the typical citizen-voter from readily observed behavior, we can frame four key objectives:

1. Residential segregation by socioeconomic class, with income a simple, workable criterion for arranging "nice neighborhoods";
2. Small local government to achieve highly responsible government and the personal value of creative political participation as well – "political fragmentation";
3. Local fiscal autonomy, in the belief that government spending is most responsibly performed when the spender must impose the requisite taxes;
4. Minimum public service standards and redistribution of income in the name of both humanitarianism and equality of opportunity.

We can easily imagine an arrangement where the first three objectives are achieved: residential clusters of similar income households, exhausting the full land area of a small municipality and supported almost wholly by a local property tax. With fiscal capacity lowest and public service needs highest in the poorer political subdivisions, minimum public service standards will, however, be sacrificed. Or we can imagine, instead, a comprehensive system of fiscal transfers from above that redistributes tax money raised throughout the area to places in the area where the public service needs are greatest, arranged by either the state or federal government. If the grants-in-aid have few strings attached ("block grants"), then the current pattern of residential segregation and reasonably significant small local government would be retained with minimum public service standards, although local fiscal autonomy would be lost. The Heller-Pechman proposal to share federal income tax surpluses with the states and localities expresses this pattern.

A third possibility, metropolitan area-wide government, still commands a devoted following despite its unpopularity with the electorate. Only small local government would have to be sacrificed, at least in part, as the more significant functions are performed and/or financed at the area-wide level. Expenditure decisions would be kept more closely tied to taxation decisions and the tax decision is also closer to home than under the grant-in-aid arrangement. But the expenditure-service decisions drift upward and must be made for a larger and more heterogeneous population; therefore the highly indivisible public services, such as justice, police protection, and education are more likely to be compromises that slightly misfit everyone, so the argument runs.

A fourth path would be to sacrifice income-homogeneous communities at least at the level of political incorporation if not at the neighborhood or grade-school district level. (The income-homogeneous high school district would, however, have to go in the majority of the suburbs where there is only one such district.) It is safe to say that a ground-swell of popular support for mixing income classes within small municipalities is not in the offing, certainly not in the suburbs — at any grain. Moreover, while a number of New Town designs have talked vaguely of income-balanced population mixes, the proof of the pudding will be in the digesting of even small lumps of poverty.

The citizen-voter is, unfortunately, either unaware of or refuses to face the simple fact that he can have at most only three of these four objectives in anything approaching reasonably full measure and he must sacrifice the fourth, or trade off significant amounts of the three most cherished to achieve a minimal quantity of the fourth. For example, our current practice is to try to hold fast to "nice neighborhoods" and "grass roots democracy" and fiscal autonomy and then to find minimum public service levels slipping away in the poorer municipalities. Reluctantly we transfer financial responsibility for the poor to higher levels of government, first to the state as in the shared state income or sales tax for education and then to the federal government, as in the poverty program. As more and more strings become attached to these grants-in-aid of local programs designed to equalize opportunity, local government becomes more nominal in respect to the more significant functions and political participation more illusory. All that is truly left untouched is the "nice neighborhood," the latest version of "Fortress America."

While this may not be the best formulation of the great trade-off between political and economic democracy, the need is less to toy endlessly with the conceptual framework and more to measure the "elasticities of substitution" that are implicit within this reasonably well understood framework. How large would local governments have to be in our politically fragmented large metropolitan areas to mix income classes, given our current housing practices? Some preliminary study of the Detroit metropolitan area indicates that little averaging out of the rich and poor occurs short of the county level, but most of the inter-area variation in income is removed at the county level (Thompson, 1965, Chapter 9). But this conclusion does not apply to many other large metropolitan areas, where substantial inequality transcends the county level.

How fast is political participation lost with the enlarged scale of local government? How does one, moreover, balance the loss of close control over a relatively impotent, small local government whose jurisdiction is inadequate to deal effectively with the problem (e.g., air or water pollution) against less control over a larger and more competent consolidated government?

On what scale does one translate differentials in educational services into corresponding degrees of equality (inequality) of opportunity? Is the concept of minimum public service standards consistent with the concept of equality of opportunity when even outright equal services would leave the slum child still disadvantaged? How do we make rational evaluation and implementation of "reverse discrimination"?

Rationalizing the Spatial Pattern of Local Government

Political fragmentation of our large metropolitan areas may be most serious in matters of equity and equal opportunity, but its effects on urban efficiency have not gone unnoticed. The original sin of political fragmentation, in the eyes of those favoring metropolitan area consolidation in government, was the sacrifice of potential internal economies of scale. Jealously independent municipalities replicate endless numbers of small, high-unit-cost facilities in place of having an area-wide, least-cost public monopoly. The contrast in scale between local public services in water, sewers and mass transit and broad regional privately-produced, publicly-regulated gas and electric utilities is very sharp and, to many, very damning.

A sophisticated defense of political fragmentation has, however, arisen; internal economies of scale – the technical efficiency of achieving the highest output from a given input – can be sought and found externally by small municipalities (Ostrum, Tiebout and Warren, 1961). Water supply and sewage disposal, the only two public services for which substantial scale economies have been tentatively identified, can be purchased from large, efficient producers, such as the county or private enterprise. Alternatively, many small municipalities could, through negotiation, develop an efficient joint operation. The rationalization of the very small public economy proceeds with the argument that the presence of alternative sources of supply – a county incinerator, a privately-owned dump and the municipality's own devices – will ensure that the low costs of volume operations will be passed on to the small municipal buyers through "competition."

There is ample reason for pause here, for significant internal economies of scale are more substitutive than complementary with competition. If the political subdivisions are very small and significant scale economies do not extend to the full extent of the regional market, then efficiency and "competition" may be joined short of area-wide monopoly. But if the scale economies are significant enough to make the rationalization of production worthwhile, they will probably extend to outputs which would supply one-half or at least one-third of the market. This leaves the defender of small local government with productive efficiency and *duopoly* or *oligopoly*, not competition. The prices administered by two or three firms are usually quite like monopoly prices.

Finally, the spatial facets of these attempts at industrial rationalization have been largely ignored. Many of the public services in mind are akin to public utility services in that distance or area coverage is an input. The service may have a high transportation cost, such as water and sewage flows, so that a given output costs less if rendered near and/or over a contiguous area and more of the customers are widely scattered afar. If contiguity is critical, then we are back to exclusive jurisdictions and spatial monopoly. And who will regulate the monopolist supplier operating outside the municipal buyer's corporate limits?

Introducing the effect of space into our analyses to local public services will greatly enrich them and greatly complicate them as well. For example, high transportation costs serve to offset internal economies of scale and act to create small spatial monopolies. Fire stations, for example, are small and scattered because the costs, in life and property, of traversing the required distance to a fire a little slower are very great (i.e., the marginal cost of time-distance rises steeply). Metropolitan consolidation would not, therefore, much change the number, size, or spacing of fire stations, although internal economies in special equipment might be achieved.

If, however, the cost or quality of a public service is a function of the degree of spatial coverage as well as the volume of output, then unit costs decrease and/or quality increases to the full extent of the market. For example, police protection and urban transportation are probably cheaper and better with increased scale right up to full area-wide monoply. Both are, in important measure, indivisible at the broad regional level, that is, they are metropolitan-area-wide "public" (or "collectively consumed") goods.

It is only a short step from degree of spatial coverage as a factor in technical efficiency to its relationship to spillovers and allocative efficiency. With growth and great size comes higher population density and greater horizontal spread – a willingness on the part of some to squeeze a little to avoid having to travel out so far from the center of activity and a willingness on the part of others to travel far to avoid squeezing. High density gives rise to inter-personal spillovers or neighborhood effects. The degree to which I care whether you drive a car, burn your garbage, paint your house, or socialize your children is a function of how close you live to me.

But the horizontal expansion of an urban area – "sprawl" – sweeps population over fixed political boundaries, hardened by difficult political annexation, and produces the now classic problem of political fragmentation. Thus, when a resident of the metropolitan area spills out automobile exhaust into the air or storm water run-off downward onto lower land, he is likely to beggar residents of another political subdivision. Density creates inter-personal spill-overs; sprawl plus fixed political boundaries turn them into inter-governmental spillovers. Wise and just prohibitions, penalties and compensating payments are hard enough to arrange within a single jurisdiction; inter-governmental spillovers defy equity.

More than inter-personal or inter-governmental equity are at issue. Misallocation of resources result, too, when part of the costs or benefits are borne by persons other than the decision-maker. Spill-out costs result in too much of an activity being undertaken because the decision-maker reaps all of the (diminishing marginal) returns but bears only part of the (rising marginal) costs. Conversely, spill-out benefits cause too little of an activity to be undertaken because the decision-maker does not value benefits others receive.

For all of our familiarity with the general nature of spillovers, we have precious little measurement. Sophisticated work has been done on spillovers in education (Hirsch, *et al.*, 1964). But some of the simplest exercises are ignored. We do not know such mundane things as what proportion of our central city library services are rendered to suburbanities, measured simply by the proportion of library cards held, books checked out, or reference requests filled. Origin-and-destination traffic surveys or other traffic counts seem to be used only to justify pouring more concrete, seldom to solve problems in allocative efficiency. We must bring to bear here the full heritage of our price theory, especially behavior and performance in imperfect markets and a fresh theory of the local public economy, especially one set in space.

URBAN PRICE POLICIES

While urban economics may in the beginning be concerned most with industry-mix and regional income analysis, with greater understanding of the complexity of the city, especially the great metropolis, emphasis will shift more to the role of price. A first piece of business would be to come to know better the prevailing set of prices that push and pull at the city's form and functioning. Most of these "prices" are implicit, unplanned and, more often than not, irrational. The local property tax, for example, is a type of price which unfortunately penalizes property improvements, even ones that spill out social benefits, such as painting a shabby house, or ones that reduce social costs, such as installing a new furnace or fireproofing an old building in a densely packed district. The property tax is nicely symmetrical and is reduced to reward owners of property which is undermaintained. Again, a zero price is charged for the use by a large, single-passenger motor vehicle of the main arteries of the city at peak hours. Granting that the motorist has paid *part* of the costs of driving at an *average-use* period through the gas tax, the extra capacity needed at peak times should be borne by the peak user in surcharges, along with the costs of traffic control, noise and pollution not ordinarily covered by gasoline tax receipts.

The second piece of business would, of course, be to rationalize the urban price system. Urban micro-economics will probably come to include a set of principles of administered pricing, not unlike the urban managerial economics of the business school curriculum. Programs in local public administration would do well to begin building an urban managerial micro-economics which sees price as a powerful tool for guiding the long-run development and day-to-day operation of cities.

We need to understand better the rationing function of price: how the demand for a temporarily (or permanently) fixed stock of a good or service can be adjusted to the supply. At any given time the supply of street, bridge, and parking space is fixed; urban economics is especially concerned with "goods" which last a long time and therefore have stocks which are very large relative to the current rate of output. Accordingly, the rationing function of price is especially important in this new field.

The central role of price is to allocate scarce resources among competing ends, so that the marginal value of any output is equal to the marginal cost of producing that output across all activities. Expressed loosely, in the long run we turn from adjusting the demand to fit a fixed supply to adjusting the supply to fit a constantly changing demand – the quantity demanded at prices which reflect costs of production. Prices which ration also serve to signal the need to reallocate resources. If the rationing price exceeds those costs of production which the user is expected to bear directly, more resources should ordinarily be allocated to that activity, and symmetrically a rationing price below the relevant costs indicates an *uneconomic* provision of that service in the current amounts. Rationing prices reveals the intensity of the users' demands: how much is it really worth to the suburbanite to sprawl over an acre lot or drive into the heart of town at rush hour? Are the citizens' cries valid economic alarums or fits of pique?

Urban managerial economics will probably also come to deal especially with "developmental pricing" analogous to "promotional pricing." Prices below cost may be used in the creation of a market for a new product or service. The hope would be that the artificially low price would stimulate consumption and that the altered *expenditure pattern* would lead in time to an altered *taste pattern*, as experience with the new service led to a fuller appreciation of it. Ultimately, the subsidy would be withdrawn, whether tastes changed sufficiently to support the new service or not. Our national parks had to be subsidized in the beginning and this subsidy could be continued on the grounds that these are "merit goods" that serve a broad social interest. But we have so educated people to the value of outdoor recreation that a large part of the costs of these parks could now be paid by a much higher set of park fees.

It is difficult, moreover, to argue that poor people arrive at the gates of Yellowstone Park in significant number, so that the redistribution of income is hardly sufficient cause to justify the subsidy. A careful study of the users and the incidence of the taxes raised to finance the national parks may even show a slight redistribution of income toward greater inequality. One of the main reasons for employing more user charges, fines, fees and other such "prices" would, in fact, be to have more control over the impact of the local public economy on the distribution of income. To the extent that local government finances public golf courses, marinas, or even museums from the revenues of the regressive local property tax, it almost certainly redistributes income toward greater inequality. User charges to finance these services would, moreover, free scarce tax money to be used to support public services which would produce a more desired set of distributional effects. In short, user charges on public marinas would permit us to build more "free" swimming pools in slum districts.

A very sophisticated urban public management might, then, begin with below-cost prices on the new rapid mass-transit facility during the promotional period of luring motorists from their automobiles. Later, if and when the facility became crowded during rush hours and after a taste for this transportation mode was well established, the "city economist" might devise a three-price structure of fares with the lowest fare for off-peak use, the middle fare for regular peak use (commuter's tickets) and the highest fare for the occasional peak-time user. Such a schedule would reflect the contribution of each class to the cost of having to carry excess capacity.

If the venture more than covered its costs of operation, the construction of additional facilities would begin. Added social benefits in the form of a cleaner, quieter city or reduced social costs of traffic control and accidents could be included in the cost/benefit accounting underlying the fare structure. But below-cost fares, taking care to count social as well as private costs, would not be set without a clear income-redistribution end in mind and not without careful comparison of the relative efficiency of using the subsidy money in alternative redistributive programs. We need, it would seem, not only a knowledge of the economy of the city, but some knowledgeable city economists as well.

6

Urban Travel Behavior

JOHN F. KAIN

☐ THIS CHAPTER IS INTENDED as a review of the new knowledge of urban travel behavior acquired since World War II. While large gaps remain and while there is much to be done in synthesizing the findings of completed research, the postwar period has been characterized by a truly phenomenal outpouring of data, empirical findings, and research on urban travel. Urban travel has proved to be an immensely difficult, complex, and interdependent set of phenomena and has stubbornly resisted efforts to comprehend it, but significant progress has been made in understanding at least its grosser dimensions.

INTRODUCTION

Most data and empirical research on urban travel is either a direct or indirect result of the large number of highly developed, well financed, and elaborate postwar home-interview origin and destination (O and D) studies carried out under the auspices of the Bureau of Public Roads (BPR). More than 200 large-scale home-interview studies (O and D) have been completed since 1944 and at least 29 areas have had two surveys during the period (Martin, Memmott, and Bone, 1961, pp. 212-214; Zettel and Carll, 1962, p. 15). Included among the over 200 study areas are 14 of the 16 SMSAs with more than 1.3 million population. Moreover, these studies have been extremely well financed. Cost of the Chicago Area Transportation Study (CATS) was reported to be 3.7 million dollars; it is anticipated that costs of the Philadelphia (Penn-

Jersey) and Boston (BRPP) studies, still to be completed, will exceed 4.5 and 4.8 million dollars respectively (Zettel and Carll, 1962, p. 15).

The earliest O and D studies were unashamedly and unabashedly highway planning studies. Minimal by-product analyses of transit were carried out only when its use might be expected to seriously affect forecasts of automobile travel. More recently political and other pressures have caused the BPR, state highway departments, and quasi-independent metropolitan area studies to be somewhat more concerned with "balanced" transportation and to give greater emphasis to land use and transportation planning for all modes. Even so, highway planning remains their predominant concern.

Large-scale travel surveys and the collection and analysis of enormous quantities of data are the most notable features of these studies. Sixty per cent or more of study budgets may be spent on data collection and processing, with the large-scale travel survey accounting for most of these costs (Zettel and Carll, 1962, p. 39). These very large travel survey costs are due to large sample sizes. Between 3 and 5 per cent of area households are surveyed in the typical O and D study. For example, in Chicago a 3.33 per cent sample of households yielded nearly 50,000 usable home interviews and a 10 per cent sample of truck registrations provided 7,346 usable truck survey interviews. "Internal" home-interview surveys are supplemented by roadside "external" surveys at the boundary (cordon) of the study area and large numbers of volume counts. In Chicago, drivers of over 73,000 highway vehicles and in excess of 5,000 railroad commuters were interviewed as they entered or left the study area (Chicago Area Transportation Study, 1959, p. 30). With only minor modifications survey questionnaires are the same for all of the over 200 home-interview studies completed since the war. Social scientists are generally highly critical of these "brute force" methods of sampling and are unanimous in the view that far too many data are collected, that much of it is the wrong or irrelevant data, and that far too few resources and too little time have been devoted to analysis and interpretation. No detailed description or critique of these studies is undertaken here because of space limitations and because excellent summaries and critiques are available elsewhere (Martin, Memmott, and Bone, 1961; Oi and Shuldiner, 1962; and Zettel and Carll, 1962).

In addition to the over 200 highway-oriented O and D studies completed since the war, there have been numerous rapid transit feasibility studies; Transit feasibility studies have generally been less well financed than highway-oriented O and D studies, have collected and analyzed much less data on urban travel, have focused on a much narrower segment of the urban travel spectrum (being largely concerned with travel to central business districts) and as a result have produced less information on travel behavior than the more numerous highway-oriented studies. Even so they have helped fill some important gaps left by the generally highway-oriented O and D studies. To the analyses produced by these transit and highway planning studies must be added the research by university faculties and other independent researchers. While these relied heavily on the data from O and D studies and therefore might be considered an indirect product of those studies, O and D surveys were often supplemented by other data sources.

Other important sources of travel data have been developed in recent years as well. Most states have conducted one or more state-wide motor vehicle use surveys which provided data on the travel habits of both urban and rural households. Cities have conducted periodic cordon counts of traffic entering their central business districts and large numbers of parking studies. More recently the BPR contracted with the Bureau of Census for two national home-interview surveys of travel behavior and with the Michigan Survey Research Center for still another (Bostick and Todd, 1966, p. 274; Lansing and Mueller, 1964). Of possibly even greater long-range significance, the 1960 Census of Population included for the first time questions on automobile availability, journey-to-work travel mode, and residents' places of work. Place of work was not very finely specified and is therefore of limited usefulness. However, it seems certain that future censuses will include a more detailed coding of work-place, a development that would greatly facilitate the analysis of the journey to work.

Most of the studies and analyses of urban travel resulting from these massive data collection and analysis activities can be divided into two kinds; (1) aggregate or descriptive, and (2) micro or behavioral analyses of travel behavior. The first can be compared to the economist's national income accounts or identities, and the second to micro-economic models of firm or household. As with economic analysis, analysis of travel behavior has proceeded on both of these fronts simultaneously, and, like economic models, while the aggregation problem has been solved in principle, a large gap remains in practice. Similarly, studies cannot always be easily classified because in many of them the two kinds of analysis tend to blur into one another. Even so, a distinction remains and is used in organizing the discussion that follows. The next section discusses descriptive or aggregate models of travel behavior and the following section takes up more behavioral or micro analyses of travel behavior.

DESCRIPTIVE AND AGGREGATE MODELS

Spatial and City Size Variations in Urban Travel

Were it not for the fact that urban transportation demands are very unevenly spread over space and time, there would be no urban transportation problem. Urban transportation services, except to a very limited extent, cannot be stored or inventoried. Excess capacity in the suburban areas is no substitute, at least in the short-run, for capacity shortages in central areas.

Numbers of trips may vary tremendously among locations as well. For example, in Detroit in 1952 (DMATS) an average of 1,522 trips were made to each acre of Central Business District (CBD) real estate; for developed land more than 12 miles from the CBD the figure is 15. Similar quantities for Pittsburgh (PATS) are 1,315 trips per acre for the CBD and 3 trips per acre for land over 12 miles from the CBD (DMATS, 1955, p. 41; PATS, 1961, pp. 55-56).

Figure 1, which graphically displays the spatial distribution of 10,212,000 person trip destinations in Chicago on an average weekday in 1956 vividly portrays the greater geographic variations in urban travel. Peaking would have been even more pronounced if only trip destinations during the morning rush hours were shown. The extreme spatial concentration of trips made to CBDs and nearby work-place areas illustrated in Figure 1 is found in all metropolitan areas, although generally to a lesser degree. It is to accommodate this morning and evening peak movement to and from CBDs that the much heralded and much debated rail rapid transit systems are being proposed in an increasing number of metropolitan areas, and for which major expansions of existing

Figure 1. Total Person Trip Destinations

The destinations of 10,212,000 person trips, on the average weekday, are distributed throughout the study area as shown in this model. The highest blocks represent 144,000 trip destinations per quarter square mile grid, the lowest blocks 5,000. The flat shaded areas represent less than 5,000 but more than 2,500.

Source: "Chicago Area Transportation Study," Vol. 1, Fig. 7, p. 25.

systems are being planned. Travel to CBDs is an especially important, if somewhat exaggerated, dimension of urban transportation planning.

Given the attention accorded tripmaking to CBDs, peak-hour cordon counts prove to be surprisingly low outside of New York (Meyer, Kain, and Wohl, 1965, pp. 84-88). New York City's evening peak period volumes, which exceed 800,000, outstrip those of its nearest rival, Chicago (less than 250,000) by a wide margin, a fact that those who would draw analogies between New York's transportation problems and those of other United States cities should keep firmly in mind. The most extensive study of traffic entering and leaving CBDs is based on an analysis of data from parking surveys conducted in the CBDs of 91 cities ranging in 1950 population from 6,912 in Paris, Ky. to 1,400,058 in St. Louis, Mo. (Gorman and Hitchcock, 1959). Gorman and Hitchcock found CBD trips per capita were greater in smaller than in larger cities, a finding also reported by Holmes (Holmes, n.d., pp. 49-50). The average number of vehicles per thousand population entering the CBD between 10 a.m. and 6 p.m. was found to range from a high of 1,107 for communities in the 5,000 to 10,000 population group, to 65 for cities of over 1,000,000 population. When interpreting these numbers it is well to keep in mind that they refer to vehicles and not people. The average number of persons per vehicle increases with population as more persons use transit and as the loading of private automobiles increases. Unfortunately, the survey lumps trucks and buses into a single category.

Cordon counts of trips entering CBDs include both trips with destinations there and those simply passing through. For years, traffic engineers have been insisting that adequate bypass or inner belt highways could eliminate a large proportion of the persons, and an even larger proportion of the vehicles, entering CBDs. If so, cordon counts of entering traffic overstate the number of potential users of transit systems serving the CBD. Gorman and Hitchcock determined that the mean proportion of through traffic was uniformly high for all population groups, ranging from a low of 48 per cent (50,000 to 100,000 population) to a high of 63 per cent (5,000 to 10,000 population). During the peak one-half hour the percentage of through traffic is even larger, ranging from a low of 60 per cent (50,000 to 100,000 population) to a high of 77 per cent (500,000 to 1,000,000 population). While the number of person-trips passing through the CBD is somewhat smaller than the number of vehicle trips, the available evidence suggests the numbers are still significant (Meyer, Kain and Wohl, 1965, p. 87).

Lest all of the above discussion of travel to CBDs give the impression that there is nothing else to urban travel behavior, it should be pointed out that tripmaking to CBDs is a small and rapidly declining proportion of metropolitan area travel. Travel to or from CBDs is only 9.2 per cent of all person trips in the area surveyed by the Chicago Study (CATS) in 1956, 9.8 per cent of all person trips in the area surveyed by the Detroit Area Traffic Study (DATS) four years earlier, and 6.5 per cent of all person trips made in the area studies by the Pittsburgh Area Transportation Study three years later (PATS). The area surveyed by metropolitan transportation studies roughly approximates the Standard Metropolitan Statistical Areas (SMSAs) at the time of the studies, with the geographic coverage of recent studies typically being greater (Smith and Associates, 1961, p. 95). Moreover, Holmes has presented data which illustrate that the proportion of "internal" trips having origins or destinations in the CBD declines with metropolitan population. This generalization is based on analysis of O and D data for 23 metropolitan areas surveyed between 1950 and 1958. In areas of under 50,000 population, an average of 22 per cent of metropolitan area trips originated in or were destined for the CBD. Mean values for the remaining population subgroups were: 14.1 per cent (50,000 - 250,000 population); 9.6 per cent, (100,000 - 250,000 population); 7.8 per cent (500,000 and 1,000,000); and 5.6 per cent (over 1 million) (Holmes, n.d., p. 52). Other research has determined that the proportion of interarea traffic (traffic originating outside of the metropolitan area) headed for or passing through the CBD declines with population size (Hansen, 1957).

An increasing number of metropolitan areas have had two comprehensive O and D studies during the postwar period. These studies are particularly valuable since they permit evaluation of changes over time in the spatial distribution of origins and destinations, mode of travel, trip generation, and other dimensions of urban travel. The most complete comparative study of changes in travel to a CBD, for Washington, D.C., concluded that: "The most important travel characteristic reflecting the change in the relative economic character of the CBD between 1948 and 1955 was the decreasing proportion of trips to the CBD in relation to total travel" (Silver,

1959, p. 153). Analysis of travel data from the 1948 and 1955 Washington surveys yielded the finding that while the total number of trips made to the CBD on an average weekday increased by roughly 10,000 (from 255,338 in 1948 to 265,659 in 1955), trips to the CBD declined from 15 per cent to 11 per cent of all intra-area trips. Daily worktrips to the CBD increased by just over 11,000, shopping trips declined by approximately 3,000, and other trips increased by just over 2,000. Even so, CBD worktrips increased by only 7 per cent as compared to an overall increase of intra-area worktrips of 27 per cent. Similarly, shopping trips within the study area increased 74 per cent between 1948 and 1955, while the number destined to the CBD decreased 9 per cent. As a result, the percentage of metropolitan area worktrips destined to the CBD decreased from 33.4 per cent in 1948, to 28.2 per cent in 1955 and the CBD's share of metropolitan area shopping trips declined from 31 per cent in 1948 to 16 per cent in 1955.

Silver's findings for changes in the composition of travel are similar in many ways to those obtained in a less extensive comparative analysis of changes in travel to the Seattle (1948 and 1961) and Tacoma (1946 and 1961) CBDs (Walker and Cowan, 1964). The most important difference between the findings for Washington, D.C. and those for Tacoma and Seattle is that while the former experienced small increases in total daily travel to the CBD, both the latter experienced substantial declines. Between 1948 and 1961 the total number of trips to the Tacoma CBD declined by 28 per cent, and transit trips declined by 65 per cent.

Seattle's CBD had very much the same experience, except that the absolute decline was for a much larger base. Person-trips to the Seattle CBD (including both internal and external trips) declined by 25 per cent between 1946 and 1961 with social-recreation and personal business trips experiencing the largest percentage declines. CBD-destined social-recreation trips fell by 50 per cent from approximately 21,000 to 10,000 per day, a finding that demonstrates the impact of private automobiles and television on the social and recreational habits of urban America during the postwar period. Personal business trips declined by 35 per cent, or from 28,000 in 1946 to 18,000 in 1961. Shopping trips to the CBD fell by 25 per cent; this is a figure nearly identical to the overall percentage decline in travel to the Seattle CBD. The 11 per cent reduction in worktrips to the CBD is smallest of any of the major categories; even so this amounted to an average of 8,000 trips a day. In the aggregate, approximately 43,000 fewer persons entered the Seattle CBD on a typical weekday in 1961 than in 1946.

Despite these very large declines, auto travel to the CBD increased. Thus, all of the losses in CBD travel accrued to transit, which lost 62 per cent and 48,000 of its passengers during the 15 year period. Temporary distortions of travel habits caused by World War II should be kept in mind in interpreting these findings. World War II controls caused a temporary expansion of transit use everywhere, and the figures for Seattle in 1948 probably still include many wartime "captive" transit users.

TIME AND TRIP PURPOSE PROFILES

Since the composition of travel by trip purposes differs markedly over the day, and since understanding these composition effects is central to explaining urban travel behavior and predicting its future level and composition, time and trip purpose profiles are best discussed simultaneously. Table 1 presents the proportion of trips made by the residents of 12 metropolitan areas by trip purpose at the destination.

Roughly 40 per cent of all urban trips in the 12 study areas are made to home. Trips to work are the second largest category, averaging 20 per cent of all trips, a fact that goes a long way toward explaining the great attention given the journey to work in studies of urban travel behavior. Since each trip to work must have a corresponding trip from work, roughly 40 per cent of all trips either begin or end at a workplace. Actually, the quantitative importance of trips to and from work is exaggerated somewhat by the convention, followed in nearly all of the older O and D studies, of not collecting information on walking trips, except to work.

Walk-to-work trips and work-at-home "trips" are a significant proportion of all worktrips. According to the 1960 Census of Population, 10 per cent of all employed residents of urban areas walked to work and an additional 2.9 per cent worked at home. This compares favorably with the 5.2 per cent who used railroad, subway, or elevated to reach work and the 10.9 per cent who used a bus or streetcar to reach work (U.S. Bureau of the Census, 1963). These walking millions are all but ignored in discussions

TABLE 1. TRIPS BY URBAN RESIDENTS ACCORDING TO PURPOSE

URBAN AREA (Year)	Per Cent of Trips to: HOME	WORK	BUSINESS	SHOPPING	SOCIAL-RECREATIONAL	SCHOOL	OTHER	ALL PURPOSES
Chicago (1956)	43.5	20.5	12.4	5.5	12.8	1.9	3.4	100.0
Detroit (1953)	39.5	23.5	6.9	8.2	12.1	3.0	6.8	100.0
Washington (1955)	41.7	23.4	6.6	8.2	7.1	4.4	8.6	100.0
Pittsburgh (1958)	43.4	21.0	13.5	8.4	7.9	5.8	0.0	100.0
St. Louis (1957)	40.5	20.8	6.0	10.5	12.3	3.0	6.9	100.0
Houston (1953)	40.3	18.9	7.1	10.1	10.8	4.9	7.9	100.0
Kansas City (1957)	38.4	20.6	6.7	9.9	12.9	2.8	8.7	100.0
Phoenix (1957)	37.2	18.2	7.9	11.5	11.2	5.0	9.0	100.0
Nashville (1959)	37.6	19.1	6.5	10.5	13.6	3.3	9.4	100.0
Fort Lauderdale (1959)	38.6	17.2	11.7	13.8	12.9	0.4	5.4	100.0
Charlotte (1958)	36.6	21.9	7.5	9.0	12.8	2.8	9.4	100.0
Reno (1955)	38.6	16.9	11.2	10.4	14.3	0.3	8.3	100.0
Average Per Cent —	39.6	20.2	8.7	9.7	11.7	3.1	7.0	100.0

SOURCE: Wilbur Smith and Associates, "Future Highways and Urban Growth," New Haven, Connecticut, February 1961, p. 81.

of urban transportation. Yet changes in their behavior potentially could have as large an impact on the demand for urban highways as the much discussed massive shift away from transit. Data for Philadelphia indicate a decline in the percentage of walkers from 23 per cent in 1934 to 9 per cent in 1956 (Lapin, 1964, p. 201.)

Very similar trip purpose proportions were obtained by Curran and Stegmaier (1958) in their ambitious analysis of travel patterns in 50 cities. The surveys analyzed by Curran and Stegmaier are for an earlier period, with the latest being 1951, and almost one-third were conducted during the later part of World War II and the year following. Curran and Stegmaier use a somewhat less detailed classification of trip purposes. Specifically, they combine the work and business trips into a single work-and-business category, and school and other trips into a single "miscellaneous" category. Allowing for these definitional differences the 50 city averages are quite similar to the 12 area average in Table 1: home, 40.8 per cent; work and business, 27.9 per cent; shopping, 7.5 per cent; and miscellaneous, 7.5 per cent.

Nonwork trips are spread rather uniformly throughout daylight and evening hours, whereas trips to and from work are concentrated within a few peak hours. The proportionally much greater contribution of trips to and from work to the peak demand on urban transportation capacity represents an even more important explanation for the emphasis given the journey to work. Worktrips are also longer than most other trip purposes. Relative trip lengths by trip purpose in Chicago are probably not atypical. Chicago worktrips averaged 5.3 miles as compared to an average of 2.8 miles for shopping trips and 4.3 miles for social-recreational trips (CATS, 1959, p. 38). Thus, worktrips are the most numerous trip purpose (excepting trips to home), and have the longest average trip length; as a result, they are proportionally an even larger part of total miles traveled, and are concentrated in a few hours of peak demand for transportation capacity.

Over 80 per cent of all trips either begin or end at home. This fact has caused urban transportation studies to focus a substantial share of their effort on the analysis of "home-based" travel. For the 12 areas listed, 88 per cent of all trips are home-based and of these an average of 34 per cent either begin or end at work. Social-recreational trips, which account for 21 per cent, and shopping trips, which account for 17 per cent of home-based trips, are the next two largest trip purpose categories (Smith and Associates, 1961, p. 83).

MODE OF TRAVEL

Private automobile travel dominates non-commuter travel in all but the very largest city (Curran and Stegmaier, 1958, p. 109; Meyer, Kain and Wohl, 1965, pp. 88-91). Commuting is a much more complex matter. Where the costs of private automobile operation are not too high, either in money or in traffic congestion, commuters may prefer the automobile; elsewhere they will probably find public transportation more attractive. Rising incomes will presumably work to the advantage of auto commuting.

The greater use of transit for trips to the CBD and its declining importance even there has been pointed out in several studies (Smith and Associates, 1961; Meyer, Kain and Wohl, 1965, pp. 85-99; Gorman and Hitchcock, 1959; Silver, 1959; Walker and Cowan, 1964). Transit is used most often for worktrips and least often for social-recreational trips. In the 12 areas listed in Table 1, 15.2 per cent of all worktrips are made by transit; the percentage of business and shopping trips is 7.8 per cent and the percentage of social-recreational trips made by transit in the 12 cities is 5.3 per cent (Smith and Associates, 1961, pp. 348-350).

Even so, these data understate just how specialized in purpose transit travel has become. During the postwar period the decline of transit use has been most rapid in off-peak trips, such as shopping and social-recreational trips. A recent Detroit study of central city residential areas determined that while worktrips declined by 6 per cent between 1953 and 1962, bus trips to work declined 32 per cent, and shopping trips by bus declined by 64 per cent. Similarly, although social-recreational trips rose 1 per cent, the number of such trips by transit declined 62 per cent (Mayer and Smock, 1963).

Trip purpose specialization for rapid transit and commuter railroads is specially pronounced. For example, 74 per cent of the inbound trips made from 14 outlying rapid transit stations in Philadelphia were worktrips. Even more outbound passengers from seven in-city railroad stations, 81 per cent, were returning to home from work. When long-haul trips are omitted, this figure rises to 84.1 per cent (Berryman, 1962). Similarly, in the Chicago area in 1956, 70 per cent of trips made by subway or elevated were worktrips, and 80 per cent of these worktrips were made from the central area. In short, a large and rising percentage of transit travel is made up of worktrips, particularly to the CBD, and only a small and declining percentage is composed of social-recreational, personal business, and shopping trips. This specialization in worktrips, together with the steady outward trend in urban employment locations, is the basis of much of transit's financial difficulties.

BEHAVIORAL MODELS

AUTOMOBILE OWNERSHIP

No serious study of urban travel behavior could ignore the effect of rapidly rising levels of automobile ownership. After remaining approximately constant during fifteen years of depression and war, automobile ownership per capita rose rapidly in the postwar period. While there remains considerable controversy about the effect of automobile ownership on travel behavior and about its impact on postwar development, everyone would agree it is important. Automobile ownership appears both as an independent variable and as a dependent variable in studies of travel behavior. This discussion concentrates on those analyses where automobile ownership is treated as the dependent variable, or the "effect" to be explained by other "causes."

Income, net residential density, distance from the CBD, and city or metropolitan area size are the variables most often included in studies of automobile ownership. For example, Lansing and Mueller (1964, pp. 59-62) found these to be the most important variables in their analysis of 824 household interviews collected in 33 SMSAs in 1963.

However, they concluded that the effect of income on automobile ownership (household owning at least one auto) was confined to the lower end of the income distribution, since among families with incomes of $5,000 a year and above, in the metropolitan areas studied, 90 per cent or more owned a car. Below that level, 53 per cent of those in the $3,000-$3,999 group owned cars as compared to only 27 per cent of those in the less than $2,000 group.

Bostick (1963, pp. 241-255) in a recent paper both confirms and contradicts these findings. Fully 10.4 per cent of households in the $5,000 to $5,999 income range owned no car. This percentage declined in each income group having over $5,000 until it reached a level of 1.6 per cent for the group having an income of more than $15,000 a year. Moreover, data on multiple car ownership by income group demonstrates a steady progression in the percentage of two- and three-car families as income increased, and particularly above $5,000 per year. Approximately 23 per cent of households with incomes between $6,000 and $7,499 per year owned two or more automobiles, as compared to 62 per cent of those earning over $15,000 a year. The relationship between income and car ownership exists for the ownership of three or more cars as well. An estimated 1.4 per cent of households earning between $6,000 and $7,499 a year owned three or more cars; however, the statistic for those with incomes above $15,000 a year was 14 per cent. (Bostick's data include both metropolitan and non-metropolitan areas while Lansing and Mueller's are confined to SMSA residents.)

Similarly, Lansing and Mueller determined that the per cent of the households without a car declines with distance from the metropolitan center. But they also concluded that density of neighborhood is a better predictor. Among the eleven largest SMSAs included in the survey, 47 per cent of the families in old densely-settled cities owned autos, as compared with 74 per cent of those in new low-density cities.

The authors of *Future Highways and Urban Growth* also reached similar conclusions about the effect of density and income on the level of car ownership:

> Usually there are more car owners in single-family residential areas than in high-density apartment areas. Density and income being equal, fewer cars are owned and used by persons living near the central city since areas with efficient and frequent public transit often have lower car ownership and use than areas with poor transit services. High-density areas are often in proximity to employment and commercial outlets, thereby minimizing the need for private transportation (Smith and Associates, 1961, p. 68).

The authors add that car ownership is greater in low-density communities than in high density ones, and that family size and the number of job-holding members of the family are also significant determinants of car ownership, a finding that was substantiated in research by the author (Kain, 1964a).

Given the crucial role that metropolitan transportation studies assign to car ownership in their trip-generation and modal-split models, the resources that they devote to developing explanatory and/or forecasting models for car ownership seem surprisingly small. Generally, metropolitan transportation studies treat auto ownership as an exogenous variable (a variable determined outside of the model) and rely on independent, usually simple trend, projections to give them future levels of ownership for use in their trip-generation and modal-split models. Oi and Shuldiner (1962, pp. 18-22) comment extensively on this practice, which is followed by nearly all O and D studies, and they argue the need for analyses of differences in auto ownership within metropolitan areas and for analyses which treat car ownership as a dependent variable.

A study published soon thereafter both treats automobile ownership per worker as an endogenous variable (a variable to be determined by the model) and attempts to analyze differences in auto ownership within the Detroit metropolitan area (Kain 1964a). Automobile ownership was evaluated as one of nine endogenous variables in a nine-equation econometric model. The equation system was assumed to be recursive in structure with auto ownership being affected by, but not affecting, structure type or residential density. In turn, both residential density and auto ownership were assumed to affect, but not to be affected by, the choice of worktrip travel mode (automobile or transit). Finally, elapsed travel time, the final endogenous variable in the model was assumed to be affected by, but not to affect, residential density and mode. Exogenous variables were income, a proxy variable for the price of residential space, the per cent of employed workers who were male, a measure of the number of family members employed, a measure of transit service at the workplace, and family size.

The recursive assumption used in estimating the equations discussed above might well be questioned, since it could well be argued that a decision to own an automobile should affect the choice of residential density as well as the converse. An unpublished paper by the author estimates some fully simultaneous relationships between car ownership and net residential density using data from the London Transportation Study.

Traffic in Towns, or the Buchanan Report, is the most striking example of a study which treats car ownership as an exogenous variable (Ministry of Transport, Great Britain, 1963). It borrows its forecasts of future levels of car ownership from a paper by J. C. Tanner (1962). Tanner's forecasts are modified trend forecasts estimated from time series data for Great Britain and involve an ingenious, if somewhat doubtful, application of the concept of a saturation level and a logistic curve. While *Traffic in Towns* follows the lead of United States metropolitan transportation studies in treating car ownership as exogenous, it diverges from the practice followed by those studies in one important respect. While the studies make simultaneous trend forecasts of land use, *Traffic in Towns* assumes significant modifications of historical trends. The use of trend forecasts of car ownership incorporates important trend changes in land use; the analysis also assumes important modifications of those trends, and leads to significant projection errors. The effect of these inconsistent land use and car ownership forecasts on the Report's problem definition and policy prescription are discussed in two papers by Beesley and Kain (Beesley and Kain, 1964, pp. 174-203; Kain and Beesley, 1965, pp. 163-185). To evaluate the extent of the forecast error in *Traffic in Towns,* we adapted a simple cross-section regression model estimated from data for 45 large United States central cities. This model, which makes auto ownership dependent on income and gross density, is used in forecasting car ownership under different assumptions about the future density and distribution of population and employment and income. Regression equations were estimated using both multiplicative (log-log) and additive (arithmetic) forms. There proved to be very little basis to choose between the two functional forms. The multiplicative model yielded constant elasticities of 0.24 for density and 0.72 for income, indicating that a 10 per cent increase in income would cause car ownership to increase by 7.2 per cent and that a 10 per cent increase in density would cause it to decrease by 2.4 per cent (Kain and Beesley, 1965, p. 169).

Tanner has carried out numerous analyses of car ownership using both United States and United Kingdom data. In one of his most interesting papers, he explains 84 per cent of the variance in car ownership among United Kingdom counties using average income, the percentage of workers of high social class, the percentage living in urban areas, population density, and distance north as explanatory variables (Tanner, 1962).

In two other papers, Tanner analyzes the determinants of car ownership using data on changes in per capita car ownership in United Kingdom counties and United States states for several postwar periods. His procedure is to fit simple linear regression equations, using the yearly percentage increase in per capita cars as the dependent variable and the mean level of car ownership as the independent variable. He then solves this equation for the level of car ownership per capita at a zero percentage increase in per capita car ownership. This value he interprets as the saturation level and uses it in estimating the logistic for his forecasting relationship (Tanner, 1962; Tanner, 1965). This procedure is evaluated by Kain and Beesley (1965).

Tanner (1965) also analyzes the effect of population density by fitting a multiple regression, with cars per head in each of 50 United States states as the dependent variable, and with state per capita income and population per square mile as explanatory variables. From these results he is inclined to downgrade the importance of density. In this paper, Tanner somewhat modifies the procedures used in his earlier paper by suggesting that a different saturation level may be appropriate for areas of different density. Instead of a single saturation level he offers from 0.50 per capita for rural counties, to 0.40-0.45 per capita for medium-sized towns, to 0.30-0.35 per capita for Inner London. Moreover, he adds that, "In particular classes of development, such as low-density suburban housing estates and high-density blocks of flats in cities, lower or higher values than suggested above may be appropriate, but a range of 0.25 to 0.55 probably covers the likely values" (Tanner, 1965).

TRIP GENERATION

Transportation analysts probably have devoted more time and energy to the analysis of trip generation than any other aspect of urban travel behavior. "Trip generation" refers to the number of trips produced per capita, per household, per acre, per traffic zone, per square foot of floor space or other standard unit. The Detroit Area Transportation Study (1953) is widely regarded as a watershed or landmark in the development of methodology for urban transportation studies. Its principal contribution was the development of systematic quantitative relationships between urban travel and land use and their use in combination with land use forecasts in predicting future travel. The "land use-transportation" model developed in that study has been used with minor conceptual modification and great elaboration by nearly every urban transportation study since that time. *Urban Traffic: A Function of Land Use* (1954) provided additional theoretical justification for the procedure and was highly instrumental in insuring that the techniques received widespread adoption by other transportation studies (Mitchell and Rapkin, 1954).

Much effort has been expended in calculating trip-generation rates for non-residential uses. However, traffic analysts quickly focused on the household as the most promising unit for developing trip-generation models and by far the greatest attention has been given to explaining tripmaking per household or per capita. To no small extent this was due to the much greater availability of data on households from the census and from the surveys themselves. However, Oi and Shuldiner (1962, p. 47) propose on theoretical grounds that while the analysis of land use appears to hold greater promise in explaining the *spatial distribution* of travel the household appears more promising for analysis of the total *volume* of travel.

Oi and Shuldiner's detailed analysis of origin-and-destination data from Chicago, Detroit, and Modesto is probably the most comprehensive treatment of the subject available. They concluded that the two most important determinants of trip-generation rates by households were household size and car ownership and that, between them, they accounted for a substantial proportion of the variance among households in reported trip frequency. Six other explanatory variables were also investigated: (1) CBD distance, (2) population density, (3) income or other indicators of wealth, (4) occupational status of household head, (5) social area indexes, notably an urbanization index, and (6) dwelling-unit type. Of these, CBD distance and dwelling unit type were found to have only negligible effects on average trip frequencies. Both income and occupation exhibited statistically significant associations with trips per dwelling unit, even when family size and car ownership were held fixed. However, they concluded that the magnitude of the partial associations were relatively small when compared to the responses in trip frequencies due to changes in family size or car ownership. Finally, both density and the urbanization index were determined to have significant negative correlations with trip generation rates.

Mertz and Hamner (1957) in a multiple regression analysis of resident tripmaking per dwelling unit for 200 District of Columbia census tracts also found car ownership to be especially important. In addition, the authors evaluated the effects of net population density (population per net residential acre), distance from the CBD, and family income. Both simple and multiple regressions were estimated. While the simple correlations between trips per dwelling unit and each explanatory variable were all high and had the correct signs (automobile ownership, – 0.83; population density, – 0.72; income 0.66; and distance from the CBD, 0.58) the explanatory variables were highly intercorrelated. Standard errors are not presented for the regression coefficients, but the paper does contain an elaborate analysis of the variance explained by various subsets of explanatory variables. From this the authors concluded that automobile ownership is by far the most important explanatory variable. The coefficient of multiple determination (R^2) obtained from all four variables is 0.74; auto ownership alone explains 68 per cent. Adding population density to auto ownership the equation adds only about 4 per cent to the total explained variance and a further adding of distance from the CBD and income increases the total explained variance less than one per cent more.

This analysis leads the authors to discount the importance of density and the remaining variables and to rely on car ownership alone. "The analysis shows that automobile ownership alone is definitely significant. When the effect of automobile ownership is taken out, the increment added by population density is of doubtful significance" (Mertz and Hamner, 1957, p. 147). Yet it seems plausible that density might affect tripmaking above and beyond its effect on car ownership. Despite the fact that income increases the explained variance by only a small amount when added to a regression including income, it significantly reduces the magnitude of the regression coefficient (R) for automobile ownership as Equations 1 and 2 demonstrate:

$$(1) \quad T = 2.88 + 4.50A \qquad R = 0.827$$

$$(2) \quad T = 3.80 + 3.79A - 0.0033\,D \qquad R = 0.835$$

where T is the mean number of resident vehicular trips per dwelling unit, A is the mean car ownership per dwelling unit, and D is population per net residential acre. Moreover, if the question is asked the other way around (the effect of adding automobile ownership to a regression equation including density), automobile ownership adds only 21 per cent to an explained variance of 52 per cent by density alone, and if it is added to an equation including both income and density it adds only 7 per cent. Obviously, there is a large interaction representing the joint effects of density and automobile ownership. The appropriate question is not "how much additional variance is explained by adding explanatory variables in any order," but "what is the appropriate model, and does the available sample permit reliable parameter estimates?" The Mertz-Hamner paper, one of the best and most careful studies of trip generation, clearly illustrates an error which characterizes most analyses of travel behavior. Too much emphasis is placed on obtaining the best empirical fit or in replicating observed behavior, and too little on determining, specifying and estimating the correct structural relationship.

Using data from 1948 and 1955 O and D surveys for Washington, D. C., Sharpe, Hansen, and Hamner (1958) test the stability over time of the Mertz-Hamner model. To test the Mertz-Hamner relationship between trip generation and car ownership, the authors both used a model estimated from 1948 data to forecast 1955 trip generation and reestimated the relationship using 1955 data. The authors replicated the Mertz-Hamner analysis with one important difference: the dependent variable was changed from car ownership per household to cars owned per 100 persons. The authors make no comment about changing the dependent variables and in fact treat the matter as of no consequence. Yet other studies of trip generation have found family size to be an important explanatory variable (Oi and Shuldiner, 1962; Lansing and Mueller, 1964, pp. 52-68). The question of the change in dependent variable aside, the study's findings are highly interesting. Only the intercept changed from 0.9 to 0.6; the slope coefficient was identical in both years. As a result, when the model estimated from 1948 data is used in forecasting 1955 values, it systematically overestimates 1955 tripmaking.

The authors' explanation of this result is rather remarkable. They note that while average automobile ownership increased from 21 to 29 automobiles per hundred persons, (an increase of 35 per cent) the average number of trips remained relatively constant.

Commenting on this and the uniform shift in the regression line, the authors state:

> The explanation, therefore, for the shift in the regression lines appears to be the increase in automobile ownership. This, in effect, means that during the seven-year interval the numerical relationship between the two variables changed due to the increase in automobile ownership in 1955, but the relative association between the two variables, as indicated by the correlation coefficients, remained almost constant (Sharpe, Hansen and Hamner, 1958, p. 97).

Misspecification of the trip-generation model would seem to be a more plausible explanation. For example, a smaller increase in tripmaking would have been obtained from Equation 2 if car ownership had increased without affecting net residential density, or if the increase in the former had been larger than the decrease in the latter. It is unfortunate that the authors overlooked the opportunity to investigate the reliability of the alternative forecasting models included in the Mertz and Hamner paper, since this could have provided significant information on the true structural relationships. The paper also includes a detailed analysis of the relationships between average (a) resident tripmaking per dwelling, and (b) non-residential trips per dwelling unit for the same census tracts. Using the same four variables as in the Mertz and Hamner study, the authors found no relationship between distance from the CBD and the ratio of resident and total trips per dwelling unit, but they did determine that the ratio was correlated with tract income, population density, and automobile ownership.

Curran and Stegmaier (1958, p. 118) also studied trip generation and determined that total and automobile trips per dwelling unit varied inversely with metropolitan area population, while mass-transit trips per dwelling unit varied with population. Trips per dwelling unit were found to vary from 6.60 per dwelling unit for areas with less than 50,000 population, to 5.44 for areas in the 250,000-500,000 population group, to 5.03 in the over one million population group. Of the 6.60 trips per dwelling unit, 3.73 were in the over one million population group 1.62 were made as auto driver, 0.91 as an auto or taxi passenger, and 2.50 as a mass-transit passenger. The proportions were just reversed in the under 50,000 population group. Of the 6.60 trips per dwelling unit, 3.73 were made as an auto driver, 2.10 as an automobile or taxi passenger, and

0.85 as a mass transit passenger (Curran and Stegmaier, p. 120). The relationship between population size and the use of mass transit has been investigated in its own right (Schnore, 1962).

A more recent study also concludes that trips per capita decline as the metropolitan area population increases, and adds that a similar result holds for increasing gross population density (Levinson and Wynn, 1962, pp. 1-31). These findings are based on free-hand regression lines drawn for a sample of 12 areas ranging in population from 4,800,000 (Chicago) to 81,000 (Reno, Nevada). There is no attempt to estimate the independent effects of population size and density, and visual examination of the scatter diagrams identifies large deviations from the regression lines that are ignored by the authors.

Lansing and Mueller (1964) include a fairly extensive analysis of trip generation in their analysis of urban travel behavior. Tabulations of trips per family by city size support the previously noted relationships between city size, density and trip generation. Two size categories, the largest 11 and 22 smaller SMSAs, are used, with the former being divided into old cities and new cities. Families living in the smaller SMSAs averaged 5.4 trips per day. Trip generation rates were nearly as high, 5.0 per family per day, in the new large SMSAs, but those in the old large SMSAs numbered only 2.7 per day. Three measures of density were analyzed, and all were correlated with trip generation. The Lansing-Mueller monograph is the only published study which includes data on lot size for single family homes. Trips per family were found to increase as single-family lot size increased. An average of 4.6 trips per day were made from lots of less than one-tenth of an acre; the statistic for lots of one acre was about 6.8 trips per day. Lansing and Mueller also give more prominence to income than previous studies of trip generation. This is probably because most other studies were forced to rely on less satisfactory measures of income.

Despite the obvious importance of family income in determining all aspects of travel behavior, O and D surveys did not obtain information on family income in their surveys until recently. Therefore, researchers relying on O and D data either had to match census tract income to travel data or construct an income variable from the rather gross occupation data (one digit) collected by the surveys. Lansing and Mueller found that families with incomes below $2,000 make less than one-third the number of trips of those with a mean level of income of $6,000. In contrast, those with incomes over $15,000 average 8.3 trips. These large differences among income groups are associated, of course, with differences in automobile ownership and location of residence. Still it would seem that a fully specified model of household behavior would be more likely to treat income as a determinant of automobile ownership and residential location than the converse.

Lansing and Mueller's findings for family size corroborate Oi and Shuldiner's. The mean number of trips were found to increase at a rate of approximately 2.5 trips per additional adult. In addition, families with more school-age children made more trips than those with fewer. Average daily tripmaking by families with no children in school was 4.2, a statistic that rises to 5.6 and more for those with one or more children in school.

Families without a car make less than half as many trips (1.7 per day) as families owning one car (4.5 per day); the average number is still greater for families with two cars (7.2 per day), and is greater still (9.2) for families owning three or more cars. Lansing and Mueller are careful to point out that the relationships described above are simple bivariate relationships and that the explanatory variables themeselves are complexly interrelated. Still the Lansing-Mueller findings confirm those reported in previous studies and, more importantly, they provide information on the effect of several variables either ignored or studied less intensively in previous studies.

Residential Location and the Journey to Work

Research on residential location and the journey to work are so closely intertwined that it is neither sensible nor desirable to attempt to disentangle them. Journey-to-work costs are the most important explanatory variable found in most theoretical models of residential location (Alonso, 1960; Alonso, 1964; Kain, 1962; Kain, 1965; Mohring, 1961; Muth, 1961; and Wingo, 1961). Nearly all theories of residential location emphasize the importance of a transportation cost versus site rent trade-off in determining the residential choices of households within metropolitan areas. Quantity of residential space consumed by households plays an important role in determining the extent of location cost or location rent savings by households, and therefore the distance workers will be willing to commute. Hoover and Vernon, (1959) aptly characterize this trade-off as "spacious living versus easy access." Several earlier studies, although presenting less elaborate theories of residential location, proposed the worktrip cost versus housing cost trade-off as a promising research hypothesis (Schnore, 1954; Row and Jurkat, 1959).

Herbert and Stevens (1960) extended this concept of a location rent-transportation cost and suggested the use of a linear program model for simultaneously determining residential location and the journey to work. Penn-Jersey has discussed use of a formulation of this kind in a regional growth model (Harris, 1963). A simpler linear programming formulation, one that simply minimizes journey-to-work travel time for subgroups of workers stratified by income, automobile availability, and race has been tested in the Buffalo, N.Y. area (Hamburg, Guinn, Lathrop, and Hemmens, 1965). Home-to-work functions are key elements in computer simulation models (Lowry, 1964; Goldner and Graybeal, 1965).

Given the emphasis placed on housing cost savings, it should come as no surprise that several studies have found the length of the journey to work to be related to residential density and/or structure type (Meyer, Kain and Wohl, 1965, Chapter 6; Kain, 1962; Kain and Beesley, 1965; Hoover and Vernon, 1959, pp. 153-182). However, use of residential density or structure type in explaining journey-to-work and residential location behavior can be objected to on much the same grounds as use of automobile ownership in trip generation and modal-split models, i.e., that residential space consumption, residential density, or structure type are themselves intervening variables or else simultaneously determined with the journey to work. The theoretical works referred to previously, suggest the desirability of looking to income, household characteristics that may determine preferences for lower residential densities and transport prices as more fundamental determinants of residential location.

Despite the fact that family income was not obtained in home-interview O and D surveys until very recently, nearly everyone who has thought seriously about residential location and the journey to work considers it an extremely important explanatory variable. In the theoretical models of residential location referred to previously lower residential density (greater consumption of residential space) is usually regarded as a superior good (one whose consumption rises with income). Thus, higher income, *ceteris paribus,* should cause workers to reside farther from their workplaces, at least in those situations where the cost of residential space per unit decreases with distance from the workplace. On this basis high income workers would be expected to live farther from their workplaces and to make longer work trips than low income workers. But there is an offset. It has been suggested that the valuation which households place on time spent in making the journey to work is also likely to rise with income. *Ceteris paribus,* this would cause worktrip length to decline with income. Very little reliable information exists which would permit definitive statements about the value placed on travel time by income level. However, there are some useful theoretical discussions (Moses, 1962; Moses and Williamson, 1963; Wingo, 1961) and Beesley (1965) has published some interesting empirical findings. Most theoretical studies assume that workers value travel time at their marginal wage rate. Since marginal wage rates are seldom available, most empirical studies requiring a value of time (for example, investment cost-benefit analysis) use average wages. Beesley's tentative findings suggest that the valuation workers place on travel time does increase with income. However, his findings also indicate workers on the average value journey-to-work travel time at only about a third of their average wage, although this proportion appears to increase somewhat with income. Beesley (1965, p. 182) notes this finding is generally consistent with that of a recent United States study based on an analysis of free and toll roads (Claffey, 1961).

Empirical findings on the relationship between worktrip length and family or worker income suggest that location rent savings generally outweigh any higher valuation of travel time by higher income workers, since travel time and distance traveled generally increase with income (Meyer, Kain and Wohl, 1965, pp. 119-130; Kain, 1962, pp. 148-150; Kain 1965; Hoover and Vernon, 1959, pp. 166-176; Lowry, 1964, pp. 65-67). Lapin (1964, p. 50) presents data on the median time-length of worktrips in the city of Philadelphia and the Philadelphia SMSA in 1956 and while his data show some tendency for travel time to increase with income he notes that the extreme income groups (less than \$2,000 and over \$10,000 in 1956) make the shortest trips. Of the two, the higher income group has much the shorter median. This result could be due to higher time valuations for very high income groups.

However, it should be pointed out that higher income workers have other ways of reducing their travel time besides living near their work. Specifically they can substitute faster, but more expensive, travel modes for slower and cheaper ones. Driving experiments conducted during the peak of the evening rush hour in the 25 largest cities in the mid-1950s showed that outbound auto traffic averaged about 20 mph in most of the cities. The average by transit, using the busiest transit routes in the same cities, was about 13 mph (Bello, 1958, p. 58). Using average speeds of 20 mph (auto) and 13 mph (transit) a commuter making a 30 minute trip could live 6.5 miles from work if he went by transit or 10 miles from work if he went by auto. Numerous studies report the greater use of faster and more expensive travel modes by higher income workers and/or workers employed in occupations having higher average incomes (Hill and Von Cube, 1963; Bostick, 1963, p. 258; Kain, 1965; Meyer, Kain and Wohl, 1965; pp. 138-42; Bostick and Todd, 1966, p. 275; Lansing and Mueller, 1964, pp. 69-95). These studies also indicate that trips by more expensive and faster travel modes are longer in miles, but that the travel time difference is much smaller. For most centrally-employed workers choosing to live at medium and low density, housing cost savings from commuting longer distances appear to be large enough to pay the higher costs of faster journey-to-work travel modes. In addition, relative travel time by alternative travel modes and choice of residential density are themselves closely related (Meyer, Kain and Wohl, 1965, Chapters 6 and 10; Kain, 1964b).

Under most circumstances, journey-to-work travel time by transit depends on the density of the residential neighborhood and the location of the workplace. Transit service may be very frequent and fast in high- to medium-density neighborhoods and at centrally located workplaces. However, transit service is frequently altogether unavailable in low-density neighborhoods and at suburban workplaces. Workers employed at suburban workplaces will often have no choice but to commute by private automobile or to live within walking distance.

Moreover, once a worker has decided to commute by private auto, the incremental costs of driving slightly farther are very low and there is no impediment (at least in terms of the journey to work) to his choosing a still lower density neighborhood. Increases in family size, and particularly the presence of school-age children, have been found to increase residential space consumption and to lead to longer journeys to work (Lansing and Mueller, 1964, pp. 15-75; Kain, 1962, pp. 150-154; Kain, 1964a). It is no accident that the stereotype of the long-distance commuter is a family man with a station wagon and large mortgage.

Studies of the journey to work have also provided evidence on differences in the length of worktrips by males and females. Regardless of workplace location, female workers make shorter worktrips and live nearer to their work than male workers. The probable explanation is that women more often are secondary wage earners and their lower paying jobs provide them with less incentive to make long trips; in addition their frequent domestic responsibilities may cause them to spend less time traveling to and from work. When the female is a primary, or the sole, wage earner, she typically belongs to a household with modest preferences for residential space or low incomes, both of which form residence in higher density neighborhoods and structures and residence near work. Finally, women more often use transit or walk to work than men, an additional consideration which works against choosing a residence far from work (Meyer, Kain, and Wohl, 1965, pp. 119-130; Kain, 1962; Kain, 1964a).

Location of workplace both in terms of the size of the metropolitan area and the location within a particular metropolitan area has long been recognized as an important determinant of residential location. Carroll (1952) observed a difference in the journey to work and residential location behavior of workers employed in the CBD and at outlying workplaces. He concluded that the residential distribution of workers employed in the CBD approximated the distribution of the population for the entire area, but that the residences of persons employed in off-center or peripheral workplaces were concentrated near their places of work. Further evidence of this was provided by the Detroit study which examined work travel to the CBD and to four outlying plants (DMATS, 1955, pp. 95-97). Other research has indicated that as workplace distance from the central business district increases, worktrip length decreases for all family size and income groups (Meyer, Kain, and Wohl, 1965, pp. 109-119; Kain, 1964a; Kain, 1962). A related finding is that household consumption of residential space at every income and family-size level increases as the workplace's distance from the CBD increases (Kain, 1962; Kain, 1964a; Meyer, Kain and Wohl, 1965, p. 126). Precisely this result would be expected if the price of residential space declined with distance from the CBD. Increases in average density as metropolitan area size increases are also consistent with this hypothesis.

Postwar suburbanization of employment has caused an increased concern with travel patterns from outlying workplace areas. Two of the best studies of travel from outlying workplaces are a survey of employees along Boston's Route 128 and a study of outlying workplace areas in suburban Chicago based on CATS data (Bone and Wohl, 1959; and Taaffe, Garner, and Yates, 1964).

RACIAL SEGREGATION AND THE JOURNEY TO WORK

Given the well-documented extent of racial segregation in United States metropolitan areas and its obviously great impact on the residence choices of Negroes, it is surprising that more attention has not been given to race in studies of travel behavior. Very few analyses of travel behavior by race have been published and with the exception of one study the subject has been all but ignored by metropolitan transportation studies (Hamburg, Guinn, Lathrop and Hemmens, 1965).

Comparisons of Negro and white worktrips indicate that housing market segregation greatly affects the travel behavior of both groups and particularly that of Negroes. In most metropolitan areas, virtually all Negro residents are confined to a single massive ghetto, usually located within the central city near the CBD. A few metropolitan areas have one or more much smaller, but still significant, outlying Negro residential areas, and some older Southern metropolitan areas have a more dispersed pattern of nonwhite residence, although these appear to be rapidly moving towards the ghetto model. In those instances where all, or nearly all, Negroes are limited to a single part of the metropolitan area, one end of the worktrip is fixed for Negroes. Regardless of where they work, Negroes reside in the ghetto. When work is found in distant suburban areas, Negroes are forced to commute long distances to and from centrally located Negro residence areas. Nor can their behavior be explained by low income alone. Low-income whites employed in outlying areas invariably live in the same outlying suburban areas as those in which they work, and, in fact, they generally live closer to their workplaces than do higher income whites (Meyer, Kain, and Wohl, 1965, Chapter 7). Low income Negro workers employed in central areas tend to live near their workplace since these are usually located in or near the ghetto. Under these circumstances their behavior more closely resembles that of low-income whites employed in central areas, who tend to live nearer work than whites with higher income.

Racial segregation of Negroes almost certainly affects the travel behavior of centrally employed whites as well, by forcing them to commute greater distances than they would in the absence of racial segregation. In general, the evidence is that discrimination forces minority groups to do a disproportionate amount of cross-hauling and "reverse commuting." Research on Negro travel behavior also indicates that the determinants of nonwhite travel and residential behavior do not appear essentially different from those of whites, except for the constraints imposed by housing segregation (Kain, 1965; Meyer, Kain and Wohl, 1965, pp. 144-171).

Moreover, the bifurcation of the transit market caused by racial segregation adds to the difficulties of providing efficient transit service for metropolitan areas. Housing segregation creates a need for several more-or-less independent and yet duplicating systems. A system is needed to transport central city white "captive" transit users (low-income, childless, and elderly white households) between high-density origins and other high-density destinations. An entirely different system is needed for ghetto Negroes. Finally, a third system is needed to transport centrally employed whites through the steadily expanding ghetto to white garrison suburbs. Since the distances between home and work are so great and steadily growing, this white commuter system usually must be high performance (special purpose and expensive) and subsidized (Kain, 1966).

Recently the McCone Report on the Watts riots pointed to inadequate transportation as a major cause of high Negro unemployment and made subsidized and vastly improved public transit from Watts one of its major recommendations (The Governor's Commission on the Los Angeles Riots, 1965, pp. 65-68). Some limited research findings indicate that housing segregation clearly affects the spatial distribution, with travel costs and other factors causing Negroes to be underrepresented in outlying workplace areas and other employment centers distant from the ghetto. This same research even suggests that housing segregation may be a cause of Negro unemployment (Kain, 1964b; Kain, 1966). As employment, and particularly manufacturing employment, continues to shift towards outlying areas, the implications for Negro employment could be severe.

TRANSIT USE AND CHOICE OF MODE

Studies of modal choice can be divided into two groups, those that include travel-time ratios between competing modes as an explanatory variable and those that do not. Most of the former studies have been produced as part of transit feasibility studies, although at least one metropolitan transportation study plans to use travel time ratios in its modal-split models (Basmacian and Schmidt, 1964). Use of travel-time ratios in transit feasibility studies is not particularly surprising, since proponents of new rapid transit systems contend that the much higher performance speeds of these new systems will attract riders from other modes.

As noted above, transit feasibility studies have generally collected less data and performed fewer analyses of travel behavior than metropolitan transportation studies. To a limited degree, this has been changing in recent years and the more recent transit feasibility studies have devoted somewhat greater amounts of resources to the analysis of travel behavior. Rather sophisticated models have been developed for the National Capital Transportation Agency (NCTA), the Metropolitan Boston Transportation Authority (MBTA), and the Metropolitan Toronto Planning Board.

The most elaborate travel time ratio modal-split model is probably that developed for the NCTA (Hill and Von Cube, 1963; Traffic Research Corporation, 1962; Deen, Mertz, and Irwin, 1963; Sosslau, Heanue, and Balek, 1964). The NCTA modal-split model might be likened to an analysis of variance procedure. Interzonal trips by transit and auto are first divided into worktrips and non-worktrips and then further stratified by (1) travel cost ratio, (2) service ratio, and (3) income subgroups. These stratifications yield 80 individual subgroups for each trip purpose (worktrips and non-worktrips). Observed modal-split percentages for each of these

80 subgroups are then regressed on the travel time ratio.

As noted previously, transit feasibility studies place their primary emphasis on relative travel time because it is the variable that is expected to be most effected by the construction of new rapid transit systems. The authors of the NCTA model conclude that:

> Within each set of stratified relationships the effects of time, cost, service, and income can be seen quite clearly. Generally, it can be seen that the slope of the curves increases for increasing values of cost ratio, service ratio and economic status. That is, as public transit become relatively less and less competitive in terms of travel time, demand for its use falls off more quickly among prosperous people and those paying relatively low transit fares continue to use transit in fairly large proportions. By the same token, these curves show that high percentages of travelers are using public transit for trips in which it is fairly competitive with the private automobile in terms of travel time and excess time, even though transit is relatively expensive and/or the travelers in question are of high economic status (Hill and Von Cube, 1963, p. 86).

Metropolitan transportation studies have usually not included travel time ratios in their modal-split models. The modal-split model, developed in the Pittsburgh study, though somewhat more elaborate than most, is essentially like those generally found in most highway O and D studies.

In the Pittsburgh study, separate relationships are developed to explain and predict transit travel to and from the CBD (PATS 1961, pp. 50-53; Schwartz, 1961). Transit services to and from the Pittsburgh CBD, as in most other cities, are quantitatively and qualitatively very different from those for most remaining parts of the urban area. Similarly, the availability and cost of automobile parking usually differs sharply from other parts of the metropolitan area. Rather than attempting to model these cost and service differentials, urban transportation studies invariably follow the expedient of developing separate modal-split models for transit travel to CBDs and to the remainder of the area.

Remaining transit usage is stratified according to school trips and local trips. In Pittsburgh these three categories of transit use accounted for appproximately equal proportions of all transit usage: CBD trips, 33 per cent; school trips, 32 per cent; and local trips, 35 per cent. As a proportion of all tripmaking in each category, CBD transit trips amounted to 56 per cent of all travel to and from the CBD and school transit trips amounted to 64 per cent of all school trips; but local transit trips accounted for only 10 per cent of local (non-CBD, non-school) travel.

Metropolitan transportation studies nearly always conclude that automobile ownership is the single most important determinant of transit and automobile use, and automobile ownership plays an especially prominent part in the modal-split models developed by all urban transportation studies. The authors of the Pittsburgh model placed considerable emphasis on the importance of "captive" transit riders in explaining transit use. They determined that 85 per cent of the 474,000 Pittsburgh daily transit trips are made by persons who either cannot drive a car, who do not own a car, or for whom the family car is unavailable when they need it. Moreover, four-fifths of 400,000 "captive" transit trips are accounted for by non-drivers. From these findings the authors of the PATS study conclude: "Auto ownership and availability is, in fact, the principal determinant of the traveler's choice of mode" (PATS, 1961, p. 52).

PATS introduced automobile ownership into its modal-split model by stratifying tripmakers into either car owning or non-car owning households. Net residential density, the remaining variable included in the PATS modal-split model, is used as the sole explanatory variable in equations stratified by trip purpose and automobile ownership.

History and Geography

HISTORY AND GEOGRAPHY ARE the disciplines considered in the fourth pair of chapters. Charles N. Glaab provides "Historical Perspective on Urban Development Schemes," and Harold M. Mayer treats some of the relations between "Urban Geography and City and Metropolitan Planning."

Urban history is a relatively new field of inquiry. As we observed in Chapter 1, most writings in urban history can be classified as local history, and "most local studies only assume wider significance when their subject is itself important by virtue of its size and political status, or because of the outstanding events and historical personalities associated with it." Glaab's chapter takes another tack; it is a balanced consideration of something seemingly generic in American urban growth. As he observes, "One of the most important activities associated with the history of cities in America is the promotion of economic enterprise by organized public and private groups within urban communities."

Those of us who are inclined to regard public and private urban development schemes as post-World War II phenomena need the historical perspective provided by Glaab. Efforts to attract industry, for example, can be seen in dozens of late nineteenth-century cities. Such "modern" devices as the creation of industrial parks, municipal bonding, tax deferment, and the provision of virtually free buildings all have their historical antecedents in the promotional activities of city governments and urban-based private associations of yesteryear.

In Chapter 7, Glaab provides concrete historical evidence to back up his general assertions. For example, "From the early years of American colonial urban development until about 1910, at which time most of the major cities that are part of our national urban network had been founded and were on their way to becoming well established, rivalry among competing urban centers for transportation and for commercial and manufacturing enterprises constituted a central theme of American urban history." With respect to transportation, he has developed this notion and documented it in detail in his excellent monograph on *Kansas City and the Railroads: Community Policy in the Growth of a Regional Metropolis* (Glaab, 1962).

In the course of his chapter, Glaab casts a wider net, considering American cities from coast to coast, reviewing some of the more notable efforts aimed at enhancing the local community's economic standing. At least two distinct eras are identified:

> *In the closing years of the nineteenth century, a definite shift took place in the character of urban promotion. For the older emphasis on commercial facilities, transportation, and the establishment of new urban sites was substituted a concern on the part of established cities with the attraction of manufacturing and industrial enterprises. The completion of a national transportation system, the location of the major urban sites in relation to this system, and increasing legal restrictions on municipal investment in private companies all tended to limit the customary kind of boosting of potential new cities associated with early and mid-nineteenth century urban development.*

This kind of promotion was initially conducted under private auspices. After 1930, however, Glaab contends that there began a trend for local governments rather than private business groups to manage development programs. "The most important period for the use of municipal developmental corporations occurred after World War II," he says, "particularly in communities seeking to convert local economies tied to war production."

In contrast to urban history, urban geography is a well established field. Mayer's chapter is essentially a follow-up to two of his previous essays: "Urban Geography" in *American Geography: Inventory and Prospect* (Mayer, 1954) and "A Survey of Urban Geography" in *The Study of Urbanization* (Mayer, 1965). This time, however, he focuses upon applied aspects of his field, and he is particularly concerned to show the relevance of geographic research for urban planning in the United States. Again, the emphasis is upon developments since World War II.

Mayer begins by locating geography as a discipline concerned with cities and other forms of human occupancy:

> *Geography, as a social science, is primarily concerned with the spatial patterns of man and society on the earth, just as history is concerned with the temporal patterns. Like history, it may, in a sense, be said to have no distinctive subject matter; the philosophy and methods of investigation of a problem make it geographic, rather than the substantive delimitation.*

He goes on to treat a number of specific topics about which geographers have made significant contributions. These include the study of functional relations between cities and between urban nodes and their complementary regions or hinterlands; the analysis of the economic base of urban areas; the functional classification of cities; and the study of cities as "central places." Mayer also provides an enlightening discussion of environmental risks wherein he indicates the natural constraints to which human activities and occupancy patterns are subject. In this context, he also deals with such man-made environmental hazards as air and water pollution.

He points up some of the ways in which geographers already have made very direct contributions to more rational policy planning:

> *Recent geographic studies have been useful in such widely diverse fields as (1) planning the location and service programs of an urban church organization, (2) recommending job-training programs in the schools which may vary within different communities of the same city, (3) suggesting local variations in the methods to be used in achieving school integration in accordance with various criteria for bounding school districts, and (4) determining the kinds of industries which should be encouraged to utilize internal differences in labor force characteristics within a city.*

Mayer concludes Chapter 8 with a list of some future research priorities that can be developed in the light of a very practical criterion — their importance from the standpoint of policy planning in cities and metropolitan areas. He advocates a reconsideration of the very concept of the metropolitan area, especially in view of the growing importance of the "megalopolis." He also feels that geographers can make a distinctive contribution in the field of inter-racial relations. "By describing the direction and rate of racial change," he holds, "the urban geographer may assist in predicting changes and thus help the planner to achieve policy recommendations that may be workable." Another promising field of investigation — at the little-explored borders between geography and psychology and urban aesthetics — is the perception of the city environment. Finally, major opportunities exist for geographers to contribute to planning by virtue of their expertise in graphic and cartographic representation. Technological advances, especially since World War II, mean that we can assemble and process vast amounts of data that are potentially useful to both the geographer and the planner.

—L.F.S.

7

Historical Perspective on Urban Development Schemes

CHARLES N. GLAAB

☐ ONE OF THE MOST IMPORTANT ACTIVITIES associated with the history of cities in America is the promotion of economic enterprise by organized public and private groups within urban communities. When observed from the standpoint of the present, the pattern of city location within the United States urban network seems in accord with "natural" factors of location, but in reality when historical perspective is brought to bear on the problem of city location, it is clear that the character of promotional activity within aspiring urban centers was frequently influential in determining, within sometimes rather broad limits, which community became a successful urban enterprise and which remained a failure.

Moreover, the promotional activities of American cities often provided a means of capital accumulation that initially furthered general economic growth in an undeveloped country and later provided the means for the stimulation of economic activity in newer sections of the nation. From the early years of American colonial urban development until about 1910, at which time most of the major cities that are part of our national urban network had been founded and were on their way to becoming well established, rivalry among competing urban centers for transportation and for commercial and manufacturing enterprises constituted a central

---

AUTHOR'S NOTE: *Most of this chapter's text is based on primary historical materials which I have not tried to cite in detail. The references cited are mainly secondary sources that have become available since World War II.*

theme of American urban history. Although after 1910 the emphasis in urban promotion had shifted from the establishment of new cities to the improvement of the economic welfare of successful urban centers, urban development schemes remained one of the chief concerns of urban leaders. In the years after World War II in particular, the attraction of industry and other enterprise to cities became a highly technical and highly professionalized aspect of modern urban planning.

EARLY URBAN PROMOTION

In some aspects, urban promotion dates back to the first days of municipal life in America. Leaders in colonial towns, operating in carefully protected local markets in accord with medieval ideas of regulation, extended subsidies in the form of land and houses for skilled artisans, bonuses to certain kinds of industries, and immunities from municipal taxation – devices that became a standard part of urban promotion. It was not until after the founding of the new nation, however, that organized promotion became a dominant activity of municipalities.

In the early years of the nineteenth century, as settlement into the west expanded, older eastern cities began competing for control of vast hinterlands, and this competition took the form of organized development of transportation projects. A Bostonian writing in 1816, at the beginning of an era of great urbanization, accurately examined the kind of cities developing in the United States and analyzed the rivalry among the eastern ports for commercial control of hinterlands. Baltimore was "struggling with Philadelphia to obtain the preference of the western country." Philadelphia, while losing some of its business to New York, had turned its attention to the west and to the organization of a variety of manufacturing projects. New York, anticipating the effects of its canal between the Hudson River and the Great Lakes, was "probably destined to become the greatest commercial emporium in the United States." As did many others, the writer recognized the key feature in a developing metropolitan drama – rivalry among established eastern centers competing for transportation to the interior (Glaab and Brown, 1966, p. 28).

Forms of Promotion

The immediate impetus for the intense rivalry among eastern seaboard cities was the building of the Erie Canal connecting New York City to the Great Lakes by way of the Hudson River. The highly profitable state-constructed enterprise, completed in 1825, greatly stimulated the growth of New York as an exporting port for agricultural products and caused rival cities to try to duplicate the success. The Maysville Road veto of May 27, 1838, which killed a stock subscription of $150,000 by the Federal government to a private turnpike company, had ended an era of substantial Federal support of public transportation schemes and led to a complex system of financing major transportation efforts in which states, counties, municipalities and private interests participated — a system that has frequently been termed "mixed enterprise." It should be emphasized, as Carter Goodrich and others have demonstrated, that there was no general opposition in the United States in this period to the principle of governmental participation in developmental projects; there was only debate over which units of government should participate and the means by which government aid should be extended (Goodrich, 1960, *passim*).

In the period before 1860, local governments contributed approximately a quarter of the total amount of governmental aid to transportation enterprises. In some instances the amount of municipal support was impressive. Baltimore's investment was larger than that of many state governments. The cities of Portland, Maine; Louisville, Kentucky; and Mobile, Alabama all extended more aid than the states in which they were located (Goodrich, 1960, pp. 162-163). In their attempts to obtain transportation, cities could employ a variety of approaches — direct municipal construction and ownership, subsidies of various kinds, and, most commonly, stock purchases in private companies. The method employed as well as the kind of transportation plan supported reflected not only the requirements of state legislation but also varying circumstances within the communities themselves. Julius Rubin, in a detailed study of the responses of Boston, Baltimore, and Philadelphia to the Erie Canal, has emphasized that the varying decisions as to whether to support canal or railroad in the respective cities reflected differences in the character of leadership and the social structures of the three communities.

The decisions also reflected the varying capacities of promotional groups successfully to dramatize their programs and thereby gain the necessary community support. Philadelphia supported a cumbersome combination of canal and railroad – the Main Line – which proved slow, expensive, and which ultimately represented a promotional failure. Boston leaders temporized and delayed waiting to see whether or not railroads would prove themselves suitable for American conditions. Baltimore leaders enthusiastically endorsed the transportation innovation and began at an early date energetically to marshal local funds for extensive railroad projects to benefit their city (Rubin, 1961).

RAILROAD PROMOTION IN BALTIMORE

Baltimore provides an excellent example of large-scale promotion of transportation enterprises by nineteenth-century cities. Local business leaders, after sending a delegation to England to inspect the Stockton and Darlington railroad opened in 1825, decided that railroads rather than canals offered the most potential benefits to cities even though railroads had not been tested under American conditions. During 1827 they rallied support for their Baltimore and Ohio Railroad Company in the city and elsewhere. Because of their capacity to establish community confidence in their abilities to carry through their ambitious proposal, they were able to gain endorsement of their plan for municipal investment in their company, even though the building of a railroad at this time represented a revolutionary idea, and their program was subject to the kind of doubting attacks evoked by any dramatic technological change. As so frequently occurred with successful promotions in the nineteenth century, the Baltimore leaders were able to create a frenetic community enthusiasm for their project; the presence of "railroad mania," as it was frequently referred to in contemporary sources, was a common occurrence in cities developing transportation projects. An observer described the enthusiasm aroused by the initial sale of stock in the Baltimore and Ohio, which the company encouraged primarily as a means of obtaining public support for large municipal investment:

> There came a scene which almost beggars descriptions. By this time public excitement had gone far beyond fever heat and reached

> the boiling point. Everybody wanted stock . . . Before a survey had been made – before common sense had been consulted, even, the possession of stock in any quantity was regarded as provision for old age and great was the scramble to obtain it (Rubin, 1961, p. 75).

In addition to creating the kind of community emotional climate necessary to gain support for large-scale municipal investment plans, Baltimore leaders also established an organizational framework for the promotion of local railroad enterprises. Often during this period of local railroad promotion, private associations performed quasi-governmental functions in cooperation with regular municipal governmental agencies. In Baltimore, the Joint Committee on Internal Improvements of the City Council provided the kind of special organizational unit necessary for the coordination of local promotional enterprise. The committee's 1836 report set forth the position that sustained local promotion during this period of expansive economic development: "Whether the city of Baltimore is to be reduced to a place of comparative insignificance in a commercial point of view, or to assume a position, equal if not superior to that of any other city in the Union" (Goodrich, 1960, pp. 85-86).

In the period before the Civil War, which marked the end of a phase of nineteenth-century promotion, Baltimore committed more than 13 million dollars of municipal funds in the form of stock subscriptions and loans to the Baltimore and Ohio and other railroad projects. Baltimore planned its railroad program with a high degree of responsibility, managed it in a financially responsible fashion, and, during the years before 1860, devoted more funds to its transportation program than did any other American city. The policy of extending extensive aid in the form of stock subscriptions and loans was continued in the years after the Civil War but on a diminished scale; the 6 million dollars provided in municipal aid between 1864 and 1886 was less than half the amount extended before the war. Detailed examination of the financial aspects of this extensive program of municipal support of private enterprise indicated that the city's support of railroads was a successful urban developmental scheme. The city's early commercial foundations were sustained and strengthened through an extensive system of interior transportation connections. Although missing an excellent opportunity to sell its large Baltimore and Ohio holdings at a substantial profit, the city eventually probably broke even on the liquidation of its investments in railroads (Goodrich, 1960, pp. 239-241).

MUNICIPAL RAILROAD OWNERSHIP IN CINCINNATI

The Baltimore plan of stock purchase in private railroad companies represented the most common form of nineteenth-century municipal development scheme for obtaining transportation. There were, however, urban experiments in actual municipal ownership of railroads. Often leaders in aspiring towns and cities organized an elaborate set of local "paper" railroad companies as an advertising device or as a means of bargaining with established railroad companies. But serious efforts at municipal building and operation of railroads also occurred in the nineteenth century. Troy, New York, built the Schenectady and Troy Railroad, completed in 1842 at a cost of $700,000, as part of an unsuccessful effort to compete with Albany. The road failed to obtain the anticipated traffic and was eventually sold at a loss.

A more important experiment in municipal ownership was that of Cincinnati. At the close of the Civil War, Cincinnati leaders found their city steadily losing trade to rivals, particularly Louisville, and decided a railroad to the south was essential to maintain the city's position. Sufficient private funds for the project could not be raised, and the Ohio constitution of 1851 blocked the customary procedure of extending loans, subscriptions, or donations to private corporations. Acting in bold fashion, city leaders were able to establish the legal position that the constitutional prohibition did not extend to the city's building a railroad on its own account. Representatives from the City Council, the Board of Trade, and the Chamber of Commerce obtained enabling state legislation for the organization of a railroad company, and a Board of Trustees was placed in charge of the project. Eventually the city spent 18 million dollars for construction and $300,000 for a terminal at Cincinnati in completing the 334-mile line to Chattanooga in 1880. The railroad was then leased to a private company and quickly became a successful carrier. The exact financial return to the city on its investment cannot be ascertained, but the railroad proved to be a highly successful developmental project which promoted Cincinnati's growth (Goodrich, 1960, pp. 239-241).

City Promotion and Western Railroads

In the years after 1950 the rivalry among eastern cities, which had been important in the development of a transportation system into the interior, was transferred to the west, and the basic conditions of urban promotion were altered. In the early part of the nineteenth century, local governmental support had been the means for the creation of new private transportation companies. Now the process became one of municipalities bargaining with well established railroad corporations seeking to extend their lines into new areas.

Railroads were not bound by topography, by the paths of river commerce, or by natural trade patterns. Within limits, they could be built anywhere, and railroad leaders were willing to bargain with competing communities in newer areas to obtain the best possible deal in stock subscriptions, bond issues, and right-of-ways. Accordingly, it was sometimes possible for towns with limited natural advantages to triumph over more favored rivals for the prize of local or regional urban dominance. Numerous cities in the west and south owe their importance to the fact that energetic urban promoters through superior community organization and superior propagandizing were able to persuade railroad officials to build lines to their particular locales. Western railroads such as the Illinois Central and the Chicago, Burlington, and Quincy perfected bargaining with local communities into a fine art and were able to realize considerable profit from promotional programs that emphasized the development of town sites. The recognition by railroad officials that "nothing can be realized from any locality after they are sure of the road," as one of them put it, led to intricate negotiations over bond issues, stock subscriptions, and other concessions, which posed a major task for community leaders.

Western Promotional Ideology

During this great era of urban promotion and rivalry western writers and promoters, as part of their efforts to build support for the claim of the particular urban site with which they identified their fortunes, worked out involved geographic theories of location that emphasized the inevitability of some locale becoming the site of a great future city. These ideas played an important part in sustaining local promotional programs. Jesup W. Scott (1799-1873), a Toledo newspaperman and promoter, won considerable attention for a series of articles in the 1840s and 1850s designed to show that the future metropolises of America would be found in the interior particularly along the Great Lakes (Glaab, 1964). William Gilpin (1813-1894), with theories derived from the German geographer Alexander von Humboldt, in the 1850s became a national authority on the nature of the American West.

Gilpin devoted a good deal of his attention to speculations on the location of the great central city. In accord to some extent with his own material interests, he first located it near Independence, Missouri, then at Kansas City, and finally late in his career (after he had moved farther west) at Denver, Colorado. Notions of geographic inevitability expressed by Scott, Gilpin, and numerous other writers, which emphasized that this point or that point must be the site of a great city, were woven into the promotional efforts of urban leaders. They provided ideological foundations on which to build the enthusiasm which sustained community efforts to raise bond issues, extend municipal aid to railroads, and to gain support for other local developmental projects. Without this powerful tool for the dramatization of the importance of an individual urban site, community promoters could not have so frequently obtained the near unanimity of sentiment characteristic of nineteenth century local promotional programs.

Urban Promotion in the Growth of Kansas City as a Railroad Center

The relationship between ideology, community effort, and local promotion has been studied in detail in the rise of Kansas City, Missouri, as a western railroad center (Glaab, 1962). This case study illuminates some of the general themes that were a part of nineteenth-century urban development schemes in new regions. The settlement of Kansas City began as a relatively unimportant western trading depot and for the first fifteen years of its existence was little more than a collection of warehouses and general stores near the juncture of the Kansas and Missouri rivers. The settlement functioned as an entrepôt of the river-caravan trade – a place where cargoes could be transferred from steamboat to wagon for shipment to scattered points of a distant western hinterland.

After the opening of Kansas Territory and the movement of large numbers of settlers into the region, a group of local promoters set out to build a regional city through obtaining railroads. Despite a well organized local program, by the time of the Civil War Kansas City was not yet connected to the railroads being built across Missouri; Leavenworth, Kansas, a few miles to the north seemed a much more promising site for the future great regional city. But after a period of near disaster for the community during the war, a few property holders in Kansas City revived their program as railroad building began again in the region. Using municipal investments in their paper railroad companies, local bond issues, and blocks of potentially valuable real estate, the Kansas City leaders were able to persuade officials of the Hannibal and St. Joseph to connect with a transcontinental branch being built in Kansas — the Union Pacific, Eastern Division (later the Kansas Pacific) — by way of Kansas City rather than by way of Leavenworth. In part, they were able to complete their negotiations because of the unity for their program they had established within the community. Through years of careful agitation in terms of the Gilpin vision, they had been able to identify their aims and aspirations with the broader central meaning of the city. The Hannibal and St. Joseph's building of a railroad bridge at Kansas City — the first across the Missouri River — assured the city's rapid development. Within a decade Kansas City had eclipsed its rivals in the region, and had established its regional metropolitan position.

Other Western Cities and Transportation Programs

Urban promotion was also significant in the foundation and early growth of many of the major American cities that developed with the completion of the railroad network into the Rocky Mountain and Far West regions. After William Larimer helped to bring about unity among competing promoters in the mining settlement at Denver in 1860 and became its "Donating Agent," the community moved rapidly to provide real estate for those who would build the urban institutions necessary for a successful city-building enterprise — hotels, newspapers, general stores, and mills. When it appeared that the town's promising hopes would be destroyed by the decision of the Union Pacific Railroad to build to the north by way of Cheyenne, Wyoming, community leaders organized an effective local railroad program which not only provided a northward connection to the Union Pacific but also opened new mineral areas to the south, and in general assured the city's regional importance. In all their promotional programs, Denver leaders consistently demonstrated a good deal of zeal and skill. For example, the location of a United States mint at Denver, which provided official recognition of the city's regional status, owed a great deal to local organizational activity.

The relative positions of Portland, Oregon, and Seattle and Tacoma, Washington, as urban centers of the Pacific Northwest were also substantially affected by the character of local promotion. Portland, the oldest of the communities which had gotten its start through the utilization of good natural port facilities, followed a conservative railroad policy that permitted the rise of the two rivals in Washington. Despite the support of Tacoma's interests by officials of the Northern Pacific railroad, Seattle, through local organization of competing railroad projects, was eventually able to obtain the necessary transcontinental connections to assure its leadership over Tacoma. It is significant that both the "Kansas City Spirit" and the "Seattle Spirit," which were locally considered as the reason for the communities' respective railroad victories, became effective community symbols which could be appealed to by local leaders at a later date to gain support for other developmental plans.

Urban Promotion in Smaller Cities (Wichita, Kansas)

The influence of nineteenth-century urban promotion, although evident in the growth of larger cities, can often be more precisely delineated in the histories of smaller urban centers which may not have achieved metropolitan status but which nonetheless were successful urban enterprises. Wichita, Kansas, supplies a good example. In 1868 urban speculators established a town site on the route of cattle drives from Texas to railheads in Kansas. Although the location was 80 miles from a railroad and had no particular natural advantages, promoters began advertising the virtues of the site and managed through raising a community bond issue of $200,000 to persuade officials of the Atchison, Topeka, and Santa Fe Railroad to build a branch toward their town. Even more importantly, they persuaded Joseph G. McCoy, the leader in the Kansas cattle marketing industry, to transfer his operations from Abilene to Wichita. Within a few years, Wichita had become a booming cow town.

With the decline of the open range drives, Wichita leaders faced a period of hardship, but through vigorous advertising of the "Peerless Princess of the Plains" were able to attract substantial investment in flour milling, the manufacture of farm machinery, and other industries. In the twentieth century, the same kind of vigorous promotional techniques were applied to the development of local oil and airplane industries. Although Wichita lacked substantial natural advantages, at each stage of its development, local leaders had been willing to support the community projects necessary to growth (Green, 1957, pp. 148-166).

NINETEENTH-CENTURY PROMOTIONAL FAILURES

The history of American cities tends to emphasize successful ventures in city building and seldom considers the failures and partial failures of community enterprise that doomed a number of once promising places to oblivion or second rank. Norfolk, Virginia, with unsurpassed natural port facilities, seemed in the early part of the nineteenth century to be potentially a great city, but support for transportation projects that might have made the city the center of a unified railroad system into the interior came too late, and Baltimore maintained control of what might have been Norfolk's hinterland. In the 1850s, Superior, Wisconsin, attracted national attention as a site of a great future metropolis of the interior, but the failure of outside investors in the city to agree on promotional programs led to its becoming the lesser community of a middle-sized urban complex. Galena, Illinois, once appeared to be one of the most promising cities of the state, but after lead supplies in the region began to run out, local leaders were unable to obtain necessary railroad connections to maintain their city building goals. Galveston, Texas, an important pre-Civil War port on the Gulf of Mexico and a magic name in the writings of early western urban promoters, failed to take advantage of the possibilities of railroads and lost its position to Houston. Numerous small lumber, mining, commercial, and manufacturing cities throughout the west did not diversify their economies at the proper time or were unable to profit from opportunities exploited by more energetic rival communities. Rather consistently in the nineteenth century, the problematic element of the quality and character of local promotion affected the location of important American cities and their relative positions within the national urban network.

EARLY URBAN PROMOTION BY ESTABLISHED CITIES

In the closing years of the nineteenth century, a definite shift took place in the character of urban promotion. For the older emphasis on commercial facilities, transportation, and the establishment of new urban sites was substituted a concern on the part of established cities with the attraction of manufacturing and industrial enterprises. The completion of a national transportation system, the location of the major urban sites in relation to this system, and increasing legal restrictions on municipal investment in private companies all tended to limit the customary kind of boosting of potential new cities associated with early and mid-nineteenth century urban development. Now business leaders in established cities sought to protect their investments in an area through the systematic encouragement of local industrial development (Moes, 1962, pp. 113-114).

AGENCIES OF PROMOTION

In general, this kind of promotion was conducted by private business organizations within cities – boards of trade, chambers of commerce, and trade associations – an approach that evolved early in the history of American urban growth. Commercial clubs of one kind and another had existed in American cities from the colonial period. In the pre-Civil War era of urban rivalry over transportation, these private associations had frequently been important coordinating agencies in local developmental programs. By 1858, there were ten chambers of commerce and twenty boards of trade in the United States, most of them performing some type of promotional role (Sturges, 1915, pp. 41-42). In the Midwest, boards of trade organized in Buffalo (1844), Detroit (1847), Cleveland and Chicago (1848), and Milwaukee (1849) helped to organize local programs for roads and railroads, sponsored promotional excursions by merchants, and sent drummers and runners into trade areas in dispute with other cities (Still, 1941, p. 199). The Kansas City Chamber of Commerce, organized in 1856, advanced the comprehensive kind of program typical of many aspiring cities. In addition to planning and managing the entire local railroad program, the Chamber also initiated efforts to persuade the Federal government to make the city a starting point for mail service to the Far West; to improve river navigation facilities; to obtain charters from the state for local insurance and banking companies; and to establish new European trade connections by way of the Gulf of Mexico (Glaab, 1962, pp. 55-56).

By the mid-1850s there was some change in tone discernible in statements of local promotional aims in American cities. Now it was argued that commerce alone could not make a city great; also needed were manufacturers and the programs to attract them. The Cleveland *Leader,* for example, asserted in 1856 that "no thinking man with capital will stop here when we have only commerce to sustain us. A manufacturing town gives a man full scope for his ambition" (Still, 1941, p. 199). The newspaper proposed the raising of popular subscriptions to manufacturing enterprises and the reduction of real-estate prices to induce manufacturers to invest in the area. The outbreak of the Civil War ended this early phase of manufacturing promotion, and only a few of the pre-Civil War community business organizations survived in American cities. But the extension of telegraph connections during the war and the completion of the Atlantic Cable in 1866 greatly expanded long-distance trade possibilities and encouraged the rapid formation of new commercial exchanges and clubs as a means of coordinating trade information. Although many of these new business organizations were still concerned primarily with commerce, several began turning their attentions to the attraction of manufacturers (Sturges, 1915, pp. 42-43).

PROMOTION OF MANUFACTURERS IN MILWAUKEE, WISCONSIN

The Chamber of Commerce of Milwaukee, Wisconsin, was one of the earliest to move toward a program of systematic manufacturing promotion. In the early 1870s, the Chamber organized a Committee on Commerce and Manufactures, which established a fund of $860 to promote industrial growth. The Chamber's list of city advantages published in 1871 emphasized industrial benefits – cheap land near the waterfront, low construction costs, low taxes, freedom from municipal debt, and a high quality labor force. In 1879, the Chamber joined a local Merchants' Association and the city council to sponsor an industrial exposition that was opened in 1881. The exposition was held annually for the next twenty-one years and inspired similar exhibitions in St. Louis, Chicago, and Minneapolis.

Out of agitation for a "central bureau of information" to promote the city emerged a new organization, the Association for the Advancement of Milwaukee, whose primary aim was "to advertise to the world the advantages which the city had to manufacturers seeking new locations." The Association sponsored programs to provide free rents to manufacturers for a period, free industrial sites, and local capital investment. Subsidies were obtained for a number of manufacturing companies and a score of new industries were attracted to the city as part of an effort, according to a local newspaper, to enable the city to fulfill its destiny as "the manufacturing metropolis of our boundless West." During this period, Milwaukee promotional announcements emphasized the theme that was part of the new approach of several cities:

> It is not enough to sit in a comfortable counting-room and write a letter now and then inviting some enterprise to come . . . ; the manufactories should be urged to come; we should go out and "compel them to come in." This other manufacturing cities are doing with results profitable to themselves . . . There must be tangible money inducement which hitherto Milwaukee has been unable to offer through lack of specific organization to this end (Still, 1948, p. 349).

NEW TECHNIQUES OF MANUFACTURING PROMOTION

Late in the century, American cities began developing more specialized techniques of promotion. The permanent Commercial Museum – designed to exhibit local industrial products – was established in 1894 in Philadelphia and adopted in San Francisco, St. Louis, and Boston. The Cleveland Board of Trade in 1892 set up an industrial promotion committee which led to the board's reorganization as a chamber of commerce a year later. The Cleveland Chamber of Commerce hired a full-time secretary, developed a number of new welfare functions, and became a prototype in its organization for twentieth-century chambers.

By the turn of the century, the value in urban promotion of trade conventions, exhibitions, and elaborate publications to advertise local advantages was accepted in a number of American cities as several hundred boards and chambers had emerged throughout the nation (McKelvey, 1963, pp. 43-44). The emphasis in this period was primarily on private organization of promotion, on "free enterprise," even though the identification of chambers with the interests of cities led them to support movements to curtail monopolies, particularly in public utilities. The Merchants' and Manufacturers' Association indicated the basic point of view of these promotional agencies when it asserted in 1908 that American cities had found

> ... that the enterprise and energy of individuals can be considerably augmented by co-operation of commercial, industrial, and professional factors. There are opportunities for promotion of local interests in every community — opportunities which cannot be fostered by single individuals on the one hand, nor by the municipal government on the other (Still, 1948, p. 345).

Urban Promotion in the Post-Civil War South

A dynamic agency in the industrialization and general economic growth of the south in the period after the Civil War was, as in other underdeveloped areas, the city itself. The south, particularly after the end of Reconstruction in 1877, experienced the same kind of town promotion and rivalry that had been a part of the growth of the west, with the "wildest plunging" in "brand new towns or cities yet to be established." But by this time, with the national pattern of city location more rigid, the possibilities in the customary city-building enterprise were limited, and from the beginning of the rise of the "New South," the emphasis in urban promotion was on the attraction of industry. It was a period when "even country villages were making their efforts to secure investors who would transform them overnight into metropolises ..." (Lemmon, 1966, p. 264). Although a number of factors influenced the general industrialization of the south, the actions of individual communities could affect the precise location of a given factory or company. Moreover, advertising, bond issues, and other promotional efforts probably contributed, at least in a limited way, to the total extent of southern industrial development in this period.

Southern cities in the late nineteenth and early twentieth century to a large extent led the nation in the extensive utilization of old methods of promotion and in the development of new approaches to the problem of community development. The device of the industrial exposition was particularly emphasized during the early years of the New South's industrialization; the World's Industrial Cotton Culturist Exposition at New Orleans in 1883-1884; the Cotton States and Industrial Exposition at Nashville in 1897; the meeting of the Southern Industrial League at Atlanta in July, 1900 were among the better known examples of this frequently used tool of urban promotion.

As was the case in other parts of the country, southern cities in the late nineteenth century conducted their promotional activities through private business organizations. In August, 1888, a Chamber of Commerce was organized in Raleigh, North Carolina with the express intent of securing additional industries for the community. Similar organizations were established in a number of cities in the 1880s and later, including Lynchburg, Virginia; Greensboro, North Carolina; Atlanta and Macon, Georgia; New Orleans, Louisiana; and Houston, Galveston, and San Antonio, Texas. A primary concern of southern chambers – and an emphasis somewhat distinctive from that of their counterparts in the north – was improvement in the quality of basic municipal services such as water, electricity, and transportation as part of other inducements to manufacturers to settle in a locale. This program involved chambers in the activity of organizing community support for bond issues, just as in an earlier period such groups had been instrumental in gaining popular endorsement of financial concessions to railroads. And they were frequently as effective as the early groups promoting transportation improvements. The Atlanta Chamber, which took charge of obtaining a necessary two-third's popular majority for a 3 million dollar bond issue for municipal improvements, managed to get an 84 per cent turnout of the city's registered voters with only 66 votes cast against the measure (Doonan, 1914, p. 11).

In the late nineteenth century, southern cities moved toward systematic advertising programs emphasizing the advantages of a particular locality. Generally these were cast in terms of the old boosters' doctrine of inevitability. "It is absolutely certain," a Raleigh newspaper observed, "that Raleigh is destined to be a large and important manufacturing center" (Lemmon, 1966, p. 212). Both municipal governments and private business organizations attempted to make their city known by purchasing advertising space in northern newspapers and nationally circulated magazines. In 1908 the Commercial Club of Knoxville, Tennessee, for example, spent $10,000 in advertising the city in both northern and southern newspapers and magazines.

By 1926 most of the major cities in the south were spending substantial sums annually on advertisements. A survey of that year revealed that of 50 cities that engaged in advertising 18 were located in the south; $260,000 by Atlanta, Georgia; $250,000 by St. Petersburg, Florida; $350,000 by Miami, Florida; and $100,000 by Ashville, North Carolina, were among the higher expenditures. In the 1920s southern cities also began purchasing radio time for advertising purposes, and by 1929 three municipally owned radio stations – in Dallas, Texas, and Jacksonville and Pensacola, Florida – were in operation in the south. In addition to making extensive use of older traditional methods of urban promotion, southern cities were often at the forefront in the development of the new approaches to urban promotion that emerged in the twentieth century.

TWENTIETH-CENTURY URBAN PROMOTION

The task of urban leaders promoting city development in the twentieth century was essentially the same as it had been in the past – to organize community support for programs that would convince outside investors to support the interests of a given locality. But there were significant shifts in approach and emphasis:

1. A concern with establishing and retaining industry rather than the attraction of transportation connections.

2. A tendency to establish more elaborate promotional and developmental organizations to take the place of the simple promotional committees of chambers of commerce and other private business organizations.

3. A wider and more varied range of inducements to potential outside investors including tax concessions, formalized local investment plans, industrial parks, and comprehensive loan programs.

4. A trend beginning in the 1930s for local governments rather than private business groups to manage development programs.

INDUSTRIAL DEVELOPMENT COMPANIES

In the early years of the twentieth century, American cities began to evolve systematic industrial development plans which emphasized the use of formally constituted industrial development corporations. As early as 1910, La Crosse, Wisconsin, had established such an organization, the Industrial Association of La Crosse. Shortly thereafter, the community development plans of three cities – Davenport, Iowa; Scranton, Pennsylvania; and Little Rock, Arkansas – attracted considerable national attention.

The Davenport Plan

Of the three, the Davenport plan was the most elaborate; four local groups were involved in the plan, three concerned with the attraction of industry and the fourth with the improvements of farm areas in the county in which Davenport was located. The Commercial Club of Davenport established committees to improve local business conditions, enlarge markets, and promote the city as a site for conventions. The Greater Davenport Committee took charge of providing advertising material on the city's advantages for manufacturers and also contacted industrial prospects. After investigation by this group, a manufacturer might be referred to the Davenport Industrial Development Company, which could purchase stocks and bonds in the manufacturing enterprise and could recommend that local private investors purchase stock in it. Through this program several industries were attracted to the city between 1910 and 1914.

The Little Rock Plan

The Little Rock developmental plans centered on the donation of idle land for the purpose of attracting industry. The Chamber of Commerce then sold the land through low-down-payment, low-interest loans, and the funds collected from these sales were deposited with an Industrial Development Committee, elected by the Chamber's Board of Governors. The committee was empowered to make stock investments in manufacturing concerns interested in the city and in some instances might extend direct bonuses.

The Scranton Plan

The Scranton Industrial Development Company, organized in 1914, sold $10 shares that paid an interest of 5 per cent. To insure the rapid sale of the stock, local banks agreed to make loans on the stock up to 80 per cent of value; in addition, payment for the shares could be stretched out over five years. All revenues derived from the sale of stock were invested in new industries brought to the community. The Industrial Development Company, whose directors were elected by the 19 banks and trust companies in the city, worked closely with the Manufacturers' Committee of the Board of Trade in recommending private purchases of stock in new companies locating in the city.

The launching of the stock sale in the Scranton development company in 1914 recalled the efforts to arouse support for local railroad stock and bond issues in the preceding century. An organized force of businessmen canvassed the city the day before a fund-raising banquet. Large cards with the slogan "A Million for Scranton's Factories" appeared throughout the city on streetcars and in store windows. Automobiles carried pennants, and 10,000 booster buttons were distributed. Newspapers carried full-page advertisements for the campaign. In part, because of the generation of this kind of enthusiasm, the subscription sales reached the million dollar mark by the eighth day and over a million and a quarter dollars were subscribed by the end of the tenth day.

The Louisville Industrial Foundation

One of the best known of the local developmental corporations of this period was established in Louisville, Kentucky. The Louisville Industrial Foundation was founded in 1916 at a time when local business conditions were badly depressed, and local leaders developed a plan for a "Million-Dollar Factory Fund" to offer low interest loans to manufacturers who could not obtain capital at the same rate elsewhere. The enterprise, though it may not have been a complete success as a financial venture since there were a few failures to repay loans and lengthy deferment in payments, did prove a successful local developmental program. By 1945, the foundation had attracted 44 manufacturing enterprises whose operations greatly expanded the economy of the city. In addition to operating the revolving loan fund, the Industrial Foundation also compiled briefs on land sites for factories, answered business inquiries, and supplied data on the Louisville area (Moes, 1962, pp. 51-53).

Development Corporations in the Recent Period

During the relatively prosperous period of the 1920s the organization of developmental corporations by cities slowed down considerably, but during the depression years of the 1930s, when numerous cities faced the crisis of losing a key industry, the approach again became popular. When Manchester, New Hampshire, in 1936, faced liquidation of its largest enterprise, the Amoskeag Manufacturing Company, local business leaders quickly organized a developmental corporation, Amoskeag Industries Incorporated. The corporation purchased the property, set up four textile mills, three of which were successful, and by the time of World War II had disposed of all the remaining industrial space.

The most important period for the use of municipal developmental corporations occurred after World War II, particularly in communities seeking to convert local economies tied to war production. In Texas, for example, only 18 community developmental corporations were established before 1953, but at least 27 more were organized from 1953 to 1955. In New England, approximately 75 corporations were formed between 1912 and 1956 with 34 of them organized in the last four years of the period. A Department of Commerce survey of 1958 found that a majority of the 1,800 local developmental corporations had been established in the preceding five years. These new developmental corporations were primarily to be found in smaller cities, many of them in the south. In addition to stock purchases, they offered a variety of other concessions to potential investors — free sites, tax exemptions, free use of buildings, and free utilities.

Industrial Surveys

In the same period that the developmental corporation technique was being developed, cities moved to supply technical information to potential investors through industrial surveys. The Chamber of Commerce of Cincinnati indicated the new approach when it asserted in 1914 that it was trying to get away from the usual "hot air" approach praising all aspects of a community. Instead the Chamber compiled data on traffic, housing, education, rental rates, living costs, sources of raw material, markets, and similar information. The Chamber also provided detailed maps of industrial locations in the city and published monographs on specific aspects of the city of interest to investors.

Industrial Districts

Another new technique of promotion that emerged early in the century, with an effort in Chicago in 1908, was the development of industrial districts and industrial parks. Briefly defined, the planned industrial district was a "subdivided tract of land, suitably located with reference to transportation routes, and adequately provided with utilities, and that is restricted and promoted solely for industrial use." Industrial parks were comparable except that the term was sometimes loosely applied to undeveloped tracts of land which the owner chose to call an industrial park simply as a promotional technique. Similar to the developmental corporation, the planned industrial district experienced its greatest popularity after World War II, with at least 80 per cent of those in existence in 1963 having been established after 1948 (Whitlach, 1963, pp. 1-2).

Municipal Bonding

One of the more significant changes in methods of urban promotion in the twentieth century was the re-establishment during the 1930s of the practice of using municipal bonds to finance private manufacturing projects. This revived an approach that had been employed in building internal improvements in the nineteenth century but which generally had been made illegal in the late nineteenth century as a result of reaction to the excesses that had frequently occurred in the support of railroads by local governments. The use of municipal bonding had the effect of shifting promotional activities from private organizations back to local government.

The most important action in reviving this practice occurred in 1936 in Mississippi, where during the depression farm income had fallen to 185 million dollars a year as compared to industrial income of a mere 14 million dollars. As part of Governor Hugh White's "Balancing Agriculture with Industry Program," cities were empowered to issue bonds, to buy land, to erect factory buildings, and to purchase equipment. Eight communities took advantage of the measure between 1936 and 1939 with effective results. The largest effort was made by Natchez in 1939 when the community bonded itself for $300,000 to provide the facilities for a large tire manufacturing company. The city built the factory and leased it to the company at a rate of $50 a month for the first five years, after which the company had the option to buy the plant, and the business would then be placed on the tax rolls. In addition, the city provided water, sewerage, and road facilities while the manufacturer agreed to install at least $500,000 worth of equipment in the plant, to insure the factory, and to keep the building in proper repair. The practice of municipal bonding was also authorized in Tennessee where 18 towns and cities in the late 1930s issued general bonds for factory construction ranging in amount from $20,000 to $110,000. By 1964, 28 states had authorized some type of municipal bonding, and 17 states had actually used the device. From 1936 to 1964 more than a half-billion dollars had been issued in municipal bonds, 95 per cent of the amount in the south. While the practice did not in itself cause any fundamental change in overall patterns of industrial location, it did provide an important promotional tool which could be used to benefit the individual community willing to support ambitious programs to attract enterprise (Gooding, 1964, pp. 2-7).

New Governmental Agencies

As part of their participation in attracting industry through bond issues, tax concessions, and other subsidies, municipal governments in the post-World War II period established departments of industrial promotion, often with substantial budgets for advertising the city. These departments carried a variety of names — Department of Economic Development, Department of Industrial Development, or Department of Industrial Recovery. Their heads became in effect expert "city salesmen" who often travelled around the country selling the "local story." In spite of a new emphasis on the technical aspects of promotion — on precise data and specialized information — there was an element of a very old enthusiasm still present in recent promotional efforts. William Fay, president of the Chamber of Commerce of Rochester, New York, echoed the theme that had been central to the history of urban promotion in America in speaking to a group of local business and governmental leaders in 1959:

> You are going to help us sell Rochester to plant location executives all over the country.
>
> Yes, you gentlemen, *can* and we are confident you *will*, be missionaries for our community — selling the gospel of Rochester wherever you go. You know from experience that nothing sells like face-to-face persuasion.

CONCLUSION

The urban promoter and booster — as exemplified by Beriah Sellers or George Babbitt — has often been critically portrayed in American culture, and in fact has served as a stock representative of a supposed American narrowness, provincialism, and vainglory. Yet, one of the more dynamic and vital aspects of the history of American urban growth — although it has received limited historical consideration — has been the systematic and organized promotion of enterprise by the representatives of American cities. Although patterns of city location and industrial development in America have been influenced by a variety of complex economic factors, the efforts of urban communities, from colonial times to the present, to obtain enterprises has been one of the fundamental historical forces shaping the character of American economic and urban growth.

8

Urban Geography and City and Metropolitan Planning

HAROLD M. MAYER

☐ CITY AND METROPOLITAN PLANNING HAS, in recent years, utilized many of the concepts and methods of geography, an old academic discipline which has itself undergone rapid evolution. More and more geographers are applying their backgrounds in the discipline to the service of urban society through the field of planning, and are finding stimulating and productive careers as staff members of planning agencies and as consultants to governmental organizations, business firms, and institutions which are concerned with problems of location, spatial organization, and urban development. Geographers in academic institutions are to a major extent addressing their research programs to problems of cities and urban society (see, for example, Mayer, 1963). Behind this accelerating movement is a long tradition of urban studies in geography, paralleling those in the other social sciences.

This chapter deals with geography's potential contribution to policy planning. Other useful – and much longer – surveys of some comparable topics have recently become available (Haggett, 1966; Murphy, 1966). In general, however, the present resumé deals with geographic developments only since World War II.

AUTHOR'S NOTE: *For a longer list of references to the geographical literature see Harold M. Mayer, "A Survey of Urban Geography," in Philip M. Hauser and Leo F. Schnore (editors),* The Study of Urbanization *(New York: John Wiley, 1965), pp. 81-114.*

GEOGRAPHY AS A SOCIAL SCIENCE

Geography, as a social science, is primarily concerned with the spatial patterns of man and society on the earth, just as history is concerned with the temporal patterns. Like history, it may, in a sense, be said to have no distinctive subject matter; the philosophy and methods of investigation of a problem make it geographic, rather than the substantive delimitation. Although some American geographers are primarily concerned with the physical world and the locational interrelations among physical elements of the environment from place to place, in the United States, in contrast to many other parts of the world, geographers have in recent decades tended to abandon to other disciplines primary emphasis upon the patterns of spatial interrelations among landforms, soils, climates, and other purely physical phenomena, and have increasingly turned to problems of the human occupancy of regions as their principal concern. Most American geographers are human geographers, rather than physical geographers; they are concerned with man and society on the earth; with the patterns of localization of man, his structures, his societies, and his culture; with the interrelations of these to the physical stage upon which the drama of human relations takes place; with the reciprocal relations of man and the environment, both physical and cultural, tangible and intangible, as those relations exhibit resemblances and differences from place to place. In its primary concern with spatial patterns, geography occupies a distinctive place among the social sciences.

Any phenomena which are non-ubiquitous – which are localized or which vary in intensity from place to place – are amenable to and potentially the subject of geographic investigation. Geographers, like all scientists, are concerned with associations among phenomena, and they seek explanations of the relationships among variables; their special concern is those variables the coincidence of which is spatially associated, whether positively or negatively. A generation or two ago, some geographers were seeking the end of the rainbow of environmental determinism; now virtually all geographers accept the axiom that man is faced with a great variety of choices in the ways in which he utilizes the opportunities offered to him by the environment, and that the choices are influenced by such cultural forces as history, tradition, economic and political systems, as well as by the rather elastic limits of the environment.

Given sufficient incentive, there are few absolute limits to what man can do with, and within, any or all of the environments within which he lives and works.

GEOGRAPHY AND URBAN ENVIRONMENTS

It is reasonable, therefore, that geographers are very interested in urban environments (within which an inceasing proportion of the population carries on its activities) and in the processes by which man and society can modify those environments. Variations in the social environment between and within cities and metropolitan areas, no less than variations in physical settings, are of geographic concern. The processes of adaptation to and modification of those environments – the process of planning – are therefore, of vital concern to the geographer, who is increasingly devoting his talents not only to the study of the roles of planning, but also to active participation in planning, as a professional. A recent survey of the backgrounds of the membership of the American Institute of Planners revealed that nearly 10 per cent of those belonging to that organization are geographers, as well as planners, or have substantial background in the field of geography.

Geographers are concerned with cities and metropolitan areas as elements of the cultural landscape; as nodal regions within which specialized functions are concentrated; as centers of the origin and diffusion of innovations; as environments within which an increasing proportion of the population lives and works. Each of these aspects has been the subject of significant geographic research, both theoretical and applied.

Until recently, a preponderant proportion of geographic research was descriptive, empirical, and *inductive*. From a large mass of studies of individual cities and portions of cities, generalizations concerning urban settlement, growth, form, and functional organization were developed. Lately, and especially within the last decade, much geographic urban research has been *deductive*, involving the development of generalized models of urban morphology and physiology, commonly with the use of sophisticated statistical and mathematical techniques (for a survey of urban geography through the early 1950s, see Mayer, 1954; for most of the rest of the decade, see Mayer and Kohn, 1959). A key feature of more recent work, then, has been the testing of generalized models in application to specific situations (Mayer, 1965; Berry, 1965).

Both the deductive and inductive approaches to geographic understanding of cities and metropolitan areas involve field investigation, including mapping of phenomena and their mutual spatial associations. Census and other statistical sources characteristically do not present data for areal units which are of maximum value for geographic study; the best areal units vary with the immediate purposes and objectives of the study. Geographers, however, have been active in the development of areal units for statistical purposes, as well as in the evolution of processes of regional delimitation. The Geography Division of the U.S. Bureau of the Census, for example, developed the concept of the "Urbanized Area" which has become a standard statistical unit, and the same division had major responsibility for the criteria and delimitation of the Standard Metropolitan Statistical Areas of the United States. A committee in which geographers are playing leading roles is currently engaged in the process of re-examination of the concepts and criteria for delimitation of such nodal regions for tabulation and presentation of a wide variety of statistics.

FUNCTIONAL RELATIONS

A major concern of urban geography is the nature and extent of functional relationships between cities, and between urban nodes and their respective complementary regions or hinterlands. These relationships constitute continua between two scales: (1) the *internal*, in which the focus is upon areal variations in forms, structures, and functions within cities and metropolitan regions; (2) the reciprocal relations between cities and metropolitan regions and their *external* service areas. The former is expressed in the internal arrangement of land uses, facilities, and traffic flows *within* the urban areas, and the latter in flows of people and goods, money and credit *among* cities and *between* cities and their respective regions. Thus, there are two aspects of the urban scene of equal concern to geographers: the *static*, involving fixed locations, and the *dynamic*, involving spatial interaction, or the movement of people, goods, and ideas. Both of these aspects, in turn, may be investigated in the *present*, representing a cross-section in time (chorology), in the *past* (historical geography, or "sequent occupance"), and in the *future*.

The geography of the future may be studied in terms of projection of past trends, including extrapolation of rates of change (projection), and in the framework of prospective results of organized intervention in the processes of urban growth and development (planning), the former furnishing a base line from which to evaluate possible effects of the latter. The geographer and the planner have common interests in such problems as: socioeconomic segregation and integration; effects of areas of jurisdiction and political boundaries upon the evolution of the forms, functions, and internal organization of cities and urban regions; localization of employment opportunities; the effects of changes in transportation technology and routes upon urban growth; spatial differences in the kinds, qualities and availability of housing; relations of urban activities to air and water pollution; and the relations between urban functions and forms and the aesthetic qualities of the environment.

THE ECONOMIC BASE

A major concern of urban geography, as of planning, is the economic support of cities. Cities are almost always multifunctional, but in almost every instance the principal urban functions are economic in nature. The locational patterns of economic activities, and the forces behind these patterns, therefore, have been the subjects of many and varied geographic studies, constituting a major portion of the urban geographic literature.

Since cities are focal or nodal areas, their economic bases depend upon flows to and from their respective service areas or complementary regions. While the economist is primarily interested in the flows of money and credit and their role in the creation and sustaining of employment, the geographer is also interested in such flows, but primarily in the physical flows of people and goods. An important aspect of urban and regional geography is the study of the physical facilities for effectuating such flows, i.e., the transportation routes and terminals. Geographers have traditionally been engaged in investigations of trade flows at the international scale; indeed, the first modern doctoral dissertation in geography in the United States, submitted in 1903, was a study of the patterns of international shipping and the potential influence of the Panama Canal. Studies of ports have engaged the attention of many geographers, (1) partly because the flows through ports, as the gateways of regions, are indicative of the economic bases of the regions and nations which constitute their hinterlands; (2) partly because international trade statistics, including the movements through individual ports, are more readily available in many instances than are comparable statistics on domestic flows; and (3) partly because the port facilities themselves constitute major elements of the geographic patterns of their respective urban areas. Delimitation of port hinterlands furnished precedent for later concepts of the complementary regions served by trade centers and for other central-place functions; this was basic to the development of central-place theory, a major contribution of modern economic geography to understanding of the functions, numbers, sizes, and spacings of cities (see Berry and Pred, 1965).

The Need for Flow Data

Unfortunately, much potentially useful research on flows is inhibited or prevented by lack of adequate data. Because available data are generally more adequate for it than for other forms of movement, water-borne commerce has been subjected to earlier and more intensive geographic research than has other flow phenomena. Even for water traffic, however, data are partly unsatisfactory; while many nations publish information on movements through ports, the landward origins and destinations are rarely available.

For intercity land transportation, freight flow information is generally unsatisfactory; very seldom are data available for geographically meaningful areas. The best we can do on railroad freight traffic data for the United States, for example, is commodity information for entire railroad systems, or for state-to-state movements by commodities based upon the published 1 per cent waybill samples. Neither the railroad system information nor the state-to-state information is of much help to the city or metropolitan planner. Consequently, the volume of research on American railroad traffic flow patterns is relatively small. For air and pipeline movements, much more adequate data are regularly published, and, especially for the former mode, many significant geographic traffic flow studies have been made.

in such widely diverse fields as (1) planning the location and service programs of an urban church organization, (2) recommending job-training programs in the schools which may vary within different communities of the same city, (3) suggesting local variations in the methods to be used in achieving school integration in accordance with various criteria for bounding school districts, and (4) determining the kinds of industries which should be encouraged to utilize internal differences in labor force characteristics within a city.

The urban geographer, perhaps more than those in any other discipline, is always aware of the uniqueness of location, and of the fact that any grouping of locations for descriptive or analytical purposes is very apt to obscure significant differences between and among them. No two cities are alike, and no two areas within a city are alike, yet we must categorize locations, classify them, and group them into regions of similarity and into nodal regions if we are to reach any useful generalizations. Geographers thus approach their problems both inductively and deductively, checking one approach against the other; some prefer to start with empirical observation in the field, others with generalized models to be checked by observation. As in the other social sciences, the empiricists and the theoreticians represent two points on a continuum.

Other Useful Concepts

Among the general concepts of urban growth, structure, and internal differentiation which geographers, borrowing in part from other disciplines, have found to be useful in their applications to planning are: (1) the balance of centrifugal and centripetal forces, stated by Charles C. Colby, after Johann Heinrich von Thünen, Richard M. Hurd, and the sociologists' concepts of "invasion" and "succession"; (2) the density gradient and the stratification of land uses and densities in accordance with their ability to benefit from and hence pay for centrality, after Robert Murray Haig, Ernest W. Burgess, Richard U. Ratcliff, and others; (3) the competition among alternative central places and functions, developed by William J. Reilly, Walter Christaller, Edward L. Ullman, Brian J. L. Berry, and many others; (4) general concepts of location of economic activities along the lines developed by Alfred Weber, August Lösch, Walter Isard, and others in many disciplines; and

(5) the concepts of "natural areas" and "neighborhood units" as propounded by sociologists and planners. Each of these concepts has been tested by many empirical geographic studies, and each has been found to be useful for both descriptive and predictive purposes within more or less limited areas.

CROSS-CULTURAL COMPARISONS

Geographers are acutely aware of the dangers of cross-cultural comparisons and analogies; many of the descriptive generalizations regarding the forms, structures, and internal differentiation patterns within American cities are not completely applicable to non-American, and particularly not to "non-Western" cities (Ginsburg, 1965a). A few examples will suffice. The notion developed by the Chicago School of sociology, that slums and blighted areas are particularly characteristic of zones surrounding the cores of cities, is not generally applicable in Latin America; there the areas adjacent to central business districts have been generally the residential areas for the well-to-do, while the slums have characteristically developed on the slopes and uplands beyond the reach of public utilities. The typical negative exponential curve of density in American cities is true in the cities of Western Europe only in those portions developed since the advent of mechanized transportation; there is a tendency for more uniform densities in the older portions of cities, commonly once contained within walls, developed before the mid-nineteenth century. The "urban sprawl" characteristic of American and many West European metropolitan areas is much better contained in some other parts of the world where the automobile is not ubiquitous.

Many urban geographers specialize in non-American regions, such as some who concentrate their attention on African cities, Central European cities, Far Eastern cities, and so forth. There is a need for increased emphasis upon cross-cultural comparative studies of cities and metropolitan areas, better to determine which characteristics and attributes of cities represent cultural variables and which are relatively independent of cultural differences.

SOME RESEARCH PRIORITIES

What are some of the potentially useful geographic studies of cities, with special reference to American cities and metropolitan areas, that can be made by geographers in the next decade or two which would have utility in city and metropolitan planning?

THE METROPOLITAN AREA

One direction which future geographic urban research might usefully take is toward a reconsideration of the concept of the metropolitan area. Just as the older idea that the city is a closed unit, a discrete functioning entity, is obsolete, so is the idea that the metropolitan area can be considered as a viable unit. In the 1960 Census, two clusters of Standard Metropolitan Statistical Areas were recombined as so-called Standard Consolidated Areas, but these, in turn, constitute only portions of larger megalopolitan agglomerations. With the virtual ubiquity of the automobile and the spread of expressways, especially with the near-completion of the federal interstate highway system, urban areas and rural areas are no longer distinctive and discrete units, and metropolitan areas overlap. This was recognized by Jean Gottmann, who defined and delimited the northeastern "Megalopolis" (Gottmann, 1961). Congress has also recognized it in legislation to develop experiments in high-speed ground transportation in the "Northeast Corridor," but the phenomenon of intermetropolitan coalescence was recognized much earlier by Patrick Geddes, Lewis Mumford, Benton MacKaye, Jerome Pickard, and many others.

Geographers can contribute much-needed research in developing criteria for defining and delimiting urbanized areas of significant application in planning; the federal statistical agencies recognize the need for this and have set up a study committee which may revise the concepts of the metropolitan area (SMSA, or Standard Metropolitan Statistical Area) and the Urbanized Area prior to the next decennial census.

Similarly, metropolitan planning is perhaps the weakest link in the planning chain; lacking metropolitan government in most areas, it is necessary to determine and then to "sell" to the public and to the public officials the idea that many problems transcend arbitrary boundaries, and that metropolitan planning need not depend on metropolitan government where the latter is, at least for a time, politically unfeasible.

Beginnings have been made at the federal level in the "701" planning assistance program to metropolitan areas, in the matching-grant provision for acquisition of open space where unit areas larger than those of individual local governments are encouraged to do comprehensive planning, in the federal activities in air and water pollution reduction, and in the mandatory provisions for joint planning, as a prerequisite for federal aid, of metropolitan land uses and transportation facilities. Determination of the extent and boundaries of such super-urban areas is essentially a geographic problem, and it is one of considerable urgency.

Race Relations

Another set of current problems in which geographic research can make substantial contributions to planning policy is in the field of interracial relations. Although there are relatively few studies by urban geographers of patterns of racial distribution within cities, interest in such studies is increasing, and a few geographers are specializing in it. Much can be done in the investigation of the characteristics of neighborhoods, and even blocks, in the process of changing racial occupancy, with reference to their physical and socioeconomic characteristics, the rate of turnover, and the direction and rate of movement of the racial enclaves.

The directions and rates of assimilation are amenable to useful geographic investigation. School integration, in turn, must be coordinated with neighborhood integration; in large cities where areas of minority racial occupancy are considerably larger than the service areas of individual schools, the latter inevitably have a population composition reflecting that of the total area. Gerrymandering of the school district boundaries to achieve integration constitutes a makeshift and very temporary solution. By describing the direction and rate of racial change, the urban geographer may assist in predicting changes and thus help the planner to achieve policy recommendations that may be workable. Few geographers have been involved in local research relating population composition and change to school service areas, although an increasing number are conducting studies of service areas of churches, hospitals and medical services, and, of course, retail stores and shopping center locations.

Perception of Environment

Another promising field of investigation for urban geographers is in the perception of environment. As mentioned previously, several geographic studies have been made of the problems of perception of environmental hazards, particularly of the catastrophic type, but much more subtle is the problem of perception of the aesthetics of the environment. What constitutes beauty in an urban setting? How much open space and recreational area is really required in cities and neighborhoods with various socioeconomic compositions? In fact, does the neighborhood really exist as a social organization, and, if so, how universally does it transcend social, economic, religious, and ethnic differences as expressed in the spatial distribution of population groups? Are neighborhoods necessary? Since they are forms of spatial organization, these problems should be of geographic concern, yet very few geographers have conducted research in the field of neighborhood organization.

GRAPHICS AND CARTOGRAPHICS: OUR WORLD FROM THE AIR

Major opportunities exist for geographers to contribute to planning in the field of graphic and cartographic representation. Geographers are very much interested in the uses of computers and modern print-out techniques for the production of statistical maps and cartograms; the potentialities are tremendous for utilization of statistics and the portrayal of statistical relationships in the form of large quantities of maps for synoptic study, also with use of automatic methods. In addition, many of the conventional methods of urban land-use mapping fall short of requirements in densely built-up areas of cities where multiple uses are made of individual parcels and individual buildings; new methods of three-dimensional cartographic representation of structures and their uses are required.

Among the most spectacular technological achievements of the past decade, and the most promising for the next, is the development of mapping and remote sensing of the earth's environments from orbiting artificial satellites. Recent achievements in intercontinental communication by satellite, in improvements in planimetric mapping through better position plotting, in more accurate navigation, and in continuous weather mapping by satellite, are well known. All of these achievements are resulting in changes in the geographic patterns of urban activities, and some may change the competitive situations among cities by changing the competitive significance of their locations. For example, the Port of Montreal, formerly closed in winter, is now open the year 'round, in part because the information transmitted from satellites on weather and ice conditions in the lower St. Lawrence have facilitated winter navigation through the ice fields. This has led to consternation on the part of Canadian ports of the Maritime Provinces, who depended upon winter ocean traffic for a major part of their economic base. Similarly, resort activities in Florida and the Caribbean area are safer in autumn because of the greater accuracy with which hurricanes can be traced as the result of satellite photography. Former hazards which were detrimental to the economic base of the region are now substantially reduced.

Mapping programs, in urban areas as elsewhere, can be greatly speeded up and reduced in cost by the use of satellites. "Real time" mapping of many urban phenomena will be possible by use of remote sensing devices, including not only photography, but also chemical and radio sensing. Traffic flows and their diurnal variations can potentially be studied and mapped by continuous use of remote sensing, including time-lapse photographs, chemical sensing and thermal sensing of vehicular emissions, and other methods. The result is that, within a relatively few years, elaborate ground surveys of traffic flows and origin-destination studies may either be unnecessary or can be greatly expedited. Sources of air and water pollution may be instantly detected for entire urban areas, and enforcement of anti-pollution measures made much more effective. Air-photo coverage of entire metropolitan areas can be made as frequently as desired at greatly lowered cost; continuous inventories of structures and land uses will be possible in the not very distant future by remote sensing from orbiting satellites.

The "hardware" produced by modern technology, in short, can produce and process vast amounts of data of potential value to both the geographer and the planner. To utilize these data effectively in the development of policy recommendations, the geographer, like other social scientists, must work in partnership with the planner. He must refine and carry forward a body of general concepts or models of city patterns, structure, and functional organization. This will form a framework within which both inductive and deductive research, methodological, theoretical, and empirical, can proceed, directed toward better understanding of cities and metropolitan areas and urban ways of life. Such understandings are indispensable prerequisites to policy planning.

Political Science and Political Sociology

THE LAST TWO CHAPTERS in Part I are by Norton E. Long, who deals with "Politicial Science and the City," and by Robert R. Alford, who discusses "The Comparative Study of Urban Politics."

Long's chapter is a veritable *tour de force,* ranging broadly over a number of problems — from the prospects for local government reorganization through the question of who "really" governs contemporary metropolitan areas to the dilemmas confronting today's civil rights leadership. In every case, Chapter 9 brings the penetrating insight of one of our most imaginative political scientists to bear on crucial issues. Long is clearly not afraid to raise the embarrassing question, and in a pointed way.

The chapter defies easy summary, but a few highlights may be noted. The matter of community power — or "Who Governs?" — receives extended treatment. Closely related is the dilemma faced by Martin Luther King and his colleagues in the civil rights movement. It is Long's contention that "An ironic effect of the 'community power structure' literature has been to teach civil rights leaders to seek a confrontation with a putative white power structure . . . What the civil rights leaders are asking for and what a general government of wide local jurisdiction would have to face is the politics of role redistribution, or social politics."

The role of the federal government in this area and others is then given Long's sharp scrutiny. "The political logic of a nation," he contends, "leads to a thrust to create a nationally appropriate system of local government." The deficiencies of local government are only too clear to political scientists, but the remedies are not all that obvious. They engender a politics of limited commitment. "Clearly what local government can be asked to perform depends on the loyalties that it can mobilize. Technical expertise, finance, and jurisdiction are not enough." As Long concludes, "For some time to come the job may be such that national leadership and national power will have to fill the vacuum of effective local leadership and local commitment."

Chapter 10 turns to a systematic review by a political sociologist of five major works by political scientists. All five are comparative studies carried out in the United States since World War II. The feature of this chapter that raises it above the level of the ordinary book review is Alford's use of a consistent analytical scheme in his examination of recent research in his field.

He begins by pointing to the "dependent variables" that have been identified:

> *There have been three principal objects of study in the area of comparative urban politics: decisions, policies, and roles of government. A* decision *is a particular act by a local government agency or other authoritative group. A* policy *is a series of decisions of a certain type, any one of which has a certain probability determined by the consistency of the policy, its legality, and support by political and economic forces. A* role of government *is a commitment to certain types of policies, established formally by law or informally by means of the dominance of groups in a community holding certain political values and goals.*

Alford then goes on to identfy the kinds of "independent variables" that have been used in various efforts to explain the consequences or correlates of decisions, policies, and governmental roles. He sees them as falling into one or another of four broad classes of factors: situational, structural, cultural, and environmental. A *situational* factor is one pertaining to the particular sequence of events, together with the balance of political and social forces, bearing upon and determining a particular decision. *Structural* factors include both long-term "situations" and relatively unchanging elements of the society and polity. Examples of the latter are the community's economic base, its social and economic composition, the number and type of organizations present with potentially significant political roles, the legal powers of local and non-local government officials, and the composition of population in terms of such relatively stable characteristics as age and social class. *Cultural* factors are the value commitments of various groups within the community as a whole, expressed through laws and politics. Examples include the preferred ranges of governmental action, the accepted "legitimacy" of the demands of particular groups, and the types of pressures upon government that are locally regarded as proper and appropriate. Finally, *environmental* factors comprise a residual class; they include all those relevant factors that affect the local community's political system despite their operation outside its immediate boundaries.

After elaborating on this analytical scheme, Alford goes on to apply it to the recent work of Robert Presthus, Robert C. Wood, Robert E. Agger, Charles R. Adrian, and Oliver P. Williams, together with their various colleagues. The scheme serves — at one and the same time — as (1) a means of summarizing an enormous amount of detailed information about the various communities under study, and (2) a framework for critical analysis.

Alford concludes that the particular objects of study — the "dependent variables" — tend to be associated with the use of certain "independent variables" or causal factors.

> *Those who have studied particular decisions have usually sought their explanation in situational factors. Policies have usually been explained by structural factors and roles of government by cultural ones. Because of limitations of resources, few studies have systematically taken environmental factors into account.*

Alford's review brings to the forefront certain important possibilities for future comparative studies of urban politics.

— *L.F.S.*

9

Political Science and the City

NORTON E. LONG

☐ POLITICAL SCIENCE HAS been concerned with prescription for the city at least since the time of James Bryce. While the discipline has made some progress in tolerance since the earlier dogmas of reform, it has shown only fitful concern with making explicit the hypotheses underlying its prescriptions and submitting them to empirical test. Despite his optimism, Lawrence J. R. Herson's strictures in his essay on "The Lost World of Municipal Government" seem still applicable (Herson, 1957). To be sure, his swallow, the Banfield-Wilson *City Politics* (1963) has had its Brycean ethos theory subjected to a rather convincing and statistically elegant mauling by Raymond E. Wolfinger and John Osgood Field, and one might hope that this latter effort portends some sustained endeavor (Wolfinger and Field, 1966).

More to the point and less encouraging is the recent pamphlet on *Modernizing Local Government* published by the Committee for Economic Development. There is virtually nothing in the recommendations of this tract that does not fully accord with the conventional wisdom of the municipal texts against which Herson levelled his critique. This might be a matter of little concern to political science were it not for the fact that the CED advisory committee contains many of the discipline's most illustrious students of local government (Committee for Economic Development, 1966).

The prescriptions of political scientists for the city (and indeed for local government generally) are of a piece with classical organization theory. As Charles S. Hyneman has pointed out, that theory was, as applied to administrative reform, an adventure into theology and metaphysics (Hyneman, 1941). As such, it had the benefit of not depending on evidence. Its more candid advocates confessed its primary appeal to be aesthetic. Local government reform in its most recent variants depends on the self-evident virtues of the single executive, the small legislature and the suppositious economies of scale. Functions dictate areas and the areas thus dictated hopefully coincide and produce general governments of technical and political problem-solving competence and motivation. In administrative reorganization we have grown wary of the easy logic of boxes and lines. We have even learned from the unintended experimentation of urban renewal that slum neighborhoods have human structure that may represent social capital. But political science has yet to come to grips with the socioeconomic requisites for an effective self-governing community.

THE POLITICS OF LOCAL GOVERNMENT

There is an easy assumption that all right-thinking men will see the desirability of certain levels of service performance and the consequent necessity of local governments including within their jurisdictions sufficient resources and territory to achieve the indicated performance levels. Police, schools, and planning all become matters of scale sufficient to permit professionalism and the scope for its appropriate realization. Thus, the politics of local government is that of satisfying the public goods requirements of a set of citizen-customers whose demands differ only because of their ignorance and selfishness. A homogenized middle-class culture will ever more pervasively dictate a standard market basket of public goods. The logic of providing these goods efficiently will dictate the least-cost means of their production and distribution as readily as for that of any other business. Indeed Robert C. Wood found in his *1400 Governments* that if you knew median income and density, you had a better predictor of the market basket of public goods than any of the customary political factors provided (Wood, 1961). However, this may represent the special case of homogenization of public demand in the New York metropolitan area. Examples of wide variation in the composition of the public goods market basket still abound and cry out for study, as Aaron Wildavsky has pointed out (Wildavsky, 1964).

What may really lie behind the assumption of a nearly self-evident bundle of municipal services is a mobile middle-class executive culture that demands the same civic amenities as it moves from place to place up the corporate hierarchy. Deficiencies in local government might be remedied if some reputable chain like the Holiday Inn were to take on the achievement of a standardized quality product. This commercial ideal is in a way realized in the mobile mid-career executive suburb presided over by a city manager host with a proper sense for maintaining tax yield through satisfied customers. The service orientation in local government studies has led to a reduction of citizenship to consumership. The citizen-consumer votes with his feet as he transfers his custom from some municipal Gimbel's to some municipal Macy's. In doing so he may feel a certain satisfaction in subjecting the municipal entrepreneurs to the rigors of the laws of supply and demand. Indeed, Ostrum and his colleagues have seen in the citizen-consumer an agent of the invisible hand that has turned the nation's metropolitan areas into a wondrous array of land uses where many tastes may be met (Ostrum, *et al.*, 1961).

The rhetoric of the CED's *Modernizing Local Government* might apply equally well to argument over the comparative merits of the corner grocery and the supermarket. In both cases efficiency is contrasted with what is purported to be an anachronism. Power and competence are taken as self-evident grounds for the euthanasia of the great majority of local governments which are blithely to be consigned to the dust bin of history. Indeed, if they have no more justification for continued existence than the one-room school house with which they are often compared, it is not surprising that the argument carries conviction. But while arguments of scale and competence are persuasive for those who share a common object, they miss the mark when addressed to an audience whose views are widely divergent. Even a poorly supported confessional school may better serve the ends of its sponsors than one meeting all the criteria of the National Education Association that neglects or repudiates its major objective. The concept of service standards becomes a deceptively "value neutral" way of imposing one's own values. How do we distinguish betwen the vested political flotsam of a rural and booster past and institutions that breathe the breath of political life? The corner grocery is obsolete only when its customers so regard it. The country town, the undersized county, and

Robert C. Wood's "republic in miniature" all have their customers and, for them, these units may have values not entered in the CED calculus.

Despite the long history of metropolitan attempts and failures, there seems as yet little concern with the politics of constitution-making. Some inkling of the problems of and conditions for integrating separated political entities has penetrated from international relations. Karl Deutsch's work on communications has been given specific application to metropolitan areas (Deutsch, 1964.) Matthew Holden has treated metropolitan politics as a system of diplomacy (Holden, 1964). In *Metropolitics,* Scott Greer also identifies some of the key individual and institutional actors in metropolitan agitation and the definitions and motivations that provide some understanding of their behavior (Greer, 1963). Case studies by Edward Sofen, Henry J. Schmandt and Daniel R. Grant (among others) have begun to provide an empirical base for a comparative study of the metropolitan process (Sofen, 1963; Schmandt, *et al.,* 1961; Grant, 1955; Grant, 1964). But there still is no careful attempt to piece together the wealth of experience that now is at least partially recorded. In *The Metropolis,* John C. Bollens and Henry J. Schmandt have provided a useful handbook that gives ready reference to a wide range of data and contains some shrewd observations based on much experience (Bollens and Schmandt, 1965). Even this has not yet worked its way into the conventional wisdom.

Like administrative reorganization, local government reorganization seems to assume that the problems confronted are technical, structural, and resource problems. That is, if you have the area requisite to handle the engineering and planning, the money to pay for implementation and a businesslike governmental structure, you have it made. Americans are like their kids. All are capable of playing sandlot baseball, all are socialized to it and ready to do so when the game and the new park in which it is to be played have been defined for them. If only one can somehow get the bigger ballfield created, the players will shape up. There is a good deal of evidence for the existence of a free-floating political technology that stood Americans well in the colonies and the settling of the West. Daniel J. Boorstin, in *The Americans,* has paid tribute to the government of the wagon train, the claim club and the mining camp (Boorstin, 1958). Do-it-yourself government has a long history in the United States and has served a useful purpose. However, the purpose it served was usually highly limited. The Jeffersonian sovereign individual bulked large in governments that resembled conferences of sovereign states with secession an acknowledged right. Anwar Syed, in his interesting little volume on *The Political Theory of American Local Government,* has dealt with the Jeffersonian doctrine and its dialectic with Madisonian, Hamiltonian and latter-day aristocratic and nationalistic concepts (Syed, 1966). It might seem odd that a Jeffersonian confidence in the simplicity of government should be evinced by so patently an aristocratic an institution as the CED. A Burkean piety toward the institutional *status quo* would appear more appropriate. There is almost a Jacobin contempt for the local political inheritance as an "edifice of mud." Perhaps the wholesale reorganization proposals may be defended as Madisonian attempts to enlarge the public views and blunt the force of faction by submerging the ward republics in a metropolitan federalism which in its turn would replicate the success of Philadelphia. But this is to make the matter more sophisticated than the facts would warrant. What is involved is the simple faith that big government will encompass big resources and challenge big men to do big things.

This faith survives in the face of a great deal of contrary evidence. The success story of Toronto is the nearest to justification that exists. Frederick Gardiner is almost an ideal type of the big man doing big things in a big government. Yet the achievements of this Canadian Bob Moses were all of the brick-and-mortar variety. As Frank Smallwood and Dean Albert Rose of the University of Toronto's School of Social Work have pointed out, the miracle of Toronto became ever less miraculous as its metropolitan government turned to social politics and the problems of fiscal redistribution (Smallwood, 1963; Rose, 1965). Agreement can somehow be reached on highways, sewers and water, and many construction problems. Especially, agreement can be reached as long as the consequences of brick-and-mortar government do not seriously affect the social *status quo.* However, when metropolitan politics seriously aspires to social politics, its lack of effective leadership and consent for such basic purposes becomes painfully apparent.

American government has been largely based on placing its fundamental politics out of the reach of its formal politics. This is what Marxists mean by their claim that *bourgeois* democracy is a fraud. Indeed, until experience in the nineteenth century disproved it, it had always been thought that political democracy entailed social democracy. Much anguish was suffered by conservatives in American state conventions who feared that removing the property qualification from the franchise must lead to an agrarian law and the abolition of debt. As Louis Hartz point out, American liberals taking their cue from their European counterparts were continually prophesying social revolution and as continually being proven wrong. Hartz's explanation – taking off from de Tocqueville – that lacking feudalism to instruct our *bourgeoisie* in class consciousness, we lacked the means to instruct a class conscious proletariat, is ingenious if less than completely convincing (Hartz, 1955).

Jefferson's sovereign individual could believe his government weak and to be kept weak because so much of it was hidden from view. Reacting against the overt use of British government for class and individual enrichment, the Jeffersonian put his faith in a formal government restricted to the Lockean remedy for the inconveniences of the state of nature. Identification of the state of nature with *laissez faire* obscured the powerful and essentially political workings of the laws of property, contract, debt, and currency. The two most important institutions for the authoritative allocation of values, the economy and the school, came to be largely outside the scope of the formal institutions of government. This significantly trivialized formal government, all the more so at the local level where the remaining vital functions of foreign relations and war had been removed. How weak the institutions of Jeffersonian government were is illustrated by the near loss of the West through Washington's difficulty in mobilizing a mere 3,000 troops for the national government to check the Indians.

WHO GOVERNS?

Howard M. Brotz and others have wondered how the hierarchies of society, government, and business could for long remain in separate hands (Brotz, 1959). It seemed absurd that first-class political citizens should be second-class economic or social citizens. Politics, wealth, and status should coalesce. Yet, the researches of Robert A. Dahl in New Haven and the studies of others have documented this trifurcation of the bases of power. First the old

Congregational elite is pushed aside by a rising new business class in business, then in politics; then the business class is pushed out of politics by rising ethnics and ultimately the separation of society, business and politics with differentiated elites is attained. The studies of Dahl and many political scientists have been directed toward the examination of the leadership structure of the local community. The title of his book – *Who Governs?* – was in a sense dictated by Floyd Hunter and the late C. Wright Mills who claimed to have found some tightly integrated power structure that calls the shots (Dahl, 1961; Hunter, 1953; Mills, 1956). Dahl's work tends to show that the Hunter "ruling elite" model has none of the universality its author claimed for it. A somewhat bootless debate has gone on between and among political scientists and political sociologists as to the existence of pluralism or monism in the elite structure. What is sorely lacking is any carefully collected empirical evidence as to what difference it makes and to whom that one or another elite structure should obtain.

Pluralist theory seems to take for granted implicitly a premise that underlies much of the writings of the late V. O. Key, Jr. It is assumed that if there is a pluralism of elites, the elites will compete and, in a formal democratic framework of elections, they will be forced to provide significant representation to any numerically important part of the electorate. Revisionist work such as that contained in the volume of Jacob and Vines is calling some of Key's assumptions into question at the state level (Jacob and Vines, 1965). It would be interesting to know what differences and to whom the answer to the question "Who Governs?" makes. At present we are not much further than knowing that what Hunter and perhaps Mills took to be a universal may be only a particular and exceptional case. Nelson W. Polsby's point that the decisions of community decision-makers so far studied have about them an air of inconsequentiality is one that goes ill with the assumed importance of the actors and their actions (Polsby, 1963). Thus, Hunter's Atlanta businessmen strove mightily to create a world trade center in their town and Dahl's mayor-as-folk-hero, Richard C. Lee, persuaded Republican businessmen to abandon their scruples and accept a federal subsidy to remain in New Haven.

Robert E. Agger, Daniel Goldrich and Bert E. Swanson have introduced notions about community leaders' ideology and its importance for local politics (Agger, Goldrich, and Swanson, 1964).

The capacity to define the situation is clearly one of the most important elements of ruling and if Aristotle is right, the ideology of the rulers not only limits and directs their behavior but provides the basis for their legitimacy as well. The existence of competing ideologies may well be an important basis for pluralism resulting in significant electoral competition. A single elite, at least ideologically homogenous, may have a division of labor among it and even cooked into it ethnic and other new elements. The monism that counts may be that of the "definition of the situation" rather than the elite structure. As long as Irish and Italians accept the social and political system, their entrance into the elite structure may mean no more and as much as the rise of the self-made man in business. Their defense of the attained status may be as passionate and their example a celebration of the reality of the claim to an open society.

Peter H. Rossi makes a point of the low status of the politician at the local level as an inhibitor on powerful programmatic action (Rossi, 1960). They just cannot take themselves and are not taken by others sufficiently seriously to do much. The picture presented by Arthur J. Vidich and Joseph Bensman reinforces this (Vidich and Bensman, 1958), and Oliver P. Williams and Charles R. Adrian have a typology of communities in which status of community leaders is an important variable (Williams and Adrian, 1963). Using Aristotelian analysis, it would seem that there are at least three important claims to legitimacy in the American local community: social, business, and votes. It would be worth studying what the consequences are when the bases of legitimacy are combined or separated. One suspects that, in the great days of Chicago when its merchant princes were competing with St. Louis for railways and territory, these bases were in the same hands and that perhaps in Dahl's sense the rate of resource utilization was high. One suspects also that the disaster studies might show that those communities that made the best comeback were able, at least temporarily, to pool their bases of legitimacy in a leadership embracing them all. While the *union sacrée* of the United Fund seems something of a do-gooding ritual, it is the way in which the community routinely achieves unified action for resource mobilization and presumably would for extraordinary resource mobilization.

James S. Coleman's *Community Conflict* is a promising beginning at developing sociological concepts of explanatory power and research interest (Coleman, 1957). As Rossi points out, Coleman's conception of continuous and discontinuous elites and the consequence of this state of affairs for the management of conflict is of great potential value (Rossi, 1960). This is the kind of concept that directs research fruitfully and of which we have all too few. Unfortunately, like many another urban researcher, Coleman has not enlisted for the duration. However, his recent work in education may presage a return to the field.

A further useful hint about elites and the issues they represent as a problem of scale is given in the work of James C. Coke. Coke set himself the interesting question of whether the smaller metropolitan area was beset by the same problems as the larger, and, if so, why the issues were not articulated. His findings showed that the problems of housing blight and central business district decay were all present but failed to emerge in public discussion. His explanation lay in the phenomenon of scale. Until a community reached a certain size, its population of concerned experts, architects, planners, and the like was insufficient to support the specialized voluntary associations needed to agitate a class of issues (Coke, 1962). One suspects that, just as the small town is unlikely to support a brain surgeon or even a heart specialist, a similar lack of specialization occurs elsewhere. It would be interesting to know what is the threshold size for a civil liberties union, a citizens' housing council and other specialized public interest organizations. Of equal interest would be the characteristics of those communities that do and those that do not support these organizations and differentially support various mixes of them. The differing value structures of communities are surely related to the representation of these values in its associational life. At the institutional level, Vidich and Bensman type a few important actors and change agents for the small town in their portrait of the school principal, the extension agent, and other state officials. Some more adequate data on different mixes of voluntary associations and other institutional and individual actors might help to illustrate differences in scale in community definitions and decisions.

One major observable community change related to changes in elite structure is the role of the police in the handling of strikes. In the 1920s and early 1930s, R. R. R. Brooks and other students of labor portrayed an almost universal pattern of shop owner and police action on behalf of employers (Brooks, 1937). Today, in

Gary, an erstwhile citadel of U. S. Steel, a strike would more likely see the police siding with workers rather than employers. This would seem to be a difference that makes a difference. How much of a difference it really makes to employers' earnings is a matter of controversy. Some University of Chicago economists have so small an opinion of union power as compared with market forces that they would deny it any. For the individuals and their status, there would still seem a difference of measurable magnitude. While we have abundant data on strikes, we have little on comparative community response and response over time. This would seem a dimension with which one might measure what difference to whom it makes "Who Governs?"

The question "Who Governs?" has proved in the end rather less interesting than expected. In a sense it has been a blind alley arising from the obsession with when can it be shown that "A" has power over "B" and the understandable desire to refute the social science fiction of C. Wright Mills and Floyd Hunter. In a paper on "The Power of Power," James G. March has paid his respects to its lack of profit (March, 1966). Dahl, by identifying power with cause, has probably given it the only useful meaning it can have. Polsby's point about the inconsequentiality of the community decisions that have been studied leads to questioning the importance of the decisions generally made by the decision-makers (Polsby, 1963). This could lead to looking at the process of governing and its consequences rather than at the consequences of the specific acts of prestigious personages with top roles in the system.

THE MISFORTUNE OF MARX

It is the misfortune of Marx that because he referred to the state as the executive committee of the *bourgeoisie* that he should have been interpreted as asserting that there was in reality an executive committee of the *bourgeoisie* and that it was all-powerful. Quite the contrary. For Marx, the capitalist system was essentially planless and the capitalists as a class were doomed precisely because they could not plan. Marx saw the paradox of a very powerful system capped by highly rewarded but essentially powerless capitalists — conspicuous, wealthy but driven cogs in a social machine they did not control. Because the social system rewards them so well, it is assumed that the capitalists control it. Marx knew better. They even have a horror of controlling it, for this would not only admit responsibility for its functioning but also in so doing assure its transformation. Urban political scientists need to go to school with Marx and learn how a powerful system can operate with largely powerless individuals.

An ironic effect of the "community power structure" literature has been to teach civil rights leaders to seek a confrontation with a putative white power structure. Following the vulgar Marxism of Floyd Hunter and C. Wright Mills, Negro leaders have tried to bring to terms the local executive committee of the *bourgeoisie.* Given the attributions accorded this entity they have no doubt that it could if it would accord them their demands. Thus, Martin Luther King could conclude his marches in Chicago with a so-called "summit meeting" with businessmen, politicians, and clergymen and claim a meaningful open-occupancy pact. However symbolically important the meeting, it would be the grossest delusion to suppose that the assemblage of civic leaders and politicians he met with could, even if they would, accord him open occupancy. It is doubtful if this "white power structure" had any such conviction of its magical efficacy. Even though this power structure is composed of men of wealth hundreds of times as great as that of Negroes and white ethnics, there is no ready way for them to translate their wealth, even if they were willing, into a structure that could produce the massive changes in behavior King's demands require.

What King is asking for is the creation – in reality – of Hunter's and Mills' mythical executive committee of the *bourgeoisie.* King is not alone in asking for a government with power to govern. His desire to hold Mayor Richard Daley responsible for housing in Cicero is the very guts of a meaningful demand for metropolitan government. In this demand for a general government with the power to govern generally, King joins Paul Ylvisaker and the CED. One wonders whether the sponsors of the CED proposals will stay the course when they find that the general government they advocate may attend to more than the removal of middle-class inconveniences such as smog, unsightly streams, traffic jams, lack of open space, and crime in the streets.

What the civil rights leaders are asking for and what a general government of wide local jurisdiction would have to face is the politics of role redistribution, or social politics. In its bluntest form this politics is opening up access to the opportunity structure to Negroes. The stratification system in the United States depends on the charmed circle, housing, education, jobs, matrimony, income, and again housing unless your income is discriminated against. This stratification system is now open to attack through its dependence on the key relationship between housing and education. As the society has become increasingly middle class it has increasingly turned to public goods for a growing part of its consumption. This is most apparent in the case of schools. Given the critical importance of schools to access in the society, their class segregation is critical to the maintenance of the stratification system.

THE ROLE OF THE FEDERAL GOVERNMENT

The society has two conflicting norms – (1) that of equality among citizens and (2) that of differential reward for achievement. These norms did not seriously conflict in a laissez-faire society where consumption was mainly in the private sector and rationed by price. Now that a middle-class society is turning more and more to public goods consumption, it faces the problem of how to give effect to unequal incomes among equal citizens. The answer has been segregation of public goods consumption through suburbanization. Of course, differential neighborhood services are an old story in the central city, but there they have come under increasing attack. The suburb is the Northern way to insure separate and unequal. It has the advantage of being legal. If housing, education, jobs, and matrimony are to remain a charmed circle among formally equal citizens in an era of public goods, there is a powerful logic behind the existing metropolitan fragmentation and the basis for considerable resistance to the creation of really general governments. The logic of general governments gains its force not only from the split personality of a public that is or was pro-civil rights in Washington and segregationist locally, but also from the growing demand for effective action on the physical problems of air and water pollution, transportation and general land-use planning. The solution of physical problems that cut across local political boundaries seems to require a degree of common coordinated action that is extraordinarily difficult to attain in the absence of a general local government to effectuate it. The federal government, after spending billions in shoring up the local *status quo* and having a powerful unintended impact on the nation's urban areas, is increasingly concerned to coordinate that impact in the service of rational, planned goals. Robert H. Connery and Richard H. Leach have shown this dramatically (Connery and Leach, 1960). Indeed, the creation of the Department of Housing and Urban Development was viewed by many as a step toward creating a national ministry of local government that would use its carrot and stick to bring about metropolitan planning that would become in effect metropolitan government. While set back by the stringencies of the Vietnam war, this development may be only delayed.

The federal government never had any qualms about intervening forcefully and intimately in the lives of the nation's farmers, even creating local governments around its extension agents. It has shown a much worse conscience about meddling with the urban resident who is now its major constituent. We are not a decade from debate as to whether power to spend money for the general welfare permitted a welfare state and even if it did, whether this were not un-American. We are only gradually beginning to accept the social-democratic turn of our erstwhile "pure" political democracy. But the turn seems to be decisively taken ever since the passage of the Employment Act of 1948. As the federal government becomes more concerned with its urban constituency, it inevitably becomes concerned with the local counterpart institutions through which it chooses or is constitutionally compelled to act. Having for long acted piecemeal through a variety of state and local unifunctional agencies, the federal government has come to realize the importance of overall local coordination if its resources are to have their desired effect. The political logic of a nation leads to a thrust to create a nationally appropriate system of local government. Such a system, by setting up local governments responsive to the range of problems and the mix of population that are nationally salient, would provide a superior counterpart local government to the present agents of the *status quo*.

The national thrust is probably the most enduring and powerful factor making for change in our system of local government. War and foreign relations apart, our most important politics will be urban, and urban politics will be social politics. It was unexpected that a middle-class society should radically increase its demand for public goods. If this continues (and it seems likely) the political allocation of values may become as important or even more important than the market. A middle-class social democracy is a new animal whose anatomy has received little attention from the political scientist. Milovan Djilas in his book on *The New Class* has suggested some of the less pleasant outlines (Djilas, 1957). As previously pointed out, we are presently achieving unequal consumption of public goods among formally equal citizens by suburban segregation. Given gross inequalities of income, some way to their appropriate recognition has to be found. In the Soviet Union this can be done through special institutional perquisites. We have scarcely begun to think about how we shall organize our public goods, middle-class social democracy. Oddly, the demand on Washington's part for a powerful general local government is motivated by the hope that such a government would both provide a rational regional plan and the muscle to coordinate the presently uncoordinated federal impacts. This delegation downward of the job is partly rationalized by deference to local self-determination, but seems even more to represent federal despair of effective presidential coordination.

THE DEFICIENCIES OF LOCAL GOVERNMENT

Widespread physical problems transcending existing local jurisdictions, together with inadequate resources and the problems of social politics, all point up the deficiencies of existing local government. Meeting these emerging objectives requires what Edward C. Banfield has called a great increase in the "burden" of government (Banfield, 1961). Local governments, if they are to deal effectively with the array of problems that are now proposed to be thrust upon them when reorganized, will have to mobilize fiscal and human resources in an unprecedented fashion. Is there reason to believe that a reorganized local government with extensive territory and simplified and centralized government structure would be capable of the tasks assigned them? We have had an anemic local politics carried on by low-status politicians neither taken seriously nor taking themselves seriously. Such power as they were able to muster through the patronage political machine has been largely dissipated and replaced through a media politics even less capable of serious political work. Our major methods of authoritatively allocating values are the market and the school. Both of these are supposed to be beyond the soiled hand of politics. Now the thrust of the civil rights movement is forcing social politics to the surface and revealing, as in the pathetic "summit meeting" of Chicago, the incompetence of our politics to handle this kind of issue.

The problem of political power is often treated as if it were solved by the adequacy of the territory to the technical problem, the adequacy of the territory's fiscal resources to the technical problem, and the adequacy of the territory's political structure to the technical problem. Planners usually fail to recognize that plans are policies and policies, if they are to be more than art for art's sake, require politics to give them life. All the objects that are salient on our urban front require massive resource mobilization and some of them require massive change in deeply etched human habits. The objectives of urban change require a thorough political analysis of the kinds and amounts of behavioral change their successful attainment would necessitate, and of the political resources that would have to be amassed to bring about the changes. Little enough realistic consideration is given to the political requirements of local government reorganization. The sad history of metropolitan reform is filled with brave efforts of adventurous businessmen armed with the research of political scientists, funded by Ford, and supported by the media, that have failed ingloriously. This history is little studied for its lessons and these remain largely unapplied to the problems of maintaining life in the new organization. The desperate struggle of metropolitan Miami just to remain alive is a warning that one does not live happily ever after and indeed has no assurance of even living.

Herson's complaint about the separation of the political science of local government from the general body of the discipline is still appropriate. We are perhaps not as euphoric over the model charter as the National Municipal League but we are well nigh as innocent of concern for the political requisites of metropolitan reform and the operation of any newly created general government. Our past experience has shown not only the great difficulties in mobilizing reform against the vested interests of the *status quo,* the difficulty of moving from charter drafting to campaign, but the even greater difficulty of mobilizing sustained interest in the job of tackling tough problems with new tools. A lesson from the underdeveloped countries should teach us that gaining independence is one thing, creating and running a new government another. The more important the objects of the new government, the more serious the need to mobilize adequate political power for their attainment. Legal power, even legally taxable resources, are not automatically political power translatable into means of attaining objectives.

The simple recipe, "big territory, big resources, big government, big men, big things" may seem an unfair caricature of current doctrine but it has an all too familiar ring. We need to ask why the big cities of New York, Chicago, and Los Angeles are unable to mobilize big resources, to secure big men, and to do big things. Is it because they lack the blessings of the model charter? Are the resources within their jurisdiction inadequate or exhausted? Is the talent peculiarly short? It would seem that most of the supposed requisites for meeting our major problems are to a large degree present in some of our major cities. Yet these cities are not notable for their solution of the problems about which complaints are made. Perhaps the requisites of the standard formula, if indeed requisites, are necessary but not sufficient conditions for solving our problems. Scale and appropriate government organization and powers may be no more than the entrance ticket to the solutions we seek.

WHAT IS OUR PROBLEM?

If we are frank, we have to admit that the degree of our problem is in the greatest dispute. From Mitchell Gordon's *Sick Cities* (1965) to the cool appraisals of Raymond Vernon and Edward C. Banfield there is a gulf. Even in an area so seemingly objectively observable as housing, Bernard Frieden has shown that conditions for most of us, even in the central city, have dramatically improved (Frieden, 1964). Vernon diagnoses our urban discontents as largely the artifact of the articulate upper-income suburbanite's discontent with his journey to work (Vernon, 1962). The revolution of Negro expectations and the belated discovery of the poor do add another dimension to what might be defined as an essentially middle-class *malaise*. Indeed if most of us are now urban and if we were never before so prosperous, it is difficult to reconcile the municipal doom and gloom with the affluent society. To be sure, an unintended by-product of the affluent society is the production of more and more waste that taxes the limited disposal capacities of air, land, and water. Indeed solid waste disposal has become a major industry and bids fair to stand near the top of municipal costs. Still for the white ethnics, the workers, and the lower-middle class, the postwar years have brought dramatic improvements in their life style. The clamor about the city, except for the occasional ills of traffic and smog, must seem rhetorically overdrawn. Save perhaps for the Goldwater issue of "crime in the streets," they are little touched by the middle-class sense of guilt and perhaps only a little more by the frantic call to save downtown. In the imaginative exercise of depicting the condition of our cities stable dependable measurements would be a help. Raymond A. Bauer's *Social Indicators* might introduce objective comparisons into a wide-open field (Bauer, 1966). However, the political realist must admit that, in the absence of institutionalized sources of programmatic leadership, the American political system is moved by crisis, whether real or imaginary. The production of artificial crisis is in all probability the price we pay for media politics rather than party politics.

But Watts is real enough, in all conscience, and so is a young Chicago hoodlum waving a swastika flag as the symbol of white power. Despite the affluence of the middle class, the white lower-middle class and white workers are ridden by anxiety. They feel insecure in status, housing, and even jobs. In a society blessed with a war-heated economy, with unemployment below 4 per cent, we should be well able to concede the elbow room Negro aspirations require. The wealthy liberals of Winnetka can sign open-occupancy petitions with a noble sense of assurance not shared by the white ethnics who literally fight for their turf. The Winnetkans only danger is that Sammy Davis, Jr. might choose to live there. This is perhaps not too great a price to pay for demonstrating the reality of their convictions. The likelihood of CED proponents of general governments succeeding with white ethnics where Mayor Richard Daley has failed seems slight. For them, housing and jobs and status are still scarce and precarious. Nor has Daley had better success with Negroes who resent his failures, despite his accomplishments. Perhaps the proponents of general governments do not really expect to do more than Toronto. Indeed, they probably define the problems to be solved as technical — above conflict — and as not requiring political solution.

There are those among the Negroes who see the interest in general-purpose governments as a device to dilute or emasculate black power by submerging the central city in the white suburbs. The cynical feel that rather than see the white-owned central business district threatened with a tax squeeze by a Negro-dominated city government, the "white power structure" will induce the suburbs and the state legislature to rescue it from its peril. Some sanguine souls even feel that a Negro mayor, such as Cleveland might have had, could disabuse whites just as John F. Kennedy disabused Protestants of an imaginary danger. The new Massachusetts senator who violates the mores by both being black and having a white wife will give partial test to the theory.

The interest in a general-purpose local government on the part of business leaders might seem merely of a piece with their post-Civil War opposition to a central government of whose control they cannot be sure. They may well be confident that a congeries of Los Angeles would be preferable to what we have now. Certainly without well organized political parties, a Los Angeles can be managed. Beyond the Moses type of public works a Los Angeles is unlikely to do much. Local political parties divorced from the national parties have not proved notably successful. To mobilize the resources necessary to carry through regional land use planning, a regional transport grid, industrial development, and the social politics of education, housing, and welfare is beyond the capacity of a blue-ribbon city council, a city manager, and a professional bureaucracy. The range of objects intended for local action would, if undertaken nationally, amount to a planned economy. Political scientists may subscribe to general-purpose governments because they share Jefferson's and de Tocqueville's estimate of the importance of local governments to a free society and feel that only by forcing local governments to become significant can they be given life. It may be that the political theorists of this change hope to produce their political following after the fact. The federal constitution has lent support to the view that a government once created can grow its own support. Indeed, it may be claimed that the political framework is needed to provide even the opportunity for an appropriate political consciousness.

POLITICS OF LIMITED COMMITMENT

What is worrisome about American local governments is a fact pointed out by Scott Greer: they engender a politics of limited commitment (Greer, 1963). In Jefferson's view the hierarchy of loyalties was town, state, and federal government. Today it is clearly the reverse. The problem of structuring a general local government is that of producing citizens. We think that because we have legal citizens we have citizens with identification and commitment enough to run a government sufficient to handle serious political issues. Instead we have a set of consumers of a localized brand of public goods with some good will ready to transfer their custom when the costs get high or some one offers a better price. Indeed, at times some of our legal citizens resemble a Goth with a vote as a battle axe, readier to loot and despoil than support and sacrifice for the city. What is true of the nation, and but doubtfully true of the states, is clearly more aspiration than reality as it applies to local government. Max Weber said that the city ceased to exist when the citizens ceased to man the walls. The walls our citizens man are those of the nation; elsewhere we have become civic birds of passage with transient and shallow-rooted loyalties. The technical reorganizers of local government need to consider the power of attainable local loyalties to sustain the political tasks they place upon their loyalties. The nation is not the strongest unit of our government because of its taxing power. It has the strongest taxing power because it is the strongest unit. This is the one unit for which people voluntarily die. We have been so bemused by our heritage of federalism that we have not asked what kind of local government with what commitment to it can one have in a nation. Clearly what local government can be asked to perform depends on the loyalties that it can mobilize. Technical expertise, finance, and jurisdiction are not enough.

If we have become a nation, and reversed the Jeffersonian hierarchy of loyalties, what place is there for significant local self-government? Are our real divisions to become so many convenient areas of national administration with perhaps a dash of Philip Selznick's coopted local elite to ease the job? (See Selznick, 1949.) The answer is by no means as clear as one might wish. How far the states will be revitalized by reapportionment remains to be seen. Even a Heller plan, transferring painlessly collected national revenue, might merely weaken state capacity to assume burdens. There may be truth in the maxim that without the moral capacity for self-taxation a people is incapable of self-government. Certainly a leadership that cannot carry tax measures is unlikely to deal with other urgent and unpopular measures.

What seems clearest is a trend in all nation-states to limit the costs of centralization by delegation and to seek escape from centralized paralysis by allowing scope for local spontaneity and creativity. Even in the Soviet Union, concern with local self-direction is manifest. In Yugoslavia the concern has become well-nigh pathological. As we have emerged as an urban nation, we have begun to require an urban government responsive to a mix of problems that is nationally salient, and the mix of values to which the national government is responsive. Restructuring along this line is under way. When it is achieved, a better division of labor may be achieved. In the meantime, it will not be possible to delegate the toughest problems downward. It may be a hell of a way to run a railroad to have to send paratroopers to Little Rock and marshals to Mississippi, but that way the railroad runs as a national majority wishes it run. For some time to come the job may be such that national leadership and national power will have to fill the vacuum of effective local leadership and local commitment.

10

The Comparative Study of Urban Politics

ROBERT R. ALFORD

☐ THE COMPARATIVE STUDIES OF URBAN politics that have been done focus on rather different social and political processes and explain them by selected sets of factors. It is the purpose of this chapter to place certain of these studies within a scheme which will allow assessment of where the field stands and where further work might be fruitful.

Several major books have been chosen for analysis, each with a different focus falling, sometimes uncomfortably, within the scheme. Robert Presthus' *Men at the Top* is a study of power structure and culture as manifested in several decisions made in two small New York communities. Robert Wood's *1400 Governments* is a study of the structural factors affecting policies of revenues and expenditures in local governments of 22 counties within New York, New Jersey, and Connecticut. Oliver Williams' (with others) *Suburban Differences and Metropolitan Policies* is a study of structural and cultural factors affecting policies in 238 Pennsylvania local governments. Oliver Williams and Charles Adrian's *Four Cities* is a study of the cultural factors (commitments to conceptions of the proper role of government) underlying policies in four middle-sized Michigan cities. Robert E. Agger's (with others) *The Rulers and the Ruled* is a study of cultural and situational factors as they change over time in their effect upon decisions. These were chosen because they are major works, representing important aspects of the entire field of study. No attempt will be made here to cite all of the relevant additional books and articles, because the purpose of this chapter is not bibliographic but analytical. The procedure will be to summarize each book briefly and then consider how it treats its object of study and its explanatory frame of reference.

AN ANALYTICAL SCHEME

There have been three principal objects of study in the area of comparative urban politics: decisions, policies and roles of government. A *decision* is a particular act by a local government agency or other authoritative group. A *policy* is a series of decisions of a certain type, any one of which has a certain probability determined by the consistency of the policy, its legality, and support by political and economic forces. A *role of government* is a commitment to certain types of policies, established formally by law or informally by means of the dominance of groups in a community holding certain political values and goals.

Several classes of factors have been used to explain or to show the consequences and correlates of decisions, policies and governmental roles: situational, structural, cultural, and environmental. A *situational* factor is one pertaining to the particular sequence of events and balance of political and social forces bearing upon and determining a particular decision. Incumbent leadership, the strategies used, the motivations of participants, the coincidence of one decision with another, are all situational factors which determine the outcome of a particular decision-making process.

Structural factors include both long-term "situations" and relatively unchanging elements of the society and polity. What this means is that there are important subcategories of structural factors, which we do not have space to analyze here. The economic base of the community, its social and economic composition, the number and type of organizations which exist that play potential political roles, the legal power of governmental officials, the distribution of population in a community by class, age, and other characteristics, the amount of land reserve, are only a few examples of the many possible structural factors which for any given period of time are relatively constant. Clearly they differ considerably in their degree of permanence. Whether a chamber of commerce exists at the time that a decision is made may be regarded as a marginal case; the proportion of college educated persons in the community is far more stable than the existence of a particular organization, although the general density of organizations may be quite stable. Structural factors thus establish the framework within which situations for action arise, although the outcomes of those actions may in turn alter the structure.

Cultural factors are the value commitments of groups within the community as a whole, expressed through laws and policies. Preferred ranges of governmental action, the legitimacy of the demands of various groups, the types of pressures upon government regarded as appropriate, the norms attached to political participation, are examples of cultural factors.

Environmental factors are those which, for convenience, are considered to operate outside the boundaries of the community political system although affecting it. We shall not be able systematically to consider environmental factors in this chapter.

Structural factors may be regarded as those which are at least potentially quantifiable (e.g., size, density, mobility, unemployment, number of organizations) but which have an influence independent of their cultural content. Cultural factors are those which are qualitative in their intrinsic character (e.g., the strength and pervasiveness of norms, the degree of group solidarity) despite the fact that some quantitative indicators might be constructed to measure parts of their meaning.

Structural and cultural factors have consequences for community life which, at any given point in time, produce events that have no connection with the political system. If these events occur regularly, they become processes of various kinds – e.g., crime rates and divorce rates. Depending on situational factors, one or another such process may become important in the strategies and alliances of leadership. The crime rate may become visible after a particularly heinous murder. But the reason for the distinction between events and decisions is to make explicit the fact that there are many processes going on at any time which have no relation to the political system, and yet are potentially "available" to political actors, depending upon strategic considerations. Since the processes are not random, but depend upon structural and cultural features of the community, they must be taken into account in any systematic attempt at comparative political studies.

Also to be emphasized is that a number of processes taking place even within "government," however defined, may not be either a decision or a policy, in the sense that any person or group intends them to happen. Unanticipated consequences of structural and cultural factors, whether internal or external to government or politics, may occur and have great consequences for subsequent decision and policy processes, and yet have no purposeful relation to present decision and policy processes. The effects of increasing the size of a police department, for example, may be to decrease the span of control by central policy makers, and to increase the individual patrolman's area of discretion, without anyone intending it to happen. Such consequences of change impinge on policy in ways which have to be understood in order to explain what actually happens, but would be excluded from a mode of analysis which treats only consciously intended policies and decisions.

Figure 1 presents a graphic picture of this analytical scheme.

Each of the variables shown in the scheme can be regarded as a class of either independent or dependent variables. We cannot here deal with all of the complexities of these relationships, but must deal only with the general categories: the dependent variables of decisions and policies and the independent variables of situational, structural and cultural factors.

The regional, state, and national environment within which decisions are made and with which decision-makers must reckon also has situational, structural, and cultural components, but we cannot include these systematically, partly because no existing study has dealt with them. The economic base of the community is a constant at a given point in time — industrial composition, market position, employment stability and composition. Historically, the economic base of a given local political unit depends upon the environment — a given community will become economically differentiated by the various market and locational forces dealt with in studies of regional economics. How and why given concentrations of economic activities become marked off into political units depends on the relative advantages seen by local leaders at crucial decision-making points, and upon the successes of the strategies used in conflicts between various groups benefiting from or injured by a given political structure and boundaries.

Given a particular economic base, consequences follow for the demographic changes and composition of a city. Clearly the occupational and educational composition of a city, and its income distribution, are influenced by its economic base — the industrial

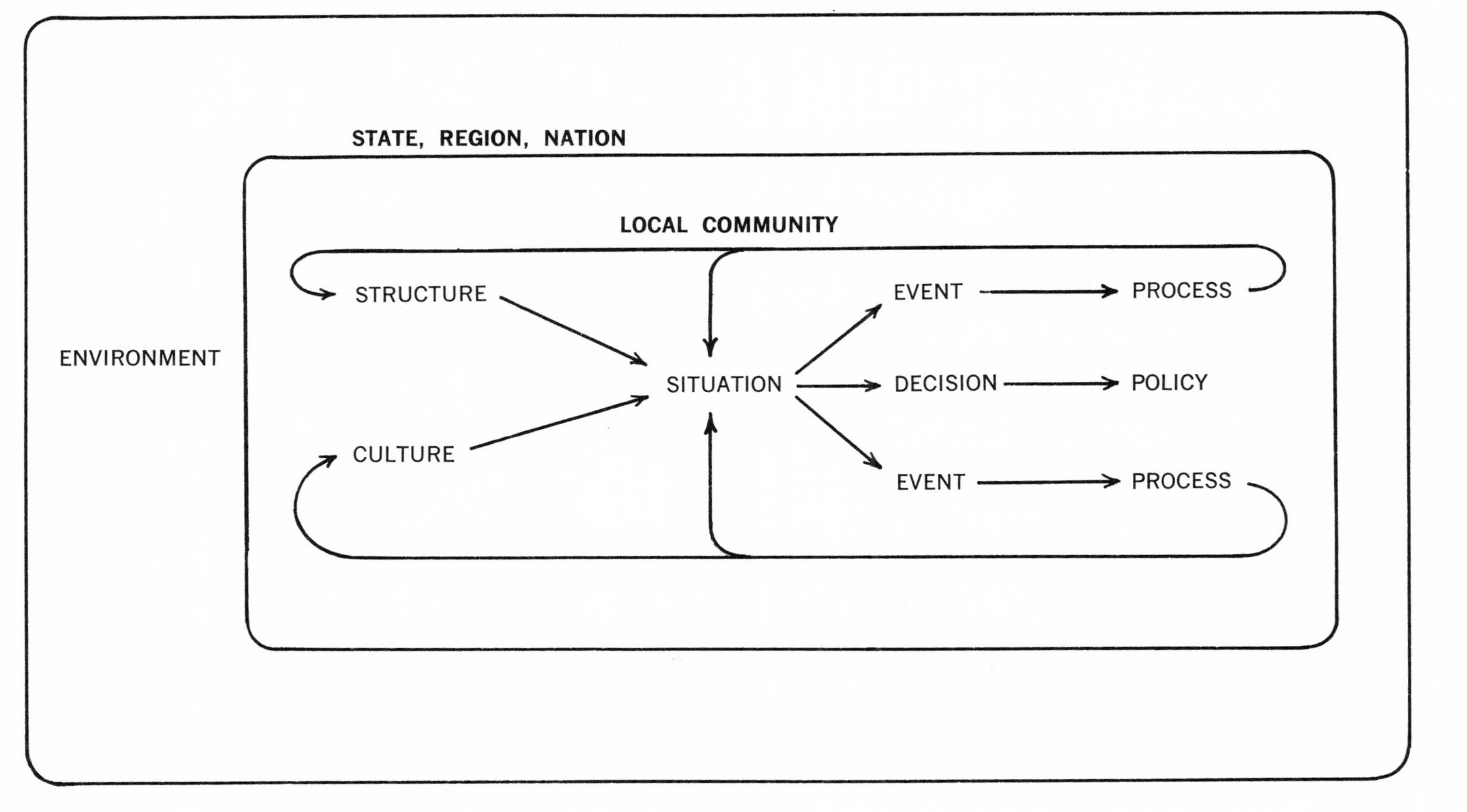
STATE, REGION, NATION
LOCAL COMMUNITY
ENVIRONMENT
STRUCTURE
CULTURE
SITUATION
EVENT
PROCESS
DECISION
POLICY
EVENT
PROCESS

and service "mix" of the city's economy. Given the technological level of development in the nation at a given time, the level of economic growth of its industries is also determined, and therefore its population growth or decline. These factors in turn, by influencing the income structure of the population, will affect the proportion of home owners, population density and distribution (which in particular areas will be influenced by the particular climatic and geographic features of the land).

The previous factors will influence at any given time the political and social structure of the city. Given a certain income and occupational composition, racial and ethnic mixture, and political and economic values, a class structure will develop, as well as organizations expressing the needs and demands of various groups in the community, neighborhood groupings, and other forms of social organization.

The "problems" facing city government at any given point in time will be determined by the history of the city – its past social composition and wealth and how these have been translated into public and private action to serve what are defined as the proper services performed by government and public-spirited private groups. Political structures will have emerged which reflect the balance of forces between groups with conflicting interests and values. The strength of political parties, various forms of governmental organization, electoral systems, and the state of the government bureaucracy will at any given time reflect the past victories of particular groups competing for the allocations of community resources.

Existing concurrently with these social and political structures, providing them with meaning and legitimating them, are the local political cultures of the city. The historical cumulation of community experiences, combined with the values infused from the national political culture, will provide several sets of guiding norms which constrain particular leaders or free them to act. The expectations and demands of various groups in the electorate create a climate of public opinion which at any given time opens or closes paths for political action.

At any particular time, "issues" will arise in a city. Their content and form will depend upon the particular combination of all the other factors affecting the course of political and social development of the city. Which "issues" are seen as the legitimate subject of public action will vary in different historical periods. The line between "private" and "public" action is frequently an obscure one, with private groups contributing to public goals and public agencies contributing to goals of private groups.

The outcomes of particular decision-making struggles over issues will be determined by the pattern of situational factors which exists at the time the decision is made: the incumbents in public office and their political values and skills, the strategic electoral situation, the "pileup" of issues of various kinds and the bargaining that goes on between interested parties for support, the particular national and state political situation at the given time, the resources which are able to be brought into play by activists, the visibility of the issues to the electorate, the resonance of the issues, against opinions of concerned publics, and many other factors which exist in a particular situation. All of these situational factors are conditioned by the underlying factors already summarized above: the local and national political culture, the social and political structure of the community, themselves shaped by the demographic and economic base of the community, and by the social and political environment.

Given a certain pattern of outcomes, "policies" emerge – sets of commitments to certain decisions which are set in motion by a particular outcome. One outcome may increase the chances of another and parallel outcome, other things being equal. Under certain conditions, of course, a particular outcome, if it is the result of a peculiar and unrepeated set of contingencies, may not have any impact upon future outcomes.

Once policies are settled (and clearly the conditions under which policies are reopened are an important problem), political "decisions" in the sense usually meant no longer are necessary, and routine actions may be institutionalized to carry out the policy. Administrative agencies may be created, or executive action may become routine, not requiring any legislative or judicial assent to carry out the policy. Depending upon the content of the policy, there are feedbacks to previous stages of the policy-making process. By removing certain areas of decision-making from the political process, the institutionalization of policies removes many "decisions" from the contingencies and "accidents" of the political situation in existence at any given time. Here the historical fact of the establishment of commitments must be taken into account in evaluating the nature of the political situation at a given time. Many factors which might affect the outcome of a given political struggle over an issue are not operating because the relevant actors, groups, and interests have removed themselves from the political arena by a previous victory or compromise. Thus, the establishing of a particular policy serves to affect future decision-making situations.

Decisions also change the political and economic structure of the city. By definition, a number of aspects of political and economic structure are subject to change, and the essential meaning of an open, democratic system is that a given system of allocation of resources to various groups is never final. It is always at least theoretically possible to reopen established policies embedded in the economic and political structure, even if the political and economic power of particular groups at any particular time makes basic changes difficult.

Established policies can also play an important part in controlling the demographic composition of a city, by zoning industry out or in, by restrictions on residential construction, by racial segregation, or by housing covenants and other controls designed to reinforce or change an existing economic and social composition. Once a given set of policies reflecting the interests of dominant groups is in force, it may be relatively difficult to shift, unless forces beyond the control of the locally dominant groups intervene in the form of state or national legislation, or market and other economic forces against which local leadership is relatively impotent.

The policy preferences of groups in a community are differentially transformed into effective city policies. Some groups with policy preferences are not internally cohesive enough to enable their preferences to become politically potent. If a group does achieve dominance in a community, whether by virtue of its strength, stability, and homogeneity of its preferences, or by default because of the weakness, vacillations, and heterogeneity of other groups, their preferences (and the ideologies attached to them) may become institutionalized to the point where they become part of the political culture of the community. By this is meant that governmental commitments are not easily changed by the accession of other groups to power. If this were not the case, then there would be no point in distinguishing political culture from policy preferences. City politics would merely be the arena of combat of competing interest groups, able to institute their programs at will as the aftermath of victory. There is reason to believe that this is not the case; a given set of goals and procedures established in institutionalized forms persists in spite of changes in incumbents. This is the implication, at any rate, of the conception of "roles of government" that Williams and Adrian present.

The above brief statement of the relations between the wide range of factors affecting urban policy-making is not intended to be an empirical prediction of their relative importance in any given situation. Nor is it intended to be an exhaustive summary of all the possible types of variables which might be included under one or another general class of factors. The assumption which the scheme reflects is that each class of factors has at least analytical, if not in each instance empirical, independence which requires that it be distinguished at a theoretical level. The studies summarized here have necessarily dealt with selected variables. We turn now to the five studies.

THE COMPARATIVE STUDIES

Men at the Top in Two New York Communities

Men at the Top (Presthus, 1964) is a study of two small New York communities, Edgewood and Riverview, with populations of six and ten thousand respectively. Edgewood is more Republican, richer, more homogeneous ethnically, more diversified industrially, and less given to conflict than its neighbor. Five major decisions made in each community in the previous eight years which involved the spending of more than $100,000 and affected most citizens were chosen: passage of a school bond issue (on the second try in Edgewood), attraction of a new industry, building of a new hospital, (in Edgewood) the building of a new municipal building and (in Riverview) public housing. Those individuals who contributed to the positive outcome of each decision were determined by whether or not they and others acknowledged their direct participation. The set of persons constituting the "power structure" was determined by direct participation and also by having a reputation for general influence, even if a given person had not contributed to any of the particular decisions chosen for analysis. Some

35 persons in each community were identified as leaders by these procedures in each community, and their characteristics were contrasted with those of representative samples of adults in each community.

Decisions and Situations

Participation in ten decisions regarded as "'critical incidents' which might provide an operational index of power" of an individual (Presthus, 1964, p. 91) is thus the principal empirical foundation of the study. It will be seen that the consequences of this research decision are vital.

All of the decisions studied were "positive" in the sense that something was decided. Only those persons who contributed to the specific outcome were considered to be "leaders" (i.e., to possess power). The result of this procedure guaranteed finding leaders who favored a particular outcome. That is, Presthus, by asking who participated in bringing about what actually happened, selected persons who favored the actual outcomes. Thus, of the 71 leaders in the two communities, only four opposed any of the decisions, and those four were selected because they opposed the first Edgewood school bond election which failed. (Even they changed their minds in the second election.)

The power structure thus agrees on every decision. But winners in the case of issues which did not become "decisions" are excluded from leadership. For example, a case in which Riverview trade unions exercised a veto and kept out a nonunion industry is not included as a "decision," although it clearly involved money and affected many people (Presthus, 1964, p. 82).

Power is thus defined in this study in terms of situations and decisions in the present, with power structure defined as the set of persons who purposefully contribute to positive decisions.

Policies and Structures

The economic and political structures of these communities – their economic base, private property, form of government – created situations in which it would have been difficult for any set of actors to behave differently from the way which the "logic of the structure" defined for them. A case in point was the ratification by the city council in Edgewood of the sale of city land to a new industry. Given the economic situation and the dominance of private industry, there was nothing else they could do. Presthus argues as a consequence that the city council did not have power in that situation. "When the alternatives to a given decision are so limited, it seems incorrect to accept the action as an indication of power" (Presthus, 1964, p. 105). This point seems to miss the the distinction between policies and structures, on the one hand, and decisions and situations on the other. Probably a more accurate statement would be that in fact the city council had the authority to refuse to sell the land, and supported the sale because of a *policy* of encouraging industry. They *could* have refused to sell, and under a different combination of circumstances (another situation) would indeed have refused. Possible circumstances might include a better offer, a compelling alternative usage, a temporary majority of opponents of industry. But, in fact, a majority of the council probably accepted the policy of encouraging new industry, and therefore the chances were that, in any given instance, they would have approved such a sale. Simply because they did approve does not deprive them of "power," except in the specific sense in which Presthus is using the term: positive contribution to a particular decision-making outcome. Presthus does not explicitly consider the chosen decisions to be particular instances of policies, and this failure to make such a distinction may help account for this view of power.

Presthus does characterize the communities by structural characteristics. Riverview has a lower level of organizational memberships, sharper class and economic cleavages, a more "integrated" leadership in the sense of more overlapping memberships and social contacts, than does Edgewood. All of these may be regarded as structural in the sense that they are likely to be relatively stable and persistent characteristics unless the economic base and thus social composition of the community changes drastically. Riverview thus "approximates the fragmented 'mass society' type of political community" (Presthus, 1964, p. 427). Nevertheless, Presthus says that it is more "elitist" than Riverview, because "two political and three economic leaders tended to monopolize the major decisions" (Presthus, 1964, p. 426). He argues that a fragmented community "encourages elitism" by placing a premium on "more centralized, imperative leadership" (Presthus, 1964, p. 427). This characterization raises certain question about these seemingly structural terms. If only decisions on which everyone agrees are chosen, in what sense is there a test of elitism? Can a greater role for political (elected) leaders be considered to be evidence of elitism? Since Riverview leaders also exhibit a greater preference for "public" rather than "private" decisions and Riverview party organizations are better developed than in Edgewood, the domination of political leaders would seem to be expected. These structural concepts are weakly developed, compared to those concepts which describe the situations in which consensual leadership by the ten decisions was exercised.

Presthus does begin to make the distinction between situation and structure in the concepts of potential and actual power. Potential power derives from an organizational base, and provides a "situational framework that conditions greatly the exercise of overt power" (Presthus, 1964, p. 61). The reputation of a person and his organizational memberships are used as a rough measure of his potential power, and his participation in particular decisions as the measure of his actual power, but the focus upon contributions to specific decisions by specific individuals as the defining character of "power structure" prevents the author from following up this line of investigation.

Roles of Governments and Cultures

The value commitments of groups and of the community as a whole are investigated by means of survey data on leaders and voters, with the qualitative characterization of Edgewood as more "conservative," less "active," more "consensual," interpreting and guiding the analysis. Presthus finds, for example, that Republicans in "Democratic" Riverview are more like the Democrats in Riverview than they are like the Republicans in Edgewood, and attributes this to the "accommodation" of members of each community to "dominant local political values" (Presthus, 1964, p. 320) through the mechanism of "social support" of majority values. Leader-voter differences were also found to be smaller in Edgewood than in Riverview, and this was considered to be evidence of higher "consensual validation" in Edgewood (Presthus, 1964, p. 330). And, in all class strata, political participation was higher in Edgewood (Presthus, 1964, p. 367).

The difference between a study of decisions and policies is well illustrated by another portion of the study, by Vaughn Blankenship. The effectiveness of hospital organization in the two communities was related to their power structures. He found that the more integrated the hospital leadership was into the informal organizations of the economic and political elites, the more support it received from the community. The Edgewood hospital was far less "politicized" than the Riverview hospital, which suffered accordingly from being caught in crossfires of party and class because it was far more dependent on public support. As the author puts it, Edgewood's "power structure functions effectively because it is well integrated, is able to evoke the value of 'civic responsibility,' and is composed of political and economic leaders who share many values and class qualities" (Presthus, 1964, p. 403). No specific decision was analyzed in either hospital, but rather a general policy differentiation was noted: greater versus lesser financial support and greater versus lesser willingness by residents to be hospitalized. Note that either of these measures can be regarded as sets of "decisions," by a potential financial contributor to give, or by a potential patient to allow himself to be hospitalized. The "policy" amounts to a statement of a probability that certain *rates* of these decisions will in fact be made, and the differences between communities in these rates is a measure of institutional "effectiveness" in this particular sphere. Then to relate institutional effectiveness to the level of consensual integration of the political and economic leadership is a good illustration of a study of the influence of structure upon policy.

1400 GOVERNMENTS IN THE NEW YORK METROPOLITAN REGION

This study (Wood, 1964) of the 1,467 political entities in the 22 counties of the New York metropolitan region, in three states, New York, New Jersey and Connecticut, focuses upon revenues and expenditures as related to such structural features of the community as size, industrialization, housing density, age of population, low income prevalence, residential affluence, and the proportion of residential land which is undeveloped (land reserve). The author is not concerned with the situational factors which caused any particular community to spend a given sum of money and thus he is not interested in the patterns of leadership which may be seen in a sequence of decision-making events. In effect, he assumes that if regular associations are found between the social and economic "environment" around the local political system, there will be common patterns of response regardless of the motivations and skills of leaders in any particular community. This point does not mean, of course, that the existence of effective leadership resources may not be itself correlated with structural factors.

The quantitative part of the study deals with the operating expenditures of 64 middle-sized municipalities in five New Jersey counties (all places between 10,000 and 85,000 population in Hudson, Essex, Union, Bergen, and Passaic counties). Some 20 characteristics of the communities are included in a factor analysis in an attempt to see whether a smaller number of characteristics account for variations in expenditures. Seven factors were found: size (accounting for 83 per cent of the variance), industrialization, housing density, age of the population, the prevalence of low income persons, residential affluence, and the amount of land reserve. The first four were regarded as the main factors, with the last two measuring the needs of the population for services (Wood, 1964, pp. 39-40). Size was found to be related to a "critical threshold." Below about 10,000 population, "differences in expenditure levels appear primarily a function of the availability of revenue rather than of needs and pressures." Larger size produces a "different level of expectations and capacities, and a different political process for registering public needs" (Wood, 1964, pp. 59-60). Wood emphasizes that many different forces affect spending, so that "types" of public sectors are not easily defined. "Communities may spend because they have to for reasons of population pressures; they may spend because, being large, they acquire a special bundle of public services, or being new they require heavy capital investment" (Wood, 1964, p. 64).

But even given these pressures upon the public sector created by size, industrialization and various kinds of needs, communities do not respond in the same way. Local communities can adopt different "strategies of adjustment," by manipulating tax assessments, searching for new types of local revenues, persuading their state government to change the legal limits on rates and borrowing, and creating special districts with taxing powers (Wood, 1964, pp. 74-79). Growth can be guided and controlled by zoning industry either out or in, and thus determining by political means one of the basic forces affecting expenditures.

The New York and New Jersey communities and states have adopted quite different policies regarding expenditures, taxation, and cooperative efforts. New Jersey communities spend less and both state and communities have refused to adopt new types of taxation.

Wood's principal conclusion is that municipal strategies have had little effect on the "mainstream of economic development" (Wood, 1964, p. 120) because the major economic and population forces at work shaping an area depend upon actions in the private, not the public sector. While a particular community may take actions which influence its future, from the point of view of the region, the private sector *as a whole* (as distinct from particular firms or households) is not greatly affected. An industry barred from one locality can find a reception in another. High income families can take refuge in Westchester, while mass developers can build in Nassau. "With so many different constituencies, many options are open for firms and households alike" (Wood, 1964, p. 122).

Policies and Structures

Wood finds a regular association between such structural factors as size, level of industrialization, and the age of the population, and the level of operating expenditures of a community. Once the critical decision has been made to zone out industry, or to attempt to attract new industry, or to hold population down, or to attempt to maximize growth (and these depend to a large extent upon situational factors), a community will find itself committed to certain levels of expenditures almost without regard for the ideologies and preferences of leadership.

Wood presents one basic distinction between the structure of a political economy and the private economy which seems to me untenable. He holds with Harold Lasswell that the focus of analysis shifts from "transactions" to "decisions" when one shifts from the private to the public sector. In a political economy, the basic unit of decision is not the individual producer or consumer, but the group. Resources are not allocated to the public sector by thousands of individual choices, but by a few persons speaking for voters in the name of the public interest and the general will. Voting and opinion are "rarely interpreted as an aggregation of individual attitudes," but rather in terms of ethnic, neighborhood, income and occupational groups. Institutions such as banks and labor are significant as entities in themselves. Thus, the "aspirations of groups and leaders of groups, more than the opinions of the members," are the "critical element" (Wood, 1964, p. 21). He is thus attempting to establish a difference on the basis of (1) the market, individual choices, and preferences dominating the private economy; and (2) group decisions and institutions dominating the political economy.

It seems to me that both sectors may be usefully described from both vantage points, and that the "structure" of these public versus private subsystems is not any more adequately characterized by one set of attributes than by the other. On the one hand, consumer preferences can be and are analyzed in terms of ethnic blocs, occupation, and racial types, in exactly the same way that political preferences are. On the other hand, economic decisions are no more made by thousands of consumer choices than are political decisions made by thousands of voting choices. Groups and leadership – corporate, labor, governmental – are just as "critical elements" in the determination of economic decisions as they are in the determination of political decisions.

To reverse the point, fashion and product identification operate in both economic and political spheres. On the one hand, individual economic choices do recognize the preferences of others, through the mechanisms of fashion and product identification. On the other hand, voting and opinion do exercise control over political decisions in much the same way that consumer choices do: via indirect influence over the calculations of decision-makers and in critical elections (sales) which determine the success or failure of a particular candidate (product).

Wood goes on to point out that the political economy differs from the private in that resources are obtained through budgeting, not the price mechanism, and that the products of government are "public," in the sense that they are theoretically indivisible among persons, and frequently so in practice. Whether these distinctions are any more valid cannot be discussed here, but our point is merely to show that Wood is attempting to delineate major structural features of *political* systems as a fundamental type of decision-making process which have characteristic consequences. He then goes on to show that what we have termed structural features of the population, area, and organization of the community determine to a considerable degree the gross level of public activity by local governments.

Wood is by no means unaware of the distinction between structural and situational factors. Discussing the seeming irrationality of squabbles between local governments in the New York metropolitan region, he says: "Environmental circumstances combined with an established revenue system make particular strategies and particular controversies almost certain" (Wood, 1964, p. 70). The link is clear between the structural features of social and political organization in a given period of time and the probabilities of certain situations existing which create a likelihood of certain types of issues. Wood deals in detail only with the specific actions of particular regional organizations such as the New York Port Authority, and I will not deal further with this aspect of his study.

Roles of Governments and Cultures

Although variations in political cultures of local communities are not a major focus of the book, Wood refers to this factor frequently enough to warrant some reference to his treatment.

Wood deals with three aspects of political culture: (1) the variations between communities attributable to the historical development of certain ways of doing things; (2) the pressures upon all political institutions to adopt procedures and goals which are consistent with a market economy; and (3) the ways in which local communities are influenced by their existence within a state with a particular political culture.

Dealing with the responses of local governments to the various pressures created by changing size, industrialization, and population needs, he notes that "the alternative first adopted [of the expenditure and tax levels] tends to become a governmental tradition, a political style, and even may crystallize into law" (Wood, 1964, p. 72). This point illustrates the relationship between the situational factors which led to a decision to choose a particular industry, and population composition, and the structural and cultural consequences of that decision. A course of alternative actions is made more probable or improbable, politically difficult or easy, depending on which decisions have been made in the past. Wood does not attempt to deal with any of these critical decisions in detail, because his is not a book on the path of development taken by any particular community. Historical and comparative analysis of the critical decisions which constrain future actors in a community to more limited paths of action remains an unexplored area of comparative urban politics.

The ways in which the market economy influence political decision-making are well illustrated by Wood's treatment of the regional authorities in water, transportation, and housing. As a result of his analysis, he concludes that "... the public programs expanding most rapidly in the Region are those that exhibit an operating philosophy most closely akin to a market economy." Those agencies, that is, that define needs according to individual consumers, that depend on user charges, and that try to satisfy purchasers, such as the Federal Housing Administration, highway agencies, and veterans' organizations, are the most rapidly growing and successful. They proceed on the basis of the "same philosophy of supply and demand that governs the behavior of private firms" (Wood, 1964, p. 188). Urban renewal agencies, by contrast, operate more on a "corporate concept of community, and represent a notion of public interest which is not the same as an aggregation of individual wants" *(Ibid.)*.

As Wood says, this difference is not surprising, for the "ideological environment of the Region's governments remains that of the market economy and limited government activity." Even the Regional agencies are "committed to the principle that changes in the private sector are generally for the best," and thus support the "present lines of development" *(Ibid.)*.

Again, without making this a major focus of his analysis, Wood is pointing to an important aspect of urban politics which would have to be analyzed systematically in a broader context of international comparisons. For his purpose, analysis of several metropolitan counties in the United States, this element of American political culture is a constant — a feature of the context of environment of every local community. As he puts it, "... few inhabitants of the Region, or of the nation for that matter, have ever looked to their local governments to 'optimize' or 'maximize' anything. On the contrary, people have regarded these units as necessary but not especially admirable service units, to provide programs which did not seem supportable through private enterprise" (Wood, 1964, p. 216). To put the point another way, a general aspect of American political culture is probably a commitment to individual, or at the most voluntary associational, action, rather than governmental action. The satisfaction of individual preferences and minimum public action are the norm, frequently challenged and inconsistently defended, but still the norm.

The third aspect of political culture with which Wood deals is the way in which a state creates an environment within which local communities act. He summarizes New Jersey's policies as follows:

> [Its] tax pattern reflects a reliance upon local units of government to carry out major service activities. Its state grant-in-aid programs down to the present time have been relatively modest; it has shown a disinclination to experiment with new local governmental structures; and it has sanctioned public salaries and public services at considerably lower levels than in the neighboring states (Wood, 1964, p. 28).

Wood does not attempt to explain why New Jersey is different from New York, and it is possible, of course, to find structural factors which will explain this set of policy commitments, which, in the terms we have already laid out, we would term the state political culture (i.e., a probability that certain sets of policies will exist in the future). But the fact about New Jersey municipalities which raises the whole problem of the influence of the state political culture upon their actions is that "many of the same policies have been independently adopted by the majority of the local units" (Wood, 1964, p. 114). The state does not legally constrain their actions, and in fact, Wood emphasizes the diversity of planning and zoning policies in New Jersey communities, at the same time that they share a "conservative" attitude toward spending. With respect to water policy, he points to the high degree of concern for local autonomy in New Jersey, which has made cooperation between water-using and water-supplying jurisdictions difficult (Wood, 1964, pp. 160-161). The historic pattern of each municipality "going it alone" has meant that no single water system, not even Newark's, has developed its resources enough to be able to share its water with any other (Wood, 1964, p. 167). Again, the reasons why this pattern developed are not the subjects of Wood's study, but the differences between states, which apparently exist between communities with the same size, level of industrialization, population composition – and therefore leadership resources and needs – point to the independent influence, of structural and cultural factors in the environment in urban decision-making which have not been systematically analyzed in comparative studies of urban politics.

Wood notes that different areas of the Region have developed different political styles, despite similarities of social composition: "... [M]unicipalities apparently inhabited by the same type of people, in roughly the same stage of development, have acquired individual public sectors all their own" (Wood, 1964, p. 30). Westchester County is professionalized, Hudson County has had an old-style machine system, now atrophying, Bergen has court house cliques, and these patterns cannot be explained by the attitudes of the population, which might well favor exactly the same type of government and public policies, nor by the structural factors of size, level of industrialization, or objective "needs" of the population as determined by their ages and levels of affluence. A series of critical decisions in the past produced dominance of leaders, with certain political styles, habits, and perspective, and thus established a dominant set of procedures and goals, which became the local political culture. Why Westchester has been able to keep its upper-middle-class character by restricting growth and commercial development, and why Nassau has not guided its growth like Westchester, but has adapted its "governmental structure to the new environment" rather than attempting to "shape the character of the environment itself" (Wood, 1964, p. 105) is not explained by Wood's study, but would have to be the subject of a much more detailed study of the particular community's history and would have to take into account the situational factors neglected by Wood.

Four Cities in Michigan

This study (Williams and Adrian, 1963) attempts to distinguish four "roles of government" as manifested in a variety of policies carried out by four middle-sized Michigan cities. A wide range of data are used, and the cities compared with respect to the importance which each role seems to play in each one.

The complexity of the patterns found by Williams and Adrian in their study of many diverse policies in the four cities makes it difficult quickly to summarize their conclusions. They divided various city policies into four "roles of government" (economic growth, amenities, arbitration, and traditional services) and then ranked the four cities along the four continua from high to low. Alpha and Delta were most clearly distinguished from each other with Beta and Gamma somewhere in the middle, partly because, from the nature of their "arbiter" government, they did not exhibit any clear commitment to any set of governmental policies. Because of this lack of consistency as a total system, some of the "sub-systems" in Beta and Gamma functioned like those in Alpha, being highly professionalized and committed to governmental initiative in improving city services and adding new ones, and some like those in Delta, far less professionalized and committed merely to maintaining the traditional level of city services.

During the period of their study (1948-1957), Alpha was dominated by (in contrasted to the other three cities) a stratum of professionals and well-off businessmen who were concerned with such amenities as recreation, planning, and physical attractiveness. Delta was controlled by a lower-middle-class union of city employees who enforced policies of caretaker government, emphasizing traditional services and rejecting innovations of all kinds, including professionalization of local government. The other two cities, Beta and Gamma had no definite group controlling local politics. As a consequence of a lack of dominance in Beta and Gamma of a distinctive social stratum with any set of views on the proper goals and procedures to be used by local government, both Beta and Gamma were the scenes of continuous conflicts over policies and procedures, and the city council acted mainly as arbiters of these competing claims.

In the terms we are using in this chapter, Williams and Adrian are characterizing their cities according to the dominance of a certain political subculture comprising a set of ideologies about the proper role of government, its goals and procedures, as manifested in patterns of behavior in various groups and institutions comprising local government. The four roles which they distinguish do not have the same status, since "arbitration is not, strictly speaking, a policy in the same sense as promoting economic growth, providing and securing life's amenities, or maintaining traditional services."

However, where fully developed and established as a "norm for policy determination," this mode of conducting city affairs may actually become a subculture in its own right among city leaders (p. 32). This viewpoint, when it is not merely a description of conflict between other ideologies, but becomes a set of norms in its own right, corresponds to the classic liberal democratic view of political affairs which seeks to keep government to the role of a neutral arbiter between competing interests.

Growth also may not have quite the same character as do amenities and the caretaking roles of local governments. Policies of growth are a "normal" part of almost every city's concerns, as measured, at least, by the indexes that they use: Industrial recruitment, concern for the economic health of the central business district, and a desire to annex suitable adjacent areas. Where business interests have their "normal" voice in city affairs, then such goals should be a continuous part of every city's activities. And, in fact, three of these four cities, despite their considerable differences in other goals and predominant ideologies, stress economic growth as a key role of government.

The dominance of certain political styles or cultures does not determine the outcomes of political processes. Because these are structurally similar cities (all have city managers, all are within the same state political context, all have some industry, etc.), there are general pressures for similar types of action and similar levels of services, within certain limits. That the councils in the "arbiter" cities (Beta and Gamma) were not active agents making policy means that professionals took over many decisions. (See pp. 293-297 for examples of this process.) Also, even though a certain decision was ultimately made, whether a city procrastinated or not, or whether the decision was made with much sound and fury and public debate, or quietly by administrators was an indication of its political style.

Thus, what finally is achieved — the policies in existence at any given time — is not an adequate measure of the community's political culture, but rather what is desired by various groups, what is worked for, how political struggles are conducted. Who finally does something, and what is done is an outcome of the interaction of culture, the sociopolitical structure, and situational factors of strategy, and the involvement of particular groups and individuals in particular issues.

Williams and Adrian explain some of the differences between the four cities entirely in structural terms. Thus, Delta has a ward system, while the other three cities have at-large elections for council. This, they assert, partially explains the greater role of labor unions in Delta. But where the communities have a common structure – e.g., a city manager – they explain the different functioning of the structure by the political culture, or the role of government which is accepted by dominant groups. For example, Delta had a weak commitment to the professionalization of city services. The city manager, the recreation worker, the traffic engineer, the police specialist, found their work interfered with and their recommendations ignored (pp. 223, 307). Delta voters were also "most steadfastly opposed to changes in local government costing more money" (p. 233), despite their being subjected to the lowest overall per capita tax rate of any of the four cities. This was consistent with the general attitudes of the city council. In Delta the realtors did not have to oppose tax increases, unlike Beta, because the "Delta council itself was guided by values that might be considered congenial to caretaker standards" (p. 250).

The authors suggest that "differences in consumer preferences of economic classes" account for the sharp differences in preferences for amenities in the cities. The upper-middle class allied with professionals dominated the goals of city government in Alpha, laboring groups in Delta. Gamma was more like Alpha, and these two were the only communities in which "the wealthy assumed a considerable role in the city's political life" (p. 225).

In Beta and Gamma, labelled "arbiter" government, "it was rare that either individual councilmen or the council collectively was identified with any policy or set of policies over a span of time" (p. 292). Accompanying this was considerable "unpredictability in policy decisions" and considerable vacillation (p. 293). The professional administrators, especially the manager, the plan director and the chief engineer, in certain respects "filled the vacuum" left by the council's lack of policy direction and vacillation (p. 297). Also, negotiations between contending parties (businessmen and administrators, frequently) over urban renewal and other matters (sewers, franchises) often completely bypassed the city council. The legislative body much less frequently initiated decisions in these two cities. The role of the manager was thus a difficult one in the arbiter cities. Because he did not have policy consensus behind him, and because of the weakness of the council (two related factors), he was sometimes "accused of seeking to 'control' the mayor or council" (p. 306). In spite of this, in both cities he was a "key leadership figure and a policy innovator," contrary to the classic manager ideal (p. 308).

Indicators of a concern with *amenities* as a key role of government were the quality of personnel in city government and the level of salaries. Alpha ranked highest, Delta lowest. Planning and consumer services were also considered measures of amenities. Alpha and Gamma had superior planning "programs and achievements" to Beta and Delta, according to specialists consulted (p. 205). Delta never had a professional planning department and the planning commission was made up of persons with low prestige in the community. Alpha also ranked first in most consumer services (police, traffic, fire, sewage, water, streets, recreation), and Delta last, except for its fire department and street maintenance.

By selecting four cities similar in a number of structural characteristics – size, metropolitan status, in the same state, all essentially manufacturing cities, with similar governmental structures – the authors hoped to have selected four cases of a "particular type of city" (p. 42). Nevertheless, the political styles of the communities differed, and became the major focus of the book. Precisely because the communities were chosen to be alike in ways affecting the scope of governmental activity, the presence of groups likely to be active and to hold certain sets of preferences, these differing styles or political cultures are difficult to explain in terms of the dominance which particular groups have managed to achieve historically, or by particular features of the social and political organization of the communities. I refer to trade unions, business, voluntary associations, downtown merchants, and the like, which cannot be directly related to the economic base of the community or its gross political structure. The problem of the framework for comparative analysis of urban politics is acutely visible in this study of four cities, because it is difficult to know how much importance to attach to any given difference between the cities. How much different is Alpha from Delta, in a wider context of comparison of Northern and Southern cities, industrial and nonindustrial cities, small and large cities, partisan and nonpartisan cities? Even if we accept, and there is no reason from internal evidence in the book to reject it, the differences in political styles or local cultures of these communities as real, we have little evidence which would allow us to place the cities on a larger scale of comparison to see whether the differences remain of an order which would allow us to say that they are examples of diverse types of urban politics, or only minor variants of a single type.

Suburban Differences and Metropolitan Policies

This study (Williams *et al.*, 1965) combines several of the perspectives distinguished in this chapter. Communities are characterized by their demographic composition, level of urbanization (density), and functional specialization. Differences between types of communities in their revenues and expenditures are examined. Value commitments are inferred from expenditure policies in conjunction with the social rank of the community, assumed to reflect preferences of majorities in the community. Case studies of particular decisions are chosen to illustrate the operation of situational factors intervening between the needs and resource base of a community and its policy outcomes.

The five-county sector of Southeast Pennsylvania around Philadelphia contains three and one half million people, two million of whom are in Philadelphia. There are 238 local governments. The authors studied 90 "suburbs" (contiguous municipalities around Philadelphia with a density of more than 500 per square mile), 41 "towns" (farm commercial service centers and a few industrial complexes), and 94 "townships," rural areas with low density. Suburbs, in line with the hypotheses that "areal specialization and differentiation is characteristic of urban areas" (p. 42), exhibited greater differentiation with respect to the average age of population, social rank (occupational and educational levels of the population), and property use, than the other two types of communities. Specialization with respect to social rank and age increased for the 90 suburbs between 1950 and 1960, but differences in their tax resources and wealth decreased (p. 69). The authors suggest that although differences in wealth are decreasing, social-rank factors may serve to maintain municipal differences in values as exhibited by expenditure and revenue policies (p. 71).

The overall volume of services, municipal and school revenues and expenditures, tax effort, and residential zoning, were the policies of local communities examined. The major hypothesis was that "levels of expenditures and their distributions among alternative functions of government represent policy choices reflective of community values and that these values are structured by, and correlate with, certain measurable social, economic and political attributes of a community" (Williams *et al.*, 1965, p. 77). The authors hasten to add that they do not imply that "all decisions reflect a conscious assignment of values to alternative courses of action," because the needs and resources of a community differ and have effects independent of values. Policies are thus affected by *needs* (determined by the composition of population, the space available, the size and distribution of service-demanding population), *resources* (mainly wealth), and *preferences* (how citizens wish to live). These choices generally reflect "values associated with differing life-styles" (p. 78). The study assumes that social rank and age are indicators of the values of different life-styles which will produce different sets of preferences for local government policies, and therefore influence revenue and expenditure patterns. In the terms being used here, the authors are assuming that certain demographic and social characteristics (occupation, property ownership, age) define categories of persons likely to have certain policy preferences, and that a community with a certain proportion of such persons will exhibit corresponding governmental policies. Again, they are neglecting in their statistical studies the situational factors which lead to a decision on revenues or expenditures in any particular community.

The population size of a community was found to be the characteristic most closely related to total operating expenditures. Among the suburbs, four distinct patterns were found, and four sub-types of suburbs were then distinguished, labelled Industrial and Commercial Centers, Residential High-density Suburbs, Residential- Low-density Suburbs, and Enclaves (pp. 102-103). The main findings were summarized as follows:

> . . . Industrial and Commercial Centers spend for activities that serve the needs generated by their specialized economic role in the metropolitan area. Residential Suburbs differ in expenditures according to their development pattern. Low-density Residential Suburbs have little need for most services, but do evidence concern for planning. More densely populated Residential Suburbs, regardless of their wealth or status, respond to congestion by developing more services.

> Wealth and status generate higher service demands, reflecting preferences for more and better amenities. Where young adults predominate, there is a general emphasis on low expenditures . . . (Williams *et al.*, 1965, pp. 120-124).

Although wealth and social rank (occupation and education) were themselves correlated, the two factors had different associations with expenditures. "Library expenditures were related to social rank, but not to wealth. On the other hand, municipalities with higher home values were clearly more concerned with planning and land-use controls, while no significant relationship was found between this expenditure and social rank" (p. 135).

With regard to school revenues, the most important factors associated with higher revenue were found to be the per cent of the total population in school, the market value of property per capita, and social rank. The first two factors form the basis for the state aid formula, which equalizes support for the schools up to a minimum level. But "at any level of resources and needs, higher revenues per pupil are associated with higher social rank" (p. 151). State action thus reduces the influence of "disparities in resource-need ratios," and enables the "preferences associated with populations of differing social ranks to emerge in the Suburbs, and throughout the sector, as the most discriminating characteristic affecting school expenditures" (p. 161).

Having found these gross ecological correlations between social characteristics of communities and expenditure and revenue policies, the authors go on to search for more direct evidence that the values and preferences of social groups may underlie these differences. Social rank, as they put it, "reflects and/or structures attitudes and opinions, and . . . preferences associated with the latter affects the institutional behavior of relevant political organizations – municipal and school governments" (p. 211). No systematic surveys were conducted, but two small pre-tests were run in one county on both residents and city councilmen. Three of five attitudes were found to be significantly associated with the social rank level of 16 suburbs: local-cosmopolitanism, conservatism, and ethnocentrism. Residents of high rank communities were "more oriented to national affairs, were more opposed to government activity in the economic and social sphere, and were less hostile to out-groups than residents of low social ranking communities" (p. 216).

The character of leaders was also consistent with the social rank of the community. The higher the social rank of the community, the better educated, the more likely to be in white-collar occupations, the more likely to participate in organizations was its leadership (p. 227). Since status origins are related to experiences, values, and perspectives, we might expect parallel variation in policy choices of local governments.

Decisions and Situations

In one of the few attempts to combine an analysis of situational with structural and cultural factors in the literature of comparative studies of urban politics, the authors examine two decisions by Pennsylvania counties concerning the establishment of a county health department, a "functional transfer" as they call it. The referendum was defeated in Montgomery County and passed in Bucks County, and their concern is to explain why, thus leading them to examine the situational factors of leadership activity, party involvement in the issue, and the existence of organizations likely to take a stand. The Bucks County campaign was not as well organized as Montgomery's, much less activity was generated, but there was also little opposition from parties of local officials. The referendum was successfully "kept out of politics" (Williams *et al.*, 1965, p. 273). Montgomery County, where the referendum was defeated, had not experienced as rapid and as disruptive growth as had Bucks County, so health officials had fewer examples of waste, refuse, and other health problems to point to. Opposition developed among the Republican party, local officials, newspapers and other *ad hoc* groups. The Democratic party supported it (p. 276). Within each county, growth rates and density were associated with support of the referendum, as was social rank, although less so.

This case study of a referendum election in two counties well illustrates the interplay of structural and situational factors. The defeat of the referendum and its victory elsewhere was apparently partly due to party opposition where it was defeated. But the association of the social rank of communities within each county with the level of "yes-voting" was similar in each county. Structural factors were thus associated with the *relative* level of yes-voting, situational factors with the *absolute* level. The effect of social rank was neutralized when a local party leadership opposed the referendum, regardless whether Republican or Democratic.

Leadership, in conjunction with differences in the level of urbanization (growth and density) thus made the difference in the two outcomes. The authors suggest that two structural factors linked to growth and urbanization might explain why leadership in opposition did not emerge in Bucks County. The mobile population of Bucks County was less settled into small communities and therefore may have been more receptive to centralization of government. Also, leagues of municipalities were less well developed in Bucks County and therefore an organizational base for the development of opposition did not exist (p. 285). Potential leadership with probably the same "personal stake in home rule" probably existed in both counties, but with different organizational bases from which a campaign could be mounted.

The fuzzy margins separating situational and structural factors is well illustrated by those which the authors used to explain the differences between the electoral outcomes in Bucks and Montgomery counties. Mobility and the existence of organizations clearly change, probably faster than does the economic base of a community. As the rate of community growth declines, as the social composition probably becomes more stable, organizations develop, and patterns of leadership emerge in a more or less stable network of key organizations. As this happens one would expect that patterns of coalition on issues would become more predictable, although still a particular outcome would hinge upon a unique set of situational factors, their mutual conjunction having a fairly low level of probability.

In conclusion, the authors say that a community's evaluation of its needs for services is "influenced more by differences in the tax consciousness and attitude toward government of varying social groups than by the actual amount of resources available and effort required to support high service levels" (p. 293). They found, that is, that cultural factors – the values held by social groups in communities – will be translated into public policies of taxation and expenditures over and above those effects due to structural factors of wealth, resources, and needs.

The important distinction is made between values regarded as preferences, and values regarded as "actual public policies realized through the actions of local governments" (from the Preface).

The development of economically and socially specialized areas was linked to the dominance of groups holding policy preferences which to some extent are realized in policies of local governments.

The Rulers and the Ruled

This study (Agger *et al.*, 1964) of two small Far West communities (Farmdale, population 1,500 and Oretown, population 15,000) and two middle-sized Southern cities (Metroville and Petropolis, both about 100,000) is essentially social-psychological in its approach, concepts, and conclusions. It deals almost entirely with particular decisions in particular situations, but describes these in structural and cultural terms. However, it is one of the few studies to make a serious attempt to trace changes in decision-making processes over time, and the only one to characterize the ideologies of competing leadership groups as factors in decision-making.

The authors interviewed samples of voters in each community as well as leaders chosen by their reputation for general leadership and their participation in specific decisions. Some persons in the community sample were designated "Active Influentials" if they discussed politics, went to civic meetings, took an active part (by their own admission) in a recent issue, and belonged to at least one organization whose members were themselves politically active. "Manifest Leaders" were those persons who were nominated by a panel of officers of various community organizations as being the "general leaders" of the community, excluding both nonparticipants in specified decisions and those participants who disagreed with the decision. "Latent Leaders" were those individuals who did not receive enough nominations to be part of the pool of potential Manifest Leaders, but who actually participated in decisions. Latent Leaders also included those persons from the ranks of the "Active Influentials" who were satisfied participants in one or more decisions.

Leaders were classified into ideological groups according to their conceptions of the community (whether collectivist, individualistic, or as composed of interest groups), their preferences as to "who shall rule?" (industrialists, public leaders, professionals, small businessmen, labor, minorities), their sense of cultural and socio-economic class, and their attitudes toward the legitimate method of allocating values in the community. Seven ideological groups were distinguished, based on various combinations of the various ideological components: Jeffersonian Conservatives, Orthodox Conservatives, Progressive Conservatives, Community Conservationists, Radical Rightists, Liberals, Radical Leftists, and White Supremacists. Leaders were classified into one or another ideological group and participation of an individual or group was always identified by their ideological label.

Leaders and voters act to expand or contract the scope of local government, and particular decisions affecting scope were classified into economic, social, governmental, and "civic improvement" reorganization. Detailed histories of the consequences of events in issues of each type were given for each community, showing how the balance of private versus public "space" altered. These issues moved through decision-making stages, from formulation to deliberation, to the organization of support, to authoritative consideration, and thence to an outcome. Promulgation and effectuation followed.

Four principal characteristics of decision-making processes were distinguished and used as the basis of classifying communities into different types of "power structures" and "regimes." The breadth of participation in decisions among the citizenry and the degree of ideological agreement among the leadership defined four types of power structure. The sense of electoral potency or efficacy among the electorate and the probability of effective illegitimate sanctions being used to block efforts to shift the scope of government defined four types of regimes. Breadth of participation is labelled the Mass versus Elite dimension and ideological agreement or disagreement the Consensual versus Competitive dimension of power structure. High or low sense of electoral potency differentiates Democracies (a regime attribute) into Developed and Underdeveloped, *if* the probability of illegitimate sanctions being used is low. A regime is a Guided Democracy even though the sense of electoral potency is high, if the probability of use of illegitimate sanctions is high. In an Oligarchy, the sense of potency is low and the probability of use of illegitimate sanctions is high.

Participation and influence, stages of decision-making which shift the net scope of government, the ideologies and types of leadership, power structures and regimes, are thus the main subjects of the study. Despite the seemingly structural character of these concepts, they are all social psychological in character. Actions and events are analyzed from the perspective of an actor's intentions and goals. Political participation is action *intended* to influence the scope of government (Agger *et al.*, 1964, p. 51). Power is obtained by an individual if he *purposefully* contributes to a decision and wants the outcome (Agger *et al.*, 1964, p. 59). A leader is a person who has shared in power, i.e., contributed to an outcome which he wants. Leadership groups are defined by their *beliefs*, not their behavior. Power structures and regimes are defined by *feelings* of potency, how many people purposefully contribute to an outcome.

A detailed investigation of decision-making processes in a one or two year period in each community (ranging from 1950-1952 to 1957-1958) found that Farmdale and Metroville exhibited less open, more restricted decision-making patterns than Oretown and Petropolis. In the former two communities, the administration prevented new decisions, those decisions which were made were made quietly, there were few of them, and no formal associations of businessmen or labor were active. In the latter two, the administration tried new things, there was conflict and more decisions, and formal associations were active. In addition, Negroes were more influential in one of the Southern cities, Petropolis, than in Metroville (Agger *et al.*, 1964, pp. 256-259). Correlated with these patterns were found to be higher levels of various kinds of participation by citizens in the more open systems. As a result, Oretown and Petropolis were classified as possessing Competitive Mass power structures and Developed Democratic regimes at "Time M," the moment of the study, Farmdale as a Consensual Elite power structure and a Guided Democracy, Metroville as a Competitive Mass power structure and Underdeveloped Democracy (Agger *et al.*, 1964, p. 653).

These characterizations of power structures and regimes are not permanent, however, because any of the variables comprising them can change overnight, literally, if a few leaders decide to oppose others (the power structure shifts from Consensual to Competitive) or if their sense of electoral potency drops (the regime changes from a Developed to an Underdeveloped Democracy). Because the Farmdale publisher, Mr. King, was "successfully deactivated," the regime remained a "Guided Democracy for approximately a 3-month period after Time M" (Agger *et. al.*, 1964, p. 540). The type of power structure and regime considered to be characteristic of each community was determined for each of fifteen years from 1945 to 1961 from qualitative information on the four component variables, and the changes from one type to another are the basis for the major conclusions of the study: (1) The existence of competitive electoral opportunities is not a sufficient condition for a high sense of electoral potency and a lack of illegitimate sanctions (Developed Democracy); (2) A Developed Democracy requires a group that is ideologically divergent from the prevailing leadership to aspire to office or power (Agger *et al.*, 1964, pp. 655-656); (3) Ideologically divergent leadership and wide participation (Competitive Mass power structure) encourages Developed Democracy, but is not necessary for its existence; (4) Developed Democracy is necessary for a Competitive Mass power structure; (5) If the regime is other than a Developed Democracy, the power structure will be a Consensual Elite; (6) Community Conservationist leadership groups and Conservatives have civic associations as their organizational base, because they are non-political, respectable, avoid conflict, and do not mobilize the citizenry; (7) Liberals have unions and the Democratic Party as their organizational base, and are more likely to rely on elections as the avenue for power rather than informal negotiations through civic associations (Agger *et al.*, 1964, p. 674; (8) Where "good government" has become institutionalized, strong cultural-class conflict will be generated.

Decisions and Situations

Issues and decisions were classified according to the *actors' perspectives,* not the authors': ". . . political decisional processes [are classified] on the basis of the question or questions the active participants indicate are at issue . . ." Sometimes "a decisional process is listed more than once because of multiple perspectives of participants or different perspectives of different participants" (Agger *et al.*, 1964, pp. 200-201). Also, "In the minds of active participants, certain house-keeping decisions were also economic-reorganization processes" (Agger *et al.*, 1964, p. 222).

Power was assigned by the authors to those who participated consciously in shaping outcomes and who were pleased by them. But the actors themselves and their perspectives determined the categories in which concrete issues and decisions were placed (Economic Reorganization versus Civic Improvement, for example). It would seem just as meaningful to reverse the assignment of meanings, to allow the actors themselves to assign quanta of power to themselves and others, and for the analyst to determine the categories into which to place substantive issues (cost, who is affected, the agency making the decision, the level of visibility, the degree of conflict, or a number of other possibly important classifying dimensions).

The assigning of "units" of power to individuals indicates some of the problems with the basic categories and assumptions of a situational and decisional approach to power. In a decision in Metroville to apply for a planning grant, "... some of the initial opposition in the White subcommunity was eliminated" (Agger *et al.*, 1964, p. 220). Yet, units of power could not be assigned if the "authoritative consideration" stage of the decision process had not been reached. This procedure for determining who has power is called an operational definition and yet obviously carries great theoretical weight. Because of the authors' stress upon the subjective perceptions of actors in particular situations, they do not want power to be regarded as activated or "invoked" (p. 200) until a process has reached the point where everyone must say to himself: "A decision is going to be made; which side am I on?" But if early opponents are quieted, and if they could have blocked action at a later stage (and the authors clearly distinguish these stages) why not allow them a share of the power?

Leadership and power are thus qualities of particular individuals in given events, not of persistent structural and cultural attributes of a community. Power structures and regimes are just as evanescent, because a "potentially sanctionable" person who has not realized that he has been boycotted or otherwise subjected to illegitimate sanctions, may have a sudden insight into the real situation. As a consequence, a "Guided Democracy may change to an Oligarchy in the next period" (Agger *et al.*, 1964, p. 104).

Power structures can also change from moment to moment, because they are measured by how outcomes of particular decisions accord with the preferences of participants at a given point in time. The power structure may actually disappear if no decisions are made (at the authoritative consideration stage) at any given moment. A single shift of vote, from a four-man consistent majority (on a seven-man city council, for example) to an inconsistent majority of four (because one man moves away from the majority on an issue) can shift the community power structure from a Consensual state to a Competitive one (Agger *et al.*, 1964, p. 81). Power structures also change with new decisions, with shifts in the scope of government, the entrance or withdrawal of participants, the winning or losing of different participants, the changing of preferences, or any combination of these. Thus, political change is the usual condition.

How many people must change their sense of electoral potency, how many leaders must disagree, and by how much? How many people must be illegitimately sanctioned and how effectively is not considered. The authors properly point to the difficulty of assessing these intangible properties of a community political system, but their social-psychological view of power and leadership in decision-making as almost purely due to situational factors leads them to characterize an entire community by data deriving from a non-random sample of individuals' subjective perceptions and desires in a discrete series of particular situations.

Policies and Structure

Although the book is packed with concrete details about decision-making outcomes, there is no systematic *theoretical* concern with policies, in the sense used here. Although Agger and his associates classified the specific issues in their communities into abstract types (civic improvement, economic reorganization and so forth), the occurrence and outcomes of decisions in each type were not made part of the theoretical framework, and no propositions linking their processes of decision to leadership patterns or to power structures and regimes were advanced.

Because of the discrete treatment of issues and decisions, there is no consideration of the level of consistency of decisions which might justify inferences that certain substantive policies were favored in any of the communities. None of the major hypotheses in the concluding chapter refer to the contents of decisions or to the success of participating leadership groups in gaining their ends. This lack of emphasis on policies is consistent with the procedural rather than substantive emphasis in the major variables and concepts. Power structures and regimes, for example, are defined by formal properties of procedures, such as convergence or divergence of ideologies, broad or narrow distributions of power, sense of potency, and illegitimate sanctions. What is converging, the goals of participants, what they feel potent to do, what sanctions are used, are not made part of the *theoretical* structure, although substantive detail occupies hundreds of pages. Even ideologies lack content, since they refer to conceptions of community, who shall rule, and one's sense of social or cultural class, not *what* should be decided, despite the focus on particular decisions.

Inferring the nature of the power structure from those who have won in particular decisions of the moment avoids entirely the question of resources raised by Robert A. Dahl (1961) and others: who has the "capacity" or the "potential" to exercise power – to win. Power to Agger and his associates resides in the moment of authoritative decision and is allocated or "released" to those participants who win. The authors are aware of the difficulties of this position, and at one point suggest that the analyst might want to make a "double classification" of the power structure if there is little participation in some decisions but broad participation in others (Agger *et al.*, 1964, p. 732). Surely this is the usual situation. Whenever an election is held, those voters on the winning side have power (in their definition). and thereby a "mass" power structure exists with respect to that decision. But in many noncontroversial, administrative decisions, a few men make the decision unchallenged. That decision thereby exhibits an "elite" structure. It seems highly likely that in most if not all communities both types of decisions, those involving mass participation and those involving only elite participation, occur if not simultaneously at least in close and frequent succession.

Power is defined as influence over decisions, but the groups whose power is regarded as defining the nature of the power structure of a community are defined not in terms of their influence over decisions, but rather in terms of their general ideology. Such general ideologies are probably much less subject to change than strategic decisions on particular issues. The authors want to be able to trace short-term changes of power structures and regimes, and yet the *units* they use as the basis for assessing these changes are defined in terms of long-range commitments to general ideological positions.

Roles of Governments and Cultures

Political culture enters into *The Rulers and the Ruled* in two ways, as the ideologies of leadership, and, as a consequence of the dominance of certain types of leaders, the value-commitments of the local political system. The authors make a major commitment to ideologies as a major differentiating factor in local political systems, and explicitly distinguish ideologies from interests. They claim to have actually found that

> . . . the informal political organization of ideologically differentiated groups is a necessary although insufficient condition for both extensive citizen participation in politics and intensive conflict in decision-making. Competitive ideological groups give rise to both situations, whereas the competition among groups lacking ideological interests is insufficient to produce "mass" participation or either a cohesive or conflicting character (Agger *et al.*, 1964, p. 18).

Ideological characterizations are used as the basis for predicting specific outcomes, rather unsuccessfully (see Agger, *et al.*, pp. 544, 554, 563, 565, 568, 578).

Agger gives several examples of strategic and tactical divergence within factions of a single ideological group. Yet leadership ideology remains a key classifying dimension of power structure. This has problems, even within their framework of definitions of power and ideology in terms of those who participate in outcomes and agree with them. If factions are in sharp conflict over particular decisions, one side wins, and another doesn't; power (in their terms) must be assigned to one segment of a faction and not another. Yet, the *general* ideological position of the members of the faction may not have changed at all, and thus their ideologies may still be "convergent." Given their definition of power, this situation in which one ideological group is split, and part of it wins and part loses on a given issue, does not seem well defined by the term "consensual."

To make this point is not to criticize the decision to separate consideration of factional strategy from general ideological perspectives. These are or may certainly be independent factors determining the behavior of leaders. But the analytic decision to make *ideological* convergence or divergence of leaders a main axis of classification of power structure, rather than actual cleavages between leaders over alternative decisions, which is after all the basis for the assignment of "units" of power, is puzzling.

In the terms used in this paper, ideological perspectives of leaders would better be regarded as part of the political culture, constraining the actions of persons even though their interests are in conflict with those perspectives. Agger in fact cites the example of the businessman who believes strongly that government should not interfere in the economy and who therefore does not push for governmental action even when it is in his own interests. But these long-range constraints must not be identified with considerations of tactics and strategy in particular situations. Agger *et al.* merge the two aspects of ideology and strategy by defining their basic concepts and distinctions in long-range terms (ideology, group, structure, regime) but treat their data in short-range terms, as if the latter are a test of the former. Consistencies of policy over a period of years would seem to be a better test of the dominance of the ideology of a certain group rather than the participation in particular situations of specific individuals who hold general ideas about the role of government. To infer from the participation of certain individuals who hold Progressive Conservative ideologies that this is the dominant ideology of the regime or power structure would seem to move from one level of analysis – commitments to certain goals and procedures (culture) – to quite another – tactical questions of action (situational factors).

Ideology is a component of political culture – sets of beliefs about the proper role of government which may guide behavior in the long run, but do not necessarily determine it in any particular situation. Agger *et al.* assume that ideology influences the behavior of leaders, but do not distinguish it in their theoretical framework from the individual and group advantages which would follow a given course of action, and which would influence short-range tactical alliances, and the value and policy preferences which follow from an ideological position and influence long-range strategy. Such a distinction is indeed frequently drawn in their substantive discussion of issues and decision-making processes in the four communities, as illustrated by the frequent discrepancies between the presumed ideological commitments of leaders and cliques and the alliances which they formed in particular situations.

CONCLUSIONS

I have argued that a critical distinction often ignored in studies of power and influence in urban political processes is the one between long-term and short-term factors, or what we have called here structural and cultural factors versus situational factors.

If opportunities are continually available to particular individual or groups by virtue of their positions in particular institutions, then we might refer to the conduciveness of a structure or culture to the creation of certain situations. Social and political structures may provide situations continually favoring one group with greater political access, visibility of their interests, and various resources, and consequently with greater motivations, interest, and experience. Such individuals and groups may thereby have disproportionate chances to win when their interests are at stake in a decision. Such a statement is an attempt to link the long- with the short-range aspects of factors affecting decisions, not a hypothesis about the nature of structural conduciveness. Even such a link, if established, does not tell us what is likely to happen (who will win) in a unique sequence of events. Only relatively low probabilities can be established by knowledge of the structural and cultural factors creating opportunities for action. Prediction of which individuals will get involved and which strategies will be chosen and ultimately successful in such unique situations is probably a goal with little scientific pay-off.

As we have seen, a focus upon one or another object of study has been accompanied in these studies by a parallel focus upon a certain class of explanatory or correlated variables. Those who have studied particular decisions have usually sought their explanations in situational factors. Policies have usually been explained by structural factors and roles of government by cultural ones. Because of limitations of resources, few studies have systematically taken environmental factors into account. Most studies, either tacitly or explicitly, simply regard other objects of study and associated factors as either being "constant" and therefore capable of being ignored or as beyond their resources to study.

Our intention here has not been to evaluate existing studies, but rather the field of comparative studies of urban politics as a whole. Any particular study must make certain assumptions, must exclude problems which are vital for another, and must exploit resources available at the cost of neglecting certain aspects of the problem which may well be important. To have noted that a certain book fails to deal with a certain class of factors is thus not a criticism, unless its omission was vital for the task that the author set for himself. It is hoped that this sketchy review has brought out some of the possibilities for future comparative studies.

Although a major controversy in the area has concerned the nature of "community power structure," this concept has not been treated here as a major analytic category, because of the inconsistency of meanings and operations attached to the term. It is hoped, however, that the different sets of problems dealt with under the rubric of power structure have become clearer by treating the several studies with respect to their focus upon the influence of cultural, structural and situational factors in decisions and policy-making.

Whether a power structure, for example, is defined as a set of *persons* or as a set of *institutions* which provide such political resources as property, wealth, high status, communication networks, and legality to persons is an important distinction corresponding to the distinction between situational, structural and cultural factors. If a power structure is a set of persons, then finding different people involved in different issues might lead to the conclusion that a pluralistic power structure exists. If a power structure is a set of institutions, then it may be irrelevant whether or not the same individuals are involved in different situations. The point is not that individuals who have similar resources and institutional positions will always act in the same way. Rather, the two aspects must be considered separately, and resources must not be simply viewed as attributes of individuals who choose whether or not to act on behalf of political ends in particular situations, but also as systematically allocated consequences of the institutional structure of the society and political system.

Part II

POLICY PLANNING

Expanding the Horizon of Planning

THE FIRST PAIR OF CHAPTERS in Part II of the book presents essays by Henry Fagin on "The Evolving Philosophy of Urban Planning" and by Lyle C. Fitch on "Social Planning in the Urban Cosmos." These and the remaining chapters continue to deal with the same scope of urban research that has characterized Part I. Yet the motivation is different. Where the questions investigated up to this point have emphasized urban research for the sake of knowing, Part II is concerned with research for the sake of knowing what to do. As we noted in the Preface, it is this difference that distinguishes our use of the terms *urban research* and *policy planning* in the main title.

In Chapter 11, Fagin contrasts the widespread deprecatory attitudes toward planning of the 1940s with the present prosperity of a substantial cluster of planning professions — people planning for every function, at every level, and in every part of America, to say nothing of the rest of the world. He suggests an incipient merger of persons originating in many disciplines and professions born of a need to perform public planning as an interwoven, interdependent, multifaceted activity. He reviews (1) evolving views of planners about planning and plans; (2) uses of power; (3) questions of scope and time-range; (4) hierarchies of planning agencies; (5) the planned and the unplanned; (6) the potential crucial role of the policy plan in the formulation, communication, legislation, and administration of programs; and (7) the knotty problem of plan evaluation. He reflects on the significance of the recent move toward "systems" thinking and the rise of PPBS (planning-programming-budgeting systems).

Fitch, who has been involved heavily in New York's social planning throughout most of the two decades under review, identifies two levels of social planning in Chapter 12. Broad social planning must encompass all the parts of the social organism, "including those which we customarily classify physical and economic, not to mention psychological, biological, organizational, and other categories." The other level (with which the essay mainly deals) "concentrates on economic and cultural impoverishment, while recognizing that 'human resources development' per se applies to the entire population."

Fitch describes, analizes, and interprets the same convergence and integration of the various strands of planning that Fagin notes. Fitch sees this development through the eyes of an economist-administrator charged in his career with increasingly broad policy responsibility, while Fagin sees it from his background as a traditionally trained urban planner who has come to regard development in recent years more and more comprehensively. Fitch highlights the increasing sensitivity of governmental policy planners to the mutual repercussions among individual programs in the human resources field. He cites the growth and continual elaboration of measures directed toward lifting the disadvantaged groups to an acceptable if minimal level. He also raises and debates some of the controversial issues that have been concerning social planners. For example, he asserts that despite a "large body of literature dealing with [the] problem of relating private individual choices and public choices, and many attempts . . . to construct social welfare formulas which attempt to bridge the gap, . . . these have proved fruitless as guides to social policies." This leads Fitch to a keen interest in the political processes that determine budgets and to the kinds of systems analyses that can help inform public decisions.

Later, Fitch poses two questions: (1) What degree of cultural differentiation is consistent with the somewhat contrary value of abolishing discrimination? (2) To what extent can desegregation remedy deficiencies in educational facilities, programs, and general climate? He suggests the possible conclusion that 'the main need is not for homogenization but for superior educational facilities constructed specifically to meet the needs of deprived children." Fitch concludes the section exemplifying the questions that social planning must try to resolve with the following thought: "They can be resolved, if at all, only by experimentation and research on a scale far greater than has yet been undertaken."

Fitch's essay next deals with *planning and program packaging.* He hails a "proliferation at all three levels of government of programs concerned with human resources development and with urban development generally . . ." saying that these present cities with "an embarrassing abundance — embarrassing in the sense that more is available than most cities can readily use."

Three important new social programs are examined in detail: (1) the war against poverty; (2) the New York City Human Resources Administration; and (3) the Demonstration Cities program. In a concluding section, Fitch offers this warning:

> *[T]here is a danger for social planning, if it seeks to build on precedents drawn from the physical sciences and physical planning, which are predicated on more measurable quantities and sequential, cause-and-effect relationships. Social planning deals with a world of uncertainty owing in part, but only in part, to lack of knowledge. Many things are* inherently *uncertain.*

Social planning, then, "must be based on probabilities, not certainties; with strategies to meet possible alternative developments, rather than with neatly constructed models based on known facts; and with continual rolling adjustments rather than with tidy consequences."

— *H.F.*

11

The Evolving Philosophy of Urban Planning

HENRY FAGIN

☐ VARIOUS WORDS—THEORY, STRATEGY, STRUCTURE—reflect the human propensity to seek coherence and meaning in the face of any persistent behavior that comes to assume an accepted place in man's affairs.

I have chosen the term *philosophy* in the title of this chapter, not because a formal philosophy of urban planning exists (it does not) but to underline a nascent groping that is to be heard when planners meet, and to be read between the lines of what they write. There is slowly coming into being with respect to urban planning a body of underlying general conceptions commonly if not universally shared among planners of many sorts. Not so rigorous as to warrant the name *theory* and in some ways broader in compass than that term might imply, the evolving concepts and methods of planning do seem to be crystallizing toward an implicit philosophy, with far more agreement than divergence among urban planners regarding its broad outlines.

If no authentic statement of urban planning philosophy exists today (though some recent books have made an effort), this was also true, of course, at the close of World War II, the start of the twenty-year period covered by this first *Urban Affairs Annual Review*. My interpretation of planners' outlooks, therefore, is based mainly on the impressions of one who has lived through the period and known planners and their plans, rather than on direct documentation of their theories about what they were doing. For the most part, professional planners have been too busy planning for them to write about the concepts and processes involved. Nonetheless, they have based their plans on sets of conceptions no less definite than if these had been recorded, and an evolving philosophy can validly be read into their works.

One might succinctly characterize twenty years of change in urban planning philosophy by noting a singular trend common to virtually all facets of this evolving philosophy. In 1946 the professional differences were over a series of dichotomies with people tending to stand on one side or the other: plan or process, long-range or short-range, advisory power or fourth power, general or detailed, rail or rubber, social or economic, planning or democracy. By 1966, almost all the old dichotomies have come to be regarded with far more sophistication, not as mutually exclusive contradictories but rather as points along continua that frequently turn out to be circles or multi-layered matrices. I shall make use of this similar history of various dichotomies to organize the main substance of the chapter – for each of the main elements of today's emergent philosophy counterposing the stereotyped dualities of twenty years ago.

PLANNING DEFINED

In the 1940s the term *planning* was recovering from a pratfall peculiar to recent American history. One was apt to hear arguments couched in language for or against planning, plans, or planners. The early decades of the century had generated a great vogue of municipal betterment following the "muckraking" years. Several expressions of urban planning received impetus simultaneously. These included municipal financial control and budgeting, manpower development aided by civil service, scientific management of work programming, and the design and regulation of streets, land uses, and municipal lands and structures. Engineers, landscape architects, and architects were especially prominent in the latter expression of improved municipal planning – the focus on designing the public aspects of the physical environment and regulating private aspects through zoning and the control of land subdivisions. Out of their professional vocabularies, the word *plan* came to be used in the special restricted sense natural to physical design people, and the phrase *city plan* acquired a segmental meaning recognized not only by the design professionals but also by the planners of other segments of governmental administration. Thus it was, that the planners of physical development achieved the sanction of common speech usage when they organized in 1917 as the American Institute of Planners, simultaneously dissociating themselves from an earlier collaboration with the other planners, whose work was expressed in proposals for social, economic, or political measures.

This physical bias in the connotation of *planning* was reinforced in the 1920s when the word itself became unpopular in many other circles, particularly in the business community, because of highly oppressive acts taken in the name of planning in totalitarian Russia. Only the somewhat conservative and clearly respectable professional engineers, architects, and city planners safely could describe what they were doing by the politically suspect word, planning. History repeated itself early in World War II when the Congress, terminating Roosevelt's National Resources Planning Board, solemnly abjured all future congresses from using the word "planning" in the name of any future similar federal agency.

Thus, in the common parlance of everyday language in the 1940s, urban planning bore the limitation explicitly stated in the constitution of the American Institute of Planners: planning "as expressed through the comprehensive arrangement of land use and land occupancy and the regulation thereof." For an identification of the other segments of urban planning in 1946 we must look under other labels than *planning:* budgeting, forward programming, research and development, etc. Moreover, to the extent planning implies a conscious handling of change over time, it probably is fair to say that affairs other than those closely related to the physical environment were not extensively planned in the 1940s. Rather, they were managed largely out of day-to-day or very short-range considerations.

POWERS OF THE PLANNER

A major controversy in the philosophy of planning in the 1940s was over the appropriate powers of the planner. It was agreed that planners had the special role of developing proposals for consideration and action. Some people, however, believed that the judgments of planners about matters of development should be given special status under law, to be overruled only by extraordinary vote of the local elected officials. Such notions, indeed, were written into the typical planning statutes of the day, modeled after the standard enabling acts published in the late 1920s when engineer Herbert

Hoover was U.S. Secretary of Commerce.

Two issues are imbedded in this controversy. One is whether there are some classes of decision that ought to be given to professional planners for final judgment – matters of highway curvature to transport planners, epidemic danger to public health planners, or urban aesthetics to civic designers. One might now suggest, however, that the phrase "*the* decision-makers," though illuminating in some contexts, also tends to obscure the inescapable fact that everyone is a decision-maker – and should be. We perceive hierarchies and classifications of decisions – degrees of generality, of importance, of consequence regarding the subject of a decision. And we note that it is as harmful for high-level strategic decision-makers to spend time making decisions in areas of specialized competence as for professional planners to close off major strategic options, which they sometimes conceal knowingly or unwittingly, under what appear as relatively low-level technical choices. Thus, the earlier debate over whether planning ought to be considered advisory or ought to be given decision power is giving way to a subtler and more significant inquiry about the best placement of different sorts of decisions.

The vogue of talking about *the* decision-makers slights the numerically enormous host of decisions made by everyone in an organization everyday, which in their combined impacts are fully as consequential as the small number of decisions made on matters that directly involve people high in the organizational hierarchy. Increasingly, we are learning that decision-making is diffused throughout organizations, as a few people like Chester A. Barnard suggested some years ago. To the extent that planning can help improve decisions, it too must be diffused throughout organizations.

The other definitional issue is perhaps more a matter of semantics. A great statesman is sometimes referred to as the planner or architect of a particular policy. On the other hand we more generally restrict the meaning of these latter names to the specialized work of formulating plans to be adopted and implemented by other persons and institutions. In both this sense and that of the first issue, most planners would find it anachronistic today to claim for planning that parity with the executive, legislative, and judicial branches of government that Rexford Guy Tugwell advocated twenty-eight years ago in his theory of planning as the "fourth power" (Tugwell, 1939).

SCOPE

As to the appropriate scope of urban planning, we are coming full circle back to the outlook of those early municipal reformers who, in their search for civic improvement, viewed all the handles of municipal improvement as equally useful and accessible. After half a century, the ancient minority who resisted the segmentation of public policy planning appear more in the spirit of today than their contemporaries who attempted to tear the physical from the social and economic aspects of the urban environment. It is notable that a generation after the Institute of Planners was formed, just before the demise of the National Resources Planning Board during World War II, staff director Charles W. Eliot made an unsuccessful effort to reunite the several segments of planning to achieve a concerted attack on the urban problems of post-Depression cities, but was rebuffed by his contemporaries. Moreover, there was no counter-move of persons working with social welfare or economic development programs to coalesce with the environmental planners.

The signs today, however, point strongly to a redefinition of the scope of urban planning. The segment of planning that formerly concentrated strictly on municipal fiscal management and budgeting has become increasingly concerned in the past twenty years with longer-range projection, with the substantive or program content of public expenditures, and with the interrelationships between the public and private sectors of the economy. In seeking to strengthen the economic base of their areas, the financial planners today are looking comprehensively at the whole evolving community. Influenced to a degree by practice abroad, especially in the so-called underdeveloped regions, this new outlook is beginning to coincide more and more with the conceptual framework that has been evolving in recent years among the traditionally defined urban planners. In the word "planning" that leads PPBS, the current vogue for *planning-programming-budgeting systems,* there is clear indication of an important maturing in public financial planning circles.

Something analogous has been occurring in the segment of public policy planning that customarily has revolved in fragmented fashion around problems of individual and family welfare. The separate movements of twenty years ago in housing, social security, social work, public health, job training, and similar welfare concerns are today being brought into a common focus under such terms as *human resources planning*. Furthermore, it is increasingly evident that the old separations of thinking into alleged economic, social, political, or physical realms are impediments to clarity in the development of public policy. To take just one important example, education is at the same time a key *economic* factor as in job training, a key *social* factor as in the productive use of leisure time, a key *political* factor as in election literacy, and a key factor in the physical environment – witness the portion of public investment going for school buildings.

It is true, of course, that planners of the physical environment have recognized from the beginning the need on the one hand to take account of social and economic needs and on the other hand to pay attention to the potential impacts of their proposals on non-physical elements of the community. Their creative thinking and recommendations, however, were limited to physical changes, and their agencies were fatally isolated from the places where basic social and economic policies were being hammered out.

In 1966, after some years of discussion and debate, the governing board of the American Institute of Planners, recognizing the spirit and facts of the times, voted a referendum among the 4,000 members to strike from the Institute's constitution the specific reference to land planning as being the exclusive expression of the planner's profession's sphere. This further sign of evolution in the philosophy of urban planning may presage a general integration of urban policy-making at an overall level. This development would provide a vital counterbalance to the equally significant and desirable proliferation and specialization of the specific public programs addressed to particular urban problems, with the attendant specialized planning.

Finally, the scope of planning is expanding significantly through the recognition that a great many different elements of urban administration must be integrated and projected within some sort of unified framework. In the *policy plan* concept, as developed by this author among others (Fagin, 1965) a multi-column referencing format not only provides for expressing policy for each proposed program by narrative description (as well as maps, tables, and schedules) but also calls for the specifications of annual costs of financing and operations, space and locational requirements, essential legislation and legal steps involved, personnel requirements and manpower development plans, and the interrelated private measures assumed or to be elicited. Thus, the potential scope of the plan becomes coterminous with the scope of governmental program development.

DIVISION OF LABOR IN PLANNING

Two decades ago planners concerned with how to approach urban policy development were debating the pros and cons of centralization *versus* decentralization, overall planning *versus* departmental, state *versus* local, metropolitan *versus* municipal, and other either-ors in the placement of responsibility for planning and administering urban programs. In the 1950s people began to stress the fact that most functions have *aspects* of specific kinds best handled at different places in the organizational or geographic hierarchy. It was seen increasingly that the older concept of a *division* of powers, by whole functions, written into the United States Constitution as a compromise between advocates of federal power and of states rights, had little relevance to urban life. Rather, it was perceived that the seemingly antagonistic dichotomies were in fact symbiotic poles – by another analogy two sides of the same coin. It is very much part of the current philosophy of planning to regard effective centralization and decentralization as essential to each other, not opposed. There cannot be successful central or overall policy development unless satisfactory decentralized or divisional policy is being produced at the same time. The best total body of policy is the result of the interplay of policy development throughout the hierarchy of government.

At least two major types of division are recognized as necessary: functional and geographic; and there is increasing sensitivity to the richness of both. In terms of function, a widespread reconsideration is underway. In places like New York City, this reexamination is leading to a regrouping of many functional responsibilities that had become so fragmented as to be unmanageable. The current proposals at federal, state, and local levels to collect scattered agencies that handle fragmented pieces of transportation into comprehensive transportation departments or super-departments is a case in point. Indeed, while operational considerations have played a role, it has been notably the logic of transportation planning that has insistently demonstrated the need for an integrated approach to the diverse modes of transportation and to the hitherto separate activities of planning, constructing, financing, operating, and regulating what is essentially one system for transporting people and goods.

The post-World War II years were marked by a hope that urban problems, characteristically metropolis-wide rather than merely local in existence and in interaction, might yield to metropolitan attack since municipal efforts alone had proven ineffectual. The current tendency is to view various specific problems as having geographic dimensions that differ substantially from problem to problem and from place to place. Total solution by total consolidation has few supporters today.

Whether the problems of specialization and integration are faced in regard to geography or function, the simplistic notion of a single organizational structure suitable for all matters is yielding to the more complex notion of multiple policy development frameworks. The pertinent organizational analogy, which used to be the pyramid or the layer cake, and then after Morton Grodzins the marble cake, now might be the kaleidoscope. In it, the same administrative units and the same people sometimes appear in one organizational structure and then again appear in quite different ones. A Princeton official meets in the morning as part of the New York metropolis, in the afternoon with the Philadelphia region, and in the evening with the other components of greater Trenton. The budget director sits now with accountants, treasurers, and assessors as a member of the financial management group and later with the other central policy formulating officials who specialize in the spatial, programmatic, and political dimensions of policy. He has "line" responsibilities for processing expenditure proposals and transactions, "staff" responsibilities for aspects of urban strategy. Thus, as bits in a kaleidoscope take on different aspects and roles as the contextual pattern is shifted, so with both geographic and organizational units and groups of units. These latter shift their roles from time to time in the division of labor within urban administration and the consequent division of planning responsibility to serve each deciding unit or combinations of units.

Still another early dichotomy respecting the division of labor in planning was the assertion that the concern for the triad, *long-range, general,* and *comprehensive,* is to be conceptually and organizationally separated from the daily, the detailed, and the partial. Pursuant to the stress on this kind of separation, many planners a generation ago justified a deliberate insulation of their brand of planning from the daily hurly-burly of politics, from any real responsibility for the steps from here to there, from a recognition of fine grain as well as coarse grain determinants of general policy, and from a close involvement and two-way interaction with the other planners working at different scales and in the specialized functions. Today, it is becoming widely recognized that planning permeates organizational structure. A major objective is to introduce at every level and in every function a sense of time flow, a perception of the detail in the context of the larger whole, an awareness of the integrity of each subsystem at the same time as a recognition of the functioning of the larger system as a whole.

THE CHARACTER OF THE PLAN AND THE PLANNING PROCESS

Twenty years ago the urban plan was expressed principally by a map depicting the ultimate pattern of development for an area and the public facilities essential to its functioning. I remember in the early 1950s going through a yard-high stack of master plans collected at the Regional Plan Association in New York. Of perhaps a hundred sets of local plan reports, none dealt in any way with operating budget considerations, fewer than a half dozen even mentioned capital budget requirements; and indeed one, prepard by a past-president of the American Institute of Planners, declared that the problems of financing the master plan were not properly a concern of the municipal planning agency as such.

In his book about the master plan concept, the lawyer Edward M. Bassett, a leading innovator of planning legislation in the 1920s, declared that the scope of the plan should be limited to what can be shown on a municipal map – elements like streets, sidewalks, street trees, parks, streams, lakes, public building sites, and the general districts for which private land should be zoned. A plan for the City of Oakland, California, prepared in the 1950s, epitomized this viewpoint. The entire plan was on one sheet of paper – map on one side and assumptions, goals, standards, and development principles on the reverse.

The model or archetype of this kind of plan was the nineteenth century architect's design for a building – though the city was to be constructed in slow-motion time, to be sure. The city blocks and districts corresponded to rooms and suites, the plazas and streets to lobbies and corridors. The completed city, like the finished building, was to carry out the design ideas of a single designer, though the interior decorator in the one case and the private property owner in the other would make minor variations within the set structure. To this idea of the plan of the city there was a corresponding concept of the methodology of the planner. He was the architect of the city, drawing on his personal knowledge of the situation and his intuitive design capacities to make the plan.

The current interest in policy planning as a new sort of documentation and in the closely related planning-programming-budgeting systems (PPBS) approach turns in a very different direction from traditional master map making. This approach to the urban plan views it not primarily as a graphic design but rather as a kind of loose-leaf compendium of many interrelated documents that in their entirety describe policy for the evolving community or region. Graphic plans there are; but these are incidental parts and not the primary expression of planned municipal policy.

Gone with the one-sheet one-shot city plan illusion is the conceit – happily never widespread among planners despite the full implications of our one-time theories – that a single mind or a single plan can or should control the flow of future urban development. Rather today's planners are keenly aware of the multiplicity of persons and governmental units that make important plans. It is clear enough that any attempt to render these many plans wholly consistent in intention or impact would be unreasonably costly and would be bound to fail in any event, given the extreme complexity and magnitude of urban life and the bewildering specialization of its manifold activities. What we do seek, however, is a meaningful measure of coherence among programs, a reasonable effort to forestall unnecessary interference among peoples' actions, a reduction of unanticipated consequences, a mutual strengthening of related programs by workable coordination, a tempering of all present plans by as good information as sensibly can be developed about future probabilities, taking into account known trends, expected and proposed policies, and the inherent uncertainties of life.

This awareness of the transitory nature of knowledge, of technology, of aspirations, of power coalitions leads planners today away from the earlier preoccupation with what architects call preliminary sketches and final plans. It is part of the pervasive contemporary sense of dynamics that planners are more interested in streams of change over time, sequences of events and situations, and periodically shifting patterns than in snapshots of end states, in so-called plans of ultimate development.

Planners today seek to hedge uncertain futures by gearing the costly purchase of durability to magnitudes of probability; that is, they advise relatively flexible, easily amortized and modified patterns and structures for situations hard to predict with accuracy. They move with special caution in the area of the irreversible, calling for large consensus before embarking on ways from which there is no turning back. They favor planning processes that provide for continuous feedback and adjustment in the light of experience; strategies that enable periodic modification of plans relentlessly made obsolete by the threefold sources of plan obsolescence: the unanticipatable in the flow of events; the inescapable faultiness of forecast, proposal, and execution; and the inevitable change in aspiration that is the steady companion of human experience.

To Plan or Not to Plan

As to the appropriate application of the planning process, the philosophy of today recognizes a continuum from the unplannable, through what ought not to be planned, to the things that can be attained only through highly organized and conscious planning. There is room in the philosophy of planning for elements of urban life best handled by spontaneity, others by the competitive market, others by a pricing mechanism used more extensively for governmental services, and still others by non-governmental voluntary cooperative action. The evolving philosophy recognizes situations, so well described in the writings of Charles E. Lindblom, in which overall plans would be excessively costly or unattainable in any practical sense—wherein the best outcomes are to be achieved through other than planning processes (Lindblom, 1965).

But the philosophy no less firmly asserts the presence of many elements of urban life in which an incremental or a competitive approach has proven disastrous and in which our growing capacity to plan effectively represents the more reasonable way of proceeding, with the greater probability of success. Such elements, for example, include the provision of comprehensive systems for mass transportation, air pollution control, air travel, public education, water supply, urban data management, and other services that require long lead times, large-scale development efforts, dependable cooperation, predictable coordination. Like pregnancy, some public decisions involving large systems of highly interdependent parts have an essential "to be or not to be" quality, to be embarked on totally or not at all. For these, incrementalism and "partisan mutual adjustment" can prove abortive.

Nevertheless, the very examples chosen to illustrate vital contemporary functions that demand unified handling also suggest that there are limits of reasonable integration, limits to what we may wish to comprise in any one plan. After all, there probably is no significant sense in which *all* aspects of these several gigantic systems could themselves be encompassed in a single larger formal plan. To say that mass transport should be coordinated with education has some meaning, it is true: we need educated people to plan, build, and administer public travel systems and we need public travel facilities to bring people to and from schools. It is true further that dollars spent on buses are lost to classrooms. But these examples of interrelation surely are overwhelmingly overbalanced by the huge number of variables in the educational and transport systems respectively that are quite independent of each other. It follows that for the great preponderance of the important areas of urban life, each is and should be managed within its own realm. Only the relatively few interactional elements (or the *interfaces* in current parlance) need be studied in a common setting and shaped to each other in an overall plan.

In three senses, then, we are vividly aware of the policy question facing all urban governments: What should be planned and what should not be planned? *First*, there is the sense that some systems either do not greatly need coordination (like the colors of women's dresses at a formal dinner) or are best coordinated in any event by partisan mutual adjustment (as in the case of couples on the dance floor after dinner); while other systems demand dependable and uniform conformance (true of the men's observance of white tie and tails on the same occasion).

In the *second* sense, as Lindblom also has pointed out, we endanger any plan when we load it with more elements than we currently have the dexterity or the power to manage.

Third, there is the matter of alternative modes available for carrying out many of the same functions. We *can* provide education, recreation, transportation, and commodity production by a combination of institutional modes only some of which are appropriate direct subjects of governmental planning. By institutional modes, I am referring to private businesses, largely coordinated in the market and through voluntary agreement; voluntary non-profit associations, private or with open membership; quasi-public corporations like RAND or the port authorities or AT&T; voluntary associations of governmental bodies like San Francisco's ABAG (Association of Bay Area Governments) and Philadelphia's RCEO (Regional Conference of Elected Officials); and the hierarchy of districts and general purpose governments that serve urban populations. We are today vividly aware of the advantages that accrue from our typically American maintenance of all these modes for administering urban activities, enabling experimentation and flexible selection to meet unique and changing sets of requirements.

If we have sensibly affirmed the frequent value of spontaneity and freewheeling, the limits of human capacity to comprehend, and the exceeding richness of the urban institutional fabric, we have at the same time defined an important running question, continuously part of the planner's inquiry: *What* to plan? No absolute rules divide the planned from the unplanned. Rather, a continuing review is called for of matters of public concern, with the shifting boundary kept fluid. Wherever a problem or an opportunity arises, planners today tend to look for the best combination of decision by competition and decision by policy – of spontaneous and relatively free bargaining and of coordinative, structure-imposing planning. Thus, in the last analysis one is neither *for* nor *against* planning, merely by virtue of being a professional planner. Rather, one is for a rational, experimental process for discovering what is best handled in what specific way.

There are, indeed, two distinguishable aspects of how each of us argues with himself internally which are quite similar to how we jointly handle issues in and among our organizations. Partisan mutual adjustment, to use Lindblom's phrase (Lindblom, 1965), is a pervasive way we have for coordinating a great multiplicity of interacting things. It is the major mechanism we use in political life, in the business world, and in our private spheres to work out reasonably compatible relationships among the many semi-independent areas of which our lives are fashioned.

But the processes of partisan mutual adjustment have their limitations and the human being has the capacity for another and somewhat different way of coordinating the disparate elements of life. We are capable occasionally of an act of intuition, based on a period of intensive study of a situation, in which we perceive a new way of putting things together that solves simultaneously and effectively what otherwise would entail a laborious series of only partial solutions. We do this occasionally in our private lives. We do it sometimes in the management of community affairs. It occurs at rare intervals in national policy. In the evolving philosophy of planning it is strongly asserted that we can organize the planning function in government and educate professional planners in such a way as to increase substantially the frequency and effectiveness of creative integration.

The Policy Plan Document

In recognizing tremendous interaction and interdependence among realms of modern urban life, we have identified a communication problem of gigantic magnitude. This problem is stimulating persons working independently on many different applications of planning to reach simultaneously for new means of conceiving, performing, and recording plans — means consonent with the complexity, dynamism, and interactance that typify contemporary organizational plans, whether in the business world, the realm of space science, or the area of urban government.

The virtual revolution that is occurring in the recording, processing, and retrieval of factual data is well known. So are the close similarities in data management whether in business, science, or government. What is perhaps less widely recognized is the parallel development in the systematic handling of *policy* in organizations of varied kinds. The rule book and dated memorandum continue to replace the traditional sets of procedures that used to be handed down from journeyman to apprentice only by example and by word of mouth. The ubiquitous elaborate printed manual now specifies assumptions, principles, standards, forms, and communication flows that formerly were handled more casually. Organizations no longer can afford some of the ambiguities and inconsistencies that have characterized unwritten or unclearly formulated bureau, departmental, and overall policy. Even for voluntary mutual adjustment to take place, one must be clear on what one is adjusting with and to. Especially for attempts at systematic policy integration, rigorous policy expression in writing is essential. This, then, is a period marked by an insistent, widespread demand for policy explicitness.

I have earlier noted the awareness in contemporary planning philosophy of the dispersed distribution of planning and consequent decision-making throughout the hierarchy of urban organizations. The activities that shape and serve the metropolis are federal, state, special district, and local; and they run the gamut from one-man professional establishments to huge complicated governments. The policy plan, quite aside from its function as a conceptualizing instrument, is an essential currency for that exchange of knowledge which is so necessary for the governance of modern urban communities.

The policy plan begins as a compendium of the policies of the many units (including the overall units) of the organizations that comprise the governance of an area. The juxtaposing of the many initially separate plans enables an identification of those elements of the component policies that chiefly interact across divisional lines (an identification foreshadowed and facilitated in the format of the individual plans).

The design element of the earlier architectonic approach to planning is by no means diminished in the policy planning process. Spatial relationships remain vital considerations, and their design remains a major challenge to imagination in the science and art of environmental design. But in an equally valid sense, design of a higher order than physical design also is called into play. By a combination of intuitive, trial-and-error, and decision-modeling techniques, perceptions are developed of various ways to combine the initially disparate or unrelated policy elements into mutually reinforcing combinations, into innovative *gestalts:* that is, new functional integrations with favorable properties not derivable from the mere summation of the parts.

Another important new element in contemporary planning philosophy has emerged out of the recognition that, if we search for them, a great number of possibly valid alternatives are characteristically available. This is in sharp contrast to the traditional architect's view that he alone could perceive the single right solution to the client's set of needs. The urban planner is aware today of many choices dispersed throughout the entire web of policy development, entering early and late, at all levels, and within every function. He knows that relatively few of these choices are within his special competence, that many involve a balancing of diverse group interests or even of conflicting values within individuals. The evolving planning process is moving toward the periodic involvement of technicians, laymen, professionals, and politicians at many stages of the planning cycles – not only or mainly at the end of a cycle to merely accept or reject plans prepared in remote offices reminiscent of architectural ateliers of the nineteenth century. Policy is arrived at successively by the refinement of several generations of alternatives, each new set based on further knowledge than was available earlier.

Validation of Plans

A basic proposition of the planner is: If you do this, which I recommend, the following things favorable to you will happen. Traditionally, the main validation offered was the reputation of the planner and a kind of intuitive plausibility built into the presentation of a design. To return to the architectural analogy, few clients can visualize a building at all reliably from plans; rather, laymen tend to rely on the professional judgment of their architect. But, as has been emphasized above, the predictability of a plan for an urban area is of an entirely different order of difficulty than a judgment about how someone's unbuilt house will likely function and look. Yet, as late as the 1950s, planners were still working predominantly by rule of thumb, with mountains of assumptions backed by mole hills of solid knowledge.

It is not so much that our capacity for prediction has greatly grown as that our approach has changed to reflect the fact of uncertainty. In the 1950s, a significant new approach to the testing of alternative plans was launched. As in the case of other methodological advances, no one person is responsible for the change; rather, it was, so to speak, "in the air." In the early 1950s, J. Douglas Carroll, Jr. was beginning to apply large-scale data handling techniques to the prediction of traffic movement among diverse land uses, first in Detroit and then in Chicago (Chicago Area Transportation Study, 1959, 1960, 1962); Robert B. Mitchell and Chester

Rapkin were theorizing about the relationships between land uses and urban traffic (Mitchell and Rapkin, 1954); and Alan M. Voorhees was constructing and testing a gravitational theory to explain urban movement (Voorhees, 1955). By the end of the decade, the Penn-Jersey Transportation Study had begun work on a simulation model to test the respective potential impacts over time of alternative staged bundles of public policies, especially in transportation but also in urban renewal, housing, open space, public finance, metropolitan organization, and other elements of urban policy (Fagin, 1963). That the methods did not at once become operational is less significant, I suggest, than the fact that *social* progress in planning competence was greatly expedited. The judgment of an individual professional is limited by his personal capacity and experience; but the predictive capability initiated by the explorations of the recent metropolitan studies is susceptible to an entirely different order of improvement. Each study builds on the achievements of its forerunners. The current approaches to the validation of plans are extending the reasonable prediction period significantly and are enabling the comparative consideration of substantially greater numbers of alternatives.

Moreover, run in reverse so to speak, some of the predictive models are being used now to generate design alternatives – in the Southeastern Wisconsin Regional Planning Commission studies, for example. In this process, the present situation and the operational qualities to be achieved are fed into the calculations as inputs and the several potential solutions that would satisfy the requirements are generated by the decision model. This technique, known as decision-modeling, which like simulation modeling generally is still in its infancy, promises to influence further the philosophy of urban planning. It may enable an even clearer posing of the political questions involved in urban planning.

THE EVALUATION OF URBAN PLANS

An increasing awareness of the intertwining of fact and value judgments and of technical, professional, and political prerogatives already has been highlighted. A personal reminiscence will underline the distance traveled in the short span of the recent past. In 1953 the Detroit Area Metropolitan Regional Planning Commission met to consider three major alternative patterns of future land development and to choose among these to guide future county and local land development action and regulation. The three selected alternatives had been depicted on maps of the multi-county region – growth by continued sprawl, by corridor development, and by satellite cities. A decision to promote a fourth variant – a modification dubbed "growth by planned sprawl" – was made by the commissioners duly assembled in formal meeting, and so recorded in the minutes. Upon visiting the commission offices just a year later, I was told by the Detroit city representative that he had never seen any written staff comparison of the three major alternatives. He said further, that the commission had acted so casually that some members remained unaware that a selection had in fact been made, and that no formal record existed of considerations that had led to the choice nor of the deliberations at the decisive meeting. I was, in fact, unable to reconstruct either the staff or commission rationale for the decision from any memoranda in the files. I recount this not to single out the Detroit case, but to emphasize that even in what probably was the best administered metropolitan planning program of the early 1950s, the evaluation process remained highly rudimentary. The selection appeared as casual as the conference of a house architect with a family contemplating sketches of a small home.

In the intervening time there has been a notable heightening of attention to the whole problem of urban criteria. The Goals for America studies promoted by President Eisenhower, the Regional Plan Association's Goals for the Region project in New York, the extensive Twin Cities regional studies emphasizing the identification of hierarchies of values as the foundation for urban policy development, the special 1964 volume of *The Annals* devoted to goals and standards for urban revival – all these attest to the change in outlook.

Toward More Adequate Evaluation

The expansion already noted in the scope of urban planning has challenged the planner to compare the alternative proposals he produces in more meaningful fashion than formerly appeared necessary. Twenty years ago (if I may indulge in a slight caricature) the planner typically began his work by surveying population, employment, street traffic, and land development trends, translating these into forecasts of future "wants and needs" for land and for various public facilities. He then drafted a plausible list of community development goals, which were reviewed, modified, and approved by a commission of laymen or administrative officials or both. He then designed a community land use and street pattern proposal, indicating the locations also proposed for future public installations; and he recommended the development of one or more public housing projects, recreation areas, etc., and a civic center. Sometimes he produced more than one fundamental pattern for consideration, often not. His stated criteria justifying the quantities and qualities spread out on the map were couched in such terms as *balanced, orderly, economical, efficient, coordinated.* He alleged that a recommended arrangement would secure the most appropriate use of land for each purpose throughout the municipality, taking into account the character of the topography and trends in the vicinity. Frequent were statements about achieving a maximum of something consistent with a minimum of something else – which on closer examination proved to be a kind of naive or unconscious double-talk.

The need to state criteria for urban planning much more rigorously became increasingly acute in the last decade, after about 1956, when urban planning generalists began to become involved in a massive way with two nationwide action programs: urban highways and urban renewal. Up to this point, master plans had exerted tangible impact mainly through zoning – and this only over considerable time periods in a sort of delayed effect that tended to blunt any current broad concern with what the master plan might or might not say. The hooking of highway and urban renewal decisions to the work of urban planners, however, brought the issues of planning one way or planning another out into the white heat of public controversy over subjects like relocation and the making or breaking of regional shopping centers. Moreover, planners were being asked far more specific and detailed questions about how alternative arrangements would function: the potential flows of people and goods on highways at different hours in the day; the impacts of proposals on the housing market, on racial patterns, on municipal services and taxes, on overall and sectoral productivity, on the attraction of industry, on the amenities of urban and suburban environments. People became vividly aware of the social costs of projects that disrupted neighborhoods, uprooted families and long-standing businesses, destroyed treasured views of favorite buildings and harbors and hills. They began to be as much concerned with the intangible values gained or lost as with factors readily convertible into dollar amounts of cost and benefit.

Most recently, an intensive search has been proceeding for ways of making criteria operational without unduly weighting decisions in favor of those particular considerations that are inherently quantifiable or can readily be rendered so. Moreover, a major element in the evolution of the planner's philosophy has been a determined concern to place less stress on criteria that relate mainly to quantities measuring *things* and to develop more effective operational indices describing potential impacts on *people*. In comparing alternative policy bundles for urban areas, planners are asking, for example: How many people will have to travel how far to enjoy each kind of open space? How many will have to spend various amounts of time and money to get to and from work, or school, or shopping, or museums? How many and which people will have their taxes increased by various amounts? Which businesses will be aided and which ones disadvantaged by the contemplated changes in urban structure? How will the present situation of various interest groups be affected? What will be the likely impacts on new investments in the area, or on population trends, or on political trends?

Attempts to organize answers to these sorts of difficult questions are confronting planners with analytical requirements apparently substantially more difficult than the cost-benefit and cost-effectiveness balance sheets that have aided decision-making in water management studies or even within the complex defense establishment. It is not that urban planning techniques already have mastered the problem of how to apply effective criteria to assist the choice among complicated policy alternatives. Rather, what marks this stage in the evolving philosophy of planning is the clear understanding that human values and their application to public decisions constitute an area of utmost importance to the development of urban policy. We are today hard at work to make operational the late Henry S. Churchill's enduring phrase, "the city is the people" (Churchill, 1945).

12

Social Planning in the Urban Cosmos

LYLE C. FITCH

□ THE "SOCIAL PLANNING" WHICH IS THE main topic of this chapter refers to policies and programs to raise the cultural and economic levels of certain population groups, mainly those who are not self-supporting. It is concerned largely with government action which has a direct impact on persons. Thus, it is distinguished from planning done by private groups (whether for their own benefit or that of others) and from physical and economic planning concerned primarily with the physical environment and with the productivity and growth of entire economies. And it concentrates on economic and cultural impoverishment while recognizing that "human resources development" per se applies to the entire population.

GENERAL WELFARE PLANNING

The above is a narrow definition of social planning. In the broad, all planning which aims to promote the general welfare, as contrasted to the interests of small groups, is "social." And because the social organism is an ecology – a "system" of closely interacting parts – broad social planning must encompass all the parts including those which we customarily classify as physical and economic, not to mention psychological, biological, organizational, and other categories.

Western thought in the last couple of centuries has emphasized the supremacy of individual choice as the arbiter of welfare – individuals, knowing best their own preferences, are in the best position to gratify them, having at hand those extraordinarily flexible and convenient instruments, the market and the money economy. Social action through collective or political choices has tended to be regarded as a necessary evil, since it is likely that in the provision of public services – protection, education, health, utilities, *et al.* – each individual will receive something a bit different than he would have chosen for himself; and persons who prefer not having the service at all, but have to pay for it anyway, will be completely dissatisfied. There is a large body of literature dealing with this problem of relating private individual choices and public choices, and many attempts have been made to construct social welfare formulas which attempt to bridge the gap, but these have proved fruitless as guides to social policies.

Gerhard Colm and others have pointed out that there is an essential discontinuity and noncompatibility between most public and private services, and that the demands for each are predicated on quite different principles. They do have strong common elements in that the demand in either case is largely socially derived. Even the individual choices made by most people are conditioned by the society in which they live, and most people express their individualism in only small ways.

The bridge between individual and social choices is tenuous because people do not balance off increments of private goods and services against increments of public services when they are making choices. They do not say to themselves, "I think I will take a bit more defense this year instead of painting the house," or even, "My transportation would be considerably improved if I voted to spend money on a new road rather than buying a new car."

Public or collective demand tends to be developed by a process of social interaction in which political leaders, bureaucrats, pressure groups, expressions of public opinion, and ultimately the voting booth all play a role. In the process of this interaction people come to accept the public decision after it is made, in many cases, as something which they would not change in retrospect. What happens is that in the process of social interaction, preferences shift. Of course, the machinery of choice is less than frictionless. Budget makers and legislators continually must make guesses about public preferences, or about what they will be *ex post*. And many people do not see clearly the connection between the taxes they pay and benefits they get.

The essential link between the private sector, governed by household budgets reflecting individual choices, and the public sector, governed by public budgets representing collective choices, lies in the fact that they call on the same pool of resources — manpower, material, and financial. In this broad sense they are competitive — where resources are fully employed, public services and benefits can be expanded only by decreasing private-sector purchases. But they are also complementary in the sense that many private activities depend upon a public infra-structure (the first ingredient being maintenance of law and order, the second education). The more advanced and complex the society, the more complex is the infra-structure required and the greater is the interdependence of the public and private sectors. Where resources are under-employed, government fiscal policy has the further function of increasing either private or public demand, or both.

A substantial part of the welfare-increasing activities of modern governments lies not in the provision of goods and services but in transferring incomes, in effect taxing A in order to increase the purchasing power of B — as in grants to relieve destitution. The rationale of such transfers is that they improve social welfare overall, first by increasing total satisfaction (though this is impossible to prove conclusively), second by gratifying altruistic urges and easing the public conscience (closely related to the first), and third by obviating social unrest, which is usually the most compelling immediate reason for action.

If policies respecting public expenditures cannot be derived directly from individual preference scales, by what means can we build agreement on (1) the division of resources between public and private sectors, and (2) the allocation of public-sector expenditures among the different functions which all compete for a share? The proximate answer is that this is done through the political process through which the claims and demands of the various groups who want something from government are resolved. In itself, however, the political process is a volatile and not always rational one — a game where many players with many different motivations compete for various prizes. Not all of the prizes relate to the provision of goods and services; for example, some of the players may want less regulation or less taxation from the government process, others (bureaucrats) may want more money for providing less service.

Out of the welter of conflicting claims imposed by the various players in the political game, the rational society attempts to achieve a rational allocation of resources, by which we mean resources allocated by considered judgments respecting social priorities. Throughout the twentieth century we have been evolving *means* of imposing a degree of order on the social process and making more considered judgments, toward the *end* of increasing general welfare. The instrument of the budget is the most powerful device evolved so far; it is, however, largely an in-house government device with only marginal participation by the public, and budgets thus far are largely short-term.

There is increasing acceptance of the notion that budgets should be long-term and predicated upon plans which in turn are predicated upon stated goals. Thus far, this notion has found expression mainly in physical planning and capital budgets, but planning methodology is being rapidly extended to all areas of government activity. On August 25, 1965, the President issued his now-famous directive to federal departments and agencies, directing that they install program planning and budgeting systems (PPBS) involving the definition of long-range goals and objectives, consideration and evaluation of alternative means of attaining objectives, and analysis and evaluation of performance. The Presidential interest and the ensuing work in the federal agencies has revived, at least to a degree, flagging interest in program and performance budgeting at state and local government levels.

GOALS AND GENERAL WELFARE PLANNING

Goals, the beginning point of planning and program-making, are the means of obtaining political consensus for social action, through which individual preferences and collective decisions are brought into accord. Party platforms, executive communications (State of the Union messages) and other media are means of goal-formulation and consensus-building, and it appears that these are taken with increasing seriousness as voters become more sophisticated. And increasing interest in goal-making per se is manifested by political leaders and the public; for example, in such efforts as President Eisenhower's Goals Commission, White House conferences on national policy, and citizens' commissions on goals in many cities and metropolitan areas.

Goal formulation is more than a town meeting or citizens committee type of exercise, however. In the complex modern society it requires expert analysis of population trends, development rates, applied technology, probable effects of alternative policies, and other factors. Such analyses must rest on the basic concepts of aspirations which already are widely held or which the public can be persuaded to adopt, and goals must be fitted into projections of productive capacity of the nation, region, or local area concerned.

Colm mentions *aspiration* goals, *achievement* goals, and *performance* goals. Aspiration goals are those not yet reflected in actual decisions. They exist "sometimes in articulated expressions of individuals or groups in leverage positions, but mostly as general, inarticulated 'notions'" (Colm, 1965). One purpose of analysis is to clarify vague aspirations and make them more specific, to construct alternative combinations of goals, or tentative budgets which can be related to resources potentially available for goal achievement. Aspirations spring from many sources. Colm suggests, as his point of departure, the already existing goal structure as revealed through market decisions and public budgets. Existing dissatisfactions suggest one source of aspiration goals; another is the "thinking of people in 'leverage' positions" including business, civic and political leaders, professional specialists, and so on. Technological and economic developments themselves suggest aspirations.

Some aspiration goals stem from development of technical knowledge which makes possible their achievement. Probably the greatest triumph thus far for United States social planning (broad-scale) of the twentieth century has been general acceptance, in a generation, of the goal of high-level employment and stabilization. The principal contributing factor was the development of a theory of economic control which would make goal achievement possible without impinging on the free market system in the process. The role of consensus is so well illustrated by the success thus far of American economic planning directed at the goal of high-level employment and general stability that it should afford useful clues respecting other aspects of social planning. Here I note four characteristics which help explain the success.

First is the fact that the central goal – high-level employment and stability – is simple and therefore easily understood. This greatly simplified the job of building consensus.

Second is the fact that the aspiration goal had been well cultivated during the Great Depression of the 1930s which made virtually everybody sensitive to the evil consequences of depression.

Third is the fact that the goal could be achieved by incremental measures. The planning-implementation process could be one of continual adaptation to changing circumstances by relatively small adjustments rather than of attempting to control all of the circumstances in order to produce a preconceived result. This made it possible to experiment and learn progressively, and to avoid revolutionary changes in the structure and organization of the economic system and the self-defeating complexities of the Soviet model.

Fourth, there are no serious opposing values which are offended by "full employment" policy. The main exception may be price-wage stability, but we still think or hope that these two are not in fundamental conflict. At least it was confirmed, in the late 1950s, that underemployment will not necessarily hold down wages and prices — a sort of proof in reverse.

To be sure, other gaps in our knowledge are still apparent. Thus, the federal government's policy or no-policy during the first six months of 1966 respecting the curbing of apparently incipient inflation reflected not so much the lack of national consensus that inflation-control is desirable, as the lack of a consensus among the experts — between those who believed, with the Council of Economic Advisers, that the ice was thin but would probably hold and those who believed that the nation was headed for a cold bath of inflation.

But the employment-stability goal is matched by few other broad social goals in its simplicity and clarity of purpose, its general acceptance, and a tested (though not yet fully) and growing body of theory and practice regarding goal implementation.

Respecting other broad social goals, one being the abolition of poverty, we apparently have less of a consensus and fewer data with which to set performance and achievement goals. We have less knowledge about the ramifications of various alternative implementation programs, and hence more difficulty in formulating program objectives. Paradoxically, one of the difficulties in the way of acquiring knowledge of social relationships is the increasingly rapid pace of social change, itself predicated on the "knowledge explosion" in technology.

Such obstacles do not diminish the desirability of or need for goal-making, however. General welfare goals, and planning for their achievement, are the more necessary the greater the pace of change, in order that the forces of change may be channeled into socially desirable directions and unwanted results may be foreseen and diverted. Also important is the elimination, so far as possible, of inconsistencies in policies, which now abound.

Though general welfare planning, broadly conceived, is conceptually holistic, encompassing the entire social order and the spectrum of knowledge concerning it, existing knowledge and techniques still dictate limited approaches and concentration on special subject areas such as education, health, etc. However, the areas continue to broaden as we gain further insights into various interrelationships, aided by increasingly powerful analytical tools (such as "systems analysis").

PLANNING RELATIONSHIPS

Most important has been recognition of the relationships between planning for human resources development and physical and economic planning. Public policy long tacitly assumed that human beings are divided into two classes, the prone-to-rise and the prone-to-fall, and that nothing much could be done about the latter except to provide them with bare subsistence (their plight being due to laziness, drunkenness, or other manifestations of original sin). This assumption was reinforced by the fact that most of the immigrant groups coming from Europe and the Orient brought with them strong indigenous cultures which supplied motivation and hopes for achievement. (With Japanese and Chinese and Eastern European Jewish immigrants, the drives appeared to be particularly strong.) In the melting pots of American cities, such immigrants quickly adapted to the new society (while adding to it their own special flavor) and began rising toward the top.

And it was long assumed that the automatic process of the free market, powered by thrift and the acquisitive instinct (both Divinely inspired), would assure continued economic growth and increasing prosperity for worthy individuals; temporary setbacks in the form of depressions were useful cathartics or punishments for departing from the path of economic righteousness.

Planning could therefore concentrate on the physical environment – on orderliness, efficiency and, ultimately, on aesthetic quality.

Two twentieth century developments undermined these assumptions. The first was the wholesale immigration to cities of rural groups, both Negro and white, who had long been largely alienated from the American cultural mainstream. Their own subcultures supplied insufficient motivation for achievement, rejecting middle-class values of thrift, hard work, and respect for education and property. In the Negroes, these legacies of alienation were reinforced by caste and discrimination – a systematic repelling by the whites of their attempts to enter the cultural mainstream.

The second development was the Great Depression of the 1930s, which effectively destroyed faith in the efficacy of the undirected economy. The notion of gross national product growth as a legitimate object of public concern and action took hold. And the notion also took hold, although more slowly, that human beings are potentially valuable capital whose development is too important to be left to the chance that subcultures will always interact favorably with the formal educational system predicated on middle-class cultural values and the existence of middle-class family systems. Human resources development slowly gained recognition as a subdivision in the field of planning in the 1950s and 1960s, although it of course had many earlier antecedents.

Then it became possible to see common threads in various planning categories. The physical planning answer to slums – replacement of slum dwellings with better housing – was found to be quite inadequate. Also required, it appeared, were systems of social support, concern for building and maintaining community relationships, and economic opportunity for the people involved, without which new housing quickly degenerates into new slums.

And exposure to formal education is not itself sufficient to educate many of the children coming from low-income low-culture groups which concentrate in cities. We now see, or think we see, that formal education has to be reinforced by favorable environmental conditions, which include such diverse factors as decent housing and assurance of a job at the end of the formal education process.

The socio-anthropological approach which concentrates on remaking ("acculturating") people is not enough either. That process must be reinforced by a favorable social and physical environment. No amount of acculturation will solve the problem of poverty if the people concerned have no transportation to get to places of employment, or are prohibited by discrimination from escaping the slum.

SOCIAL PLANNING AGAINST ECONOMIC AND CULTURAL POVERTY

Social planning in the narrow sense used here has emerged primarily from a growing conviction that social action can largely eliminate poverty and the causes thereof. (We will not pause here to examine the nuances of defining "poverty;" here it refers to gross and demeaning deprivation.) This is the first aspiration goal. A second and related goal is elimination of the long-standing evil of racial discrimination. While it seems clear that consensus is slowly forming around these goals, the consensus still falls far short of that behind the high-employment-and-stability goal.

Social Planning Achievement Goals

The following list of social planning goals for urban regions, compiled by Harvey S. Perloff (Perloff, 1963), are reflected in much of the federal government's recent social legislation. They are of the order of "achievement goals" (to use Colm's classification) rather than "aspiration goals."

1. To maximize the proportion of families who are self-supporting, and thus reduce dependency.

2. To increase the lifetime earning-power of individuals by measures such as health and mental health improvement, providing useful work for the handicapped and the aged, and encouraging individual entrepreneurship.

3. To provide at least minimal support for those individuals and households who cannot provide entirely for themselves.

4. To achieve all possible economy and effectiveness in the administration of welfare services.

5. To enlarge the scope for individual and small-group decision and action.

Tools of Social Planning

The job of social planning is to assemble and put to work the following kinds of tools, simultaneously and harmoniously, in proportions which will produce noticeable results. Unless results come fast and strongly enough to be noticed, social planning, defined as a conscious process of control for the purpose of obtaining conditions better than would otherwise obtain, fails.

1. Education, including training and retraining of adults.

2. Income maintenance programs for those who are economically stranded through personal incapacity or from social malfunctioning such as unemployment.

3. Social services and counseling for those who need outside personal assistance and counseling.

4. Medical services, both general and preventive, and specific remedial services.

5. The apparatus of law enforcement, penology, parole, etc. directed at the prevention of delinquency and rehabilitation of those who tend to get into trouble by committing various offenses.

6. Housing. Adequate housing has long been and still is considered a minimum essential ingredient of human resource development. Not only quality but location affects the family members' ability to hold jobs, shop, go to school, engage in recreation.

7. Employment. In the contemporary American culture, a job for everyone who wishes to work is a *sine qua non* of personal and social well-being; for males particularly, joblessness is tantamount to inability to play the male role — a form of social castration. But a job per se is no longer enough. The greatest curse of the poverty groups, particularly the Negroes, has been less one of unemployment than one of exclusion from all but low-skill, low-pay jobs offering no avenues of advancement. Career opportunities, rather than job opportunities, are needed in which individuals can advance to levels at which they can make their greatest potential contributions.

Employment has been considered to be a major concern of economic planning, but there is no point in talking about social planning without considering employment. (This underscores the point that there is no way of fencing off a set of planning concerns called social planning which are clearly distinguished from physical and economic planning.) To be a fully-effective social planning tool, employment must be created directly, if necessary, and by government, if necessary. The National Commission on Technology, Automation and Economic Progress has discussed some possible approaches (1966, pp. 35ff).

8. Measures to combat discrimination and segregation, including overt measures to enforce equal treatment in schools, housing, jobs and public facilities, and the more subtle measures of education for tolerance through such means as schools, churches and political leadership.

9. The whole set of other aspiration, achievement and performance goals (and what they imply in the way of policies and programs) directed at improving the environment, better to meet the physical and spiritual needs of the entire population. Environmental planning emphasizes efficiency and aesthetic quality — efficiency to increase productivity and ameliorate physical and psychological stress, beauty and grace to uplift the spirit. This consideration emphasizes again the integral nature of general welfare planning.

Finally, social planning could be much improved by systems of social accounts relating various magnitudes concerned with human resource development, beginning with labor force sectors classified by skills, education, employment status, income, job opportunities — and these are only a few of the demographic, economic, social, fiscal, and other data needed. The accounts should show not only balance sheet conditions at specified intervals but gains and losses over time. Such accounts would make possible analysis in depth, research on social forces and ways of using them constructively or diverting them, and developing strategies for action which cover all participating groups and activities. The analogy is that of national income accounts, which provide our principal source of information respecting the performance of the national economy and the basis for national economic policy (see Perloff, 1963 and Gross, 1965).

It has been suggested also, by Bertram Gross and others, that the President should add to his series of reports on the state of the nation and the economy a report concerned specifically with social and cultural needs, and progress in meeting them.

Development of Social Planning

Although some of the sub-systems of social planning, particularly education and health services, have been going on for years and are fairly well advanced, social planning per se is a fairly recent invention. It is the result of several influences coming together when each was running strongly.

First was the growing recognition of poverty as a problem of "cultural deprivation" of the post-World War II flood of immigrants from the south into cities, particularly northern cities. The transition from rural to urban life stirred a great awakening, as has been the case throughout history, and vociferous political demands for a better deal.

Second was the tendency to think of human skills as productive capital, expenditures on education as investment (rather than as consumption) expenditures, and the persons embodying skills as valuable resources. Human beings, except slaves, have not been so regarded in Western economic thinking until recently; rather, labor has been regarded as a resource to be purchased from the workers, like imports from a foreign country, with no need for concern as to the condition of the worker or the export country. But once workers are regarded as a productive source, their productivity – incorporated in training and physical well-being – becomes a matter of social concern (see Schultz, 1961 and Becker, 1964).

Third was the increasing attention to "systems analysis" and to program and performance budgeting. Systems analysis seeks to bring together for analytical purposes all closely interrelated variables affecting a policy or a line of action; systems approaches have been bringing new insights to social policies and programs, and uncovering their interrelationships.

Program budgeting and performance analysis seeks first to define and give priorities to goals and objectives, explore alternative means of attaining them, select the most effective and economical alternatives, and evaluate results. (For example, if social welfare expenditures are regarded as part of a system of maintaining and improving human capital rather than as grudging charity, it becomes possible to see that present welfare systems have many anti-social consequences.)

The very large investment implicit in the Great Society's commitments to abolish poverty and discrimination pose the requirement for careful management if they are not to be wasted. It is clear that more is required than additional teachers in ghetto schools, construction of low-rent housing units, additional building inspectors or social investigators. The whole structure of services and policies must be evaluated with respect to effectiveness in breaking the poverty trap. Comprehensive plans incorporating all necessary elements of the "system" have to be devised. For instance, it does no good to train people for jobs which will not exist or which will not be accessible when training is completed. Better analysis of future job requirements is needed, along with improved job-market information respecting both available workers and available jobs. Subsidized employment may be another link in the system, transportation still another.

Failure to identify central goals around which to shape programs has led to many inconsistencies in public attitudes and policies. Thus –

1. Urban redevelopment projects are designed to destroy obsolescent buildings which are the only living space that many lower-income bracket people can afford. The housing gap may be supplied in part by public housing programs, but these in the past have tended to perpetuate ghetto conditions and to be located without regard to employment opportunities open to tenants. Public housing income limitations deprive communities of natural leadership. Many projects have quickly degenerated into slums, completing the vicious circle.

2. A primary cause of poverty is low productivity, associated with educational deprivation, lack of incentive, and lack of employment opportunities. Solutions take such diverse forms as attempts at school integration which accelerate the flight of middle-class families from core cities and minimum wage legislation which further shrinks employment opportunities for unskilled workers. The flight to the suburbs has been facilitated by FHA mortgage insurance, while the Urban Renewal Administration has as one of its objectives the provision of middle-income housing which will induce families to stay.

3. Lacking the opportunity for employment, the only recourse for many people is to public welfare. But the public welfare laws are a hodgepodge of measures designed to meet particular needs of individuals and families rather than to focus on the total constellation of requirements for increasing productivity and upgrading

culture. Many features tend to perpetuate dependency conditions; for example, the requirement that the earnings of children be deducted from family welfare allotments, which strikes at the incentive to engage or even learn how to engage in productive activity.

4. Substantial effort and funds are put into education and training, but with no assurance that these will pay off in access to desirable jobs. As a result, in some areas unemployment is higher among people with high school or some high school education than among illiterates and those with only an elementary school education, simply because the latter will accept the least desirable jobs. The situation is epitomized by the comment of a Harlem youth who was "making out by running numbers:"

> I'm not going down and slave around pushing garment trucks. That's worse than being an animal. The law wouldn't let no animal get treated like that. I make out here. Ain't going down there and be treated like an animal.

SOME ISSUES OF SOCIAL PLANNING AND GOAL FORMULATION

This list can do no more than illustrate the great range of social planning issues.

Cultural Homogenization

One social planning objective, more commonly found than articulated, is the indoctrination of the poor with middle-class values and standards of conduct – a process frequently referred to by the innocuous title "acculturation." The middle-class virtues commonly mentioned are those of aspiration and the felt need for achievement, self-reliance, thrift, and respect for law, private property and middle-class moral standards generally. It is difficult to see how the groups involved can escape from poverty without accepting a large part of the middle-class culture and standards, particularly those respecting the need for achievement.

Assuming that such an acculturation process for today's bottom-rungers is feasible, as it has been with other racial and ethnic groups, the question remains as to whether minority subcultures incorporate values which should be preserved in the interests of a more colorful pluralistic society. What degree of cultural differentiation is consistent with the somewhat contrary value of abolishing discrimination?

Strengthening Subculture Family Life

Moynihan and others have put great stress on the thesis that lower-class Negro social organization tends to be matriarchal rather than familial in the middle-class sense of the word. This situation reflects the hundreds of years of degradation of the male Negro, first in slavery, then in the post-slavery caste system of the south, and more recently under the impact of unemployment and the vicious welfare systems which make family allowances depend partly on the absence of the father, and hence break up families.

One of the outcomes is that many Negro boys have no experience with aspiring, successful men – no one to emulate. Recognition of the importance of the quality and stability of family life, says Moynihan, could be the central event leading to a new era of social legislation, centering on the family rather than, as in the past, on the individual.

The thesis has been hotly rejected by many Negro spokesmen, but it appears that the rejection may be based more on the reflections it casts on the subculture than on the merits of the thesis.

Ways of Reaching Alienated Subcultures

The difficulty of breaking in from the outside has been noted by many, including Mark Battle:

> With considerable fanfare, governments, foundations and charities are spending millions to help Negroes in the urban ghettos. Yet in city after city these "action plans" bog down in confusion and disappointment. Meanwhile the ghetto spirit of revolt continues to grow . . . The truth is that the white man's programs to help the ghetto cannot succeed as expected. The legions of white lawmakers, administrators and social workers who devise and run these programs may have the best intentions, but they make a momentous mistake. They assume that White America's middle-class standards of sexual morality, parental behavior, social propriety, and economic success are universal . . . The fact is that the many Negro slum-dwellers know little and care less about middle-class morality (Battle, 1966).

Surrogates for the Middle-Class Home

The extent to which the education system is predicated upon the existence of a supporting middle-class family system has already been noted, along with the fact that such conditions do not apply to "disadvantaged" children – children who are neglected, have nowhere to go after school, are on the street with no supervision or sense of direction, who include in their behavior models the most sordid aspects of the slum. Head Start and similar programs so far have been of little more than marginal help. Question: Should there be programs designed specifically to supply as many as possible of the functions of education and supervision for which society ordinarily has looked to the family? Any such programs should be complemented by family services designed to better equip the family to understand and help the child. But in cases where the family base is weak, children's programs might occupy most of the child's waking hours. In this respect, the United States may have much to learn from the experiences of other countries such as the Soviet Union and Israel, where such intensive programs have been established to bridge the gaps between widely different cultural levels and bring young people into the cultural mainstream as rapidly as possible.

Part of such a support program can concentrate on education itself. Machlup has observed that

> Adding a few years of schooling has been proposed by many as a measure for raising productivity of the next generation. Many school reformers, however, propose to add the years at the wrong end, at the ages 15 to 18 instead of 3 to 6. Schooling ought to be provided at the earliest age, when systematic mental stimulation can still do something to increase the capacity of the mind. Children thus prepared will be able to absorb much more of what they are taught later (Machlup, 1965).

But is extended education, however important, sufficient by itself? What of the hours after school which, for middle-class children, are heavily occupied in recreation and acquiring still further skills, but which for many slum children are occupied simply in roaming the streets and imbibing the less savory aspects of slum life?

Desegregation and Education Deficiencies

To what extent can desegregation remedy deficiencies in educational facilities, programs, and general climate? Negroes rightly consider that educational facilities available to them in both south and north have been vastly inferior to those of middle-class whites. It is easy to jump to the conclusion that desegregation can remedy this situation, first by eliminating disparities in the quality of educational programs; second, and more important, by exposing culturally deprived people to middle-class influences (children learn from each other). It is the latter proposition which is at issue. There is little reason to think that children who are culturally deprived can keep pace with well-prepared children, nor will middle-class parents, white or nonwhite, consent to see their own children disadvantaged by programs based on the lowest common denominator. They will flee to the suburbs, they will put their children into private schools, but they will not stand for radical adulteration of standards. It is widely accepted, too, that culturally deprived children need special assistance which by definition is not provided to all children. This may point to the conclusion that the main need is not for homogenization but for superior educational facilities constructed specifically to meet the needs of deprived children. So far they have been getting the worst in physical facilities, quality of instruction, and educational climate; and for many, the extras such as supervised homework or even provision of a place to do homework are out of the question.

Minimum Income

Should a minimum, or foundation, income be assured to every family (including unattached individuals)? Minimal foundation income grants are now being widely advocated as a means of replacing the present hodgepodge of welfare and other income-supplementing payments; they might also replace social security and other employment compensation benefits and various kinds of subsidies, as for housing. The negative income tax, providing rebates for those whose incomes fall below a specified minimum, is one of several possible administrative devices.

The central issue, besides cost, is the fear of damage to work incentives and the encouraging of idleness. But proponents point out that there will be some contrary effect of increasing work incentives on the part of those who can begin to see, for the first time, a chance to make substantial gains through work. Present welfare programs, in effect, impose a 100 per cent tax on earnings of welfare recipients. And why, it is asked, should not the poor as well as the rich have some choice in the matter of leisure (with the poor it is usually called "idleness")? Machlup observes that measures which extend the choice of whether to work are more desirable than measures which tend to create unemployment, as minimum wage measures.

Importance of Environment

Many of the above measures involve doing things to *people.* How about *environment?* Should social planning act deliberately to eliminate segregation in urban areas, and to break up city ghettos, or should it emphasize eradicating discrimination and raising cultural and economic status, leaving desegration more largely to choice? If the former, what should planning objectives attempt to achieve in the way of greater population heterogeneity; for example, should the effort be to achieve equal ratios of white and nonwhite residents in each community? Is there merit in seeking to maintain a pluralistic society with a place for distinctive Negro culture? How would this culture be affected by planned desegregation?

These are only examples of the many questions that social planning must try to resolve. They can be resolved, if at all, only by experimentation and research on a scale far greater than has yet been undertaken. And with the increasing emphasis being given to the concerns of social planning, there must be correlative emphasis on evaluation of proposed programs already undertaken. This is a field in which the appearance of action is especially likely to be accepted as a substitute for action. But however many political values may be satisfied by otherwise ineffective programs in the short run, such programs may have little impact on poverty in the long run.

Conscious of this fact and of the vulnerability of experiments at the national level, the Office of Economic Opportunity and other federal agencies have instituted a variety of evaluation procedures and projects. But at local government levels, where much of the administrative work goes on, there is ordinarily little of the expertise needed for good evaluation or other aspects of program planning.

PLANNING AND PROGRAM PACKAGING

A proliferation at all three levels of government of programs concerned with human resources development, and with urban development generally, presents cities with an embarrassing abundance – embarrassing in the sense that more is available than most cities can readily use.

However, the existing smorgasbord of programs, each devised to meet a particular urgent problem, seldom adds up to achieving coherent central objectives. They are piecemeal and lack essential ingredients; they are administered by a great variety of administrative agencies, many of which have little to do with each other. Thus, in the federal government alone, we find crucial human resources programs under the Departments of Health, Education, and Welfare; Housing and Urban Development; Commerce (Economic Development Administration); and Labor; the Office of Economic Opportunity; and several other agencies. There are some twelve dozen grant programs, each concerned with different angles of the urban problem. In the field of training, even the experts find trouble keeping track of Youth Corps, Job Corps, MPTA (Manpower Training Act), and the numerous other training-related programs. States and localities, with much more widely proliferating jurisdictions, and specialized agencies and bureaucracies face the problem of knitting everything together into some sort of coherent picture. Hence, the words "coordination," "integration," and "cooperation" have become some of the most overworked terms in government.

A central objective of social planning is to bring a greater measure of coherence and effectiveness out of the welter of existing programs and to fill existing gaps. The first step is the redefining and simplifying of objectives – "human resources development" itself is a powerful organizing concept. It has already been suggested that clearer perspectives on central objectives could eliminate many inconsistencies and conflicts.

In part, because of the proliferation of programs, the trend of the times is toward program packaging – mobilizing resources of already on-going programs in concentrated attacks instead of scattered skirmishes. This is simple organization; what is new are the bases of organization – the broadening comprehension of integral relationships among programs – which make possible necessary simplifying generalizations.

The present trend toward government program packaging was developed and accelerated, if not invented, in the early 1960s through such agencies as the President's Committee on Delinquency, the Ford Foundation's gray area projects, and the federal government's community renewal programs launched in the Housing Act of 1961. In response to these and other stimuli a number of city (and state) governments began reorganizing themselves to cope better with their human resource problems.

Meanwhile, the human impulse toward tidy organization has been at work within the federal government with the creation of the Department of Health, Education, and Welfare (1953); the Office of Economic Opportunity (1964), placed in the Executive Office of the President with the mission in part of bringing together various human resources development programs; and a Department of Housing and Urban Development (1965).

But after all of these unifying measures, the job of putting together a comprehensive urban development program somewhat resembles that of assembling an automobile if only about half the components are available, if they could be obtained only by going to a hundred departments of a dozen stores (where some of the parts would be found to be too expensive), and if the job were to be done by a team of mechanics none of whom had ever seen an automobile and were working more-or-less independently with no set of plans.

Even under such circumstances it may be possible to get started if agreement can be reached on the purpose of the automobile, and if the mechanics can be gotten to work together in a creative way. We are now at about this stage. As an indication of what is going on, I mention three recent developments of some planning and organizational significance: the Economic Opportunity (Anti-Poverty) Act of 1964, the demonstration-cities program of 1966, and the creation (1966) of New York City's Human Resources Administration.

WAR AGAINST POVERTY

The target of the Economic Opportunity Act is poverty which "is handed down from generation to generation in a cycle of inadequate education, inadequate homes, inadequate jobs, and stunted ambitions," and that part of the poverty population – the young and others potentially capable of employment – who can take advantage of the opportunities offered. Since these are a minority of the poverty population, the war against poverty, while more than a cold war, is somewhat less than all-out.

The main provisions of the Economic Opportunity Act include:

1. *Youth programs*

   a. The Jobs Corps – training through rural conservation camps and urban residential training centers.

   b. The Neighborhood Youth Corps – work experience and training for school dropouts and those continuing in school.

   c. Work-study Program – part-time employment for students in institutions of higher education.

2. *Urban and rural community action programs*

   a. General community action program – "services, and assistance, and other activities of sufficient scope and size to give promise of eliminating poverty; these may include employment, job-training and counseling, health, vocational rehabilitation, housing, and home management, welfare, and special remedial and non-curricular educational programs."

   [The most notable feature of this section is that stipulating "maximum feasible participation of the residents of the areas and members of the groups served."]

   b. Adult basic education programs – literacy training for adults over eighteen years old.

3. *Work-experience programs* – experimental pilot projects for those on welfare to secure or obtain employment, self-support, or personal independence.

The Act has several other provisions including those creating the Office of Economic Opportunity and establishing VISTA (Volunteers In Service to America).

Finally, the Economic Opportunity Act established the Office of Economic Opportunity in the Executive Office of the President, with broad responsibilities for insuring that "all federal programs relating to the purposes of this Act are carried out in a coordinated manner." In addition, federal agencies are directed, in administering their own programs, to assist in carrying out the purposes of the Act, and directed "to give preference to any application for assistance or benefits made pursuant to community action programs organized under the Economic Opportunity Act." Pursuant to the intent of this section, devices for better-coordinated planning are being built up. For example, local economic opportunity councils are asked to comment and pass on anti-poverty projects, such as public housing projects, emanating from other agencies.

It is too early to evaluate the policies and programs ensuing from the Economic Opportunity Act. Most of the programs – education and training, assistance to small business, rural programs – are incremental or supplemental to programs already in existence under federal, state or local sponsorship. But in another sense they have raised hopes and provided opportunity for another start, as through Youth Corps and Job Corps programs, to thousands of young people. Operation Head Start for pre-kindergarten ages has focused on one of the greatest sources of deprivation – the lack of elementary training in the low-culture home and the inability of many children reaching school age to recognize simple words and concepts, carry on simple conversations, or handle simple abstractions. Though Head Start programs have been highly popular, there have been suspicions that in fact they reached more middle-income than poverty-group children. This itself is a testament to success, although it misses the planned objective of narrowing the educational gap between children of different classes.

The most significant section of the poverty program may turn out to be the section encouraging "maximum feasible participation of the residents of areas and members of the groups involved." This section addresses, perhaps in part inadvertently, the most crucial elements of the poverty subculture, political power and participation. Based on a growing body of sociological doctrine, it strengthened and accelerated movements already under way.

There are really two issues – (1) participation in program planning and administration, and (2) building political power. Political power, so the argument goes, in the last analysis must be the principal weapon of the poor and of minority groups in seeking to improve their economic status. Proponents of the thesis point to the precedent of organization and the fact that labor did not gain until it became sufficiently organized to exert strong political power. (This analogy is questionable on two counts, however. First, labor was not able to organize strongly until it received political support — in the Roosevelt Administration of the 1930s. Second, the sheer number of members was far greater proportionately than are the numbers of the poor, or of the minority groups [Negroes] most afflicted.)

The early days of the poverty program saw attempts in several cities, encouraged by OEO staff, to organize poverty groups for protest and political action. Such activity brought vociferous protests from city mayors and was de-emphasized by the Administration. Further problems were encountered in organizing participation. Initial attempts to arrange elections for the poor to sit on local community action councils produced only listless responses — the poor, it seemed, were not to be drawn into participation through the more conventional means of balloting.

Meanwhile other forces were at work. Watts, in Los Angeles, furnished further demonstration of the need for organization in the ghettos when it developed, during the 1965 riots, that there was no means for communication between government officials and the Negro community and no one to whom the rioters would listen. This and other demonstrations went some distance toward convincing mayors and other government officials of the need for means of communication with the discontented and for responsible leadership which could make communication meaningful. (It is impossible to communicate with a mob or with the clamor of voices from competing groups.)

The second development arose from participation in the action programs. Here, rather than through contrived formal polling processes, could leadership emerge. As Earl Rabb summarizes it:

> Originally, there was a tendency to define participation in terms of hiring poor people to do many of the jobs that had to be done — aids and sub-professionals who would provide a bridge between the poverty population and the programs. They would serve as living signals to the neighborhood people that they were now in fact being "invited into" the society.

> But very swiftly there came a shift in the definition of participation. The "neighborhood boards" became the focus of interest. And it was the policy-making functions of these neighborhood boards that became the important thing (Rabb, 1966).

Indigenous leadership then began taking over the organization and direction of programs. Thus an article in the *New York Times* of September 12, 1966 was headlined

> **[New York] City's Poor Excel in Leading Poor**
> **Ran More Than Half of 322 Summer**
> **Programs with 50 to be Continued**

In many areas the definition of participation is changing still further, as exemplified by Rabb's example of a western city whose progressive mayor moved to give neighborhood groups virtually complete control over neighborhood programs. This was subject, however, to some maintenance of supervision and control by a central body representing other community interests – business, labor, and the general public – over which he would have political control. But this did not satisfy those who were emerging as the "anti-poverty militants," who demanded an automatic majority control over the city-wide council, which they ultimately got.

Then it became clear that the militants "were not interested in any kind of service program for some time to come; they were interested in using *all* the available funds for the purpose of 'organizing' the people of the neighborhoods . . . not just for the purpose of planning and administering their own welfare programs, but for the purpose of expressing and implementing their needs and desires in all arenas of public life."

The same basic process has taken place or is taking place in hundreds of other communities in a variety of forms and faces. The pattern is clear: "participation" as a principle of the anti-poverty program has emerged not only or even primarily as a means of motivating people themselves occupationally and educationally, but as a value in itself. And the value is power, political power.

In these terms, however, *power* has no basis except votes and threats. Where the poor and the racial minorities do not command the votes for major power moves, they can do no better than build more effective voting enclaves which can then bring more weight to bear on the political structure. And it should be remembered that racial minorities are themselves a small minority of the poor. As for threats, they boomerang. Probably the threats implicit (and explicit) in the "black power" movements of 1965-1966 were more responsible than anything else for the negative Congressional attitude toward broadening civil rights legislation in the 1966 session.

We are driven back to the conclusion that the chief values of participation may lie in the development of leadership and skills in the subculture through indigenous leadership working with action programs, rather than seeking to build independent power bases.

The struggles for power, the kaleidoscopic patterns of community behavior and response, the lack of knowledge about what does and does not work, all explain why the anti-poverty program still was largely unplanned in the summer of 1966.

The New York City Human Resources Administration

This agency, established in 1966 by executive order of Mayor John V. Lindsay, is an obeisance to the power of human resources development as an organizing concept. In its compass are the New York City Department of Welfare, the anti-poverty agencies, the Youth Board and other youth agencies, and a unit to be concerned with education which will maintain liaison with the City Board and Department of Education.

The three principal organizing concepts of the Human Resources Administration are:

1. The need to redefine and simplify goals, objectives and programs so as to produce greater internal consistency and effectiveness, and to devise corresponding programs and strategies.

2. Emphasis on general education, training, manpower and career development, and employment opportunities, and on a system of social services and public assistance which tie in with these other programs and increase their chances of success.

3. Increased participation of residents in poor communities in developing and operating programs for their benefit. Placing with local community corporations, to be created in designated poverty areas (some 16 have been designated thus far), a wide range of

responsibility for planning and supervising administration of a number of functions having to do with social and developmental programs. Corporation governing boards would be elected by people of the community, carrying forward the notion of involvement in political life and community affairs of people who previously have been outside the political process. (See Institute of Public Administration, 1966a.)

The agency will be headed by an administrator "responsible to the mayor for overall planning and coordination of city policy on community development and community action, manpower and career development, social and youth services, and public assistance; he will also advise the mayor on public education policy, especially as it affects other human resources activities."

Three deputy administrator posts are established respectively for planning and budget, management, and community relations. The deputy for planning and budget would be responsible for the agency's overall planning and for establishing and operating a program-planning-budgeting system. The creation of this post, unique thus far in New York City administration, indicates the importance attached to the overall planning process.

The agency's structure and program thus go in two directions which up to now have generally been found to be more or less incompatible. First is the notion of imposing rationality and order on the community development process by setting up a highly structured and capable top-level planning and administrative system; second, that of increasing community involvement and participation in planning and administration by the people involved. In the past, with cities over the country, there has tended to be an inverse correlation between substantive programs and community action — where community action programs are relatively strong (as they have been previously in New York City) substantive programs are relatively weak and vice versa.

As the agency was getting organized in September of 1966, this dilemma was strikingly illustrated by a controversy in Harlem over community participation in a new intermediate school, (a controversy not yet resolved as this is written). The families of the district demanded either that the school be integrated by bringing in white pupils from the outside (a manifestly impossible condition) or that they be given an active voice in the management of the school, including a voice in the selection of administrators and teachers. When the superintendent of schools made the gesture of withdrawing the white principal and substituting a nonwhite administrator, the professional staff, including the Negro component, threatened to withdraw. When the white principal was reinstated, outside extremist forces moved in to fan the controversy.

The Demonstration-Cities Program

The demonstration-cities program, still being debated in Congress when this was written, is another thrust toward concentration of resources on specific objectives and toward comprehensive planning. The purpose of the bill is to provide machinery for organizing the resources of all federally aided programs, together with state and local programs, concerned with human resources development and urban renewal for "rebuilding or restoring entire sections and neighborhoods of slum and blighted areas" (see Chapter 20 by Robert C. Weaver for program description).

As conceived, the demonstration-cities program would almost certainly be a powerful force in stimulating more comprehensive planning and bringing together city agencies for concerted efforts. But the obstacles in the way of putting together comprehensive, well-integrated programs are still formidable — lack of basic knowledge, lack of planning talent, problems of organizing local government bureaucracies, to name a few. Some trails have been blazed, at least, by community renewal planning (provided for by the Housing Act of 1961).

Then there is the question of getting concurrence of federal agencies, from three on up, each of which would have to approve the program contemplated for them in the plan, which plan is to be prepared entirely by local agencies. The House Banking and Currency Committee version requires that the DHUD Secretary shall "insure, in conjunction with other appropriate Federal departments and agencies and at the direction of the President, maximum coordination of Federal assistance provided in connection with this title . . ." But it would appear that the Secretary's power in fact would lie in jawbone rather than muscle, and jawbone methods have difficulty resolving deep policy conflicts and getting cooperation from reluctant bureaucracies.

It would seem that programs which require the participation of a number of agencies (whether public or private) of divergent interests can be formulated most effectively and efficiently if all of the agencies participate in the planning process. This is particularly true of innovational programs requiring new types or combinations of action, where there is little in the way of experience or precedent for guidance. It is in the planning stage that alternatives can be explored, different viewpoints of various agencies and interests can be registered, and those who ultimately will have to make decisions concerning provision of funds or taking of action can be stimulated and educated. No such process is contemplated by any version of the bill thus far.

Even correction of this apparent weakness, in the opinion of some, would not solve the central problem which the demonstration-cities bill proposes to attack. James Q. Wilson observes:

> Its central problem – apart from (though related to) the obscurity as to its goals and the mystery as to its means – is that it is an effort to improve on old programs, not by changing them or by substituting a wholly new strategy, but by creating a new apparatus to show how, by "coordination" (i.e. more administration) the job can be done better. But the failures of the past sixteen years have been precisely the failures of administration – of seeking inappropriate or incompatible goals, or being unable to attain given goals, or failing to take into account the consequences of working toward these goals. Overcoming the weaknesses of administration by providing more administration is likely to succeed only if extraordinary men do the administration (Wilson, 1966).

SUMMING UP

Social planning in the United States in the mid-1960s represents many influences, strains of thought, and conflicting sentiments. On the one hand is the combination of a troubled social conscience on the race issue; the rising sense of guilt about poverty in the midst of plenty combined with the realization of the costs of poverty in terms of low productivity, delinquency, crime, and other pathological indicators; the growing recognition of the essential unity of the social fabric and the essential oneness of many kinds of problems which previously have been considered distinct. On the other hand is the overhang of deeply ingrained convictions and prejudices, stemming in part from the Puritan heritage, concerning the worthiness of the poor and damage to personal incentives of doles and subsidies; racial prejudice, particularly on the part of the working class fearing competition and intrusion from those lower down; concern about costs – all complicating the task of building national consensus.

One can speculate that much of present-day social planning stems from the need to bridge the gap between a less sophisticated and superstition-ridden age and a more sophisticated age which finds new first causes of what it perceives as social problems. But there is a danger of a disappointing failure of social planning, if it seeks to build on precedents drawn from the physical sciences and physical planning, which are predicated on more measurable quantities and sequential, cause-and-effect relationships. Social planning deals with a world of uncertainty owing in part, but only in part, to lack of knowledge. Many things are *inherently* uncertain.

The uncertainties increase with the new trend toward community involvement. Robert Weaver notes that "Congress has, in effect, set a new national standard of citizen interest and involvement that, however hazy, goes far beyond anything ever contemplated in more than a few communities prior to the antipoverty program. . . . The engagement process cannot be neatly confined to an agenda of pure planning or renewal questions."

The complexity of the variables involved in social planning suggests the question of whether there is an analogy with the economic system, where equally complex variables are pulled together into a working cosmos through the device of the market. No one has found a substitute for the market, and in numerous Socialist countries, notably the Soviet Union, planning has overreached itself in trying to replace market mechanisms with planning decisions. One may ask if social planning is similarly in danger of overreaching itself.

The credo of the democratic society is that the "better life" lies in the direction of, first, extending the range and scope of the individual choices we can make, and second, extending effective participation in community choices involving schools, recreation facilities, health, sanitation, transportation, and other benefits and services provided by the public sector. In a sense, both are antithetical to planning, if by planning we mean centrally directed change. But in another sense, social planning seeks to extend such choices; this may be its main contribution.

Accepting that individual choice and participation in social choice both are essential to the "good life," we still have the question of what should be the relative emphasis on enlarging the scope of individual decisions, and enlarging the capacity for community action (as through community action programs). It is claimed for both that they build motivation and self-respect and doubtless, under favorable circumstances, both do. But we need to know more.

Are community action programs, based on geographic concentrations of the poor — that is, on segregation — a viable base of political power? Do they tend to perpetuate segregation? If so, do the values of community action override the values of desegregation. Recent studies confirm that poverty itself is one of the greatest deterrents to social cooperation, by preoccupying each man with his own concerns and setting him against his neighbor — does this suggest that frontal assaults on poverty may produce results more quickly than will organizing community action programs?

Would direct approaches such as guaranteeing jobs for all who wish to work, and a minimal income set somewhere above a bare subsistence level, do more to promote incentives and build self-respect by affording individuals more freedom to make their own decisions? Community participation by such devices as representation of the poor on anti-poverty action agencies, and in planning and operating programs, will involve at best substantially only a relatively few of the poor, whereas direct measures to extend individual choice may reach nearly everyone. (Other devices for extending individual choice include rent subsidies, as opposed to public housing; grants for education designed to give parents more choice as to schools, etc.)

Finding better answers to such questions requires much more in the way of research to straighten out goals, objectives and programs and much more communication of social needs to physical and other planners. Perhaps the most persuasive demonstration of the need for social planning lies not so much in what it has been able to do thus far as in the conspicuous absurdities and stupidities which accrue without it.

In any case, such are the uncertainties that social planning must in the main be based on probabilities, not certainties; with strategies to meet possible alternative developments, rather than with neatly constructed models based on known facts; and with continual rolling adjustments rather than with tidy sequences.

Technology in Transition

THE SECOND PAIR OF CHAPTERS in Part II consists of essays by Britton Harris on "The New Technology and Urban Planning" and by Melvin M. Webber on "Transportation Planning for the Metropolis."

In Chapter 13, Harris considers how technology has been affecting urban planning and hazards some thoughts on where this may be leading. As he puts it, it is his "modest effort to relate the development of science and technology in our society as a whole to human social organization in the urban environment and to man's conscious control over the development of this milieu."

Harris distinguishes four main areas of scientific and technological advancement and a fifth area which may in some ways be regarded as a synthesis of the other four. "The main area of scientific advance which carries forward the industrial revolution in the second half of the twentieth century," he says, "is man's increasing *command over sources of power*." Harris calls the second area "*microprocessing . . .* the fact that increasingly the products which we use in our society are more finely processed and that frequently this processing requires the manipulation of materials at the atomic and molecular level, or to very fine measurements." A revolution in *communications and control* is the third area, and in Harris's view it "is central to one or another aspect of the other revolutions being discussed." In an intriguing aside, he suggests that "the principal impact of the technology of communication and control upon our society is only indirectly by way of information pure and simple, and much more significantly by way of the challenges and solutions which it brings to our abilities to think."

Harris's fourth type of technological change is the general area of the *life sciences.* He includes "the technologies in particular of health, medicine, and agriculture, all of which are predicated on the understanding of living processes through the various sciences of biology." The technology of *purposeful social control* is Harris's last category. He warns that "An appropriate technology must here be based on a revived social science which demonstrates that science can indeed be humanistic in content. We can then recognize that, in general, the technology of social organization is identical with the technology of planning."

Discussing the "Social Consequences of the New Technology," Harris emphasizes the social thrust "toward enormous increases in affluence and power." There follows a full treatment of developments and prospects in the technology of the urban planning process. The closing section, "The Metropolis and Technology," shifts to the substance rather than the process of urban metropolitan planning. As Harris suggests, "There is perhaps more immediacy to the resolution of problems of process than of substance, since it is apparent to me that it will take many decades of work to evolve the socially acceptable and technically feasible city of the future."

In Chapter 14, Webber addresses "Transportation Planning for the Metropolis." Like Harris, he is interested in the impacts of changing technology on the planning process, and there is a close relationship between the two essays. Webber's approach is to a narrower subject, however, for he focuses on the recent evolution of transportation policy development is a historical way and in some depth. He begins with the Highway Act of 1916 and ends with transportation studies that have not yet published the final conclusions of even their first rounds of work.

Most significant is the story of the steady growth of sophistication in transportation planning, especially since about 1954. In the 1950s metropolitan transportation came to be looked at as an activity integrally related to all the other uses of land and not merely as a separate function to be "suboptimized," i.e., to be decided within the framework mainly of transport considerations. And now, with the passage of the Housing Act of 1966, the federal government has, declared that each metropolitan area seeking federal aid for local projects shall designate a single area-wide governmental agency, cooperatively established by the governments of the entire metropolis, to which proposals for highways, transit, parks, hospitals, water and sewer systems, urban renewal — in fact about everything but schools

— must be referred for review within a single framework of metropolitan development policies.

Webber deals critically with two divergent viewpoints that he perceives in modern transportation planning. One is based on a conviction that transportation serves but does not shape the urban region. Within this first rationale, land-use studies enable a prediction of future transportation demand, but land-development processes are thought to be inevitable, predetermined by general social, economic, and logistic factors. The second viewpoint is that people can and do affect the flow of urban development by all sorts of public actions: by the specific choice and staging of highways, transit lines, park and waterfront developments, renewal activities, airports, water and sewage facilities, and other similar programs. Webber holds that decisions in these several areas, if aligned toward coherent development goals, can produce planned change in their combined effect.

Transportation planning has been the first adequately financed application of systems analysis, with large-scale data development and computers, and with mathematical model-building used for shaping policy in a fundamental sector of social life. But the same methods could be used for other sectors too. As a consequence, Webber's account has important implications for the handling of general urban development as well as transportation per se.

— H.F.

13

The New Technology and Urban Planning

BRITTON HARRIS

☐ IT HAS BEEN SAID THAT AN OLD Chinese curse is, "May your children live in interesting times." The suggestion is obviously that there is some stress involved in living in a period of rapid change and uncertainty. I agree, but within limits I find this change and uncertainty exhilarating and of genuine interest. Quite apparently, there are two connected sources of change in the present century – one depending on knowledge and one on all other social forces. I incline to the feeling that the primary source is in the explosion of knowledge (or science) together with its application to mankind and his environment (or technology). The impact of this explosion on man's age-old problems of economic well-being, social organization, and international rivalry is impressive. Changes which are occurring in these problem areas have given rise to much social, philosophical, and ethical speculation and torment, and this will undoubtedly continue for many decades. Such speculation is perhaps not very useful unless it is anchored to an understanding of the processes through which change occurs. I make here a modest effort to relate the development of science and technology in our society as a whole to human social organization in the urban environment and to man's conscious control over the development of this milieu.

THE NATURE OF THE NEW TECHNOLOGY

In order to look at this problem we need, first of all, to take a brief look at the most fundamental aspects of the development of man's control over himself and his environment, and to see why and how present changes differ in quality and quantity from the previous epoch of development. I shall distinguish four main areas of scientific and technological advancement, and a fifth area which may in some ways be regarded as a synthesis of the other four.

Power Sources

The *first* main area of scientific advance, which carries the industrial revolution forward into the second half of the twentieth century, is man's increasing command over sources of power. This advance, together with the increasing division of labor, has forced the pace of the last two centuries and brought us to the threshold of the present era. Within the last quarter-century, a basis has been laid for severing man's dependence on fossil fuels through the command over atomic processes. It is therefore now fair to say that there is no limit in the near future to the energy which society can command. At the same time, owing to the specific nature of this technology, there is also no limit to the amount of energy which can be released in very small compass; this is the basis for the military technology of atomic energy.

The positive aspects of unlimited command over energy are easy to see. In general, they have to do with processes which essentially require the application of brute force, but there are more subtle applications as well. The brute force aspects include the drastic modification of the environment through engineering works; heating and cooling large spaces; moving objects faster, farther, and in greater volume against the resistance of the environment; and the like. Such activities have an archaic flavor as an extension and magnification of the last century and are in some senses in opposition to trends in the coming era. It seems somewhat paradoxical to use gigantic amounts of energy to build dams to produce hydroelectric energy with the wealth of atomic power lying ahead of us. Power is also needed, however, for a variety of purposes of a different quality, such as the separation of new metals like titanium from their ores and the synthesis of many materials used in agriculture and construction.

The ultimate difficulty in the brute force application of expanded power sources lies in the fact that most such power is ultimately degraded into heat. As long as man was primarily dependent on solar energy and fossil fuels, there was a limit to the extent to which he could raise the temperature level of his environment. Now, the continued release of heat into the environment can continuously increase its temperature, with presently unforeseeable consquences for climate, geology, and ecology. The indefinite expansion of our utilization of energy must, therefore, ultimately be carefully considered and controlled. Fortunately, if we can decrease our absolute dependence on fossil fuels, we will offset this danger by reducing the greenhouse effect of carbon dioxide. Fortunately, also, the effect of other technological developments seems to point in the direction of de-emphasizing the importance of energy per se.

The discovery of atomic energy has been a triumph for man's understanding of nature at the finest possible scale – at the level of subatomic particles and their interactions. The era of this understanding can perhaps be considered to have begun no earlier than 1900, when the quantum theory was first suggested. At any rate, this revolution in understanding, less than a century old, is rapidly being extended into all aspects of our technological interests. The three additional technological revolutions are also profoundly influenced by this scientific change. As we discuss them, it will be well to bear in mind that, even though many of the changes which are occurring are visible at the level of the whole world environment and all human society, many of the impulses to change rest on an understanding of very small things indeed. It is also important to know that, while the energy revolution has proceeded in somewhat isolated form, the following three technologies are extremely closely interrelated.

MICROPROCESSING

Our definition of the next new technology emphasizes the inherent nature of this scientific background. For want of a generally accepted term, I shall call this *second* main area "microprocessing." What I mean to convey by this term is the fact that increasingly the products which we use in our society are more finely processed and that frequently this processing requires the manipulation of materials at the atomic and molecular level, or to very fine measurements. Insofar as an increasing proportion of human energies which are devoted to processing are devoted to microprocessing, the demand for materials and for the brute force application of energy will not rise as rapidly as the total demand for goods. Microprocessing requires higher levels of skill and more automated equipment, together with its care. Since microprocessing in many instances involves a greater division of labor and specialization, its products may require more physical movement from place to place, but this depends on the extent of vertical integration in the economy. Highly processed goods such as we are discussing have a high value in relation to weight and bulk, and the demand for them is almost indefinitely expandable by comparison with the demand for bulky items of consumption and raw materials. Consequently, the demand for high-grade transportation for goods, approaching or surpassing the levels of safety, comfort, and convenience applied to the transportation of people, is bound to increase both absolutely and relatively.

COMMUNICATION AND CONTROL

One aspect of our ability to manipulate the world at a fine grain has received special emphasis because of the unique aspects of its impact upon human society. Our ability to understand and to control the movements of electrons in networks has led to an explosion in communications and in computational capability. Taken as a package, we may call this *third* area a revolution in communication and control. The communications aspects of this change involve the wider spread of information and knowledge and the conversion of social interaction from face-to-face contact and the shipment of documents into interaction by wire and radio. Perhaps because the information-processing and feedback aspects of this communications revolution are closely related to the patterns of human thought, perhaps because the computer is in some ways analogous to the human brain, and perhaps because the revolution dramatically amplifies man's ability to think, this aspect of technological change has received special emphasis, and efforts have been made to subsume the entire transformation of our technology under this one heading. In may ways I believe that a failure to distinguish those important cases in which communication and control is *not* the essential ingredient in change, tends to blunt and weaken our analysis. For this reason, of course, I have set this revolution down as only one of five, but in many respects it is a key to all the others. It makes possible the solution of conceptually difficult and intricate problems. Through the development of cybernetics, formalizing concepts of feedback and control, means are provided for conducting many affairs with incredible precision and delicacy. Thus, communication and control is central to one or another aspect of all of the other revolutions being discussed.

In this connection, however, one more distinction needs to be made. I have spoken in particular of the importance of the analysis of difficult problems and of the processes of feedback. Each of these intimately involves strong ideas about relationships, about cause and effect. It is therefore quite improper to equate this revolution with a revolution in information, even though the technology of computers greatly facilitates the collection, transmission, and storage of such information as is needed for analysis and control. Information by itself is mute; it cannot tell us anything unless we breathe into it the life of conceptualization, or statements about relationships. It indeed follows that the principal impact of the technology of communication and control upon our society is only indirectly by way of information pure and simple and much more significantly by way of the challenges and solutions which it brings to our abilities to think.

Biological Control

The *fourth* type of technological change which I should like to distinguish is in the general area of the life sciences. This includes the technologies in particular of health, medicine, and agriculture, all of which are predicated on the understanding of living processes through the various sciences of biology. Here again, our understanding of these processes upward from the level of atoms and molecules is giving rise to tremendous advances in man's ability to control and direct the development of nature. By implication, since man is a part of nature, this provides him with a new level of influence over his own ultimate destiny.

The social implications of advances in the life sciences are perhaps more direct and more easily identified than the implications of the other technologies. Thus, when we describe some of the elements of this revolution, their effects are immediately clear. Perhaps the first and broadest developments have occurred in the field of agriculture, with increasing understanding of plant and animal genetics, plant metabolism, and pest control. Some of this knowledge has been rapidly extended to the animal, man – through the direct control of reproduction by simple chemical and mechanical means, for example. Similarly, the control of man's diseases and his aging depends on a knowledge both of the human organism and of its environment, together with the means to intervene in both. In the very near future we may expect a substantial growth in our capability to intervene directly in biological processes. We shall be able directly and purposively to alter the heredity of organisms and to intervene in and change both physiological and neurological processes in them. Thus, we will be able either greatly to improve or to derange physical and psychological health and social function in large numbers of individuals.

SOCIETAL SELF-CONTROL

The *fifth* and final area in which we may talk of a new technology is in the arena of social relations and societal organization itself. Here I use the term "technology" with some reluctance, since the title "social engineering" has always seemed a particularly repulsive one to me. Nevertheless, since the eighteenth century at least, man has always had the ambition of controlling his own progress. The idea of such effective control implies that there are means of implementation of this desire, and these means, taken collectively, might be called a technology. Perhaps my revulsion against social engineering can be traced to the fact that the enlightened ideas of this era are essentially humanistic in their aspirations and content, and we are accustomed to counterpose concepts of humanism and technology.

The technology of purposeful social control, for obvious reasons, has been very slow in its development and application. The sloth has perhaps depended largely on the fact that society and societal development are extraordinarily complex and varied and hence difficult to comprehend and control. The reluctance to accept and apply any "technological" innovations in this field may be attributed not only to a certain essential conservatism of people and institutions, but also to an unwillingness to accept crude and inadequate measures and to an individualistic and innovative intransigency which might be regarded as the direct opposite of conservatism. The technological revolutions, in communications and control and in the life sciences in particular, now lay a basis for a complete new era of discovery and invention in the techniques of societal self-control. If such a technology were to perpetuate the non- or even anti-humanistic qualities of most economic theory, of military planning, and of industrial management (where these techniques are currently visible in their most advanced form), then it would perpetuate its previous unsuccess and lack of acceptance. An appropriate technology must here be based on a revived social science which demonstrates that science can indeed be humanistic in content. We can then recognize that, in general, the technology of social organization is identical with the technology of planning. Such planning will of necessity have to accept both man and men as the measure.

I have in this section tried to outline the fundamental sources in the scientific and technological understanding of the current revolution in our existence. In so doing, I have identified five main areas of interest: the technology of power sources, the technology of microprocessing, the technology of communication and control, the technology of biological control, and the technology of societal self-control. These five categories are, as I have indicated, not the manifest variables in the world around us which are most rapidly changing and most clearly perceivable by the socially sentient observer. To denumerate them in this fashion is an attempt to define more precisely the causes of societal change, the latter phenomenon being more readily apparent but also somewhat confusing if viewed in isolation from these impelling causes. We are now hopefully in a position to give a brief review of those phenomena which, although perhaps more superficial, are for that very reason more deeply felt and widely appreciated.

THE SOCIAL CONSEQUENCES OF THE NEW TECHNOLOGY

As I have suggested in many examples above, most of the elements of these technological revolutions create at one and the same time both opportunities and dangers. This duality, like sin and salvation, may perhaps be attributed to the nature of man and human society. In any event, the technology of societal self-control lags far enough behind the other four technologies to reveal the emergence of serious problems. I will not attempt to enumerate or evaluate all of these problems but merely to adumbrate some of their essential qualities.

The essential social thrust of all modern technology is toward enormous increases in affluence and power. The man in the gray flannel suit now has health and wealth far exceeding that possessed at least by minor Oriental potentates of bygone years. Unfortunately, our accounts of history do not convey any adequate sense of the prevalence of odor, filth, disease, and danger, and most of these are left behind.

Affluence creates new levels of freedom both for the individual and society. Choices are no longer so rigidly constrained by circumstance. Thus, we may anticipate encountering and appreciating the physical and social environment on the part of individuals and families. This differentiation of individual behavior may have the effect of destabilizing the dynamics of social development and, in any event, probably complicates the problems of analysis, prediction, and control. These are already substantially more complex by virtue of the wider range of options open to man at the societal level and by virtue of his greatly augmented power to intervene in the environment, a power which immediately implies greater complexity in choices and decisions.

Without further elaboration, let it be noted that affluence and power imply a potentiality to heighten conflict between societal groups.

A side effect of affluence and of the particular nature of current technology has been the constant explosion of the world's population. A concomitant of this explosion has been the "massification" of societal organization which has over the last century altered the setting and therefore the meaning of old questions of ethics and philosophy. One cannot but wonder whether the problems of an expanding population and a mass society may not be brought to an explosive point by the freedoms which are also associated with affluence.

By their very nature the scientific and technological revolutions of this century have put their own imprint on society. The explosion of knowledge which is associated with so many aspects of human existence has led to an explosion in the knowledgeable membership of society and to increases in the specialization which may further complicate the already difficult problems of communication and consensus within the society. A special aspect of the professionalization of our productive society is the increasing gap between the haves and the have-nots — internationally, between regions, and within regions and metropolitan areas. This gap, combined with other problems referred to above, again makes for an explosive mixture and poses the most difficult of all problems in self-direction for world society.

TECHNOLOGY IN URBAN PLANNING PROCESSES

After all of these Olympian views of man's present technical capabilities and major social problems, I now wish to focus my attention primarily on the process, and later on the substance, of urban metropolitan planning. I shall treat this as a special and perhaps somewhat more manageable case of the more general problem of social self-control. As such a special case, urban metropolitan planning will affect the lives of a majority of the future population of the world, and it subsumes most social problems together with their putative solutions.

The needs for society's control over its own development are based on very simple propositions. Owing not only to the weight of tradition but also to the complexity of societal function, it has appeared both expedient and wise to decentralize a great deal of the decision-making which goes on in social and economic life. Such decentralized decision-making is the essential ingredient of freedom and of innovation. Culture, mores, laws, and regulation stand in a polar relationship to this decentralization and provide means for maintaining stability and continuity and for avoiding or resolving conflicts, without which means decentralization could lead to chaos. Over time, the autonomous and decentralized network of decisions in the society establishes its own mode of development and internal consistency, and within limits the probable future outcomes of present conditions and relations can thus be foreseen. Increasingly, society and its members, however, have their own images of a desirable future, and increasingly they are conscious of the power which we possess to move purposively toward that future. Planning arises and becomes acceptable to the society or to parts of it when the foreseeable outcomes of present states diverge in an undesirable way from these images of the possible future. Thus, planning involves purposeful design of the future through societal action.

FIVE ELEMENTS OF THE PLANNING PROCESS

From this simple-minded but not entirely obvious definition, we may perhaps conclude that there are five major elements in the planning process. (1) A "problem" is identified regarding the mismatch between aspirations and potential developments. These problems cover a wide spectrum of complexity and urgency, and the most general is the difficulty of designing and securing a better future urban environment. Solving this problem is more than "problem solving" in the ordinary sense of the term. (2) Next, a number of solutions or new courses of action are generated for consideration. This phase of planning is essentially one of design or invention and involves many more subtle difficulties than are generally recognized. (3) The third and perhaps at present the central problem of planning is, then, to predict the effects of adopting each of a selected set of designs or inventions, estimating their costs and benefits and at the same time establishing a comparative basis by predicting the conditions which would arise in the absence of new designs and new policies. (4) The fourth stage in the total planning process is the evaluation of courses of action and the selection of a most desired course for effectuation. (5) Finally, the desired course is spelled out in a program of effectuation which includes detailed budgets, project schedules, legislative enactments, public education campaigns, and perhaps a sketch of political processes. The whole effectuation procedure represents a distinct and important operating aspect of planning in contrast with the preceding four steps, which in principle may be isolated from the actions required to translate them into reality.

It is, of course, completely artificial to assume that these stages in the planning process are in fact separate. The evaluation procedures which will be used as step four enter into the process at the outset in the identification of problems, which are defined above in value terms. The evaluations to be made also influence the design of solutions and the form in which predictions are cast for evaluating purposes. The detailed political problems of effectuation enter into design, prediction, and evaluation both as constraints and as costs and benefits which must be entered into any grand accounting. Since in the future as well as in the past, decision-making in society will continue to be partially decentralized, the *effects* of policies upon private decision-making are a most important part of the calculi of design, prediction, evaluation, and effectuation.

PROBLEMS OF COMPOSITION

The outstanding problems in the planning process today are problems of composition – that is, problems of fitting together parts of the whole in order to achieve overall better solutions. These problems of composition fall into three main classes. The whole process of planning is animated by an overall conception of societal values, but in a diverse, pluralistic, and specialized society, these values are very difficult to define. The *first* problem is, therefore, to compose or combine the objectives of diverse groups and individuals, and even the internally diverse objectives of groups and individuals, into a rational and acceptable whole. The *second* problem of composition has to do with the planning process itself. This process is fragmented both functionally and geographically. Planning for transportation, land use, education, economic development, and many other functions is pursued in isolation by a variety of agencies, even within the same governmental jurisdiction. Similarly, within any metropolitan area the responsibility for the discharge of individual functions and for overall budgeting is fragmented amongst scores of local jurisdictions geographically, and governmentally between the local, state, and national levels. Composing the planning process to provide for adequate interaction and coordination between the planning for various functions and various levels of government represents a major problem. Finally, *third,* even to consider the first two aspects of composition in planning we must find means of composing our view of the metropolis as a functional system. Socially, economically, and technically it may be argued that the metropolitan system does in fact possess an essential unity and should be regarded as a whole, but that specialized views on the part of planners and academic analysts have tended to fragment and circumscribe the consideration of the metropolis and its function.

PREDICTING THE EFFECTS OF POLICIES

For reasons which I hope will become clear in the following discussion, I regard the inadequacies in the development of means of predicting the effects of policies upon the metropolis (including continuation of present policies) as a central difficulty which hinders the adequate development of the planning sciences today. It is, of course, far from the only such difficulty, but because of its central importance I shall take this as a starting point in developing the relationship of technology to the planning process. In this section as a whole, I shall be concerned mainly with the interaction between the technology of communication and control and the technology of social self-control. The influence of the technologies of power, of microprocessing, and of biological control will be taken more or less for granted, and their effects will be examined in somewhat more detail at a later point in considering the substance of planning.

Perhaps one of the most remarkable aspects of the development of modern cybernetic technology is the capacity which has been generated for dealing in a realistic way with large and complex concatenations of entities. This capability arises almost entirely out of the extension provided by the computer to man's ability to think and compute. Thus, for example, the many-body problem of Newtonian mechanics, which has for centuries resisted an analytic solution, has repeatedly been solved for specific cases and by brute force calculation in the space programs of the United States and the Soviet Union. Perhaps a little more elegantly in the field of economics Vassily Leontiev's first efforts to deal with input-output analysis required weeks of calculation to invert rather small and grossly overaggregated input-output matrices; today, using computers, we can deal as a matter of course with matrices thirty times as large and a thousand times as difficult computationally. Similarly, twenty-five years ago linear programming did not exist, but today it is routinely applied to thousands of very large problems in science and social science and in industrial and military management. All this is not to say that these new methods are highly sophisticated and represent the ultimate in excellence in scientific perfection. On the contrary, viewed by any objective standards they are perhaps extraordinarily simplistic and crude. Even with flexible computers several million times as apt as a human calculator, we still rely largely on methods which are linear. Perhaps, even *because* of the computer, we utilize brute force methods of solution of problems which in the long run may be solved with greater analytical elegance and efficiency.

The essential lesson, however, is that the greatly enlarged capabilities created by computers are being directed towards the formulation and solution of previously insoluble problems and that these problems have the nature of involving very large numbers of elements or very large amounts of computation or both. These computational characteristics of a large class of formal problems correspond in detail with the identified characteristics of large social, economic, and technical systems. We thus have the capability of developing a systematic treatment of large systems on a computationally feasible and experimental basis. This capability is giving rise on the one hand to the development of general systems theory which will hopefully generalize the results and simplify the methods, and on the other hand to very large practical applications in industry and military activity. These applications range from the control of large chemical plants and satellite trajectories to such inventory and sales problems as a large airline's reservations system. Perhaps, intermediate between general theory and very specific though complex practical applications we can place the efforts which are important to urban metropolitan planning to replicate in considerable detail the phenomena of operation, growth, and change.

If we look more closely at the process of reproducing or simulating interactions in the urban environment with a view to predicting future development, we may distinguish more clearly the reasons why computer technology is an essential element in this process and the roles which this technology plays. The size and complexity of metropolitan areas are extraordinary. Metropolitan Philadelphia contains perhaps a million parcels of land and structures, a million and a half families, and 100,000 employing establishments ranging in size from Mom-and-Pop stores to firms employing over 5,000 people.

For various purposes incidental to understanding the metropolis, there are perhaps over 300 significantly different types of economic activities, several scores of types of families, and similarly numerous classifications for structures and ancillary facilities. All of these entities engage in a large number of distinct classes of activities which are influenced by their total environment, and they interact with each other in a multitude of distinct modes. Thus, any manageable description of the modes of behavior and change in a metropolitan area must incur tremendous sacrifices in potentially relevant detail, and these sacrifices are minimized when we use an environment like a computer or the human mind with its large information storage capability. It seems likely, however, that an important aspect of the problem is the extent to which we are able consciously to follow through the interactions and repercussions in a system, since apparently many of the indirect effects of events in the metropolis are more important than some of the direct effects. Here the superior ability of the computer to remember and to compute may be advantageously utilized. In addition, the user of the computer is forced consciously to decide which interactions are to be retained, studied, and used for predictions, and which are to be omitted. The human analyst, unaided by the computer, is apt to make such decisions subconsciously as guided by preconceived notions and consciously in the interests of achieving a definition of the problem which is manageable by his own memory and computational capability. These built-in limitations of the human analyst can be partially avoided and at least explicitly examined through relating the work of the human analyst and the computer's capabilities.

Three Roles of the Computer

Looking at the matter in a slightly different light, the computer plays three distinct roles in this process. Each role is related to the others and to the human individuals, organizations, and processes which are linked to the computer technology. We are accustomed to put a merited but possibly exaggerated emphasis on the *first* of these roles, which has to do with information collection and processing. The increasing use of the computer for these purposes has made it possible for urban planning to tap the very large flow of administrative statistics which has always existed and which is currently rapidly increasing and becoming better organized. At the same time, special purpose data which has frequently been used in well understood ways in the planning process can be recorded, preserved, and made accessible more efficiently. It is, I think, becoming increasingly recognized, however, that information alone will not provide answers to problems. For example, more current and more complete information may enable us to detect in urban development divergences from a prediction or a program. This detection, however, does not answer the complex questions as to whether it is a random event or a fundamental change, whether corrective action is necessary and desirable, and what action should be taken. These questions and their answers imply both a much more profound understanding of the total process and a capability not only for gathering data but also for interpreting it than is comprehended in the definition of information pure and simple. What is needed in fact is "information about the future," and this requirement suggests the importance of analysis and prediction in addition to information handling.

At the purely analytical or even descriptive level, the computer combines with its capability of handling large information files a computational ability, the *second* role, which makes possible increasingly complex analyses of urban distributions, trends and interactions. Although internally complex, the purpose of these analyses is to extract, from an incoherent mass of data, simplicities and regularities which will be of use in furthering our understanding of the phenomena reflected in the data. For this reason, the analysis of data (which is frequently presented as an independent activity) depends in fact upon the infusion of a concept of structure and of relationships. These concepts of structure and relationships within the metropolitan region are apt to be more complex and intractable than can readily be dealt with with present-day linear and multivariate statistical methods. It is therefore probably true that we exaggerate the automaticity with which current analytical techniques permit us to organize our understanding and description of reality; but there is no question that these analytical techniques are expanding rapidly and play an important role, with major computer assistance, in the whole process of predicting future development.

Given the inadequacy of analytical techniques standing by themselves, it is quite plain that adequate prediction depends on an understanding in all relevant detail of the processes involved in urban function and change. We reflect our present understanding of these processes back into the collection of data and its preliminary analysis; and as our understanding improves, we increasingly refine these preliminary stages. Our understanding of these phenomena is, first of all, expressed in theories which define cause and effect and, second, in the concomitant design of models. In this context, models are usually truncated realizations of theory which serve as an experimental design either for testing the theories, or for testing (if the theory is considered adequate) the effects which changes in conditions will have upon development and function. The creation of adequate models based on sound theories of metropolitan development is thus the central problem in making useful predictions regarding the effects of alternative policies or the impacts of alternative technologies and social developments; and the testing of such theories is the *third* role of the computer.

Without belaboring this point or going into excessive detail, we may distinguish two main problems in the construction of successful models. *First,* and clearly foremost, the models must be based on a sound conception of the interrelationships and phenomena which are of salient importance in the metropolis. This primary precondition is all too frequently violated by considerations of expediency with respect to data availability, computational feasibility, or policy guidelines. Frequently also, the existence of previously defined mathematical models provides a lazy man's excuse for not attempting to define relationships in their "true" form. All this is not to say that practical considerations are not important; but they should not play a direct role in the formulation of theory. The *second* and distinguishable problem is indeed to undertake precisely the practical job of testing and implementing a theoretical formulation by making it operational in computer terms and by ensuring that the necessary data for its testing and use in prediction are available.

From the viewpoint of the relationship between the planning process and modern technology, we may therefore recognize at this point that a central issue is the interaction between the planner's understanding of the metropolitan environment in all its complexity and the capability of computer technology to aid in the development of predictive techniques embodied in models. These techniques must in the context of the larger planning process provide "information about the future" that is relevant to the total decision process and particularly to the evaluative phase of planning, and they must at the same time be fully realistic with regard to all significant factors and their interaction.

The developing modern social sciences, the basis of our fifth technology, have a tremendous contribution that they must yet make to the planning process. This contribution has two or three aspects of major interest. *First,* in the most elementary sense, the models which we have just been discussing will not have the necessary realism unless they deal realistically with human behavior.

We are only at the threshold of an understanding of that behavior in all its richness in the scientific sense, despite the centuries of attention which it has received in the arts and the humanities. Thus, for example, in the past ten years a sudden interest in animal territoriality on the one hand and in the psychological effects of overcrowding on the other suggests that human spatial behavior needs a complete re-examination. Quite clearly, in the *second* place, the formulation of appropriately realistic descriptions of behavior and its sources will greatly clarify the content and meaning of evaluative measures which ought to be applied to plans. *Finally*, therefore, the whole analysis of societal decision-making can be related back to the behavior of individuals and the systematic synthesis of that behavior into group activity and societal organization. The present technology for dealing with these subtle and complex issues in any context, as illustrated by the not inconsiderable achievements of Economics and Operations Research, is at present simplistic and primitive. I would suggest, however, that the emerging theory and technology in this field can be of tremendous power and richness.

TECHNOLOGY OF THE DESIGN PROCESS

The design aspects of planning have perhaps received inadequate attention in the development of a technology of decision-making. Most analytical or quasi-analytical social management sciences take a retrospective or *ex post* view of the development of new policies and new modes of societal action. Insofar as alternatives are examined, these alternatives are those which were historically articulated in the body of society prior to the point where a decision was required. Very little attention has been given to the process of innovation itself in social affairs broadly conceived, and still less attention to the consciously directed process of innovation. There is thus an assumption that innovation is latent in the status of society at any given time and that it is sufficient to examine the circumstances which encourage or hinder its development. Given the increased latitude which the affluence of present society has provided for long-term development, it should now be apparent that the design of the future can no longer be left to random innovation. This design requires conscious consideration and systematic attention, and this in turn requires the development of a technology of the design process.

In this context, the design of public policies is closely akin not only to the architectural design of buildings and spaces but also to the arts of painting, sculpture, and poetry. It differs from some of these to the extent that identifying and meeting needs is not internalized in a single person and further in the extent to which society must permanently accept, if it accepts at all, the results of the invention. But because of the similarity, it may be recognized that the policy design process in some respects is an institutional analog of creative human thought and that the technology of the computer, which is beginning to assist us in understanding these thought processes, can also assist in understanding and assisting the design processes. The essential factors of creative human thought are probably, in my view, *pattern recognition* in a highly developed form and a prodigious *combinatorial flexibility*. These two modes of thinking have proved especially recalcitrant to systematic analysis and computer representation despite their centrality in the design process; and for this reason, I would anticipate that the role of the human individual in design is much less susceptible to amplification and certainly to usurpation by machine processes. The nature of the development of science and technology, however, suggests that, insofar as continuous pressure is exerted to overcome these difficulties, the probability of a break-through which could cause me to change this statement is increased.

It might superficially appear that much of the technology of communication and control could be directly applied to urban development in the effectuation of plans. Indeed, such a prospect is held out in glowing terms by the proponents of systems methodology, which has been so successfully applied to problems of industry, the military, and space. The essential elements of this technology, applied to control, are the sensing of events in the system subject to control, the comparison of these events with a preconceived desired state of affairs or of development, and the definition of corrective action which will diminish the discrepancy. This type of system thus involves achieving control through the use of "negative feedback." It is quite apparent that in principle the information-gathering aspects of this feedback loop can now be implemented at the municipal, metropolitan, state, and national levels; but even here, the implementation involves questions of cost and questions regarding the invasion of privacy. But it is also quite clear that we do not yet have any consensus upon the information to be collected and the interpretation to be placed upon it. This unclarity reflects, first of all, our lack of agreement on metropolitan goals and, second, our lack of complete understanding of the relationships between cause and effect in the metropolitan system. Thus, we are unable to say not only in what direction the system should be made to move, but even if we were to agree on this, we can hardly say what policy levers would in fact promote change in the desired direction and no other. We are at least partly debarred from taking an experimental approach to this problem of control by the long lead-times which intervene between many metropolitan-level decisions and their consequences and by the fact that many of these decisions are irreversible. At the present time, it seems unlikely that the control of the metropolitan system can be automated like the control of the operation of an oil refinery. In fact, one might usefully distinguish between operation and design, and point out that, while the operation of the oil refinery has indeed been automated, its design has not. Imperfect design of an oil refinery undoubtedly can lead into situations where the automatic controls have no option but to shut down. An analogous situation in urban operation would return controls to the planner and to the politician in the event that an unanticipated and uncontrollable operational or developmental situation arises.

It should indeed be an objective of design of the planning process to automate the operation of controls as much as possible and to minimize the return of control to the planner and the politician. Insofar as this may be possible, their experience and ability could properly be focused on the more difficult and intractable problems of operation and plan-making. It is hardly to be expected, however, that any great level of automaticity can be achieved at an early date without much greater clarification of goals and understanding of processes. We may regard the objective of automaticity, therefore, as yet another spur in solving these problems while recognizing that they are to a considerable extent more fundamental and more immediate.

Our synopsis of the planning process has led us to relate it in many aspects to the technological revolution in communication and control which make it possible for us to consider the explicit solution of much more difficult and complex societal problems than have heretofore been self-consciously considered and resolved. We see concretely some of the ways in which the computer and its connections with the outside world can amplify man's ability to sense events, to interpret their significance, and to take actions which will tend to control his natural and social environment in desired ways. We also see some of the limitations implicit in this amplification. Amongst the most important of these limitations are our current lack of understanding of man and his associations. Thus, we see a related role for the biological sciences, and even more for the social sciences and for their associated technologies, in articulating and improving the planning process. We may now turn briefly to some of the horizons which are implied by the new technology for the city or the metropolis itself, as the object being planned.

THE METROPOLIS AND TECHNOLOGY

While the planning process itself is most closely related with those technologies dealing intimately with concepts and values, the actual functioning of the metropolis as we plan it for the future will be in turn more closely related to the technologies which have to do with the manipulation of things, and hence in particular with the technology of power sources and the technology of microprocessing. At the same time, however, the technology of communication and control plays an essentially different role here. In the planning process, one may roughly regard the technology of things as providing constraints, while the technology of values provides the means of studying the relationships among variables. In considering the functional future of the metropolis, values provide the constraints, and the manipulative technologies provide the variables.

The first consequence of our manipulative abilities is that our potential for planning the future urban environment is, by virtue of our affluence, much greater than ever before. In principle, we are now and will in the future be increasingly able to say that if what is wanted can be properly defined, it can be achieved technologically and economically. Pushing the definition of need to new limits will of course uncover conflicts of goals which cannot be immediately technologically resolved; in other words, our resources and our powers are not unlimited. I would suggest, however, that these boundaries have not been adequately explored and that when this exploration is further advanced, the dynamics of technology vill become more evident. Particular well-defined problems can ecome the object of scientific and technological exploration. In his sense, the dynamics which we have been exploring will be eversed, and technology will become a dependent rather than an ndependent variable in social development.

I have already suggested that it is possible to exaggerate the mportance of energy or power as such in reshaping the future f the metropolis. This broad statement is subject to qualification vith respect to the development of new materials and their use in ity building. It is further subject to qualification in respect of najor modifications of the environment, such as climate control. very much doubt, however, that programs of this kind will ultinately be undertaken by unleashing and harnessing new sources f energy; this represents a brute force approach which has already een demonstrated to have unforeseeable consequences for a probably recarious natural balance of forces. It seems much more sane and erhaps somewhat more likely that man's control over nature will ncreasingly involve small applications of force at strategic points. 'his use of cybernetic technology applies to the whole natural nvironment, including the biosphere, and will ultimately depend ot only on cybernetics but also on the technology of the life ciences and undoubtedly upon the use of very accurate mechanisms roduced by microprocessing. The whole process is summed up ery nicely in the contrast between the eradication of the screwfly y irradiation and the control of malaria through massive spraying f DDT and other insecticides. While these examples are contemoraneous, and while mistakes may be made in both fields, it eems likely that a finely calibrated approach to such problems is kely to be more economical, safer, and more in line with the hrust of modern technology.

An interesting analogy exists in the planning process itself which nay increasingly abandon direct controls and rely on the harnessng of "natural" social forces through the development of undertanding and cybernetic techniques.

In a slightly different view of some of these same issues, Keneth E. Boulding is quoted as saying:

> . . . man has been accustoming himself to the notion of the spherical earth and a closed sphere of human activity . . . The closed earth of the future requires economic principles which are somewhat different from those of the open earth of the past . . . I am tempted to call the

> open economy the "cowboy economy" . . . associated with reckless, exploitative, romantic and violent behavior, which is characteristic of open societies. The closed economy of the future might similarly be called the "spaceman" economy, in which the earth has become a single spaceship, without unlimited reservoirs of anything, either for extraction or for pollution, and in which, therefore, man must find his place in a cyclical ecological system which is capable of continuous reproduction of material form even though it cannot escape having inputs of energy . . . In the cowboy economy, consumption is regarded as a good thing and production likewise; and the success of the economy is measured by the amount of the throughput from the "factors of production" . . . The gross national product is a rough measure of this total throughput. . . . In the spaceman economy, what we are primarily concerned with is stock maintenance, and any technological change which results in the maintenance of a given total stock with a lessened throughput (that is, less production and consumption) is clearly a gain. This idea that both production and consumption are bad things rather than good things is very strange to economists, who have been obsessed with the income-flow concepts to the exclusion, almost, of capital-stock concepts (Resources for the Future, in press).

I can accept Boulding's comments as a bold and useful guide to policy in urban affairs as elsewhere. Two modifications, however, suggest themselves for clarity in understanding. *First*, insofar as increasingly sophisticated processing in general and microprocessing in particular increase the value of the flow of commodities without increasing the flow of energy, it is possible that we will have the benefits of both a cowboy and a spaceman economy. *Second*, Boulding's references to gross national product may slightly confuse the issue, since presumably the capital stock to which he refers provides a flow of services. Insofar as that capital stock becomes more and more long-lived, the real value of the services which it provides may be increased at minimal increases in current investment.

One of the most interesting views which seems to me to summarize the importance of a conservative balanced cybernetic and microscopic technology is a quotation from science fiction of the opinion of the people several millennia in the future who maintain that "a true machine has no moving parts." We have but to compare the relative impact of electronics and of the automobile on our environment to imagine how this simple statement as a guide to technology can create a whole new way of life.

EXIBILITY

One of the most interesting challenges facing planning and :hnology jointly is the problem of flexibility in urban metropolitan rangements. We are by now accustomed to living with the knowlge that in a period of rapid growth, increasing affluence, and :hnological change, arrangements completed in one decade are t to be out of date in the next. It is also by now quite clear that r building technology, with its emphasis on solidity and perınence, is at loggerheads with the need of the metropolitan strucre to change and adapt to new conditions. Systematic solutions to is problem at the broadest possible scale have, to the best of y knowledge, not seriously been attempted. The most obvious lution has, I believe, been called the "Dixie cup" approach to city ilding. More contemporaneously, it might be called the "beer n" or even the "used car" approach. It is simply to make strucres, facilities, and arrangements more flexible by making them eaper or more disposable. Given the ultimate restraints on our ilization of power sources and given the usefulness of the concept the spaceman's economy, I believe that this is an imperfect proach to the problem. The Dixie cup solution directly implies larger throughput of commodities and consequently offers greater zards for the pollution and devastation of the total environment. however, the ultimate solution for the good life is to be found the preservation of our capital stock, it does not follow that this pital stock must be embodied in currently accepted methods of nstruction and city-building. The technological challenge is there:e to find forms of capital which are usable and reusable but ıich are inherently flexible in their disposition and their fitting :o total urban patterns. This represents on a grand scale a subtle oblem of system compatibility which has, to my knowledge, only en seriously considered and resolved in relation to the technology telephony.

If, as is suggested by the implications of microprocessing and the implications of Boulding's spaceship analogy as well as by :ent trends in economic life, an ever-greater proportion of pernal income is to be taken in the form of services, then interesting t clouded indications may be drawn. The economic and struc:al implications in this area are not altogether clear, and much ›re research will be needed before they can be completely defined. Some of the apparent growth of services may be due specialization as between firms, so that services which previousl were performed internally are now identifiable in national statistic Still other services, such as transportation and power productio depend essentially on the chemical or nuclear transformation materials and are more akin to manufacturing in the nineteent century sense than to communication in the twentieth centur On the other hand, the increased commodity production of co sumer durables satisfies, in fact, an increased demand for service

On balance, it is probably quite sound to conclude that th services *cum* information content of personal consumption is risin This rise on the one hand is accelerated from the demand side b the increased professionalization of our society. On the other han from the supply side the technology of communications is inherentl more dynamic than the technology of fabrication and transportatio since it deals more frequently with machines which have no movin parts. The city of the future will therefore have to deal with large relative increase in the movement of information by compar son with the movement of people and goods.

This change in the relative shares of certain key activities doe however, require serious qualification. With increased affluence r lated to increased personal productive capabilities, the man of the f ture will probably be able to consume a larger volume of real physic inputs. While the share of throughput commodities in this co sumption may decline, its absolute volume may not. It may furth be anticipated that in a healthy society, where much less labor required for commodity production, a large proportion of servic may be in the form of travel, recreation, and the performing art where the movement of people and interpersonal contact may b important. The extent to which electronic communication ca substitute in these fields for personal presence and face-to-fac contact is certainly undefined. Here then is a potentially very larg and important source of demands upon the urban functional syste which may not necessarily be satisfied through the communicatio revolution pure and simple.

The illustrations that I have elaborated in the preceding par graphs must be considered sufficient in a chapter of this length illustrate the nature of the problem. We may attempt to summari and recast the nature of these salient examples very briefly. Fro the viewpoint of resources and physical powers, mankind now h the capabilities of shaping his physical environment in any desired form, although this capability is (hopefully on a temporary basis) withheld from large portions of the world. This power carries with it the concomitant ability to despoil and pollute the environment, which in the long run poses very grave dangers. The cybernetic revolution of communication and control offers the possibility of automating much of the operation of the modern city, perhaps with a reduction in energy demands and cost and certainly with a reduction in human labor and an increase in environmental control. The increasing "consumption" of information and images by the population tends to shift an emphasis from transportation in the metropolis to communications for consumption rather than control purposes. Finally, we have identified the problem of flexibility in development patterns which, it may be seen, poses a major area for future coordination between planning and technology. In attempting to address all of these problems, we can readily begin to see areas in which the dependence of plans on technology may be reversed and the moving force for social, physical, and environmental development may become the desires of man rather than the apparently random discoveries of human scientists.

CONCLUSION

Having started out to discuss in a rather direct way the impact of our modern technology on the process of urban planning and on he construction and operation of urban agglomerations, I find that have necessarily reversed my field and discussed in principle the nature of the new technology and the social matrix, including ocietal planning, in which it operates. This has proved necessary not mainly for want of a general understanding of these problems but because the resolution of the tension of forces that has been created in the last fifty years still lies in the future and is perhaps inherently unpredictable. Since many of my readers will participate directly in the resolution of these issues, I do not offer any apologies for having attempted to help orient their views of how the resolution may be achieved. There is perhaps more immediacy to the resolution of problems of process than of substance, since it is pparent to me that it will take many decades of work to evolve the socially acceptable and technically feasible city of the future.

At the heart of this evolution, however, will be an informed, wel
trained, technologically competent, and socially sensitive plannin
profession. This profession, unfortunately, does not yet exist, and it
creation is a task on which we can feasibly immediately resolv
to lengthen our recent small steps. For this reason, the rathe
extended discussion which I have given to the application of tech
nology and to the planning process itself may perhaps be con
sidered appropriate.

14

Transportation Planning for the Metropolis

IELVIN M. WEBBER

] IT IS BUT FIFTY YEARS SINCE THE Congress recognized the auto-ıobile as something more than a pleasure vehicle and enacted the Iighway Act of 1916. Following the growth curve typical also of ther fields, conceptual developments in transportation planning ere sparse during the 1920s, increased slowly during the 1930s nd 1940s, and then, following some major empirical discoveries nd conceptual clarifications during the mid-1950s, began to ac-elerate rapidly. Now, in the mid-1960s, the pace of developments extremely rapid; and we may be on the verge of a golden age f discovery and creative thought in metropolitan transportation lanning.

Of course, the so-called metropolitan problem, or even the ıetropolitan transportation problem, is not about to be "solved." aul Ylvisaker stated this clearly when he spoke to the World raffic Engineering Conference.

> . . . The art of planning in the Twentieth Century is admittedly about where the art of medicine was in the Sixteenth. If there is a difference, it is that we are much less naive than the medical scientists who began their rational assault on disease four centuries ago; we know about the intricate web of cause and effect and the subtle process of balance by which nature resists what in man's self-centered view is a total solution.
>
> We can use this sophistication to speed the development of the planning art. Not least by perfecting and exploiting nature's process of balance, and playing down the childish notion of total solutions. There

AUTHOR'S NOTE: *The author gratefully acknowledges the assistance f Lester Hoel and Joseph L. Intermaggio on an earlier version of this hapter, prepared for the National Capital Transportation Agency.*

will never be total solutions to urban problems for the simple reason that the future is never finished . . .

We ought to be talking about resolving urban problems, not about solving them . . .

Perhaps the most significant event in the recent history of transportation planning is a shift from a way of thinking that would seek a total designed solution to the transportation problems to a fresh way of thinking that sees transportation planning as but one of the ways of grappling with the evolving problems of urban life. Once an isolated, road-building effort, transportation planning is now becoming an integrated part of a larger effort to lead metropolitan development into desired directions – to accommodate the metropolitanization of the nation to the newly emerging social and economic processes that mark a society at the high-scale of development.

THE EARLY STAGES

GETTING THE FARMERS OUT OF THE MUD

Following upon nineteenth century traditions of transport-facilities planning, which had located and then built a network of canals, railroads, streetcar lines, and subways, the early twentieth century efforts were directed to locating specific routes. The major shift that came with the turn of the century was a redirection from rail facilities to roadways for individual vehicles. Indeed, transit planning in the first half of this century was almost exclusively aimed at improving operating characteristics of then-existing facilities. The new routes to be located were to serve cars and trucks.

The initial motivations in the early 1920s were to get the farmers out of the mud and to do something about reducing traffic hazards. At a time when private auto ownership was fast becoming a fact to contend with, there was little need for elaborate planning methods. The task was clear, and civil engineers were clearly the men best equipped to deal with it. Hard-surfaced roads had to be built wherever the obvious traffic demands and political pressures arose, and as soon as funds could be found. Notions of highway system, even highway network, were yet to come. Certainly "systems planning" was neither known nor needed. The concept of a planned etwork of roads was to come quickly, however, as the grid began evolve and as demand arose for links between once-separate outes.

The main financial burden lay with local government, federal d being initially limited to 7 per cent of the rural mileage of each ate. Then, with the establishment of the federally numbered ighway system in 1925, a major effort was begun to build paved oads connecting major cities. It took a long time for the small-scale, ural-oriented approach to highway planning to give way through- ut the nation to a large-scale effort to plan for urban facilities. major impetus, however, was supplied by the Regional Plan f New York and Its Environs, published in 1929, which boldly alled for a system-wide design for all urban transport facilities. s plan for a vast network of highway and transit lines was the rst product of a "systems approach" to urban transportation plan- ing in the United States. The effects were slow in being felt, how- ver. During the 1930s, increased auto ownership and use, increased peeds, and a rapid rise in trucking gave impetus to studies for xtension and modernization of highways of all sorts; but the ocus of attention remained glued to route-location studies for pecific highway links. Few transportation planners had either the me or the inclination to attempt system-wide planning.

In 1934, the Highway Act provided that 1½ per cent of the ederal funds be used for surveys, plans, and engineering and conomic investigations for future highways. From then on the Bureau of Public Roads (BPR) acquired a decisive leadership ole in promoting highway studies. The level of sophistication has teadily risen since that date, with the Bureau offering technical nd intellectual leadership in a great deal of the work that followed.

The Highway Planning Surveys, jointly sponsored by the BPR nd the states during the 1930s, were designed to inventory existing acilities and to measure existing volumes of traffic. Although the urveys were primarily devoted to rural roads, they accumulated great deal of factual information on the characteristics of all oad users. Perhaps the most striking finding was that most motor- sts were urbanites and that most people traveling on rural roads vere destined for urban areas. There was thus no escaping the act that the rural-road system was inseparable from the urban ystem, and that rural roads could not be planned in isolation.

O and D and the Shift to an Urban Orientation

During the 1930s, seeking a more sensitive method of identifyi travel habits than gross roadside counts, the BPR undertook r search on sampling methods for estimating traffic volumes. Initi tion of the origin and destination survey, now a standard traffi inventory method widely referred to as "O and D," marked a maj increase in the level of refinement in traffic analysis. The O and survey called for the construction of representative samples households, home-interviews concerning travel on a representati day, roadside checks, and refined statistical verification. Goir beyond the mere recording of travel volumes at points on the road the O and D survey was able to produce estimates of travel-desi patterns in which the surveyors could place high confidence. Tl new information told how many trips were being made from plac to place. In turn, it was hoped that a knowledge of travel desir would supply a firm basis for planning new transportation faciliti that, in turn, would effectively satisfy the surveyed demand. Whe the O and D studies were initiated, the preoccupation of roa planners was with the overwhelming backlog of highway-constru tion needs. Future highway needs were not considered of immedia concern; and designs that were fitted even to existing travel desir represented a major step forward.

The widespread application of the new and sophisticate O and D survey method had to await the end of the war, althoug the urban-travel studies were begun in earnest in 1944. The un versally accepted need for a vast postwar highway constructio program was punctuated by the phenomenal increase in aut ownership during the late 1940s and the 1950s. A firm warrar was needed to support the large expenditures that were entailec and the O and D survey had all the marks of scientifically derive certainty.

Explicitly oriented to urban transportation, the surveys marke a major shift in emphasis from the initial rural orientation of higl way planners. The surveys were intended to furnish a basis for th design of urban *highway* facilities, for neither the Bureau c Public Roads nor any state highway department was charged wit transit planning. Nevertheless, the survey method itself obligate the surveyors also to inventory urban transit usage, since person responding to the questionnaires reported their transit as well a highway trips so as to yield a controllable total. The findings of these and related studies confirmed what everyone already knew about transit patronage, of course. The curves showing trends in transit riding were all heading downward, threatening to go off the bottom of the charts, as they do in the cartoons. And, of course, the curves were interpreted to support the highway-construction programs, on the theory that fewer and fewer persons wanted public transportation.

There were some built-in shortcomings in the O and D survey and in related methods of inventorying travel habits, volumes, and spatial patterns. A survey made in 1947 may, with care, be made to yield a reasonably accurate description of travel in 1947, but it doesn't necessarily say anything about future travel. Moreover, any inventory method, however elaborate, can yield only a description of *what* goes on at the time of the inventory; it says nothing about *why* it goes on as it does. Descriptions of transit patronage, for example, were telling; but they didn't tell why patronage was dropping as it was. To be sure, a body of descriptive data in the hands of an imaginative analyst can be enriched by combination with other sorts of information. Correlation analysis can identify other variables with which the data are associated; and such correlation studies have revealed some very enlightening associations of income, family size, occupation, race, and other demographic characteristics with certain variations in travel patterns. But, still, these are descriptions rather than explanations of phenomena observed today, and highways are intended also to serve populations that will use them in the future. Reliable projection must be based on explanation, not mere description.

During the 1940s and the 1950s most transportation planners easily bypassed both the problems of futurity and the absence of explanatory theory. Those who had grown up in the conceptual traditions of civil engineering were well prepared to make professional decisions despite the absence of theory, since they were well acquainted with the stability of certain empirically observed characteristics. Structural engineers have successfully designed many complex structures relying upon the empirical measurements of the strengths of materials; a theory that would purport to explain why concrete behaves as it does is not really essential, so long as the designer can be sure how it will behave under given circumstances of loading and stress. He can be confident that, if the chemical composition and preparation conditions of two batches of concrete are the same, the performance will also be the same, whatever the time interval between the batches.

It was no surprise to the empiricist, then, when the O and D surveys revealed similar travel patterns in the various metropolitan areas. And then, when the refined descriptive measurements and comparative analyses showed that even the modal, temporal, demographic, and other specific variations were also similar from place to place at any particular time, it seemed wholly reasonable to assume that future traffic would follow the same patterns. It remained then to develop "expansion factors" that would take account of population growth and, hence, traffic growth.

In the early days, traffic was "factored up" as a direct function of population size in any two interchanging zones within a metropolis. With the later introduction of "gravity" models, distance was introduced as an added determinant of traffic interchange. Traffic was then calculated from land-use data, varying directly with the intensity of land use and inversely with the distance between zones.

Given empirically observed regularities in traffic patterns, it was assumed that these would hold into the future. Highways could therefore be properly designed, given only an O and D survey and a basis for factoring it up to some future date. For a short period of time, then, all the transportation planning pieces appeared to be in place, since the planning task was seen as no more than an assignment to install sufficient capacity to handle forecasted traffic.

EMERGENCE OF METROPOLITAN STUDIES

As the findings of the O and D surveys in the various metropolitan areas began to accumulate, a vast amount of new empirical information became available. At the same time, a wide variety of different kinds of people became involved in metropolitan studies. There had been a long and traditional interest among certain sociologists and geographers in the spatial patterns of metropolitan development, but in neither of these fields had this research remained quite respectable. Now, however, when metropolitan expansion was becoming so dominant an event in contemporary society, and when the complexity of the policy issues was becoming so apparent, more and more social scientists and behavioral scientists were attracted to the intriguing puzzles that were being posed. In the 1960s it is becoming quite respectable, if not fashionable, for men from a great many fields of inquiry to participate in "the attack on the metropolitan problem." As dual effects, we are coming to recognize the complexities of the problem and we are beginning to learn how to deal with those complexities.

Of course there had been a long-standing interest among city planners in the development patterns of metropolitan communities, but up until the beginning of the 1950s there had really been very little planning activity in the United States at this scale. To be sure, there had been New York's Tri-State Regional Plan in the late 1920s, and there had been the short-lived New York State Commission on Housing and Regional Planning that prepared a plan at about the same time for the state; and these two efforts had in turn generated numerous analogous efforts elsewhere. Metropolitan planning remained an objective of planners through the Depression, the war years, and beyond into the 1960s. By now, indeed, a few metropolitan areas have made small steps toward establishing permanently continuing metropolitan planning and governing actitivies. As we shall see later, however, most of the metropolitan planning remained an objective of planners through the Depression, 1960s has been tied to the metropolitan transportation studies.

Well financed, well staffed, and empirically oriented, the recent transportation studies produced much more information about metropolitan development than ever had been available; and this new information proved to be very valuable to all sorts of students of the metropolis. Immediately, the new data made possible detailed comparative studies of automobile versus transit usage, travel times, trip lengths, trip "purposes," directional and temporal variations in travel patterns, and so on. Now, students of urban life and urban spatial structure had some new and rich data to supplement the United States census and their own survey findings. The spate of research that followed led to a revolution in metropolitan transportation planning and in general metropolitan planning as well. No longer were we tied to personal intuitive judgments alone; the careful observations and measurements gave us a bench mark against which our preferences had now to be tested.

THE LAND-USE BOOM OF THE 1950s

Pioneering Efforts

Unquestionably, the major event in metropolitan transportation planning in the 1950s was the rediscovery that land-use patterns and travel patterns are intimately related, a fact discussed in the early 1920s, but largely neglected since. In 1954, Robert B. Mitchell and Chester Rapkin published *Urban Traffic: A Function of Land Use,* the first major clarification of this important idea (Mitchell and Rapkin, 1954). At the same time, the Detroit Metropolitan Area Transportation Study, directed by Dr. J. Douglas Carroll, Jr., was successfully applying land-use data including estimates of future land-use patterns as effective determinants of urban-travel patterns. In the same year, the San Francisco Bay Area Rapid Transit Study was independently seeking to derive travel patterns from land-use patterns. A year later Alan M. Voorhees published his prize-winning essay entitled, "The General Theory of Traffic Movement," in which he too was demonstrating that traffic patterns are consequences of land-use patterns, and that the gravity formula can be adapted for relating the two. Then, in 1956 a year later, John Rannells published his perceptive book, *The Core of the City,* in which some important conceptual clarifications were made (Rannells, 1956). This was followed in the latter years of the decade by the Chicago Area Transportation Study, where some of the most refined analyses of urban phenomena ever made were conducted.

These were primarily the contributions of city planners, who understood that transportation planning cannot be done in isolation from land-use planning and who therefore became transportation planners themselves. All of them were saying, as the Mitchell-Rapkin title had contended, that traffic is a function of land use – that traffic can be better understood and projected as a derivative of activity location-patterns. Underlying this proposition is the more general idea that urbanites, being specialists, are dependent upon other urbanites with whom they communicate. One mode of communication is travel – travel to work or to shop or to school or elsewhere. Another mode of communication is goods shipment, expressed primarily as truck and rail movements. Another mode is message-sending, through telephone, newspaper, broadcasting, and other message-handling channels. The metropolis in this context is seen as a vast communications system within which thousands of interdependent establishments – whether business firms or households or governmental agencies – interact with other establishments. Land use, then, is simply a short-hand way of identifying different kinds of establishments and, hence, different kinds of relationships – linkages – that each has with other establishments.

The effect of the Mitchell-Rapkin and the Detroit studies, particularly, was to precipitate a new approach to transportation planning. Land use was quickly recognized to be a more sensitive indicator of traffic generation than anything that had been available before. Almost overnight, transportation planners became land-use analysists as well, and land-use planners were welcomed as collaborators by transportation engineers.

LIMITATIONS OF LAND-USE INVENTORIES

The built-in dilemma of land-use inventories is of course the same as that which we noted with O and D surveys: an inventory of today's land use does not necessarily tell us anything about tomorrow's, nor does it offer any direct clues about the causes of potential change. The response to these bothersome facts has been identical to the response to the O and D inventory's "nowness." With the completion of a fairly large number of quantified land-use inventories, marked regularities among the patterns in different areas were discovered. Again it did not surprise those who were familiar with empirical regularities in structural materials and, by now, with the empirical regularities in traffic patterns, that land-use patterns in one metropolis turned out to be quite similar to land-use patterns in another. More than that, even with the little information that was available about prior patterns, it became possible to detect certain regularities in land-use pattern changes through time, however coarse the early analyses had to be. It became clear that land use, like traffic, is not capricious. Indeed, it began to appear that land-use patterns might be the consequences of the workings of something akin to natural laws. And, again, as with the natural laws governing the behavior of materials, for certain purposes it is not necessary to ask why the laws govern as they do. To apply the findings, it is only necessary to know what the consequences are; and if the consequences of the natural laws are indeed consistent, as the effects of natural law by nature are, then future land use should be readily predictable. To see what the future patterns will be, then, one need only to look at present, empirically observable patterns.

THE NEW FORMULA FOR TRANSPORTATION PLANNING

With the fortuitous development of high-speed computers at this very same time, we thus entered a period of lively investigation of land-use and traffic patterns in urban areas. In the hands of some creative and able analysts, the findings of the studies were reducible to fairly simple mathematical formulations. Now, in the mid-1960s, land-use and traffic forecasting and highway planning are becoming standardized procedures that most transportation engineers can readily learn. They call for (1) an O and D survey (or desire-line patterns synthesized via computer-based simulation models, without the expensive home-interview); (2) a quantified land-use inventory; (3) computations of the traffic-generation rates of the various land-use classes; (4) forecasts of area-wide population and employment to some future date; (5) spatial allocations of future population and employment in accordance with the empirically discovered present patterns – in effect, factoring up land use to a future date; (6) application of the traffic-generation rates to the forecasted land use, thus synthesizing future O and D travel patterns; (7) assignment of the traffic to a hypothetical highway network and testing of the ability of the net to handle the forecasted traffic volumes; (8) adjusting the net to fit the projected traffic; and then, finally, (9) constructing the network.

This strategy for metropolitan transportation planning is highly compatible with good civil engineering practice. Engineers are well equipped to handle the large volumes of data; the modes of analysis are similar to those in civil engineering; and the empiricism is of the same sort, as we have noted before, as is traditional in testing strengths of materials and designing engineering structures.

The metropolitan transportation planning task clearly calls for a high level of sophistication in data handling and in the treatment of large and complex problems. These are, of course, the traditional skills of the engineer, and he has not hesitated to take on this difficult and intricate task. Highway planning also, of course, has been one of the traditional professional assignments of civil engineering and, more recently, traffic engineering; and most of the staff in the state highway departments and in the Bureau of Public Roads are trained as engineers.

With the discovery of the vital importance of land-use projections, during the past few years, the engineers have not hesitated to invite other kinds of specialists to assist them; and it is now no longer a rarity to find urban planners, economists, geographers, sociologists, and others participating in the large metropolitan transportation studies. Because of their long-standing concern with urban land-use patterns, the urban planners in many of the metropolitan areas are called upon to prepare inventories and extrapolations of existing land use and to help evaluate the realism of land-use forecasts.

But a few urban planners have had a far more central role than that. The pioneering Detroit Area Transportation Study was directed by a group of social-science trained planners who later conducted the large-scale Chicago Area Transportation Study where the forecasting techniques were refined and made fully operational. The most advanced state of the art along this important line of development is now to be found at the seat of the earlier metropolitan and state planning efforts of the 1920s, having been transported from Chicago to New York. The up-state New York transportation studies, directed by Roger Creighton, and the Tri-State Transportation Study for the metropolitan region centered on New York City, directed by Dr. J. Douglas Carroll, Jr., have carried the techniques to a high level of technical proficiency and sophistication.

Under the impact of these and the numerous other metropolitan transportation studies that have been undertaken during the early 1960s, route planning has almost universally given way to transportation-system planning. Indeed, federal highway legislation now makes this mandatory on a "comprehensive, continuing, and cooperative" basis. The contemporary effort is to lay out coherent networks of routes interlacing the entire metropolitan territory. The exclusive focus on the highway, that dominated transportation-planning efforts throughout the first half of the century, is by now yielding fast to the conception of a "balanced transportation system," comprising some rationalized mix of auto and transit facilities. Rarely, however, is the boundary of the system under design stretched much beyond the physical transport facilities themselves. Metropolitan transportation planning has gone through a rapid and revolutionary development during the past twenty years; but it is still transportation planning, not metropolitan planning.

THE GROWING DISENCHANTMENT

METROPOLIS: MACHINE OR SOCIAL SYSTEM?

The approach to metropolitan transportation planning that is briefly outlined here and that is now becoming codified in transportation planning practice throughout the nation seems to derive from the conception of the metropolitan area as a closed mechanical system. It is assumed that if we can predict land-use patterns and hence, future travel patterns for some specified future date, we can then install sufficient transportation capacity in the appropriate places to satisfy future travel demand. This is akin to designing a part of a machine in such a way that the operations and capacities of the part will match the machine's requirements – say, to take a simple example, the design of an automobile's carburetor, with fuel-handling capacities matched to the fuel intake of the cylinders. The idea is, of course, a very familiar one in many branches of engineering, architecture, and urban planning; and it is familiar to all of us who have grown up in an industrial society.

But metropolitan areas seem not to be systems of this kind. Rather, they seem to be more like self-regulating biological systems than like mechanical systems. They maintain themselves, they grow, they somtimes reproduce, they respond to stresses, they age, and they may even die and enter the hereafter as ghost towns. Unlike the workings of a mechanical system, the inputs into the metropolitan system contribute to the system's growth and change. More than that, a change in any one of the subsystems induces changes in other subsystems, such that the characteristics of any part depend upon those of all the other parts. To add a part to the system is to change the characteristics of all other parts and indeed to change the characteristics of the new part itself.

New population arriving in a metropolis is not simply added on to previous populations; it influences the preexisting populations, itself changes, and in turn influences later development of the metropolitan area, possibly in quite different ways than did earlier immigrant populations. Similarly, the construction of a major public work, such as a new freeway or transit line, is not simply added to the existing stock of facilities. Rather, it becomes a causal input that influences all prior and later developments, possibly in quite different ways than did previously constructed facilities.

Metropolis and the Transportation System — An Interacting Process

And yet metropolitan areas are different from both mechanical and biological systems, being in some degree susceptible to willful modification through the actions of organized communities of men. Inputs to the system — new populations, new public works, new business activities, new social services, new governmental fiscal arrangements, changes in the locational preferences of establishments resulting from technological or cultural changes, and so on — can modify the patterns of future metropolitan development. Some of these influences can be deliberately controlled, most notably of course, the very transportation facilities which the planning studies are typically intended to design.

It is thus becoming clear that transportation facilities are considerably more than cogs in a metropolitan machine. They not only serve transportation demand, they also shape it. And the ways in which they do so are devious and complex, finding expression through the millions of decisions made daily by individuals and groups who deal with each other within the metropolitan setting.

Although it had apparently escaped the attention of many practioners and theorists concerned with the metropolitan transport, over a long period of time a body of theory has been accumulating in economics, seeking to account for the locational decisions of urban establishments. Currently that theory is being actively reexamined, and important refinements and elaborations are now coming forth. But, at least to our knowledge, none of these theorists has yet challenged the long-standing proposition that locational decisions of households and firms are fundamentally shaped by the costs of overcoming distance. Other variables — including the costs of density, incomes, and space and amenity preferences — are also directly at play; but the theorists are agreed that distance costs are among the major variables accounted in the locators' calculus. Because distance costs depend upon the transportation facilities and services that are available, transportation, in turn, is itself a major influence upon the spatial patterns in which urban establishments distribute themselves. This being so, it is patently clear that a change in the transportation sytsem is tantamount to a change in the locations of activities – that is, to a change in the land-use pattern – and to a change in the pattern of social and economic intercourse. In turn, a change in interaction patterns probably leads to more fundamental changes in the social and economic structure of the metropolitan community.

It is thus becoming apparent that transportation facilities are not only shaped by land-use patterns but that they are also shapers of land-use patterns. And, perhaps of even greater significance to the long-run evolution of transportation planning thought, we are now beginning to see that traffic, which is a reflection of social and economic intercourse, in turn influences and shapes patterns of social and economic intercourse. And if these propositions be valid, it then becomes clear that transportation planners are involved with a great deal more than highways and transit lines.

THE INSIGHTS IN THE EARLY 1960s

THE METROPOLITAN COMMUNITY AS A SOCIAL PROCESS

The urban planners' discomfort with the mechanistic character of transporation planning has been spreading within the engineering profession as well. Five or ten years ago, the engineer's response was one of despair; the more he planned and built, the more traffic was generated, the more congestion showed up on the counters, the more facilities were needed. The metropolitan machine seemed to have a mind of its own and, like Pinnochio, it seemed determined to break the rules that good mechanical systems are supposed to obey.

The problem is, of course, that metropolitanites do have minds of their own; and given new highways, they seem determined to use them. Unlike Pinnochio, though, they are not being mischievous. A new freeway that reduces the travel time between the central district and a suburban locale may, for the first time, make it economically feasible for a family or a business firm to move to an outlying location. Newly created ease of access within an urban area may open up opportunities for visiting friends, shops, or parks that were previously too hard to get to. Improved highway networks make trucking more competitive with the railroads. And, of course, the increasing attractivenes of the large metropolitan areas to families and firms in some measure reflects the effectiveness of the transportation system in serving the economic and social processes of the metropolitan community. New urban highways become congested because social and economic interaction is the very stuff of urban life; and, because highways are an important means of maintaining interactions, people locate themselves in places where they can take advantage of the accessibilities that the highways create.

We have been accustomed to view the metropolitan area as a static pattern of land uses interlaced by a static network of transportation lines, as these might be portrayed on a map. Even when we have viewed traffic flows, we have tended to regard flow patterns as static phenomena, as traffic counts at various stations. This photographic image is now being supplanted by a view of the metropolitan community as a social process in which people deal with other people. In the complex network of individual and group relations, traffic is but one of several processes of communication by which linkages among establishments are maintained. It is these interdependencies that make land use relevant to traffic, and it is now becoming generally understood that the most sensitive understanding of traffic generation would come from studies of these linkage patterns, rather than from empirical land-use measurements and maps alone. Whereas during the 1950s, transportation planners tended to treat land-use statistics as reified "things," they are now searching behind the superficial meanings of land use for the social processes that give "land use" its important meaning and its utility. A static *form*-view of land use and transportation is now giving way to a dynamic *process*-view.

THE METROPOLITAN COMMUNITY AS A GROWING SYSTEM

At the same time a new conception is emerging that sees the metropolitan community as a *growing system*. Traditional plan-making methods in urban planning and in public-works engineering called for a portrait of the state of affairs at some future *point* in time. Desired land-use patterns or land-use forecasts were made for some single future date, typically some twenty to twenty-five years away. The planned facilities were then fitted to the anticipated demands that would occur at the future date, in accord with the idea of a mechanical system that we have mentioned before. Even when the planners did not simply factor up existing patterns to accommodate projected trends in population and employment increase, but instead projected considerable change in the pattern, the future state of affairs was typically viewed as a static portrait at a given point in future time. Now, as we are beginning to learn something about the processes of change in metropolitan patterns, this static conception is being replaced by a view of the metropolitan area as a growing system.

THE PENN-JERSEY STUDY – OPENING A NEW FRONTIER

Simultaneously, as the theoretical work of the various groups of social scientists is being brought to the attention of transportation planners, we are learning to ask the "why" kinds of questions about urban growth, instead of the descriptive, "what, where and how much" kinds that we have traditionally dealt with. Our understanding of the complex matrix of casual relationships among the various aspects of the metropolis is increasing very rapidly now. We may already be at the stage at which we can apply multicausal models in transportation planning to replace the simple cause-and-effect models that we have used in the past. This was precisely the intent of the Penn-Jersey Transportation Study, initiated in the Philadelphia area in 1959.

There an effort was made to put our new insights to work in designing a transportation system that would best conform to a wide range of criteria. The planners sought to grapple with the metropolis as an economic, social, and political process. Traffic was understood to be an expression of the functional interdependencies among the individuals and groups living there, and the decisions to locate their establishments were seen as responses to a wide range of variables – including public actions, previously located private establishments, economic opportunity, and private preferences. Instead of projecting a future land-use pattern to some future point in time – as every previous metropolitan transportation study had done – Penn-Jersey attempted to simulate the process and the spatial patterns of growth *through* future time.

This is a decisively important step forward. Contending that the realism of a future land-use portrait can be evaluated only if we can describe and explain the sequence of steps that would create it, Penn-Jersey attempted to trace alternative sequences of future metropolitan growth patterns that would result from different combinations of public policies and from different combinations of private opportunities and preferences.

The procedures created for deriving future land-use patterns represent a major improvement in metropolitan planning technology and thought. In 1954, both the Detroit and the San Francisco land-use plans, prepared by city planners and then adopted as the bases for traffic projection, were largely intuitive expressions of the planners' best thinking concerning the desired future state of affairs. Being essentially static in concept, they were "snapshots" of land-use patterns, each at a single point in future time. The Chicago and the 1959 Washington D.C. land-use forecasts were not presented as *desired* future states of affairs, but were conceived, rather, as the most probable state at the single future design date. Although the difference between a plan and a forecast is great – the one being normative in nature, the other positivistically predictive – all four of these land use plans in common dealt with a single future date, with no explanation of the sequence of causes between the now and the then. None of them sought to derive the future state of affairs as the resultant of sequenced events. In common, they seem to have bypassed any explanation of growth processes.

The Penn-Jersey planners, deliberately assembled from a dozen disciplines, sought to attack the issues of developmental processes frontally. Tapping into the body of economic and social theory that purports to explain locational decisions of households and firms, they constructed a set of "growth models" to be used to simulate the alternative, time-sequenced processes of development that would occur under alternatively assumed market and public-policy conditions. In accord with the behavioral theories of the economists, sociologists, and political scientists, they sought to account for the effects upon individuals' locational decisions that would be generated by different hypothetical transportation systems, zoning regulations, taxation policies, and the like. They collaborated also with the City of Philadelphia in monitoring the actual impacts of experimental programs testing the reactions of daily commuters to modifications in fare structures, time schedules, and comfort levels in mass transportation services. Future land use was thus to be derived as a function of transportation and other governmentally supplied services and facilities; simultaneously, future traffic was to be derived as a function of land use and of the changing interdependencies among establishments. The intent was systematically to predict which interacting chains of events might occur, *if* governments and private decision-makers were to act one way or another. Thus, the pattern of the analysis and prediction was to test effects of alternative government actions with respect to transport and other matters by evaluating the networks of repercussions that the actions would trigger.

The Penn-Jersey charter called for the design of a regionwide transportation system. When the formulations of the economists' location theory were introduced into that task, under the research leadership of Britton Harris and Henry W. Bruck, it became apparent that transportation-directed actions are both cause and effect of a far larger spectrum of actions. Hence it became clear that transportation cannot be dealt with as though it were a separate system, susceptible to independent management. The long-sought goal of an optimum transportation system, which a few years earlier had seemed to be nearly within grasp, suddenly vanished. Transportation services and facilities now had became intrinsically valueless, so to speak. Their value lay only in the instrumental contributions they might make to the workings of the larger metropolitan system. And, because the larger metropolitan societal system is governed by intricate and subtle economic and political processes, the task of transportation planning became inseparable from the larger and more complex task of governing metropolitan development processes. Accordingly, the transportation study officials became instrumental in the formation of improved general policy making machinery for the metropolitan region. As it had been thirty years earlier in the Regional Plan for New York, transportation planning again became one instrument, among others, with which to shape metropolitan growth. At Penn-Jersey the transportation mandate became inseparable from that larger mission. The idea, no doubt, was among the things transported from New York to Penn-Jersey by Henry Fagin when he moved from the Regional Plan Association to head the Philadelphia staff.

Currently, such transportation studies as that in southeastern Wisconsin are building further onto the structure of methodology that evolved so significantly since the first massive O and D surveys of twenty years ago. Here, water supply and sanitary and storm sewer systems plans are, together with transportation, integral parts of one continuing regionwide set of policy development responsibilities.

SUMMARY AND PROSPECT

Thus, during the course of the past forty to fifty years, we have seen what has amounted to a major revolution in transportation planning. We have moved from a road construction, project orientation, through a period in which efforts were made to analyze empirical regularities in traffic patterns, to a concern for the land use traffic relationships, to the present time when transportation-system planning is becoming inseparable from metropolitan planning. As Robert B. Mitchell has so aptly put it, we now know enough to realize that coordination of highway planning and transit planning, or even coordination of transportation planning and land-use planning, is not enough. Nothing short of complete integration of the two efforts will suffice. Because we now understand that transport facilities have such important impacts on so many aspects of the metropolitan community, none of us in good conscience can any longer deal with transportation systems alone.

Whether we like it or not, all of us are involved in shaping the whole metropolitan environment and thus, in shaping the environmental conditions in which business firms will conduct their affairs and in which residents will live out their lives. Transportation planning has evolved to become an activity for planning the environment of urban life. And it is this broadened perspective that makes the undertaking so exciting and its results so important.

The Physical World and the Human Environment

TWO SIMULTANEOUS TRENDS in the post-World War II development of public planning were identified in the preface. One has been toward a proliferation of planning specializations, each increasingly narrowly focused and therefore done in greater depth and competence within its limits. The other has been toward a more systematic integration of the several types of planning that evolved independently — a unifying effort found necessary to produce acceptably coherent and mutually reinforcing programs of action.

Urban design, the main subject of Chapter 15 on "Urban Design and Urban Development," could be viewed as an expression of either trend or of both. It is a new field of specialization that concentrates on the design aspects of the urban scene and on the specifically urban aspects of the work of the several design professions. But urban design also can be regarded as an integrating activity concerned centrally with the intersection of five overlapping fields: (1) architecture at the large-scale and community-wide end of its spectrum; (2) landscape architecture practiced in the city rather than in the country; (3) civil engineering applied to the design of urban sites and districts; (4) industrial design at the macro level; and (5) land-use planning at the micro level. Urban design is studied and practiced as a field of specialization within each of these professional areas. But urban design is becoming articulated too as a new professional area in its own right — with its own theorists, researchers, students, and practitioners — even its own ethics. Above all (alas) it has also its own evolving professional jargon.

A full history of the crystallization of urban design as a new field of concentration has not yet been written, and the implications for urban development have not yet been explored systematically. In Chapter 15, a beginning is made toward clarifying both history and meaning. Given the paucity of formal published materials, the authors of the chapter, Henry Fagin and Carol H. Tarr, have drawn into a single unified framework the hitherto scattered ideas of an array of urban design experts — ideas still in a state of fluidity and search but clearly defining an important new field of public policy.

In their essay, Fagin and Tarr focus first on a series of theoretical considerations: What is urban design? What has been its historic evolution? What variations in attitudes are there toward urban design and change? How extensively should the designer become involved in changing the larger environment? How shall the perceptual form of the urban area be explored? What is the nature of urban design creativity? How may design ideas be communicated before projects are carried out? What new possibilities in design are opened up by the use of the computer to make analytical computations and to display three-dimensional forms from simple sketch inputs? Will we succeed in the search for a new vernacular in urban architecture?

Later sections cover various problems of application: the implications of the population explosion, of new technology, of changes in transportation. In presenting materials on scale, the authors of the chapter distinguish intra-city from inter-city scale. In their discussions of "taste," some experts advocate the deliberate imposition of upper-middle-class tastes on slum dwellers, while others are vigorously opposed. A final section offers policy statements on urban design and recommendations for research and action in a wide variety of directions.

Like other fields and sub-fields, urban design has its sub-sub areas of specialization. In a volume as selective as this one, all the subdivisions cannot be covered. The editors have chosen site design in housing to exemplify specialization in a typical area. Accordingly, in "Urban Housing and Site Design," Robert D. Katz examines recent trends in housing innovation. The illustrated discussion is abstracted from his recently published book entitled *Design of the Housing Site: A Critique of American Practice* (Katz, 1967).

In Chapter 16, Katz organizes his illustrated presentation of innovations in site planning first by type of location — inner city, by-passed sites and older neighborhoods, scattered locations, and outlying areas — and then by the characteristics of occupants, including the elderly and the young adults. Innovations are then distinguished by site and construction characteristics. Striking new ways of arranging parking and circulation are followed by imaginative new ways of conceiving and arranging open space. One section deals with a silent subject of our day, industrial housing and mobile homes. A set of conclusions, reached after a field survey of twenty years of postwar site plans from coast to coast, suggests to the reader how few and precious are the innovations and how great is the work ahead.

One of Katz's conclusions sums up an impression also expressed by the authors of the more general chapter on urban design. As Katz says, "Few of the site planning innovations can be regarded as breakthroughs brought about by contemporary American ingenuity." Rather, he considers them "old proposals belatedly realized, older practices rediscovered or foreign ideas imported." Fagin and Tarr similarly enumerate the major landmarks in American urban design and note wryly that most of what has been done in recent years was done at least as handsomely and imaginatively by the 1930s. Yet, to the authors of both chapters, the signs do point to an imminent change in the offing. A veritable revolution in urban design may lie just ahead.

—*H.F.*

15

Urban Design and Urban Development

HENRY FAGIN and
CAROL H. TARR

☐ THE ROOTS OF URBAN DESIGN, of course, are ancient. In America that simultaneous consideration of street and square layout and the siting of buildings which epitomizes urban design is seen in the plans of many colonial towns like Charleston and Philadelphia and New Orleans (Reps, 1965). Outstanding advances in the chief elements of urban design have come in a wide diversity of applications and have been contributed by inspired designers from many backgrounds. For example, the great 1792 plan for the new federal capital in Washington, D.C. was the work of Major Charles Pierre L'Enfant, a civil engineer-architect. The winner of the 1867 competition for the design of New York's Central Park was the landscape architect Frederick Law Olmstead. His design included very modern elements, indeed: the grade-separation of general urban traffic, pleasure traffic, bridle paths, and pedestrian walks, for example, and the provision of an exceptional variety of leisure activities to meet a wide variety of recreational tastes. The leading organizer of Chicago's 1893 World's Fair, with its innovations in urban water distribution and sanitation as well as in formal site planning, was the architect Daniel H. Burnham. Later, in 1909 Burnham created the first modern city plan for Chicago, with its imaginative reconstruction of the whole lakefront integrating land and water, open spaces, civic institutions, and private buildings into one great unified experience. The Grand Central Terminal in

---

EDITORS' NOTE: *This chapter is from a forthcoming book by Henry Fagin entitled* Urban Beauty and Public Action. *The studies and field work on which the manuscript is based were jointly financed by the University of Wisconsin and Urban America, Inc.*

New York, completed just before World War I, remains one of the most astonishing structures of the twentieth century. It incorporated such newly re-discovered ideas as *vertical zoning* (including on one site three different kinds of rail transport, an automobile highway raised above cross traffic and integrated into the architecture, a taxi tunnel – also free of cross traffic – connecting below grade, off-street loading bays, elevated glass sidewalks, and a system of ramps for pedestrians). Further, there was an integrated mixture of land uses within one *superblock* including a heavy locomotive machine shop, a major traffic interchange, light manufacturing of various sorts, retail and service establishments, a residential hotel, an office building, a theater, and New York's grandest civic concourse – all the result of the collaboration of every sort of environmental designer with the land economists and administrators of the day.

The fertile collaboration of the architect Clarence S. Stein and the landscape architect Henry Wright during the 1920s and 1930s produced a whole new vocabulary of urban design in successive innovative communities at Sunnyside, Long Island, Hillside in the Bronx, and Radburn, New Jersey. Their ideas about cluster housing, interior walkways, grouped open spaces, taming the automobile to provide safe and varied neighborhoods – ideas derived in part from English precedent – introduced in thoroughly American and contemporary terms most of the remaining basic elements of urban design used today, beyond those already noted above. The two main additions to all these ideas were the landscaped, grade-separated, split-direction expressway concept pioneered in New York's Bronx River Parkway in the 1920s and the important development, also in the 1920s, of Rockefeller Center – a commercial application of the multi-block design idea, tying a group of office buildings and theaters into a unified whole, connected below grade by pedestrian arcades and offstreet parking and truck loading facilities.

POST WORLD WAR II DEVELOPMENTS

We have recited these early landmark innovations to stress a view that the worldwide depression of the 1930s and its aftermath in World War II interrupted a brilliant process of urban design invention. We have hardly yet recovered the lost momentum despite some renewed interest in the most recent twenty years and a few exciting projects now in the construction stage. Most notable since 1946 have been *first,* the efforts of reconstruction in cities abroad like Rotterdam and Coventry and sections of London; *second,* the experiments with several generations of new towns culminating in places like Cumbernauld in England and Reston, Virginia and Columbia, Maryland in America; *third,* bold but still very limited central city reconstructions like portions of Hartford and New Haven, Connecticut; Philadelphia, Pennsylvania; and San Francisco, California; and *fourth,* the launching of an extensive dialogue among many design professionals in search of new urban design approaches suited to contemporary ways of organizing, financing, and carrying out the developmental activities that build and rebuild the modern urban fabric.

In this latter dialogue, one can observe a continuity of evolving concepts running through several key writings: (1) a paper analyzing the visual elements of the urban environment by the architect-planner Sydney Williams, given at the 1953 Annual Conference of the American Society of Planning Officials (Williams, 1953); (2) the 1958 report of a joint committee of planners and architects in New York, which advocated for the first time the creation and implementation of a municipal design plan and program for every community as an integral part of its comprehensive planning process and master plan (Fagin and Weinberg, 1958); (3) the pioneering book by Kevin Lynch on how we perceive cities, (Lynch, 1960); and (4) the papers given at a series of some 20 conferences on urban design in the past decade, extensively reviewed in the remainder of this chapter.

Particularly because the recent history of American urban design as realized in actual construction is so meager, we shall stress in this chapter the development of new and we think important *ideas* about urban design. These appear more significant to the larger discussion of urban policy in this volume than any possible recounting of accomplishments in urban design. We are confident, however, that the ideas outlined soon will take concrete form as the doubling of urban America that is essential in the remainder of this century and the equally challenging replacement of obsolete America unfold.

A DECADE OF DESIGN CONFERENCES

Since the end of World War II regular extensive discussion and interaction among design professionals has been taking place in conferences and panels specifically organized around the theme of *Urban Design.* Urban design has primarily to do with the evolving arrangements and functions among and between the three pairs of elements: whole buildings and groups of buildings, open spaces and open-space systems, and circulation pathways and transport facilities – all considered at a scale larger than the individual building project. Urban design emphasizes particularly the relationships among the many physical elements that together comprise the evolving neighborhood, community, and region.

The scale considered may vary from the grouping of buildings, open spaces, and circulation pathways in a small village neighborhood to the physical urban structure of an entire metropolitan region. Many excellent books deal in depth with aspects of urban design. The present chapter, however, makes available materials that either have never been published or have appeared hitherto only in limited form.

The discussion that follows is a kind of imaginary symposium inspired by what has been said in the course of some 20 actual symposia. The quoted excerpts have been taken from selected urban design conference proceedings in an attempt to bring together recurrent themes, topics of major concern today, and emerging concepts. Of course, this technique of reporting permits only an underscoring of recurring issues of discourse and professional concern; no pretense is implied of encompassing the full breadth or depth of conference participants' contributions. For the whole meaning of the excerpts, one must read them in their original contexts.

Because many urban design conferences have encouraged a free-wheeling type of discussion and because related ideas were expressed randomly in different places and at different times, we have organized this part of the chapter around selected concepts rather than strict chronology. Accordingly, the discussion has its own internal logic rather than strict historic fidelity.

THEORETICAL CONSIDERATIONS

WHAT IS URBAN DESIGN?

The term "urban design" has been used in the past decade to encompass the complexity of the interrelated architectural forms involved in the urban scene. Two related concepts are involved – the one a matter of physical form, the other a matter of the planning process required. The latter emphasizes the diversity of planning activities demanded to cope creatively with the dynamics of an ever-changing urban fabric responding to the forces of urbanization. The architects, landscape architects, engineers, planners, and other designers working in urban design must function within a hierarchy of scales and a continually changing element of time. In relation to architecture, urban design as described by Paul D. Spreiregen (then Project Head of the American Institute of Architect's Urban Design Program)

> . . . involves the same design elements – space, mass and activity – the components of urban form, as well as of architectural form. In architectural design, spaces are rooms, corridors, courts and halls; in urban design, spaces are streets, squares and parks. In architectural design, masses are building bulks, walls, floors, ceilings, screens and sculpture; in urban design, masses are the floor of the city, its buildings, trees, fences, screens, poles, sculpture and fountains. In architecture, activities are the uses of the various parts of a building; in urban design, the uses of the various parts of the city. But here is where the analogy becomes difficult, for the nature of design on an urban scale is quite different from design on an architectural scale. The discrepancy between the sizes of buildings and cities is so great that the design problems take on a qualitative difference as well as a quantitative one. Design actions in the city span long periods of time and many people are involved; a large-scale urban design concept must be broad enough to allow for the inevitable variables, yet be sufficiently specific and sensible to function as a rallying point for the many separate actions which compose it and translate it into real constructions (Spreiregen, 1963).

David A. Wallace (Professor of City Planning, University of Pennsylvania) underscored the process of change:

> There has been a major change in planning thinking in the last few years. The concept of the city and urbanization as a system of interrelated parts has profound implications for the way urban design is handled and the way planners and architects work within it. This leads to thinking of process rather than thinking of completion at any stage. One of the limitations of a traditional architectural background has been an end-state approach to things. Once a building was finished it was perfect and any change would automatically make it less than perfect. This is not the case in terms of cities (Harvard Graduate School of Design, 1964).

Basic to urban design is the bringing together of forces and forms of the city in an *aesthetic* synthesis. A quotation from *The City in History* by Lewis Mumford (urban philosopher) was adopted as the theme of the 1962 *Aspen International Design Conference:*

> All the sacrifices that have helped bring the city into existence come to nothing if the life that city makes possible is not its own reward. Neither augmented power nor unlimited material wealth can atone for a day that lacks a glimpse of beauty, a flash of joy, a quickening and sharing of fellowship (quoted in *Aspen International Design Conference,* 1962, p. I).

Norman Day (then Design Section Head, Twin Cities Metropolitan Planning Commission, Minneapolis) summarized *The Architect and the City* conference in 1962:

> The task seemed clearly identified: restructure the old fabric of the city without destroying its fundamental value; create a framework for a new growth capable of guiding and coordinating a thousand individual acts; design connections between old and new scales with transitional continuity; and re-examine the nature of the basic cells, the micro-scale thematic units of our lives. However, if the task was made clear, both the method and the image of the new city are blurred.
>
> That the content, the processes and activity systems of our cities must be rediscovered and expressed in physical form was the strongest recurring theme among many divergent and convergent points of view. The description and dimension of this content proved extremely elusive to the end (Day, 1962, p. 93).

Historical Summary

A brief historical summary of the development of urban design in the United States may serve to set theoretical considerations in perspective. Edmund N. Bacon (Executive Director, Philadelphia City Planning Commission) addressed the 1957 *Aspen International Design Conference:*

> From its beginning in the New England village and southern colonial town, the picture of the American city became blurred in the Nineteenth Century economic expansionist movement. A continuous stream of unrelated structures competed for the limelight, and in the competitive tumult that was the dominant note, the over-all city form was obscured. . . . A potent new vision appeared on the horizon just before the turn of the century in the form of the Chicago World's Fair. . . . The important thing was that, for the first time in the modern era, a concrete physical expression was available of the larger order, of a series of buildings in a clear and meaningful relationship with each other. This, evidently, was a thing that the Nineteenth Century had begun to yearn for, and to desire enough to actually reproduce variants of it on a small scale in permanent form. . . . As the Twentieth Century moved into its second and third decade the great new influence of the "modernists," Le Corbusier, Gropius, Mies van der Rohe, smashed away the accumulation and impedimentia of stylistic preoccupation, and set new images of light, freshness and freedom. But smashed away too, at the same time, was the image of the larger order. Most of the executed work of the three masters consisted of individual buildings in limited number, so the models they produced were sparse and separate. . . .

Bacon suggested that as we move into the second half of the twentieth century searching for indications of new influences on the development of the urban environment two major observations be considered:

> One is the action of individuals which may be symptomatic of a trend; the other is evolving governmental policies.
>
> . . . .
>
> A few, and a growing number of families are finding that the institutional richness, the freedom from transportation strains, and the close association with the cultural activities of the city core, more than outweigh for them the advantages of open space and other amenities of the suburb. . . . The second indication is the national policy as set by the action of Congress. The National Housing Act of 1949 asserted that the environment in parts of most American cities was wholly unsatisfactory, and provided one billion dollars to clear it away and to provide a new and better one.
>
> . . . .

> With the advance of urban renewal, the program has changed from the design of individual structures to the design of parts of the city. This completely changes the relationship of the designer to his problem, and of necessity, must involve the interaction of a series of different designers working for different clients in areas adjacent to one another (Bacon, 1957, pp. 1-2).

Attitudes Toward Urban Design and Change

Albert Szabo (Professor, Harvard Graduate School of Design) commented:

> I see in Urban Design an interdisciplinary concern for the whole of our urban physical environment wherein form (outer appearance) and structure (inner order) serve the needs and desires of men living in proximity and wherein the attendant advantages of proximity are maximized and the disadvantages minimized (Szabo, 1962, p. 91).

Morton Hoppenfeld (then Urban Designer, National Capital Planning Commission) in 1962 discussed urban design qualifications as "essentially a *frame of mind* or an *attitude* one holds toward the multiple acts of city building." This attitude would be based on at least four characteristics necessary to the competent urban designer: (1) "a positive attitude toward the city; a sense of involvement, a personal commitment to the city as a way of life, and urbanism as a study of man"; (2) a knowledge in depth of many fields and ability to learn continuously; (3) experience; and (4) talent. He further explored aspects of the urban design process considering "the urge to correlate" and an "equilibrium of incompletion."

> If we accept the city as a natural, constantly changing, constantly growing organism, then all individual acts of creation either as additions to or changes of the organism must correlate to the immediate environs and to the organism as a whole. . . .
>
> . . . .
>
> One of the key values of a truly good design will be its apparent completion, its apparent unity within itself but still its ability to grow, change and mesh with the rest (Hoppenfeld, 1962, p. 81).

Flexibility within time has been a recurrent theme in discussions of urban design. Lewis Mumford pointed out that time "gives to design vitality and complexity as well as change" (University of Pennsylvania Graduate School of Fine Arts, 1963, p. 8). David A. Crane (Professor of Civic Design, University of Pennsylvania) developed a similar point in what he termed "the Kaleidoscopic City of Change."

> The Dynamic City starts with a comprehensive view of the time dimension – past, present, and future – and relates it to space.... Over a long period of time change is more than replacement; forms evolve to suit entirely new purposes (Crane, 1962, p. 71).

Crane expressed skepticism of the term urban design. For him, it is not just a "profession" since it has no unique ethic, theory, or practitioners; nor is it a "method," but it is more a "scale of space or scale of time." He made a strong plea for the identification and use of similar forms derived from the necessities of the environment rather than the hackneyed focusing on perfecting of old forms. He called for the training of

> *City form-makers, city builders,... neither "heads of the team,"* nor *"experts in visual aspects,"* but versatile artists of function, the formal integration of a complex problem-solving process, the inventors of new city needs and new dimensions of city satisfaction (Crane, 1962, p. 76).

INVOLVEMENT IN THE ENVIRONMENT

Crane further developed these themes of change and involvement at a later conference:

> To influence form as a process state we need strategic tools or systems not just for designing form, but rather for designing forms which in turn design other forms which in turn lead to other acts, expanding and enriching our small powers and talents (Crane, 1963, p. 25).

He outlined three requirements of such a strategy. (1) The strategy must be *effective,* recognizing and understanding the city as a place of movement and impending motion or rest, change or permanence, and as a city of multiple participation in the city-making process. (2) The strategy must be an *art,* not a mere scientific logistic. Civic design is not just a placing of the right scale and types of public facilities at the right place and time but also "an interpretive visual representation . . . of the highest public aspirations" (Crane, 1963, p. 27). (3) The strategy must also be one of *love* Crane quoted August Heckscher:

> The question is not whether the next decades shall see building and planning: these things in one way or the other are bound to occur. The question is whether we can build with love and a sense of the values involved. . . . To contemplate the community and its works as they are, to view them without cynicism and without illusion, is to be left in a very human mood, at once marvelling and sad because of what man has made (quoted in Crane, 1963, p. 26).

August Heckscher was also a participant at the 1963 *Pennsylvania Civic Design Symposium.* His concept of the "Public Happiness" is summarized in the proceedings of that conference by another participant, James Nelson Kise.

> [Heckscher] finds the Welfare State, seeking to increase the comforts and satisfactions of private citizens, too preoccupied with things negative. He argues for another alternative which he calls the Public Happiness. In this concept of a government's role it would seek to lift men above private comforts and to give them some vision of Public Happiness. Whereas the Welfare State is concerned with necessity and survival as a level of existence, the Public Happiness is concerned with freedom, adventure, choice, and courage as a level of existence. He is careful to warn that the Public Happiness is not simply spending more money in the public sector, for that alone is not assurance of a higher civilization. Rather, he sees the greatest strength of the Public Happiness coming from the *individual's* awareness of the public sector of existence. In this way he argues not for a new society but to make coherent what exists (University of Pennsylvania Graduate School of Fine Arts, 1963, p. 13).

Heckscher describes the "interior landscape" of the contemporary citizen as lacking self-identity, moving in vagueness, lacking direct experience, and missing a sense of place:

> The result in terms of the individual personality or in terms of the psyche is a sort of boredom and vagueness and an inability of the person to get hold of life; a feeling that although we are in the midst of things we are really on the outside; that although we acquire much we possess nothing; that although we travel far we don't get anywhere (University of Pennsylvania Graduate School of Fine Arts, 1963, p. 38).

Heckscher urged the planner and the architect to help the individual by constructing an *outer* landscape "of form, of definiteness, of boundary, and of order" (University of Pennsylvania Graduate School of Fine Arts, 1963, p. 38).

> Congruity between the inner and outer order is the beginning of what I have called the Public Happiness. Once felt this congruity is the thing which sets up a sense of tensions and excitements which the individual then carries forward and which makes other parts of the physical and inner life meaningful to him (University of Pennsylvania Graduate School of Fine Arts, 1963, p. 39).

PERCEPTUAL EXPLORATION OF URBAN DESIGN

Following Professor Kevin Lynch's interest in "the perceptual form of cities," there has been concern expressed in design conferences for the psychological perceptions of the environment as well as the philosophical perception. George S. Welsh (Professor of Psychology, University of North Carolina) developed the theme that "perception of the urban environment, like any perception, must involve one or more of these various sense modalities" – sight, sound, smell, taste, touch, and kinesthetic perceptions such as temperature and motion (Welsh, 1966, p. 5). Dr. D. Wilfred Abse (Professor of Psychiatry, University of Virginia School of Medicine) approached environmental perception in terms of associationism and gestalt similarity:

> In its simplest form, associationism makes of the mind an elaborate machine responding to the environment in a causally determined way. After initial response, via sensations, to the environment ideas are linked so that the sensations acquire meaning, thus becoming percepts; and then these percepts give rise to other ideas linked together passively and mechanically according to the laws of similarity and contiguity.
>
> . . . .
>
> Psychologists, from their experiments and observations of animals and humans, have come to the view that the perceptual process is always one of actively organizing configurations, of picking out a figure from its ground, of grouping and pattern-making. . . .
>
> . . . .
>
> The law of *similarity* in Gestalt principles of organization . . . indicates that similar items (for example, those alike in form and color)

> or similar transitions (those alike in the steps separating them) tend to form groups in perception. . . . The law of *proximity* . . . indicates that perceptual groups are favored according to the nearness of the parts. . . . The law of *closure* indicates that closed areas are more stable than unclosed ones and therefore more readily form figures in perception, and the law of *continuation* indicates that perceptual organization tends to occur in such a manner that a straight line appears to continue as a straight line, and a part circle as a circle, and so on, even though many other kinds of perceptual structuring would be possible (Abse, 1966, pp. 13-14; emphasis added).

Concern for man's hectic and confused environment, already indicated in August Heckscher's remarks above, was recurrent in design conferences. Dr. Abse referred to "the noise and the overstimulation, and what is called the 'input overload'" as constituting a serious threat to both physical and mental health (Institute of Government, The University of North Carolina at Chapel Hill, 1966, p. 28). Ian McHarg (Professor of Landscape Architecture, University of Pennsylvania) pointed out that ecology is concerned with functioning interacting systems composed of organisms and their environments: there are strong parallels in the interaction of man with his city environment. In organisms and in man, density increases disease, and sensory overload and stress result from anarchic, disordered environments (McHarg, 1962, pp. 101-103).

CREATIVITY AND COMMUNICATION OF DESIGN IDEAS

Designers participating in professional conferences actively concerned themselves with the nature of creativity and the problems of communicating and implementing their design ideas. When arranging conferences, some professional groups selected a specific theme and invited interdisciplinary participants to discuss the theme from their differing perspectives – for example, *The Architect and the City* conference jointly sponsored by the American Institute of Architects and the Association of Collegiate Schools of Architecture. A specific *case study* method was adopted for the urban design conferences at the Harvard Graduate School of Design. Dean Jose Luis Sert called for this sharpening of focus when he noted that the earlier general discussions on urban design "were tending to become repetitious" (Harvard Graduate School of Design, 1959, p. 3). Still other conferences have been directly concerned with the training of designers and have approached substantive material from the viewpoint of educational organization and communication – for example the 1962 Washington University School of Architecture conference, *Education for Urban Design*, in St. Louis.

Symbolic Communication of Spatial Experience

Edmund Bacon suggested that a problem of communication stems not from lack of good will on the part of the public, but lack of "designers with an ability to present to the public significant ideas in a form which can easily be understood" (Bacon, 1963, p. 15). Bacon advocated diagrams as a physical expression for the symbolic language of design. He developed a matrix wherein columns for apprehension, representation, and realization were plotted against rows for various systems – intuitive, individual centered, single movement, and simultaneous movement systems. According to the Symposium report, "Bacon suggested that in order for a designer to communicate a design concept, the apprehension of space must go through the process of representation, which in turn becomes a means of transmitting the concept into a state of realization."

> The single movement system depended upon a unity of speed of movement by the various modes of transportation available during the period. Actually, there was very little difference whether one moved around on foot or on horseback or in a carriage. Each essentially resulted in the same basic experience of movement through space. Now, however, high speed ground movement by automobile and rail summons forth entirely new dimensions of civic design in which the rate of reception of impressions must be considered in a variety of movement systems at a single moment. Our apprehension of space has been completely revolutionized and the old individual centered, earth centered universe of man has been shattered for all time. We have in our day *simultaneous movement systems,* an understanding of which is, in my opinion, the key to civic design. Our apprehension of these systems is perfectly clear. Our representation is absolutely miserable (Bacon, 1963, p. 18).

Elsewhere, Karl Otto Schmid (urban designer, Zurich) took exception to analyzing urban design from a purely aesthetic point of view, citing the dynamic quality of the space considered and the dynamic human activity involved:

> It is therefore of primary importance that an urban designer . . . be thoroughly aware of all the criteria which qualify as a sequence of experiences for the human being in any and all relationships to this space.
>
> . . . .
>
> One of the difficulties is that no "model" can visualize very well the dynamic intensity of space. Thus the designer is usually faced with solving the problem analytically, one aspect after another (Schmid, 1966, p. 83).

Schmid defined design as "a conscious anticipation of a possible action upon the environment by means of registration in visual form" (Schmid, 1966, p. 78). Urban design introduces a fourth dimension into architecture – that of time, and rapidly changing environment outdates solutions before experimentation with them can take place:

> Thus our lack of more durable results is not only due to our lack of foresight, but is most of all the fault of old-fashioned methods in tackling problems of an over-complicated nature, the most tangible of these methods being intuition. . . . Let us not overemphasize the importance of creativeness in the design process. It is certainly important, but our traditional and confident reliance on it must be revised (Schmid, 1966, p. 79).

Philip Thiel (Professor, College of Architecture and Urban Planning, Washington University) reported some success in teaching experiences using a rudimentary system of sequence-experience notation. He pointed out that such tools exist in other fields, for example, musical notation and Labanotation for the dance (Thiel, 1962, p. 109). Thiel emphasized that the problem is not one of communicating existing forms but of expressing ideas for yet unrealized forms.

Decision Theory

Barclay G. Jones (Professor, Department of City and Regional Planning, Cornell) discussed decision-making at the Washington University *Education for Urban Design* conference. Jones posited that successful design solutions result from a combination of both the rational and the intuitive processes. Rational processes involve direct, deliberate reference to the individual's experience and direct reference to the individual's fund of knowledge and vicarious experience. Intuitive processes involve referring to knowledge and experience without conscious awareness of the way or manner in which the reference is made. "Our focus changes from one of product to one of process" (Jones, 1962, p. 128). Relevant data from experience and knowledge are fed into a prediction system

> whereby we assess the probability of events in the future, and into a value system whereby we assess the desirabilities of different kinds of events. The possibilities and desirabilities are combined and we apply some sort of decision criteria in order to arrive at a decision and a recommendation between alternative actions (Jones, 1962, p. 128).

Jones stressed that the state of nature prevailing at the time of the predetermined action will influence its future outcome and that skillful use of personal judgment is essential at each stage. "We must cease focusing our attention on *form* and give more attention to the *problem* in the hope of gaining insights as to how other creative beings have used their experience and knowledge to arrive at creative solutions" (Jones, 1962, p. 130). "As designers we must learn to think not in terms of unique solutions but in terms of superior alternatives" (Jones, 1962, p. 132). "Decision theory provides a place in the design process of a systematic means for inspecting the alternatives and removing the present practice of choice by default" (Jones, 1962, p. 138).

Uses of the Computer in Urban Design

In his foreword to the proceedings of a conference on *Architecture and the Computer,* Sanford R. Greenfield (Boston Architectural Center) summarized current computer uses:

> The most obvious examples of current use of the computer are to be found on the periphery of the architectural profession, among structural and mechanical engineers, city planners, contractors, etc. Even among architects . . . we find that the computer is mainly used in non-design areas, information retrieval, building programming, visual presentation of statistical data, and automated drafting.
>
> Professor Coons of M.I.T. demonstrated with SKETCHPAD that it is possible to communicate with the machine by drawing, a language in which architects have been trained. With SKETCHPAD, automatic

> data processing may be utilized by the profession with relatively little prior preparation and thus become a practical extension of the architect's capabilities. The Computer Graphics work of [W. A.] Fetter shows how the architect can test his visual hypothesis in a computer-created three dimensional graphic environment, through which he can move and anticipate the spatial sequences he would experience in reality (Boston Architectural Center, 1964, Foreword).

In his paper "Computer Aided Design" Steven Coons further described SKETCHPAD, a computer program developed in 1962 by Dr. Ivan Sutherland that made possible communication by means of drawings. Coons explained:

> Engineers tend to consider design process as entirely rational in terms only of carefully dimensioned graphical form and the application of analytical techniques to a concept. . . . The notion of innovative activity, of generation of the original concept, of invention, is completely lacking. . . . On the contrary, many architects . . . use the word "design" to mean only the innovative, generative, intuitive acts of conception. . . .
>
> . . . .
>
> The true and complete process of design, it seems to me, consists of an inextricable mixture of these intuitive, imaginative, cognitive processes together with analytical, mathematical, rational processes. It is the thesis of this article that humans have special skills of a high order when it comes to devising, structuring, comparing, and making penetrating and powerful qualitative judgments, but are remarkably inefficient when it comes to carrying out those rational processes that involve precise attention to intricate mazes of elaborate details. On the contrary, computing machines are extremely efficient and tireless in dealing with analytical processes, no matter how complex, but are completely inept at creative tasks. Since art and analysis are both parts of the design process, it seems only reasonable to combine the human and the computer so that each can perform a proper function (Coons, 1964, p. 26).

Coons projected that with a combination of SKETCHPAD programming and other developments now being implemented, designers a few years hence will be able to draw directly on a computer screen with a specially wired pen and to manipulate push buttons and a keyboard, thus accomplishing a high degree of complex graphic communication.

> In the sketch, let us assume that certain lines are intended to be horizontal and others vertical. When first drawn these lines are

> straight but not precisely oriented. By a push button signal, the computer interprets the crude sketch and makes appropriate changes to "true up" the drawing. The designer can at any time introduce dimensional information, to any desired degree of precision, simply by pointing to a line on the screen and typing in its desired length. At other times, he can query the computer, and cause it to measure some distance implicit in the configuration he has drawn. If this dimension does not satisfy him, he can modify it by typing on the keyboard; the computer will not only change this dimension, but will "fix up" the rest of the drawing to fit, subject always to certain controlling dimensions. If, as may happen, the constraints on the dimensions are incompatible, the computer will advise the designer of this fact. . . .
>
> . . . .
>
> The computer can also supply all the analytical computations involved in the structural requirements, adherence to building codes, zoning ordinances, population density, traffic flow, compatibility with existing buildings, and can semi-automatically prepare the working drawings and specifications, . . . with the assurance that these drawings and specifications will not only adhere strictly to the appropriate codes, but they will be mutually compatible; there will be no possibility that by oversight a water pipe and a ventilating duct interfere with one another (Coons, 1964, pp. 26-28).

Sanford Greenfield raised a provocative question in his Foreword to the *Architecture and the Computer* conference proceedings:

> It is, perhaps, ironic that SKETCHPAD and computer graphics, the two tools most readily adaptable to the architect's work, themselves pose the greatest threat to his traditional role. The conference failed to discuss this aspect and for that reason I would like to touch on it here. The role of the architect requires him to make functional decisions (analytically at best), discover visual relationships, and express both in formal terms. The use of computers suggests the possibility of simultaneous analysis of many functional variables, and the use of computer graphics makes it possible to examine visual relationships in a manner impossible with our present handicraft methods. Unless the profession educates itself to programming and computer use, might it not be possible for people outside the profession, without a basic understanding of the formal problems but with a sophisticated grasp of automatic data processing techniques, to produce competent buildings? (Boston Architectural Center, 1964, Foreword).

A statement by Serge Chermayeff (Professor of Architectural Design, Yale University) at the above quoted conference serves well as a transition between discussion of computer uses and the excerpts that follow in the section "The Search for a New Vernacular." Chermayeff pointed out the absurdity in our accelerated age of keeping up the "myth of conflict between *rationality* and *inspiration*."

> Rationality as a system of procedure does not exclude inspiration which acts as an accelerator on the path to the desired goal. Inspiration is a special moment in a rational process. The two are inseparable and complementary.
>
> . . . .
>
> Architecture seen and interpreted exclusively as an *art form* is reverting back to formalism and eclecticism which some of us had hoped to see finally abandoned as a form-making process in complex organization.
>
> . . . .
>
> The evidence seems to point toward a growing architectural lag in a period of widening and accelerating change; architects do not appear interested in or even aware of the meaning for them of scientific discoveries, technology of controls and communication, social redeployment and cultural metamorphosis. . . . Yet vast decisions have to be made, and the powers derived from rational exploitation of all available resources are immense, as is professional responsibility in relation to Environmental Design, the task of which is to manipulate them. . . . (Chermayeff, 1964, pp. 21-22).

The Search for a New Vernacular

The excerpted materials above indicate that the concept of change underlies discussion of many aspects of urban design. The city's activity patterns are changed by time; the city's physical form is changed by growth. Planning technique and building technology change. The professionals concerned with urban design reflect this change in their search for a *new vernacular;* that is, a new and pervading expression of contemporary technique and spirit as a coherence-giving element in the physical environment. Louis Kahn (architect and Professor, University of Pennsylvania) commented on contemporary architecture at a 1962 design conference:

> Law cannot be changed, law is there. You may not understand it fully, but it's there. Always there. Rule always should be considered as on trial. Rule is just made from realizations of feeling and the law. And when more is known of the law at certain times, then the rule

> must automatically change. Think of the wonderful discoveries of science today and think of how much our architecture is at a standstill. I believe our architecture looks like Renaissance buildings, simply in new materials. I do not think it looks like modern buildings. . . . It's all because the rules have really not been changed *(Aspen International Design Conference,* 1962, p. 47).

A useful example of this search for a new vernacular is suggested by architect B. V. Doshi's description of the concept of the "Main Structure" and the "Filler." If the grid of a city is the main structure, the contents of its blocks can be considered the filler. If the parts of a city which operate on a mass scale (places for meeting, shopping, communications, recreation) are considered as the main structure, then the individuals' dwellings and places of work, the elements of the human scale, become the filler. If the load bearing and service elements of an apartment tower are considered the main structure, dwelling units could be plugged in as filler by the inhabitants.

> The relation between main and filler has several properties. The main structure is always more permanent than its filler. The functions performed by the main structure are usually more exacting than the functions of the filler. In many cases the development of the filler can be left to the fluctuations of the market and to the whims and special desires of individuals *(Aspen International Design Conference,* 1962, p. 65).

The search for a new vernacular may take the form of rejecting identified principles as does Jesse Reichek (Professor of Design, Department of Architecture, University of California, Berkeley) in his paper "Questions Concerning Urban Design Principles."

> Our teachers have told us what their teachers have told them, that our compositions must have unity. It seems not to matter that our present state of understanding of the urb tells us that the activity systems we are dealing with are not composed states but are process states. We are in constant search of unifying devices — building material, building heights, street furniture, colors and textures, signs, architectural styles, etc. — as if unity corresponds to our real experience.
>
> In fact, we have gathered a whole pot full of devices which we use to achieve *good* urban design. . . . Open civic spaces (plazas, squares, parks) express urbanity. Varied building types protect us against monotony. Distinctive communities give us our identity and sharp boundaries our sense of place. Vistas — open and closed, short

> and long – give us the spatial experiences we need. Landmarks provide us with our orientation, symbolically and physically. Pedestrian ways give us the human scale we want, the exercise we need, and a means of rejecting the automobile we love.
>
> . . . .
>
> The principles that we have been using no longer have any claim to being fundamental truths, since they do not relate to anything in our contemporary life experiences. The devices we have been using for establishing an order for our experiences are not in accord with the pluralistic and ambiguous nature of our existence and the patterns of our behavior. Our problem is to provide a spatial system that will facilitate an activity system that is diverse in its parts, equivocal in its structure, changing in time, and divergent in purpose (Reichek, 1962, pp. 102-103).

Aldo van Eyck (avant-garde Dutch architect) denounced urbanistic art that springs "from any but the most fundamental consideration of the fact of men living in groups on particular occasions and at particular times. The challenge of today's architects is that they must produce vernacular cities in a scale and at a pace that is not related to vernacular building" (van Eyck, 1962, p. 177).

> It is up to architecture to provide a built frame work – to set the stage as it were – for the twin phenomenon of the individual and the collective without resorting to arbitrary accentuation of either one at the expense of the other, i.e. without warping the meaning of either, since no basic twin phenomenon can be split into incompatible polarities without the halves forfeiting whatever they stand for. This points toward the necessity of reconciling the idea *unity* with the idea *diversity* in architectural terms or, more precisely to achieve the one by means of the other [emphasis added].
>
> . . . .
>
> The time has come to conceive of architecture urbanistically and urbanism architecturally.
>
> . . . .
>
> Now what does this imply with respect to place and place's twin sister occasion? (For space in the image of man is place and time in the image of man is occasion.) Split apart by the schizophrenic mechanism of deterministic one-track thinking, time and space remain frozen abstractions. . . . Place and occasion constitute each other's realization in human terms. Since man is both the subject and object of architecture, it follows that its primary job is to provide the former for the sake of the latter. Since, furthermore, place and occasion imply

participation in what exists, lack of place – and thus of occasion – will cause loss of identity, isolation and frustration.

. . . .

A houselike city and a citylike house should, I think, be thought of as a configuration of intermediary places clearly defined. This does not imply continual transition or endless postponement with respect to place and occasion. On the contrary, it implies a break away from the contemporary concept . . . of spatial continuity and the tendency to erase every articulation between spaces, i.e. between outside and inside, between one space and another. Instead, I suggest articulation of transition by means of defined inbetween places which induce simultaneous awareness of what is significant on either side. An inbetween place in this sense provides the common ground where conflicting polarities can again become twin phenomena (van Eyck, 1962, pp. 178-181).

PROBLEMS OF APPLICATION

The foregoing theoretical considerations of urban design have been complex. The problems of applying these theories to the functioning physical city further magnify these complexities. Nevertheless, even the best theory has to be put to work, sooner or later. The comments excerpted below have been chosen to illustrate some contemporary approaches to the problems of application.

Elements of Change

The Population Explosion

Percival Goodman (Professor, School of Architecture, Columbia University) underscored four issues raised by the current population explosion that are of primary importance to modern urban planning in his paper for the Washington University conference on *Education for Urban Design.*

(1) *Increased population.* Goodman suggested that the city planner be given a basic principle: "*maximum use of minimum land*" (Goodman, 1962, p. 18). (2) *Automation and technological efficiency.* Goodman called for serious planning for the leisure resulting from the shortened work week. Game courts are not

sufficient. Thoughtful planning must make provisions for creative use of free time. (3) *Transporation and instant communication.* He called for a reconsideration of urban design, providing for types of transportation other than the automobile. (4) *Giantism.* Goodman also discussed the problem of keeping society and the individual in human scale as increased population tends to increase organization toward larger combines and greater centralization.

Technology

Similar considerations were discussed by Aaron Fleisher (Professor, Department of City and Regional Planning, Massachusetts Institute of Technology) in his paper "Technology and Urban Form." Fleisher posed the questions: "Are there physical limits to growth?" and "Will changes in communications, occupations, and transportation favor any particular pattern of density?" He considered technological capabilities for supplying and distributing food and electrical power "adequate for the future – though not capable of indefinite extension" (Fleisher, 1962, p. 98). New sources of water (the sea) must be developed, and chemical control of wastes can be managed. Transportation facilities may change technologically – aircraft capable of vertical take-off and landing and vehicles running at faster speeds on automatically controlled rights-of-way. Technology will not, however, alleviate the resultant urban congestion, although an elaboration of controls may help:

> Local congestion, however, is not a technological problem. The patterns of density within a city appear to be largely independent of technological development (Fleisher, 1966, p. 52).

Transportation

Historically, roads have been determiners of urban form. The proliferation of the automobile (and the roads that service it) has occasioned voluminous debate among architects, engineers, and planners. There are those who advocate the total elimination of the auto from the urban scene; there are others who seek creative design solutions to the already acute and increasingly complex problems of transportation. It is beyond the scope of this collection of conference excerpts to do justice to the transportation debate itself, however.

As an element of urban design, the road was cited by David Crane as a *fundamental* form-maker. He described the road functioning as a carrier; defining areas and fulfilling a city-building function; serving as a space for fulfilling services, for housing equipment, and for facilitating the needs of human activity; and revealing intelligence about the city (Crane, 1962, p. 70).

The road is also the means of egress from the city and the urban scale and leads out into the larger scale of the region. Thomas W. Mackesey (Vice Provost, Cornell University) said in his summary of *The Architect and the City* conference:

> Of course the most obvious evil of today's city is motor traffic, but the problems are far greater than the central issue of moving and storing. The motor car has destroyed the ancient concept of the city as a social and political entity and it has created in its place the urbanized region (Mackesey, 1962, p. 106).

THE HIERARCHY OF SCALES

A major development in the thinking of urban design professionals over the past decade has been the emerging recognition of the importance of distinguishing a hierarchy of scales. The increasing mobility of man expands the limits of his environment. Planners and designers of the city feel a need to reconsider the definition of the range and scope of that which is considered the urban area. This major consideration of inter-city scale introduces vastly expanded dimensions to the older problem of intra-city scale — the relationship of individual buildings and groups of buildings to their function, to their site, and to each other. Beyond the lot is the street, neighborhood, district, municipality, county, region, state, nation, continent, world.

Intra-city Scale

The composition of scales within the city is a classic consideration of urban design. An example of this concern can be found in Edmund N. Bacon's description of the *greenway system:*

> Willo von Moltke and I, aided by some suggestions of Louis Kahn, think we have rediscovered a principle which may give the key to the problem of design at this scale. . . . In approaching the design of a

> neighborhood needing urban renewal under this method, which we call the "Greenway System," we regard the job as one of collaboration between the architect and the planner. The planner's work is to devise a basic design structure consisting of a system of public open space, focusing on significant local landmarks and having a meaningful relationship with the *principal* buildings of the new development projects. This system provides a means for getting about on foot in such a way that the walker is exposed to a series of space experiences in designed sequence, opening and closing of spaces, sunny and shaded spaces, spaces for movement and for rest, with changing textures underfoot. It provides vistas of significant local institutions, settings for structures important functionally or symbolically, visual relationships between elements of the community. It provides a basic design structure, a system for the larger order, which throws into meaningful relationship the *essential* elements of the composition of the designers of the various new projects which make up the neighborhood, producing an over-all civic unity but still allowing great freedom of expression in the greater part of the individual projects (Bacon, 1957, p. 4).

At the intra-city level, scale can apply to the individual building. Wolf Von Eckardt (architecture critic) pointed out at the Harvard Graduate School of Design 1964 conference the need for both "background and foreground architecture" (Von Eckardt, 1964). He went on to comment that while people need buildings that satisfy their aspirations for monumentality, there is no need to make a monument out of a parking garage.

Paul Rudolph (architect, New Haven) discussed the hierarchy of building types in an environment as a stylistic responsibility of the architect:

> We do need symbols of State, perhaps of the church, of gateways to the city, etc., but by and large these things become relatively small in terms of their bulk in relationship to housing, to places of finance, and so forth. . . . We cannot really change programmatically the fact that ninety-five per cent of the buildings, of the inhabitable space, are basically a series of cubes and rectangles. But the buildings at the top of the hierarchy need to be dominant ones and need to be in a sense the single story ones, if you like, the true monuments. . . . Our problem is, of course, that we tend to treat all buildings as if they were at the head of the hierarchy. Now the difficulty comes that certain types of buildings which should be very far down on the hierarchy scale are — quite often become the dominant element simply because the people concerned with the really important buildings don't truly make them dominant (*Aspen International Design Conference,* 1964, p. 38).

Inter-city Scales

The inter-city or multi-city scale is expressed in another hierarchy of terms: metropolis, urban region, megalopolis, economic region, etc. In 1956, Garrett Eckbo (Professor of Landscape Architecture, University of California, Berkeley) called attention to the expanding hierarchy of scales as seen in terms of the continuous quality of the landscape.

> In the most final analysis the landscape is indivisible. It stretches from ocean to ocean, and its limits are those of human vision and motion, and such physical obstacles as may exist or be established. The landscape is everything an individual can see from a given station point or circulation route, colored by everything he has seen before and everything he has heard or read about it. This landscape, especially in the more developed urban areas, is compounded of many separate parcels of real estate, and of all the multiple disconnected decisions made by different people at different times on those different parcels. This is the basic process of landscape design in the large sense. The problem of how to unify and co-ordinate these multiple decisions so as to produce a unified and harmonious community landscape is being tackled today by planners and redevelopers, but tomorrow it will be ours. Once the proper relation between over-all control and democratic processes is worked out, the community landscape will become a physical design problem. Its solution will require major re-orientation by all the design and planning professions (*Aspen International Design Conference*, 1956, p. 6).

Christopher Tunnard (Professor of City Planning, Yale University) in his paper "The Roads We Travel" commented in 1958:

> Recent decades have witnessed the emergence of a radically new pattern of human settlement in America. Older, high-density urban places are being encircled by areas of low-density urban use, which cover vast amounts of space and merge into one another.... These rapidly growing areas differ from the old suburbs in many ways, one of them being that they are not compact in their physical form, but scattered, and another that their economic and social activities are oriented toward several regional centers at once (Tunnard, 1958, p. 1).

The following excerpts are indicative of the widespread attention coming to focus on inter-city environmental concerns. Architect Victor Gruen in a paper entitled "Environmental Architecture" said:

> The mission of architecture in these times of mass production, mass consumption, population explosion and urban growth lies in a completely different area than in historic times. Architecture must widen its horizons; it must switch its attention from the individual structure to the entire man-made environment (Gruen, 1962, p. 97).

Morton Hoppenfeld:

> Urban design practice has no scale: we do not limit the role of the designer. We must continually appreciate that as the project changes in size from neighborhood to the urban region the design elements change in kind from the tree to the watershed, from the width of the street to the mode of travel, and with these changes in design elements must come a corresponding change in the designer's knowledge and abilities (Hoppenfeld, 1962, p. 86).

Lewis Mumford called for the maintaining of the individual character of the community within the large-scale organization:

> The largest urban assemblage must be on a regional scale and even on this scale, the local richness must be constantly present. The largest of world capitals should symbolize the world as a whole. Small communities should also have some of the characteristics that belong to the world, they must not love their isolation or segregation but become part of the complex interrelationships that we are developing throughout the world. Part of the life of any community should be associated with the wider life beyond (University of Pennsylvania Graduate School of Fine Arts, 1963, p. 6).

Paul Spreiregen:

> There is a new palette of urban design now developing. This new palette is as different from our older palette as Varese is from Bach. We may be designing soon with economic policy, hierarchical circulation network, a water-resources plan, or micro-climates – plus, of course, our older palette. We are at one of the most exciting thresholds of urban design in history (Harvard Graduate School of Design, 1964).

Matthew Rockwell (Executive Director, Northeastern Illinois Planning Commission):

> The new suburbia (which I choose to call the city-region) can be the guided product of comprehensive metropolitan planning, . . . the most dramatic shaper of the planning process can be the predominating natural resources of any particular area. . . . Natural resources of

> a metropolitan area are its foundational determinants, and . . . basic proposals for growth of the area stem from these determinants (U. S. White House Conference, 1965, pp. 448-449).

Patrick Horsbrugh (Professor of Architecture, University of Texas) called for the creation of a new environmental concern; for a new kind of collaboration and interdisciplinary design organization bringing together the landscape architect, industrial designer, architect, planner, and certain medical specialists for a better balanced design effort at all the scales of the environment from the individual block, the street, the neighborhood, the community, the metropolis, all the way up the scale of environment to the region and the climate (University of Wisconsin, Department of Urban and Regional Planning, 1965, pp. 9-10).

An entire Harvard Graduate School of Design conference in 1962 was devoted to inter-city growth. Frederick Gutheim (journalist and consultant on urban affairs) addressed the conference:

> The design of inter-urban areas, what happens between cities and as large metropolitan areas grow, has become a cardinal problem of urban design, an art and a profession that is barely five years old. Recent advances in aesthetics have made the principles of architectural design applicable to large urban areas as our definitions of perception have changed. Now the earlier preoccupation with microdesign must be supplemented by an interest more wholly new and less derived from it than our recent concern with the design of central business districts and urban redevelopment projects — the macrodesign of large metropolitan areas (Gutheim, 1962, p. 98).

Gutheim outlined the four alternative patterns of growth examined by the conference.

> (1) *New Towns.* The experience of the greenbelt towns of the prewar decade and the orientation of our most distinguished urban philosophers, such as Lewis Mumford, have strongly predisposed us toward this plan, and the scale of present day home building has produced many variations of the so-called garden cities. . . . Fifteen new towns in Britain . . . have now established themselves as commercial successes, but this limited program has not provided an effective means of coping with the growth of metropolitan London, and it has now been abandoned as an official policy. One of the reasons for its abandonment was a failure — in which design has at least a partial responsibility — to create satisfactory living requirements of urban scale in the new towns. How much of this is due to

the earlier ideas of the appropriate size of new towns (from 50,000–80,000 population), how much to their character as industrial suburbs, and how much to physical and socio-economic design still needs explanation. . . .

(2) *Inter-City Corridors.* The possibility of reconstructing new urban areas by the expectation that transportation facilities will dominate their form is a dubious contention that smacks of a once-held belief that control of industrial development and location would similarly control urban growth and form. In an age of universal personal transportation, the strong structuring influence which transportation had in 1905, when the New York subways were being built, is unlikely. Nor, from their present position on the sidelines, will planners be able to force new urban masses into uneconomic locations at extra cost. . . . Corridor growth also invites some skepticism with respect to control over open spaces between the spokes. . . .

(3) *Concentrated Growth.* The pattern keeps the town together as a single unit, with all the practical advantages from the social, economic, and managerial points of view. It is the traditional way in which towns grow, and all that appears necessary is to improve the process rather than to start something radically new. . . . [But suburban development with low-density residential areas, large lot industries, shopping centers] has obstructed any organic relation between new development and the redevelopment of older cities [presenting a conflict which must be resolved by design]. . . .

(4) *Rationalized Sprawl.* . . . If we put aside the cultural apparatus of conventional urban design, the older image of the city, . . . perhaps we can tackle freshly the job of harnessing these new forces [the inherently decentralized influence of the automobile, vacuum tube, and modern technology] . . . and creating a new urban form. . . . Accepting low densities and transportation difficulties that are inseparable from them, is it possible that the large public costs involved in the patterns of development we find in New Jersey and California may be overbalanced by lower private costs and greater living satisfactions in the eyes of their citizens? (Gutheim, 1962, pp. 98-99).

Robert C. Weaver (then Administrator, Housing and Home Finance Agency) pointed out in 1962 that additional problems arise from the lack of governmental units at the metropolitan and regional level. Such elements of urban environment as population explosion, transportation, inadequate representation of urban (and especially suburban) people in state legislatures, physical environment and aesthetic values:

[These elements of] urban environment in terms of problems do not coincide in their geographical distribution and their geographic intensity with our units of government *(Aspen International Design Conference,* 1962, p. 1).

DESIGN AND SOCIAL RESPONSIBILITY

Another recurrent theme in urban design conferences has been a realization of the social responsibility of the designer. Jack Meltzer (Director, Center for Urban Studies, University of Chicago) stated that urban design should not be approached in aesthetic terms alone. Design does not stand apart but is an expression of political, economic, and social forces.

> The visual appearance of the environment should be the result of such form-giving elements as equitable social environment, workable productive environment, and safety of transportation (University of Wisconsin, Department of Urban and Regional Planning, 1965, p. 11).

In discussing the philosophy of the Housing and Home Finance Agency at the 1962 Aspen conference, Robert C. Weaver quoted from one of his earlier speeches:

> A large part of urban population, the lower income, the minority groups, the elderly, and the lower middle class, live largely where they have to, not where they want to, because no provision has been made for their needs except in the slums and blighted areas where no one else wants to go. As urban populations expand, compression in the living space and standards of these neglected groups mounts and with these pressures goes serious and critical deterioration of the social health and moral standards of the entire urban community. . . . Cities are more than a set of structures and facilities for those who live and visit there, and as we build and rebuild our urban areas we must build into them something more than the means of living. They must also create a way of life. We must strive to give them pleasantness, a sense of dignity and inspiration and excitement and a character that becomes reflected in the culture and creative activities of the people who live there *(Aspen International Design Conference,* 1962, p. 4).

At a 1964 conference as chairman of a panel on Residential Neighborhoods and the Urban Core, William Conklin (architect and Partner, Whittlesey and Conklin) said:

> Urban renewal is really but a battleground in the larger urban revolution. This revolution . . . is a social and economic one and not

> really an architectural one, and yet our frequent answer is only in terms of physical form. "Good urban design" runs the danger of being an admirable form with an unknown function (Harvard Graduate School of Design, 1964).

He raised several questions related to social policy as well as to design policy:

> (1) Are we re-establishing a sense of community in the modern life that will occur in the newly rebuilt residential areas?
>
> . . . .
>
> (2) Do our plans and planning procedures really cherish and insure diversity? . . . Financing procedures, real estate market pressures, and zoning all tend to increase the segregation of people by age, income level, and other factors, as well as race – into one-class city neighborhoods. Do we hold the value of diversity strongly enough to be willing to endorse procedures which will guarantee that our cities will be rebuilt with this ethic and social value built in?
>
> (3) Are the mechanisms of urban renewal and our urban design goals really in tune with the stated purpose of urban renewal: "To provide decent housing for every American," as stated in the introduction to the 1949 Act? (Harvard Graduate School of Design, 1964).

In the proceedings of the *White House Conference on Natural Beauty* the report of the Townscape Panel, chaired by Edmund Bacon, declared:

> The panel also wished to put special stress upon the new provisions of the proposed 1965 legislation pertaining both to urban beautification and the development of neighborhood centers, as these provisions can be applied to impoverished areas of cities. These programs, limited as they are in funds and scope, should be particularly directed to the poorest areas of cities, to insure that all American families share in the effort to beautify our townscape (U.S. White House Conference, 1965, p. 634).

Taste-making

The interaction of design policy and social policy thus entails discovery and interpretation of the social, economic, and political goals and needs of the public. It also raises a concomitant question of the responsibility and opportunity of the urban designer as a *taste-maker*. A background paper for the Residential Neighborhoods and the Urban Core panel cited above asked:

> How does the middle-class urban designer find out about the values and needs of a population that is completely foreign to him? What is the meaning of design in these terms? In trying to get an expression of local views, how does one get representation of the inarticulate rather than of the middle class? (Harvard Graduate School of Design, 1964).

Roger Montgomery (Professor of Architecture, Washington University) discussed the urban designer as a former of public taste at the *University of Wisconsin Urban America Project Conference*. His comments were summarized as follows:

> Taste is not an *a priori* platonic ideal but a component of life style, a result of social upbringing. There exists a disparity between the high taste of design professionals and the mass taste of an affluent society. It would be possible to set some design standards embodying upper-middle class canons of current taste as goals toward which architectural control standards operate and then consider how the people who administer them and live in them react (University of Wisconsin, Department of Urban and Regional Planning, 1965, p. 11).

An expression of caution about upper-middle class canons was offered by June King McFee (Director, Institute of Community Art Studies, University of Oregon) at another 1965 University of Wisconsin Conference on *The Education of Children and Adults in Aesthetic Awareness of the Environment of Man*. Mrs. McFee stressed the need for a "shift that needs to be made in our thinking . . . that something . . . well designed according to our tastes will have meaning to other people as well. We are extremely egocentric as a people, seeing the world only through our own eyes and through our own ethclass values" (McFee, 1965, p. 18). (*Ethclass* is a new term used by the sociologist Milton M. Gordon to describe the ethnic groups within the different economic strata of society.)

Morton Hoppenfeld touched on the point of the designer's responsibility:

> Part of the concept of local government is the issue of community goals and aspirations which the electorate expresses in one way or another. It is the designer's responsibility to work toward them, at times to try and influence them, but never to be out of touch with them (Hoppenfeld, 1962, p. 85).

Wolf Von Eckardt approached the problem in a different respect in his Aspen, 1964 talk on designing without the traditional restraints:

> The restraints of the technology are gone, . . . the restraints of the material are gone, . . . so we are reduced to find the restraints in our own conscience. . . . The discriminating client [represented a form of restraint which is superseded by the designer being] asked to perform for the non-taste of the average masses *(Aspen International Design Conference,* 1964, p. 9).

LEGISLATING DESIGN

Proceedings of urban design conferences also reflect current concern over the question of legislating design. To avoid misinterpretation of the following excerpted comments, a distinction must be considered between strict, inflexible, mathematical zoning and the current trend toward a more flexible, creative shaping of urban development that is becoming the dominant goal of urban design as a discipline. The key to this emergent philosophy of design control is yet another hierarchy of scales that must be considered in legislating design. That which may represent individual freedom on a single lot might become chaos on the scale of a metropolitan region. It is interesting to note, however, that the studies directed by the architect Harvey Wiley Corbett and published in New York's Regional Plan of 1928 clearly foreshadow this present development. The fundamental ideas were applied to proposals for major districts, avenues, and waterfronts.

David Crane addressed the hierarchy concept of the several scales each requiring design in his reference to "The City of A Thousand Designers."

> Once cities were produced by a complementary overlapping of three form-making disciplines: popular use of a consistent regional vernacular; style-giving and pace-setting of architects; and concrete skeletal constructions of kings and their Haussmanns. Each of these kinds of form-makers has . . . dissolved. The vernacular and the architect have gained access to too many techniques and half-truths and but few values, and have thus lost the regional or problem-solving attitudes. Behind pretexts of catering to private enterprise, local governments interfere with private design of private facilities through a thousand obscure regulations. Whereas uncoordinated cacophony is the present

result of the Thousand Designers, music might come if local government and professionals would announce the tune (Crane, 1962, p. 72).

Municipal zoning has been the major expression in the past of the community level of design imposing its constraints on the primary level, the design of the ultimate building on the lot. Robert C. Weaver condemned the rigidity of outmoded zoning:

> What sort of requirements are we going to make about the physical structures in which we live? Are we going to see them perverted as zoning has been perverted? First, zoning was an instrument to protect the development of our areas of living and housing, and now it is being used to complicate them, very often, by setting such high standards as to prevent any sort of sound and economic utilization of the land, and also to exclude all but those of one particular class (*Aspen International Design Conference,* 1962, p. 1).

Similarly, William Slayton in 1963 (as Commissioner, Urban Renewal Administration, Housing and Home Finance Agency) said:

> Our cities in the past 20 to 30 years have developed under the zoning ordinance, . . . and indeed zoning *has* prevented unwise growth in many ways. But the zoning ordinance is a negative control, prohibiting undesirable uses and controlling by mathematical formula form, shape, height, and relation to other structures and uses. It must depend upon rules that apply universally to all varieties of size and shape of parcels. It cannot circumvent the happenstance of parcelization. It is a limited, negative, non-creative mechanism for controlling city development. But urban renewal . . . can create its own parcels. Urban renewal *need* not be bound by mathematical controls on density, set backs, side yards, etc. – urban renewal permits the city to look positively at the setting of the structures and their relationship and consequently to judge the development in terms of design and function – not in terms of meeting mathematical formulas (Slayton, 1963).

Lewis Mumford warned: "Our pre-occupation with standardized forms, regimented in space, suppressing variety could overthrow the values, social life, and the culture that the city brought into existence" (University of Pennsylvania Graduate School of Design, 1963, p. 6).

Two of the Harvard urban design conferences contain particularly relevant discussion. The 1959 conference considered design of large-scale residential sectors; the 1964 conference was organized around the theme: the role of government in the form and animation of the urban core. Dean Jose Luis Sert addressed the 1959 conference:

> This is a conference upon Urban Design and upon a special aspect of Urban Design – the residential sector. . . . It is not a general conference upon city planning. Neither is it a conference to frame new zoning regulations and building by-laws. This does not mean that any of us wish to deny the vital importance of these fields. We are, I think, conscious that the specialized framework of legislative and administrative regulation is essential to implement any proposals we may make. But as a result of two previous conferences and one panel meeting we believe that certain crucial problems have now been sifted out, and the decisions must be taken upon these by us as responsible designers, *before* the lawyers and administrators can start to do their work (Harvard Graduate School of Design, 1959, p. 5).

At the 1964 Harvard urban design conference the panel on the Government Center and the Urban Core noted the changing concept of the role of government. Government was considered more pervasive now with increased responsibility in shaping the urban core. No longer does private enterprise initiate and government respond; the positions are reversed. At this same conference Hideo Sasaki (Chairman, Landscape Architecture, Harvard University) commented:

> At one time excessive controls of zoning and other types of regulations tended to direct design solutions into a predetermined format. This was done on such an extensive scale, and with so little design consideration that the process led to the kind of amorphous environment that we are now resisting. However, controls in themselves are not necessarily bad, because design means working within certain limitations and relationships which are sometimes financial, sometimes of program, and sometimes of regulations on height, mass, etc. (Harvard Graduate School of Design, 1964).

Garrett Eckbo in the Townscape Panel at the 1965 White House Conference suggested:

> We have to concentrate on the autonomy and responsibility of the designer. The city has to become a client of good design. We are going to have to remove a lot of arbitrary, negative restrictions which limit the design process on the theory that it is not reliable. Standards, codes, rules and regulations are essentially efforts to bypass design. Instead of these, we must obtain competent personnel to perform design and require them to police themselves in a responsible way (U.S. White House Conference, 1965, p. 85).

Richard F. Babcock (Attorney, Chicago) discussing architectural controls in terms of the rights of the individual made an interesting distinction between evolved and imposed neighborhood context. His comments were summarized as follows:

> The police power may be used to maintain or preserve the existing aesthetic quality of an area for which the governing body feels that a change in character would be undesirable, but the police power should not be used to create such an area. The police power should not be used to cause the owner of an individual piece of property or the designer of an individual structure to change his view of what he wants to do unless the property or structure has been hallowed by history. This power should be reserved for environments already in being but not applied to the creation of new environments (University of Wisconsin, Department of Urban and Regional Planning, 1965, p. 10).

Historical Preservation

Babcock suggested that it was not merely the right but the duty of the government to preserve those efforts of man which by any definition would be recognized as a significant contribution to an area (University of Wisconsin, Department of Urban and Regional Planning, 1965, p. 10). Excerpts from other conferences attest to the increasing national concern for the significance, preservation, and use of historical areas and landmarks. Gordon Gray (Chairman, National Trust for Historic Preservation) at the White House Conference called for:

> A national survey to inventory landmarks of all types and grades of historic, architectural and unique community value . . . with accompanying legal protection. . . . We should continue to develop and protect historic districts in our urban areas. Compensation should be paid to private owners for losses incurred in preserving certified landmarks. Other devices should include tax relief . . . and scenic easements. Restraining covenants should be placed on historic properties, and an increasing number of them should be brought into public ownership. The FHA bank loan system should be revised. Zoning ordinances need strengthening. . . . favorable governmental and administrative policies should be codified and enacted into legislation. Federal support and assistance should be given to the National Trust as . . . a program is needed to guide adaptive uses, and to stimulate private philanthropy (U.S. White House Conference, 1965, pp. 79-80).

Patrick Horsbrugh also urged that the effort be more than just preservation:

> To the greatest possible extent, buildings remaining from earlier periods when techniques and aesthetic principles were different from today's should be used as part of the fabric of the evolving environment (University of Wisconsin, Department of Urban and Regional Planning, 1965).

A positive approach was suggested by Christopher Tunnard in discussion on the Water and Waterfronts Panel of the White House Conference:

> Paradoxically, the very existence of decay on the waterfront gives Americans a second chance to improve its appearance and amenities. Although there is still competition for land on the water's edge, the existence of decay is evidence that certain older uses are no longer necessary there and that we should be thinking seriously of the kind of uses which should replace them. (U.S. White House Conference, 1965, p. 155).

Tunnard called for the establishment of urban waterfront districts along the lines of the soil conservation districts.

POLICY STATEMENTS AND POSITIVE DIRECTIONS

Excerpts of discussions from urban design conference proceedings presented in the two previous sections were chosen to reflect (1) theoretical considerations involved in urban design, and (2) some problems that arise in the implementation of urban design. The focus of the following selected excerpts is more specifically on statements of policy by governmental agencies and on recurrent recommendations by professionals involved in urban design. These recommendations are primarily concerned with two subjects: the programming and carrying out of specific steps toward the realization of urban design and the education of the public to appreciate and demand a higher quality of urban environment.

Policy Statements

Robert C. Weaver described the federal role in urban design in a major address to the Harvard urban design conference organized around the theme: "The role of government in the form and animation of the urban core."

> My stated position on our role in the field of design has been that the Federal Government cannot and should not establish standards of taste or dictate design. But I have also held that we have positive responsibility to encourage local communities to concern themselves with the best in modern planning and design and to support and stimulate the enlistment of our most creative talents in re-shaping our changing cities (Weaver, 1964).

He outlined the progress made between 1961 and 1964 in Housing and Home Finance Agency programs to encourage more imaginative and creative design. Weaver described the three major programs of HHFA: (1) Public Housing Administration; (2) Urban Renewal Administration; and (3) Federal Housing Administration. Federal involvement varies from program to program; but Weaver expressed "not only a legitimate interest, but an inescapable responsibility for encouraging more appealing and better functioning urban environments" (Weaver, 1964).

The *Public Housing Administration* has held regional seminars to encourage better design in public housing involving architects, local public housing authorities' staffs, National Association of Housing and Redevelopment Officials, and the American Institute of Architects; it has established more effective communication with the AIA; it has revised outdated architects' contract and fee schedules; and it has revised the Low-Rent Manual, replacing restrictive requirements with guidelines allowing room for innovation.

The *Urban Renewal Administration* has also emphasized the importance of design. URA has initiated a series of publications and memoranda delineating the agency's policy position on high quality design as a basic objective of the program, encouraged design competitions for redevelopment, encouraged experimentation in design, and established substitution of good design for maximum land prices as the major criterion for selecting developers. "These efforts have produced an awareness of and an environment conducive to good design which has been greatly enhanced by participation of outstanding architects" (Weaver, 1964).

The *Federal Housing Administration* has encouraged design improvements that increase the livability of individual family housing and multifamily dwellings (through, for example, noise control research and encouragement of common open space), and it has sponsored design competitions:

> These efforts to recognize and encourage outstanding design have been so successfully received that I am pleased to announce that we have determined to make this policy agency-wide. Our constituents will soon announce design awards covering all HHFA programs, including urban renewal, public housing, elderly and college housing, and public facilities, as well as as private housing already recognized by the FHA (Weaver, 1964).

Weaver quoted from an earlier speech in which he had said, "We should give the 'd' for 'design' at least equal standing with the 'd' for 'dollar' in the development of our urban areas" (*Aspen International Design Conference*, 1962, p. 4).

In his paper "Design Considerations in Urban Renewal" William Slayton emphasized the importance of design:

> What is done in these next several decades will have a tremendous impact upon our cities in terms of their function, their shape, their form, their appearance. What is done in the next several decades will last for a long, long time, and one should not accept lightly the responsibility that has been thrust upon him. . . . My concern is that in our frenetic activity to clear areas, to rehabilitate houses, to sell land, to be sure that plans are adopted, and to see that construction gets under way, we may not recognize the enormity of this responsibility (Slayton, 1962).

And more recently in 1965, Slayton said:

> Good urban design, after all, means more than a few urban renewal projects. And commitment to good urban design means more than hiring a good architect although that is very important. We now have a commitment from President Johnson himself. Recently he said: "There is much the Federal Government can do, through a range of specific programs, and as a force for public education. But a beautiful America will require the effort of government at every level, of business, and of private groups. Above all, it will require the concern and action of individual citizens . . . determined to improve the quality of their surroundings, resisting blight, demanding and building beauty for themselves and their children."
>
> How can we carry out this commitment? . . . The most important way is for the city to see itself as a client — for the public officials to see themselves as clients — public clients. There is a great deal that the city does and much that it can do through its public officials,

> its commissioners, directors, department heads, to see and recognize the city as a client in the field of urban design. Good urban design cannot be produced without a good client. It is the client who must make the final decision on what is to be built, its cost, its location, and even its character. He also writes the program and selects the designer. Thus, in a very real sense, the client is the creator, for in his hands lie the determinants, the decisionary limitations within which the designer must operate. . . . So this is the first order of business: education of the public official as client, to achieve a commitment of the public official to good urban design (Slayton, 1965).

The Urban Renewal Administration issued two special technical bulletins in February and in May, 1965 stressing design review and design objectives in renewal projects. These bulletins are intended as guides to aid local developers to realize improved design quality (U.S. Urban Renewal Administration, 1965). Federal support for these and other policies was strengthened by the establishment of a Department of Housing and Urban Development (HUD) to succeed the HHFA and the appointment of Robert C. Weaver as Secretary in January, 1966.

RECURRENT RECOMMENDATIONS

Experimentation

Frequent reference was made by designers to the need for experimentation, both in questions of design and in terms of overcoming expense. The permanence of city building and the fact that errors endure have been pointed out in earlier excerpts. But even within the major restraint of the dominance of what already exists, planners and architects registered a plea for experimentation.

Oskar Stonorov (architect, Philadelphia) suggested:

> I think that public housing, from the point of view of family housing, or the elderly or whatever it is, is the most important tool with which to bring about technological progress. I think that public housing is the one thing we can use for experimentation. In public housing we have sufficient funds and tax subsidies by which we can experiment in terms of plans, amenities, and all the things people need. . . . I am asking whether we should not think about testing out what America is capable of by suggesting to Dr. Weaver that he and his complete staff would make a powerful experiment in five metropolitan centers

> . . . of technology, social and human engineering and finance engineering, so that at the end of five years we would have some examples of urban environment which we could consider set a standard for our country at this moment in time. . . . We could look and judge and say: these are the things we ought to do and these are the things we ought not to do (Harvard Graduate School of Design, 1964).

Commenting recently on this excerpt, Stonorov wrote: "This in essence was put into a memorandum one month later and presented to President Johnson by Walter Reuther and became the Demonstration Cities Program."

In 1962, M. Justin Herman (Executive Director, San Francisco Revelopment Agency) noted a need for an "experimental vehicle for doing the unconventional – for trying out new ideas." He suggested that of the vast sums of money involved in renewal a small percentage could be devoted to "a special category of projects that do not have to meet the norm" *(Aspen International Design Conference,* 1962, p. 78). It is interesting to note a corollary excerpt from Weaver's 1964 Harvard address: "And only a few months ago, Commissioner Brownstein announced an allowance of one per cent for art work in multi-family FHA-insured developments" (Weaver, 1964).

Discussion also called for a more efficient use of scarce and expensive design skills in limiting expense through the repeated use of prototype design ideas. That this should be a process of artful reproduction, not mere quantitative multiplication was suggested earlier by David Crane:

> In this category there is an obligation to produce demonstrable examples proving that certain objectives can be achieved. One example is the present contract with Carl Koch and Associates who have been encouraged to team with a developer to design and build three prototype projects encompassing at least a total of five-hundred units. From this will come the proof that better designed houses at far lower prices can be produced in Boston. It is essential to achieve this in order to meet the long-range goal of the development program: to produce ten thousand units of housing (Crane, 1963, p. 28).

At the 1964 Harvard conference Carl Koch (architect, Carl Koch and Associates, Boston) commented:

> We tried to provide a framework with sufficient standardization for industry to apply itself to producing elements in sufficient quantity

> and still leave sufficient freedom to relate the project to the facts of a particular neighborhood. This framework could provide the architect with the opportunity of concentration upon building a good environment. The problem is that no one with power is really concerned to get costs way down. Industry is ready to go to work if they get big enough orders, but if you cannot give them a big order you cannot get a low price (Harvard Graduate School of Design, 1964).

Design Programs and Implementation Programs

Two distinct concepts involving the word *program* have been extensively discussed. One refers to the technical term used by architects to describe the client's requirements in verbal language before a design is visualized. The other refers to the sequence of steps required to carry out a design project so as to make it real.

The successful *White House Conference on Natural Beauty* held in May, 1965 was indicative of the growing national concern for the quality of the environment. A strong policy recommendation on programming, a vital echo of the 1958 joint New York report cited above, emerged from the Townscape Panel of that conference:

> Every city should develop a comprehensive design plan embracing elements of the environment, as part of its comprehensive planning program. The Federal Government should require that such design planning be developed in comprehensive planning before Federal development funds are released to a city or urban county. Every American community must have an organizational framework for performing the functions of sound environmental design. Where such a framework does not now exist, it should be created as soon as possible. In some cases, it might be feasible to establish a special agency to oversee all elements of design in city development. In every case, the function of urban design must be performed in an effective and comprehensive fashion (U.S. White House Conference, 1965, p. 635).

It is encouraging to note the emergence of governmental leadership in the enunciation of design-oriented policy statements. A plea for this positive endorsement had been registered at earlier design conferences. In 1962, Peter Blake (Editor, *Architectural Forum*) described an "architecture of abdication" in the face of blocks to creating a coherent architectural environment in America. He feared that the designers might give up, despairing the use of architecture as a force for unity in the face of the existing obstacles:

> Now, these are the three most serious obstacles to creating a decent architectural environment in America: the unrestricted speculation with land, . . . ridiculous tax policies, . . . and the absence of leadership at governmental level (*Aspen International Design Conference,* 1962, pp. 96-98).

Even earlier, concern had been registered in 1959 by a panel chaired by David Wallace at the Harvard conference concerned with large-scale residential sectors:

> Potential local sponsors have shown interest in urban renewal often above their actual ability to envision and design adequate urban patterns and to cope with the financial problems of urban development. The panel felt that the widening sponsorship posed a need for new techniques in agency programming.
>
> The immediate prospect of many proposals from diverse sponsors forces upon the local community the long neglected responsibility of determining the overall community context into which individual projects – large and small, housing and non-housing – can be fitted (Harvard Graduate School of Design, 1959, p. 27).

Concern about the development of better design programs and more effective programs to implement urban design goals has been a recurrent conference discussion theme with particular emphasis on the need for the early involvement of urban designers. Morton Hoppenfeld discussed programming at a 1962 conference and at the same time offered a most illuminating comment about the meaning of inter-disciplinary collaboration in planning:

> One of the most distinguishing aspects of urban design . . . is the fact that the urban designer seldom has a program given, but, instead, usually designs toward the evolution of a program.
>
> . . . .
>
> To many, a program is simply a statement of physical and functional objectives or limitations described in terms of land uses, building coverage, number of units, building types, etc. When so seen they describe to the average architect a range of architectonic forms permissible – but in reality, and more significantly, a program describes a life style. Whether explicit or implicit the program is a description in the broader sense of the way people will live and use the particular fragment of the city under design.
>
> . . . .
>
> Programs . . . should in fact evolve through many of the specialists involved in urban planning-building such as the sociologist who can

> describe reasonable population structures for a given community; the economist who can relate the land uses to economic productivity; the politician who can judge the feasibility; the administrator who can establish the strategy and timing. In among these must come the designer who will inject his own formal objectives, the formal implications of what others suggest and the human implications of what might be a formal solution of a formal imperative to a given site and symbolic situation. The designer must be part and parcel of the program-making process – sometimes to dominate, other times only to mitigate – but always in at the formulative stages of the program, lest his design be, in fact, created by those with no concept of the end product (Hoppenfeld, 1962, pp. 83-84).

August Heckscher also called for the integration of the designer in the earliest possible stages, a practice followed in industry with respect to the industrial designer (University of Pennsylvania, Graduate School of Fine Arts, 1963, p. 45). G. Holmes Perkins (Dean, School of Fine Arts, University of Pennsylvania) concurred:

> The architect must participate in the programming. . . . It is in the program process that many decisions are made that you later complain about, where densities are set, where segregation of uses is established. You must understand the design repercussions of the economic, political or social decisions which are proposed and advise as the expert in this area (Perkins, 1962, p. 95).

Garrett Eckbo, participating in the Townscape panel at the White House Conference, also addressed this point:

> Quality today can only be produced by the full use of the conscious design process. This is more than a planning process, although it includes planning; it also involves positive, creative action. . . . It is essential that the design process be invoked at the beginning and not come after many decisions have been made. It must encompass the total area under consideration and must be involved with the continuity of space and time (U.S. White House Conference, 1965, p. 85).

An example of the process of an urban design study was brilliantly outlined by Charles Blessing (Director of City Planning, Detroit) at the 1962 National Association of Housing and Redevelopment Officials conference.

> The special design group will consider the following major problems roughly in the order suggested.

First will be the collection of information in depth on the existing design resources in the city, with emphasis on the center city boulevard area. This survey will have to do with salient physical, social, cultural, historical, and economic characteristics. . . . An effort will be made to identify all significant positive physical design resources and negative disadvantages as they exist at present, at all scales, ranging from the central business district, with its skyscrapers, to the many individual churches in the center city, which have a design influence on their immediate area and on a larger area surrounding them. The design impact of significant commercial and industrial buildings located throughout the city and contributing importantly to its present texture and fabric will be evaluated – attention will not only be given to the three-dimensional aspects of the buildings in the city, but to the two-dimensional open space plan, which includes, importantly, the major and minor recreation areas and the new open lands represented by the wide expressway rights-of-way, as well as present and future institutional open area.

In addition the study will include a qualitative investigation of attitudes, perceptions, impressions, and opinions of both the general public and those in the highly skilled design professions of architecture, landscape architecture, engineering, and the allied fine arts.

Having in hand these two basic types of surveys, it will be the responsibility of the urban design staff to prepare an analysis and a program that will identify and rate significant urban design sources, establishing reasonable priorities with reference to urban renewal criteria, and to develop procedures for implementing better design, enforcing reasonable design standards through realistic controls, such as architectural and site planning controls.

Based on the above survey and analysis, the development of comprehensive three-dimensional design plans will be undertaken, keyed to the general master plan and realistic in terms of what may be accomplished during the coming two or three decades. These design proposals will be tested in relation to the complex interaction of economic and social factors, and the value of good design will be tested in relation to general market responses and to the public's growing commitment to develop a city that is at once functional, efficient, and aesthetically challenging (Blessing, 1962, p. 373).

Weiming Lu (Principal Planner, Minneapolis Planning Commission) summarized the goals of an urban design program in his paper "A More Attractive and Livable Minneapolis."

We are preparing a new "design framework" which will: ensure diversity, safety, comfort, efficiency and resilience in our city; harmonize natural and man-made forms in our city to project a vivid, coherent, and meaningful image to both residents and visitors; give individual designers specific meaningful guidance to their work in an over-all city context, yet not be rigid; be specific enough to solve problems of today and general enough to meet the needs of tomorrow; be imaginative enough to inspire the creativity of designers to make the most of their talents, yet realistic enough to attract the confidence of farsighted builders, and to persuade them to dedicate their energies to its execution; enable public improvement to serve as an effective incentive for private investment.

Above all, it must not be purely visionary, but yet it must have vision. We are constructing a "design process" which will: ensure coordinated, effective decision-making processes in both the public and private sectors of our city so that the "design framework" just outlined can be carried out; provide all the necessary legislative tools which will help us prevent ugliness, vulgarity, and squalor, and to search for beauty and grace in city design; enable us to program our capital improvement properly, and to search for quality as well as quantity in city building (Lu, 1966).

Education and Raising Aesthetic Expectation

A consensus existed among design professionals that education of the public as well as of the designer to an awareness of the urban environment and a concomitant elevating of the level of public demand for urban beauty were primary needs. M. Justin Herman said:

> I think there is no single way to educate a community. The educators themselves work at it and need to do more. I made a suggestion to the AIA . . . in which I said that I thought AIA ought to set up a service, perhaps through the newspapers, whereby a team of different but competent critics of the urban scene could be invited into a community and provide a critique on that community and what it looked like. . . . I think one of the most important influences on a community is its awareness that it doesn't really look very good to other people, and, maybe, that it doesn't look very good to itself *(Aspen International Design Conference,* 1962, p. 77).

Joseph C. Sloane (Professor of Art, University of North Carolina) also discussed the low aesthetic expectation on the part of the public. He suggested that builders often "choose banal but safe architects." Perhaps the only solution is to seek "gradual creation in each metropolis of an influential group of persons to whom beauty is a vital concern" (Sloane, 1966, p. 41).

Practicing members of the design professions as well as the public must be educated to a higher level of expectations in terms of urban design. The Townscape Panel at the White House Conference reported:

> The panel recommends that the professional societies concerned create, with Federal aid, a National Urban Design Center. Such a center would coordinate the work of architects, planners, landscape architects, industrial and interior designers, manufacturers and research corporations – with all who contribute to total townscape design. The center would also coordinate the needs of all agencies of Federal, State, and local government who post signs, specify materials and fixtures, determine spaces and relationships and uses. The Federal Government should assist, through grants and other types of aid in the establishment of a National Design Center and support its activities and educational program in the same manner as it assists the Highway Research Board (U.S. White House Conference, 1965, p. 635).

Earlier, a panel chaired by Preston Andrade at the 1959 Harvard urban design conference had reported:

> Of still more importance is the conscious development of a set of positive steps to improve the quality of urban design through better training for personnel motivated to apply their skills through government service and private practice, through efforts to develop and evaluate experimental projects, through efforts to provide citizen education programs on changing concepts of urban design, and finally, through a comparison of the effects of criteria used in urban design concepts and schemes in a number of cities (Harvard Graduate School of Design, 1959, p. 26).

A concluding excerpt from the Townscape Panel of the White House conference serves to summarize the need for the education and elevation of aesthetic expectation on the part of everyone involved in the evolution of our urban communities:

> We must develop in the youth of the Nation a greater awareness of and sensitivity to all aspects of the environment and what every citizen can do to insure its development and maintenance. Perhaps most important, we must involve young people in the actual development of a stimulating environment. Programs to accomplish these objectives should be established and administered locally, but with aid from both private industry and the Federal Government.
>
> There must also be a nationwide program of education for our urban leadership, public and private. Many of the conditions which are blighting our cities today are the result of ignorance, apathy, and neglect. These are forces which can be dispelled, and education can

be our major weapon in this task. Such a program should be initiated immediately, with the help of Federal, State, and local funds as well as contributions from foundations and private industries. It should be aimed not only at mayors, city councilmen, county supervisors, boards of education, zoning and building commissions and planning boards, but also at the heads of private industry such as insurance companies and other large industries which bring to bear powerful influences on the urban environment. All must be made to see most clearly their responsibilities, as leaders, in the development of a more stimulating environment (U.S. White House Conference, 1965, pp. 634-635).

16

Urban Housing and Site Design

ROBERT D. KATZ

☐ EVER SINCE *The New Yorker* Magazine was involved in a law suit in the 1920s over the proposed criticism of a newly erected skyscraper, there has been a dearth of published research evaluating the quality of architectural and site planning design. The goal of the study from which the materials of this chapter are drawn is threefold: to identify factors, both technical and procedural, essential to high quality residential site planning; to document current practices throughout the United States; and where appropriate, to recommend ways of improving site planning. The focus is on design and its relation to livability.

In the course of the study, extensive field work was undertaken with major emphasis on the metropolitan areas where the greatest amount of housing is being built. During the field work phase, two objectives were pursued with special interest:

1. Investigation of development factors and physical characteristics influencing the quality of site planning of multifamily housing projects.

2. Investigation of single-family housing to determine ways of increasing intensity without sacrificing livability.

EDITORS' NOTE: *This chapter was abstracted from a recently published book by Robert D. Katz entitled* Design of the Housing Site: A Critique of American Practice. *The studies and field work which formed the basis for the book were jointly financed by the Federal Housing Administration under its Technical Studies Program, by the Urban Renewal Administration, and by a contribution from the Mobile Homes Manufacturers Association. The accompanying illustrations (unless otherwise indicated) were photographed by the author.*

The conclusions listed below are the most important ones of the study. Their order does not indicate any priority, but instead follows the organization of the larger report from which the chapter is drawn.

1. The bulk of current site planning in the United States is of mediocre quality. Exceptions are random since they do not seem to fall into any discernible geographic pattern or relate to any particular housing program. Good practice is attributable to a combination of skillful designers and motivated developers.

2. Open space voids are receiving disproportionately less design study than structural masses. The result is that sites lack spatial organization even though individual building façades may be pleasing.

3. Failure to plan open space for use causes waste of land.

4. Multifamily housing offers little real privacy. Usable private outdoor spaces are not provided. In addition, interior privacy is jeopardized by uncontrolled access to communal outdoor areas.

5. In lay and official circles, multifamily housing is considered a poor second to living in or owning a single-family detached house. This opinion discourages efforts to improve the quality of design for multifamily housing.

6. Mobile home parks are generally of uninspired design because for the most part neither the homes nor the parks are designed by professionals and because community attitudes toward mobile homes are derisive.

7. Generally little effort is made in advance of occupancy to determine the needs of tenants of multifamily housing. Design decisions take inadequate account of family differences in size, type, and values.

8. Traditional concepts of single-use planning dominate and prevent many efforts to mix uses and housing types on a single site. Lack of variety produces monotonous physical appearances and also precludes any focal points for social activities.

9. An examination of site neighborhoods should be a precondition for plan approval. Site plans are often prepared and evaluated with little respect for project environments.

10. Efforts should be made to attract more talented designers into public service by offering them positions with substantial responsibilities. Government employment is not held in high esteem by most design professionals.

11. Design review by qualified permanent staff or consultants should be mandatory for all federally aided programs.

12. Existing regulations should be revised to minimize inconsistencies and bureaucratic complexities, and to place the emphasis on design goals instead of quantitative measures.

13. Less overriding concern with risks and more financing of site planning experiments are needed.

14. Discussion of design shortcomings should be as common as publicity of good design. Professional criticism of site planning and housing is rare.

SITE PLANNING INNOVATIONS

We have had to discard the assumption that imagination and innovation are synonymous with extravagance and waste (Weaver, 1964).

Few of the site planning innovations discussed in this chapter can be regarded as breakthroughs brought about by contemporary American ingenuity. Most fit into one of the following three categories: old proposals which did not materialize until recently, practices which were once common and are being rediscovered, or borrowings from foreign experience.

To date in the United States, there has been little boldness of thought or action in the field of site planning and housing development. The chief reason is a lack of incentive and not a lack of tools or talent. Many distinguished individuals and groups of professionals have recognized this fact and are calling for measures to supply motivation. The Panel on Housing of the Office of Science and Technology, part of the executive office of the President of the United States, concluded in 1963 that it was

> necessary . . . to increase Government expenditures in support of research and experimentation in housing, [and that] . . . by revamping and expanding the roles which Government plays in the support of research and experimentation in housing, the Government can,

> if it so desires, stimulate the national economy and, at the same time, enable the nation to realize the benefits of its scientific and technical capabilities by creating better housing and a better living environment for all its citizens (U.S. Office of Science and Technology, 1963).

What constitutes a true innovation in the nature of housing environment is subjective. As interpreted by the President's Panel, variance in building codes and employment of different building materials would be considered innovations. However, under the definition established for this study, modifications of current prevailing practice would not be regarded as innovative *unless* they had some promise of influencing the fundamental nature of site design.

For convenience of discussion, the innovations that are cited here are grouped by *Location, Occupant Characteristics,* and *Site and Construction Characteristics.* Examples include developments which have been completed, are under construction, or are in the planning stage.

INNOVATIONS BY LOCATION

Inner-city Areas

The most significant innovations near city centers integrate housing, recreation, and commerce on a single site. The impetus for the construction of such projects has come from several quarters: urban renewal programs designed to increase the attractiveness of formerly neglected core areas, reaction against single-use land planning which discourages combinations of housing and commercial establishments, and the desire to meet the growing demand for in-town housing. For many families, particularly those with grown children, the attractiveness of suburban sites has diminished. Many want proximity to public transportation as well as to offices, commercial centers, and entertainment and cultural facilities. Housing projects in core areas which have best filled these special demands are the most successful.

One of the most publicized inner-city projects is the Marina City complex in Chicago (Figures 1 and 2). In a few short years, its cylindrical towers have become a city landmark. It combines many innovations on a site of less than five acres: integration of

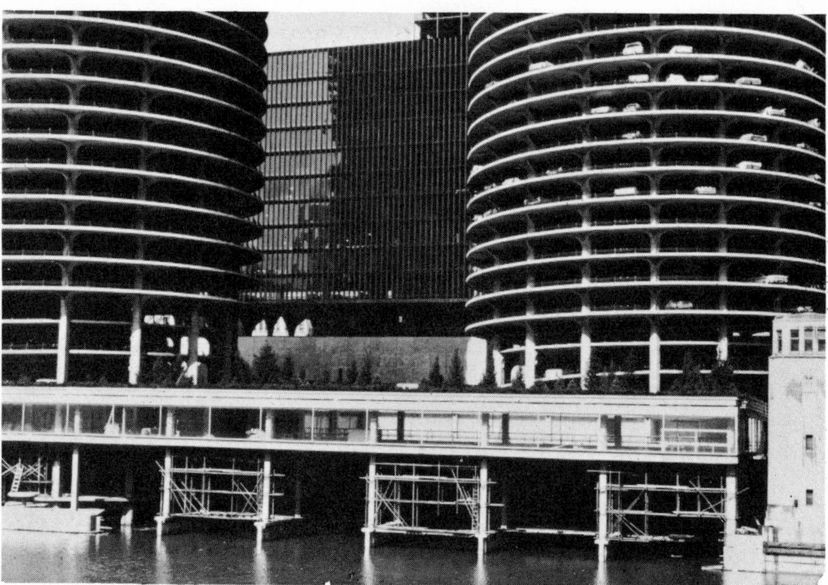

Photograph By Russell V. Keune
Figure 1. Marina City, Chicago, Illinois

Figure 2. Marina City, Chicago, Illinois
Photograph By Russell V. Keune

functions on a single site, proximity to the center of the city, automobile storage on the lower floors of a residential structure, convenient mass transportation (bus service on adjoining streets and potentially water-taxi service on the Chicago River), and modern structural forms. There are generous balconies, indoor recreation and convenience facilities (for example, swimming pool, health club, bowling alleys, restaurants, commissary, newsstand), a skating rink, and a marina for 700 small boats. On the same site there is also an office building. The shortcoming of Marina City is its ground space planning. This matches neither the quality of the architecture nor the concept of integrating uses. The spaces between the buildings appear to be unplanned voids, without any specific function in mind (other than traffic routes and the skating rink).

Another interesting Chicago project is Outer Drive East, the initial building of a large planned complex of residential towers, office buildings, and commercial facilities bordering Lake Michigan (Figure 3). Right now, it consists of a single apartment tower with

Figure 3. Outer Drive East Apartments, Chicago, Illinois

an adjoining restaurant and swimming pool. Like Marina City, it is close to employment, shopping, cultural resources, and the water. Also like Marina City, it cannot boast of any innovations in site development. What is most innovative about Outer Drive East is the fact that it utilizes the air rights of a rail yard. Following this lead, many more residential sites may be located over the countless railroad tracks that cross and penetrate the hearts of American cities, particularly as ownership of air rights is better defined.

Additional potential sites for residential structures exist over public facilities such as highways, piers, and parking fields. It has been estimated that in New York alone, in the five city boroughs, air rights over public facilities could provide for an estimated one-quarter of a million apartment units housing one million people. In fact, the first such project, Bridge Apartments, has already been built over the highway approach to the George Washington Bridge (Figures 4 and 5). The site also contains a bus terminal and adjoins a subway station, providing a convenient interchange point between

Figure 4. Bridge Apartments, New York, New York

Figure 5. Bridge Apartments, New York, New York

local and regional transportation networks. Other roadbeds offer opportunities as sites for residential as well as commercial buildings that could rise on paved decks or structures supported by columns anchored between the lanes of traffic. At some sites housing could be an integral part of the traffic movement system – a linear development in which housing and related activities would be a planned part of the highway, and where access from the road would lead directly into parking structures attached to residential buildings. Traditional attitudes toward mixing housing and highways will have to be reexamined before such schemes become a reality, however.

Commercial Wharf in Boston is yet another illustration of how a public facility, a pier in this case, may be combined with residential development (Figure 6). Commercial Wharf, a solid masonry nineteenth-century building, has been renovated and refurbished inside to house shops and offices at ground level and apartments on the upper floors. It is only part of a total Atlantic Avenue water front renewal scheme that eventually will combine residential, commercial, office, cultural, and recreational facilities with the existing shipping facilities of this area. Following this example in Boston, builders of transient housing are erecting new hotels and motor inns overlooking other busy city ports.

Figure 6. Commercial Wharf, Boston, Massachusetts

By-passed Sites and Older Neighborhoods

In many cities, land once thought to be unserviceable for residential development is being put to use by the imaginative planning of sites. In Cincinnati, for example, slopes heretofore by-passed because they were considered too steep for economical and safe construction are today choice residential properties with magnificent views of the city center and the Ohio Valley (Figure 7). Steel and reinforced concrete construction make it possible to build hillside property by anchoring foundations to the rock behind the face of the slope. Expensive earth moving to create level terraces is not required. Depending upon the road system and the grades at individual sites, hillside properties can be approached from the top, bottom, or intermediate levels; the steepest portion of the site may be used as a parking garage with interior ramps serving to connect the various road levels.

Where residential buildings are constructed on steep terrain, it is not always feasible to provide usable individual and communal open space at ground level without resorting to terrace levels. Most

Figure 7. Mt. Adams Area, Cincinnati, Ohio

of the hillside construction viewed during this study consisted of individual buildings, not groups of structures; no extensive planning of open space in the form of galleries or decks was observed. For the single building on the small steep site, the common space is frequently provided in the form of rooftop gardens. A few luxury apartments have rooftop swimming pools.

At a San Francisco Bay site, steep grade and waterfront land meet at a single location barely large enough to accommodate a cluster of buildings (Figures 8 and 9). Since site planning under

Figure 8. Côte d'Azur, Sausalito, California

these circumstances is more a matter of creating land than manipulating existing elements, the task of designing safe accessways to buildings and usable open space at this site was very difficult. Access to dwelling units in the buildings is obtainable at two levels – from rooftops (where automobiles are parked) and from the lower water level (where boats are docked).

Figure 9. Côte d'Azur, Sausalito, California

When new housing is interspersed in older, established residential neighborhoods, it sometimes gives a false impression of being innovative simply because of the contrast with the existing surroundings. Such housing and site types are often not so much new to a city as they are new to a particular neighborhood. What is mistaken for an innovation may be a thoughtful conversion of single-family into multiple-occupancy dwellings or a return to housing types once in vogue such as town- and court-houses. Many reemerging housing types permit higher densities than the detached single-family dwelling and at the same time stress privacy for the dwelling. The court-house faces in on its own contained space. Other innovative types turn a solid wall to the street or a fence to neighboring properties to screen gardens and patios that are designed for the exclusive use of a number of attached dwelling units.

Scattered Locations

The use of scattered sites, now being tested in numerous localities by local public housing authorities, offers great promise. It is a means, probably the best means to date, of eliminating housing monotony while still retaining the financial benefits of repetitive design. Under this plan, many small sites, separated by a number of intervening blocks, are developed with identical buildings; however, the physical separation of the structures breaks up what would otherwise be a big, dull "housing project" (Figure 10). Where these "vest pocket projects" contain more than one building, there is an opportunity for achitectural diversity. This scattering of buildings throughout a community can result in social mixture as well as physical variety and should prove successful on both grounds.

Figure 10. Wayne Low-Rent Public Housing, Wayne, Michigan

Outlying Areas

The potential for innovations in terms of both design and social mix is greatest in totally new towns. In the area of design, planners can:

1. support the adoption of new regulations which will permit the testing of new theories of design;

2. provide a variety of accommodations, interspersed throughout the town;

3. cluster individual buildings related to one another to create tight urban cores;

4. experiment with new building forms generated by circulation systems; and

5. devise new modes of transportation for residential areas.

Many new cities have been built around the world during the past twenty years, but the record in the United States is a meager one. Although there are many pseudo "new towns" in the United States, these are generally nothing more than large developments of conventional housing types laid out in traditional subdivisions, with the addition of a few multifamily buildings and shops to attract new residents. Since the Greenbelt Towns of the 1930s, Reston and Columbia, both in the Washington, D.C. area, are the only two in the United States which contain truly original concepts.

Reston's first village (encompassing only a fraction of the planned ten-and-one-half-mile city) is nearing completion. The site was carefully planned and many successful innovations are already evident. The multifamily dwelling areas have choice locations rather than "leftover" ones. The natural amenities of the new land have been preserved and some new landscape features have been added, the most spectacular of which is a 36-acre lake. At the head of the lake is a village center with commercial, residential, and community facilities all in one compact grouping (Figures 11 and 12). The residential clusters around the lake have separate identities but are interconnected by a series of circulation routes for automobiles, bicycles, and pedestrians (Figures 13, 14, 15, and 16). The successful integration of housing and open spaces is the most refreshing of all the innovations of Reston. Though incomplete at the time of this writing, the village center already impresses the visitor with its animation and sense of purpose that is so lacking in most housing areas.

Figure 11. Reston, Reston, Virginia

Figure 12. Reston, Reston, Virginia

Figure 13. Reston, Reston, Virginia

Figure 14. Reston, Reston, Virginia

Figure 15. Reston, Reston, Virginia

Figure 16. Reston, Reston, Virginia

The city of Columbia is still in the planning stage, but if building follows blueprints, residents will enjoy a satisfying physical and social environment plus an outstanding public transportation system. Designers anticipate a variety of transportation modes including minibuses, which will be within walking distance of the majority of dwelling units.

At Reston and Columbia land has been reserved for industrial parks. In the future, many of the residents will be able to work near their homes, even within walking and bicycling distance for some. These towns, with their clustered single-family housing and multifamily apartments will have populations of sufficient size to support a range of community facilities at the very outset. This policy of high net density planning satisfies demands for suburban living without the usual responsibilities of home ownership and provides focal points for both the multiple- and single-family housing by on-site commercial, educational, and recreational facilities. The innovative site planning concepts are more related to the integrated land use planning of the entire community than to specific building sites in both towns. The compact development — in sharp contrast with other recent large projects on the outskirts of metropolitan areas — and the willingness to plan for other than automobile traffic makes Reston and Columbia bright spots on today's housing scene.

INNOVATIONS BY OCCUPANT CHARACTERISTICS

Housing for the Elderly

Increased longevity has focused attention on the problems and needs of the elderly. Housing built especially for them by both private and public developers is commonplace. Since this segment of the population is not homogeneous, several distinct types of projects are emerging which differ to the extent that residents are dependent upon medical and nursing care. Best known, perhaps, are the retirement communities where the residents are almost entirely self-sufficient and not dependent upon medical care to any unusual extent. The most striking characteristic of retirement communities is the stress placed on recreational and communal facilities — golf courses, club houses, swimming pools, shuffleboard courts, and flower gardens (Figure 17).

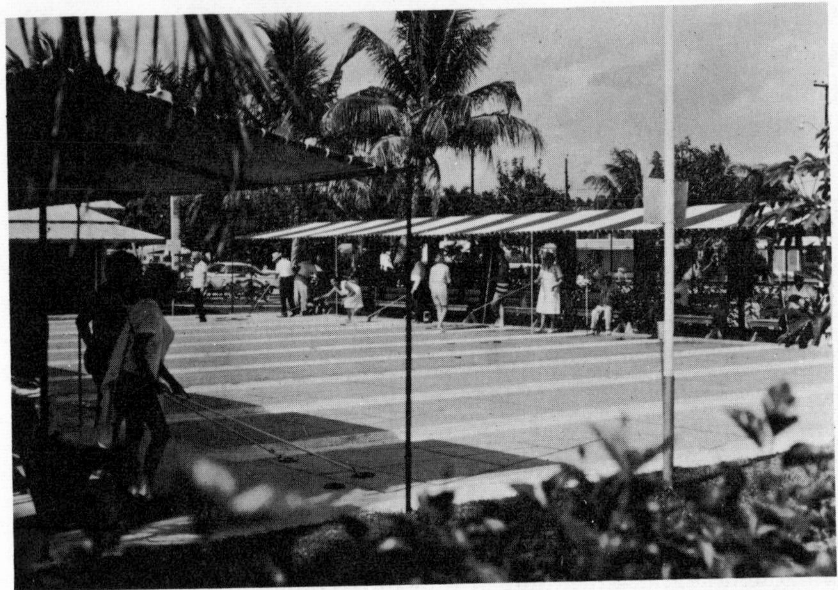

Figure 17. Park City Mobile Home Estates, Fort Lauderdale, Florida

Photograph By Russell V. Keune

Since residents are generally either couples or single persons without children, variety in dwelling types and site planning becomes an exercise in the distribution of identical or very similar structures and the arrangement of open space flow between buildings. The most satisfactory designs are the ones in which the community facilities are convenient but not so close that they detract from the privacy of the dwelling units and in which on-site automobile circulation is replaced by some other form of transportation. In warm climates, small electrically powered trains or individually owned golf carts or both solve the transportation problem at several sites. In northern cities, the communities tend to be small and compact, with individual buildings connected by covered walkways leading to the dining or recreation hall and other communal areas.

Housing for Young Adults

Site planning of multifamily housing designed for occupancy by young adults, both married and single, reflects the special tastes and characteristics of this segment of the population. Among these are high mobility and a high degree of social interaction with contemporaries. The accommodation of automobiles and communal recreational facilities is very important in site layout programs. Parking ratios are often required in excess of one space per dwelling. The closer the parking lot to the buildings, the better. It is this handling of the automobile plus the design of the units themselves that makes much of the housing for younger people indistinguishable from motels. Often privacy is of low priority at these sites, in spite of the fact that there are differences in the housing needs for persons within the same age group. Inclusion of communal recreation facilities such as swimming pools and barbecue pits is generally more important than provision of private outdoor space (Figure 18). Even private areas such as patios often are either extensions of public walkways or they open directly off the living rooms of the apartments. Since young married couples have either no children or youngsters of preschool age, schools play no significant part in housing location and community planning. The most successful sites are those which do not try to attract both older families and young couples but concentrate instead on catering to this style of group living, that young people apparently prefer.

Figure 18. Turtle Creek Village, Dallas, Texas

INNOVATIONS BY SITE AND CONSTRUCTION CHARACTERISTICS

Parking and Circulation Systems on Site

Interior parking in multifamily residential structures is a fairly recent innovation that has proven advantages. Drivers can park their cars in garages without having to leave shelter to reach their own apartments. Moreover, because cars are off the street and thus shielded from view, site appearance benefits.

Integration of parking into a dwelling structure can be achieved in a number of ways. Cars may be stored in the base of a structure, in decks above ground level, below grade in basement areas, or in a split system – both above and below grade (Figure 19). The structural system for garage floors and residential floors may vary and could result in column spacing that is not suited equally well for both types of floor plans. An alternative is to place the cars in a separate building connected by pedestrian passageways to the residential structure (Figure 20).

Figure 19. Atlanta Towers, Atlanta, Georgia

Figure 20. Executive Towers, Phoenix, Arizona

For some time there has been a recognized need for "the combination of complete convenience in the use of the automobile and a peaceful escape from its dangers" (Stein, 1957, p. 189). The cluster principle, which facilitates saving of streets by eliminating repetitive driveways and minor residential streets, and the superblock, which keeps the automobile out of the heart of community open spaces, are two ways of meeting this dual need. Neither is new. Clustering was introduced with the Radburn plan of 1928; the superblock scheme, also introduced at Radburn, was developed fully at Baldwin Hills Village in 1941. A variation of these plans is achieved at Swan Lake Mobile Home Park in Mira Loma, California (Figures 21,

Figure 21. Swan Lake, Mira Loma, California

Photograph By Russell V. Keune

Figure 22. Swan Lake, Mira Loma, California *Photograph by Russell V. Keune*

22, and 23). Automobiles are not permitted in the residential areas of this adults-only park. Instead, they are parked in a lot at the main entrance to the 128-acre site. (A few homes at the periphery of the site have private parking areas.) At this point, the resident can obtain an electrically powered golf cart and proceed to his home or elsewhere on the site. Each mobile home site has a small shelter

Figure 23. Swan Lake, Mira Loma, California *Photograph by Russell V. Keune*

where the cart is parked. Since all internal pathways are scaled to cart size, a great deal of space is saved. This space, that would otherwise be required for streets of ordinary width, is devoted to augmenting the open space around individual homes. In addition to this saving of space, the noise and traffic generally associated with automobiles are considerably reduced if not entirely eliminated by the use of carts.

Open Space

Many innovations in open space planning as a system represent a breakaway from the traditional block and lot building patterns. Cluster development, the common green, greenways, superblocks, and planned unit developments all lend themselves to a diversified utilization of open space (Figures 24 and 25). They deviate from convention by (1) pooling some private spaces for communal purposes, and (2) connecting the communal spaces to create a continuous flow of space, or greenway, through a site.

Figure 24. Willits West, Birmingham, Michigan

Figure 25. Willits West, Birmingham, Michigan

Greenways can be used as golf courses and riding and hiking trails. In their most highly developed state, the greenways are connected to off-site open space systems, forming a continuous flow of space throughout a community. It is possible for pedestrian networks to lead in an unbroken ribbon from residences to schools, to major parks, and to other community facilities. At major crossroads, underpasses or overpasses ensure safety from vehicular traffic.

In theory, common open space is a form of land conservation. Regional and local sites of outstanding natural beauty can be saved for communal use. The pooling of private lands can result in a net saving of land area per dwelling unit if the size of the common open space is less than the total "contribution" of the individual lots. What has happened in practice, however, is that some developers have used this technique as an excuse to bypass open space standards and then have reneged, with the consequence that they have failed to provide adequate space for either private or public use. In some locations, such as at the FHA experimental subdivision in Salinas, California, there is no evidence that any communal open spaces have been allocated to supplement the small, private enclosed yards on each house site. Although very small lots and no communal open space may mean a savings to home buyers, this initial financial gain ultimately may be offset by a corresponding decline in neighborhood livability.

In view of the numbers of apartment complexes being constructed on small land parcels throughout the country, it would seem reasonable to exploit as fully as possible open spaces above ground level. To date, however, little experimentation has taken place. The few exceptions are rooftop plazas and gallery corridors. At Reston there are rooftop plazas designed over parking garages that serve as areas for passive recreation as well as "street" fronts for some of the town-houses (see Figure 15 above).

Most of the "sidewalks in the sky" that have been built are little more than wide access corridors to apartments, rather than pleasant places for recreation. Enclosed by wire screening for safety purposes, they give the impression of cages – anything but inviting. Unless more attractive materials can be found to make them safe for children, access galleries might better be planned exclusively for adult use. This is the case at Victoria Plaza, a public housing project in San Antonio, Texas, where these corridors are wide enough to be used as sitting areas (Figure 26). A worthwhile consideration would be to go one step further and design outdoor corridors to be accessible from private balconies, somewhat analogous to the relationship between common greens and private patios at ground level.

The rooftop patios at Capitol Park in Washington, D.C., are examples of excellent use of outdoor space above grade (Figure 27). They combine esthetics, function, and safety. They are large, private, made of handsome materials; and they command a spectacular view of the city. As a consequence, they are truly outdoor extensions of the living rooms of the apartments that occupy the top floors of the buildings. In fact they are reached directly from the living rooms below by spiral staircases (Figure 28). They also constitute a secondary means of egress from the apartments because they connect with a public stair tower at the rooftop level. This staircase in turn is used by all the residents in the building to gain access to that portion of the roof which is set aside for communal use.

Figure 26. Victoria Plaza, San Antonio, Texas

Figure 27. Capitol Park, Washington, D.C.

Figure 28. Capitol Park, Washington, D.C.

Industrial Houses

The field of industrial housing, with the exception of mobile homes, has demonstrated little originality in site planning and development. The experiments that are underway in this field deal mainly with building materials and not so much with relationships of structure to ground. The Monsanto House, that was first designed in 1955 and later exhibited at the 1964-65 New York World's Fair, for example, is innovative only with respect to materials and construction techniques. It rises from a central service core, and the living wings cantilever out over the ground. This design has potential for innovations in site planning because it covers only a very small portion of ground.

The mobile home industry has several interesting designs for high-density mobile-home complexes. One of these is the use of factory produced mobile homes as cores of larger single-story structures. In some instances a simple wooden roof structure is built, under which the mobile-home unit is parked (Figure 29). The roof extends out over the mobile home so as to provide cover for a carport on one side and a patio on the other. In more elaborate units,

Figure 29. Apache Wells Mobile Home Country Club, Mesa, Arizona *Photograph By Russell V. Keune*

Figure 30. The Oasis Mobile Home Park, Scottsdale, Arizona *Photograph By Russell V. Keune*

actual enclosed rooms are built under the roof, but these may not be insulated as in a conventional house or equipped with heat or water (Figure 30). The utilities are all contained in the mobile home which is inserted into the structure but can be removed, should the owner wish to relocate his movable house without its shell.

Somewhat the same principle is now being tested for multistory structures. Factory-manufactured units would be transported to a building site, either in sections or as completely self-contained

Figure 31. Factory Prefabricated Multifamily Housing
Illustration By Ronald Goodfellow and Ken Fryar Associates

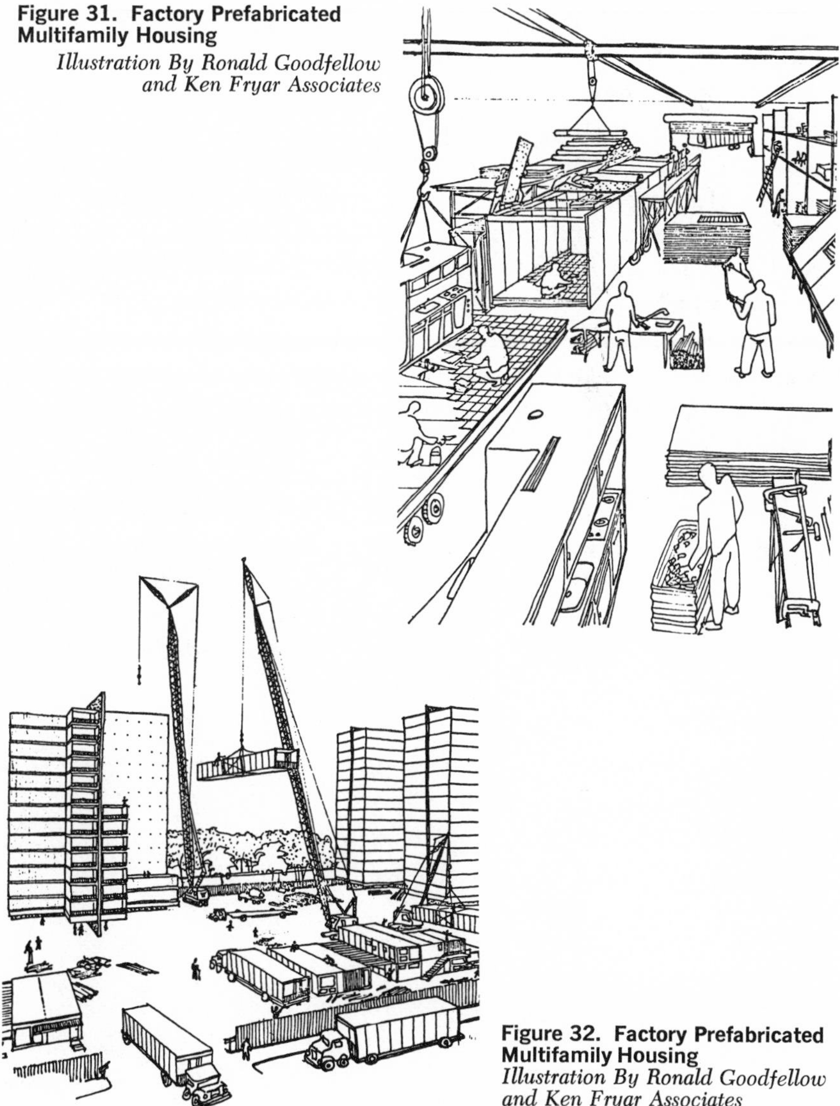

Figure 32. Factory Prefabricated Multifamily Housing
Illustration By Ronald Goodfellow and Ken Fryar Associates

apartment units, and then hoisted by crane into slots in a skeleton superstructure (Figures 31 and 32). Obviously, major modifications in the design of the mobile home as we know it today would be necessary, and the superstructure would have to contain vertical and horizontal circulation as well as utilities for the individual units. But these requirements present no difficulties considering the sophistication of modern technology. In other schemes, mass-produced dwellings would be part of clusters, raised to various levels by a system of ramps or sited at ground level. In each of these proposals there are many opportunities for site planning innovations to accompany the structural and material experiments.

In Canada, Western Europe, and the United States, experiments are underway with what are labeled megastructures – individual units connected so that a whole community is contained in a single building. Housing complexes of this magnitude contain unified systems for circulation and utilities. Some examples of megastructures are Moshe Safdie's Habitat 67, to be built for the Montreal Fair, and Pelli and Lumsden's award-winning Urban Nucleus.

At the scale of the individual house, attempts are underway to design dwellings with greater flexibility by such means as interior partitions and exterior annexes which can be readily added or collapsed. The British Ministry of Housing and Local Government, in a 1961 report, called for more investigation of an "adaptable house" to serve changing family needs over time more effectively than the traditional model (Great Britain, Ministry of Housing and Local Government, 1961, p. 9). For American builders, flexibility seems to lie in the direction of some sort of cellular component house design which combines the best of mobile homes and conventional housing.

Policy and Action

THE FOURTH PAIR OF CHAPTERS in Part II shifts emphasis from the creation of urban policy to its fruition, with essays by Robert T. Daland on "Public Administration and Urban Policy" and by William L. C. Wheaton on "Moving From Plan to Reality."

Daland traces changes in the conceptual relationships of Public Administration and Planning, two inseparable professional specializations that happen to have evolved separately. These two professions

> *represent the core of the two processes . . . urban administration and urban policy-making. The recent trends in relationships between these two processes involve both (1) the continual development of new and specialized facets of technical activity and knowledge and (2) the tendency increasingly to integrate and articulate these new specialties. While the articulation . . . has not yet been achieved, it is clear that it is high on the urban agenda.*

Daland suggests how planning or developmental policy-making has gradually shifted goals. At first, action

> *was intended to prevent chaos on the periphery of the growing urban area by adopting measures to insure the continuance of the "orderly" pattern already developed within the city. . . . The second line of action . . . was intended to prevent the spread of blight or of generally lower standard conditions into high class areas . . . and next came public housing and slum clearance programs. [But] the affluence of American society became less evenly rather than more evenly spread in a geographical sense . . . When the significance of this trend sank home, spurred recently by constantly rising rates of*

> *mass violent unrest, it became clear that urban policy required "development." This involves efforts to produce change in the basic economic and social structure of the great urban areas. . . .*

In discussing how the technology of urban policy and administration has been changing to meet the newer goals, Daland describes once again the astonishing proliferation of experts that has been occurring, and he then shows the key role of systematic urban information systems in making it possible to deal realistically with urban magnitude and complexity.

Certain new pressures are affecting the role of the generalist planner, notably: (1) our tremendously increased ability to move things, people, energy, and communications; (2) the proliferation of federal and state programs; and (3) contemporary social science research and thinking. Daland divides the latter into new decision-making insights and insights into the political context of public planning. A lively section deals with the impacts of "incrementalist" doctrine on overall planning. A concluding section dealing with "Administration and Organization for Urban Planning" ends with the following thought: "It is because urban politics has become development politics that urban planning goals have changed, and in turn, [so has] organization for urban planning."

In Chapter 18, Wheaton looks at some of the same developments Daland has treated, but with an emphasis on the processes by which plans are carried out. Of city plans prior to World War II he says: "The powers available for carrying out these plans were limited to the exercise of the police power, chiefly through zoning, building codes, and subdivision codes, the power of condemnation for public works, the power to spend for traditional public works, and the power to inform and exhort." But an impressive set of new powers has evolved. Following Fitch, Wheaton declares flatly that "These resources are now broad enough in scope to carry out any plan yet prepared and published by any city in the United States."

After describing the institutional framework within which plans are carried out in municipal government, Wheaton comes to an extended discussion of a vital new development, "The Mixed Enterprise Institution." These corporations "carry out phases of a development program utilizing both public and private resources, managerial skills, leadership, and incentives. . . . Their success has been copied on a sufficiently widespread basis so that they now constitute a major category of institutions to execute plans, and appear in one form or another in almost every city." Despite Wheaton's recognition of the ubiquity of such mixed-enterprise institutions, there appears to have been little documentation to date of their existence, let alone their accomplishments. Wheaton here provides an important beginning.

The indispensable role of civic leadership in politics and administration is highlighted next. It is made clear that the great accomplishments of certain cities are directly traceable to particular men who originated, inspired, and led movements for change. Furthermore, the emergence of a new class of civic servants has occurred, viz., "professional manipulators who administer the federal aids, the local powers, the private investment incentives, and the political processes necessary to carry out urban development programs."

Wheaton, too, is impressed with changes in the scope of planning. "The national attention now directed toward program budgeting, and toward poverty programs, the recent proposals for the reorganization of human services in New York City, and President Johnson's Demonstration Cities proposal — each of these may contribute toward, first, the coalescence of planning to make it comprehensive and later, that direction or coordination of action which is the main concern of this chapter."

— *H.F.*

17

Public Administration and Urban Policy

ROBERT T. DALAND

□ IN ORDER TO COMMENT ON RECENT TRENDS in the relation of public administration to urban policy-making it is necessary to begin with a considerably extended time perspective. We now recognize that at the turn of the century policy-making was clearly regarded as the province of the elected representative, while administration was ideally the technical implementation of that will. The two functions were to be kept as separate as possible. By the decade of the 1940s, however, the new view had become so widely approved that many subtle inter-relationships necessarily and properly existed between the two processes, despite a considerable disagreement over what, precisely, these were or should be. The myth that policy and administration are basically separate processes is still voiced in responsible quarters; but this is the result of institutional or strategic convenience (John Porter East, 1965).

The important point to emphasize, however, is that while urban policy-making and administration are inseparable, they are also *different*. In fact, we are suggesting that over the long run both policy-development (planning) and administrative roles are becoming increasingly specialized and distinctive, while at the same time increasingly integrated. In 1900 there was no city manager profession, much less an urban planning profession. By 1947 both were virile young professions – managers and other urban administrators having something of a headstart. The planners were in the position of winning themselves recognition as a profession. It was functional for this objective to take a highly independent, non-political, technical stance which was represented by the central tool of planners of that day, the master plan. This institutional strategy kept administrators and planners at arm's length, each with his separate governing board. In the review we are about to make of developments of the past two decades, we will not confine ourselves narrowly to developments within the manager and planner professions. They do, however, represent the core of the two processes with which we are concerned: urban administration and urban policy-making. The recent trends in relationships between these two processes involve both (1) the continual development of new and specialized facets of technical activity and knowledge, and (2) the tendency increasingly to integrate and articulate these new specialities. While full articulation of urban administration and policy-development processes has not yet been achieved, it is clear that it is high on the urban agenda.

The general developments alluded to tend to fall into the following four categories, which we shall review: (1) developmental policy-making, (2) the technology of urban policy-development and administration, (3) the changing role of the generalist planner, and (4) changes in organization for urban planning.

DEVELOPMENTAL POLICY-MAKING

During the past two decades perhaps the greatest change that has come to urban planning and policy-making has been the least noticed and studied. The goals of planning have changed. The change is clearly observable if we think in historical terms. The city beautiful movement sought to create a better looking façade for the city. Urban problems were basic however, and during several decades two lines of action became prevalent. The first was intended to prevent chaos on the periphery of the growing urban area by adopting measures to insure the continuance of the "orderly" pattern already developed within the city. Zoning and subdivision controls served this purpose, often combined with extraterritorial jurisdiction so that the controls might be exercised beyond existing city limits. Projections were made as to future growth and this provided a basis for calculating the need for future public works. These strategies were intended to extend the *status quo*.

The second line of action began earlier but was less effective. This was intended to prevent the spread of blight or of generally lower standard conditions into high class areas. Building codes were created for this purpose, and eventually housing codes. The early efforts were not effective, however; and next came attempts to meet the problem through public housing and slum clearance programs. Their failure, in turn, led directly to a new development-oriented goal for planning. Urban policy now required innovation. Cities were considered underdeveloped in the same sense as the underdeveloped nations. That is, either the economy was not producing sufficiently to raise or even to maintain the standard of living of all the city dwellers, or the benefits of the economy were not being evenly distributed. In the underdeveloped nations both of these conditions are typical. In our cities, however, the problem became rather more complex. Precisely through the efforts to prevent the central city's blight from spreading, autonomous suburban governments erected barriers – sustained by the system of real estate transfers – against the "pollution" from the central city. Since production units were parts of grand corporations of nationwide extent, there was no necessary correlation of costs and benefits of production within a given geographical area. The affluence of American society became less evenly rather than more evenly spread in a geographical sense, despite national social security legislation and progressive taxation which tended to counter this trend.

When the significance of the trend sank home, spurred recently by constantly rising rates of mass violent unrest, it became clear that urban policy required "development." This involves efforts to produce change in the basic economic and social structure of the great urban areas. These changes not only involve urban renewal and all of its related programs, discussed elsewhere in this chapter, but attention to the kind of an economic base that will increase affluence and keep it at home. Originally "new industry" was thought sufficient to do the job. Latterly we have realized that it is the type of industry, its location, and its relation to the rest of the economy that is relevant. Even more recently we have realized that urban costs follow urban profits so that we must calculate the costs of public works, education, recreation, public health, and other services that people manning units of industrial expansion will require. Development therefore means (1) understanding the complexity of the socioeconomic equation, and (2) administering a set of controls which will produce change in a healthy direction. These requirements have produced a "regional science" with its analytical techniques.

It has been suggested that the experience of national development in the emerging nations is relevant. True as this is, the lessons of national development have not been reflected in urban policy-making. National planning depends on macro-economic analysis which is highly developed; but new administrative systems are required for national development. The pathology of the older administrative systems has been documented by Albert Waterston (Waterston, 1965). A number of proposals for new systems for administration of national development are before us. Two good examples are those of Saul Katz and Bertram Gross (Katz, 1965; Katz, 1966; and Gross, 1964). These imply that a larger number of variables must be subject to control than is typically the case in the United States urban areas. National development plans, where they have been effective, involve a greater degree of governmental intervention in the economy than is current in the United States urban planning; a greater penetration of the planners into the implementation process; and a greater degree of coordination of plans as between national, regional, and local levels of government. The United States government has been much more quick to require comprehensive national plans as a condition to aid in foreign countries than it has vis-a-vis domestic urban planning.

Urban planning is becoming developmentalist not only in the sense that it seeks to move toward an improved socioeconomic structure, but also in the sense of partnership with the developmental activities of private entities in the community, particularly business. More and more of the decisions of the community are of the partly public, partly private character. The most obvious case is the urban renewal program which is a partnership that can result in an ultimately privately owned project, as well as in a public one or a mixed ownership development. The same partnership is apparent in other areas such as transportation, utilities, hospitals and even manufacturing plants, which may operate from municipally owned, leased buildings. Other examples are industrial and research parks, such as the famous Research Triangle Park in the Carolina Piedmont, which represents a development oriented, deliberate change process in which three cities, three counties, and the state participated along with a variety of private profit and non-profit corporations.

To summarize, development oriented policy-making attempts, through governmental activities, to change the essential character of an urban environment in order to accommodate *all* the needs of the citizenry. This is in sharp contrast to older policies, still widely prevalent, of protecting the *status quo*, moving away from the problems of urban life (to the suburbs) and pushing the diseases of urban society into enclaves from which they cannot spread, but where they are allowed to fester. Urban development policies will have matured with the realization that there is no escape from urbanity and that urbanity must be made not only tolerable but positively desirable, while at the same time the policies are made to encompass all of the urban functions. This is in sharp contrast to notions of confining blight, pouring pollution into the neighboring river, permitting a system of personal mobility which poisons the air, or pushing undesirable industries and lurid forms of recreation across the municipal boundary. The new urban renewal, mass transit, and human relations programs are the portents of development oriented policy-making.

THE TECHNOLOGY OF URBAN POLICY DEVELOPMENT AND ADMINISTRATION

The most obvious recent trend in urban policy-development and administration is the rapid increase of new technologies and bodies of expertise that are being brought to bear. This may be due in part to mere borrowing of available techniques from other areas which have pioneered them; but more importantly it is due to the change in the goals of planning just discussed. The goals are broader. A new urban form must be designed. This trend may be expressed in terms of the specialization of planners, new concepts of systems and operations research, and the creation of urban information systems.

The Proliferation of Experts

As urban government has acquired new functions to perform, it has of necessity employed specialists in each new area. It is in the nature of this process, happening at all levels of government, that in addition to experts in the new functions, other new coordinative and staff roles must be added so that the resulting administrative machine may be monitored and directed toward the common goals of the community.

The function of the formal planning staff has broadened immeasurably during the past two decades in a similar way. From the time when the land use planner was thought of as the unique core of the profession and as the real generalistic planner, we have moved to a situation where the distinction between the policy planning activities of the planning staff and of the top "planners" in the operating departments is an increasingly hazy one. We now have economic planners, transportation planners, renewal planners, land planners, human resources planners, public works planners, recreation planners, site planners, housing planners, and administrative planners, just to mention the more obvious types. On the way are new specialists like planning educators, public investment planners, systems planners, and even political planners. The last named, of course, will be called community relations planners. The point is not that planning in these areas has not previously been done. Rather, it is that we are developing a new and more complex makeup within the planning department itself, with the result that its relations throughout the administrative hierarchy and the community are multiplied greatly. There is more two-way communication at the technical level in a wider variety of areas than ever before. This trend has not been documented in detail, but it is familiar to those who frequent planning and administrative offices.

What has happened to the generalist planner in all this? The need for the generalist seems greater than ever since it would be logical for him to coordinate the work of the specialist planners, and this approach is frequently advocated. In fact, however, the roles of top planning directors vary considerably, chiefly along the continuous dimension of operating as a staff coordinator at one extreme as against liaison with the governmental environment and the community at the other extreme. The proper education for the generalist planner, therefore, is still very much an open question. Our conclusions on this subject are explored in a later section of this chapter.

Systems and Operations Analysis

The notion of the "system" is an ancient one in the physical science field, but its use in the social realm is much more recent. Systems analysis for the purpose of solving practical problems has been employed in both private and public administration for some decades. In public administration it was the Defense Department which first made extensive use of systems analysis. The technique clearly has practical application wherever the organization itself controls the system in question. The logical services of the military or the manufacturing processes of industry may be thought of as essentially closed systems. When the system concept came to the cities, however, its application was much more complicated and often baffling due to the presence of exogenous forces, which constantly affected the system, as well as to the relatively rapid change processes that constantly took place. This has been well pointed out by Belknap and Schussheim (Belknap and Schussheim, 1965, pp. 3-16). It is true that the exogenous forces can be dealt with on a system basis when all the systems which relate to each other are fully understood, but we are far from penetrating these complexities. In short, we do not have accurate models of the urban system as a whole.

What we do have may be described at three levels. At the *first*, the theoretical level, academic theorists in economics and regional science, in urban sociology, and in political science are attempting to define and measure relevant system variables. We may dismiss this level for present purposes, except to observe that the dissemination of a popularized model, such as the monolithic political power structure model, tends to make actors on the urban stage behave as though the model were in fact reality. This is an unnerving development to the scientific analyst and suggests the distance we still have to go.

At the opposite extreme, the *second* level, we find micro-system analysis in both public administration and planning. There are various examples such as cost-benefit analysis of specific proposed projects employed by both planners and administrators. Perhaps the most notable development has been the use of programming and scheduling procedures which provide a planning element in "routine" administration which has been heretofore missing. The first of these procedures is the "critical path method" (CPM) developed in 1958 by a group of engineers who sought to employ computers in planning. The second was developed for the same purpose shortly afterwards by the Navy and is called the "program evaluation and review technique" (PERT). The two, independently created, were so similar that they have now merged into one system. Essentially the program in question is divided into its component processes. These are represented graphically on a chart with arrows indicating how each component of the program relates to the others, including particularly the time relationship. Observation of the diagram, when it has been constructed, reveals what is the critical operation at any given time in order to achieve the program goals with minimum time and effort. The end-on-end series of critical operations constitute the critical path. This technique is skillfully summarized in *Program Development and Administration* issued by the International City Managers Association (ICMA, 1965, pp. 41-48). It has been used to advantage in urban budgeting (Wahl, 1964, pp. 29-33). In 1962 it was applied successfully to preparation of the Community Renewal Program in Philadelphia (ICMA, 1965, pp. 32-40). This development is a specific illustration of the general thesis of this chapter, that administration and planning are becoming more closely integrated. Both professions are using the same technique of micro-system analysis.

Between these two extremes of the theoretical and the applied, we find the *third* level, the whole exciting area of operations research as a sort of middle-level systems analysis. Operations research relies on the construction of models, the quantification of variables, and the use of Electronic Data Processing (EDP) to manipulate the models. The object is to provide a quantitative basis for decision-making. Operations research has made real contributions in situations where many of the relevant variables are subject to control, where few variables are not subject to control, where variables are quantifiable for measurement purposes, and where the variables in the system tend to persist over time. It involves problem-solving in the sense of analysis, forecasting, and extracting generalizations from the data (Ronayne, 1963, pp. 227-234).

A variety of specific techniques have been employed. One of the earlier ones is *queuing*, a means of processing efficiently elements with uncertain times of arrival. *Probability* theory is used to achieve such purposes as reducing idle facilities, permitting minimum inventory, and achieving efficient use of manpower. *Monte Carlo* involves a trial and error method of making repeated calculations in order to arrive at the most effective solution to a problem. This is particularly useful when there is a minimum of previous experience on which to rely. *Linear programming* is increasingly used in planning operations. It can be used, for example, to maximize a predetermined goal in the presence of limited resources of specified kinds. The problem is to find the proper mix of resource use. Linear programming involves a straight-line relationship among variables. If this situation does not exist, *dynamic programming* can be used, a more complex technique. *Game theory* is concerned with selecting the best strategy in a conflict situation. While it has no tested application in planning or administration as yet, a further theoretical development along these lines could be of immense utility, so far as the professional is concerned, in filling the information gap represented by the political factors in urban policy-making.

Finally, *simulation* is employed in both administration and urban planning. A model (a simplified abstraction of some real situation) is constructed of the relevant variables; and the simulation is effected by running the model through the computer. In one application, for instance, one of the variables is changed for each computer run in order to see what change is produced with each combination. When one significant variable is observed changing in the real world, one can use simulation to gauge the likely long-run effect. A similar change in the model will indicate the consequence of the change in real life. The Port of New York Authority has used this technique effectively to develop improved traffic control measures. In planning, Arthur Maass and Maynard Hufschmidt have constructed a model of a hypothetical river basin system, manipulating twelve variables (Maass *et al.*, 1962, pp. 247-559). While simulation is normally associated with the computer, it should be noted that experiments have been conducted in *actor simulation* of political decision-making processes in urban communities at M.I.T., Tufts, the University of North Carolina, and more recently at other universities (Scott, Lucas, and Lucas, 1966, pp. 119-158). The further development and analysis of actor simulation will be necessary if we are to begin to deal systematically with the poltico-psychological elements in urban policy-making through quantifiable variables.

Urban Information Systems

While the above types of operations and systems analysis represent the beginnings of a system of decision-making for urban areas, we have not stressed the obvious point that any decision system must be built on great quantities of relevant information.

Urban information systems, relying heavily on EDP, are in their infancy, though some significant developments suggest that major breakthroughs are imminent in this area.

While systems analysis and operations research techniques seem equally applicable to planning and to administrative implementation, the same is not true of information systems. The consensus is that different kinds of information are required for planning and for administrative management (Grundstein, 1966, pp. 21-32; and Mindlin, 1963, pp. 209-218). It is naive to think that simply gathering every kind of information and placing it in a central data bank will solve management and planning problems. The encouraging part of the question, however, is the tremendous increase in our capacity to process and to store information and then to retrieve it. This ability is a development of the past decade, and it is only in its incipient stages. What we are just beginning to realize is that an urban information system will be effective in proportion to our ability to feed useful information to the right place at the right time. The central data bank is only a solution for those with time to spend, in effect, "in the library." Computer technology is or soon will be at the point where it is possible to transmit a variety of kinds of information from one computer to another. Thus, it is no longer a question of centralized versus decentralized computer operations in a major urban area. It is a question of employing standardized computer languages so that the planner's computer can draw from a central data bank, or from any of the computers employed in the operating agencies, and vice versa.

It is quite possible that the real bottlenecks will be (1) knowing what data to gather and in what form, (2) devising a way of standardizing data collection over entire metropolitan areas, and (3) convincing political actors to permit the monitoring of public attitudes and the use of this information for planning purposes. In an integrated metropolitan decision system for planning and management, this last element would be crucial since it would permit the quantification of some of the political variables. Once these bottlenecks are broken, an exciting new era of urban development could emerge. First, a new "information environment" would exist, potentially for all public and private interests alike, as Lowden Wingo has suggested (Wingo, 1966, pp. 143-151). With this new environment, behaviors would begin to change, following the new levels of information available. One can imagine a much heavier reliance on the "partisan mutual adjustment" of which Charles E. Lindblom speaks (Lindblom, 1965). Such a system would no doubt strengthen existing trends toward incremental decision-making as well as bring the planning system and the management control system into even closer relationships than is now the case (we return to both of these points below).

We must descend from this vision to consider what evidence exists that the vision sometime may be reality. Data collection was cited as a major bottleneck, despite the outpouring of recent information on urban problems. Administrators have long used EDP for specific operations in overhead management, collecting data on personnel, materiel, and finances as a basis for expediting routine tasks. In program areas the uses of EDP by the U.S. Census, labor statistics, Veterans' Administration Insurance, and other programs are well known. In engineering for space, in nuclear energy, in weather forecasting, and in highway engineering other uses of EDP are far advanced. In urban government such applications are not far advanced, though some cities like New Orleans have used computers for a variety of purposes such as accounting for appropriations, payrolls, and taxes. In general, however, local government records are not automated, they are not in a form useful to agencies other than the one which collects them, and they are not standardized from one jurisdiction to another, even when these overlap geographically. To be sure, efforts are underway to remedy this situation.

The Urban Renewal Administration has given some demonstration grants which involve experiments in establishing metropolitan data centers. The most notable is the center located in Tulsa, which is intended to assemble data necessary for an urban decision-making system utilizing data in such fields as planning, renewal, urban economics, sociology, geography, engineering, and administration. In June of 1965 the National League of Cities sponsored a conference on a system of urban observatories, some dimensions of which are already developing at the universities participating in the conference – Wisconsin, Harvard, M.I.T., and Rutgers. The Urban Development Bill of 1966 contained a proposal for the establishment of a series of Urban Information Centers. Grants for this purpose, under the bill, would be made to states and metropolitan area-wide agencies. With federal financing this particular bottleneck could begin to crack.

The storage and retrieval of data has long been a major challenge. Certain kinds of routine, management-oriented data can readily be stored and retrieved through EDP, as has been noted. More complex types of information, such as books for example, are a difficult matter. Yet planners require all kinds of information in their research activities. The first breakthrough in this field came as the result of the cooperation of a variety of agencies; it is known as URBANDOC, which refers to computerized documentation and information retrieval of urban planning and renewal literature. The project was assisted by grants from the Urban Renewal Administration and the Taconic Foundation; and it involved the cooperation of the American Institute of Planners, New York Public Library, the Council of Planning Librarians, Institute of Public Administration, IBM, and the New York Department of City Planing. An experimental model system of document storage and retrieval has been created, based on a carefully selected 200 item test library, and the reports of progress are most encouraging.

A large number of computer applications in urban planning have already proven successful. These include major studies of transportation, urban renewal, land use, central business district uses – horizontal and vertical – population, housing, employment, vital statistics, zoning, and subdivision control, among other topics (Lamoureaux, 1961). Finally, the technology of computers talking to computers has proven workable. For example, in the Research Triangle of North Carolina a central computer at the Research Triangle Park is connected with computers at the three universities in the area as well as with other research installations. The purpose of these connections is not primarily to disseminate data but rather to enable any single computer to engage in complex programming and computations according to instructions sent from other computers in the system. This will make it possible to engage in complex research at any of the institutions. This system will soon be extended to the other colleges of the state.

NEW PRESSURES AND THE ROLE OF THE GENERALIST PLANNER

Just as the goals and techniques of planners within the governmental structure have been changing, the *roles* of the planner within the system are changing as well. One might simplify by saying that planners who used to create plans are now coordinating decisions. The decisions they are coordinating are primarily those of a developmental type. We have already noted that the techniques contributing to planning decisions (that is, decisions about matters subject to planning) have proliferated and become highly specialized. This in itself requires the conscious mixing together of information derived from complex processes. But, as a result of several forces, planning is now coordinative in a much broader sense than this.

The first of these forces is the "mobiletic revolution" as Bertram M. Gross has described it (Gross, 1966, p. 4), which refers to our tremendously increased ability to be mobile in terms of things, people, energy, and communications. Concurrent with the mobiletic revolution, and presumably a part of it, is the greatly increased scale of non-governmental organizational forms of all kinds. It is perhaps a paradox that while more and more of the activity of the human race takes place in cities, the importance of the city boundary has waned. It has become much more permeable. What happens in cities is increasingly dependent on decisions made in decision centers of giant corporations, foundations, governments, unions, social movements, and even international organizations of various sorts. All of these transcend municipal boundaries. Yet the city is the seat of culture and the engine of progress, we are told. More of our people live in cities every day. The dilemma resolves itself insofar as the urban governments are able to mold the exogenous forces which play upon them and the things they directly control into an acceptable physical and social system. This requires coordination of the most professionally competent type.

PROLIFERATION OF FEDERAL AND STATE PROGRAMS

While we cannot, in the space available, refer to all of the exogenous forces which impinge on the work of urban policy-making, we can approximate this by tracing recent trends in urban policy of the United States government. Many of the other forces are expressed through the channel of federal action. During World War II large sums were spent in urban areas impacted by booming war activities. These aids have continued in one form or another, but with relatively little impact on urban administration and policy in general. What is notable is that the aids were administered by the local governments without detailed federal controls. New schools were built and new sewers constructed in the usual way.

Far more important were the landmark housing acts. The original act was passed in 1937, and it was further developed through major amendments in 1949, 1954, 1961, and 1965. The 1966 Urban Development Bill seeks to continue the process of innovation. The original acts were only a foretaste of the revolution in urban administration and policy-making that was to come. Public housing originally created a new urban entity, the housing authority, and a new program somewhat distant from the "regular" city government. When the slums did not disappear, a new program – slum clearance and redevelopment – was adopted. This new program required a variety of techniques to be applied successively before the new area was "redeveloped." A new type of local authority was created to handle land acquisition, clearance, project planning, and reconstruction. Now it appeared that housing was not alone the necessary object of treatment. Related facilities became involved, including commercial centers and industrial installations. The program soon became known as urban renewal, and other new processes became involved, such as residential and commercial relocation. New procedures were added to the old, including more planning, the "workable program," and the application of rehabilitation to areas not needing total renewal. (See Chapter 20 by Robert Weaver for the details of the federally assisted programs.)

By this time it was apparent that coordination of a variety of local and federal programs was needed in order to prosecute renewal effectively. Local code enforcement, local public works programs, local service programs, federal home loans, federal urban highway aids, public housing programs all had to be coordinated if urban renewal projects were to succeed. The city itself had to assume this role. Next, therefore, came the Community Renewal Program (CRP) officially described as :

> . . . a method for assessing in broad terms the community's overall needs for urban renewal and developing a stage program for action to meet these needs, commensurate with the resources available to the community. The CRP covers the entire community, including both residential and nonresidential areas, and takes into consideration renewal activities which may be undertaken either with or without Federal assistance (U.S. URA, 1963, p. 1).

The CRP is an extension of general planning, grants for which are available only when general planning as prescribed in the urban renewal manual is in progress. The CRP was not originally a prerequisite for other aid when adopted in 1959, but it is increasingly expected by the URA. With the federal government saying that planning precedent to urban renewal and other aids must be comprehensive rather than project-oriented, the problem of urban planning became more complex. The CRP policy does not provide for aid for transportation planning, now covered by other department grants and grants from the Bureau of Public Roads; nor does it aid activities sponsored by the Area Redevelopment Administration. It does require that cognizance be taken of these planning-related activities however.

The federal programs not only stimulated but required planning activity in every aided city. A more and more crucial kind of planning datum was knowledge of the thickening federal manuals. Key expertise in the urban renewal program was the ability to predict responses of the federal bureaucracy and to represent the city's case to maximum advantage when a new interpretation was pending – an interpretation which was soon to become encased in the manual. The cities were not merely pawns in the game; but their planners, administrators, mayors, and political friends employed their persuasive skills through all available channels when the time came to amend the legislation itself. This required another sort of planning, with its rather pale reflection in the state capitols where authority to proceed under federal grants had to be enacted into law.

By 1960 the relation of the cities to the federal government was not unlike that developed years before between state health, welfare, and other agencies relying heavily on federal aids. Manual-oriented grant-in-aid programs had blossomed with some tendency to proliferate local grant-administering agencies. After 1960 new urban programs were added even more rapidly, partly under the stimulus of the Housing and Home Finance Agency, the precursor of the newly created Department of Housing and Urban Development (HUD). These new programs included aid for urban mass transportation, purchase of open space, urban beautification, rent supplements for certain low-income families, low interest loans for certain families in renewal programs, park renovation, and establishment of neighborhood centers. A variety of programs of other departments and agencies are relevant to solution of urban problems: the Civil Rights Act, Medicare, aid to education, and the Economic Opportunity Act are perhaps the most notable.

The broader consequences of these new policies have been evaluated in detail by Roscoe Martin in *The Cities and The Federal System* (Martin, 1965). He argues the position that the cities have emerged as a new partner in the federal system as a result of these increasing direct relationships. Only the tremendous efforts diverted to space programs and the Viet Nam war have prevented the consummation of a genuine revolution in federal urban policy. The new urban policy is, moreover, a self-conscious one. President Johnson has called it "creative federalism," perhaps to distinguish it from "cooperative federalism" and the "new federalism" of the 1930s and the 1940s. It is important to recognize that creative federalism is not merely a quantitative increase in direct federal-local relations. A very new qualitative change presently is emerging, its ideology best expressed by spokesmen of HUD in connection with statements supporting the Housing and Urban Development Bill of 1966. This new ideology is founded on the idea that the national government is responsible for developing and administering a "Federal strategy for urban development" (Weaver, 1965, p. 6). In contrast to the single shot, specific objective programs of the past, the new approach is characterized by three qualities – flexibility, coordination, and creativity.

Secretary Weaver and Under Secretary Wood constantly reiterate the variety of programs available as tools from which cities can select the appropriate combination with which to attack their particular urban problems. Significantly, the HUD officials not only emphasize the programs of HUD but also the urban oriented activities of other agencies. As a result of the wide variety of activities in which a city may join with the federal government, the second element, coordination, becomes crucial. Repeated emphasis has been given to the need for comprehensive development, integrated growth patterns, concentration of resources, mobilization of resources, balanced growth of the urban environment, and similar phrases. Finally, an increasing emphasis is being placed on innovation, ingenuity, and inventiveness as being essential for creating new solutions to unresolved problems.

In order to implement this kind of creative federalism in the urban areas, three specific techniques have been advanced, and others can be expected. The *first* of these specific techniques has been developing over a period of years. It is the reliance on local plans to coordinate multi-source programs. By the end of 1965 Robert Weaver could cite twelve federal grant-in-aid urban programs (of more than 120 that have been identified) which required planning as a condition to the grant. These included programs for urban mass transportation, sewer and water facilities, open space land, neighborhood facilities, urban beautification, urban renewal, Federal Housing Agency (FHA), mortgage insurance for land development, grants for advance acquisition of land, advances for public works planning, land acquisition for outdoor recreation under the land and water conservation programs, airport aid, waste treatment plants, and education and health facilities. Several of these are not programs of HUD, and the list is not exhaustive. (Weaver, 1965, p. 7). The justification for the planning requirement, in Weaver's words

> . . . is to direct and coordinate Federal urban assistance programs in order to gain the maximum impact from the Federal investment in urban areas. Planning requirements help create the intergovernmental channel essential to a concerted, orderly, and rational attack on a wide range of urban development problems. To be effective, planning obviously must be part of the total urban development process – planning without active, fully funded development programs is little more than an intellectual exercise. We will continue to stress the need for planning to be action oriented, to be an effective guide for the functional programs being assisted (Weaver, 1965, pp. 7-8).

The *second* technique is embodied in the Demonstration Cities legislation before Congress in 1966. This approach is based on the idea that the elements needed to attack urban problems are already at hand in the cities, and that what is needed is coordination and federal funds to support demonstrations that will show how a coordinative approach can work. To this end, the city would select a large target area. Federal funds would finance 90 per cent of the initial planning for the demonstration program and would also finance 80 per cent of the *local share* of the various existing federal programs to be involved in the target area. The 80 per cent would be *in addition* to the grants regularly available. What is particularly notable about the Demonstration Cities Act is that the 80 per cent contribution would be totally *unearmarked,* except that it would have to be spent within the demonstration program objectives.

This innovation would begin to reverse the "manual" approach which is now so prevalent. Instead of the manual, HUD would provide a "Federal Coordinator" in the city who would assist in the meshing of the federal programs.

The *third* technique is the metropolitan planning program. This proposal would provide federal grants of up to 20 per cent of the cost of construction of projects which significantly effect the growth of metropolitan areas – like transportation, water and sewer, and recreation facilities. The aid would only be given to metropolitan areas which had established area-wide comprehensive planning and programming. Allied to this proposal is the "Metropolitan Desk" which refers to an HUD provided resident coordinator for federal programs in the metropolitan area as described in detail by Robert Aleshire of the Advisory Commission on Intergovernmental Relations (Aleshire, 1966, pp. 87-95). The functions of the metropolitan desk would in itself be a matter for experimentation, but presumably would include providing information, stimulating local participation in metropolitan problems, generating ideas, and serving as a "convener" for planning or conflict resolution purposes. This proposal has found considerably more support from among federal officials who would be involved than from governors and mayors, who continue to be suspicious of it.

Whatever the fate of the federal coordination devices, the proliferation of federal urban aids will increasingly require the city to integrate the federally presented opportunities into a city planning program. If the city is part of a complex metropolitan area, this need for coordination will have a multi-municipal spatial dimension in addition to the program dimension. That is, coordination with the federal programs will be complicated by the need to coordinate with other governments in the metropolitan area. In addition to this, a number of states have programs and agencies with which the cities must deal. Urban planning assistance is a traditional program by now in most states. Furthermore, Rhode Island, Alaska, New York, New Jersey, and Pennsylvania have departments of urban affairs. In 1965 California established a Department of Housing and Community Development. All of these exogenous influences – mostly stimulants coming in the form of cash incentives – must be coordinated by the local urban planner if he is to exploit all the opportunities for the development of his community. In this context, when we say "planner" we include renewal coordinators and other functionaries who have specialized a portion of the planner's total role.

Social Science and the Policy Decision Process

The expansion of the planner's function from one of narrow technical calculations to coordinative relations with a variety of administrative entities, however, is by no means the only change in his role during the past twenty years. Another major source of change stems from contemporary social science research and thinking. We may divide this into two major categories: decision-making insights and insights into the political context of public planning.

The planner's early model of rational decision-making was allied to that of the engineer and architect who manipulated physical objects subject to a limited number of variables. By the 1950s urban planners had begun to employ quantitative data from economics and demography. These additions fit very well into the rational decision model that has since been described as *synoptic*. Very generally, this model was based on the notion that policy-making was or could be based on specific goals. These goals were of different sorts, but it was possible to measure their social values approximately. Planning constituted studies of all possible means of maximizing these goals and the selection of that combination of means which produced the greatest social utility. Political processes only interfered with this rational-scientific method of planning. Planners admitted that it was proper for political authorities to take the product and adopt it or not, but the making of the plan itself was not a part of the political process. The product of the planner, then, was a technical one, frequently a master plan for the city.

More recently the synoptic approach has been attacked on the grounds that it is not in fact rational for specific reasons. The case has been expressed at greatest length by Braybrooke and Lindblom (Braybrooke and Lindblom, 1963). Man has only limited capacity to understand the complexities involved in social planning. The information at his command is limited. Analysis of the kind demanded by the model would be excessively costly. No measures had in fact been operationalized with which to compare differing (and often conflicting) goals. Systems undergoing analysis are subject to change from endogenous and exogenous forces which tends to render any analysis obsolete before it can be implemented. The dissimilarity of problem situations makes it difficult to employ past analyses and experience. In place of the synoptic model, Lindblom has suggested a strategy of disjointed-incrementalism. Essentially this involves making limited decisions on problems as they present themselves and in terms of the best information available.

Now, the two systems are not as analytically distinct as one might think, since choices must still be made between values that cannot be measured, but the strategy of the planner or policy-maker is deeply affected by the new approach. The present author is suggesting that planners are in fact becoming coordinators of a variety of forces at play in the urban area. Lindblom's analysis attacks even the rationality of central coordination, arguing that *partisan* (self-seeking) *mutual adjustment* is not only prevalent and practicable, but rational as well (Lindblom, 1965).

The effect of the debate between the relationalists and the incrementalists, clearly, has been to increase the respectability of that professional planning which does not require a comprehensive general plan as an end product but justifies itself on the basis of marginal impacts on a set of strong forces within the area only partially understood and even less subject to control.

A *second* product of the social scientist which has been avidly consumed by the professional planner has been the "power structure" literature. Since the job of the planner is to produce (or prevent) change through governmental action, his function by its very nature is a political one. The students of urban politics have shown that decisions in urban politics are made on the basis of the use of power—however monolithically or pluralistically exercised—and not on the basis of an abstract model of a better community. The role of the planner in the political process and his attitude toward it has been the subject of increasing analysis (Daland and Parker, 1962; and Meyerson and Banfield, 1965; Altshuler, 1965). Most planners today recognize that plans to be useful must be implemented and to be implemented must be politically acceptable. It is now respectable for the planner to verbalize his understanding of the urban power structure. The area of controversy has moved from whether planning is a part of the political process to the precise political role of the planner. No consensus seems to have appeared on where the planner should be as between simply operating within the existing political norms and acting to change those norms. In a series of investigations at the University of North Carolina the precise role seemed to be related to the personality of the planner, the history of the planner's role in the city in question, and to the age of the planner. Younger planners tend to see a greater role in political innovation. While little empirical evidence has been assembled to show that the planner's role is increasingly being politicised, the increasing number of writings by planners and others on the subject is suggestive. One of the more interesting strands of thought has been advanced by Paul Davidoff who advocates the establishment of "majority" and "minority" staffs in planning departments as a contribution to political pluralism (Davidoff, 1965, p. 335).

In summary, the strands which combine to force the urban planner into a coordinative — which is to say administrative — role, include the specialization of knowledge and expertise both within and outside the planning staff, the proliferation of state and particularly national urban programs, the doctrine of incrementalism in decision-making, and recognition that implementation requires political action at some level.

ADMINISTRATION AND ORGANIZATION FOR URBAN PLANNING

As the goals, techniques, and roles of planners have been changing in urban areas, organization for planning has changed, though this change has lagged behind the other developments. We need not dwell at length on a subject which is by now much discussed and obvious. Two decades ago Robert Walker seems to have opened the debate in his doctoral dissertation, later published as *The Planning Function in Urban Government* (Walker, 1941). He attacked the validity of the independent planning commission as a proper organizational home for what was to him an integral part of the process of governmental administration. The debate was joined for many years and still continues. The planning commission and the zoning board had become written into the laws of most states following the model act born in the Department of Commerce in 1928. For years the planning commissions and city councils went their separate ways. Where planning was implemented, it was not through city management but through the less direct operations of influentials of the community, often the Chamber of Commerce.

During the 1940s capital budgeting became prominent in urban budgeting practice and for the first time planners and budget administrators came face to face – at least in some cities. Often enough the capital portion of the budget was prepared in the planning office and the final figures were incorporated by the budgeteers in their document. Yet, the suspicion of planners on the part of managers and budgeteers continued. City management began to develop program and performance budgeting for operating programs, and to engage in activities suspiciously like planning, while not called planning. But the courtship never really started until the advent of urban renewal. This process demanded cooperation among planners, management staff, and operating departments. Even though organizationally there were four or five semi-autonomous agencies operating in housing, renewal, utility systems, planning, and zoning in addition to the departments under the municipal executive, this cooperation was still necessary.

Increasingly the answer has come through the device either of creating a new administrative entity, a development coordinator or of administrative reorganization to create a department of development, or sometimes both. The urgent need to coordinate through one of these means resulted from the simple fact that in order to get the maximum of outside (federal and state) funds, urban renewal had to be under one directing head. With reorganization, current budget expenditures could probably provide the local resources with which to match federal funds; without coordination there would be substantial losses. While many authorities have urged the integration of planning and urban development activities into the city administrative hierarchy (Walker, Fagin, Duggar, and Perloff for example), there is also evidence that integrated structure *in fact* improves performance. In a study of relocation programs, this point has been emphasized by Harry R. Reynolds (Reynolds, 1964, pp. 14-20). When legal authority remained dispersed due to state law, the development coordinator was the usual instrument, as in Baltimore, Philadelphia, Boston, Chicago, Pittsburgh, and San Francisco. Other cities moved to create a regular line department, like Milwaukee, Syracuse, Buffalo, Cincinnati, and Cleveland (Moravitz, 1964).

Where departments were formed, they had varying collections of the renewal-relevant agencies – with or without planning. At present the organization for planning and planning implementation is in a great state of flux. The trend is undeniable, however, that formal planning tends to move away from the old commission and into the orbit of regular urban management agencies under the municipal executive. Jerome Kaufman has recently reported this tendency from the perspective of the planning commission (Kaufman, 1966, pp. 221-227). While only a few planning commissions have disappeared completely, their functions have been receding rapidly. Frequently they have been relegated to an advisory role. Some remain chiefly as sounding boards or as a device for public opinion inputs. This is not to say that multi-member bodies are about to disappear from the planning scene. In fact, they appear to be on the increase so far as numbers are concerned in the sense that the old boards continue while the newer renewal and housing authorities are created. In addition, there has been a rapid proliferation of citizen groups and metropolitan affairs non-profit corporations, which have sometimes exercised strong leadership in planning (Mathewson, 1965). These competitors to official planning bodies contribute even further to the weakening of the planning commission.

While such bodies frequently perform valuable services for planning, they are not preventing the integration of the professional planning staff into the city administration. Whether overall planning will settle in the office of the executive with the operating aspects of development administration in a line department (which seems likely), or whether planning will fragment into various locations within the city hierarchy depending on the specialty in question, cannot be predicted with accuracy. The solidarity of the profession as expressed through the American Institute of Planners, and reinforced by increasingly generalist-oriented planning schools, however, suggests that "planners" will remain together in a planning staff distinct from the coordinators of development. If this proves to be the case in the long run, the role of the planner may not continue to be coordinative but may become more technical. This development can already be noted in some large cities despite a *general* tendency for the planner to be a coordinator today. This matter will be affected materially by the distribution of planning responsibility as between metropolitan level instrumentalities and the municipality. With significant planning developing at the metropolitan level, which has already happened in transportation planning, for example, the municipal planner will continue to be a coordinator with the metro staff to a significant degree. Whether the federal contacts will eventually move from municipalities to metropolitan authorities or governments is another variable which it would be hazardous to predict. The present trend is to stimulate metropolitan planning institutions, but this has so far proven one of the difficult tasks of institution-building in the United States.

We would be remiss not to notice the motivation for the change in planning and development organization in the political sense. Where reorganization has occurred, in most cases it has not been the planner who has instigated it. Rather, it has been the municipal executive, typically a strong mayor. It is because urban politics has become development politics that urban planning goals have changed, and in their turn, organization for urban planning.

IMPLICATIONS

Walter Lippmann says that "the problem of governing a great city like New York is by all odds the most important, the most pressing, and the most unavoidable domestic problem we have to face" (Lippmann, 1965, p. A13). Frederic N. Cleaveland, in a critique of Congress' approach to urban problems, notes the contrast between the efforts from the White House to deal meaningfully with urban problems and the inadequacy of Congress to meet the challenge (Cleaveland, 1966, pp. 289-307). It seems clear that urban problems will become more critical and that neither the states nor Congress are capable of significant action. This action must come from the White House or from the metropolitan areas themselves. With respect to the latter alternative, Frank Smallwood has pointed out that the United States style of creating metropolitan institutions is considerably less effective than that of the British or the Canadians (Smallwood, 1965, pp. 191-197). Federal government pressure is what will change the institutions of metropolitan America. If one wishes to avoid having urban policy made in Washington, policy-making roles within structured policy-making systems of decision will have to be clarified locally if indeed, it is not already too late.

Already the municipalities are losing their relevance as centers of decision for major urban policy, due to their limited controls over what goes on within their boundaries. Bertram Gross says that "The conversion of large metropoli into megalopoli administers the *coup de grace* to the vision of the true-bounded urban region with a local government capable of unified action throughout the area" (Gross, 1966, p. 4). Should this seem pessimistic to some, we need to work the harder on the development of the technology of urban-regional decision systems, wherever the final political decision may rest. As this occurs, the planning generalist near that authoritative decision center will find that technical information becomes more and more marginal to his role. The number of specialties will be beyond his ability to master. He will be concerned with the outputs of more and more mechanized decision systems, and he will increasingly be able to deal with the political system on the basis of specific information as to how it works. On the other hand, he will be closely tied to the administrative system that implements urban development and for which his staff will constitute a crucial input. He will also require regular feedback from a system which monitors administrative activity to make sure that this becomes data for the various planning specialists under his supervision. Nothing resembling this planning-communications-administrative system is at hand, but significant steps toward almost all of the elements of such a system have been taken within the past two decades, as we have tried to show.

18

Moving from Plan to Reality

WILLIAM L. C. WHEATON

☐ DURING THE TWENTY-YEAR PERIOD 1945-1965, there has been a rapid growth in the scope of planning, in the evolution of institutions for the execution of planned programs of urban development, and in the resources of money, legal power, public opinion, and personnel required to make planning operational in American society. At the beginning of the period, the scope, powers and institutions for planning, despite a long and slow prior evolution, were narrow and limited, largely lacking influence in public policy. By the end of the period it is possible to enumerate powers and programs and provide examples of the use of a broad complement of these resources in many cities. These resources are now broad enough in scope to carry out any plan yet prepared and published by any city in the United States. Financial limitations remain, of course, and the application of all of the methods now available has been spotty. No city exhibits a complete program, and no city has produced a complete plan. Most important, planning for metropolitan areas remains in the state of advocacy or early experimentation, and the execution of metropolitan plans has nowhere begun. In view of the enormous progress made within cities, however, it is fair to anticipate an equally rapid evolution of metropolitan powers in the decade ahead.

PLANNING AND ACTION IN 1945

Prior to World War II, the scope of city planning was almost entirely limited to physical land use and public community facilities planning. The milestone plans of the preceding decades, those for the New York and Philadelphia regions, confined their attention to land use, transportation facilities, parks and recreation, educational facilities, utilities, and other physical works. The powers available for carrying out these plans were limited to the exercise of the police power, chiefly through zoning, building codes, and subdivision codes, the power of condemnation for public works, the power to spend for traditional public works, and the power to inform and exhort. A reading either of the plans of those days (Regional Planning Federation of the Philadelphia Tri-State District, 1932) or of the texts on planning (Segoe *et al.*, 1941) confirms this fact. Although the power to tax is mentioned, its effective use to secure planned physical development objectives was virtually unknown. Capital budgets as a means of coordinating the provision of public works were widely discussed, but only in New York City and a few other places were there beginning attempts to use this device.

More strikingly, prior to 1940 the plans and the texts deal exclusively with economic development as essential to the community, but propose few actions except discussion to correct any economic deficiencies found or to alter the course of economic development. In the spirit of the 1920s, this extremely conservative posture could be understood. At the end of the 1930s, it is almost incomprehensible – a testimony to the conservatism of planning institutions and practice. Similarly, although the plans refer extensively to inventories of housing condition and programs to clear slums or to rehabilitate blighted areas, the only means mentioned for the execution of any resulting plans is the public housing program authorized by the Congress in 1937. The enforcement of codes is scarcely mentioned. The idea of planning for employment, social security, human welfare, the renewal or reconstruction of cities, or other now widely accepted social goals, does not appear in city planning literature.

This conservatism is all the more striking because in the decade of the 1930s, the National Resources Planning Board (NRPB) was engaged in the development of methods and the exploration of goals in all of these fields. It published reports on full employment, social security, medical care, manpower development and education, housing and renewal, technology, natural resource conservation, transportation, recreation, and leisure; and it enunciated goals in each of these fields. Further, it conducted experiments in several cities with the development of local goals and methods which resulted, subsequent to its demise, in the publication of a far-sighted document, *Action for Cities – A Guide for Community Planning*

(American Municipal Association, 1943). In *Action for Cities,* the result of the NRPB's thinking about city planning, a far broader concept of the goals and scope of planning is enumerated, including goals for economic development and employment, education and cultural development, leisure and physical development. But here again, the means to be employed are largely confined to the traditional means concerned with land use planning and physical development, the programming of public service programs, public facilities and, insofar as the private economy is concerned, research, information, and advocacy.

THE EVOLUTION OF POWERS

During the next twenty years, programs were to be devised and carried out in almost every major city of the United States to implement the type of planning that the NRPB suggested but on which the plans of the period are silent. Thus, the subsequent period was one of rapid evolution from a state in which public responsibility was assumed to extend only to the provision of a framework within which private enterprise and initiative could operate, through successive stages, to its present state. The expansion occurred during the 1930s, largely at the initiative of the federal government, first in the provision of a broader range of services and of human relief. Later the national responsibility for maintaining full employment through public works, and without altering the private economy, was added. Local government rarely accepted direct responsibility in this field. Still later, the public, and especially the national, responsibility for providing financial aids and incentives for private initiative was added to the accepted roster of public powers, particularly through the Reconstruction Finance Corporation, the Home Owners' Loan Corporation, and the Federal Housing Administration. These were ingenious methods for public intervention into the private economy in the form of "aids" which were painless, highly acceptable to the recipient, and susceptible of classification within the rhetoric of the free enterprise system. Only after World War II, however, did there emerge a public acceptance of public initiative and participation in mixed enterprises, largely through urban renewal and housing but secondarily in economic development, which has by now clearly created the mixed enterprise society.

This striking development has occurred largely through the broadening of our national and local concepts of the power to spend and the appropriate fields for government expenditure. But it has been accompanied by a somewhat less dramatic evolution in judicial interpretation, a broadening of the construction of the police power and of the power of condemnation. Certainly the most important field of expansion was in urban renewal, where the federal government withdrew from the exercise of condemnation powers in the Louisville case *(U.S. v. Certain Lands in the City of Louisville*, 1935) rather than press its claims and thereafter relied upon state and local powers in this field. During and immediately after World War II, however, state courts widely upheld the power of local agencies to condemn land for the purpose of eliminating slums. These powers were steadily expanded in the next decade until the United States Supreme Court could hold that it was legal for cities to condemn land for the purpose of clearing slums or achieving beauty, for the provision of private housing, industrial development, or any other purpose which a legislature had authorized *(Berman v. Parker*, 1954). The parallel acceptance of the power of local public agencies to purchase and later to condemn land for purposes of industrial development, particularly in depressed areas, opened the field to the widest public action in the reconstruction of cities.

A similar evolution in the police power was occurring year by year. While building codes and tenement laws had been adopted nearly a quarter of a century earlier, in the period following World War II these concepts were extended, in the form of housing codes, to the enforcement of minimum standards of maintenance and occupancy of dwellings. The liability of landlords and owners has been extended to countenance, in the state of New York, the refusal to pay rent and the establishment by judicial or administrative action of receiverships through which properties could in effect be seized where not maintained in accordance with law. Under New York law tenants can be either relieved of their obligation to pay rent or permitted to pay rent into a public or private receivers' fund to be used for the maintenance, repair, and rehabilitation of the substandard structure.

There has been a similar, but less dramatic evolution in the powers available for the regulation of land use and new development. Subdivision approvals may now require that a developer set aside parts of his development for public recreational use and schools, or make payments into a fund for the acquisition of sites for such purposes. Space and density standards, clearly unnecessary for public health but merely desired by a local community, ostensibly for the maintenance of property values or amenity, have been widely accepted by the courts, and agricultural zones too have been accepted, thus enlarging the power to regulate land use far beyond the limits which would have been accepted in the 1920s or the 1930s. On the other hand, a gap remains in regulatory powers between the permissible regulation that does not constitute a taking and therefore does not require compensation and the regulation that manifestly constitutes a taking and for which there are no means for compensation. There has, however, been much experimentation with the purchase or condemnation of a part of a fee as in special easements on scenic highways, around park entrances, and the like. While proposals of means to close these regulatory gaps have been widely discussed, none has been enacted or tested on a general basis (Strong, 1965).

The most dramatic evolution in the means for the implementation of plans, however, has occurred in the expansion of the power to spend and lend for public purposes. Here an enormous proliferation has occurred, largely upon the initiative of the federal government, which now has authorized more than 100 programs of lending or grants-in-aid to state and local governments, public and private corporations, businesses and individuals, for a very wide range of purposes (U.S. Senate Committee on Government Operations, 1966). Since most of these programs have been authorized at the behest of state or local governments, and many, if not most, are channeled through state and local agencies, there has become available a wide range of granting and lending powers to encourage or permit urban renewal, economic development, business expansion, the improvement of health, education, welfare, recreation, and business services, and to protect or aid agriculture, natural resources, transportation including highways, navigation, transit, rapid transit services, aviation and shipping — in short, for a relatively full complement of public and private services and facilities.

The states have shared in this expansion but to a considerably lesser degree. Their contributions to the financing of education and highways in particular have grown enormously in the post World War II period. But several states have authorized and aggressively pursued programs of aid to business and local economic development and a few states have authorized public loans or grants to public, private, or semi-private (non-profit) housing or for urban renewal activities of various sorts. Aside from these fields the role of the states has to date been largely one of authorizing local governments to engage in new activities, either with their own funds or with those provided by the federal government.

INVENTORY OF DEVELOPMENT POWERS

As a result of this evolution, the complement of powers available to local governments with the cooperation of the states and the federal government is now relatively complete. These powers have been used principally in the major central cities and more rarely in suburban areas. Probably no city has used them all. This enumeration is not intended to be exhaustive but rather to illustrate the range of powers available.

Among the *regulatory* powers, for instance, local governments exercise control over land use through zoning; over the quality, design, and facilities of building through building and housing codes; over the spacing of buildings, the provision of public space, streets, and utilities through subdivision codes; and indeed over the design of dwellings in some communities and in most redevelopment areas through design control ordinances or covenants attached to the sale of land and through conditions on zoning changes or subdivision approvals. These controls may be exercised over almost any type of building. A municipality may even require the incorporation of a community association to own, operate and maintain open space as a condition of the approval of the subdivision plan or building permit.

In renewal areas, land may be condemned, buildings demolished, and the area re-planned and sold for public, private, or cooperative use, for residential or non-residential purposes. In connection with a sale of renewal lands, almost any feature of the planning, construction, operation, or maintenance of the resulting facility can be subjected to public regulation through covenants or other conditions; and land price may be adjusted upward or downward in the light of design conditions, social objectives, or other desired public policies. Taxes may be partially abated where desirable or necessary to secure the achievement of the intended purpose; and land may be sold for entirely profit-making and unregulated purposes or to chosen improvement corporations, either public or private, with any degree of public financial participation, control, regulation, or participation in management. In the residential field, subsidies are available both for public housing and, to a limited extent, for private housing.

Outside of areas requiring full-scale reconstruction, the same powers are available for the clearance and rehabilitation of scattered dwellings or other blighted structures, even for non-conforming uses. Rehabilitation may be required under code enforcement; or, as mentioned earlier, covenants may be imposed on resale. Buildings can be exempted from a blanket condemnation if owners will agree to specific rehabilitation terms, and where owners are unwilling or financially unable, public agencies may intervene, rehabilitate, and sell or lease the rehabilitated structures. Recently adopted federal aids for rent subsidies in privately owned housing considerably expand the effectual powers of local agencies to rehouse low-income families in the private market.

Quite similar powers have been used with respect to non-residential areas – industrial districts, shopping centers, and the like – particularly in connection with economic development programs. Public agencies may acquire land and build factories for sale or lease to private industry, with or without federal aids, tax advantages, interest rate amortization benefits, or local tax concessions. Public agencies have used similar powers to create recreational facilities, shopping centers, convention and cultural centers, and the like. Special aids are available in the vicinity of or for such institutions as universities and hospitals.

In planning for recreation areas and open space, in addition to the traditional powers of purchase or condemnation of land for public use, local agencies have experimentally and on a limited basis begun to use zoning powers, covenants, easements, and the acquisition of partial fees to preserve selected recreational, open space, amenity, natural resource, or other features.

Probably the largest volume of expenditures has been made to date in the fields of transportation, education, and health. Public expenditures are universal for highways of all types, usually with federal and state aid, and such funds are now becoming common to subsidize, purchase, or operate transit facilities, ports, airports, heliports, ferries, buses, and hovercraft. Further, public ownership of the subsidized facilities is not necessary; and various arrangements have been devised to subsidize publicly owned but privately operated facilities or privately owned and publicly operated facilities, to purchase compliance with performance standards by private agencies, and in other ways to impose public policy controls upon private operations or facilities.

Education and health are traditional areas of government operation. What is notable here is *first*, the proliferation of specialized facilities and services to solve both broad general problems and highly specialized needs and *second*, the growth in the overall magnitude of services offered. Educational facilities for pre-school children and facilities for adult recreation and for physically handicapped, mentally handicapped, culturally deprived, and other special groups have become widely accepted.

This discussion has largely stressed the provision of physical facilities. It should be noted that in many instances the *services* that are the purpose for which a facility is built are also aided and that many types of services requiring no special facilities may be aided. Thus, during the period under consideration, welfare, social security, aid for dependent children, old age and survivors insurance, and direct relief aids to persons and families have been enormously expanded. These have been supplemented by a broad range of guidance and counseling services. Most importantly, in the field of employment services, programs have been developed to identify the unemployed and the potentially employable and their particular needs – programs to engage in or support vocational training, retraining, job finding and placement, and other services to encourage more active and effective participation in employment by the individuals served. A whole new category of welfare services is in the process of evolution under the aegis of poverty programs, including the provision of legal services for the poor; the organization of neighborhood groups for community action, welfare, or morale purposes; and a score of other types of action intended to rehabilitate individuals, families and groups, modify the institutions which serve them, secure public acceptance or toleration of their different life styles, and in other ways adjust the people to the environment or the environment to the people or both. Through these programs, the promotion of the general welfare has reached limits far beyond those conceived either by the Constitution or by the most advanced thinkers of the 1930s (cf. Seligman, 1965; Silberman, 1965).

THE INSTITUTIONAL FRAMEWORK OF LOCAL GOVERNMENT

The institutional framework of local government has expanded rapidly to conduct the enormously proliferating and expanding programs of aid to development. Perhaps the most significant and extensive institutional expansion occurred in the newly established redevelopment authorities, variously titled, which were formed in almost every major city and became the primary agencies for the administration of renewal programs. As the concept of urban renewal expanded from its prewar genesis in public housing projects to early postwar clearance and reconstruction of spot areas, later to rehabilitation of designated areas, and finally to a range of treatments for almost every part of the city, the functions of redevelopment authorities expanded. These programs now included not merely clearance and reconstruction but also code enforcement, the provision of public works, and later the improvement of public services. Thus, the original special purpose administrative vehicle quickly outgrew its intended functions and began to approach more nearly the totality of development functions of city government. This led in turn to the establishment of combined housing and redevelopment agencies, which often included code enforcement and public works construction activities, traditional powers of municipal government. The first of these reorganizations was conducted in Baltimore in 1956 (Baltimore Urban Renewal Study Board, 1956).

But the scope of urban development activities could not be confined even within the framework of municipal government. Industrial development corporations, educational programs and therefore school boards, mass transit and highway facilities, for instance, became recognized as essential functions in urban development and renewal. The need to coordinate these programs – often programs conducted by special districts, authorities, or independent agencies – reached far beyond the traditional functions of municipal government. Indeed, they reached all the way to the state capital, where special aids might be available for one function or another, and to Washington, where funds for modifications in programs were often critical to their development.

This evolution in programs led to the appointment of municipal development coordinators who became, in effect, deputy mayors for development and renewal. Having the confidence of the mayor, they were in effect his agent, armed with not only the full set of powers of municipal government but also with the political influence of the mayor as the individual most symbolic of the community interest. Philadelphia, New Haven, Boston, Pittsburgh, Chicago, St. Louis, and San Francisco, to name a few, have adopted the development coordinator devices. In each case the coordinator also has some direct operating responsibilities. The logic of making this deputy mayor for development the head also of an operating department for urban development has expressed itself in only a few major cities. In Milwaukee, such a department comprises the functions ordinarily assigned to the housing authority, the redevelopment authority, the city planning agency, and real estate and city property operations, as well as conservation and rehabilitation programs. The formal organization may vary. In some instances, special authorities have been liquidated and been made into municipal departments. But more commonly, the former boards and commissions continue to exist under the chairmanship of the development coordinator or development department head. By virtue of some overlapping membership, the central body keeps effective control over the major functions, though the legal entity of the former special districts remain, with somewhat greater administrative and financial powers than are ordinarily accorded municipal departments. The most massive of these organizations is that recently proposed for the city of New York. It would consolidate some eight municipal departments and agencies into a single Housing Planning Development Agency directly responsible to the Mayor (Institute of Public Administration, New York, 1966b).

If the trend of the future is toward a consolidation of development functions in a single department of municipal government, there has nevertheless been an enormous proliferation of special districts and authorities. In part, this reflects a continuation and expansion of prewar agencies, particularly in the field of transit, bridges, ports, and schools. During the postwar period, industrial development, airport, water, higher education, parking, culture, convention, and sports functions have been organized under special authorities or districts, often for the sole purpose of evading local debt limits or permitting private participation in the financing and management of these special functions outside of the financial, personnel, and procedural restraints of municipal government.

These special districts and authorities continue to proliferate, even as in some central cities the trend toward consolidation in development departments emerges. In the absence of quantitative estimates, it is to be assumed that the proliferation in the smaller cities, still in the early stages of expanding these activities, outweighs the tendency toward consolidation. The larger cities, which have already explored the proliferation route, are now engaged in efforts to achieve coordination and consolidation. Further, it should be noted that federal aid programs have often provided powerful incentives for the proliferation of special authorities. Indeed, they made housing and redevelopment authorities almost mandatory. After 1960 the federal government directed attention to conditions requiring coordination, and recently the Congress has recognized the need for eliminating incentives toward proliferation, largely as a result of the studies and policy recommendations of the Advisory Commission on Intergovernmental Relations (Advisory Commission on Intergovernmental Relations, 1964).

The institutions of local government concerned with human development appear to be going through a similar process of proliferation, leading to the necessity for coordination and perhaps ultimately toward consolidation. New York City's creation of a Human Resources Administration is a major manifestation of this latter trend. The major special district in all parts of the United States and in cities of all sizes is the school district, which is almost entirely independent of municipal control. While there have been state-wide movements, some of considerable influence, to consolidate smaller independent school systems, there has been no similar movement to date to incorporate them into the structure of municipal government. In other fields, new programs in health, education, and welfare have spawned new forms of special districts to deal with specialized hospitals, regional hospital and health systems, higher education (especially community colleges), and specialized welfare services. The most notable source of proliferation in recent years has arisen as a result of so-called poverty programs. These have generated the creation and quasi-public agencies to handle new programs of welfare, community organization, education, job training, job finding and placement, and the like. Crude attempts at coordination have been sought through local poverty boards, variously titled, which include representatives of local governments, private agencies, and representatives of the affected areas or populations. While the establishment of new public, semi-public, and private agencies continues unabated at the moment, it is foreseeable that the trend toward coordination will eventually dominate the trend toward proliferation.

Finally, the development of community renewal programs (CRPs) may prove to be a source of coordinative pressure. Since essentially the CRPs require the joint programming of physical development and human development activities, they must necessarily involve the central government and the special district governments, public agencies, and private agencies in a programming process. To date, CRPs have been conducted by special staffs and under the guidance of inter-agency committees. To the extent that community renewal programs become a continuing function of local government, however, one would anticipate their ultimate establishment as a staff function in municipal government.

THE MIXED ENTERPRISE INSTITUTION

A significant feature of the new action programs has been the development of mixed enterprise corporations to carry out phases of a development program utilizing both public and private resources, managerial skills, leadership, and incentives. These new types of enterprise have been typically pragmatic innovations, pursuant to no organized philosophy. But their success has been copied on a sufficiently widespread basis so that they now constitute a major category of institutions to execute plans and appear in one form or another in almost every city. They had their roots in the non-profit corporations fostered in some depressed areas during the 1930s as a means either to take over closed factory buildings and reopen them on a "nest" factory basis or, in the South, to attract new industry with tax concessions, free plants, and the like. In the 1950s, these precedents were expanded to attain industrial development in renewal areas, institutional development, housing, transportation, cultural and sport activities of various types, and other objectives critical to the execution of programs of renewal or development.

It should be noted that the actual organization of the new mixed enterprises is quite varied. Often they are little more than privately financed, non-profit corporations on whose boards of directors sit public members, usually appointed by the mayor. In other instances, however, not only the control but the capital may be mixed; i.e., there may be both public equity or loan funds and private equity or loan funds. We can discover illustrations of private capital with public control, a device common in the financing of stadiums and cultural centers, and public capital with private control, in the same field, for instance. An analogous and closely related development is the evolution of special districts, following the early example of the New York Port Authority and now including airport, parking, and transit authorities, exhibiting similar control and financing features.

Among the cities having the most fully developed of these devices, Philadelphia is probably outstanding (Roseman and Wheaton, 1966). Its Philadelphia Industrial Development Corporation (PIDC) was initiated by, in effect, the contribution of a former airport site owned by the city. Capital from the sale of this land for industrial purposes was put in a revolving fund to enable PIDC to acquire additional land so that there could be a revolving pool of the land available to attract industry. The powers of the Philadelphia Redevelopment Authority are used to condemn properties, where necessary. The authority can sell land at a negotiated price to the corporation, which in turn can negotiate sales to the ultimate users. Thus, public subsidy funds can intervene through the redevelopment authority where clearance and write-down are necessary. In other instances, the revolving fund may provide all of the necessary capital for the purchase of land, with or without condemnation. The corporation is also authorized to build, and builds and leases, plants for manufacturers under favorable terms, taking advantage of both the lower interest rates available under public financing and the tax benefits conferred on private corporations by leasing plants financed by others. In the industrial development field, similar corporations are now quite widespread, particularly in the Northeast, the Middle Atlantic states, and the South.

Another type of corporation is commonly organized for renewal purposes. The Old Philadelphia Corporation may be typical of this form of enterprise. Organized with private capital to promote the redevelopment of the Society Hill section of Philadelphia, it hired a high-priced staff; and it organized to expedite public actions; provide incidental support and promotional support for private activities; provide legal, consulting and financial services to developers; and the like. It has served as a technical consultant to public agencies, particularly the Redevolpment Authority, and as a private consultant to would-be developers, thus serving to bring the two together in agreement on development actions. In addition, corporations of this type are sometimes empowered to purchase, rehabilitate, and sell or lease buildings or to build new buildings. A similar organization, the West Philadelphia Corporation, created by the several universities and hospitals in the West Philadelphia Redevelopment Area, serves as their agent for the purchase of land for common purposes, the building of buildings for common purposes, and the pooling of their resources to acquire and maintain planning services. It, in turn, has spun off a separate building corporation for the financing, construction, and management of a Science Center. The latter will lease laboratory space to research and development firms, conduct certain educational activities, and otherwise promote scientific development to serve the combined purposes of the sponsoring institutions and the city. In most of these types of corporations, the public is represented by appointees of the city. Purchase, planning, and action programs are conducted in a goldfish bowl; and both plans and transactions are in effect legitimized by the consent of the otherwise contending parties interested in the area.

Philadelphia has moved still further in the creation of the South East Pennsylvania Transportation Authority (SEPACT), organized at the initiative of the City of Philadelphia but later reorganized under state act. SEPACT, an agency representing the city of Philadelphia and the surrounding counties, has the function of subsidizing the operations of commuter railroads. Here, the city felt that its stake in maintaining rapid transit to the central business district justified the utilization of subsidy funds. These are used to purchase the agreement of the railroads to stay in business and to finance the additional costs of maintaining minimum standards of service for the customers while at the same time reducing fares. After a period of experimentation and testing, SEPACT received the power to acquire commuter lines and to lease facilities of the railroads and subsidize or operate them to maintain a comprehensive system of transit. Other examples of somewhat similar relationships have been the inadvertent result of receiverships.

In the field of housing, the mixture of private and public powers and funds has proceeded at a rapid pace, beginning at the national level with the Reconstruction Finance Corporation and the Home Owners' Loan Corporation, both of which made federal loans to private, limited-profit or non-profit housing corporations in the 1930s. The New York State 1938 Redevelopment Company's Act authorized the establishment of private, limited corporations and conferred upon them the power of eminent domain and the right to receive tax concessions. New York State Mitchell-Lama Housing Corporations may receive state and private loans, are usually privately organized on a limited-profit basis, but may also be organized at the initiative of public agencies. The Federal National Mortgage Association may make similar loans to non-profit and cooperative housing corporations; and the Urban Renewal Administration may extend loans to local redevelopment agencies for the purchase, rehabilitation, and sale of properties in redevelopment areas. Thus, public loans are available either to private, limited-profit corporations, or to public agencies; and private agencies may use private or public funds with all of the permutations and combinations that are possible in between. Pittsburgh, under the auspices of Pittsburgh Action Housing, a private, philanthropically supported group, has chartered corporations for the building of demonstration projects and communities; for the organization, financing and conduct of neighborhood rehabilitation efforts; and for other similar purposes. In several communities, banking groups have organized special loan funds, with or without governmental aid, to pool risks involved in high-risk loans in rehabilitation areas.

The most recent development among mixed enterprises has occurred in the field of poverty programs. Beginning with New Haven's Community Progress, Inc. – a private corporation representing public and private welfare, health, and education agencies and the municipal government – the principle has been extended to many cities. These corporations are a chosen agent through which municipal, private, and federal poverty program funds are channeled to a variety of specialized agencies for the conduct of education, health, recreation, vocational training, job-finding, and neighborhood organization purposes characteristic of poverty programs. As in the case of the development enterprises, the essential administrative characteristic is the creation of an instrumentality through which the freedom of action of private corporations can be brought into play by means of an institution that can represent both public and private agencies and draw upon funds from both public and private sources.

CIVIC LEADERSHIP IN POLITICS AND ADMINISTRATION

The intiative for the new planning-in-action programs has come from a variety of sources, usually civic and reformist in temper. In Philadelphia, for instance, a business leadership group, the Greater Philadelphia Movement, constituted an important initiating force toward civic reform and action to improve the economic base and the cultural vitality of the city. It was joined by the half-century-old Philadelphia Housing Association, a Red Feather agency with an unusually vigorous combination of young leaders from the professions, academic life, and business. These in turn led to the organization of the Citizens Council on City Planning, which brought together a similar group best characterized by the terminology, "eggheads and professionals." The varied proposals for action by these initiators of reform soon brought to public attention a group of young, vigorous, potential political and business leaders. The alliance of these elements led in turn to the political reform movements that brought Mayor (later Senator) Joseph Clark and Mayor Richardson Dilworth into power and revitalized municipal government, planning, and renewal programs.

This alliance of professional and business leaders brought into the service of the municipality intellectual talent and civic dedication that had almost totally neglected municipal affairs for the preceding two generations. Once the door to City Hall was open, these brilliant and imaginative leaders could make the vigorous, inventive contributions to civic affairs which led to the explosive growth of new institutions and brought younger leaders of enormous talents into public service. They soon peopled the city agencies, developed contacts with private foundations, sought out the university resources, and evoked the support in the business community necessary for comprehensive civic reform and the development of the mixed enterprises previously described. Some analysts have questioned whether these coalitions could maintain their initial vigor and political following against the more pedestrian but full-time attack of older political machines, whose concern was power for its own sake, jobs, and other more menial objectives. While the new movements will doubtless be subjected to considerable fluctuation in strength, they have unquestionably brought into play substantial new elements of power, initiative, and imaginative leadership.

A new group of strong mayors, found in cities throughout the nation, often have provided the leadership for reform and the actions necessary to bridge the gap between planning and accomplishment. Richard Lee of New Haven and Jerome Cavanaugh of Detroit are conspicuous illustrations of this new type of political leadership. Clark and Dilworth of Philadelphia have been mentioned. Mayor Raymond Tucker of St. Louis might be cited as another example. Occasionally, these leaders presumably carry a large share of the burden for planning and action. In the New Haven case, for instance, there has never been conspicuous, organized private civic leadership backing the program of Mayor Lee. An elaborate civic council constructed and staffed in City Hall performs the review and endorsement functions (to the extent that they are performed) that elsewhere are performed by independent private, civic, and other groups. In Philadelphia, the independence of these broader constituencies has helped to keep City Hall "honest" and to maintain the vigor of action programs even when political leadership had transferred back into the hands of those, associated with the old political machines, who are less deeply or effectively committed to the scale or vigor of action characteristic of Clark and Dilworth.

In other cities, old guard mayors have adopted the new tactics of reform; cooperated with, supported, or accepted the leadership of the civic groups; and achieved similar results. Thus, Mayor David Lawrence of Pittsburgh, later Governor of Pennsylvania, could hardly be called a reform mayor, but he found an identity of interest between business leadership and organized labor and brought them into a coalition that could mount one of the most vigorous of civic programs in renewal, housing, transportation, planning, and industrial development. Mayor Daly of Chicago, certainly an old-school professional politician, has demonstrated a similar capacity to bring into play the organizations representing an alliance of business and civic leadership and labor; and thus he obtained the consensus necessary to mount programs that are scarcely distinguishable from those conducted by reform mayors.

From this welter of new institutions, new programs, and new initiators, there has emerged a class of civic servants distinctly different from the earlier ones. These are the professional manipulators who administer the federal aids, the local powers, the private investment incentives, and the political processes necessary to carry out urban development programs. Jack Robin and James Pease of Pittsburgh, William Rafsky of Philadelphia, Edward Logue of New Haven and later Boston, and John Duba of Chicago are nationally known professional leaders in this field of endeavor. Each started out as an adviser to a strong mayor and quickly acquired a knowledge of the political processes, the technical processes, the investment functions, and the other forces which when properly assembled could rebuild major parts of the city. Each became a chief executive officer for urban development. Each in turn ultimately came to be appointed municipal development coordinator representing the mayor – otherwise without formal power but achieving something more than mere ordination. Each has come to be in charge not only of housing and renewal but also of parking, transportation, city planning, and other functions. Thus there has emerged, in a score or more of cities, a class of executive who may or may not have achieved the formal title of development coordinator but appears to have carried out very similar functions.

Having demonstrated their ability to "put the pieces together" in effective and broad scale action programs, these new executives develop considerable autonomy. They may survive a change of mayoralty and continue in office with their powers unimpaired. Such changes have occurred in San Francisco, St. Louis, and Philadelphia. They may move from a municipal position to a position of leadership in one of the new mixed enterprises or civic agencies and still retain a large measure of the power and leadership they acquired in public office. They may even move from city to city, bringing into play in a new environment the same skills which they have successfully demonstrated in another city. Thus, Jack Robin could successfully transfer from Pittsburgh to Philadelphia to Calcutta and Edward Logue from New Haven to Boston. Perhaps this transferability of skill demonstrates more conclusively than any other phenomenon that what we are describing is a general case rather than a series of specific instances. The development coordinators have, in fact, more than charisma to sell. They can assemble the professional and technical talent, the legal and intellectual skills; they can utilize the political powers and the informal influences necessary to maintain an effective working force of public and private agencies directed toward urban development. If it is necessary to revise federal legislation, to develop a new package of aids to meet a new need, or to secure new state legislation, they have a demonstrated ability to manage these functions. When it is necessary to engineer consent from the business, labor, civic, and political community and to make accommodations with labor or minority groups, they have demonstrated ability to handle the negotiations, make the accommodations, and adjust the programs so that action may proceed without interminable delays, endless bargaining, or the plain failure to act so characteristic of other cities.

Finally, it should be noted that a similar evolution appears to be in process in the field of poverty programs, where a new class of highly skilled civic executives appears to be emerging. Perhaps the most conspicuous example is Mitchell Sviridoff of New Haven, recently appointed Human Resources Administrator by Mayor John Lindsay of New York City, who has demonstrated a remarkable ability to energize public and private resources through public and private instrumentalities and to devise and manage programs for human renewal analogous to renewal programs in physical development. The greater involvement of the client groups in these programs, a result of legislative and ideological commitment to "maximum involvement of the poor," may have momentarily obscured the development of executive leadership in this field and may have delayed the creation of viable instrumentalities and programs. But there appears to be little doubt that a similar evolution is in progress.

THE SCOPE OF PLANNING

If the powers of government to execute plans have expanded dramatically during the period 1945-1965, the enlargement of the professionally recognized scope of planning has proceeded at a slower pace. It is notable that no city planning agency has yet embraced the scope of planning defined by Robert Walker in the early 1940s, or anticipated by the studies and the statements of objectives of the NRPB (Walker, 1941). Most city planning agencies continue to atttend at best to comprehensive physical development planning; more commonly, they deal only with land use and community facilities planning, often even omitting the three largest sectors within this narrow field – education, transportation, and urban renewal – leaving these to specialized planning and administering agencies. No city planning agency appears to have brought forth a plan for education, for health services, or for economic development.

Despite the failure fully to embrace comprehensive planning, the scope of development plans has grown steadily. The Cincinnati Master Plan of 1948, a milestone effort of that era, delineated areas for clearance and renewal, a significant departure, and it contained detailed plans for the reconstruction of the central business district. Although it could be claimed that these features were no innovation, since they were also contained in Burnham's plan for Chicago of 1909, in Cincinnati the proposal dealt with publicly planned changes in private land use, to be executed through the new public renewal powers. The Cleveland Plan of 1950, which followed shortly, also delineates rehabilitation and conservation areas; and the Chicago Residential Land Use Plan of 1946 attempts to forecast the condition of areas twenty years in the future and the treatments through which they will have gone, or will then require.

Fifteen years later the treatment of these topics in the Philadelphia plan of 1960 (Philadelphia City Planning Commission, 1960) shows considerably greater depth and sophistication. This plan refers to rates of change in land use, shows a considerable elaboration of treatment methods, forecasts the changes in land use that will result from treatment of conditions, and calculates in some detail the prospective losses to the housing stock that will result from various programs of rehabilitation, partial clearance, and complete clearance. But further, the Philadelphia plan sets industrial and other employment goals for the city and proposes massive changes in land use, chiefly from residential to industrial, to enable the city to achieve these employment targets. The plan was not the innovative document, for the operating programs toward these ends were already in existence. But the plan specifies goals and traces the land use and transportation implications. Thus, the plan illustrates a shift within the period from the timid, laissez-faire premises of the prewar period to the affirmative statement of employment targets with means for their implementation.

The Philadelphia plan illustrates another significant expansion of the scope of planning by suggesting the goal of equalization of average family income as between different *areas* of the city. This section of the plan is on the borderline between a mere projection and a statement of goals. There is no detailed exposition of the means to be used to achieve the projected and quantified objectives, except as these are implicit in the treatment of housing quality objectives and retail space needs. Nevertheless, to deal with differences of family income and to project a narrowing of the sub-area differences is in itself a milestone.

Further, the Philadelphia plan projects the public investment costs of executing the plan by class of facility required. Equally important, it provides a means of measuring progress toward carrying out this aspect of the plan – the even rate capital expenditure chart. In estimating these costs, Philadelphia builds upon precedents established earlier in several smaller area plans of the Pittsburgh Regional Planning Association, which projected capital requirements, operating costs, and tax rates (Pittsburgh Regional Planning Association, 1955).

The Philadelphia estimates present the anomaly that the target time periods for capital investments do not coincide with the time periods for projected population and land use. They do not deal with school investment, the hidden half of local government. Nevertheless, the very act of estimating requirements in detail moves decisively in the direction of capital programming and suggests that there is an intention to move from plan to reality.

Another illustration of the trend toward affirmative economic planning is presented by the Stockton, California plan of 1965 (Arthur D. Little, Inc.). This plan contains an input-output model of the Stockton economy, which reveals the interdependencies between sectors of the economy and between the public and private sectors. It therefore reveals deficiencies, under given conditions of economic growth, in the secondary and public sectors, and it identifies targets for treatment within the economy.

Some of the community renewal programs move in the direction of a further incorporation of social and economic features into city plans. The Philadelphia Community Renewal Program has treated social services in some depth; but others, such as those of New

Haven, Chicago, and San Francisco, largely direct their attention to physical, land use, and capital requirements for public and private facilities.

On the other hand, specialized planning for these essential services of the city is conducted by their special agencies in varied ways. There have been comprehensive statements of policy with respect to transportation and segmental transportation plans of extraordinary high quality (e.g., Philadelphia Urban Traffic and Transportation Board, 1956). Major beginnings for that group of services which has been conceived to be relevant to the elimination of poverty and deprivation have been launched.

Efforts to coordinate the physical development universe with the human development universe at the local government level have scarcely begun. Some of the work done in the New York City Administrator's Office, especially during the years when Luther Gulick, Lyle Fitch, and Henry Cohen were associated with that office, moved in the direction of program budgeting for the allocation of resources of the community to the solutions of its problems in a more comprehensive way. Some efforts, as in the New York and Pittsburgh metropolitan studies, became directly concerned with the totality of public and private investment or employment. But nowhere have these been brought together into a comprehensive plan or program. Nowhere have they been brought together in a series of coordinated actions which might be described under the rubric of moving from planning to action in a comprehensive way. The national attention now directed toward program budgeting, the national concern now directed toward poverty programs, the recent proposals for the reorganization of human services and of physical development services in New York City, and President Johnson's Demonstration Cities proposal – each of these may contribute toward, first, the coalescence of planning to make it comprehensive and later, that direction or coordination of action which is the main concern of this chapter.

METROPOLITAN AREA INSTITUTIONS

Despite a decade of attention and a host of special studies, there has not yet emerged a capacity to translate metropolitan plans into action comparable to that which has characterized central city government. Repeated proposals for a federated metropolitan layer of government have thus far largely failed to produce agencies, powers, or personnel capable of moving effectively from plans to fulfillment.

The postwar period has been characterized by an enormous proliferation of local governments, many of them small incorporated suburban communities, and by major reliance upon the creation of special districts to provide special services. There has been a secondary tendency for county governments to assume some of the functions of municipalities, to broaden their range of services, and to provide special services on a district basis for special charges. The most extreme example of this phenomenon is the package of municipal services offered by Los Angeles County under the so-called "Lakewood Plan." Another notable trend in the development of metropolitan institutions has been the shift of financial responsibility for certain service functions from the local to the state and federal governments. There have also been tendencies toward the establishment of metropolitan-wide special districts in the fields of airports, transportation, water supply, sewerage, and air pollution among others, to handle new problems or functions. Reference will be made to these subsequently.

If there has been a failure in the evolution of multi-purpose metropolitan action agencies, there has been a vigorous growth among agencies concerned with planning. First it should be noted that federal grants for planning activated professionally skilled planners in all parts of the country and led to the development of numerous local, city, county, and metropolitan plans for physical development. While the scope of these plans has tended to follow the minimum prescriptions of the federal grant-in-aid manual, their sheer geographic extent has brought some form of planning to nearly all the urbanized areas of the country. The metropolitan-level planning agencies at the end of World War II were generally weak, powerless, largely advisory, understaffed, and uninfluential. In a few metropolitan areas having the longest traditions of metropolitan planning, the agency was established by state law; and it included representatives of counties, municipalities, and special districts and had some ties to the local government operating agencies that had the power to act. These ties, however, have been so weak that these efforts at official metropolitan planning have been only slightly more influential than the efforts in those metropolitan areas where the only area-wide planning agency was a private instrumentality.

Federal legislation and incentives, however, have recently created a new class of agencies with new potentials for planning and for influence on action. These agencies have arisen in response to the grants-in-aid authorized under Section 701 of the Housing Act of 1954, the Highway Act of 1962, the Open Space provisions of Title VII of the Housing Act of 1961, and other acts. The first of these initially merely granted matching funds for local and metropolitan planning, though subsequent amendment provided sustaining grants for continuous metropolitan planning. The second, most significantly, required that by July, 1965, metropolitan areas must have a metropolitan planning process under way to qualify for further federal highway grant funds. The third offered 10 per cent higher grants for the acquisition of open space where the grants were associated with a metropolitan planning or administering agency. Finally, for several years the Advisory Commission on Intergovernmental Relations has had under consideration proposals introduced by Senator Muskie for the greater integration of various separate federal planning requirements. These proposals were incorporated in the Demonstration Cities and Metropolitan Development Act of 1966. They impose metropolitan planning requirements as a precondition to the receipt of applications for federal grants in a variety of fields – including transportation, transit, open space, sewer, water, and certain health and educational grants. Thus, cumulatively and within a period of less than a decade, the national Congress has moved decisively to create incentives – virtually requirements – for the establishment of metropolitan planning agencies.

The most significant of these, though still seriously inadequate, have emerged in the highway transportation field where metropolitan transportation planning agencies have been widely created. In some instances, as for example in the Los Angeles Transportation Study (LARTS), the planning agency has been a legal fiction created by the State Highway Department and offering membership on advisory commission, but no powers, to participating local governments which sign a contract saying that they are engaging in metropolitan planning. In other cases, like the Penn-Jersey Transportation Study, there has been a serious effort to create a new instrumentality by interstate compact, governed by a representative body including appointees from municipalities, counties, state highway and state planning agencies, and with voting and non-voting representation from the major federal agencies concerned, the Bureau of Public Roads and the Department of Housing and Urban Development. In San Francisco, the comparable body, the Bay Area Transportation Study (BATS), established by state law, embodies a representation formula including not only the general units of government – cities, counties, and the state – but also special districts such as the Golden Gate Bridge Authority and others importantly concerned with transportation.

Coincident with the development of these specialized transportation agencies, there has been an evolution of loosely federated local government representative bodies. In the Philadelphia area, the Regional Council of Elected Officials (RCEO) was convened at the joint initiative of the Penn-Jersey Transportation Study and a philanthropically supported regional research agency named Penjerdel. RCEO has emerged as a loosely representative annual conference of municipal and county elected officials, with a more tightly organized smaller council and executive committee. Far more vigorously in the San Francisco region, the Association of Bay Area Governments (ABAG) has been created by joint compact of the local governments under the Joint Exercise of Powers Act of the state. It contains representatives of the local governments of the metropolitan area, cities and counties, with a nominally full complement of planning powers. The association has debated issues with fervor, partly in response to pressures from the state and threats of state action if local governments demonstrated their inability to act on metropolitan problems. While it is yet to be demonstrated whether ABAG can reach agreement or withstand the pressures of disagreement under its present charter, there is no question that it has moved halfway in this direction in the creation of a federal government of limited powers. Elsewhere the combined impact of federal incentives mentioned and of local concern with metropolitan problems has created scores of metropolitan planning agencies ranging from those with fairly close connections with local governments and fairly adequate communication machinery, as in the case of the Southeast Wisconsin Regional Planning Commission or the Twin Cities Planning Commission, to agencies with very little connection and very little communication with branches of local government that execute programs.

Federal and state pressures may quickly procure a rapid evolution in metropolitan planning. The availability of federal grants-in-aid will create substantial incentives for the establishment of staffs and of machinery for the assembly of information, exchange of viewpoints, and decision. The principle of differential grants for metropolitan functions will certainly be enlarged so that metropolitan systems will receive larger proportional grants than purely local facilities. There is also a re-examination in many states of the proliferating special districts that now conduct those limited functions already administered on a metropolitan basis – air pollution control, port development, transportation, and in rare instances higher education. California's Local Agency Formation Commissions are moving rapidly in this direction. Thus, we may expect within the decade the creation of both plans and instrumentalities for action, although the powers and the plans remain largely to be explored.

CONCLUSION

Dramatic changes have occurred in the relationship between planning and action in the postwar period. To describe them accurately, we must consider changes both in the scope of planning and in the competence for execution. Prior to World War II, city plans were limited largely to land use and public works plans. Few means existed to carry out even the very narrow objectives commonly stated. In the subsequent twenty years, the powers available to local governments have expanded enormously. The previous constraints of law and public opinion have largely disappeared. Powers are now available to carry out almost any conceivable plan for municipal physical development. Administrative institutions and leadership capacity have been developed in many cities, though almost no city has developed the full range of institutions, programs, and resources which have been displayed in some of the leading cities. The programs of New Haven and Philadelphia are probably the most fully developed, but even these lack features found in Boston, Baltimore, and elsewhere.

At the same time, the scope of planning has expanded to embrace economic and social plans. These have rarely been embodied in truly comprehensive plans. While extensive powers exist and additional resources are being made available almost daily through federal grants-in-aid, these programs do not yet display the richness and the range of powers available to influence physical development. Nor has the progress of planning for these services matched that shown in recent years in the improvement of techniques for the earlier tradition of physical development planning. And finally, the wedding of economic, social, and physical planning into something which might be called *planning for facilities and services* has yet to occur. The new concepts of planning and programming have made their beginnings here, however, and a comparably rapid expansion in planning method may be expected to ensue, coincident with the expansion of operating programs.

World and Nation

THE FINAL PAIR OF CHAPTERS consists of essays by Ernest Weissmann on "The Role of the United Nations in Urban Research and Planning" and by Robert C. Weaver on "The Evolving Goals of the Department of Housing and Urban Development."

Weissmann's essay is a truly stirring document, written immediately after the end of a tour of duty on the staff of the United Nations that spanned just about the entire post-World War II period that is the subject of this book. Taking issue with the general sense of economic and cultural affluence that pervades most American writings — in which poverty appears to be a concern for a steadily shrinking part of the nation — Weissmann rivets our attention on "the explosive character of the current world-wide crisis [that] has only begun to be recognized in the recent debates of several international bodies."

> *In the struggle to create new capacities, we have become so preoccupied with economics that we often lose sight of the wider meaning of development: the creation of new qualities of life. . . . In the meantime, shanty towns, slums, and urban decay are spreading. In many metropolitan areas they already shelter one-quarter to one-half of the population. . . . Some 60 million people are added to the world's population every year. This annual figure will become 125 million in the year 2000, when 6 billion people are expected to live on this planet, and two-thirds of them may be urban. An urban environment tolerable in physical and in socioeconomic terms will have to be built in the last third of this century for thirteen times as many people as in the previous 150 years. To do it, construction will have to average almost forty times that of the present — a rate of construction inconceivable even in the highly industrialized af-*

> *fluent countries. . . . Unless resources and measures adequate to the challenge of the task at hand are devised and put into action quickly, the United Nations and its member governments will have presided over what may be the beginning of a* far-reaching *disintegration of industrial society.*

Against the background of these somber reflections, Weissmann provides a detailed account of the gradual realization by the UN and its organizations of the immensity of the world problem that we confront. He also outlines the step-by-step evolution of UN programs aimed to reverse what appears to be a disastrous tide. His essay supplies a veritable index and guide to what has been done, what is being done, and what must be done. A paradoxical sentence in Weissmann's essay also suggests a bridge to the final chapter of the book: "Indeed, the creation of a livable physical, social, and moral environment precisely in the affluent part of the world may become the major social issue of this century, commanding highest priority and attention by the United Nations and the governments concerned."

In Chapter 20, Secretary Weaver — who is responsible for just this outcome — relates the evolving goals of his vital federal department. In so doing, he delineates a twenty-year emergence of concern and action in the world's most affluent nation. Echoing the spirit of Weissmann's plea, Weaver writes: "It is our goal to reconstruct the physical and social fabric of the American urban environment so that it will contribute toward a better life for groups of all income levels, all age levels, and all racial characteristics or religious beliefs. We must also improve the economic lot of the disadvantaged by utilizing the unemployed poor to help in the rehabilitation and rebuilding of their homes and neighborhoods."

Recognizing how intergovernmental relationships in the past frequently blocked fruitful action, Weaver places stress on the need for "creative federalism." "The entire concept of 'creative federalism'," he says, "calls for cooperation between Washington and states and local communities and involves not only public bodies but private leadership and private industry as well."

Following a description of the present and prospective "urban condition," Weaver tries to show how the creation of the new Department of Housing and Urban Development might provide a symbol for the rallying and focusing of federal programs irrespective of department or agency. "The overridding purpose is to assist in the orderly growth and development of the nation's urban areas; this requires that a complex of programs be directed under a single set of policies and with maximum staff coordination."

After depicting the mission of his department, Weaver discusses its changing goals. "In general, policies have been evolving toward a greater stress on creating employment opportunities and tailoring education to specific vocational needs and on providing more low- and moderate-income housing, rather than simply tearing down slum buildings and putting up highrise monuments of luxury apartments or office buildings." A key passage relates to the trend in policy planning, already noted in several of the essays, toward recommendations in the social and economic spheres as well as the physical:

> *The past tendency has been to approach a many-faceted environmental situation with a physical solution. The old approach was to eradicate the problems of the slumdweller by removing the slums. Today, urban renewal funds may be used for diagnostic interviews and referral services to social agencies for project site occupants.*

Finally, recognizing the importance of the metropolitan areas in dealing with urban problems, Weaver proposes a dramatic strengthening of the capacities of metropolitan areas to handle area-wide problems and to coordinate the actions of functional districts and local governmental units within them.

—H.F.

19

The Role of the United Nations in Urban Research and Planning

ERNEST WEISSMANN

□ THE MANY SOCIAL PROBLEMS WHICH can be traced back to the growing urban crisis have caught and held the attention of the entire group of the United Nations Organizations ever since their establishment. But the explosive character of the current worldwide crisis has only begun to be recognized in the recent debates of several international bodies. In spite of considerable progress since the war, the economies and productivity of the less industrialized countries remain insufficient and seem to be less and less capable of sustaining the lives that better health and sanitation are saving. The highly accelerated population growth is running so far ahead of the more elusive economic growth (more demanding in terms of resources and therefore also desperately slow) that many refer to it as an "explosion," thus connoting the fear it inspires in the more timid minds among planners and statesmen. As the gap between economic and demographic growth widens in most developing countries, their urban crisis also grows more intensive and more widespread. While in the highly developed countries comparatively moderate population movements and a steady and relatively high rate of economic growth tend to create new urban jobs at a higher rate than ever, many industrializing countries appear to be already "over"-urbanized: their urban economics cannot

---

EDITOR'S NOTE: *The author recently retired as Director of the United Nations Center for Housing, Building and Planning, and is now Adviser to the Center. The views expressed in this paper reflect the author's own views and not necessarily those of the United Nations.*

employ all men and women seeking work, whether they are rural migrants, urban unemployed, or young people come of age. What is the role of the international community in coping with the urban crisis in the world? Is it ready to assume a major role in this crucial area of development? How do the United Nations Organizations cooperate? What may the future bring?

THE URBAN CRISIS AND ITS MEANING FOR DEVELOPMENT

At this stage in the development of our industrializing society, the city has become the essential environment in which economic capacities are expanded or impeded and human and social qualities of life are enlarged or frustrated. Nevertheless, as yet the city's crucial importance has not been sufficiently realized. Development planners have not yet fully assessed its role as the major medium of development. In the struggle to create new capacities, we have become so preoccupied with economics that we often lose sight of the wider meaning of development: the creation of new qualities of life. Recently, however, the purist economic approach has begun to change. Improving the human condition is now widely believed to be necessary for both a balanced and a sufficiently rapid economic growth. Unfortunately, development doctrine is far ahead of national policy; it is a long step from theory and resolution to allocation of resources. In the meantime, shanty towns, slums, and urban decay are spreading. In many metropolitan areas they already shelter one-quarter to one-half of the population. The rural migrant often has no choice but to squat in settlements he must build for himself overnight. He cannot afford the minimum legal standard of housing; and ironically he does not, therefore, qualify for aid by his adopted new community.

Some 60 million people are added to the world's population every year. This annual figure will become 125 million in the year 2000, when 6 billion people are expected to live on this planet, and two-thirds of them may be urban. An urban environment tolerable in physical and in socioeconomic terms will have to be be built in the last third of this century for thirteen times as many people as in the previous 150 years. To do it, construction will have to average almost forty times that of the present – a rate of construction inconceivable even in the highly industrialized affluent countries.

Looking now not at the needs but at the resources, however, we find that only 25 African, Asian, and Latin American countries had in the 1950s an annual per capita income exceeding $200. And these combined had less than 10 per cent of the population of the three continents. While their per capita output grew between 1960 and 1962 by barely $5, the per capita output in the world's industrial countries as a group rose by $100. In Latin America, for example, population grows annually at the rate of 2.5 to 3 per cent and urbanization at 4 to 6 per cent. But the so-called "marginal populations" in the slums and shanty towns agglomerate at the staggering rate of 12 to 15 per cent per year. At the same time, however, gross national product of some countries averages an annual growth of not more than 2 per cent. As a consequence, living conditions continue to decline rapidly.

In the mature industrial cultures, urbanization does not any more express itself in sheer size and explosive growth, but rather in new demands stemming from a new mode of living. This fundamental change manifests itself, for instance, in the massive emergence of the private motor car and of suburbia; in important population shifts inside metropolitan regions; and in the urgent need for readjustment and rationalization of physical arrangements within and without the city limits proper. In addition, a strong international migratory movement is also developing. In Europe, for instance, migrant labor now shifts from the low-income countries in the south to the affluent north, where they perform the hard, unpleasant jobs discarded by natives now upgraded to better paying, more agreeable work. Germany has more than 1 million "guest workers," France employs 1.5 million, Britain at least 800,000; and in Switzerland one out of every three employed persons is foreign. This is yet another reflection and impact of the adverse terms of modern trade on the human condition of the underdeveloped world, whose levels of income and standards of decency remain extremely low. Most migrants live away from their families, isolated from the local population in virtual ghettos, in shanty towns, barracks, and in the slum sections, of big cities.

The highly industrialized countries are slow to act, and the developing nations lack the necessary resources. But failure to act has already created an *acute urban crisis* in every part of the world.

Squatter towns are a common feature of the developing countries, and destructive riots due to less than tolerable housing conditions are erupting periodically in the slums of some of the affluent countries. The crisis is complex. It is deeply rooted in world economic and world trade patterns. It has, therefore, become a worldwide problem, insoluble in terms of national economies and national planning alone. Obviously, all available and potential resources of every nation must be fully mobilized. But the size and urgency of the job to be done and the resources needed to do it in the developing pre-industrial countries imply that massive external assistance, both technical and financial, will be required. Therefore, the problems are different in the two situations in substance, in size, in intensity, in the rate of change – growth or decline – and in terms of measures and resources required to deal with them. But quick and massive action is needed everywhere. For unless resources and measures adequate to the challenge of the task at hand are devised and put into action quickly, the United Nations and its member governments will have presided over what may be the beginnings of a *far-reaching* disintegration of industrial society.

The United Nations established, as a quantitative annual target for housing and urban growth in the developing countries, the construction of 10 dwellings and attendant urban services and facilities for every 1,000 inhabitants, amounting to a total of some 24 million units in 1965 and 27 million in 1975. But due to slow economic and industrial growth, and specifically to low levels of building technology, the present rate of building in many developing countries is as low as 2 dwellings for every 1,000 inhabitants. Even so, the developing countries currently use between 15 and 25 per cent of the investment resources available for physical capital formation for residential construction. Another 15 to 20 per cent is being absorbed by essential urban services and facilities. Thus, while one-third to one-half of these resources go into housing and urban development, no measurable impact is made on the growing crisis: even this heavy investment usually does not add more than between 2 and 3 per cent to the existing dwelling stock.

Against this background, the concern of governments and the international community has shifted from isolated aspects of housing or building or town planning to the causes and consequences of our current urban explosion and the concept of comprehensive environmental development as part of general development. Now, out of an earnest preoccupation with these matters, a body of doctrine and experience is gradually emerging; and we could perhaps agree that it is not the lack of ideas, or facts, or institutions that is preventing action in the presence of the worldwide crisis. What mainly is missing are the resources needed to demonstrate convincingly their feasibility. For example, the United Nations has conceived the idea of pilot projects as a means of transferring knowledge and of adapting practical experiences by showing with the help of *external* resources the possibility of using *local* resources for massive and sustained action. Unfortunately, the existing procedures to initiate international aid and the weak response of the affluent nations remain insufficient for the job at hand; and we are still very far away from the creation of an adequate international fund or pool of resources and skills for this purpose.

A basic change of attitudes and values concerning development is now needed. We are still prepared to accept a restrictive economic philosophy born in an era of scarcity when "social" development had to be limited to what was "unavoidably" required for attaining the desired economic goals. But now the world has reached the threshold of plenty. Can we still be guided by an obsolete economic concept of national balances in the midst of a paralyzing economic imbalance between the rich and the poor nations? The dilemma for the affluent nations has now become to define the levels of living they desire as a society in realistic and human relationship to the contribution they are willing to make toward creating a viable world economy, thus wiping out the remnants of an obsolete economic relationship created by colonialism; or to continue to arm and "police" in the vain hope of isolating themselves from human suffering and inevitable social change.

The introduction to the first UN Report on the World Social Situation (United Nations, 1957a) refers to historian Toynbee's thought that a far-reaching change, inconceivable only a short while ago, was taking place in the outlook on world problems. It is now being recognized that all people must manage to live together and share the resources of the earth; that the general impoverishment of any area is a matter of concern to all areas; and that the technical experience, knowledge, and wealth of our society must somehow aid communities that are as yet less advanced and less well-equipped. Indeed, it has been suggested that our century may be remembered in future centuries not as an age of political conflicts or technical invention, but as an age in which society dared to think of the welfare of the whole human race as a practicable objective.

The highly developed nations have yet to recognize the full impact of their relative affluence and how the worldwide urban crisis will come to affect them. In fact, in some of them social problems and physical congestion may soon reach the point of no return unless they learn how to use their high and ever-rising productivity both for their own continued well-being and for the attainment of an economically and socially tranquil world. The United Nations could provide the leadership essential to shift the emphasis from a purely economic to a human approach to development policy and planning. The yardstick of growth could then be progress in the human condition – a focus on income and social and individual welfare and on the ease, the comfort, and the convenience of our physical environment. Indeed, the creation of a livable physical, social, and moral environment precisely in the affluent part of the world may become the major social issue of this century, commanding highest priority and attention by the United Nations and the governments concerned.

The world is spending annually between 150 and 200 billion dollars for armaments. Five countries are putting up four-fifths of these funds, and many developing countries also feel compelled to divert considerable resources from productive investment to armaments. United Nations' studies and reports on the economic and social consequences of disarmaments, prepared for the Economic and Social Council, concluded that controlled disarmament would be an unalloyed blessing for the world. Some of the equipment, installations, and institutions, and most of the funds and skills now used for the world's military establishments and for the research, development, and production of arms are quite suitable for the job to be done in urban reconstruction and development. Is it not conceivable that in the not-too-distant future some of these resources may be combined to create an international pool to be used in this constructive way? Even a *tenth* of these "public" resources and funds, if diverted to urban improvement, would exceed the total existing system of international and bilateral assistance grants. If resources released from armaments were channeled into large-scale urban reconstruction and regional development as a basis for further economic and social progress, and actual increase in employment could be obtained instead of the widely feared loss of employment through a shift from armaments to other activities in mechanized and automated industry, agriculture, and services. This is inherent in the very nature of present technology in building, utilities, and communal services since for every dollar spent for urban development, housing, and the building of new towns and regional facilities, significantly more labor is needed than in any other field of development.

GROWING INTERNATIONAL ACTIVITY

As the concern of governments about housing and urban affairs increased in the postwar period, the United Nations and its *specialized agencies* inquired into various facets of housing, building, and planning. A long-range program of proposed concerted action in this field has gradually evolved. To date, however, the efforts have served mainly the two-fold purpose of highlighting the chief areas of need and of clarifying the respective roles of the many participating agencies. It is impossible to escape the conclusion that, for the most part, the separate programs of the various organizations have been marginal rather than central to housing and urban development and largely unrelated one to the other. Agencies have become involved in particular housing, building, and planning activities principally through their interest in such matters as vocational training, environmental sanitation, the wider use of forest products, or rural resettlement rather than in the building or financing of actual living accommodations. This is not said for the purpose of criticizing the agencies concerned but rather to indicate why there has not yet been anything like a full frontal attack on the world's community and housing development problem. Indeed, there is no intergovernmental agency in existence — either within the United Nations family or outside it — that has the attack on this problem as its principal *raison d'être*. Instead, we find a number of agencies with other principal interests or concerns engaging peripherally in activities that are related more or less directly to the housing and urban development field. The importance of these peripheral activities is undeniable; they make, unquestionably, an important contribution to the building up of an infrastructure of knowledge, skill, and understanding required to produce a viable community development policy and program in the developing countries. But, this having been acknowledged, it still must be said that no intergovernmental agency has come into existence to date with the sole or even main purpose of promoting improved housing and urban conditions throughout the world. The inevitable result, as in so many other areas of effort, is that what is everyone's partial interest tends to become no one's full responsibility justifying the provision of necessary resources in funds and manpower.

Existing Institutional Responsibilities

The respective roles of the various specialized agencies and of the United Nations in the field of housing, community development, and related activities were spelled out in the constitutional instruments of the agencies themselves, in their various declarations on the subject from time to time, and more particularly in the long-range Program of Concerted International Action initiated in 1959.

The *International Labor Organization*'s (ILO) principal interest and concern in the field is with the vocational training of building workers, productivity in the building industry, cooperative housing, and advice to governments respecting workers' housing policies. The *World Health Organization* (WHO) is probably the most active of the specialized agencies in programs related directly or indirectly to housing and urban development. WHO is interested principally in the health aspects of housing, and in

> the improvement of environmental hygiene and sanitation, including the development on sound lines of urban and rural planning and of housing schemes.... The Organization's interest in housing is not limited to those elements which are important in preventing death and disease: it encompasses a broader sphere, including mental health and social well-being.... It recognizes that the hygiene of housing cannot be considered in isolation but should be treated as one of a multiplicity of environmental health problems associated with physical and social planning and development (World Health Organization, 1961).

The *United Nations Educational, Scientific and Cultural Organization's* (UNESCO) areas of interest relate to building and planning rather than to housing. But they are clearly marginal, involving concern with school building research; with studies of the social and psychological effect of mass housing and urbanization; and with seismological research in earthquake-prone areas in relation to building codes, housing policies, and building materials. The *Food and Agriculture Organization* (FAO) through its Home Economics Branch participates actively in measures designed to improve conditions of rural life. FAO's other principal point of contact with the housing field arises from its promotion of the wider use of forest products and other natural fibrous materials in the building industries of individual countries. Closely related to the work of FAO and the United Nations is the undertaking, launched in 1961, known as the *World Food Program*. Its basic purpose is to receive contributions of food supplies from countries with surpluses of certain commodities, and to furnish these surplus foods free to needy areas of the world, under safeguards designed to ensure that the distribution does not interfere unduly with the normal commercial channels of trade. The connection between this program and the field of housing, building, and planning is that it can stimulate and encourage housing and related projects in the recipient countries. This involves sometimes the direct use of food as part of the wages paid to workers on housing and urban development projects — thus lessening the burden of construction costs for the recipient country. Alternatively, when the surplus food is supplied under arrangements permitting its sale by the recipient country, local currency proceeds from such sale may be utilized, on a counterpart funds or similar basis, for housing construction projects.

The *International Bank for Reconstruction and Development* (IBRD) to which some have turned in the hope that it would assume leadership and initiative in the financing of housing and urban development, has remained warily aloof from involvement up to the present time, though it has provided limited support for the development of building industries. Prospects, on the face of it, are slightly more promising when one turns to the bank's companion agency, the *International Development Association*. IDA has been given wider scope than IBRD for the support of projects holding a high priority in the development plans of an applicant country, even though such projects do not normally qualify under the bank's more restrictive criteria. This makes it possible for IDA to consider high priority projects in such fields as education and water supply and even pilot housing projects. Both IDA and IBRD are now committing funds to approved projects in the fields of education and water supply. Here, the bank appears to have accepted the view that education and health contribute directly to productivity. So far as can be determined, however, it does not yet accept this view in respect of housing; no pilot housing project has yet been approved.

The *International Finance Corporation* (IFC) is another agency established under the wing of the World Bank. It assists in setting up development banks and in providing international financing, jointly with private investment capital, for the creation or expansion of industries in developing countries to produce locally what would otherwise have to be imported. IFC has made through its investment decisions a significant and practical contribution to the housing, building, and planning program of several countries by providing support for a number of new or enlarged industrial ventures in the building materials field.

The UN *Special Fund* is interested in preinvestment projects, such as building research and housing institutes through which substantial reductions in the cost of housing construction might be achieved and scarce resources released for other urgent purposes. In addition the fund has already approved preinvestment surveys for urban and regional development, pilot projects for housing improvement and developments, and centers and institutions concerned with urban and physical planning. The participation of the special fund in such projects is rapidly increasing as governments of the developing countries formulate their policies and programs in housing and in urban and regional development and building.

The most recent development in the evolutionary process of assistance has been the 1964 creation of the United Nations Development Program (UNDP), which merged two separate programs existing at that time: the Expanded Program for Technical Assistance, established in 1949, and the Special Fund, created in 1958. In addition to direct assistance to governments in the different economic and social aspects of development, certain governments also contribute the services of volunteer personnel to be used in approved programs and projects (United Nations, 1966). The United Nations also assists governments, at their request, by providing on a temporary basis the services of qualified persons to perform duties of an executive or operational character as servants of these governments. All other personnel provided through UNDP serve in an advisory capacity. Finally, governments, non-governmental organizations, and individuals may contribute funds into trust accounts for the financing of assistance projects additional to the continuing UN technical cooperation programs.

While the amounts being expended through any one channel of the United Nations family may not be large, it seems clear that when all sources are taken together, substantial amounts of technical and financial support are gradually being mobilized and made available at the international level for programs prerequisite to and part of the infrastructure of comprehensive rational housing and urban development programs. But, even though progress continues to be made along all these lines, the central problem still remains — how to assist the developing countries to generate or mobilize the massive quantities of domestic and international capital required to overcome their increasing housing and community development deficits.

Over the years, as the United Nations and the specialized agencies have endeavored to correlate the separate bits and pieces of activity related to housing, building, and planning in which they have become involved. A general agreement has evolved to the effect that, since housing activity is not central to the programs and purposes of any one of the specialized agencies, the United Nations *Secretariat* should assume the role of leadership and coordination in this field. For a good many years, in a good many quarters, doubts existed as to whether housing and community development comprised truly an appropriate field for international action as distinct from regional or local. To the extent that an international role was visualized at all, this was approached hesitantly and with considerable misgiving, partially at least because of the instinctive realization that the enormity of the problem, if tackled directly, could swallow up the entire resources of even the strongest of the international organizations operating in the postwar era.

Neither the agencies nor the United Nations Organization itself have had more than token resources in terms of money and manpower to devote to work in this field. It is not surprising, therefore, that no cohesive or truly unified program in the field of housing, building, and planning has emerged. We can point to a number of countries that have solidly based and well-established *national* housing and urban development programs. It has been possible for a few countries to correlate in reasonably adequate fashion the various "bits and pieces" of what is being done, to "ration scarcity" in a rational and orderly fashion, and to avoid inordinate waste through overlap or duplication in the limited resources available. It would, of course, be too much to expect – and unreasonable to hope for – the same degree of coherent effort in the *international* field, in respect to housing or any other matter, that is possible within a national administration under the best of circumstances. In the international field, responsibility and control of policy and resources is vested in "separate but equal" international organizations, responsible to separate and independent governing bodies, albeit dedicated to a common general purpose and committed to working together in a common cause. The procedures under which they operate leave much more of the initiative for policy and program in the hands of the constituent membership – and correspondingly less in the hands of the central secretariat – than is the case in most national contexts (United Nations, 1966).

PREPARING FOR INTERNATIONAL STUDY AND ACTION

This, in short, has been the shape of the urban crisis and its meaning for development, and these have been the organizations and resources of the international community available to deal with it. Clearly, both the resources and the organizations remain grossly inadequate to the task. Yet it is important to see that great strides have been made in the two decades since the first discussion of the housing problem in the General Assembly in 1946 and the formulation of the Universal Declaration of Human Rights in 1948. Both recognized the importance of housing and urbanism in international efforts to raise the standards of living of large populations throughout the world. As early as 1949, the Economic and Social Council (ECOSOC) initiated a first international program in the field of housing and town and country planning. This was to be carried out jointly by the United Nations and its specialized agencies: ILO, FAO, UNESCO, and WHO. The leadership responsibility for housing and town and country planning was implicitly vested in the United Nations and its Council and in the Social Commission (SOCOM) and its secretariat, the Department of Social Affairs.

ACTION PROGRAM

A second phase of development of the international program was marked by the establishment in 1952-1953 of a definite program of action. This was highly influenced by the growing interest of the whole international community in housing and urban matters—an interest born out of the recognition by many governments of the continuously developing crises in their national housing programs despite the large resources being devoted to these programs. In this phase of the program, housing and community improvement problems were beginning to be related to general economic activity; and training of personnel, coordination of research, and exchanges of information were recognized as essential functions of international assistance to governments. In order to achieve a sufficiently broad and inclusive set of objectives, the United Nations in 1953 recommended that governments, especially in the less-developed countries, should accelerate the establishment of appropriate ministries or special national "housing" agencies where these did not yet exist, and should strengthen any agencies that still had only limited scope and resources.

A further and even more comprehensive development of the program became necessary as a consequence of the multiple problems created by the worldwide massive shift of populations from rural to urban areas, especially after 1946. In this connection, the need for a more effective integration of economic and social development was inescapably perceived and pointed out. This need was particularly acute in the less-industrialized countries, lacking the economic and technological resources available in the highly developed areas. By 1955, the Social Commission, therefore, emphasized and the Council endorsed an extension of the housing and community development program so as to relate physical (environmental) planning to the other problems of urbanization and regional development, and to general plans for national economic and social development. This extension included, *inter alia,* regional environmental planning as a means to integrate national and local development programs within a given area. It was recognized that the less-developed countries, in particular, faced overwhelming problems of rapid urbanization which were running ahead of employment opportunities and amenities emanating from industrial and urban development. In this context, the study of social aspects of housing and community improvement and the mobilization of self-help were considered particularly important. Conversely, housing, building, and planning as a cluster of economic activities were accorded an important position within the framework of United Nations studies on industrialization.

Lessons of Early Programs

International experience, even in just the first postwar decade, gained from studies, conferences, seminars, and from direct assistance to governments, made it possible to note a number of significant developments in the several parts of the world. Generally speaking at least three factors came to light which should make it unnecessary for the developing countries to repeat the costly mistakes made in the now highly developed countries during their industrial revolutions – mistakes which some countries even today have not yet overcome and which continue to expose large groups of their populations in the lowest income brackets to slum conditions of the worst order. In the *first* place, present day technology and science offer a wider range of possibilities for the geographic distribution of production, people, and settlements and for higher levels of living for larger populations than was possible in the nineteenth century. *Secondly,* there is now a definite share of government and public responsibility in the development process in all countries. *Thirdly,* a wealth of information has been assembled by scientists and practitioners throughout the world on the various aspects of industrialization, urbanization, and social and cultural change.

With respect to housing and environmental development, experience at the time pointed to the following developments, some directly influenced by the international program already underway (United Nations, 1957b).

1. Governments were assuming an increasing responsibility for the direction and financing of housing and community improvement as part of their policy and programming for general social and economic development.

2. In many countries practical action by central as well as local housing agencies was being geared to the national economic potential.

3. Resources in materials, plant, manpower, and funds needed for current and future housing programs were being assessed in the light of their contribution to full employment and social betterment in the highly industrialized countries and to economic growth and better living conditions in the developing countries.

4. Concerted efforts were being made to mobilize available resources for housing programs, including the direct contribution of future householders through cooperation and self-help methods.

5. Governments were creating special agencies for the financing of housing from public sources and establishing or strengthening institutions whose purpose was to mobilize and channel savings into the housing field.

6. Governments in some countries were introducing specific fiscal measures to provide funds for housing and community improvement programs.

7. Rent policy and related assistance to low-income groups were being considered increasingly as part of general social policy.

8. Governments formulating national housing policies and programs were relying in a substantial number of cases on information about policies and methods that had been successful elsewhere and on practical advice based on common experience of countries with similar conditions.

9. In a number of nations, governments were actively fostering the development of the building industry in order to reduce construction costs; and trade among countries in construction equipment, building materials, and related industrial products was being promoted.

10. It was being recognized that provision of adequate housing and community facilities must accompany, if not precede, the development of resources if serious obstacles to economic activity and high social cost of haphazard urbanization were to be avoided.

11. In most of the less industrialized countries, development programs emphasizing a more rapid improvement in living standards had been enacted or were being formulated.

12. A number of large new cities, as well as smaller satellite communities, were being planned and built in different parts of the world, and attempts were being made to create self-sufficient neighborhoods in existing towns *inter alia* in order to reintroduce community cohesion.

13. Vocational training of labor and technicians, needed to increase the efficiency of the building and building materials industries, was being stepped up in many developing countries.

14. A number of national and regionally based institutes had been or were being established to undertake training and comprehensive research on the social, economic, and technological aspects of housing, building, and planning in different parts of the world.

The above developments indicated that certain progress had been achieved through the formulation of policies, the establishment of programs, and the initiation of action in the fields of low-cost housing, physical planning, and training and research. The fact remained, nevertheless, that the situation was *deteriorating* in most countries and would no doubt grow worse unless more practical and more adequate ways and means were found to cope with it. The wealth of knowledge and techniques which had become available as a result of recent efforts by governments and international organizations led necessarily to the conclusion that there was a growing need for simultaneous and concerted action on all essential fronts – be they economic, social, technological, environmental, cultural, administrative, or educational.

THE SHIFT TOWARD A COMPREHENSIVE APPROACH

International activities by the family of United Nations Organizations in the first years were largely *functional* or segmental in approach. That is, studies in specific fields (for example, housing finance, urban land policies, tropical housing, etc.) were pursued to define general methods and techniques that might assist governments to develop policies, programs, and action in these particular aspects of the total problem. As has already been noted, this approach was instrumental in creating a considerable pool of knowledge and has no doubt played an important role in initiating national action and in supporting technical assistance activities. Nevertheless, in view of the rapidly worsening world situation, the question arose whether a more comprehensive approach, dealing with all the main essential aspects of environmental development as they affect large categories of the population, might not be more effective.

The inevitable conclusion was that the problem must be approached within the larger context of the growing urban-rural imbalance. It was not sufficient any longer to investigate isolated facets of the problem; and there was a pressing need to apply all experience gained to improve action for achieving a more equitable balance between conditions in town and country in terms of physical environment. A change, therefore, from a functional to a *group-oriented* approach seemed to be called for, directed toward the specific needs of people living respectively in the urban and the rural areas, the lower-income groups as well as the middle class.

Such an approach could be reflected in two ways. In the *first* place, for proven programs direct action could be undertaken in close collaboration with governments, as part of technical assistance programs, with a view to applying already available knowledge through pilot operations and demonstrations. In the *second* place, where sufficient knowledge was still lacking, action would have to be supported by further studies. From a substantative point of view it was suggested, therefore, that direct action be applied particularly in the fields of (a) mobilization of the future householders' resources; (b) development of the building industry; and (c) regional planning and development. As to certain social aspects of housing which as yet were lacking attention because priority in the past had been given to technological, administrative, and economic aspects, comprehensive studies and research were suggested to precede action. This approach was embodied in the long-range International Program of Concerted Action in the field of Housing and Related Facilities, established in 1959.

AD HOC GROUP OF EXPERTS ON HOUSING AND URBAN DEVELOPMENT

The ensuing wider interest in housing and urban affairs, on the part of the international organizations, together with the rapidly growing number of requests by governments for international assistance in this field, made it possible for the Social Commission to suggest that the Council assign to a group of experts the task of advising on two major matters: one, "the place of programs for the extension of housing and basic community facilities within national development programs, and the relationship of these programs and national programs and policies for urban development and regional planning;" the other, "the successful techniques for mobilizing national resources for the extension of low-cost housing and urban development, as well as the appropriate methods for expanding and effectively utilizing international resources which may become available for the extension of housing and related community facilities." This international body, composed of experts from Ethiopia, France, India, Israel, Japan, Peru, Tunisia, United States of America, Union of Soviet Socialist Republics, and Yugoslavia, met early in 1962.

The group noted more than 30 joint projects in housing and urban development being undertaken by the United Nations and the pertinent specialized agencies, planned for the period 1962-1965. They found that adequate coordination machinery existed at the level of the international secretariats in the form of the Administrative Committee on Coordination's *Inter-Agency Working Group on Housing and Related Community Facilities*. However, the experts also noted that there was no special body at the intergovernmental level to ensure continuing consideration of problems and programs in the field of housing and urban development and to act as a center for the exchange of information on practical experience and the results of research. They therefore recommended strengthening the existing staff establishment of the United Nations and the creation of a body, such as that outlined above, to act as a clearinghouse for the assistance rendered by the United Nations, by regional economic commissions, by specialized agencies, by governments active through multilateral and bilateral arrangements, and by other international organizations and financial institutions.

In its report (United Nations, 1962) the group attempted to show, against the background of rapid urbanization and the urgent need for rural improvement, the main social and economic problems involved in housing and urban and regional development. The group also considered appropriate methods of integrating the programs with national development programs and of taking advantage of progress in science and technological developments in the construction and building-material industries. The heavy national investment – public, cooperative, and private – already being made in housing and urban development was analyzed by the group, which also suggested techniques for the better use of available resources and for mobilizing additional resources not yet used but likely to prove effective. Emphasis was laid in these suggestions on the role of savings and the use of self-help, mutual aid, and other methods of cooperation in housing and urban development.

The group explicitly recognized the magnitude of the problem and the limited resources available for its solution. It felt, however, that scientific and technological progress offer the necessary means for a rational distribution of people and settlements in urban and rural areas and for higher levels of living, provided that national and local governments take appropriate steps in partnership with the people. The group of experts felt that combined and sustained efforts of national governments and international organizations, including substantial technical and financial aid not only in economic development but also in housing and urban development, can produce important results in this decade.

The terms *housing, community facilities,* and *urban development* as used by the group of experts connote the physical environment of contemporary society. This embraces all parts of a residential community and its location within a given geographical area; the roads, public services, and utilities which serve the community; its relation by means of transport to other structures, scenes, and activities of contemporary society; and the general physical pattern to which all these conform. Housing thus constitutes the physical environment in which the family, the society's basic unit, must develop. Its improvement represents a tangible and visible expression of a rise in the general level of living. From the family's perspective, however, housing is not "shelter" or "household facilities" alone, but comprises a number of facilities, services, and utilities that link the individual and his family to the community and the community to the region in which it grows and progresses.

Housing and urban development are, in fact, activities where social and economic programs meet. These programs are essential for both; and in practice they may be major factors for balanced development in the setting of accelerated urbanization. The provision of adequate housing and urban and regional development is accordingly nothing less than the provision of the physical framework in which man's human, social, economic, and cultural resources are released, enriched, and integrated.

The group drew up a number of recommendations covering all aspects of its findings including essential action programs. In the field of research, evaluation, and information the group made the following recommendations:

(a) Surveys should be geared to the particular types of action programs envisaged and to regional conditions, peculiarities, and priorities.

(b) The planning, organization, and execution of housing and urban development programs must be based on a continuing process of research and appraisal of the essential social, economic, physical, and administrative factors influencing this broad field of development, with a view to their integration in a concerted effort.

(c) Countries should continually seek greater efficiency in the use of employed, underemployed, and potential resources by means of research, experimentation, and evaluation of approaches, methods, and techniques and by an effective coordination of inter-sectoral planning, programming, and executive activities at the different levels of government.

(d) Developing countries should have as an immediate goal the fuller and more efficient use of an abundant resource such as labor and technical and administrative personnel and the training of adequate cadres for their housing and urban and regional development programs at all stages.

(e) A particularly important aspect of research and evaluation is to ascertain at all stages of development whether external resources are required, and if they are, how the latter can assist most in attaining the goals set by national policies in housing, urbanization, and general social and economic development.

(f) Basic conditions for centrally beneficial exchanges of information, experiences, and personnel exist and, therefore, the United Nations should assume the function of an international clearinghouse in these fields as a matter of urgency and as an important aid to economic, social, and physical development.

To strengthen United Nations action, the experts proposed the following ways of expanding international resources:

(a) There is considerable scope and need for intensified international action in the fields of statistical methods, operational surveys, and evaluation to assist governments in introducing and improving techniques for assessing housing and other communal deficiencies and requirements.

(b) International assistance in housing, building, and planning should be given in accordance with sound criteria for social and economic progress, an equitable geographic distribution, and the strict interest of the recipient country; it should be so used as to contribute permanently and continuously to the solution of housing and related problems.

(c) The developing countries should create or designate a central national unit as a point of contact for international assistance in housing and urban development; this unit should advise those giving aid on the types and location of projects that might be undertaken with international resources in harmony with general economic and social development programs, and it should provide the facilities and services required for their success.

(d) The United Nations should give encouragement to the development of internal government insurance schemes to insure savings and mortgages; and it should also explore the use of international and other aids, credit devices, financing of essential trade in equipment and materials, as well as the training of local cadres to expand the supply of housing, particularly for low income families in the developing countries.

(e) A United Nations fund or pool of equipment, technical services, and financial resources should be established on the basis of the response by Member States to General Assembly resolution 1508(XV) [on pilot projects, discussed above].

(f) To facilitate the exchange of experience and ensure coordination of financing from national and external sources, the unit of the United Nations Secretariat dealing with housing, building, urban and regional development at UN Headquarters should be strengthened and endowed with sufficient resources to cope with such of the tasks envisaged as part of the *Development Decade* as may be approved by the Economic and Social Council.

(g) A permanent organ such as a Standing Committee similar to the Committee for Industrial Development, or a Commission, or a permanent Group of Experts should be established within the United Nations Organization, comprising high-level experts in housing, urban and regional development, building and building-materials industries, and social and economic development. Such an organ could meet in rotation in various countries to: facilitate the exchange and dissemination of experience and information on the results of research; plan and program the assistance, pre-investment aid, and investment resources to be provided by the suggested fund or pool; and facilitate the coordination of international aid in housing and urban development from all sources.

(h) A higher contribution from all countries in funds, equipment, materials, and services for pilot and demonstration projects in low-cost housing, in urban development, in the manufacture of building materials, and in construction is essential to strengthen United

Nations aid to the developing countries, where the crisis in housing and urban conditions is assuming dramatic and serious proportions.

(i) The United Nations, where feasible, should be prepared to aid and take a positive role in the initiation and development of physical plans in cases involving projects of regional development between countries.

Based on these recommendations, the Social Commission proposed in the spring of 1962 and the Council approved in July of the same year the establishment of a Committee on Housing, Building, and Planning. In welcoming the establishment of the committee, the General Assembly recommended that its membership be increased from 18 to 21. Later, in 1966, the membership of the committee was again increased to 28, so as to provide for higher representation of the developing countries.

The committee's terms of reference were set out by the Council as follows:

(a) Examination of reports concerning technical assistance activities in the field of housing, related community facilities, and physical planning.

(b) Recommendations to the Economic and Social Council for appropriate coordination of these programs among the various United Nations bodies including the regional economic commissions and with other international agencies.

(c) Recommendations to governments, through the Council, on appropriate priorities and program emphasis in the field of housing and related community facilities and physical planning.

(d) Promotion of research and of the exchange and dissemination of experience and information in these fields, with special reference to the needs of underdeveloped countries.

(e) Development of proposals for consideration by appropriate United Nations bodies and others on such matters as financing of home construction and ownership, provision of land for homes and community facilities at reasonable cost, designs suitable for low-cost housing in different climates and cultures, improved building materials and their better use, and ways of promoting acceptance and adoption of efficient organizational and building techniques.

(f) Development of means and methods for the increased utilization of the regional economic commissions in this field.

In addition the Council invited the regional economic commissions to strengthen their activities in this field and to cooperate fully with the new committee. Each regional commission headquarters could serve as a sort of "Crossroads Africa," "Crossroads Asia," and "Crossroads Latin America" in respect to housing, building, and planning activities carried on under expert international—or even national—auspices for that region. Thus, the beginnings of an institutional framework were set for a more effective international action.

UNITED NATIONS CENTER FOR HOUSING, BUILDING, AND PLANNING

The Committee on Housing, Building, and Planning met for the first time early in 1963, and subsequently in New York in 1964 and 1965 and in Geneva in 1966. In its four sessions to date, it has devoted much of its attention to the specific topics in its terms of reference. Throughout the four sessions, the committee's undivided attention was centered on the urgent need of ensuring that the "proper share" of international resources be channeled into the area of environmental development and that appropriate organizational arrangements be made for an unhampered development of international action in this essential area of development. While housing and urban development has been declared by the General Assembly and the Council as one of several priority or impact programs among the objectives of the current United Nations Development Decade, to date there has been little consistency between these professions and the realities of budgetary provisions of funds and personnel allocated to realize its objectives. There is a similar gap between the committee's views and proposals concerning the institutional structure required to carry out the program and the slowness with which it is being implemented.

Various suggestions have been advanced from time to time as to the auspices under which the work in housing, building, and planning should be continued, inside or outside the United Nations Secretariat. A report on coordination and organization prepared for the Secretary General in 1963 by George F. Davidson, Bureau of Government Organization of Council, stated that no fully satisfactory solution could be devised to date (United Nations, 1963b).

Davidson further felt that the prima facie case for a separate specialized agency was, in theory at least, a good one if the professions of the Development Decade are to be taken at their full face value and if it was seriously intended to develop a major intergovernmental program in the housing and urban development field as part of the economic "forward thrust." Previous experience, however, with other attempts to establish new specialized agencies – for example, a specialized agency in the social welfare field – in his view gave little encouragement. His report, therefore, favored the following arrangement:

> (a) Re-establishment of the Housing, Building, and Planning Branch, outside the Bureau of Social Affairs but within the United Nations Secretariat, as a separate and more fully self-contained housing, building, and planning center (like the Water Resources Center and the Industrial Development Center).
>
> (b) Establishment of the post of head of the new housing, building, and planning center at the director level, reporting directly to the Under-Secretary for Economic and Social Affairs.
>
> (c) Closer linkage of the work of the housing, building, and planning center with that of the Industrial Development Center and with the economic side of the United Nations Secretariat, in addition to the existing close link of the social development program of the United Nations.

The Committee debated the issue in 1964 at its second session. It voted on the two alternatives of establishing either (a) an independent center as defined by Consultant Davidson as a first step towards a consistent and expanding UN program in the area of environmental development, housing, and building; or (b) a full-fledged independent international specialized agency within the family of United Nations organizations. Neither option received decisive support. In the words of the committee's report, "These votes were only a reflection of the difference in views as to the methods to be followed in obtaining a much desired objective" (United Nations, 1964). A third resolution sponsored by the authors of both alternative proposals, was then adopted unanimously urging the Secretary General to give priority to the establishment of the center. While the Council approved the creation of the center in July, 1964, its actual establishment even on a modest scale did not occur until almost a year later in late June, 1965. Also, it remained (and still is at this writing) part of the Bureau of Social Affairs.

Nevertheless, the establishment of the committee and the center, the rapid growth of aid to countries under the United Nations Development Program, and the recent approval by the Council of the proposal to create in India an International Institute for Documentation on Housing, Building, and Planning are encouraging steps. Together, they are beginning to provide a new set of instruments available to the international community for tackling the mountainous problem of striking a balance within the frame of general development between achieving environmental development with its economic, social, and industrial counterparts, as well as achieving their integration. The first and only assistance project of the United Nations in housing (1951) had dealt with certain rural social aspects. In sharp contrast, 73 countries and territories received *technical aid* in 1965 from the United Nations alone. Of these, 20 were African, 19 Asian, 6 European, 20 Latin American, 6 Middle Eastern, and 2 in Oceania. Of the 170 projects completed, underway, or started in 1965, 48 were in Africa, 48 in Asia, 8 in Europe, 48 in Latin America, 15 in the Middle East, and 3 in Oceania. The total contribution of the United Nations for this aid amounted to 2¼ million U.S. dollars. As of February 1966, the United Nations Special Fund had committed 8⅓ million U.S. dollars for 9 projects in 9 countries, against government counterpart commitments amounting to 11½ million U.S. dollars. The UN World Food Program allocated to date more than 5 million U.S. dollars for projects assisting in environmental development.

An example of the trend toward comprehensive development is the reconstruction of the capital of Macedonia, Skopje — a city of 200,000 destroyed by an earthquake on July 26, 1963. In October, 1965, the plans for a new Skopje were put on exhibition, marking the beginning of the process of their formal adoption by legislative bodies concerned in November. This was done in the presence of the International Board of Consultants, jointly established by the United Nations and the Government of Yugoslavia to review all reconstruction plans and advise on their implementation. A combination of techniques ranged from computer programming for emergency shelter, social surveys, and employment and income projections for housing programming, to feasibility studies for transport and the infrastructure. These techniques were applied simultaneously and at a sufficient scale to permit elaboration of the comprehensive new urban and regional plans in a comparatively short time. The reconstruction planning for Skopje is unique in several other aspects: UNESCO has provided aid in the area of earth science; ILO in large-scale training of building skills; WHO in the area of health and sanitation; and UNICEF in children's welfare. Experiences of many lands were applied. United Nations aid contributed a more effective use of material, technical, and financial aid from national and external sources; and the World Food Program provided the essential extra rations for the builders and planners during the first emergency. In many ways, this undertaking has become a symbol of international solidarity as envisaged by the General Assembly of the United Nations.

The committee felt ever since its first session that there was a need to assemble, collate, and evaluate information on practical measures and on research in environmental development. In connection with the International Cooperation Year, a similar suggestion was forwarded by the Committee on Housing and Urban Development at the White House Conference on 1965, envisaging a USA-financed international laboratory institute in urban development, located in the United States of America and serving the world. France, Israel, Italy, and Japan outlined broad terms of reference for an "international center on environmental development" which included the full scope of earlier proposals for conducting and disseminating research.

With respect to cooperative arrangements, the sponsors stressed particularly the relationship of the proposed center for environmental development with:

(a) Other centers and institutes in the economic, social, technological, and administrative fields operating under the auspices of the United Nations.

(b) The existing national centers and institutions of research and learning in these fields and in the different areas of environmental development.

(c) The existing regional centers on housing, building, and planning and the regional centers to be established in the developing areas of the world.

(d) The international professional organizations interested in the entire field of competence of the proposed center or on specific aspects of environmental development (United Nations, 1963a).

After three years of debate, the final version of the proposal (in July, 1966) changed the center's name to *International Institute for Documentation in Housing, Building, and Planning* and eliminated from its terms of reference any mention of research, including documentary research which still figured in the committee's proposals of 1965. Thus, one of the gaps still remaining in the current institutional framework for international action is the organization under UN auspices and securing of international cooperation in environmental development research encompassing the different aspects of housing, building, and planning – economic, social, physical, and technical as well as administrative, legal, and fiscal.

In the meantime, the committee and the center are in the process of projecting a long term program of international action consistent with the pivotal role this area holds in general development. In this, however, they are faced with the usual and painful dilemma of resources failing to match the needs. Instead of being able to indulge in the luxury of constructing a logical and balanced design for research and action that *ought* to be undertaken, they must respond to the most pressing needs of the developing countries as these needs emerge from requests for direct aid. Since most of the center's resources must continue to be absorbed by the different forms of assistance, the long term program may well have to continue focusing on practical action; that is, on technical cooperation, on assistance to preinvestment planning and feasibility studies, on aid and advice on sources of financing, and on a modicum of research deriving principally from these activities and essential to them.

As developing countries have increasingly recognized and demonstrated by the types of technical assistance they request, it is extremely important to relate internationally assisted programs to the level of development reached in the particular region involved. As a result, international aid for housing and environmental development will have to concentrate on certain functional areas in each of the major developing regions. In *Africa,* emphasis might be placed on technological improvement and institutional machinery in the building field. In *Asia* and the *Far East,* emphasis is needed on the problems of rapid urbanization, including formulating policies and plans for urban land development, coping with squatter settlements, determining industrial location, and promoting regional development. In *Latin America,* emphasis might be proper on the institutional infrastructure necessary to consolidate the considerable technical progress already achieved and to improve the efficiency of overall investment. This will require assistance in housing policy and planning, financial policy, and the administrative and legal framework necessary to carry out large-scale physical improvement programs.

In addition, a new type of international assistance to countries faced with problems of large-scale, rapid transition from rural-agricultural to urban-industrial societies is planned. This will involve an approach to urban development that has only recently been recognized as both necessary and desirable in many developing countries. The essential ingredient in this approach is the relationship among and between urbanization, environmental development – that is, the physical structures and services necessary for community life – and overall national development. Recognizing that all these elements are interdependent, projects might focus on a common aspect of the many functional sectors involved in the urbanization process, that is, the physical and locational requirements of environmental development. The specific objectives for the short- and medium-term would be to assist each interested country (a) to formulate a policy for environmental planning that fits fully into national and regional development efforts; (b) to establish the institutional and administrative framework necessary to plan, finance, and execute integrated environmental development programs (including the facilities to train national personnel and to collect and evaluate necessary information); (c) to undertake comprehensive demonstration projects involving physical, social, and economic planning and investment that illustrate the feasibility and desirability of integrating environmental development with national and regional development programs. Such projects would not only make a significant impact themselves, but would also help to bridge the gap between the familiar, single-purpose technical assistance projects and preinvestment projects.

This latter type of demonstration project would require the concerted efforts of several United Nations agencies. It might include the following elements: (1) planning and providing the physical requirements for surplus labor migrating to areas designated for new industries as part of a decentralization plan; (2) devising methods to relate the financial, administrative, and physical requirements for environmental development to projected industrial investments; (3) estimating direct and indirect economies of alternative forms and sizes of new urban concentration, particularly where these concentrations are significantly affected by investment decisions in the public sector; (4) determining what combinations of physical, social, and economic investments are most effective to encourage individuals to migrate to a particular area; (5) establishing and supporting both administrative structure and training and research institutions to provide the personnel and data collection and processing facilities necessary to undertake integrated physical and socioeconomic planning and development.

A proposal which contains some of the elements just outlined is currently being considered. This project would involve the joint efforts of the Government of Peru, the Inter-American Development Bank, the World Health Organization, the United Nations Special Fund, and the Center for Housing, Building, and Planning. The objectives would be *first*, to establish an experimental neighborhood unit for persons of different income levels that is integrally related to an industrial complex on the outskirts of Lima as well as to the national development plan; *second*, to develop techniques for rehabilitating existing neighborhoods and dwelling units; *third*, to provide the physical, social, and economic environment necessary for the absorption in developing areas selected for settlement of the rural migrants who would otherwise gravitate towards new or existing squatter settlements that often fail to offer community amenities and employment opportunities.

This program will require a level of resources substantially above that which can be expected through existing channels; and new methods for resource mobilization will have to be instituted. To support such a program a truly interdisciplinary approach to research and a good deal of research will be required. This will serve not only as a tool for practical action and for the evaluation of its effectiveness but also as a means of strengthening the dialogue among the economic, social, environmental, and administrative disciplines involved in the total human advance. And it will provide a needed method of developing new criteria and yardsticks capable of measuring the effectiveness of practical action and the promise of new approaches in terms of human progress, welfare, and tranquility.

20

The Evolving Goals of the Department of Housing and Urban Development

ROBERT C. WEAVER

☐ OUR MOST CRITICAL DOMESTIC PROBLEM is improving the quality of urban life for all Americans.

President Johnson, in his March, 1965 message to Congress on the Problems and Future of the Central City and its Suburbs stated that the

> core of this problem [of the cities] . . . is people and the quality of the lives they lead. We want to build not just housing units, but neighborhoods; not just to construct schools, but to educate children; not just to raise income, but to create beauty and end the poisoning of our environment. The modern city can be the most ruthless enemy of the good life, or it can be its servant. The choice is up to this generation of Americans. For this is truly the time of decision for the American city.

It is our goal to reconstruct the physical and social fabric of the American urban environment so that it will contribute toward a better life for groups of all income levels, all age levels, and all racial characteristics or religious beliefs. We must also improve the economic lot of the disadvantaged by utilizing the unemployed poor to help in the rehabilitation and rebuilding of their homes and neighborhoods.

This is an ambitious goal, but one that we can and must achieve in this generation.

"Creative federalism," I believe, will further this goal. The entire concept of "creative federalism" calls for cooperation between Washington and states and local communities, and involves not only public bodies but private leadership and private industry as well.

Many of the problems of our rapid urban growth have their roots in the economy and technology of the private industries and households. Governments at various levels have to exercise powers of suasion, cooperation, and regulation to overcome these problems. In order to mount concerted efforts to overcome urban problems, the new Department of Housing and Urban Development will work with all its resources to provide leadership in necessary joint ventures of the federal government with local and state governments and private interests.

"Creative federalism" differs from the old-style "dual federalism." Under the old system it was thought that nation and state and community were divided by specific jurisdictional barriers. For many problems which overlapped jurisdictions or didn't fall directly into one or the other, there seemed to be no solution. In response to this, a cooperative federalism developed, bringing together activities of shared responsibility through the device of federal grants-in-aid. The effectiveness of cooperative federalism has been hindered by the belief that expansion of power which is exerted at one level of government reduced the power in another. More recently though, the concept of power as a non-static, non-fixed quantity has emerged: the creative response from all levels of government, and both the public and private sectors, galvanizes the federally assisted sector into positive action. One important aspect of the federal role, however, stresses local initiative and local solutions; another responsibility of the federal government is to bring about a thorough awareness of the urban problems.

This is a time for innovation and experimentation. In quantitative terms, the increases over the next thirty-five years – by the year 2000 – will double our urban needs for housing, and housing is only one in a complex of urban concerns. Subsequently in this chapter I will outline the goals of the Department of Housing and Urban Development and our present thinking and programs toward attaining these goals.

THE URBAN CONDITION

Cities and suburbs are both facing financial troubles, due to increased demand for and cost of services. Local taxes are running about 140 per cent higher than in 1950; state taxes are also rising.

Residents and city administrations each find themselves in a spiral: the cities to provide increasing required services and the residents to pay the increased taxes. There is a need for more housing (particularly to serve the lower end of the income scale), more hospitals, more and better quality schools, more recreation facilities, more sewerage and water facilities.

The vast migrations from the farms to the city, and the flight of some parts of the city population to the suburbs, has brought the urban population to 135 million people, comprising 70 per cent of the total United States population of 193 million, as of 1965.

It is not only the large cities which find themselves caught in these pressures of the movement to urban areas. Small communities are confronted with rising costs of public services and facilities, and have their pockets of blight and slums. Federal grants, loans, and technical assistance are aimed at cities of all sizes.

In the field of housing alone, as we enter the 1970s, we will need over 2 million new units annually. Ten million additional children will require schools, welfare and health facilities will be needed for 5 million more senior citizens, transportation facilities for the daily movement of 200 million people, and highway and parking places will be required for 80 million automobiles.

Urban population will double as will the amount of land in urban use within the next forty years; that is, the equivalent of rebuilding the entire urban United States will have to be accomplished by the turn of the century. If the trends of the past continue into the future, the Census Bureau estimates that by 1970 the population will reach 214 million, and by 1980 the United States will have a population of 260 million. In less than fifty years, the year 2010, the population may reach 400 million.

Coupled with the growth of population is the significant rate of migration from rural to urban areas. The proportion of the population that lives in urban areas is expected to rise from 70 to 85 per cent. However, this population will be dispersed over a wider urban area – i.e., the cities and their suburbs will expand. Although the 70 per cent of our present population which is urban is living on only one and one-half per cent of the country's land area, the rate at which land is being consumed for urban uses is increasing. To illustrate, in some metropolitan areas land is being urbanized at the rate of 200 acres for every 1,000 inhabitants, whereas only a generation ago the rate was 70 acres per 1,000 population.

In the central cities within the metropolitan areas the population components have changed. Readers of this volume are well acquainted with the outflow of the middle-income groups and the influx of low-income, minority and rural groups. One consequence has been that the need for public facilities and services – including low-income housing, efficient mass transit, health and welfare services, and public education – has multiplied. The necessary fiscal requirements have also multiplied. The federal government has responded to these local fiscal frustrations by increased aid. The Committee for Economic Development recently reported:

> From 1952 to fiscal 1964 Federal aids to local units quadrupled. Federal aids to the states also nearly quadrupled, permitting them in turn to increase their support to localities . . . The Federal budget for fiscal 1967 proposed further increases in aids to states and local units of 50% above fiscal 1964. There is no visible prospect of significant future deviation from established trends.

The states draw 20 per cent of their total annual revenues from the federal government. The extent of increase in the federal contribution to local government is indicated by the fact that federal grants-in-aid to local units and state governments totaled 7 million dollars in 1902, 116 million dollars in 1927, jumped to over 2½ billion dollars in 1952, and over 10 billion dollars by 1964. Federal grants-in-aid budgeted for fiscal 1966-1967 total over 14½ billion dollars for both urban and non-urban areas (Committee for Economic Development, 1966, page 10). The proportion of total local budget revenue received from the federal government has obviously multiplied many times over.

Direct federal programs, as well as intergovernmental grants-in-aid, also include a variety of activities vital to the city. An analysis of the estimated magnitude of all federal financial commitments with significant urban or metropolitan development impact – Veterans Administration and Small Business Administration loans, for example – produces a total of over 28 billion dollars for fiscal 1965-1966. Even excluding the housing insurance and guarantee programs, the total federal involvement in urban community development and improving the condition of the urban population reached nearly 17 billion dollars in the year. Included in these figures are substantial portions of the urban renewal, public housing, health and educational facilities, urban transportation, and anti-poverty programs of the Office of Economic Opportuntiy. The educational facilities and anti-poverty programs each are slated to have more than twice the funds in urban areas as urban renewal. This allocation reflects a changing composition of federal emphasis for effectively working together on the cities' ills. It is well recognized that urban renewal alone cannot solve the cities' problems, just as clearing out slums doesn't necessarily alleviate the problems of the slum dwellers. A more massive attack on the roots of the dilemma must include higher educational achievement through the provision of varied opportunities, job training, counseling, and employment to raise the aspirations of deprived youth.

DEPARTMENT AS A SYMBOL

The effective recognition that ours is an urban society is marked by departmental status for the federal government's various housing and urban affairs programs. An "urban society" is not limited to the cities themselves. It includes the metropolitan areas which encompass cities and suburbs. Within thirty-five years our population will number 350 million and four-fifths will reside in metropolitan areas. As recently pointed out by Joseph Alsop, however, the cities are the major sources, the heart of our general prosperity, and we cannot afford to let them remain diseased and growing still worse.

There will be a great need, therefore, to conserve the central cities of our urban metropolitan areas. We must identify and support the development of the central city economic and social functions and activities that are needed to serve the metropolitan region. Both the cities and the suburbs – the present and new ones – will be needed to accommodate the growth in population. Planning for area-wide development can help us achieve an appropriate balance of viable functions in cities and suburbs. The encouragement and assistance of such planning is both symbol and substance of the interests of a Department of Housing and Urban Development.

The proposal to grant departmental status to the federal agency dealing with housing had been deliberated before Congress for ten years. During this time the problems had increased quantitatively and in the complexity of their interrelationships.

President Johnson, in his March 2, 1965 message to Congress on the cities stated:

> Our urban problems are of a scope and magnitude that demand representation at the highest level of government. The Housing and Home Finance Agency was created two decades ago. It has taken on many new programs . . . Much of our hopes for American progress will depend on the effectiveness with which these programs are carried forward. These problems are already in the front rank of national concern and interest. They deserve to be in the front rank of government as well.

Congress declared that the general welfare and security of the nation requires, as a matter of national purpose, the sound development of our urban communities and metropolitan areas, where the vast majority of the citizens live and work.

Therefore, Congress determined that the establishment of an executive department was desirable (1) to achieve the best leadership for administration of the principal programs of the federal government which provide assistance for housing and for the development of the nation's communities; (2) to assist the President in achieving maximum coordination of federal activities that have a major effect upon urban, suburban, or metropolitan development; (3) to encourage the solution of the problems of housing and urban development and mass transportation through state, county, town, village or other local and private action (including promotion of interstate, regional, and metropolitan cooperation); (4) to encourage the maximum contributions that may be made by vigorous private homebuilding and mortgage lending industries to housing, urban development, and the national economy; and (5) to provide for full consideration at the national level, of the needs and interests of the nation's communities and their people.

By law the Secretary is required to advise the President with respect to the coordination of federal programs and activities relating to housing and urban development; develop and recommend to the President policies for fostering the orderly growth and development of the nation's urban areas; provide technical assistance and information, including a clearinghouse service to aid state, county, town, village, or other local governments in developing solutions to community and metropolitan development problems; consult and cooperate with state governors and state agencies (including holding informal public hearings when necessary to develop solutions to metropolitan problems and encouraging effective regional cooperation); encourage comprehensive planning by the state and local governments with a view toward coordinating federal, state and local development activities; encourage and cooperate with private enterprise to serve as large a part as it can of the nation's housing and urban development needs; and conduct continuing studies of housing and urban development problems.

The Department has been organized with three basic objectives:

1. to redesign the existing structure so that it can deal efficiently and thoroughly with the problems of urban America;

2. to provide strong decision-making authority in the field, through the regional offices;

3. to prepare a sound management framework through which an innovative approach, the proposed Demonstration Cities Program, can be carried out successfully.

The overriding purpose is to assist in the orderly growth and development of the nation's urban areas; this requires that a complex of programs be directed under a single set of policies and with maximum staff coordination. The Department's functions have been regrouped to place emphasis on meeting modern and future urban needs; strong leadership is achieved at the national level by assignment of groups of related programs and functions to the various Assistant Secretaries with an aim of melding Department efforts on both the physical and social fronts. The Department will work closely with other federal departments in dealing with urban problems such as health, education, and highways.

MISSION OF THE DEPARTMENT

Under the aegis of the new legislative charter creating the Department and its organizational structure, HUD's concerns beyond housing are established. By name and intent, it is not only a Department of Housing, but of Housing and Urban Development. As such, it will work on a firmer basis with other federal departments and agencies with programs bearing on urban and community development.

There has been a considerable expansion in the number of federal programs significantly affecting urban development and administered by various agencies and departments. Twenty-one programs existed in 1951; by 1962 the number of federal programs had grown to 43; and they had increased to 70 by 1966. Within the Department of Health, Education and Welfare alone, 25 programs are involved. The Office of Education administers grant-in-aid programs for education of low-income families, library services and construction, adult basic education, community services and continuing education programs, guidance counseling and testing, the college work-study program, higher education academic facilities, and vocational education. Rehabilitation services are provided for the handicapped through the Vocational Rehabilitation Administration. The Public Health Service gives grants-in-aid for the construction of hospital and medical facilities, community mental health centers and services, and special health services for the aged and chronically ill; and it also administers the Clean Air Act. The Water Pollution Control Administration, which was recently transferred to the Department of Interior, provides technical and financial aid for waste treatment plants.

Central to a comprehensive approach to the poverty sector of our cities are the Welfare Administration's programs. A listing is a sort of Geiger counter to ghetto problems: aid to dependent children, child welfare services (including foster home and day care), maternal and child health services, medical assistance to the aged, aid to the blind, and aid to the permanently and totally disabled.

Even some of the programs administered by the Department of Agriculture – the food stamp program and school lunches – are vitally concerned with the urban poor. The construction of highways aided through the Public Roads Administration in the Department of Commerce is probably one of the chief determinants of urban form. The Department of Commerce also is involved in public work grants through the Economic Development Administration. The Neighborhood Youth Corps and other training projects are under the aegis of the Department of Labor; the Office of Economic Opportunity operates the Community Action Programs and work experience programs.

The coordination of federal policies and programs relating to urban development will be strengthened by our cabinet-level department. A continuing evaluation of relationships among programs within the Department, as well as those administered by other agencies, will be undertaken to eliminate conflicts and promote the best allocation of national resources through use in a coordinated manner. These coordinating functions will be the responsibility of an Assistant Secretary for Intergovernmental Relations and Demonstrations, who has an office devoted to Intergovernmental Relations and Urban Program Coordination.

By Executive Order No. 11297, issued by the President on August 11, 1966, the Secretary of HUD was given primary responsibility to insure better coordination of federal programs in urban areas. At present there are more than a dozen agencies, in addition to HUD, whose programs affect the health, welfare, economic opportunity, and general environment of the city dweller. These include anti-poverty, hospitals, schools, highways, and parks.

This mandate to the Secretary is a further specification of the Secretary's responsibility, previously mentioned, to provide leadership in coordinating federal programs affecting urban areas and to advise the President and recommend policies for his consideration. The Executive order reads, in part:

> All who are concerned . . . must work in close harmony and with common purposes and policies. The Order does not relieve any Agency of the responsibilities it now has. It will help strengthen the responsiveness of these Agencies to meet needs of the City.

The meetings that will be convened by HUD to implement this order will serve several functions. They will serve as a forum to consider mutual problems and to promote cooperation among the various federal departments and agencies. Assistance will be provided to state governments toward solving metropolitan development problems and encouraging regional cooperation. The intergovernmental coordination required in working towards the solution of problems of particular states and metropolitan areas can be expedited.

In addition to harmonizing at the federal level, HUD is working toward more effective federal relations with city, county, and state governments. One specific device is the contemplated clearinghouse service to aid local governments in solving metropolitan and community problems. The Office of Intergovernmental Relations and Urban Program Coordination will be responsible for coordination with cities, counties, and states and for liaison with other departments on the federal level. Presently in the thinking stage is the establishment of "metropolitan desks" to give concerted attention to the particular land use, employment, and economic problems in these areas. The Urban Program Coordination branch will launch two newly authorized programs, community development training and city planning fellowships program, when the Congress appropriates funds to activate them. As I stated recently:

> The Department will provide the opportunity for more effectively massing our resources where they can do the most good, and for achieving a much higher measure of coordination between many different urban programs than ever before. It will be the major instrument for directing the developing Federal strategy for city redevelopment and growth.

The Departmental organization also provides for an Office of Economic and Market Analysis which will work toward the development of a comprehensive market analysis format to serve all the operative housing and urban land disposition programs in HUD. Through coordinated efforts and common data bases, consistency in program views and policies in local markets can be achieved. This will help to bring about a balanced supply of housing for local areas, promote stable growth of housing construction in local markets, and avoid overbuilding of particular classes of housing through HUD programs.

THE EVOLVING GOALS

Efforts to improve particular parts and activities of the cities and to maintain their economic and fiscal viability date back to the 1930s. Local governments have sought solutions to specific problems with the assistance of federal programs designed to deal with the specific problems. More recently, some governors and state legislatures have established offices to deal with urban and metropolitan problems.

Federal assistance programs have been initiated in both the physical and social realms: public housing, urban renewal, mortgage insurance, rehabilitation loans, planning assistance, hospital construction, community facilities construction, aids to education, transportation loans and grants, waste treatment plant construction, youth job training, and community action programs. To varying degrees each of these has made progress toward the solution of individual problems, but frequently without relating one problem to another, without focusing clearly on cause-and-effect relationships. In more recent years there has been some attack on the slum problems themselves instead of the symptoms: measures such as job training for unemployed youngsters rather than recruiting additional police for street patrol, and providing day-care centers to help working mothers rather than increasing direct welfare payments. In general, policies have been evolving toward a greater stress on creating employment opportunities and tailoring education to specific vocational needs and on providing more low- and moderate-income housing, rather than simply tearing down slum buildings and putting up high-rise monuments of luxury apartments or office buildings.

However, each of these programs has been directed toward a single problem and the solution to one has frequently been the cause of another. Downtown merchants have benefitted from an urban renewal project, but there might not be sufficient low-income housing. A welfare program might support a family but provide no incentive for vocational training.

Second, through experience we have learned that even where a city utilizes many federal aids it may not coordinate their effects. Local plans frequently are detailed but not sufficiently comprehensive to make the best use of federal-aid programs. For example, the location of a federally assisted public hospital should be planned in relation to the location of low-income and mass transit facilities. In addition, resources may be spread too thin over several neighborhoods, leaving for example, a lack of adequate parks and recreational facilities in high density residential areas.

Third, in general the past tendency has been to approach a many-faceted environmental situation with a physical solution. The old approach was to eradicate the problem of the slumdweller by removing the slums. Today, urban renewal funds may be used for diagnostic interviews and referral services to social agencies for project site occupants.

Fourth, the central cities have found themselves in a vicious fiscal cycle. Municipal tax revenues increased by 43 per cent between 1954 and 1963, but indebtedness grew by 119 per cent. A city's tax increases to finance increased services may drive its more affluent citizens to the suburbs. A greater burden on industry lessens the city's attractiveness to existing and potential industry. The result is that the city is left with its poor, those most in need of but least able to pay for municipal services.

In 1965, President Johnson appointed a task force to examine the shortcomings of federal programs and make recommendations for immediate action. The result was the proposal for a "Demonstration Cities Program," presently pending in Congress. Essentially it is geared to demonstrate what a coordinated, concentrated, massively funded attack on the physical and social problems of the slums can accomplish. Vital to the program is evidence from the city of readiness to organize all of its resources to help itself. A proposal from any city must meet certain criteria, but the means for meeting them are flexible, to encourage the imaginativeness of the city and the creativity of the proposals in meeting the physical and social problems of slums. The cities will have to "produce."

Title I of the proposed 1966 Housing and Urban Development Act provides funds for both planning and program activity under the Demonstration Cities Program. Planning will be on an 80 per cent federal grant basis with the city paying the other 20 per cent. The bill authorizes 12 million for each of two years.

Actual program assistance provides aid in addition to that already received by cities under categorical federal grant-in-aid programs. The supplementary aid is computed on the basis of local contributions to federal programs involved in the Demonstration Cities Program, and can be up to a maximum of 80 per cent of the total non-federal contributions under existing federal grant-in-aid programs being carried out as part of the Demonstration Cities Program. The 80 per cent grant funds may be used to supplement the local contribution under ongoing federally assisted programs or for any other activity that is part of an approved demonstration cities program. Local self-help thus is recognized as a criterion for federal aid; i.e., a community may be rewarded by receiving supplemental grants up to 80 per cent of non-federal contributions. Program assistance of 900 million dollars is provided for a two-year period in the bill passed by the Senate on August 19, 1966.

The purpose of the bill is to provide additional financial and technical assistance to enable cities of various sizes to plan and implement programs to rebuild large slum and blighted areas and to expand and improve services to the people living in these areas.

By participating in the program a city's share in federal programs will have greater impact on the slums. By approaching a complex problem with an arsenal of correctives, bolstered by federal aids beyond those of the total of individual programs, a much greater impact will be achieved. As Representative Patman said when he introduced the legislation:

> The persistence of widespread urban slums and blight, the concentration of persons of low income in older urban areas, and the unmet needs for additional housing and community facilities and services arising from rapid expansion of our urban population have resulted in a marked deterioration in the environment of large numbers of our people while the Nation as a whole prospers.

The locally prepared programs will be designed to rebuild entire sections and neighborhoods of slum and blighted areas through concentrating and coordinating all available federal and local aid and private local resources.

Entire neighborhoods of slums and blighted areas will be rebuilt, according to a locally prepared and scheduled program, approved by HUD and utilizing all available federal and local aids, including local private resources. Eligibility will be dependent on several criteria:

1. The program must be of sufficient magnitude in social and physical aspects to
   (a) remove or arrest blight in entire neighborhoods or sections,
   (b) provide a substantial increase in the number of low and middle-income dwelling units,
   (c) make marked progress in serving the poor and disadvantaged in terms of reducing educational disadvantages, disease and unemployment,
   (d) make a substantial impact on the sound development of the city.

2. The rebuilding or restoration must contribute to a well-balanced city with adequate public facilities, commercial facilities, housing for all income levels, and transportation to employment centers.

3. Provision must be made for educational and social services for the poor and disadvantaged, citizen involvement, and employing the residents.

4. There must be adequate local resources and appropriate administrative machinery to finance and carry out the program.

5. There must be a relocation plan for displaced individuals, families, business concerns and non-profit organizations.

6. Maximum opportunity in the choice of housing must be built into the program.

It is hoped that a high standard of design will be applied; that local regulations are or can be modified to be consistent with the program's objectives; that improved technology and cost-reduction techniques will be encouraged; that housing segregation will be discouraged; and that the program will be consistent with comprehensive planning for the entire urban area.

Whether lauding the program as ambitious or criticizing it as overambitious, it is a needed strategy in the campaign against the decline of portions of our cities. There is probably no doctrinaire approach or single solution to these problems. Since the removal of blight, the provision of low-income housing, and the employment of project and area residents are all criteria, the program invites massive housing rehabilitation efforts. It can provide the opportunity for a much sought-after breakthrough in housing rehabilitation. The organization and economy that is possible in large-scale efforts could be made applicable to housing rehabilitation. Successful rehabilitation can help achieve our goal of adequate standard housing for all families in less time, with less need for new land sites and, hopefully, at lower cost than through the provision of new housing for all who do not have standard housing.

REORIENTATION

The goals of HUD have evolved to their present form in recognition of different problems, or problems viewed differently in relation to each other. We have also developed a more urgent sense of timing. The recent riots in Los Angeles, New York, Chicago and Philadelphia point out two lessons: (1) We can not always wait for the "long run," certain ameliorative actions must be taken now; and (2) There is an urgency to work on removing the basic causes of, rather than the symptoms of, poverty and despair in the slums. Many of the works of this Department, together with programs of HEW and the Office of Economic Opportunity, are moving in this direction.

The present trend in our housing policy dates back to 1961, when President Kennedy's Message on Housing asked for expansion of the housing programs and revitalizing the urban and metropolitan areas. The Housing Act subsequently passed by Congress included programs for several aspects up to then neglected on the federal level. Programs were enacted for grants for urban mass transportation demonstrations, open space land, the provision of low-interest rate loans to small communities, public facilities construction, and new FHA programs for home rehabilitation and experimental housing, as well as a new low-interest rate mortgage insurance program for low- and moderate-income families.

There are discernible changes in the ways in which we have approached urban problems. In the urban renewal program, we are modifying the emphases from clearance toward rehabilitation, from redevelopment for luxury apartments to rehabilitation for moderate- and low-income families. Relocation payments have gone up, as has the amount of housing available at lower rents. Perhaps most significantly, fewer families are being dislocated as a much larger proportion of new housing in redevelopment areas is available to low- and moderate-income families. Also, low-interest rehabilitation loans and grants are now available.

In dealing with neighborhood deterioration, more flexible tools have been adopted such as rent supplements, code enforcement projects, leasing and purchase of rehabilitated housing for low-rent public housing use, and the construction of neighborhood centers as focal points for the area's renewal efforts.

THE NEED FOR AREA-WIDE PLANNING COORDINATION

With the increasing percentage of our population residing in metropolitan areas, and the consequent change in population mix in the central cities and surrounding suburbs, the need for metropolitan-wide planning has become crucial. In response to this, many of the programs administered by HUD now require comprehensive area-wide planning as a prerequisite for grants. These programs include open space grants, grants for sewer and water facilities, advance land acquisition, mass transit facilities, urban beautification, and advance public works grants.

In the pending 1966 Housing and Urban Development Act, Title II underlines this trend of encouraging metropolitan planning and coordination by local governments by authorizing supplementary federal grants to state and local public bodies for metropolitan development projects. An incentive grant of up to 20 per cent of the cost of a metropolitan development project, generally of a public works nature, could be added to the basic grant. The effect of this is to give a bonus in addition to the regular federal grants if the responsible public body shows that the project location, service capacity, and scheduling are in conformance with metropolitan planning. The number of Standard Metropolitan Statistical Areas (SMSAs), defined by the Bureau of the Budget as an area in and around a city of at least 50,000 population, now totals 224. As recently as 1950 there were only 168 SMSAs, and in 1960, 212 SMSAs. These Standard Metropolitan Statistical Areas accounted for 23.6 million of the 28.0 million population increase between 1950 and 1960. Significantly, three-fourths of the 23.6 million population increase in metropolitan areas took place outside of the central cities.

Within the central cities as compared to the suburbs, there is a proportionately higher incidence of particular strata: the elderly, the unemployed, broken families, working wives, nonwhites, the under-educated, and those with low incomes. This pattern is frequently aggravated by the expansion and removal of industry to neighboring suburbs, which narrows economic opportunity in the city.

One indication of the burgeoning growth in the suburbs is the recent construction activity. During the decade of the 1950s, some 8.5 million 1-4 family homes were constructed in SMSAs, of which 2.6 million were built in the central cities and 5.9 million, or 70 per cent in the suburbs. This trend continued in the period 1960 to 1965, when suburban construction comprised 72 per cent.

Apartment construction has recently revealed the same pattern. In comparing 1960 to 1964, multifamily housing units authorized inside central cities of 100,000 population almost doubled; for the fringe areas surrounding these cities, the multiplying factor was 2.6. The rate of increase is certainly greater in the suburban areas, and even more pronounced in the larger SMSAs.

A comparable shift in non-residential construction is noted. During the period 1960 to 1965, 83 per cent of permits issued for industrial buildings were for construction within SMSAs; within that percentage, 51 per cent took place outside central cities as compared with 32 per cent within central cities.

The growth of retail trade in the suburbs shows the same pattern. Of the 6.3 billion dollar cost of stores and other mercantile buildings constructed during 1960 through 1965 in SMSAs, 3.3 billion dollars, or 52 per cent are located in the suburbs.

The effect of this growth of the suburbs is the decline of certain job opportunities – notably retail employment and industrial employment – in the central cities. As a result, the large numbers of unskilled in-migrants to central cities from rural areas have found a lack of employment opportunity near the central city neighborhoods in which they can obtain housing that they can afford. Mass transit facilities to reach the suburbs are either lacking or too expensive and time consuming. Therefore, the ghettos of the minority groups and other poor are perpetuated in the central cities.

To the extent that the middle-class suburbanites must attract unskilled workers from the city for retail and other services, the costs are increased by virtue of the transportation and time involved. The suburban areas also are the places where there are many overlapping governmental jurisdictions providing different public services. One area may be part of a school district and a sanitation district for some purposes, and under the jurisdiction of a county or town government for other purposes.

The consequences of many jurisdictions include fractionated policy-making and either no coordination or only paper coordination in such mutual matters as transportation planning, public works construction, and land-use planning.

Within HUD's structure there is an Assistant Secretary concerned with metropolitan development. This includes public works planning; metropolitan area planning coordination; mass transportation programs; advance acquisition of land; open space land and urban beautification programs; and sewer and water facilities. By establishing all of these programs under one Assistant Secretary, consistent comprehensive planning and development of urban areas can be encouraged. More rational land use and more efficient services will, thus, be provided in metropolitan areas.

The Department has also made a start in assisting the development of better planned large new subdivisions, under authority of

Title X of the National Housing Act which permits FHA mortgage insurance of land development loans, enacted in 1965. To be eligible for mortgage insurance, the development must, among other requirements, meet the following criteria:

> The land development shall be undertaken in accordance with an overall development plan, appropriate to the scope and character of the undertaking, which
>
> 1. has received all governmental approvals required by State or local law or by the Federal Housing Commissioner;
> 2. is acceptable to the Commissioner as providing reasonable assurance that the land development will contribute to good living conditions in the area being developed, which area (a) will have a sound economic base and a long economic life, (b) will be characterized by sound land-use patterns, and (c) will include or be served by such shopping, school, recreational, transportation and other facilities as the Commissioner deems adequate or necessary; and
> 3. is consistent with a comprehensive plan which covers, or with comprehensive planning being carried on for, the area in which the land is situated, and which meets criteria established by the Secretary for such plans.

Land development with FHA mortgage insurance is only a beginning, however, in policies and programs that must be evolved to handle rationally the urban population growth of the next few decades, which will be concentrated in metropolitan areas. This Administration has proposed New Communities legislation, and it is my hope that such a program will be enacted within a few years. It would permit the use of low-cost outlying land to provide a balanced supply of housing for all income groups outside of central cities. At the same time, it would reduce the upward pressure on the prices of close-in land.

Under the urban planning assistance program (section 701) financial assistance is available for metropolitan comprehensive planning. In addition, we are beginning a research program aimed at developing new techniques of metropolitan planning and implementation. Research includes a project on the selection and use of economic and social data in urban planning; a study designed to aid public officials in developing land banks and land-use controls; an evaluation of several computerized data-processing systems for use in urban planning; a report on the efficacy of architectural controls including the European experience; and the development of techniques for sewage and water system development in metropolitan areas.

THE NEEDS OF THE FUTURE

At a 1963 conference in Washington, the late Catherine Bauer Wurster surveyed the status of professionals' and academicians' concern with the cities. She indicated that we have achieved a greater degree of sophistication.

> A generation of experience with mortgage insurance and public housing, zoning and master plans, slum clearance and renewal, professional city administration and the unfulfilled need for unified metropolitan action, has made us sadder but considerably wiser. We are less prone to believe in simple cure-alls . . . (Wurster, 1963, p. 172).

But we do believe that we now have a better knowledge of the problems and a better understanding of the causes. The establishment of the Department and President Johnson's frequent statements regarding its importance demonstrate a commitment toward providing a wider range of choice in housing and making our cities economically viable and aesthetically satisfying. Much headway has been made in securing the necessary financial and professional resources, although much still remains to be done on this score.

For the future our task is to intelligently and consciously shape metropolitan growth, offering true choice in housing accommodations, loosening the ghetto noose, and providing for social as well as physical needs, so that a better urban life is provided for all citizens.

Bibliography

A

ABSE, D. WILFRED. "Some Psychologic and Psychoanalytic Aspects of Perception," in Robert E. Stipe (editor), *Perception and Environment: Foundations of Urban Design,* Proceedings of a 1962 Seminar on Urban Design (Chapel Hill: The Institute of Government, The University of North Carolina, 1966), pp. 11-16.

ABU-LUGHOD, JANET. "Migrant Adjustment to City Life: The Egyptian Case," *American Journal of Sociology,* 67 (July, 1961), pp. 22-32.

ADAMS, ROBERT McC. "The Origin of Cities," *Scientific American,* 203 (September, 1960), pp. 153-172.

ADAMS, ROBERT McC. *The Evolution of Urban Society: Early Mesopotamia and Prehispanic Mexico* (Chicago: Aldine, 1966).

ADAMS, WARREN T. "Factors Influencing Mass-Transit and Automobile Travel in Urban Areas," *Public Roads,* 30 (December, 1959), pp. 256-260.

ADVISORY COMMISSION ON INTERGOVERNMENTAL RELATIONS. *Impact of Federal Urban Development Programs on Local Government Organziation and Planning* (Washington, D.C.: The Advisory Commission on Intergovernmental Relations, January, 1964).

ADVISORY COUNCIL ON PUBLIC WELFARE, WELFARE ADMINISTRATION. *Having the Power, We Have the Duty* (Washington, D.C.: U.S. Department of Health, Education, and Welfare, June 29, 1966).

AGGER, ROBERT E., DANIEL GOLDRICH, AND BERT E. SWANSON. *The Rulers and The Ruled* (New York: John Wiley, 1964).

ALESHIRE, ROBERT A. "The Metropolitan Desk: A New Technique in Program Teamwork," *Public Administration Review,* 26 (June, 1966), pp. 87-95.

ALMOND, CLOPPER, JR. "Origins and Relation to Agriculture of Industrial Workers in Kingsport, Tennessee," *Journal of Farm Economics,* 38 (1956), pp. 828-836.

ALONSO, WILLIAM. "A Theory of the Urban Land Market," *Papers and Proceedings of the Regional Science Association,* 6 (1960), pp. 149-157.

ALONSO, WILLIAM. *Location and Land Use* (Cambridge, Massachusetts: Harvard University Press, 1964).

ALTSHULER, ALAN. *The City Planning Process: A Political Analysis* (Ithaca, New York: Cornell University Press, 1965).

AMERICAN MUNICIPAL ASSOCIATION. *Action for Cities* (Chicago: Public Administration Service, 1943).

ANDERSON, NELS. *The Hobo: The Sociology of the Homeless Man* (Chicago: University of Chicago Press, 1923).

ASPEN INTERNATIONAL DESIGN CONFERENCE: *Conference Papers* (Aspen, Colorado: Aspen International Design Conference, 1956).

ASPEN INTERNATIONAL DESIGN CONFERENCE: *Conference Papers* (Aspen, Colorado: Aspen International Design Conference, 1962).

ASPEN INTERNATIONAL DESIGN CONFERENCE: *Conference Papers* (Aspen, Colorado: Aspen International Design Conference, 1964).

AUBREY, HENRY G. "Small Industry in Economic Development," *Social Research,* 18 (September, 1951), pp. 269-312.

AXELROD, MORRIS. "Urban Structure and Social Participation," *American Sociological Review,* 21 (February, 1956), pp. 13-18.

B

BACON, EDMUND N. "Design and Changing Values," in *Seventh Aspen International Design Conference: Conference Papers,* June, 1957 (Aspen, Colorado: Aspen International Design Conference, 1957), pp. 1-5.

BACON, EDMUND N. "Ordering Principles in Civic Design," in *Civic Design Symposium I: Emerging Forces and Forms in the City Today* (Philadelphia: Graduate School of Fine Arts, University of Pennsylvania, January, 1963), pp. 14-23.

BAIRD, ANDREW W., AND WILFRED C. BAILEY. *Farmers Moving Out of Agriculture,* Mississippi State University Agricultural Experiment Station Bulletin 568 (October, 1958).

BALL, ROBERT M. "Is Poverty Necessary?," *Social Security Bulletin,* 28 (August, 1965), pp. 18-24.

BALTIMORE URBAN RENEWAL STUDY BOARD. *Report of the Urban Renewal Study Board to Mayor Thomas D'Alesandro* (Baltimore: Baltimore Urban Renewal Study Board, 1956).

BANFIELD, EDWARD C. "The Political Implications of Metropolitan Growth," *Daedalus,* 90 (Winter, 1961), pp. 61-78.

BANFIELD, EDWARD C., AND JAMES Q. WILSON. *City Politics* (Cambridge, Massachusetts: Harvard University Press, 1963).

BARNETT, H. G., LEONARD BROOM, BERNARD J. SIEGEL, EVON Z. VOGT, AND JAMES B. WATSON. "Acculturation: An Exploratory Formulation," *American Anthropologist,* 56 (December, 1954), pp. 973-1002.

BARR, SHERMAN. "The Indigenous Worker: What He Is Not, What He Can Be," Paper prepared for Council on Social Work Education Fourteenth Annual Program Meeting, New York, January 27, 1966.

BASMACIYAN, HERMAN, AND JAMES W. SCHMIDT, "Development and Application of a Modal Split Model for the Puget Sound Region," Staff Report No. 12 (Seattle, Washington: Puget Sound Transportation Study, 1964). (Mimeographed.)

BATTLE, MARK. "The White Man Can't Help the Black Ghetto," *Saturday Evening Post,* 239 (January 29, 1966), pp. 10-17.

BAUER, PETER T., AND BASIL S. YAMEY. *The Economics of Underdeveloped Countries* (Chicago: University of Chicago Press, 1963).

BAUER, RAYMOND A., (editor). *Social Indicators* (Cambridge, Massachusetts: Massachusetts Institute of Technology Press, 1966).

BECKER, GARY S. *Human Capital* (New York: Columbia University Press, 1964).

BEERS, HOWARD W., AND CATHERINE HEFLIN. *Rural People in the City,* Kentucky Agricultural Experiment Station Bulletin (July, 1945), 19 pp.

BEESLEY, M. E. "The Value of Time Spent in Travelling: Some New Evidence," *Economica,* 32 (May, 1965), pp. 174-185.

BEESLEY, M. E., AND JOHN F. KAIN. "Urban Form, Car Ownership, and Public Policy: An Appraisal of Traffic in Towns," *Urban Studies,* 1 (November, 1964), pp. 174-203.

BELKNAP, GEORGE, AND MORTON SCHUSSHEIM. "Urban Research from a Federal Standpoint," *Urban Affairs Quarterly,* 1 (September, 1965), pp. 3-16.

BELLO, FRANCIS "The City and the Car," in The Editors of *Fortune* (editors), *The Exploding Metropolis* (Garden City, New York: Doubleday, 1958), pp. 53-80.

BENEWITZ, MAURICE. "Migrant and Non-Migrant Occupational Patterns," *Industrial Labor Relations Review,* 9 (January, 1956), pp. 235-240.

Berman versus Parker, 348 U.S. 26 (1954).

BERRY, BRIAN J. L. "City Size Distribution and Economic Development," *Economic Development and Cultural Change,* 9 (July, 1961), pp. 573-588.

BERRY, BRIAN J. L. "Research Frontiers in Urban Geography," in Philip M. Hauser and Leo F. Schnore (editors), *The Study of Urbanization* (New York: John Wiley, 1965), pp. 403-430.

BERRY, BRIAN J. L., AND ALLEN PRED. *Central Place Studies: A Bibliography of Theory and Applications, Including Supplement Through 1964* (Philadelphia: Regional Science Research Institute, 1965).

BERRYMAN, RUSSEL G. "Mass Transportation Post Card Survey," Penn-Jersey Transportation Study, Paper No. 16 (Philadelphia: Penn-Jersey Transportation Study, May, 1962). (Mimeographed.)

BLESSING, CHARLES. "The Planner's Role in Bringing Better Urban Design into City Rebuilding," in Conference Proceedings of the Seventh National Working Conference on Urban Renewal, National Association of Housing and Redevelopment Officials, July 9, 1962, *Journal of Housing,* 19 (September 14, 1962), pp. 371-374.

BLUMBERG, LEONARD, AND ROBERT BELL. "Urban Migration and Kinship Ties," *Social Problems,* 6 (Spring, 1959), pp. 328-333.

BOLLENS, JOHN C., AND HENRY J. SCHMANDT. *The Metropolis: Its People, Politics, and Economic Life* (New York: Harper and Row, 1965).

BONE, A. J., AND M. WOHL. "Massachusetts Route 128 Impact Study," in *Highway Research Board Bulletin* (Washington, D.C.: Highway Research Board of the National Academy of Sciences-National Research Council, 1959), pp. 34-38.

BOORSTIN, DANIEL J. *The Americans: The Colonial Experience* (New York: Random House, 1958).

BORRIE, WILFRED D. *The Cultural Integration of Immigrants,* A Survey Based upon the Papers and Proceedings of the UNESCO Conference on the Cultural Integration of Immigrants held in Havana, Cuba, April, 1956 (Paris: UNESCO, 1959).

BOSTICK, THURLEY, A. "The Automobile in American Daily Life," *Public Roads* 32 (December, 1963), pp. 241-255.

BOSTICK, THURLEY A., AND THOMAS R. TODD. "Travel Habits in Cities of 100,000 or More," *Public Roads,* 33 (February, 1966), pp. 274-276.

BOSTON ARCHITECTURAL CENTER. *Architecture and the Computer:* Proceedings of the First Boston Architectural Center Conference, December 5, 1964 (Boston: Boston Architectural Center, 1964).

BOYCE, DAVID E. "The Effect of Direction and Length of Person Trips on Urban Travel Patterns," *Journal of Regional Science,* 6 (No. 1, 1965), pp. 65-80.

BRAIDWOOD, ROBERT J., AND GORDON R. WILLEY (editors). *Courses Toward Urban Life: Archeological Considerations of Some Cultural Alternates* (Chicago: Aldine, 1962).

BRAYBROOKE, DAVID, AND CHARLES E. LINDBLOM. *A Strategy of Decision: Policy Evaluation as a Social Process* (New York: The Free Press of Glencoe, 1963).
BRIGGS, ASA. *Victorian Cities* (London: Odhams, 1963).
BROOKS, ROBERT R. R. *When Labor Organizes* (New Haven: Yale University Press, 1937).
BROOM, LEONARD, AND JOHN I. KITSUSE. "The Validation of Acculturation: A Condition to Ethnic Assimilation," *American Anthropologist*, 57 (February, 1955), pp. 44-48.
BROTZ, HOWARD M. "Social Stratification and the Political Order," *American Journal of Sociology*, 64 (May, 1959), pp. 571-578.
BUTTERWORTH, DOUGLAS S. "A Study of the Urbanization Process Among Mixtec Migrants from Tilantengo in Mexico City," *American Indigena*, 22 (1962), pp. 257-274.

C

CARROLL, J. DOUGLAS, JR. "The Relation of Homes to Work Places and the Spatial Patterns of Cities," *Social Forces*, 30 (March, 1952), pp. 271-282.
CARROLL, J. DOUGLAS, JR., AND H. W. BEVIS. "Predicting Local Travel in Urban Regions," *Papers and Proceedings of the Regional Science Association*, 3 (1957), pp. 183-197.
CHERMAYEFF, SERGE. "Luncheon Address," in *Architecture and the Computer:* Proceedings of the First Boston Architectural Center Conference, December 5, 1964 (Boston: Boston Architectural Center, 1964), pp. 21-22.
CHICAGO AREA TRANSPORTATION STUDY. *Final Report*, Vol. 1 (Chicago: Western Engraving and Embossing Co., December, 1959).
CHICAGO AREA TRANSPORTATION STUDY. *Data Projections*, Vol. 2. (Chicago: Western Engraving and Embossing Co., July, 1960).
CHICAGO AREA TRANSPORTATION STUDY. *Transportation Plan*, Vol. 3 (Chicago: Western Engraving and Embossing Co., April, 1962).
CHILDE, V. GORDON. "The Urban Revolution," *Town Planning Review*, 21 (April, 1950), pp. 3-17.
CHRISTALLER, WALTER. *Die Zentralen Orte in Süddeutschland* (Jena: Gustav Fischer Verlag, 1933).
CHRISTALLER, WALTER. *Central Places in Southern Germany*, translated by Carlisle W. Baskin (Englewood Cliffs, New Jersey: Prentice-Hall, Inc., 1966).
CHURCHILL, HENRY S. *The City Is the People* (New York: Reynal and Hitchcock, 1945).
CLAFFEY, P. J. "Characteristics of Travel on Toll Roads and Comparable Free Roads for Highway Benefit Studies," *Highway Research Board Bulletin*, No. 306 (Washington, D.C.: Highway Research Board of the National Academy of Sciences-National Research Council, 1961).
CLARK, COLIN. *The Conditions of Economic Progress* (London: Macmillan, 1940).
CLEAVELAND, FREDERIC N. "Congress and Urban Problems: Legislating for Urban Areas," *Journal of Politics*, 28 (May, 1966), pp. 289-307.
CLINARD, MARSHALL B. *Slums and Community Development: Experiments in Self-Help* (New York: Free Press, 1966).
COALE, ANSLEY J., AND EDGAR M. HOOVER. *Population Growth and Economic Development* (Princeton, New Jersey: Princeton University Press, 1960).
COKE, JAMES C. "The Lesser Metropolitan Areas of Illinois," *Illinois Government* 13 (November, 1962).

COLEMAN, JAMES S. *Community Conflict* (Glencoe, Illinois: Free Press, 1957).

COLM, GERHARD. "National Goals Analysis and Marginal Utility Economics," *Finanzarchiv*, 24 (July, 1965), p. 212.

COMMITTEE FOR ECONOMIC DEVELOPMENT. *Modernizing Local Government* (New York: Committee for Economic Development, 1966).

CONNERY, ROBERT H., AND RICHARD H. LEACH. *The Federal Government and Metropolitan Areas* (Cambridge, Massachusetts: Harvard University Press, 1960).

COONS, STEVEN. "Computer Aided Design," in *Architecture and the Computer:* Proceedings of the First Boston Architectural Center Conference, December 5, 1964 (Boston: Boston Architectural Center, 1964), pp. 26-28.

COTTRELL, W. F., "Of Time and the Railroader," *American Sociological Review*, 4 (April, 1939), pp. 190-198.

COWAN, GARY R., AND JOHN R. WALKER. "Rationale for Trip Production – General Analysis," Staff Report No. 6 (Seattle, Washington: Puget Sound Transportation Study, 1964). (Mimeographed.)

CRANE, DAVID A. "Education for City Form-Makers, Not Cosmeticians," in Jerry Goldberg, Roger Montgomery, and William Weismantel (editors), *Education for Urban Design: Proceedings of a Conference*, January 8-10, 1962 (St. Louis, Missouri: School of Architecture, Washington University, 1962), pp. 63-78. (Mimeographed.)

CRANE, DAVID A. "Civic Design as the Effective Strategy of Civic Love and Expression," in *Civic Design Symposium I: Emerging Forces and Forms in the City Today* (Philadelphia: Graduate School of Fine Arts, University of Pennsylvania, January, 1963), pp. 24-31.

CRESSEY, PAUL G. *The Taxi-Dance Hall* (Chicago: University of Chicago Press, 1932).

CURRAN, FRANK B., AND JOSEPH T. STEGMAIER. "Travel Patterns in 50 Cities," *Public Roads*, 30 (December, 1958), pp. 105-123.

D

DAHL, ROBERT A. *Who Governs? Democracy and Power in an American City* (New Haven: Yale University Press, 1961).

DALAND, ROBERT T., AND JOHN A. PARKER. "The Roles of the Planner in Urban Development," in F. Stuart Chapin and Shirley F. Weiss (editors), *Urban Growth Dynamics in a Regional Cluster of Cities* (New York: John Wiley, 1962), pp. 188-225.

DALTON, MELVILLE. "Conflicts Between Staff and Line Managerial Officers," *American Sociological Review*, 15 (June, 1950), pp. 342-351.

DAVIDOFF, PAUL. "Advocacy and Pluralism in Planning," *Journal of the American Institute of Planners*, 31 (November, 1965), p. 335.

DAVIDSON, BASIL. *The Lost Cities of Africa* (Boston: Little, Brown, 1959).

DAVIS, FRED. "The Cabdriver and His Fare: Facets of a Fleeting Relationship," *American Journal of Sociology*, 65 (September, 1959), pp. 158-165.

DAVIS, KINGSLEY. "Foreword: Urban Research and Its Significance," in Jack P. Gibbs (editor), *Urban Research Methods* (Princeton, New Jersey: D. Van Nostrand, 1961), pp. xi-xxii.

DAVIS, KINGSLEY. "The Urbanization of the Human Population," *Scientific American*, 213 (September, 1965), pp. 41-53.

DAWSON, PHILIP, AND SAM B. WARNER, JR. "A Selection of Works Relating to the History of Cities," in Oscar Handlin and John Burchard (editors), *The*

Historian and the City (Cambridge, Massachusetts: The Massachusetts Institute of Technology Press and Harvard University Press, 1963), pp. 270-290.

DAY, NORMAN. "Introduction," in Norman Day (editor), *The Architect and the City:* The 1962 American Institute of Architects-American Association of Collegiate Schools of Architecture Seminar Papers, Part 1, *Journal of Architectural Education,* 17 (November, 1962), p. 93.

DEAN, LOIS. "Minersville: A Study in Socio-Economic Stagnation," *Human Organization,* 24 (Fall, 1965), pp. 254-261.

DEEN, THOMAS B., WILLIAM L. MERTZ, AND NEAL A. IRWIN. "Application of A Modal Split Model to Travel Estimates for the Washington Area," Highway Research Record 38: *Travel Forecasting,* Publication No. 1158 (Washington, D.C.: Highway Research Board of the National Academy of Sciences-National Research Council, 1963).

DEPARTMENT OF SOCIAL ANTHROPOLOGY, UNIVERSITY OF EDINBURGH. *African Urbanization: A Reading List of Selected Books, Articles and Reports* (London: International African Institute, 1965).

DESAI, I. P. "Caste and Family," *Economic Weekly,* No. 6 (1954), pp. 249-254.

DETROIT METROPOLITAN AREA TRAFFIC STUDY. *Report on the Detroit Metropolitan Area Traffic Study,* Part 1: *Data Summary and Interpretation* (Lansing, Michigan: Speaker-Hines and Thomas Inc., 1955).

DETROIT METROPOLITAN AREA TRAFFIC STUDY. *Report on the Detroit Metropolitan Area Traffic Study,* Part 2: *Future Traffic and a Long Range Expressway Plan* (Lansing, Michigan: Speaker-Hines and Thomas Inc., 1956).

DEUTSCH, KARL. "Transaction Flows as Indicators of Political Cohesion," in Philip E. Jacob and James V. Toscano (editors), *The Integration of Political Communities* (Philadelphia: Lippincott, 1964), pp. 75-97.

DICKINSON, ROBERT E. *City and Region: A Geographical Interpretation* (London: Routledge & Kegan Paul Ltd., and New York: Humanities Press, 1964).

DJILAS, MILOVAN. *The New Class: An Analysis of the Communist System* (New York: Praeger, 1957).

DOOB, LEONARD W. "An Introduction to the Psychology of Acculturation," *The Journal of Social Psychology,* 45 (May, 1957), pp. 143-160.

DOONAN, GEORGE W. "Commercial Organizations in Southern and Western Cities," U. S. Bureau of Foreign and Domestic Commerce, *Special Agents Series,* No. 79, 1914.

DORE, R. P. *City Life in Japan* (Berkeley and Los Angeles: University of California Press, 1958).

DORE, R. P. "Agricultural Improvement in Japan: 1870-1900," in Thomas C. Smith (editor), "City and Village in Japan," *Economic Development and Cultural Change,* 9 (October, 1960), Supplement pp. 1-28.

DRAKE, ST. CLAIR. "The Social and Economic Status of the Negro in the United States," *Daedalus,* 94 (Fall, 1965), pp. 771-814.

DUNCAN, BEVERLY. "Factors in Work-Resistance Separation: Wage and Salary Workers, Chicago, 1951," *American Sociological Review,* 21 (February, 1956), pp. 48-56.

DUNCAN, BEVERLY, AND OTIS DUDLEY DUNCAN. "The Measurement of Intra-City Locational and Residential Patterns," *Journal of Regional Science,* 2 (Fall, 1960), pp. 37-54.

DUNCAN, OTIS DUDLEY. "Social Organization and the Ecosystem," in Robert E. L. Faris (editor), *Handbook of Modern Sociology* (Chicago: Rand McNally, 1964), pp. 36-82.

DUNCAN, OTIS DUDLEY. "Occupation Trends and Patterns of Net Mobility in the United States," *Demography,* Vol. 3, No. 1 (1966), pp. 1-18.

DURKHEIM, EMILE. *The Division of Labor in Society,* translated by George Simpson (New York: MacMillan, 1933).

DYNES, RUSSELL. "Rurality, Migration, and Sectarianism," *Rural Sociology,* 21 (March, 1956), pp. 25-28.

E

EAST, JOHN PORTER. *Council-Manager Government: The Political Thought of Its Founder, Richard S. Childs* (Chapel Hill: University of North Carolina Press, 1965).

ECKAUS, R. S. "Economic Criteria for Education and Training," *Review of Economics and Statistics,* 46 (May, 1964), pp. 181-190.

EISENSTADT, SAMUEL N. "Analysis of Patterns of Immigration and Absorption of Immigrants," *Population Studies,* 7 (November, 1953), pp. 167-180.

EISENSTADT, SAMUEL N. *The Absorption of Immigrants* (London: Routledge and Kegan Paul, 1954).

ENNEN, EDITH. "Les Differénts types de formation des villes européennes," *Le Moyen Age,* 4th Serie-tome xi, 62 (1956), pp. 397-411.

F

FAGIN, HENRY. "The Penn-Jersey Transportation Study – The Launching of a Permanent Regional Planning Process," *Journal of the American Institute of Planners,* 29 (February, 1963), pp. 126-131.

FAGIN, HENRY. *The Policies Plan: Instrumentality for a Community Dialogue* (Pittsburgh: Institute of Local Government, Graduate School of Public and International Affairs, University of Pittsburgh, 1965).

FAGIN, HENRY, AND ROBERT C. WEINBERG. *Planning and Community Appearance* (New York: Regional Plan Association, Inc., 1958).

FEIN, RASHI. "An Economic and Social Profile of the Negro American," *Daedalus,* 94 (Fall, 1965), pp. 815-856.

FISHER, ALLEN G. B. "Production, Primary, Secondary and Tertiary," *Economic Record,* 15 (February, 1939), pp. 24-30.

FISHER, BERENICE. "Industrial Education in the United States," unpublished Ph.D. dissertation, School of Education, University of California, Berkeley, 1965.

FLEISHER, AARON. "Technology and Urban Form," in Norman Day (editor), *The Architect and the City:* The 1962 American Institute of Architects-American Association of Collegiate Schools of Architecture Seminar Papers, Part 1, *Journal of Architectural Education,* 17 (November, 1962), pp. 96-98.

FLEISHER, AARON. "Technology and Urban Form," in Marcus Whiffen (editor), *The Architect and the City* (Cambridge, Massachusetts: Massachusetts Institute of Technology Press, 1969), pp. 37-52.

FOOTE, NELSON N., JANET ABU-LUGHOD, MARY MIX FOLEY, AND LOUIS WINNICK. *Housing Choices and Housing Constraints* (New York: McGraw-Hill, 1960).

FORM, WILLIAM H., AND JULIUS RIVERA. "The Place of Returning Migrants in a Stratification System," *Rural Sociology,* 23 (September, 1958), pp. 286-297.

FRAZIER, E. FRANKLIN. *The Negro Family in the United States* (Chicago: University of Chicago Press, 1931).

FREEDMAN, RONALD. *Recent Migration to Chicago* (Chicago: University of Chicago Press, 1950).

FREEDMAN, RONALD, AND DEBORAH FREEDMAN. "Farm-Reared Elements in the Non-Farm Population," *Rural Sociology,* 21 (March, 1956), pp. 50-61.

FREEMAN-GRENVILLE, G. S. P. *Medieval History of the Coast of Tanganyika* (London: Oxford University Press, 1962).

FRIEDEN, BERNARD J. *The Future of Old Neighborhoods: Rebuilding for a Changing Population* (Cambridge, Massachusetts: Massachusetts Institute of Technology Press, 1964).

G

GANS, HERBERT. "Urbanism and Suburbanism as Ways of Life," in Arnold Rose (editor) *Human Behavior and Social Processes* (Boston: Houghton, Mifflin, 1952), pp. 625-648.

GANS, HERBERT. *The Urban Villagers* (New York: Free Press, 1962).

GIBBS, JACK P., (editor). *Urban Research Methods* (Princeton, New Jersey: D. Van Nostrand, 1961).

GIBBS, JACK P., AND LEO F. SCHNORE. "Metropolitan Growth: An International Study," *American Journal of Sociology,* 66 (September, 1960), pp. 160-170.

GINSBURG, NORTON S. "Urban Geography and 'Non-Western' Areas," in Philip M. Hauser and Leo F. Schnore (editors), *The Study of Urbanization* (New York: John Wiley, 1965a), pp. 311-346.

GINSBURG, NORTON S. "The International Conference on 'The Study of Urbanization'," Social Science Research Council *Items,* 19 (December, 1965b), pp. 49-50.

GLAAB, CHARLES N. "Visions of Metropolis: William Gilpin and Theories of City Growth in the American West," *Wisconsin Magazine of History,* 45 (Autumn, 1961), pp. 21-31.

GLAAB, CHARLES N. *Kansas City and the Railroads: Community Policy in the Growth of a Regional Metropolis* (Madison: The State Historical Society of Wisconsin, 1962).

GLABB, CHARLES N. "Jesup W. Scott and a West of Cities," *Ohio History,* 73 (Winter, 1964), pp. 4-12.

GLAAB, CHARLES N., AND A. THEODORE BROWN. *A History of Urban America* (New York: The Macmillan Company, 1966).

GLASER, BARNEY. "The Use of Secondary Analysis by the Independent Researcher," *American Behavioral Scientist,* 6 (June, 1963), pp. 11-14.

GLASER, BARNEY, AND ANSELM L. STRAUSS. *Awareness of Dying* (Chicago: Aldine, 1965).

GLASER, BARNEY, AND ANSELM L. STRAUSS. *The Discovery of Grounded Theory: Strategies for Qualitative Research* (Chicago: Aldine, 1966).

GLAZER, NATHAN, AND DANIEL PATRICK MOYNIHAN. *Beyond the Melting Pot: The Negroes, Puerto Ricans, Jews, Italians, and Irish of New York City* (Cambridge, Massachusetts: Massachusetts Institute of Technology Press, 1964).

GOLDBERG, DAVID. "The Fertility of Two-Generation Urbanites," *Population Studies,* 12 (March, 1959), pp. 214-222.

GOLDHAMER, HERBERT, AND ANDREW MARSHALL. *Psychosis and Civilization* (Glencoe, Illinois: Free Press, 1953).

GOLDNER, WILLIAM, AND RONALD S. GRAYBEAL. *The Bay Area Simulation Study: Pilot Model of Santa Clara County and Some Applications,* paper prepared for the Annual Meetings of the Western Section, Regional Science Association, Monterey, California, January 29, 1965 (Berkeley, California: Center for Real Estate and Urban Economics, Institute of Urban and Regional Development, University of California, 1965).

DE GONZALEZ, NANCIE L. SOLIEN. "Black Carib Adaptation to a Latin Urban Milieu," *Social and Economic Studies,* 14 (September, 1965), pp. 272-278.

GOODING, EDWIN C. "New War Between the States: Part 3, Municipal Bonding for Private Industry," *New England Business Review* (July, 1964), pp. 2-7.

GOODMAN, PERCIVAL. "The Population Explosion as It Affects Teaching of Urban Design and Architecture," in Jerry Goldberg, Roger Montgomery, and William Weismantel (editors), *Education for Urban Design: Proceedings of a Conference,* January 8-10, 1962 (St. Louis, Missouri: School of Architecture, Washington University, 1962), pp. 14-24. (Mimeographed.)

GOODRICH, CARTER. *Government Promotion of American Canals and Railroads, 1800-1900* (New York: Columbia University Press, 1960).

GORDON, MARGARET S. *The Economics of Welfare Policies* (New York: Columbia University Press, 1963).

GORDON, MITCHELL. *Sick Cities* (Baltimore: Penquin Books, 1965).

GORMAN, DAVID A., AND STEDMAN HITCHCOCK. "Characteristics of Traffic Entering and Leaving the Central Business District," *Public Roads,* 30 (August, 1959), pp. 213-220.

GOTTMANN, JEAN. *Megalopolis: The Urbanized Northeastern Seaboard of the United States* (New York: Twentieth Century Fund, 1961).

GOULDNER, ALVIN, AND HELEN GOULDNER. *Modern Sociology* (New York: Harcourt, Brace and World, 1963).

GOVERNOR'S COMMISSION ON THE LOS ANGELES RIOTS. *Violence in the City – An End or a Beginning?* (Los Angeles: Governor's Commission on the Los Angeles Riots, December, 1965).

GRANT, DANIEL R. "Urban and Suburban Nashville: A Case Study in Metropolitanism," *Journal of Politics,* 17 (February, 1955), pp. 82-99.

GRANT, DANIEL R. "Metropolitics and Professional Political Leadership: The Case of Nashville," *Annals of the American Academy of Political and Social Science,* 353 (May, 1964), pp. 72-83.

GREAT BRITAIN, MINISTRY OF HOUSING AND LOCAL GOVERNMENT. *Homes for Today and Tomorrow* (London: Her Majesty's Stationary Office, 1961).

GREEN, CONSTANCE MCL. *American Cities in the Growth of the Nation* (New York: John De Graf, 1957).

GREENHUT, MELVIN. *Plant Location in Theory and Practice* (Chapel Hill: University of North Carolina Press, 1956).

GREER, SCOTT. *Metropolitics: A Study of Political Culture* (New York: John Wiley, 1963).

GRIFFIN, ROSCOE. "Appalachian Newcomers in Cincinnati," *The Southern Appalachian Region: A Survey* (Lexington: University of Kentucky Press, 1962), pp. 79-84.

GRODZINS, MORTON. *The Metropolitan Area as a Racial Problem* (Pittsburgh: University of Pittsburgh Press, 1959).

GROSS, BERTRAM M. *Activating National Plans,* occasional paper, Comparative Administration Group (Bloomington, Indiana: American Society for Public Administration, 1964).

GROSS, BERTRAM M. "Social State of the Union," *Trans-action,* 3 (November-December, 1965), pp. 14-17.

GROSS, BERTRAM M. *Space-Time and Post-Industrial Society,* occasional paper, Comparative Administration Group (Bloomington, Indiana: American Society for Public Administration, 1966).

GRUEN, VICTOR. "Environmental Architecture" in Norman Day (editor), *The Architect and the City:* The 1962 American Institute of Architects-American Association of Collegiate Schools of Architecture Seminar Papers, Part II, *Journal of Architectural Education,* 17 (December, 1962), pp. 96-97.

GRUNDSTEIN, NATHAN D. "Urban Information Systems and Urban Management Decisions and Control," *Urban Affairs Quarterly,* 1 (June, 1966), pp. 21-32.

Gutheim, Frederick. "The Next 50 Million Americans – Where Will They Live?," in "Designing Inter-City Growth: Harvard's Sixth Urban Design Conference," *Progressive Architecture* (August, 1962), pp. 98-99.

Gutman, Robert, and Francine F. Rabinovitz. "The Relevance of Domestic Urban Studies to International Urban Research," *Urban Affairs Quarterly,* 1 (June, 1966), pp. 45-64.

H

Hadden, Jeffrey K., and Edgar F. Borgatta. *American Cities: Their Social Characteristics* (Chicago: Rand McNally, 1965).

Hagen, Everett E. *On the Theory of Social Change* (Homewood, Illinois: The Dorsey Press, Inc., 1962).

Haggett, Peter. *Locational Analysis in Human Geography* (New York: St. Martin's Press, 1966).

Hamburg, John R. "The Relationships of Distance, Residential Density, Relative Income and Car Ownership to Average Trip Frequency as Reported at Households in the Detroit Area," *The Detroit Area Traffic Study,* 1954. (Mimeographed.)

Hamburg, John R., Charles R. Guinn, George T. Lathrop, and George C. Hemmens. "Linear Programming Test of Journey-to-Work Minimization," Highway Research Record 102: *Urban Transportation Planning Techniques and Concepts* (Washington, D.C.: Highway Research Board of the National Academy of Sciences-National Research Council, 1965), pp. 155-158.

Handlin, Oscar. "The Modern City as a Field of Historical Study," in Oscar Handlin and John Burchard (editors), *The Historian and the City* (Cambridge, Massachusetts: Massachusetts Institute of Technology Press and Harvard University Press, 1963), pp. 1-26.

Hansen, Walter G. "Traffic Approaching Cities," *Public Roads,* 31 (April, 1957), pp. 155-158.

Hansen, Walter G. "How Accessibility Shapes Land Use," *Journal of the American Institute of Planners,* 33 (May, 1959), pp. 73-77.

Harper, B. C. S., and H. M. Edwards. "Generation of Person Trips by Areas within the Central Business District," Highway Research Board Bulletin 253: *Traffic Origin-and Destination Studies,* Publication 762 (Washington, D.C.: Highway Research Board of the National Academy of Sciences-National Research Council, 1960), pp. 44-54.

Harris, Britton. "Urbanization Policy in India," *Papers and Proceedings of the Regional Science Association,* 5 (1959), pp. 181-203.

Harris, Britton. "Linear Programming and the Projecting of Land Use," Penn-Jersey Paper No. 20, Penn-Jersey Transportation Study, Philadelphia, 1963.

Harris, Britton (editor). "Urban Development Models: New Tools for Planning," special issue of the *Journal of the American Institute of Planners,* 31 (May, 1965), pp. 90-182.

Harris, Britton. *Comprehensive Transportation Planning:* Report to the California State Office of Planning (Berkeley: Center for Planning and Development Research, University of California, 1966a).

Harris, Britton. *Urban Transportation Planning, Philosophy of Approach* (Philadelphia: Institute for Environmental Studies, University of Pennsylvania, 1966b).

HARTZ, LOUIS. *The Liberal Tradition in America: An Interpretation of American Political Thought Since the Revolution* (New York: Harcourt, Brace and World, 1955).

HARVARD GRADUATE SCHOOL OF DESIGN. *Third Urban Design Conference:* General Report of Proceedings (Cambridge, Massachusetts: Graduate School of Design, Harvard University, April, 1959). (Mimeographed.)

HARVARD GRADUATE SCHOOL OF DESIGN. *Proceedings of the Eighth Urban Design Conference:* The Role of Government in the Form and Animation of the Urban Core, May 1-2, 1964 (Cambridge, Massachusetts: Graduate School of Design, Harvard University, 1964). (Unpaginated).

HAUSER, PHILIP M. (editor). *Handbook for Social Research in Urban Areas* (Paris: UNESCO, 1965a).

HAUSER, PHILIP M. "Urbanization: An Overview," in Philip M. Hauser and Leo F. Schnore (editors), *The Study of Urbanization* (New York: John Wiley, 1965b), pp. 1-47.

HAUSER, PHILIP M. "Demographic Factors in the Integration of the Negro," *Daedalus,* 94 (Fall, 1965c), pp. 847-877.

HAUSER, PHILIP M., AND LEO F. SCHNORE (editors). *The Study of Urbanization* (New York: John Wiley, 1965).

HECKSCHER, AUGUST. *The Public Happiness* (New York: Atheneum, 1962).

HERBERT, JOHN D., AND BENJAMIN H. STEVENS. "A Model for the Distribution of Residential Activity in Urban Areas," *Journal of Regional Science,* 2 (Fall, 1960), pp. 21-36.

HERRING, HARRIET L. "The Outside Employer in the Southern Industrial Pattern," *Social Forces,* 18 (October, 1939), pp. 115-126.

HERSON, LAWRENCE J. R. "The Lost World of Municipal Government," *American Political Science Review,* 51 (June, 1957), pp. 330-345.

HIBBERT, A. M. "The Origins of the Medieval Town Patriciate," *Past and Present,* 3 (February, 1953), pp. 15-27.

HILL, DONALD M., AND HANS G. VON CUBE. "Development of A Model for Forecasting Travel Mode Choice in Urban Areas," Highway Research Record 38: *Travel Forecasting,* Publication No. 1158 (Washington, D.C.: Highway Research Board of the National Academy of Sciences-National Research Council, 1963), pp. 78-97.

HIRSCH, WERNER Z., ELBERT W. SEGELHORST, AND MORTON J. MARCUS. *Spillover of Public Education Costs and Benefits* (Los Angeles: Institute of Government and Public Affairs, University of California, 1964).

HOLDEN, MATTHEW, JR. "The Governance of the Metropolis as a Problem in Diplomacy," *Journal of Politics,* 26 (August, 1964), pp. 627-647.

HOLLINGSHEAD, A. B. *Elmtown's Youth* (New York: John Wiley, 1948).

HOLMES, EDWARD H. "Highway Transportation," *U.S. Transportation, Resources, Performance, and Problems,* Publication 841-S (Washington, D.C.: National Academy of Sciences-National Research Council, n.d.), pp. 1-87.

HOLTON, RICHARD H. "Changing Demand and Consumption," in Wilbert E. Moore and Arnold S. Feldman (editors), *Labor Commitment and Social Change in Developing Areas* (New York: Social Science Research Council, 1960), pp. 201-216.

HOOVER, EDGAR M., AND RAYMOND VERNON. *Anatomy of a Metropolis* (Cambridge, Massachusetts: Harvard University Press, 1959).

HOPE, JOHN. "Industrial Integration of Negroes: The Upgrading Process," *Human Organization,* 11 (1952), pp. 5-14.

HOPPENFELD, MORTON. "Some Significant Aspects of the Practice and Teaching of Urban Design," in Jerry Goldberg, Roger Montgomery, and William Weismantel (editors), *Education for Urban Design: Proceedings of a Conference,* January 8-10, 1962 (St. Louis, Missouri: School of Architecture, Washington University, 1962), pp. 79-90. (Mimeographed.)

HOSELITZ, BERT F. "The Role of Cities in the Economic Growth of Underdeveloped Countries," *Journal of Political Economy,* 61 (June, 1953), pp. 195-208.

Hoselitz, Bert F. *Sociological Aspects of Economic Growth* (Glencoe, Illinois: Free Press, 1960).

Hughes, Helen. *News and the Human Interest Story* (Chicago: University of Chicago Press, 1940).

Hunter, Floyd. *Host Community and Air Force Base,* Air Force Base Project Technical Report No. 8 (Maxwell Air Force, Alabama: Research Institute, Human Research, 1952).

Hunter, Floyd. *Community Power Structure: A Study of Decision Makers* (Chapel Hill, University of North Carolina Press, 1953).

Hurt, Wesley R., Jr. "The Urbanization of the Yankton Indians," *Human Organization,* 20 (Winter, 1961-1962), pp. 226-231.

Hyneman, Charles S. "Administrative Reorganization," in A. N. Christensen and E. M. Kirkpatrick, *The People, Politics, and the Politician: Readings in American Government* (New York: H. H. Holt and Co., 1941), pp. 483-491.

I

International African Institute. *Social Implications of Industrialization and Urbanization in Africa South of the Sahara* (Paris: UNESCO, 1956).

International City Managers' Association. *Program Development and Administration,* Appendix D by James J. O'Brien (Chicago: International City Managers' Association, 1965).

Institute of Government, The University of North Carolina, Robert E. Stipe (editor). *Perception and Environment: Foundations of Urban Design,* Proceedings of a 1962 Seminar on Urban Design (Chapel Hill: The Institute of Government, The University of North Carolina, 1966).

Institute of Public Administration. "Developing New York City's Human Resources," a report to Mayor John V. Lindsay (New York: Institute of Public Administration, June, 1966a).

Institute of Public Administration. "Let There Be Commitment: A Housing Planning and Development Program for New York City," a report to Mayor John V. Lindsay (New York: Institute of Public Administration, 1966b).

Isard, Walter. *Location and Space-Economy: A General Theory Relating to Industrial Location, Market Areas, Land Use, Trade, and Urban Structure* (Cambridge, Massachusetts and New York: The Technology Press of Massachusetts Institute of Technology and John Wiley, 1956).

Isard, Walter. *Methods of Regional Analysis: An Introduction to Regional Science* (Cambridge, Massachusetts and New York: The Technology Press of Massachusetts Institute of Technology and John Wiley, 1960).

J

Jackson, John N. *Surveys for Town and Country Planning* (London: Hutchinson University Library, 1963).

Jacob, Herbert, and Kenneth N. Vines (editors). *Politics in the American States: A Comparative Analysis* (Boston: Little, Brown and Co., 1965).

Jaffe, A. J., and Koya Azumi. "The Birth Rate and Cottage Industries in Underdeveloped Countries," *Economic Development and Cultural Change,* 9 (October, 1960), pp. 52-63.

Janowitz, Morris. *The Community Press in a Community Setting* (New York: Free Press, 1952).

Jonassen, Christen T. "Cultural Variables in the Ecology of an Ethnic Group," *American Sociological Review,* 14 (February, 1949), pp. 32-41.

Jones, Barclay G. "Teaching Urban Decision as A Decision-making Process," in Jerry Goldberg, Roger Montgomery, and William Weismantel (editors), *Education for Urban Design:* Proceedings of a Conference, January 8-10, 1962 (St. Louis, Missouri: School of Architecture, Washington University, 1962), pp. 121-139. (Mimeographed).

Jones, Frank E. "A Sociological Perspective on Immigrant Adjustment," *Social Forces,* 35 (October, 1956), pp. 39-47.

Jurkat, Ernest H. "Land Use in Traffic Planning," *Traffic Quarterly,* 11 (April 1957), pp. 151-163.

K

Kahl, Joseph A. "Some Social Concomitants of Industrialization and Urbanization," *Human Organization,* 18 (Summer, 1959), pp. 53-74.

Kain, John F. "The Journey-to-Work as a Determinant of Residential Location," *Papers and Proceedings of the Regional Science Association,* 9 (1962), pp. 137-160.

Kain, John F. "A Contribution to the Urban Transporation Debate: An Econometric Model of Urban Residential and Travel Behavior," *The Review of Economics and Statistics,* 46 (February, 1964a), pp. 55-64.

Kain, John F. "The Effect of the Ghetto on the Distribution and Level of Nonwhite Employment in Urban Areas," *Proceedings of the Social Statistics Section, American Statistical Association* (Washington, D.C.: American Statistical Association, 1964b), pp. 260-272.

Kain, John F. "The Commuting and Residential Decisions of Central Business District Workers," *Transportation Economics* (New York: National Bureau of Economic Research, 1965), pp. 245-273.

Kain, John F. "The Big Cities' Big Problem," *Challenge* (September-October, 1966), pp. 5-8.

Kain, John F., and M. E. Beesley. "Forecasting Car Ownership and Use," *Urban Studies,* 2 (November, 1965), pp. 163-185.

Kantner, John. *The Relationship between Accessibility and Socio-Economic Status of Residential Lands, Flint, Michigan* (Ann Arbor, Michigan: Institute for Human Adjustment, University of Michigan, 1948). (Mimeographed.)

Katz, Robert D. *Design of the Housing Site: A Critique of American Practice* (Urbana, Illinois: Department of Urban Planning, College of Fine and Applied Arts, University of Illinois, 1966).

Katz, Saul M. *A Systems Approach to Development Administration,* Papers in Comparative Administration, Special Series: No. 6 (Washington, D.C.: Comparative Administration Group, American Society for Public Administration, 1965).

Katz, Saul M. *Guide to Modernizing Administration for National Development* (Pittsburgh: University of Pittsburgh Press, 1966).

Kaufman, Jerome L. "Changes Sweep Local Planning Commissions," *Public Management,* 48 (August, 1966), pp. 221-227.

KILLIAN, LEWIS M. "The Adjustment of Southern White Migrants to Northern Urban Norms," *Social Forces,* 32 (October, 1953), pp. 66-69.

KNOWLTON, CLARK S. "Patron-Peon Pattern Among the Spanish Americans of New Mexico," *Social Forces,* 40 (October, 1962), pp. 12-17.

KOLB, WILLIAM L. "The Social Structure and Functions of Cities," *Economic Development and Cultural Change,* 3 (October, 1954), pp. 30-46.

KRAELING, CARL H., AND ROBERT MCC. ADAMS (editors). *City Invincible: A Symposium on Urbanization and Cultural Development in the Ancient Near East* (Chicago: University of Chicago Press, 1960).

KUPER, HILDA (editor). *Urbanization and Migration in West Africa* (Berkeley: University of California Press, 1965).

KUZNETS, SIMON. *Modern Economic Growth: Rate, Structure, and Spread* (New Haven: Yale University Press, 1966).

L

LAMOUREAUX, JEANNETTE. "Applications of Automatic Data Processing Methods to Urban Planning Studies," unpublished Master's thesis, University of North Carolina, 1961.

LAMPARD, ERIC E. "The History of Cities in the Economically Advanced Areas," *Economic Development and Cultural Change,* 3 (January, 1955), pp. 81-136.

LAMPARD, ERIC E. "Urbanization and Social Change," in Oscar Handlin and John Burchard (editors), *The Historian and the City* (Cambridge, Massachusetts: The Massachusetts Institute of Technology Press and Harvard University Press, 1963), pp. 225-247.

LAMPARD, ERIC E. "Historical Aspects of Urbanization," in Philip M. Hauser and Leo F. Schnore (editors), *The Study of Urbanization* (New York: John Wiley, 1965), pp. 519-554.

LAMPARD, ERIC E., AND LEO F. SCHNORE. "Urbanization Problems," in *Research Needs for Development Assistance Programs* (Washington, D.C.: The Brookings Institution, 1961), pp. 1-63.

LAMPMAN, ROBERT J. "Negative Rates Income Taxation," paper prepared for Office of Economic Opportunity, August, 1965, reproduced by the National Association of Social Workers, February, 1966.

LANSING, JOHN BAND, AND EVA MUELLER, WITH NANCY BARTH. *Residential Location and Urban Mobility* (Ann Arbor, Michigan: Survey Research Center, University of Michigan, 1964).

LAPIN, HOWARD S. *Structuring the Journey to Work* (Philadelphia: University of Pennsylvania Press, 1964).

LAZARSFELD, PAUL F. AND ROBERT K. MERTON. "Friendship as Social Process," in Morrie Berger, Theodore Abel, and Charles H. Page (editors), *Freedom and Control in Modern Society* (New York: Nostrand Co., 1954), pp. 18-66.

LEIBENSTEIN, HARVEY. *Economic Backwardness and Economic Growth* (New York: John Wiley, 1957).

LEMMON, SARAH. "Raleigh – An Example of the New South," *North Carolina Historical Review,* 53 (1966), pp. 261-285.

LEVINSON, HERBERT S., AND F. HOUSTON WYNN. "Some Aspects of Future Transportation in Urban Areas," Highway Research Board Bulletin 326: *Urban Transportation Demand and Coordination* (Washington, D.C.: Highway Research Board of the National Academy of Sciences-National Research Council, 1962).

LEWIS, OSCAR. "Urbanization Without Breakdown: A Case Study," *Scientific Monthly,* 75 (July, 1952), pp. 31-41.

LIEBERSON, STANLEY. "The Impact of Residential Segregation on Ethnic Assimilation," *Social Forces,* 40 (October, 1961), pp. 52-57.

LINDBLOM, CHARLES E. *The Intelligence of Democracy: Decision Making through Mutual Adjustment* (New York: Free Press of Glencoe, 1965).

LIPPMANN, WALTER. "The Dog that Didn't Bark," *The Washington Post* (D.C.), November 2, 1965, p. A 13.

LIPSET, SEYMOUR MARTIN. "Social Mobility and Urbanization," *Rural Sociology,* 20 (September-December, 1955), pp. 221-228.

LITTLE, ARTHUR D., INC. *Stockton Community Renewal Policies and Programs* (San Francisco: Arthur D. Little, Inc., 1965).

LITTLE, KENNETH L. "The Role of Voluntary Associations in West African Urbanization," *American Anthropologist,* 59 (August, 1957), pp. 579-596.

LITTLE, KENNETH L. *West African Urbanization: A Study of Voluntary Associations in Social Change* (Cambridge: Cambridge University Press, 1965).

LOEWENSTEIN, LOUIS K. *The Location of Residences and Work Places in Urban Areas* (New York: The Scarecrow Press, 1965).

LONG, NORTON E. "The Local Community as an Ecology of Games," *American Journal of Sociology,* 64 (November, 1958), pp. 251-261.

LOPATA, HELEN. "The Secondary Features of a Primary Relationship," *Human Organization,* 24 (Summer, 1965), pp. 116-123.

LOPEZ, ROBERT S. "The Crossroads Within the Wall," in Oscar Handlin and John Burchard (editors), *The Historian and the City* (Cambridge, Massachusetts: Massachusetts Institute of Technology Press and Harvard University Press, 1963), pp. 27-43.

LOWRY, IRA S. "Residential Location in Urban Areas," unpublished Ph.D. dissertation, Department of Economics, University of California at Berkeley, 1960.

LOWRY, IRA S. *A Model of Metropolis,* Memorandum RM-4035-RC (Santa Monica, California: The Rand Corporation, 1964).

LU, WEIMING, "A More Attractive and Livable Minneapolis," paper prepared for National Association of Housing and Redevelopment Officials-American Society of Planning Officials-Department of Housing and Urban Development Workshop on Community Renewal Program, February 1, 1966, Chicago, Illinois. (Mimeographed.)

LYNCH, KEVIN. *The Image of the City* (Cambridge, Massachusetts: The Technology Press of Massachusetts Institute of Technology and Harvard University Press, 1960).

M

MAAS, ARTHUR, *et al. Design of Water and Resource Systems* (Cambridge, Massachusetts: Harvard University Press, 1962).

MCCLELLAND, DAVID C. *The Achieving Society* (Princeton, New Jersey: D. Van Nostrand, 1961).

MCDONAGH, EDWARD. "Attitudes Toward Ethnic Farm Workers in Coachella Valley," *Sociology and Social Research,* 40 (November-December, 1955), pp. 10-18.

MCFEE, JUNE KING. "Poverty and Urban Aesthetics," paper prepared for a conference on "The Education of Children and Adults in Aesthetic Awareness of the Environment of Man," Department of Art and Art Education, The Univeristy of Wisconsin, Madison, October 28-30, 1965. (Mimeographed).

McHARG, IAN. "The Ecology of the City," in Norman Day (editor), *The Architect and the City:* The 1962 American Institute of Architects-American Association of Collegiate Schools of Architecture Seminar Papers, Part 1, *Journal of Architectural Education,* 17 (November, 1962), pp. 101-103.

MACHLUP, FRITZ. "The War on Poverty," in Margaret S. Gordon (editor), *Poverty in America:* Proceedings of a National Conference held at the University of California, Berkeley, February 26-28, 1965 (San Francisco: Chandler Publishing Company, 1965).

McKELVEY, BLAKE. *The Urbanization of America, 1860-1915* (New Brunswick, New Jersey: Rutgers University Press, 1963).

MACKESEY, THOMAS W. "Summation for the Seminar," in Norman Day (editor), *The Architect and the City:* The 1962 American Institute of Architects-American Association of Collegiate Schools of Architecture Seminar Papers, Part 2, *Journal of Architectural Education,* 17 (December, 1962), p. 106.

MADDOX, H. "The Assimilation of Negroes in a Dockland Area in Britain," *Sociological Review,* 8 (July, 1960), pp. 5-15.

MARCH, JAMES G. "The Power of Power," in David Easton (editor), *Varieties of Political Theory* (New York: Prentice-Hall, 1966), pp. 39-70.

MARTIN, B. V., F. W. MEMMOTT, AND A. J. BONE. "Principles and Techniques of Predicting Future Demand for Urban Area Transportation," R63-1, Research Report No. 38, Massachusetts Institute of Technology, Cambridge, Massachusetts, 1961.

MARTIN, ROSCOE. *The Cities and the Federal System* (New York: Atherton Press, 1965).

MATHEWSON, KENT. "Broader Horizons," *National Civic Review,* 54 (March, 1965), pp. 136-144.

MAYER, ALBERT J., AND SUE M. SMOCK. "Public Response to Increased Bus Service," paper presented at the Annual Meetings of the Highway Research Board of the National Academy of Sciences-National Research Council, Washington, D.C., 1963.

MAYER, HAROLD M. "Urban Geography," in Preston E. James and Clarence F. Jones (editors), *American Geography: Inventory and Prospect* (Syracuse: Syracuse University Press, 1954), pp. 142-166.

MAYER, HAROLD M. "Urban Geography and Urban Transportation Planning," *Traffic Quarterly,* 17 (October, 1963), pp. 610-631.

MAYER, HAROLD M. "A Survey of Urban Geography," in Philip M. Hauser and Leo F. Schnore (editors), *The Study of Urbanization* (New York: John Wiley, 1965), pp. 81-114.

MAYER, HAROLD M., AND CLYDE F. KOHN (editors). *Readings in Urban Geography* (Chicago: University of Chicago Press, 1959).

MAYER, PHILIP. "Migrancy and the Study of Africans in Town," *American Anthropologist,* 64 (June, 1962), pp. 576-592.

MEHTA, SURINDER K. "A Comparative Analysis of the Industrial Structure of the Labor Force of Burma and the United States," *Economic Development and Cultural Change,* 9 (January, 1961), pp. 164-179.

MERRIAM, IDA C. "Social Welfare Expenditures, 1964-65," *Social Security Bulletin,* 28 (October, 1965), pp. 3-16.

MERTZ, WILLIAM L. "A Study of Traffic Characteristics in Suburban Residential Areas," *Public Roads,* 29 (August, 1957), pp. 208-212.

MERTZ, WILLIAM L., AND LAMELLE B. HAMNER. "A Study of Factors Related to Urban Travel," *Public Roads,* 29 (April, 1957), pp. 170-175.

MEYER, JOHN R., JOHN F. KAIN, AND MARTIN WOHL. *The Urban Transportation Problem* (Cambridge, Massachusetts: Harvard University Press, 1965).

MEYERSON, MARTIN AND EDWARD C. BANFIELD. *Politics, Planning and the Public Interest* (Glencoe, Illinois: Free Press, 1955).

MICHELSON, WILLIAM. "Use of Social Statistics in Estimating Auto Ownership," paper presented to the OD Committe at the 43rd Annual Meeting of the Highway Research Board of the National Academy of Sciences-National Research Council, Washington, D.C., January, 1964.

MILLER, HERMAN P. *Rich Man, Poor Man* (New York: Thomas Y. Crowell Co., 1964).

MILLER, HERMAN P. *Poverty American Style* (Belmont, California: Wadsworth Publishing Company, 1966).

MILLER, S. M., AND MARTIN REIN. "The War on Poverty: Perspective and Prospects," in Ben B. Seligman (editor), *Poverty as a Public Issue* (New York: Free Press, 1965).

MILLS, C. WRIGHT. "The Professional Ideology of Social Pathologists," *American Journal of Sociology,* 49 (September, 1943), pp. 165-180.

MILLS, C. WRIGHT. *The Power Elite* (New York: Oxford University Press, 1956).

MINDLIN, ALBERT. "Problems of the Urban Government Statistician," *Public Administration Review,* 23 (December, 1963), pp. 209-218.

MINISTRY OF TRANSPORT, GREAT BRITAIN. *Traffic in Towns: A Study of the Long Term Problems of Traffic in Urban Areas,* Reports of the Steering and Working Group appointed by the Minister of Transport, Great Britain (London: Her Majesty's Stationery Office, 1963).

MITCHELL, ROBERT B., AND CHESTER RAPKIN. *Urban Traffic: A Function of Land Use* (New York: Columbia University Press, 1954).

MOES, JOHN E. *Local Subsidies for Industry* (Chapel Hill: University of North Carolina, 1962).

MOHRING, HERBERT. "Land Values and the Measurement of Highway Benefits," *Journal of Political Economy,* 69 (June, 1961), pp. 236-249.

MOORE, WILBERT E. *Industrialization and Labor* (Ithaca, New York: Cornell University Press, 1951).

MOORE, WILBERT E. "The Adaptation of African Labor Systems to Social Change," in Melville J. Herskovits and Mitchell Harwitz (editors), *Economic Transition in Africa* (Evanston, Illinois: Northwestern University Press, 1964), pp. 277-298.

MORAVITZ, FRANCIS E. "Municipal Organization for Urban Development," unpublished Master's thesis, University of North Carolina, 1964.

MORRILL, W. T. "Immigrants and Associations: The Ibo in 20th Century Calabar," *Comparative Studies in Society and History,* 5 (1963), pp. 424-448.

MOSER, C. A., AND WOLF SCOTT. *British Towns: A Statistical Study of Their Social and Economic Differences* (Edinburgh and London: Oliver and Boyd, 1961).

MOSES, LEON N. "Income, Leisure, and Wage Pressure," *The Economic Journal* 72 (June, 1962), pp. 320-334.

MOSES, LEON N., AND HAROLD F. WILLIAMSON, JR. "Value of Time, Choice of Mode, and the Subsidy Issue in Urban Transportation," *Journal of Political Economy,* 71 (June, 1963), pp. 247-264.

MOYNIHAN, DANIEL P. "Employment, Income, and the Ordeal of the Negro Family," *Daedalus,* 94 (Fall, 1965a), pp. 745-770.

MOYNIHAN, DANIEL P. "A Family Policy for the Nation," *America,* 113 (September, 19, 1965b), p. 201.

MUMFORD, LEWIS. *The City in History* (New York: Harcourt, Brace and World, 1961).

MURPHY, RAYMOND D. *The American City: An Urban Geography* (New York: McGraw-Hill, 1966).

MUTH, RICHARD F. "The Spatial Structure of the Housing Market," *Papers and Proceedings of the Regional Science Association,* 7 (1961), pp. 207-220.

N

NATIONAL COMMISSION ON TECHNOLOGY, AUTOMATION AND ECONOMIC PROGRESS. *Technology and the American Economy,* Vol. 1 (Washington, D.C.: U.S. Government Printing Office, February, 1966).

NICHOLSON, MEREDITH. "Indianapolis: A City of Homes," *Atlantic Monthly,* 93 (June, 1940), pp. 836-845.

O

OFFICE OF PLANNING AND RESEARCH, U.S. DEPARTMENT OF LABOR. *The Negro Family* (Washington, D.C.: U.S. Department of Labor, March, 1965).

OI, WALTER, AND PAUL SHULDINER. *An Analysis of Urban Transportation Demands,* published for the Transportation Center, Northwestern University (Evanston, Illinois: Northwestern University Press, 1962).

OMARI, THOMPSON P. "Factors Associated with Urban Adjustment of Rural Southern Migrants," *Social Forces,* 35 (1956), pp. 47-53.

OSTRUM, VINCENT, CHARLES M. TIEBOUT, AND ROBERT WARREN. "The Organization of Government in Metropolitan Areas: A Theoretical Inquiry," *The American Political Science Review,* 55 (December, 1961), pp. 831-842.

OWEN, WILFRED. *The Metropolitan Transportation Problem* (Washington, D.C.: The Brookings Institution, 1956).

OWEN, WILFRED. *Cities in the Motor Age* (New York: The Viking Press, 1959).

P

PARK, ROBERT E. "The City: Suggestions for the Investigation of Human Behavior in the Urban Environment," *American Journal of Sociology,* 20 (March, 1916), pp. 577-612.

PATTEN, THOMAS H., JR., "The Industrial Integration of the Negro," *Phylon,* 24 (Winter, 1963), pp. 334-352.

PATTERSON, SHEILA. *Dark Strangers: A Sociological Study of the Absorption of a Recent West Indian Migrant Group in Brixton, South London* (Bloomington: Indiana University Press, 1964).

PEARSE, A. "Some Characteristics of Urbanization in the City of Rio de Janeiro," in Philip M. Hauser (editor), *Urbanization in Latin America* (New York: International Documents Service, 1961), pp. 191-205.

PENN-JERSEY TRANSPORTATION STUDY. *Prospectus* (Harrisburg: Pennsylvania Highway Department, December, 1959).

PERKINS, G. HOLMES. "Keynote Address," in Norman Day (editor), *The Architect and the City:* The 1962 American Institute of Architects-American Association of Collegiate Schools of Architecture Seminar Papers, Part 1, *Journal of Architectural Education,* 17 (November, 1962), pp. 94-96.

PERLOFF, HARVEY S., EDGAR S. DUNN, JR., ERIC E. Lampard, and Richard F. Muth. *Regions, Resources and Economic Growth* (Baltimore: Johns Hopkins Press for Resources for the Future, 1960).

PERLOFF, HARVEY S. "Social Planning in the Metropolis," in Leonard J. Duhl (editor), *The Urban Condition: People and Policy in the Metropolis* (New York: Basic Books, Inc., 1963), pp. 331-347.

PETERSON, CLAIRE L., AND THOMAS J. SCHEFF. "Theory, Method and Findings in the Study of Acculturation: A Review," *International Review of Community Development*, 13-14 (1965), pp. 155-176.

PHILADELPHIA CITY PLANNING COMMISSION. *Comprehensive Plan 1960* (Philadelphia City Planning Commission, 1960).

PHILADELPHIA URBAN TRAFFIC AND TRANSPORTATION BOARD. *Plan and Program, 1955* (Philadelphia: Urban Traffic and Transportation Board, April, 1956).

PIRENNE, HENRI. *Medieval Cities: Their Origins and the Revival of Trade*, translated by Frank D. Halsey (Princeton, New Jersey: Princeton University Press, 1925).

PITTS, FOREST B., (editor). *Urban Systems and Economic Development: Papers and Proceedings* (Eugene: University of Oregon School of Business Administration, 1962).

PITTSBURGH AREA TRANSPORTATION STUDY. *Study Findings*, Vol. 1 (Pittsburgh: Pittsburgh Area Transportation Study, November, 1961).

PITTSBURGH REGIONAL PLANNING ASSOCIATION. *Lower Turtle Creek Valley* (Pittsburgh: The Pittsburgh Regional Planning Association, March, 1955).

POLSBY, NELSON W. *Community Power and Political Theory* (New Haven: Yale University Press, 1963).

POSTON, MICHAEL M., E. E. RICH, AND EDWARD MILLER (editors). *The Cambridge Economic History*, Vol. 3, *Economic Organization and Policies in the Middle Ages* (Cambridge: Cambridge University Press, 1963).

PRESTHUS, ROBERT V. *Men at the Top: A Study in Community Power* (New York: Oxford University Press, 1964).

R

RABB, EARL. "What War and Which Poverty?," *The Public Interest*, 3 (Spring, 1966), pp. 45-56.

RANNELLS, JOHN. *The Core of the City: A Pilot Study of Changing Land Uses in Central Business Districts* (New York: Columbia University Press, 1956).

REGIONAL PLAN ASSOCIATION OF NEW YORK. *Regional Plan of New York and Its Environs* (New York: Regional Plan Association, 1929).

REGIONAL PLANNING FEDERATION OF THE PHILADELPHIA TRI-STATE DISTRICT. *Regional Plan of the Philadelphia Tri-State District* (Philadelphia: Regional Planning Federation of the Philadelphia Tri-State District, 1932).

REICHEK, JESSE. "Questions Concerning Urban Design Principles," in Norman Day (editor), *The Architect and the City:* The 1962 American Institute of Architects-American Association of Collegiate Schools of Architecture Seminar Papers, Part 2, *Journal of Architectural Education*, 17 (December, 1962), pp. 102-103.

REILLY, WILLIAM J. *Methods for the Study of Retail Relationships*, Bulletin No. 2944 (Austin: University of Texas, 1929).

REISS, ALBERT J., JR. "An Analysis of Urban Phenomena," in Robert Fisher (editor), *The Metropolis in Modern Life* (Garden City, New York: Doubleday, 1955), pp. 41-49.

REISS, ALBERT J., JR. "The Sociology of Urban Life: 1946-56," in Paul K. Hatt and Albert J. Reiss, Jr. (editors), *Cities and Society: The Revised Reader in Urban Sociology* (New York: Free Press, 1957), pp. 3-15.

REISS, ALBERT J., JR. "Rural-Urban and Status Differences in Interpersonal Contacts," *American Journal of Sociology,* 65 (September, 1959), pp. 182-195.

REISS, ALBERT J., JR. "Urbanization," in Julius Gould and William L. Kolb (editors), *A Dictionary of the Social Sciences* (New York: Free Press, 1964), p. 738.

REPS, JOHN W. *The Making of Urban America: A History of City Planning in the United States* (Princeton, New Jersey: Princeton University Press, 1965).

RESOURCES FOR THE FUTURE. *Environmental Quality in a Growing Economy* (Washington, D.C.: Resources for the Future, in press).

REYNOLDS, HARRY R. "Local Government Structure in Urban Planning, Renewal, and Relocation," *Public Administration Review,* 24 (March, 1964), pp. 14-20.

REYNOLDS, ROBERT L. *Europe Emerges: Transition Toward an Industrial World-Wide Society, 600-1750* (Madison: University of Wisconsin Press, 1961).

RICHARDSON, ALAN. "The Assimilation of British Immigrants in a Western Australian Community," Research Group for European Migration Problems, REMP Bulletin, 9 (January-June, 1961), p. 20.

RONAYNE, MAURICE F. "Operations Research Can Help Public Administrators in Decision-Making," *International Review of Administrative Sciences,* 29, No. 3 (1963), pp. 227-234.

ROSE, ALBERT. "The Role of Government in Promoting Social Change," in Murray Silverman (editor), *Proceedings* of a Conference sponsored by the Columbia University School of Social Work, Arden House, New York, November, 1965.

ROSEMAN, CYRIL B., AND WILLIAM L. C. WHEATON. *Metropolitan Decision-Making in the Philadelphia Region,* MMS (Berkeley: Institute of Governmental Studies University of California, 1966).

ROSSI, PETER H. *Social Science and Community Action* (East Lansing: Michigan State University, 1960).

ROSTOW, WALT W. *The Stages of Economic Growth, A Non-Communist Manifesto* (Cambridge: Cambridge University Press, 1960).

ROW, ARTHUR, AND ERNEST JURKAT. "The Economic Forces Shaping Land Use Patterns," *Journal of the American Institute of Planners,* 25 (May, 1959).

RUBIN, JULIUS. *Canal or Railroad? Imitation and Innovation in the Response to the Erie Canal in Philadelphia, Baltimore, and Boston* (Philadelphia: The American Philosophical Society, 1961).

RUBIN, MORTON. "Migration Patterns of Negroes from a Rural Northeastern Mississippi Community," *Social Forces,* 39 (October, 1960), pp. 59-66.

RUDE, GEORGE F. *The Crowd in History: A Study of Popular Disturbances in France and England, 1730-1848* (New York: John Wiley, 1964).

S

St. Louis Metropolitan Area Transportation Study 1957-70-80 (St. Louis, Missouri: W. C. Gilman and Co., 1959).

SCHEFF, THOMAS J. "Changes in Public and Private Language among Spanish-Speaking Migrants to an Industrial City," *Migraciones Internacionales,* 3 (1965), pp. 78-85.

SCHMANDT, HENRY J., PAUL G. STEINBICKER, AND GEORGE D. WENDEL. *Metropolitan Reform in St. Louis, a Case Study* (New York: Holt, Rinehart and Winston, 1961).

SCHMID, KARL OTTO. "A Philosophy of Urban Design," in Robert E. Stipe (editor), *Perception and Environment: Foundations of Urban Design,* Proceedings of a 1962 Seminar on Urban Design (Chapel Hill, The Institute of Government, The University of North Carolina, 1966), pp. 77-86.

SCHMIDT, JAMES W. "Modal Split Rationale," Staff Report No. 11, Puget Sound Transportation Study, Seattle, Washington, 1964. (Mimegraphed.)

SCHMIDT, ROBERT E., AND M. EARL CAMPBELL. *Highway Traffic Estimation* (Saugatuck, Connecticut: The ENO Foundation for Traffic Control, 1956).

SCHNEIDER, MORTON. "Gravity Models and Trip Distribution Theory," *Papers and Proceedings of the Regional Science Association,* 5 (1959), pp. 51-56.

SCHNORE, LEO F. "The Separation of Home and Work: A Problem for Human Ecology," *Social Forces,* 32 (May, 1954), pp. 336-343.

SCHNORE, LEO F. "The Journey to Work in 1975," in Donald J. Bogue (editor), *Applications of Demography: The Population Situation in the United States in 1975* (Oxford, Ohio and Chicago: Scripps Foundation for Research in Population Problems, Miami University, and Population Research and Training Center, University of Chicago, 1957), pp. 73-75.

SCHNORE, LEO F. "Social Problems in the Underdeveloped Areas: An Ecological View," *Social Problems,* 8 (Winter, 1960-1961), pp. 182-201.

SCHNORE, LEO F. "The Use of Public Transportation in Urban Areas," *Traffic Quarterly,* 16 (October, 1962), pp. 488-498.

SCHNORE, LEO F. *The Urban Scene: Human Ecology and Demography* (New York: Free Press, 1965).

SCHNORE, LEO F., AND HARRY SHARP. "Racial Changes in Metropolitan Areas, 1950-1960," *Social Forces,* 41 (March, 1963), pp. 247-253.

SCHULTZ, THEODORE W. "Investment in Human Capital," *American Economic Review,* 51 (March, 1961), pp. 1-17.

SCHWARTZ, ARTHUR. "Forecasting Transit Use," Highway Research Board Bulletin 297, Publication No. 924 (Washington, D.C.: Highway Research Board of the National Academy of Sciences-National Research Council, 1961), pp. 18-35.

DE SCHWEINITZ, KARL. *England's Road to Social Security* (New York: A. S. Barnes and Company, 1961).

SCOTT, ANDREW, WILLIAM LUCAS, AND TRUDI LUCAS. *Simulation and National Development* (New York: John Wiley, 1966).

SCUDDER, RICHARD, AND C. ARNOLD ANDERSON. "Migration and Vertical Occupational Mobility," *American Sociological Review,* 19 (June, 1954), pp. 329-334.

SEGOE, LADISLAS, *et al. Local Planning Administration* (Chicago: International City Managers' Association, 1941).

SELIGMAN, BEN, (editor). *Poverty As a Public Issue* (New York: Free Press, 1965).

SELZNICK, PHILIP. *TVA and the Grass Roots* (Berkeley and Los Angeles: University California Press, 1949).

SENTER, DONOVAN, AND FLORENCE HAWLEY. "The Grammar School as the Basic Acculturating Influence for Native New Mexicans," *Social Forces,* 24 (May, 1946), pp. 398-407.

SEXTON, PATRICIA. *Education and Income: Inequalities of Opportunity in Our Public Schools* (New York: Viking Press, 1961).

SHANNON, LYLE W. "Goals and Values in Agricultural Policy and Acceptable Rates of Change," in *Goals and Values in Agricultural Policy* (Ames: Iowa State University Press, 1961a), pp. 260-284.

SHANNON, LYLE W. "Occupational and Residential Adjustment of Rural Migrants," in *Labor Mobility and Population in Agriculture* (Ames: Iowa State University Press, 1961b), pp. 122-150.

SHANNON, LYLE W. "The Public's Perception of Social Welfare Agencies and Organizations in an Industrial Community," *Journal of Negro Education,* (Summer, 1963), pp. 276-285.

SHANNON, LYLE W., AND ELAINE M. KRASS. "The Urban Adjustment of Immigrants: The Relationship of Education to Occupation and Total Family Income," *Pacific Sociological Review,* 6 (Spring, 1963), pp. 37-42.

SHANNON, LYLE W., AND ELAINE M. KRASS. "The Economic Absorption of Inmigrant Laborers in a Northern Industrial Community," *American Journal of Economics and Sociology,* 23 (January, 1964), pp. 65-84.

SHARP, HARRY, AND LEO F. SCHNORE, "The Changing Color Composition of Metropolitan Areas," *Land Economics,* 38 (May, 1962), pp. 169-185.

SHARPE, GORDON B., WALTER G. HANSEN, AND LAMELLE B. HAMNER. "Factors Affecting Trip Generation of Residential Land Uses," *Public Roads,* 30 (October, 1958), pp. 88-89.

SHAW, CLIFFORD R., AND HENRY MCKAY. *Delinquency Areas* (Chicago: University of Chicago Press, 1929).

SHELDON, ELEANOR B., AND RAYMOND A. GLAZIER. *Pupils and Schools in New York City* (New York: Russell Sage Foundation, 1955).

SHIBUTANI, TOMATSU. "Reference Groups as Perspectives," *American Journal of Sociology,* 60 (May, 1955), pp. 562-569.

SHULDINER, PAUL M. "Trip Generation and the Home," paper presented at the 41st Annual Meeting of the Highway Research Board (Washington, D.C.: Highway Research Board of the National Academy of Sciences-National Research Council, January, 1962).

SILBERMAN, CHARLES. "The Mixed-Up War on Poverty," *Fortune,* 72 (August, 1965), pp. 156-161.

SILVER, JACOB. "Trends in Travel to the Central Business District by Residents of the Washington, D.C. Metropolitan Area, 1948 and 1955," *Public Roads,* 30 (April, 1959), pp. 153-176.

SILVER, JACOB, AND WALTER G. HANSEN. "Characteristics of Travel to a Regional Shopping Center," *Public Roads,* 31 (December, 1960), pp. 101-108.

SIMMONS, OZZIE G. "The Mutual Images and Expectations of Anglo-Americans and Mexican-Americans," *Daedalus,* 90 (Spring, 1961), pp. 286-299.

SIMMS, RUTH P. *Urbanization in West Africa: A Review of Current Literature* (Evanston, Illinois: Northwestern University Press, 1965).

SJOBERG, GIDEON. "Comparative Urban Sociology," in Robert K. Merton, Leonard Broom, and Leonard S. Cottrell, Jr. (editors), *Sociology Today* (New York: Basic Books, 1959), pp. 334-359.

SLAYTON, WILLIAM L. "Design Considerations in Urban Renewal," paper prepared for the National Association of Housing and Redevelopment Officials' Annual Conference on Urban Renewal, July 9, 1962, Eugene, Oregon, School of Architecture and Allied Arts, University of Oregon. (Mimeographed.)

SLAYTON, WILLIAM L. "Design Goals for Urban Renewal," paper prepared for the Reed College Conference on Urban Development, May 2, 1963, Portland, Oregon. (Mimeographed.)

SLAYTON, WILLIAM L. "Toward Excellence in Urban Design," paper prepared for Joint Meeting of the Architectural League of New York and the School of Architecture, Columbia University, April 29, 1965, New York. (Mimeographed.)

SLOANE, JOSEPH C. "Beauty and Anti-Beauty in the American City," in Robert E. Stipe (editor), *Perception and Environment: Foundations of Urban Design,* Proceedings of a 1962 Seminar on Urban Design (Chapel Hill: The Institute of Government, The University of North Carolina, 1966), pp. 35-41.

SMALLWOOD, FRANK. *Metro Toronto: A Decade Later* (Toronto: Bureau of Municipal Research, 1963).

Smallwood, Frank. "Guiding Urban Change," *National Civic Review,* 54 (April, 1965), pp. 191-197.

Smith, Joel, William H. Form, and Gregory P. Stone. "Local Intimacy in a Middle-Sized City," *American Journal of Sociology,* 60 (November, 1954), pp. 276-284.

Smith, Thomas C., (editor). "City and Village in Japan," *Economic Development and Cultural Change,* 9 (October, 1960), Supplement.

Smith, Wilbur, and Associates. *Future Highways and Urban Growth* (New Haven: Wilbur Smith and Associates, 1961).

Social Science Research Council. Report of the Interuniversity Summer Research Seminar on Acculturation, 1953, in Leonard Broom, Bernard J. Siegel, Evon Z. Vogt, and James B. Watson, "Acculturation: An Exploratory Formulation," *American Anthropologist,* 56 (December, 1954), pp. 973-1002.

Sofen, Edward. *The Miami Metropolitan Experiment* (Bloomington: Indiana University Press, 1963).

Sosslau, Arthur B., Keven E. Heanue, and Arthur J. Balek. "Evaluation of a New Modal Split Procedure," *Public Roads,* 33 (April, 1964), pp. 5-19.

Southeastern Wisconsin Regional Planning Commission. *Regional Planning Program Prospectus* (Waukesha: Southeastern Wisconsin Regional Planning Commission, April, 1962).

Spiro, Melford. "The Acculturation of American Ethnic Groups," *American Anthropologist,* 57 (December, 1955), pp. 1240-1252.

Spreiregen, Paul D. "The Practice of Urban Design: Some Basic Principles," in "Urban Design: The Architecture of Towns and Cities," *American Institute of Architects Journal,* 39 (June, 1963), pp. 59-74.

Srole, Leo, Thomas S. Longner, Stanley T. Michael, Marvin K. Opler, and Thomas A. C. Rennie. *Mental Health in the Metropolis: The Midtown Manhattan Study,* I (New York: McGraw-Hill, 1962).

Stein, Clarence S. *Toward New Towns for America* (New York: Reinhold, 1957).

Still, Bayrd. "Patterns of Mid-Nineteenth Century Urbanization in the Middle West," *Mississippi Valley Historical Review,* 28 (September, 1941), pp. 187-206.

Still, Bayrd. *Milwaukee: The History of a City* (Madison: The State Historical Society of Wisconsin, 1948).

Stone, Gregory. "City Shoppers and Urban Identification," *American Journal of Sociology,* 60 (July, 1954), pp. 36-45.

Strauss, Anselm L. *Images of the American City* (New York: Free Press, 1961).

Strong, Ann Louise. *Open Space for Urban America* (Washington, D.C.: U.S. Urban Renewal Administration, 1965).

Sturges, Kenneth. *American Chambers of Commerce* (New York; Moffat, Park and Company, 1915).

Sutherland, Edwin H. *Principles of Criminology* (Philadelphia: J. B. Lippincott, 1939), third edition.

Sutherland, Edwin H. "Development of the Theory [of Differential Association]," in Albert K. Cohen, Alfred R. Lindesmith, and Karl F. Schuessler (editors), *The Sutherland Papers* (Bloomington: Indiana University Press, 1956), pp. 13-29.

Syed, Anwar H. *The Political Theory of American Local Government* (New York: Random House, 1966).

Szabo, Albert. "Urban Design in the Formative Stage of Architectural Education," in Jerry Goldberg, Roger Montgomery, and William Weismantel (editors), *Education for Urban Design: Proceedings of a Conference,* January 8-10, 1962 (St. Louis, Missouri: School of Architecture, Washington University, 1962), pp. 91-100. (Mimeographed.)

T

TAAFFE, EDWARD J., BARRY J. GARNER, AND MAURICE H. YATES. *The Peripheral Journey-to-Work* (Evanston, Illinois: Northwestern University Press, 1964).

TAFT, RONALD. "Shared Frame of Reference Concept Applied to the Assimilation of Immigrants," *Human Relations,* 6 (February, 1953), pp. 45-55.

TANNER, J. C. "Forecasts of Future Numbers of Vehicles in Great Britain," *Roads and Road Construction,* 40 (September, 1962), pp. 263-274.

TANNER, J. C. "Forecasts of Vehicle Ownership in Great Britain," *Roads and Road Construction,* 43 (November, 1965), pp. 341-347; and *Roads and Road Construction,* 43 (December, 1965), pp. 371-376.

THIEL, PHILIP. "Space, Sequence and a Syllabus," in Jerry Goldberg, Roger Montgomery, and William Weismantel (editors), *Education for Urban Design: Proceedings of a Conference,* January 8-10, 1962 (St. Louis, Missouri: School of Architecture, Washington University, 1962), pp. 101-120. (Mimeographed.)

THOMPSON, WILBUR R. *A Preface to Urban Economics* (Baltimore: Johns Hopkins Press for Resources for the Future, 1965).

THOMPSON, WILBUR R. "Urban Economic Development," in Werner Z. Hirsch (editor), *Regional Accounts for Policy Decisions* (Baltimore: Johns Hopkins Press for Resources for the Future, 1966), pp. 81-121.

THRASHER, FREDERICK. *The Gang* (Chicago: University of Chicago Press, 1927).

TIKHOMIROV, MIKHAIL N. *The Towns of Ancient Russia* (Moscow: Foreign Languages Publishing House, 1959).

TILLY, CHARLES. *Migration to an American City,* Agricultural Experiment Station and Division of Urban Affairs, University of Delaware, April, 1965.

TITMUSS, RICHARD M. *Income Distribution and Social Change* (Toronto, Canada: University of Toronto Press, 1962).

TITMUSS, RICHARD M. "The Role of Redistribution in Social Policy," *Social Security Bulletin,* 28 (June, 1965), pp. 14-40.

TOMAZINIS, ANTHONY R. *An Introduction to Urban Transportation Planning: Emerging Techniques and Theories* (Philadelphia: Institute for Environmental Studies, University of Pennsylvania, 1966).

TRAFFIC RESEARCH CORPORATION. "A Model for Estimating Travel Mode Usage in Washington, D.C.," Vols. 5 and 6, Traffic Research Corporation, July, 1962.

TRI-STATE TRANSPORTATION COMMITTEE. *Prospectus* (New York: Tri-State Transportation Committee, April, 1962).

TRI-STATE TRANSPORTATION COMMITTEE. *Revised Long Range Work Program* (New York: Tri-State Transportation Committee, August 11, 1964).

TUGWELL, REXFORD GUY. "The Fourth Power," *Planning and Civic Comment,* 5 (April-June, 1939) pp. 1-31.

TUNNARD, CHRISTOPHER. "The Roads We Travel," in *Aspen International Design Conference: Conference Papers* (Aspen, Colorado: Aspen International Design Conference, 1958), pp. 1-7.

TURNER, RALPH H. "Migration to a Medium Sized American City: Attitudes, Motives, and Personal Characteristics Revealed by Open-end Interview Methodology," *Journal of Social Psychology,* 30 (1949), pp. 229-249.

TWIN CITIES METROPOLITAN PLANNING COMMISSION. *Meeting the Challenge of Metropolitan Growth* (Minneapolis: Twin Cities Metropolitan Planning Commission, January, 1963).

U

UNITED NATIONS, ECONOMIC AND SOCIAL COUNCIL. *Report on the World Social Situation,* Doc. No. E/CN.5/324/Rev. 1., UN Sales No. 57.IV.3 (New York: United Nations, 1957a).

UNITED NATIONS, ECONOMIC AND SOCIAL COUNCIL. *Financing of Housing and Community Improvement Programmes,* Doc. No. E/CN.5/323 (New York: United Nations, 1957b).

UNITED NATIONS, DEPARTMENT OF ECONOMIC AND SOCIAL AFFAIRS. *Report of the Ad Hoc Group of Experts on Housing and Urban Development,* Doc. No. E/CN.5/367/Rev. 1; UN Sales No. 63 IV. 1 (New York: United Nations, 1962).

UNITED NATIONS, ECONOMIC AND SOCIAL COUNCIL. *Report of the Committee on Housing, Building, and Planning,* Report of the First Session, Doc. No. E/3719. Rev. 1 (New York: United Nations, 1963a).

UNITED NATIONS, ECONOMIC AND SOCIAL COUNCIL. George F. Davidson, *Report on Organizational Arrangements in the Field of Housing, Building, and Planning,* Doc. No. E/C.6/24 (New York: United National, 1963b).

UNITED NATIONS, ECONOMIC AND SOCIAL COUNCIL. *Report of the Committee on Housing, Building, and Planning,* Report of the Second Session, Doc. No. E/3858 (New York: United Nations, 1964).

UNITED NATIONS, ECONOMIC AND SOCIAL COUNCIL. *The United Nations Development Programme in Housing, Building and Planning,* Doc. No. E/C.6/ 54, and Add. 1, Add. 2, Add. 3 (New York: United Nations, 1966).

U.S. BUREAU OF THE CENSUS. *Statistical Abstract of the United States: 1963,* (Eighty-fourth edition), (Washington, D.C.: U.S. Government Printing Office, 1963).

U.S. DEPARTMENT OF HEALTH, EDUCATION AND WELFARE. *Hearings of the Federal Advisory Council on Public Welfare* (Washington, D.C.: Welfare Administration, 1966).

U.S. OFFICE OF SCIENCE AND TECHNOLOGY. Subpanel on Housing, Executive Office of the President, a Report from the Subpanel on Housing to the Panel on Civilian Technology (Washington, D.C.: U.S. Government Printing Office, 1963).

U.S. SENATE COMMITTEE ON GOVERNMENT OPERATIONS. *Catalogue of Federal Aids to State and Local Governments,* Second Supplement, January 10, 1966 (Washington, D.C.: U.S. Government Printing Office, 1966).

U.S. URBAN RENEWAL ADMINISTRATION. *Community Renewal Program Policy* (Washington, D.C.: Urban Renewal Administration, 1963).

U.S. URBAN RENEWAL ADMINISTRATION. *Design Review in Urban Renewal,* Technical Guide 15 (Washington, D.C.: U.S. Government Printing Office, February, 1965).

U.S. URBAN RENEWAL ADMINISTRATION. *Design Objectives In Urban Renewal Documents,* Technical Guide 16 (Washington, D.C.: U.S. Government Printing Office, May, 1965).

United States versus Certain Lands in the City of Louisville. 78F. (Second), 684 (1935).

U.S. WHITE HOUSE CONFERENCE. *Beauty for America: Proceedings of the White House Conference on Natural Beauty,* May 24-25, 1965 (Washington, D.C.: U.S. Government Printing Office, 1965).

UNIVERSITY OF PENNSYLVANIA GRADUATE SCHOOL OF FINE ARTS. *Civic Design Symposium I: Emerging Forces and Forms in the City Today* (Philadelphia: Graduate School of Fine Arts, University of Pennsylvania, January, 1963).

UNIVERSITY OF WISCONSIN, DEPARTMENT OF URBAN AND REGIONAL PLANNING, HENRY FAGIN (editor). *Urban America Project Conference: Proceedings,* December 3-4, 1965 (Madison: Department of Urban and Regional Planning, University of Wisconsin, 1965). (Mimeographed.)

USEEM, JOHN, PIERRE TANGENT, AND RUTH HILL USEEM. "Stratification in a Prairie Town," *American Sociological Review,* 7 (June, 1942), pp. 331-342.

V

VAN EYCK, ALDO. "Twin Phenomena and Inbetween Place," in Jerry Goldberg, Roger Montgomery, and William Weismantel (editors), *Education for Urban Design: Proceedings of a Conference,* January 8-10, 1962 (St. Louis, Missouri: School of Architecture, Washington University, 1962), pp. 178-195. (Mimeographed.)

VERNON, RAYMOND. *The Myth and Reality of Our Urban Problems* (Cambridge, Massachusetts: Joint Center for Urban Studies of the Massachusetts Institute of Technology and Harvard University, 1962).

VIDICH, ARTHUR J., AND JOSEPH BENSMAN. *Small Town in Mass Society* (Princeton, New Jersey: Princeton University Press, 1958).

VON ECKARDT, WOLF. "Architectural Commentary on Boston Today and Tomorrow," in *Proceedings of the Eighth Urban Design Conference: The Role of Government in the Form and Animation of the Urban Core,* May 1-2, 1964 (Cambridge, Massachusetts: Graduate School of Design, Harvard University 1964). (Unpaginated.)

VON GRUNEBAUM, GUSTAVE E. *Islam: Essays in the Nature and Growth of a Cultural Tradition,* Memoir No. 81, (Menasha, Wisconsin: American Anthropological Association, 1955).

VOORHEES, ALAN M. "A General Theory of Traffic Movement," *Institute of Traffic Engineers, Proceedings,* 25 (1955), pp. 46-56.

VOORHEES, ALAN M., CHARLES F. BARNES, JR., AND FRANCIS E. COLEMAN. "Traffic Patterns and Land Use Alternatives," paper presented at the Highway Research Board 41st Annual Meeting (Washington, D.C.: Highway Research Board of the National Academy of Sciences-National Research Council, January, 1962). (Mimeographed.)

VOORHEES, ALAN M., SALVATORE J. BELLOMO, JOSEPH L. SCHOFER, AND DONALD E. CLEVELAND. "Factors in Work Trip Lengths," paper presented at the 45th Annual Meeting, Highway Research Board (Washington, D.C.: Highway Research Board of the National Academy of Sciences-National Research Council, January, 1966). (Mimeographed.)

VOORHEES, ALAN M., AND ROBERT MORRIS. "Estimating and Forecasting Travel for Baltimore by Use of a Mathematical Model," Highway Research Board Bulletin 224: *Trip Characteristics and Traffic Assignment* (Washington, D.C.: Highway Research Board of the National Academy of Sciences-National Research Council, 1959), pp. 105-114.

W

WAHL, RICHARD P. "PERT Controls Budget Preparation," *Public Management,* 46 (February, 1964), pp. 29-33.

WALKER, JOHN R. "Social Status of the Head of Household and Trip Generation from Home," paper presented at the Highway Research Board 44th Annual

Meeting (Washington, D.C.: Highway Research Board of the National Academy of Sciences-National Research Council, January, 1965).

WALKER, JOHN R., AND GARY R. COWAN. "Comparisons of Previous Seattle and Tacoma Origin and Destination Surveys with 1961 Puget Sound Regional Transportation Study Data," Staff Report No. 3 (revised), Puget Sound Regional Transportation Study, Seattle, Washington, March 1964. (Mimeographed.)

WALKER, ROBERT. *The Planning Function in Urban Government* (Chicago: University of Chicago Press, 1941).

Wall Street Journal, September 2, 1964.

WARNER, SAM B., JR. *Streetcar Suburbs* (Cambridge, Massachusetts: Harvard University Press and Massachusetts Institute of Technology Press, 1962).

WARNER, STANLEY LEON. *Stochastic Choice of Mode in Urban Travel: A Study in Binary Choice* (Evanston, Illinois: Northwestern University Press, 1962).

WARNER, W. LLOYD. *The Living and the Dead* (New Haven: Yale University Press, 1959).

WARNER, W. LLOYD, AND LEO SROLE. *The Social System of American Ethnic Groups* (New Haven: Yale University Press, 1945).

WATERSTON, ALBERT. *Development Planning: Lessons of Experience* (Baltimore: Johns Hopkins Press, 1965).

WEAVER, ROBERT C. "The Federal Government's Concern For Urban Design," in *Proceedings of the Eighth Urban Design Conference: The Role of Government in the Form and Animation of the Urban Core,* May 1-2, 1964 (Cambridge, Massachusetts: Graduate School of Design, Harvard University, 1964). (Unpaginated.)

WEAVER, ROBERT C. "The Emerging Urban Environment," an Address, 1965 American Institute of Architects' Student Forum, Washington, D.C., November 22, 1965.

WEBER, ADNA F. *The Growth of Cities in the Nineteenth Century: A Study in Statistics* (New York: Macmillan, 1899).

WELSH, GEORGE S. "The Perception of Our Urban Environment," in Robert E. Stripe (editor), *Perception and Environment: Foundations of Urban Design,* Proceedings of a 1962 Seminar on Urban Design (Chapel Hill: The Institute of Government, University of North Carolina, 1966), pp. 3-10.

WELSH, WILLARD. *Hutchinson, A Prairie Town in Kansas* (copyright by author, 1946).

WEST, J. *Plainville, U.S.A.* (New York: Columbia University Press, 1945).

WHEATLEY, PAUL. "What the Greatness of a City Is Said to Be," *Pacific Viewpoint,* 4 (September, 1963), pp. 163-188.

WHITE, WILLIAM A. "Ever See Emporia?," in Helen O. Mahin (editor), *The Editor and His People* (New York: Macmillan, 1924).

WHITE, WILLIAM A. "The Country Newspaper," in Henry S. Canby (editor), *Harper Essays* (New York: Harper and Bros., 1927).

WHITLACH, GEORGE I. *Industrial Districts: Their Planning and Development* (Atlanta: Georgia Institute of Technology, 1963).

WILDAVSKY, AARON B. *The Politics of the Budgetary Process* (Boston: Little, Brown, 1964).

WILLIAMS, OLIVER P., AND CHARLES R. ADRIAN. *Four Cities: A Study of Comparative Policy Making* (Philadelphia: University of Pennsylvania Press, 1963).

WILLIAMS, OLIVER P., HAROLD HERMAN, CHARLES S. LIEBMAN, AND THOMAS R. DYE. *Suburban Differences and Metropolitan Policies* (Philadelphia: University of Pennsylvania Press, 1965).

WILLIAMS, ROBIN, JR., JOHN P. DEAN, AND EDWARD A. SUCHMAN. *Strangers Next Door* (Englewood Cliffs, New Jersey: Prentice Hall, 1964).

WILLIAMS, SYDNEY. "Urban Aesthetics," in *Planning 1953* (Chicago: American Society of Planning Officials, 1953), pp. 56-61.

WILLIAMSON, JEFFREY G. "Ante Bellum Urbanization in the American Northeast," *Journal of Economic History,* 25 (December, 1965), pp. 592-608.

WILSON, JAMES Q. "The War on Cities," *The Public Interest,* No. 3 (Spring, 1966), pp. 27-44.

WINDHAM, GERALD O. "Urban Identification of Rural Migrants," *Mississippi Quarterly,* 14 (Spring, 1961), pp. 78-89.

WINGO, LOWDON, JR. *Transportation and Urban Land* (Washington, D.C.: Resources for the Future, Inc., 1961).

WINGO, LOWDON, JR. "Urban Renewal Strategy for Information Analysis," *Journal of the American Institute of Planners,* 32 (May, 1966), pp. 143-151.

WIRTH, LOUIS. *The Ghetto* (Chicago: University of Chicago Press, 1928).

WIRTH, LOUIS. "Urbanism as a Way of Life," *American Journal of Sociology,* 44 (July, 1938), pp. 1-24.

WOLF, ELEANOR P. "The Baxter Area: A New Trend in Neighborhood Change?," *Phylon,* 26 (Winter, 1965), pp. 344-353.

WOLF, ELEANOR P. AND CHARLES N. LEBEAUX. "Out-of-School Negro Youth from '515' Families," *Studies in Change and Renewal in an Urban Community,* Vol. 2 (Detroit: Wayne State University, 1965), pp. 259-272.

WOLFINGER, RAYMOND E., AND JOHN OSGOOD FIELD. "Political Ethos and the Structure of City Government," *American Political Science Review,* 60 (June, 1966), pp. 306-326.

WOOD, ROBERT C. *1400 Governments: The Political Economy of the New York Metropolitan Region* (Cambridge, Massachusetts: Harvard University Press, 1961).

WOOD, ROBERT C. *1400 Governments: The Political Economy of the New York Metropolitan Region* (Garden City, New York: Anchor Books, Doubleday, 1964).

WORLD HEALTH ORGANIZATION. *Expert Committee on the Public Health Aspects of Housing,* First Report, WHO Technical Report Series No. 225 (Geneva: World Health Organization, 1961).

WURSTER, CATHERINE BAUER. "Summary Remarks at the Administrator's Conference on Urban Problems and Needs of Urban Expansion," in *Urban Expansion-Problems and Needs,* (Washington, D.C.: Housing and Home Finance Agency, April, 1963), pp. 171-174.

WYNN, F. HOUSTON. "Intracity Traffic Movements," Highway Research Board Bulletin 119: *Factors Influencing Travel Patterns* (Washington, D.C.: Highway Research Board of the National Academy of Sciences-National Research Council, 1956), pp. 63-68.

Z

ZETTEL, RICHARD M., AND RICHARD R. CARLL. *Summary Review of Major Metropolitan Transportation Studies in the United States* (Berkeley: Institute of Transportation and Traffic Engineering, University of California, 1962).

ZIMMER, BASIL G. "Participation of Migrants in Urban Structures," *American Sociological Review,* 20 (April, 1955), pp. 218-224.

ZIMMER, BASIL G. "Farm Background and Urban Participation," *American Journal of Sociology,* 61 (March, 1956), pp. 470-475.

ZORBAUGH, HARVEY W. *The Gold Coast and the Slum* (Chicago: University of Chicago Press, 1929).

The Authors...

ROBERT R. ALFORD is Professor of Sociology at the University of Wisconsin (Madison). Dr. Alford received his Ph. D. in sociology from the University of California (Berkeley). He is currently Visiting Professor in the Department of Government, University of Essex (England). He is the author of *Party and Society: The Anglo-American Democracies* (Rand McNally, 1963) and has written a number of articles and reviews for professional journals in the fields of sociology, political science, and public administration. He is engaged in a comparative analysis of politics in four Wisconsin cities.

ROBERT T. DALAND is currently Professor of Political Science at the University of North Carolina (Chapel Hill). He received his Ph.D. in Political Science from the University of Wisconsin in 1952. He has taught at the University of Alabama, Connecticut College, University of Southern California, and was Ford Faculty Fellow at the University of California. He was formerly Director of the Regional Extension in Urban Studies of the University of North Carolina. Among the articles he has contributed to various journals is the landmark essay "Political Science and the Study of Urbanism" in *American Political Science Review,* June, 1957. He is co-author of "The Roles of the Planner in Urban Development" in F. Stuart

Chapin and Shirley F. Weiss (editors), *Urban Growth Dynamics in a Regional Cluster of Cities* (John Wiley, 1962).

HENRY FAGIN is Professor of Planning at the University of Wisconsin (Madison). He has been an active member of the planning profession ever since he received his B. Arch. and M.S. in planning at Columbia University in 1937 and 1938 – serving over 15 years as planning or executive director for Jersey City, Northern Westchester, New York's Regional Plan Association, and the Penn-Jersey Transportation Study. He has been a research professor in the Political Science Department at the University of California (Berkeley), was co-author of *Planning and Community Appearance* (Regional Plan Association, 1958), and author of *The Policies Plan: Instrumentality for a Community Dialogue* (Graduate School of Public and International Affairs, University of Pittsburgh, 1965), as well as over 30 articles published in books, monographs, and journals. He has been a Registered Architect for the past 25 years, was a member of the American Institute of Architects and is a member of the American Society for Public Administration and the American Institute of Planners. CAROL H. TARR, co-editor (with Professor Fagin) of Chapter 15, also served as editorial associate for the book as a whole – with special responsibility for compilation of the volume's comprehensive bibliography.

LYLE C. FITCH is President of the Institute of Public Administration, New York City. Formerly New York's City Administrator, he is now supervising projects abroad concerned with urban govenmentral planning and administration in India, Venezuela, Peru, and Nigeria. He has served as a consultant to numerous governments and agencies in the United States, including the U.S. Departments of Commerce and of Housing and Urban Development, the Housing and Home Finance Agency, the Committee for Economic Development, and various local and state governmental agencies. A graduate of Nebraska State College, he received his Ph.D. in Economics at Columbia University in 1946 and has taught at Columbia and at Wesleyan (Middleton, Connecticut). He was senior author of *Urban Transportation and Public Policy* (Chandler Publishing Co., 1964), and has published numerous books and papers in the fields of urbanism, economics, and administration.

CHARLES N. GLAAB is Professor of History, and Chairman of the Department of History, at the University of Wisconsin (Milwaukee). He received his Ph. D. in history from the University of Missouri, and has taught at Kansas State University. He was associated with the University of Chicago's History of Kansas City Project from 1956 to 1958, and is the author of *Kansas City and the Railroads: Community Policy in the Growth of a Regional Metropolis* (State Historical Society of Wisconsin, 1962). Dr. Glaab is also the editor of *The American City: A Documentary History* (Dorsey Press, 1963). He contributed "The Historian and the American City: A Bibliographic Survey" to Philip M. Hauser and Leo F. Schnore (editors), *The Study of Urbanization* (John Wiley, 1965).

BRITTON HARRIS is currently Professor of City and Regional Planning at the University of Pennsylvania and is conducting research at the University's Institute for Environmental Studies. A graduate of Wesleyan, he received his advanced degree in Planning at the University of Chicago. He was formerly Research Coordinator of the Penn-Jersey Transportation Study, and has done extensive research, writing, and advising on the mathematical simulation of urban phenomena. He was editor of the May, 1965 special issue of the *Journal of the American Institute of Planners* on "Urban Development Models: New Tools for Planning."

JOHN F. KAIN is Associate Professor of Economics, Harvard University, and a member of the Harvard - M. I. T. Joint Center for Urban Studies. He received his Ph. D. in economics from the University of California (Berkeley). Dr. Kain has served as a consultant to the Rand Corporation and to the Department of Housing and Urban Development. He is the author of *The Journey-to-Work as a Determinant of Residential Location Behavior* (Rand Corporation, 1961) and a co-author of *An Econometric Model of Metropolitan Development* (Rand Corporation, 1962), *Suburbanization of Employment and Population, 1948-1975* (Rand Corporation, 1963), and *The Urban Transportation Problem* (Harvard University Press, 1965). He has also contributed articles to such publications as *Urban Studies, The Review of Economics and Statistics, Challenge,* and the *Papers and Proceedings of the Regional Science Association.*

ROBERT D. KATZ is Associate Professor of Urban Design, Departments of Urban Planning and Architecture, University of Illinois.

He is currently concluding a sabbatical year investigating the designer's role in publicly assisted housing in selected European countries under the sponsorship of the Graham Foundation for Advanced Studies in the Fine Arts and the American Institute of Architects. He has served as a consultant to the U.S. Public Housing Administration. His most recent book is entitled *Design of the Housing Site: A Critique of American Practice* (Department of Urban Planning, College of Fine and Applied Arts, University of Illinois, 1967).

ERIC E. LAMPARD is Professor of History and Adjunct Professor of Urban and Regional Planning at the University of Wisconsin (Madison). He received his Ph. D. in history from the University of Wisconsin and has taught at Smith College. He is a co-author of *Regions, Resources, and Economic Growth* (Johns Hopkins Press, 1960). He has written a number of influential articles on urban topics, including "The History of Cities in the Economically Advanced Areas," *Economic Development and Cultural Change* (January, 1955), and "American Historians and the Study of Urbanization," *American Historical Review* (October, 1961). Dr. Lampard's essays include "Urbanization and Social Change," in Oscar Handlin and John Burchard (editors), *The Historian and the City* (The M. I. T. Press and Harvard University Press, 1963), and "Historical Aspects of Urbanization," in Philip M. Hauser and Leo F. Schnore (editors), *The Study of Urbanization* (John Wiley, 1965). He is currently working on a natural history of urbanization.

NORTON E. LONG is Professor of Community Government and Chairman of the Department of Politics at Brandeis University. He received his Ph. D. in political science at Harvard University. He has taught at a large number of colleges and universities, including Mount Holyoke, Queens, Oberlin, Michigan, Michigan State, Texas, Western Reserve, and Northwestern. Dr. Long is the author of a very influential essay on "The Local Community as an Ecology of Games," which appeared in the *American Journal of Sociology* (November, 1958). A collection of his papers, edited by Charles Press, was published as *The Polity* (Rand McNally, 1962), and he has recently contributed an essay on "Local Government and Renewal Policies" to James Q. Wilson (editor), *Urban Renewal: The Record and the Controversy* (M. I. T. Press, 1966).

HAROLD M. MAYER is Professor of Geography at the University of Chicago. He received his Ph. D. in geography from the University of Chicago. He has served as a Zoning Specialist for the Chicago Land Use Survey and as research director for the Philadelphia and Chicago Planning Commissions. He has taught at Northwestern, the University of Pennsylvania, and the University of Auckland (New Zealand). He is the author of *The Port of Chicago and the St. Lawrence Seaway* (University of Chicago Press, 1957) and co-editor of *Readings in Urban Geography* (University of Chicago Press, 1959). Dr. Mayer's articles and essays include "Urban Geography" and "Transportation Geography" in Preston E. James and Clarence L. Jones (editors), *American Geography: Inventory and Prospect* (Syracuse University Press, 1954), "A Survey of Urban Geography," in Philip M. Hauser and Leo F. Schnore (editors), *The Study of Urbanization* (John Wiley, 1965), and "The Pull of Land and Space," in Jean Gottmann and Robert A. Harper (editors), *Metropolis on the Move: Geographers Look at Urban Sprawl* (John Wiley, 1967).

LEO F. SCHNORE is Professor of Sociology and Adjunct Professor of Urban and Regional Planning at the University of Wisconsin (Madison). He received his Ph. D. in sociology from the University of Michigan. He is the author of *The Urban Scene: Human Ecology and Demography* (Free Press, 1965) and co-editor of *The Study of Urbanization* (John Wiley, 1965). Dr. Schnore has contributed over 50 articles on urban topics to various professional journals. In addition, he has served on the editorial boards of the *American Sociological Review, Land Economics,* and *Trans-action.* He has taught at Brown University, Michigan State University, and the University of California (Berkeley). His current research deals with historical aspects of urbanization in the United States.

LYLE W. SHANNON is Professor and Chairman of the Department of Sociology and Anthropology at the University of Iowa. He received his Ph. D. in sociology at the University of Washington (Seattle), and has taught at the University of Washington and the University of Wisconsin (Madison). He is the editor of *Underdeveloped Areas* (Harper and Brothers, 1957), and a contributor of a large number of articles to such publications as the *Journal of Human Relations,* the *Journal of Negro Education, Pacific Sociological Review,* and the *American Journal of Economics and Sociology.* Among his recent articles growing out of his work on the assimilation of migrants is "Occupational and Residential Adjustment of Rural Migrants" in *Labor Mobility and Population in Agriculture* (Iowa State University Press, 1961). With MAGDALINE SHANNON, he is currently co-editing a revised and enlarged edition of *Underdeveloped Areas.*

ANSELM L. STRAUSS is a sociologist with the School of Nursing at the University of California Medical Center (San Francisco). He received his Ph. D. in sociology at the University of Chicago, and has taught at Lawrence College, Indiana University, and the University of Chicago. He is the author or co-author of a number of books, including *Social Psychology* (Dryden Press, 1949 and 1956), *Mirrors and Masks: The Search for Identity* (Free Press, 1959), *Images of the American City* (Free Press, 1961), *Awareness of Dying* (Aldine, 1965), and *The Discovery of Grounded Theory: Strategies for Qualitative Research* (Aldine, 1966). Dr. Strauss has also contributed numerous articles and reviews to such journals as *Child Development,* the *American Journal of Sociology,* and the *American Sociological Review.*

WILBUR R. THOMPSON is Professor of Economics at Wayne State University. He received his Ph. D. in economics from the University of Michigan. He has been a Research Associate with the Committee on Urban Economics, Resources for the Future, Inc. He is the co-author of *An Econometric Model of State Postwar Industrial Development* (Wayne State University Press, 1959), and the author of *A Preface to Urban Economics* (Johns Hopkins Press, 1965). He also contributed "Urban Economic Growth and Development in a National System of Cities" to Philip M. Hauser and Leo F. Schnore (editors), *The Study of Urbanization* (John Wiley, 1965). Other articles by Dr. Thompson have appeared in such journals as *Land Economics, The Review of Economics and Statistics,* and *Papers and Proceedings of the Regional Science Association.*

ROBERT C. WEAVER is Secretary of the U. S. Department of Housing and Urban Development. He received his Ph.D. from Harvard University in 1934, and has served in many capacities in governmental agencies including Adviser on Negro Affairs to the Department of Interior, Consultant to the Tennessee Valley Authority, Director of Negro Manpower Service of the War Manpower Commission, Chairman of Housing for New York, and – prior to his selection to head the newly formed HUD and join the Cabinet – he was Administrator of the Housing and Home Finance Agency. He is the author of *The Urban Complex* (Doubleday, 1964) and "Major Factors in Urban Planning" in Leonard J. Duhl (editor), *The Urban Condition* (Basic Books, 1963).

MELVIN M. WEBBER is Professor of City Planning at the University of California (Berkeley) and is currently serving as Acting Chairman, Center for Planning and Development Research, Institute of Urban and Regional Development, there. He was formerly Senior Metropolitan Planner with Parsons, Brinckerhoff, Hall and Macdonald for the San Francisco Bay Area Rapid Transit Study. He holds degrees in economics and sociology from the University of Texas and in city planning from the University of California (Berkeley). He has written in the areas of metropolitan transportation planning, metropolitan spatial structure, and planning theory. He is editor of *Explorations in Urban Structure* (University of Pennsylvania Press, 1964) and was formerly editor of the *Journal of the American Institute of Planners.*

ERNEST WEISSMANN, until his retirement in 1966, was Director of the United Nations Centre for Housing, Building and Planning. He is now Inter-regional Adviser for the United Nations and a planning consultant. He received his architectural degree from the University of Zagreb, Yugoslavia, and worked in the *atelier* of Le Corbusier. After World War II he was Secretary of Housing and Town Planning for the Economic Commission for Europe in Geneva, on the staff of the United Nations Relief Administration in Washington, D.C., and in 1950 joined the permanent staff on the United Nations. He has written numerous reports and articles including "The Urban Crisis – Its Meaning for Development" *(UN Monthly Chronicle,* Vol. III, No. 4, April, 1966) and "Population, Urban Growth, and Regional Development" *(UN World Population Conference,* 1965, WPC/WP/480.1).

WILLIAM L. C. WHEATON is currently Director of the Institute of Urban and Regional Development, College of Environmental Design, University of California (Berkeley). He received his Ph.D. in Political Science at the University of Chicago in 1952. In addition to serving as Chairman of the Department of City and Regional

Planning at Harvard University and Director of the Institute of Urban Studies at the University of Pennsylvania, he has been a consultant on public housing to the U.S. Government and to the cities of Boston, Worcester, Philadelphia, Baltimore, the East River Project, and the states of New York and Massachusetts. In addition to many articles, Dr. Wheaton co-authored *Housing, People and Cities* (McGraw-Hill, 1962) and co-edited *Urban Housing* (Free Press, 1966).

ELEANOR P. WOLF is an Associate Professor of Sociology at Wayne State University. She received her Ph. D. in sociology from Wayne State University and has been a staff sociologist at the Merrill-Palmer Institute. She has contributed articles to such journals as *Phylon, Social Problems,* and *The Journal of Social Issues.* CHARLES N. LEBEAUX is a Professor in the School of Social Work at Wayne State University. He received M. S. W. and Ph. D. degrees from the University of Michigan, and he has taught at the University of Arizona. Dr. Lebeaux is probably best known as co-author of *Industrial Society and Social Welfare* (Russell Sage Foundation, 1958).